CASSELL'S
TALES OF ENDURANCE

FERGUS FLEMING

Weidenfeld & Nicolson
LONDON

First published in Great Britain in 2004 by
Weidenfeld & Nicholson
Wellington House
125 Strand
London WC2R 0BB

British Library Cataloguing in Publication Data
A catalogue record for this book is available
from the British Library

ISBN 0-304-35747-2

Typeset and printed in Great Britain by
Butler and Tanner Ltd, Frome and London

www.orionbooks.co.uk

CONTENTS

ILLUSTRATIONS

An Inuit settlement: John Ross's Arctic voyage of 1829–33. Bridgeman Art
Library/Stapleton Collection

James Clark Ross claims Antarctica's Possession Island for Britain, 1841.
Bridgeman Art Library/Scott Polar Research Institute, Cambridge

The note found at Victory Point by Franklin searchers in 1859. Scott Polar
Research Institute, Cambridge

Robert O'Hara Burke and William Wills after their 1860–1 crossing of
Australia. Mary Evans Picture Library

Samuel Baker, big-game hunter and explorer of the Nile. (1864–5). Corbis/
Hulton-Deutsch Collection

The apparition that greeted Edward Whymper following the Matterhorn
disaster, 1865. Mary Evans Picture Library

Charles Francis Hall's winter funeral, 1872. Private Collection

George Tyson's separation from the *Polaris,* 1872. Private Collection

The wreck of the *Hansa,* 1869. Corbis/Bettmann

David Livingstone surprised by a lion. (1858–64). Bridgeman Art Library/
Stapleton Collection

Between pages 342 and 343

Life in the tent: Julius von Payer's exploration of Franz Josef Land, 1874.
Mary Evans Picture Library

The wintering of HMS *Alert* at Floeberg Beach, 1875. Corbis/Hulton-Deutsch
Collection

Adolphus Greely, leader of the US expedition to Ellesmere Island.
(1881–4). Corbis

Fridtjof Nansen at Cape Flora, 1895. Royal Geographical Society

Salomon Andrée's *Eagle* fails to reach the North Pole, 1897. Mary Evans Picture
Library

Fernand Foureau, conqueror of the Sahara. (1899–1900). Roger Viollet/Rex Features

The *Stella Polare* caught by an ice ridge, 1899. Private Collection

Robert Peary and Francis Cook dispute their right to the North Pole, 1909.
Bridgeman Art Library/Archives Chaumet

Robert Falcon Scott (centre) and party at the South Pole, January 1912. Scott
Polar Research Institute, Cambridge

Roald Amundsen, who reached the South Pole before Scott on 14 December
1911. Corbis/Bettmann

Douglas Mawson, leader of another expedition to Antartica 1911–13.
Bridgeman Art Library/Private Collection

Ernest Shackleton's men hack a passage through the Weddell Sea, 1915.
Scott Polar Research Institute, Cambridge

The *Italia* before the start to the North Pole, 23 May 1928. Scott Polar Research
Institute, Cambridge

George Mallory and Edward Norton on Everest in 1922. Bridgeman Art Library/
Stapleton Collection

PREFACE

The lion's share of the credit for *Cassell's Tales of Endurance* must go to my excellent editor Richard Milbank. It was he who came up with the concept, the title and the format. My lesser contribution was to suggest that it be structured as a sort-of history of exploration – and then, of course, to write it.

A sort-of history needs sort-of boundaries. They were drawn thus: it should start in about the 14th–15th centuries, with the birth of exploration literature; it should end in the 1920s, when the combustion engine transformed the raw nature of the quest; it should be divided into three 'Ages', equating roughly to the Renaissance, Enlightenment and Industrial eras; and the yarns within it should be both ripping and important. There the problems started. So many explorers did exciting things, and so many of their journeys can be interpreted as important. How to choose? The 'greats' had to be included – Marco Polo, Magellan, Shackleton, Scott & Co. – but thereafter the options were endless. After much deliberation it was agreed that geographical discovery should be paramount. So out went individuals such as Bligh and Bartlett, who endured much (very rippingly) yet discovered little; out, too, went a host of travellers who were keen observers and chroniclers but who did not break new ground. Still, the list of candidates was dauntingly long. Should one include Barth, Richardson, Laperrine and Lenz in Africa? In the Arctic, Steffansen, Rasmusssen and Nordenskjold? How about Hedin, Przhevalsky and Stein in Asia? What was one to do with Flinders, Sturt and Tasman in Australia? Which of the Central and South American conquistadores was most noteworthy? They all had the makings of a good story. It would have been possible, I suppose, to impose an order of seniority, to apply topographical quotas or to regiment them in some other fashion. In the end I just picked the ones I liked best.

The final selection will probably infuriate adventure afficionados and historians alike. Where are the Arabs, Greeks, the Chinese and the Vikings? Where are the quirky people that nobody has heard of? Where are the many women travellers whose exploits have long been underestimated? Not here, I am afraid – well, not much, at any rate. This is not to say they are unworthy; it is simply that they either didn't meet the spec. or weren't as exciting as the many others that did. More serious, perhaps, is the lack of balance between discoverer and 'discovered'. Many histories (like this one) treat native people as bit players: they arrive from the wings, shake their spears, then trudge offstage to await their next call. It is a distorted picture. Not only were they integral to the process of Western exploration – whether obstructing the white man or, more often, helping him – but they were occasionally explorers themselves. Whenever they had a chance they wrote clear, perceptive and sometimes beautiful narratives of the time they spent with the interloper. I am sorry that their stories cannot be told here.

In researching this compilation I have (embarrassing to admit) often found myself consulting my own books. Some tales may therefore seem familiar, but I hope they are none the duller for the retelling. While crediting myself I must also acknowledge the many other authors upon whose wisdom I have drawn. Without notes it is hard to allocate precisely my indebtedness, but the bibliography contains a list of secondary sources that have been more than helpful. Their titles are in most cases self-explanatory and I recommend them to anyone who wants to read in greater depth about any particular explorer. I would also like to thank my agent, Gillon Aitken; Rosie Anderson, Richard Milbank and Neil Wenborn at Cassells; and the staffs of the Bodleian Library (Oxford), the British Library, Gloucestershire Libraries, the Kensington and Chelsea Library, the London Library, the Royal Geographical Society, the School of Oriental and African Studies and the Scott Polar Research Institute (Cambridge).

Traditionally, every preface contains an apology for the author's lack of narrative prowess, poor organisational skills, general incompetence and so on. Here, therefore, is a quote from George Steller, naturalist and surgeon to Vitus Bering 1741–2, that says it all: 'As to the style and arrangement of matter, the pressure of duties does not permit me to spend too much time in perfecting any one thing ... I therefore set out my porridge in carefully made earthen vessels. If the vessel is an offence to any one, he will perform for me and others a most friendly service if he will pour it all into a gold or silver urn.'

· PART 1 ·

THE AGE OF RECONNAISSANCE

THE AGE OF RECONNAISSANCE

Vilhjalmur Stefansson, the 20th-century author and explorer, famously described exploration as a meaningless pursuit. How could anyone claim to have discovered new territories when, with the exception of Antarctica and possibly the northern Arctic islands, humans had already walked, at one time or another, over every landmass on the globe? 'The great tales which we are able to present are those of rediscovery,' he wrote. 'Our very best stories are lucky when they are no worse than second-best.' Theoretically he was correct. Yet the history of exploration is not just that of people breaking new ground; it is also that of people *writing* about breaking new ground. With no means to describe their experiences, how could explorers explain what they had seen and where they had been? Without the written word, they were trees falling in the forest, unheard and unseen. The fall of the Roman Empire in 476 AD, for example, plunged Europe into a limbo: fragments of knowledge survived in monastic libraries, but for more than half a millennium it was as if the intellectual slate had been wiped clean. It was this very absence of records that gave birth to a surge of discovery which started in approximately the 14th century AD and did not abate for another 600 years.

There had been explorers and geographers aplenty in the past. In the 4th century BC, the Greek traveller Herodotus wrote a description of the world, drawing partly on his own voyages through the Mediterranean and partly on those of traders whom he had encountered en route. (For his trouble he was dubbed 'The Prince of Liars'.) In 340 BC another Greek, Pytheas of Massilia, claimed to have travelled beyond the Arctic Circle, and although he may have reached Iceland his reports of a land even further north called Ultima Thule, where there was constant ice and the sun shone 24 hours a day, were probably fabricated. In 980 AD the Vikings (who had trading links with Greece and the Middle East) found a place that fitted Pytheas's description of Ultima Thule when they landed in Greenland. Twenty years later Leif Ericsson and other Greenland colonists accidentally discovered North America. Their discoveries survived in oral tradition, later to be transcribed as the Icelandic sagas. To most Europeans, however, it was as if none of this had happened. So complete was the collapse of knowledge following the demise of Rome, and so restricted the availability of information during the Dark Ages, that they had only the haziest notion of what lay beyond their borders.

Information arrived slowly and in dribbles. For a short time during the 13th century the Mongol conquests made it possible for travellers to cross the overland routes to China in relative safety. Men like the French cleric William of Rubruk and the Venetian merchant Marco Polo spent several years in the Far East, returning with astounding tales of the wealth it contained. But with the disintegration of the Mongol Empire the Far East became inaccessible, and for more than a hundred years Europe's only recourse was conjecture. The reports of travellers like Polo (themselves of dubious accuracy) were greeted with the same approval as those of Sir John Mandeville, whose fictitious 14th-century *Travels* described men with heads in their chests and eyes in their foreheads. In an age of hypothesis nothing could be ruled out.

By the dawn of the 15th century Europe occupied a position of unique geographical ignorance. Islamic merchants had already established colonies as far afield as Madagascar and China, using maps and navigational instruments far more advanced than those in Europe. The Chinese, in turn, thanks to a series of expeditions under Admiral Zheng He during the early 1400s, had created a maritime network that extended from Japan (and possibly America) to East Africa, across which they sailed in the largest, most sophisticated ships in the world. To these two civilizations the concept of exploration was, if not exactly meaningless, something that did not concern them overmuch, for the simple reason that they knew, more or less, where everything was and where to obtain the goods they needed. In the grand scheme of things Europe was a crude and impoverished outpost of the known world – a fact of which its rulers and merchants were painfully aware. It was this sense of combined inferiority and frustration that made 'discovery' a peculiarly European phenomenon.

The first problem European explorers faced was a basic one: where were they? Navigators had mapped the Mediterranean, the coasts of northern Europe and the Black Sea, using compasses to produce surprisingly accurate charts intersected by rhumb lines. Of the lands beyond these shores, however, they had minimal information. Where the rhumb lines stopped theology started, giving rise to *mappaemundi*, or 'maps of the world', that had nothing to do with cartography and everything to do with the Bible. Typically they followed a T–O pattern, the O being the circle of the globe, within which swam three continents: Asia (at the top), with Europe and Africa lying beneath it. The T was the waterways that separated them: the upright, between Europe and Africa, was the Mediterranean; the crosspieces were the rivers Nile and Don. Each of the continents was supposed to belong to one of Noah's three sons and, to reinforce the point, Asia was often portrayed with a mountain atop which balanced a tiny ark. The schematic simplicity fooled nobody: Europe's captains recognized that the earth was spherical and that if one sailed beyond a certain distance one would not fall off the edge. But for all they knew about their place in the world, they might as well have relied on the *mappaemundi*. It was commonly held, for example, that anyone venturing south of the equator would be boiled alive.

Europe's notion of discovery was tightly focused. Its rulers were intrigued by the theories of mapmakers and by reports of travellers such as Polo and Mandeville, but they had no particular desire to find new lands; what they wanted to do was reach the old; all they wanted from them was spice. A trader's handbook of the time listed more than 288 luxury substances, ranging from silk and cotton to sugar and wax, precious stones, dyes and perfumes, but it was spice that commanded the highest premium – and not because it was a luxury but because it was an essential. Thanks to a shortage of winter fodder, Europeans had to kill most of their livestock before Christmas and, despite salting, the carcases soon became putrid. Spices were necessary to disguise the meat's rank flavour, Indian pepper being the most basic requirement, followed by mace from Ceylon and cinnamon, mace and nutmeg from the Moluccas, in present-day Indonesia. These things were available from Venice and Genoa, which had a monopoly on trade with Egypt; Egypt, in turn, controlled all trade from the Far East. The mark-up was incredible: spices that sold for 3 Venetian ducats in India fetched 68 in Cairo and twice that much by the time it reached Venice. If mariners could bypass the middlemen and take a short-cut to China their fortunes were assured. All they had to do was find where that short-cut was.

Surprisingly, the answer was supplied by the Middle East. For centuries the repository of classical learning, in 1406 or thereabouts it divulged Ptolemy's *Geography*. A geographer of the second century AD, Claudius Ptolemaeus – to give him his Latin name – had not only drawn a map of the known world but had given it a scale, flattening the globe into a series of east–west lines (latitude) and north–south lines (longitude). His map was accurate within the Mediterranean but fuzzy thereafter; and although navigators could follow his latitude, they had no means of calculating the longitude. Nevertheless, armed with his map, Europe saw ways of avoiding the Muslim stranglehold. They were threefold: one could sail north over the Pole; west across the Atlantic; or east via a point where Africa might or might not end. Following the Aristotelian argument that 51 per cent of the world's surface had to be above water to stop it from sinking, and that a southern landmass must therefore exist to keep the globe in balance, Ptolemy had connected Africa to a continent that reached to the South Pole. While accepting everything else Ptolemy said, Europeans were sceptical about his view of Africa. They agreed that a southern continent might exist, but they preferred that it be separate and that Africa be a large blob, extending not very far south, around which they could sail to China, avoiding the 'torrid zones' below the equator. One nation in particular thought the African route held promise: Portugal.

In the 15th century Portugal was one of the smallest, most impoverished countries in Europe. It had barely one million inhabitants, of whom only 200 or so could be called educated. Yet it had a seafaring tradition and, above all, rulers of vision. Prince Henry the Navigator, and later Kings John II and Manoel I, pursued a policy of expansion that made it, for a while, the world's greatest mercantile nation. Portuguese trading stations sprouted along the coast of Africa, west, south and east; they flourished in Arabia, India and, above all, the spice islands of the East Indies, disrupting the Muslim monopoly that had hitherto prevailed. The wealth that accrued was unbelievable. Pepper, for example, sold in Lisbon for 40 times its price in India, and up to 2,900 tons of the stuff arrived every year. However, fortune came at a cost: roughly half the 2,400 men who sailed annually for the east died either along the way or from tropical diseases once they had arrived. By some calculations, a tenth of the country's population – or more than half its able-bodied workforce – perished in the quest. But the potential gain was worth the risk. According to the feudal system that operated not only in Portugal but in the whole of Iberia, a man had little chance of obtaining land unless he was an eldest son or a court favourite. For those favoured neither by birth nor position, the colonies were the only escape.

While benefiting from spices, Portuguese merchants also instigated a less palatable trade in slaves. Seized in Africa, they were auctioned locally before being transported either to Portugal or to one of its overseas possessions. At first they were deposited on Madeira to work the island's sugar plantations; but after the discovery and colonization of Brazil they were shipped to the other side of the Atlantic. Even hardened travellers were upset by the process. One man wrote vividly of the way in which families were divided to suit the tastes and wallets of prospective bidders: 'As often as they had placed them in one part the sons, seeing their fathers in another, rose with great energy and rushed over to them; the mothers clasped their other children in their arms, and threw themselves flat on the ground with them; receiving blows with little pity for their own flesh, if only they might not be torn from them.' But abhorrence could not be allowed to stand in the way of profit. From 1448, when the first group of 200 Africans came under the hammer, Portugal's imperial and domestic economy relied on slave labour for almost 400 years. Other nations followed suit, Britain, France and Spain in particular making free use of Africa's population. It was not until the 1800s, by which time sailors could smell a slave ship long before they saw it, that popular revulsion brought the trade to an end.

Spain, no less than Portugal, was determined to reach China, but it chose a different route. In 1492 Christopher Columbus took one of the greatest risks ever: he sailed west across the Atlantic. To explorers of every nationality, Arab and European alike, the Atlantic was horrible – the 'green sea of darkness', it was called. Using Ptolemy's map, and his own calculations, Columbus decided that China could be no more than a few weeks' journey from Spain. He found instead the West Indies – which he thought was an offshoot of Japan. Revered today as the discoverer of America, Columbus was in fact nothing of the sort. The nearest he came to the mainland was when he saw, from a distance, the mouth of the Orinoco. The true discoverers were the hundreds of conquistadores who came in his wake: men like Cortés in Mexico, Pizarro in Peru, De Soto and Coronado in Texas and Louisiana, who surged inland in search of gold and silver.

The Spanish conquest of America was swift, brutal and extremely profitable. It was also never-ending and, to some, frankly tiresome. As one 16th-century chronicler wrote, 'Oh God, what excessive labours for a life as short as man's!' But God smiled upon the conquistadores because, as they thought, they were doing His work. Their aims – and those of Europe as a whole – were encapsulated by Bernal Díaz, a conquistador who wrote openly about the reasons he went to America: 'to serve God and His Majesty, to give light to those who were in the darkness, and to grow rich, as all men desire to do'. Here was the be-all and end-all of exploration: to make money and to spread the word.

Evangelism was pronounced in the Americas, large tracts of land being handed to missionaries from one of the many Holy Orders in which Europe abounded, but it was no less urgent elsewhere. In the 12th century a letter had reached the Pope, purporting to come from a Christian ruler named Prester John. Without explaining precisely where his kingdom was, other than somewhere to the east, John wrote that he commanded a powerful army and was willing to combat the Muslim threat. It was a hoax, emanating probably from a Greek or Byzantine cleric, but it pandered artfully to Europe's sense of insecurity. One of the first signs of Europe's rebirth came in the 12th century, when its rulers formed an alliance to seize the Holy Land for Christianity. Initially they were successful, conquering the entire eastern Mediterranean seaboard. But the occupation of Outremer, as they called it, was short-lived. Bit by bit, the Muslims regained control of the lost territory until, by the time Marco Polo left for China in 1271, there was only one small Crusader kingdom clinging to Jerusalem; when he returned in 1295 that too had been overwhelmed. The loss was not easily forgotten: every captain who sailed east thereafter did so in the hope of finding Prester John. When Vasco da Gama reached India in 1498, for example, he was asked why he had made the long journey. 'We come,' he replied, 'in search of Christians and spices.' But Prester John was not to be found in India or Asia. In the end, with some disappointment, explorers decided that the only possible candidate was the king of Ethiopia, who was indeed a Christian, although an impoverished and powerless one. They gave the puzzled man a medal to confirm his status and let the matter drop.

Iberia's successes left northern Europe at a disadvantage. Excluded by papal decree from encroaching on either the West or East Indies, England, Holland and France sought their own routes to China. Three possible avenues presented themselves: the first, and shortest, was to sail directly over the North Pole, following the widely held belief that it comprised an open, temperate sea surrounded by ice. Should the pack ice prove impenetrable (as it did), there remained two other possibilities: to follow its southern fringes either east or west. The North-East Passage, running above Siberia, was for a while considered the most promising. After several disastrous attempts, however, navigators and merchants went in search of the North-West Passage.* This too eluded them, but it produced an unexpected side benefit: the colonization of North America. In 1609, after a remarkable journey in search of both the North-East and North-West Passages, the English navigator Henry Hudson claimed the future New York for his Dutch paymasters. His discovery prompted others to sail west, among them Sir Walter Raleigh, who established a colony on the east coast at a place he named Virginia. The colony failed, but it was soon replaced by others. In the interim Europe was transformed by exotic plants – tobacco, pumpkins and potatoes – that Raleigh had transplanted from the New World. After a while northern Europeans gave not a fig for the papal decree that had split the world between Spain and Portugal. They went forth and conquered. Soon it was hard to distinguish between explorers and buccaneers, men like Sir Francis Drake not only circumnavigating the world but shelling every Iberian settlement and ship they encountered.

By the 17th century Europeans had ascertained the presence and rough outline of every habitable continent – including Australia, whose southern coast, along with the northern tip of New Zealand, was charted by Abel Janszoon Tasman between 1642 and 1644 – and, thanks to the printing press, had made their discoveries available to anyone who could read. No longer were they the ignoramuses of the world; they were its masters. In the past 300 years their continent had experienced a revival so comprehensive that it was hard to equate it with the place that had believed in men with no heads and a self-basting equator. They had asserted their authority in every discipline from art to astronomy, and in large measure they had done so because of explorers. The wealth, the knowledge and even the plants that early travellers brought home contributed to Europe's revival. Encapsulating the mood of what would later be dubbed the Renaissance, an Italian scholar wrote: 'Thank God it has been permitted to us to be born in this new age, so full of hope and promise.'

---

* To put their obsession in context, both the North-East and North-West Passages still occupy businessmen today. From Europe to Japan, the sea journey through the Suez Canal is 11,000 miles long and takes 35 days. The same trip via the North-East Passage is 7,000 miles and takes 22 days. In an age when the Suez Canal did not exist, and when it took several months to reach the Far East via the Cape of Good Hope, these northern routes must have seemed exquisitely tempting.

Marco Polo (1271–95)

'The greatest joy a man can have is victory: to conquer one's enemy's armies, to pursue them, to deprive them of their possessions, to reduce their families to tears, to ride on their horses, and to make love to their wives and daughters.' Whether Genghis Khan actually said these words is uncertain. There is no doubt, however, that they represented a philosophy to which he subscribed wholeheartedly. In 1207 he led his horsemen out of Mongolia on the most ambitious and brutal programme of conquest the world has ever seen. The rapidity with which the Mongols advanced was astonishing: by 1223 they had overrun Persia and were ensconced in the Crimean Peninsula; by 1241 they had conquered Moscow, defeated the Poles, swept through Moravia and Silesia, and occupied Hungary; by 1261 they had taken Syria and were at the borders of Egypt; 19 years later, turning in their tracks, they completed the conquest of China, bringing a nation of 90 million people under their control. In due course they occupied northern India, and were only prevented from taking Japan – where they deployed gunpowder artillery for the first time in history – by a storm that wrecked their fleet and entered Japanese legend as the 'Divine Wind', or *kamikaze*.

The Mongols relied for their success on mobility, tactical skill and, above all, ferocity. Wherever they went they slaughtered indiscriminately, casualties rising as they drove a terrified populace before them: 700,000 died at Merv, 1,600,000 at Herat, 1,747,000 at Nishapur. No quarter was given, no prisoners taken. At Nishapur the survivors were decapitated, and pyramids made of their skulls – one each for men, women and children. Even the dogs and cats were killed. Then the buildings were razed. The city simply ceased to exist. If the numbers of dead were exaggerated, it served the Mongols' needs very satisfactorily, for this was a holocaust based on fear. There was no refuge to be found even in religion: when Baghdad fell, among the two million deaths recorded by one 14th-century historian was that of the Caliph, spiritual leader of Islam. As Genghis sneered, 'I am the flail of God. If you had not committed great sins, God would not have sent a punishment like me upon you.'

By 1260 the Mongols had created the largest land-based empire in the history of the world, stretching from the Pacific to the Dnieper River and

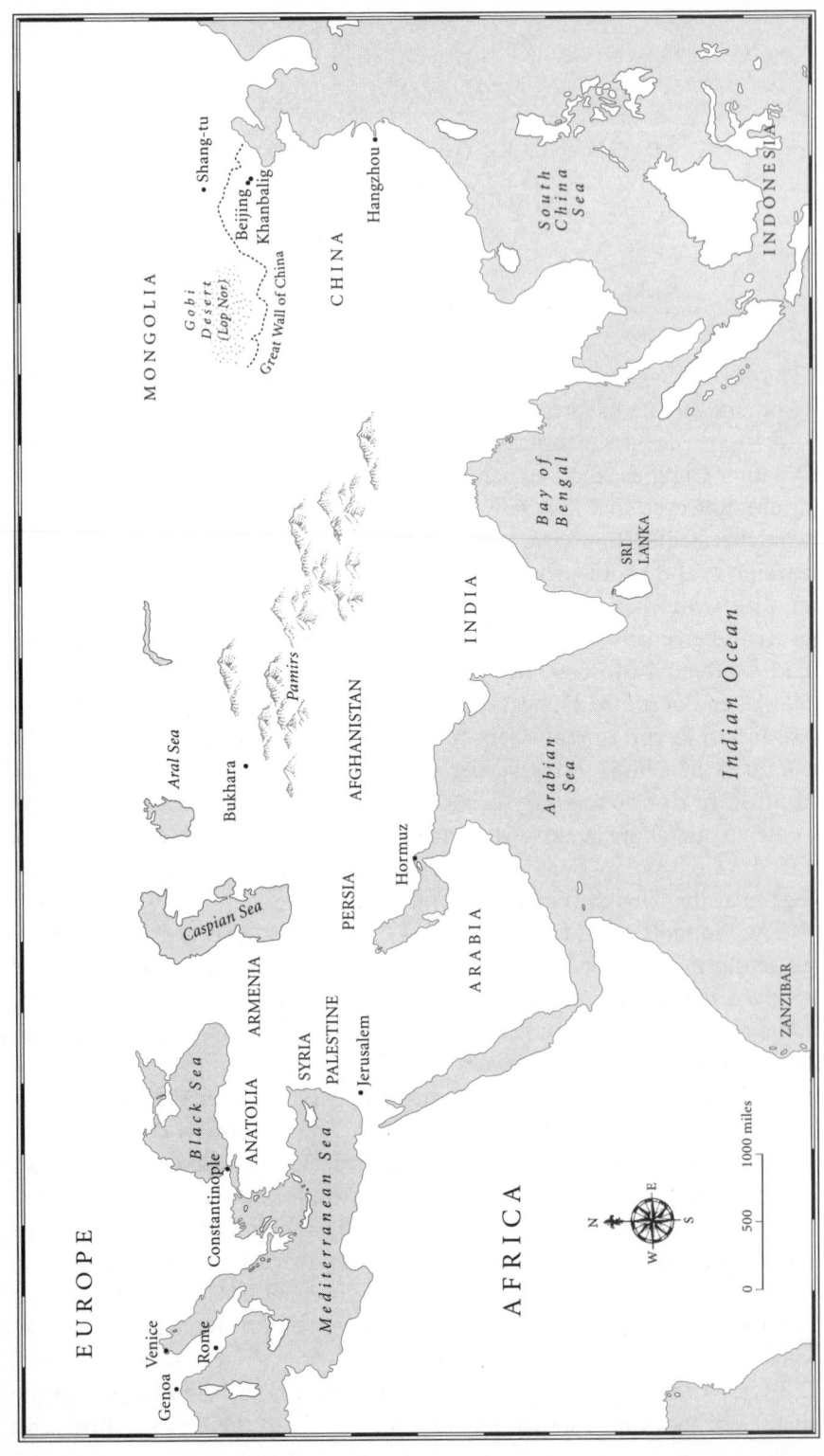

from Siberia to the Straits of Malacca. It was not a particularly cohesive empire, being divided into autonomous khanates, the two largest being the Ilkhanate of Persia and the Empire of the Great Khan, which comprised China and the Mongolian heartland. Nor did it last very long: by the 14th century the various khans had asserted their independence, adopted the customs of the civilizations they had overrrun, and soon all was much as it had been before. For a short while in the mid-13th century, however, Asia was united in a terror-inspired Pax Mongolica that allowed unprecedented freedom of movement. It was now possible for Europeans to travel unhindered to the easternmost parts of the continent – an opportunity they did not hesitate to seize. Among the first were two Franciscan missionaries, Giovanni di Piano Carpini, who left for the Empire of the Great Khan in 1245, and William of Rubruk, who followed him eight years later. They made no converts and found, to their surprise, that the Mongols already knew about Christianity, there being a sizeable community of Nestorians, as well as several Europeans who had either been taken captive or had made their own way to the Khan's court,* but they did return with written records of their journey. Possibly inspired by these accounts, two Venetian merchants, the brothers Niccolo and Maffeo Polo, embarked in 1260 for the Far East.

The Polos sailed to the Mongol-controlled Crimea – where there existed a small Venetian colony, one of whose members was the Polos' brother, Marco the Elder – then proceeded via the Volga to Bukhara. Here they spent three years before hitching a ride with a diplomatic mission on its way from the Ilkhanate to the Empire of the Great Khan. It was not a chance encounter. News of their presence had already aroused the curiosity of the Great Khan – by this time Kubilai, grandson of Genghis – and he had sent emissaries to his cousin in Persia to offer the strangers safe conduct to the east, because he 'had never seen any Latin and very much wanted to meet one'. Thus, the two Venetians found themselves in the Mongol capital of Khanbalig, near modern Beijing. It was an impressive city, whose walls were 30 feet high, 60 feet wide, and had a circumference of 24 miles. They were greeted with affability by the Khan, who grilled them for a full year on the political and religious state of Europe. When it came to Christianity he was curious but sceptical. 'Why should I become a Christian?' he asked. 'You can see for yourselves that the Christians who live in these parts are so ignorant that they cannot do anything, while these idolaters can do what they like. When I sit at table they can send cups out in the middle of the hall, full of wine or anything else, straight to my hand without anyone touching them, when I wish to drink. They can send bad weather packing in any direction they choose. And as you know, their idols talk and tell them whatever they want to know.'

---

* The émigrés included the nephew of an English bishop, a Frenchwoman from Lorraine who cooked Guillaume de Roubrouk's meals, and a Parisian silversmith named Boucher, who constructed an ornate automatic alcohol fountain of such complexity that it never worked and required the insertion of a small person to operate its mechanism from within.

The Mongols were essentially shamanistic, but Kubilai was a broad-minded man, tolerant of the religions that flourished in his empire and willing to accept whichever proved the most effective. But he worried that Christianity might not work. As he told the Venetians: 'My barons and others who do not believe in Christ would ask me, "Whatever are you thinking of, getting baptised and adopting the faith of Christ? Have you seen any virtues or miracles to his credit?"' He therefore ordered the Polos to lead an ambassador to the Pope. What the Great Khan would appreciate was 'up to one hundred men learned in the Christian religion, well versed in the seven arts and skilled to argue and demonstrate plainly to idolaters and those of other religions that their religion is utterly mistaken'. He asked, too, for some oil from the lamp in Jerusalem's Church of the Holy Sepulchre. The passports he gave them indicated the wealth and power at his disposal: they instructed all citizens to give the bearers free passage on pain of death, they measured 12 inches by 3 and they were made of solid gold.

The Polos reached Rome without the emissary, who had fallen ill on the way, and by 1271 were once again on their way to China. They had no trouble obtaining holy oil from Jerusalem, but the hundred learned men were beyond the Pope's means – there were barely that many in the whole of Europe – so they accepted instead two friars, Brother William and Brother Nicholas. They also took Niccolo's 16-year-old son Marco. Travelling through Palestine, Syria and Turkey, the party reached Armenia, where the friars turned back, appalled by the rigours of the journey and the hazards that lay ahead. With now only the holy oil to show for their efforts, the Polos struck south into Persia.

Although the Pax Mongolica had largely eliminated the wars and border squabbles which hampered trade with China, it was still a considerable feat to cross from one side of Asia to the other. The continent was so vast, its terrain on occasion so inhospitable and its facilities so rudimentary that few people braved the whole traverse. Marco Polo, who was to become the expedition's chronicler, described vividly the conditions they met: 'Here merchants travelling from one country to another have to cope with extensive deserts: dry, barren sandy regions where no grass or fodder suitable for horses is to be found. Freshwater wells and springs lie so far apart that travellers must make long marches if their beasts are to get anything to drink.' The Polo family eschewed horses in favour of asses – 'fast, steady and cheaper to keep' – on which they reached the Gulf port of Hormuz. The place was hot, unhealthy and decrepit, and the ships so ramshackle that they refused to sail in them, catching instead a caravan through central Asia. Again they plodded through deserts, spending seven days at a time without meeting a well, until they reached the foothills of the Pamirs.

Marco Polo was impressed: 'These mountains are so high that it takes a man a full day, from dawn to dusk, to climb them from the bottom to the top.' He had fallen ill and, like 19th-century consumptives who flocked to the Alps, he too found relief in the highlands. 'The air on the high tops is so pure and healthy that if any town-dweller falls ill with even the most severe kind of fever, all he has to do is go up into the mountains and a few days' rest there will restore him to complete health. I, Messer Marco, can vouch for this from personal experience.' At the top of the Pamir plateau Marco Polo was frightened by a strange phenomenon: fires burned less brightly than before, their flames had an unnatural colour and they took longer to cook a meal. At 15,600 feet Polo was experiencing the effects of altitude. Five centuries later, this would become an accepted fact of Alpine exploration, scientists measuring the height of mountains by how long it took to boil a kettle. At the time, Polo put it down to the severe cold.

He did not like the journey into Afghanistan, describing the inhabitants as 'utter savages, living entirely by the chase and dressed in the skins of beasts. They are thoroughly bad.' Nor did he relish his passage through the Lop Nor, or Gobi Desert: 'This desert is reported to be so long that it would take a year to go from end to end; and at the narrowest point it takes a month to cross it. It consists entirely of mountains and sand and valleys. There is nothing at all to eat ... When a man is riding through this desert by night and for some reason – falling asleep, or anything else – he gets separated from his companions and wants to rejoin them, he hears spirit voices talking to him as if they were his companions, sometimes even calling him by name. Often these voices lure him away from the path and he never finds it again, and many travellers have got lost and died because of this ... Because of all this, groups of travellers make a point of sticking close together. Before they go to sleep they put up a sign pointing in the direction in which they want to travel.' From the Gobi, however, it was not far to the Great Wall of China, and from there it was a straightforward passage to Kubilai's summer residence, Shang-tu.

Kubilai accepted their gift of holy oil, along with various letters they had brought from the Pope, and if he was disappointed not to receive the hundred Christian savants he did not let it show. Indeed, according to Marco Polo, he was so pleased to see the Venetians that he gave them royal treatment and promoted them to 'a place of honour above the other barons'. And later, in a remarkable twist, he made them his personal roving ambassadors, charged with the task of reporting on his domains. At one point they led an expedition to Sri Lanka and the spice islands of Indonesia. Or so, at least, Marco Polo claimed. In the account he later published of their stay in China he would exaggerate, dissemble and occasionally lie: his statement that he became governor of Hang-chow province, for example, is almost certainly untrue; in all likelihood he did not visit personally many of the places he said he had; nor are his tales corroborated by any existing Mongol or Chinese source. But whatever the exact truth, it seems that the Polos came in close contact with the Khan and that under his aegis they travelled widely throughout the Far East. It was a job that occupied them for the next 17 years. Marco Polo, who professed to speak four languages, recorded it all.

He was amazed by the marvels he encountered. One was a strange ore, found on the fringes of the Gobi, that was battered and washed until it produced little fibres that were then woven into cloth. It was a seemingly indestructible material, and to clean it all one had to do was throw it in the fire. Marco Polo called it 'salamander' – nowadays it is better known as asbestos. Another wonder was a black, combustible stone. 'These stones keep a fire going better than wood,' he wrote. 'If you put them on the fire in the evening and see that they are well alight, they will continue to burn all night, so that you will find them still glowing in the morning.' He was referring to coal, a substance familiar to northern Europeans – Londoners had been generating a heavy smog for many decades – but completely new to the Polos. He was struck, too, by the plethora of bath-houses these stones were used to heat: 'there is no one who does not visit a bath-house at least three times a week – in winter, every day if he can manage it'. No less surprising was the use of paper currency, made from mulberry bark. 'With these pieces of paper they can buy anything and pay for anything,' wrote Polo. 'You might as well say [the Khan] has mastered the art of alchemy.' He described, too, porcelain bowls 'of incomparable beauty', and the protracted manner in which they were made: 'These dishes are made of a crumbly earth or clay which is dug as though from a mine. Stacked in huge mounds, it is then left for thirty or forty years exposed to the wind, rain and sun. By this time the earth is so refined that dishes made from it are of a pale blue tint with a very brilliant sheen. You must understand that when a man makes a mound of this earth he does so for his heirs; it takes so long to mature that he cannot hope to draw any profit from it himself or to put it to use, but the son who succeeds him will reap the benefit.' And then there was the postal system, by which messages could be delivered across the empire with an efficiency simply unknown in Europe. The very slowest class of letter, carried by runners between relay posts three miles apart, took 24 hours to cover a distance that would normally take ten days. Second-class post went on horseback, switching hands every 25 miles. And first-class was carried non-stop by a single rider who sounded a horn when he was approaching a relay stage, giving the occupants just time to bring out a new mount. In this manner, according to Polo, a man could cover 250–300 miles a day. To emphasize the sheer scale and wealth of the Great Khan's empire he recorded that more than 1,000 cartloads of silk arrived at Khanbalig every day.

As for the Khan himself, Polo could barely find the superlatives to describe his lifestyle. The palace at Khanbalig had four gates, guarded by 1,000 men apiece. The royal quarters blazed with gold, silver and lacquer, and held a dining hall capable of seating 6,000 people. At state banquets, such as Kubilai's birthday (28 September), a further 40,000 guests spilled out into the surrounding courtyards. 'The number of chambers is quite bewildering. The whole palace is at once so immense and so well constructed that no one in the world, granted that he had the resources, could imagine any improvement in design or execution.' Its landscaped grounds contained an arboretum of evergreen trees, selected by Kubilai himself, that had been uprooted from around the empire and carried there by elephant. To give them extra lustre he covered the man-made hills on which they were planted with lumps of lapis lazuli. In June Kubilai took his court *en masse* to Shang-tu, their departure in August being marked by a ceremony involving the entire imperial stud – the mares, all of them white, numbered more than 10,000. The royal hunt – in fact, a form of military exercise – comprised two groups of 10,000 riders, each accompanied by 5,000 hounds, who manoeuvred in formations across the countryside. When hawking – a sport that he loved – the Khan travelled in a gold-lined portable hunting-lodge, carried by four elephants and equipped with a trapdoor so that he could loose his birds without rising from his bed. In his private parks he released trained tigers to chase deer to feed the falcons. His harem was selected by talent scouts from an initial group of 'some four or five hundred, more or less', who were then whittled down in a series of beauty contests, the finalists being handed to court officials' wives 'to observe them carefully at night in their chambers to make sure that they are virgins and not blemished or defective in any member, that they sleep sweetly without snoring, and that their breath is sweet and they give out no unpleasant odour'. The chosen few were then sent to the Khan's chambers in groups of six, to be replaced after three days with a new quota.

On and on Polo went. He clearly admired Kubilai and, equally clearly, he inflated statistics to support the Great Khan's magnificence. He also tried to link him to the mythical Christian kingdom ruled by Prester John. But his account was not a complete fabrication. Even allowing for distortions, there emerges a picture of a ruler so powerful, and a civilization so advanced, that 13th-century Europe seemed barbaric by comparison. At one point Polo remarked that 'all the world's great potentates put together do not have such riches as belong to the Great Khan alone'. In this he was probably correct.

Between the hero-worship and the legend-spinning, Polo's narrative included acute descriptions of people and places. There was Kubilai Khan himself: a plump man of moderate height whose complexion was 'fair and ruddy like a rose, the eyes black and handsome, the nose shapely and set squarely in place'. In the south he reported the explosive sounds that bamboos made when they were burned. He told how the inhabitants of Hang-chow loved lakes and boating, and how the Burmese built magnificent pagodas and were addicted to tattooing. He described a battle between Mongol horsemen and a rebel army equipped with elephants. He tried valiantly to interpret the Buddhist philosophy of reincarnation. He recorded how the people of the north drank kumiss (fermented mare's milk), how the Chinese preferred rice wine and how the people of Sumatra collected wine straight from the toddy-palm. And, in mercantile fashion, he listed the goods produced by each region and how much they sold for.

To what extent the elder Polos accompanied Marco in his wanderings is unknown. Probably they went about their own commercial business, with or without the precocious youngster. And probably, too, at the end of 17 years, it was their pressure that persuaded Marco finally to abandon China. Kubilai was reluctant to let them go, 'But when the Great Khan saw that Messer Niccolo and Messer Maffeo and Messer Marco were ready to leave, he ordered all three to be brought into his presence. He then gave them two gold tablets proclaiming that they might travel freely through his realm, and that wherever they went they should receive provisions for themselves and their attendants. He entrusted them with a message for the Pope and the kings of France and Spain, and the other kings of Christendom.' In the end, they had no need of the passports: the Ilkhan of Persia had requested a wife from the Great Khan's court, and Kubilai allowed her to join the party.

The overland route being blocked by internecine wars, they travelled by sea. In true style, Kubilai gave them a fleet of 14 ships grander than anything they had seen in their lives. The Venetian ships to which the Polos were accustomed were sturdy but small, designed for the Mediterranean and Black Seas. These, however, were huge ocean-going junks, whose holds were capacious enough to contain not only provisions for a two-year journey but every item of value the Polos had accumulated during their stay. The importance of this last could not be exaggerated. If they had had to travel overland the Polos would have lost most of their goods to regional taxes, extortion and robbery. Now they were being offered a ticket to Persia that allowed them to avoid the usual duties and that was, above all, free.

Packed with profitable cargo, and carrying not just the Polos and the Ilkhan's future wife but a reserve princess in case the first one died, the fleet left for Persia. As was universal seafaring practice, it sailed close to the shore, which allowed Polo to add further exotic touches to his journal. He described the coasts of Sri Lanka, India and Arabia, and pretended also that he had been to Zanzibar and Madagascar, which he said was the end of the world, the winds being so strong that once a ship sailed south it could never return. He reported, too, on a pair of strange islands in the Indian Ocean, one inhabited by men, the other by women, whose populations conjoined between March and May to procreate, then separated again, the children being brought up on Female Island until they were 14, whereupon they were separated according to their sex.

For some reason – either disease, piracy, local wars or shipwreck – the Great Khan's fleet lost 540 men and several vessels during the journey. The Polos, however, were among the survivors and eventually docked at Hormuz, which they found as vile as the last time they had been there. They had expected to deliver the princesses and then withdraw swiftly to Venice. But it was not to be. The Ilkhan had died during their voyage, and his successor did not want the Chinese princesses. He told the Polos to take the women to the Ilkhan's son, who was currently on the northern border. They did so,

Marco Polo adding another extravagant chapter to his journal, including a brief description of the Arctic Circle ('a region where there is perpetual darkness'), then travelled overland to the Black Sea, from where they caught a ship to Constantinople, finally reaching home in 1295.

Clad in unfamiliar clothes, accompanied by Mongol slaves, and bearing the goods they had acquired in the Far East, the Polos must have caused a stir, even in a cosmopolitan trading city such as Venice. Legends would later arise, telling how they were at first mistaken for tramps until they opened the seams of their robes to reveal strings of precious stones. Little is known for certain, however, about either their arrival or their subsequent fates. The only ascertainable facts concerning Marco Polo are that he was captured a year or two later at sea, in a battle between the Genoese and Venetian fleets, and was not released until May 1299. During his time in prison he met a professional writer, Rusticiano of Pisa, with whom he collaborated to produce an account of his stay in the Empire of the Great Khan. It was called, immodestly but not inaccurately, *A Description of the World*. The book was mocked for its exaggerations – by 1305 Polo's inflated figures had already earned him the nickname *Il Milione* ('The Million') – but when its author died in 1324, at the age of 70, he refused to retract anything. On the contrary, he insisted that 'I never told the half of what I saw'.

Marco Polo's *Description* became the most influential work of its age. By the time of his death the Pax Mongolica had expired, Cathay (as Europeans called China) was once again an unreachable country, and for several centuries his book was the most comprehensive source of information on the Far East. Merchants, adventurers and mapmakers drew upon it, accepting fact and fiction indiscriminately. It was the bedrock upon which European exploration was built. As Polo explained in his last sentence, 'I believe it was God's will that we should return, so that men might know the things that are in the world, since ... there was never man yet, Christian or Saracen, Tartar or Pagan, who explored so much of the world as Messer Marco, son of Messer Niccolo, great and noble citizen of the city of Venice.'

The wanderings of Ibn Battuta (1325–55)

When the Prophet Mohammed died, on 8 June 632, he left as his legacy one of the fastest growing religions of the millennium. By the 14th century Islam had taken root in countries as far afield as Spain and the East Indies, creating not exactly an empire but a network of kingdoms united by a single faith. Wherever a traveller went within the Dar al-Islam, or 'Home of Islam', he could expect to find the same laws, the same religious ceremonies, the same customs and often the same food and clothes. Unlike Europe, which in the same period was an insular, ignorant and frequently barbaric place, the Islamic world was cosmopolitan, civilized and above all well-travelled: every believer was encouraged to make, at least once in a lifetime, the *hajj*, or pilgrimage, to Mecca; and year by year Muslim merchants established new trade links with the east, assisted by navigators whose maps and instruments were of unrivalled sophistication. Yet for all this homogeneity, and for all the to-ing and fro-ing, inhabitants at either end of the Dar al-Islam knew remarkably little about each other. The situation changed, almost accidentally, when, in 1325, a 21-year-old legal student left Tangier to make the *hajj*. His name was Abu Abdullah Mohammed ibn Battuta.

There were two ways to make the *hajj*. The first, and most spiritually rewarding, was to go on foot. The second, and most realistic – also the safer – was to go by ship or by camel. Ibn Battuta chose the latter, travelling with a caravan of pilgrims across North Africa to the Middle East. Ibn Battuta appears to have been a charming man, who impressed people wherever he went with his piety, his intellectual curiosity and his affability. (He acquired two wives during his trip across the Maghreb.) He also demonstrated a remarkable inability to stick to his chosen course, taking sudden detours whenever they presented themselves, and refusing to retrack on the grounds that it was best 'never to travel the same route for a second time'. It was in Egypt that his *hajj* took its first unexpected turn.

Thanks to its domination of the Far Eastern spice trade, and the stability conferred by its powerful Mamluk rulers, Egypt was then the richest nation in the Middle East. In fact, it virtually *was* the Middle East, its dominions extending not only along the Nile but as far north as Syria. With 600,000 inhabitants, the capital Cairo was the most populous city west of China – its population was 15 times that of London – and as one Italian traveller wrote in 1384, more people lived in a single street than in the whole of Florence. The port of Alexandria was the grandest in the Mediterranean, with not one but two spacious harbours – the eastern for Christian ships, the western for Muslim – separated by the towering Pharos lighthouse, one of the seven wonders of the ancient world, whose beam was visible several miles out to sea. As for the Nile, it was probably the most profitable river on the globe: the silt deposited by its annual flood supported myriad farmers; and for merchants who landed in the Red Sea it offered the quickest and easiest means of getting their spices to Alexandria.

Ibn Battuta had never seen anything like it. 'There is a continuous series of bazaars from the city of Alexandria to Cairo,' he wrote. 'Cities and villages succeed one another along its banks without interruption and have no equal in the inhabited world, nor is any river known whose basin is so intensively cultivated as that of the Nile. There is no river on earth but it, which is called a sea.' Because of its geographical situation and its prosperity, Egypt became the bulletin board of the Dar al-Islam, a place where merchants and religious men from around the world met to exchange their news. Here one might encounter traders from the east coast of Africa, from the newly established Delhi Sultanate in India, from the East Indies and beyond. Wherever Muslim merchants went, news of their discoveries reached Cairo within a year or two.

Ibn Battuta's home town of Tangier was also a trading port, but compared to Alexandria it appeared ridiculously insignificant. In his charming way – and thanks to the tradition of hospitality that pervaded the Dar al-Islam – he found quarters with a revered Sufi ascetic. Casually, the man mentioned that he had three friends, two in India, one in China, whom he thought Ibn Battuta might like to visit. Looking back on the remark, Ibn Battuta wrote, 'I was amazed by his prediction, and the idea of these countries having been cast into my mind, my wanderings never ceased'. First, however, he had to complete his *hajj*. He travelled to the Red Sea where, his passage to Arabia being blocked by local wars, he retreated to Cairo and took the main highway to Damascus (where he acquired a third wife), before catching a caravan south to Mecca. From Syria the road south led through deserts and mountains, whose climate was both extreme and unpredictable: one year 100 pilgrims died of exposure to the winter cold; another year 3,000 perished from heat and thirst; in yet another a whole caravan was swamped by sandstorms. His own party survived the crossing, but even so he judged it a 'fearsome wilderness'. He spent several months studying in Mecca and then, for no reason other than curiosity, joined a caravan to Mesopotamia (modern Iraq).

Swollen by pilgrims returning on foot, the convoy left Mecca on 17 November 1326. It was so enormous that 'Anyone who left the caravan for a natural want and had no mark by which to guide himself to his place could not find

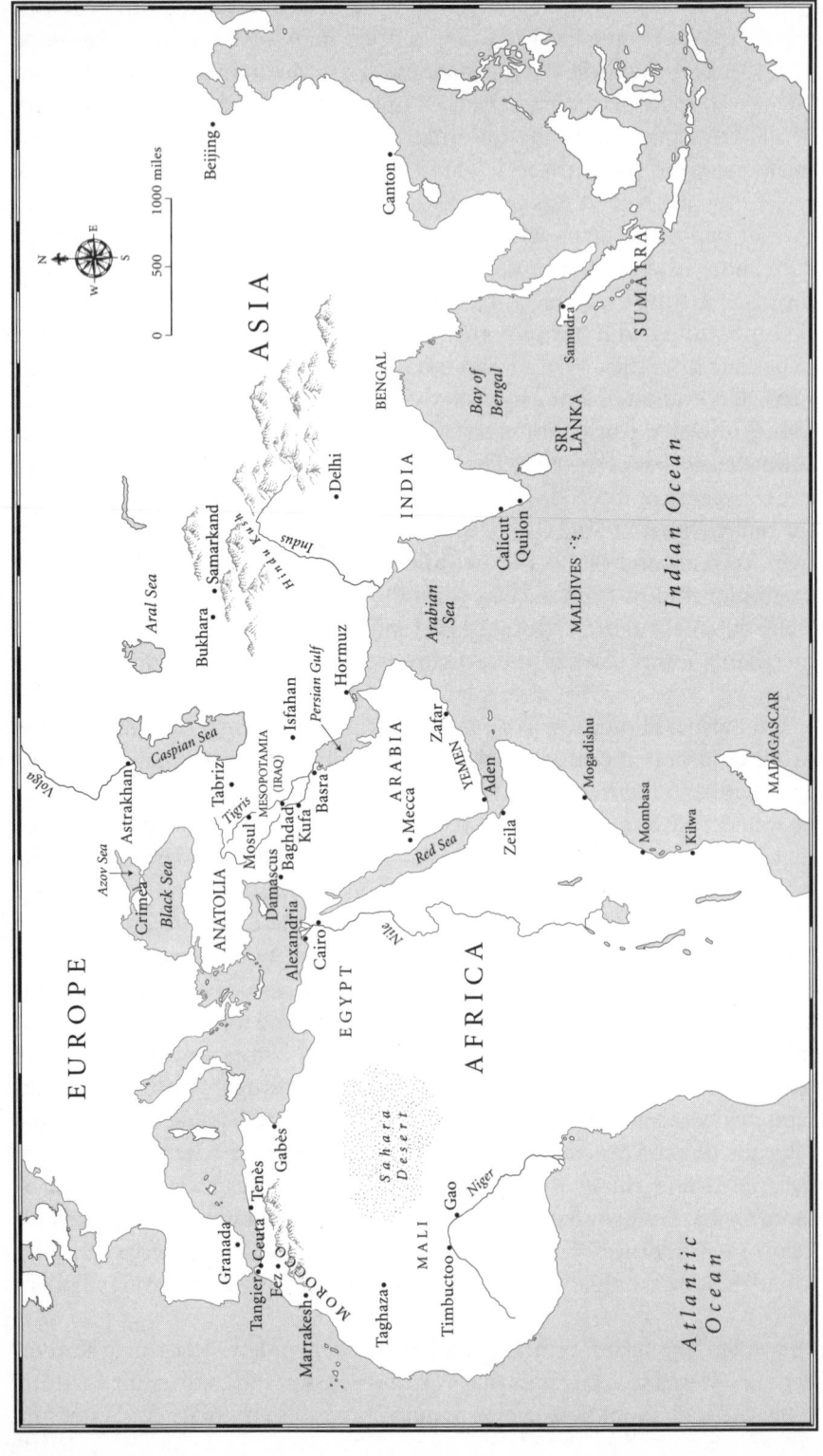

it again for the vast number of people'. Ibn Battuta was not among the foot travellers, having persuaded an official to buy him one half of a double camel litter. Thus ensconced, he revelled in their journey through the Arabian Peninsula. The landscape was hostile, but they were well equipped to face it. They carried enough water, they had 'great supplies of luxuries', the poorer members were given free water, food and medicine, and after their *hajj* everyone felt illuminated – not only spiritually but literally since, travelling by night to avoid the heat, they lit torches 'so that you saw the countryside gleaming with light and the darkness turned into radiant day'. After 44 days this gigantic glow-worm of humanity emerged on the other side of the desert, to be greeted by the citizens of Kufa bearing fresh supplies of bread, dates and fruit.

Mesopotamia fell within the Mongol Ilkhanate, whose ruler had recently decreed – to the dismay of Christian deputations from Rome and Byzantium – that his realm should adopt Islam. As a result, Ibn Battuta was shown extravagant hospitality by officials keen to demonstrate their enthusiasm for the new religion. It was not just his personability that attracted them but the fact that he spoke Arabic and could recite the Koran in its original, purest form. Under their protection he visited Basra, Baghdad, Isfahan, Tabriz and other venerable centres – marvelling at how these once great cities were still in ruins from the Mongol invasions of more than a century ago – before travelling up the Tigris to Mosul and then returning to Mecca. In the course of a year he had covered more than 4,000 miles. And he had done it all for no other reason than that, as he explained, he 'thought it a good plan'. It was a phrase that would become the leitmotif of 30 years' wanderings. Almost as soon as he reached Mecca, in late 1327, another 'good plan' presented itself: instead of returning to Morocco, he would go to the Delhi Sultanate.

The current Sultan of Delhi, Mohammed Tughluq, was a volatile, non-conformist autocrat, who had recently annexed most of India. But although wealthy beyond imagination, his empire lacked sophistication. Therefore, in a blunt-spoken way, he advertised for Islamic poets, theologians, judges and men of letters to join his court. They came in their hundreds, drawn both by the legendary generosity of the Sultan and by the near certainty of being promoted to a high position. Ibn Battuta decided to join the throng but, in habitual fashion, he went about it in the longest and most circuitous manner possible. Accompanied by a friend named Abdullah al-Tuzri, he sailed down the Red Sea, touching at ports such as Aden and Zeila – 'the dirtiest, most disagreeable, and most stinking town in the world' – then rounded the Horn of Africa and proceeded to the ports of Mogadishu, Mombasa and Kilwa, sailing almost as far south as Madagascar.

East Africa was the frontier zone of the Dar al-Islam: a region of great natural wealth, scarcely touched by Islamic civilization save for one or two outposts on the coast from which a small number of adventurers launched sporadic campaigns against the unbelievers of the interior. The merchants' houses were large and airy, with running water, all amenities and inconceivably colourful gardens, but outside the grand, three-storey mansions with their fountained courtyards everything was basic. The ports were frontier settlements which existed solely for the processing of gold, ivory, ostrich feathers, animal pelts and, above all, slaves, all of which were taken to the Middle East by dhow – fragile but flexible vessels whose hulls were constructed not of overlapping, iron-nailed strakes but of abutting boards sewn together by lengths of coconut fibre. While generally approving of the way in which these ports conducted themselves, Ibn Battuta had the city-dweller's contempt for life in the wilds. In Mogadishu he partook of a meal that comprised copious amounts of meat poured over ghee-fried rice, unripe bananas in milk and a dish of sour milk with ginger, mangoes, pickled lemons and chilli. Observing the way his hosts tucked in, he wrote: 'A single person [here] eats as much as a whole company of us would eat, as a matter of habit, and they are corpulent and fat in the extreme.'

Ibn Battuta's aim had been to catch the monsoon winds from Africa to India, but he changed his mind. If he went by sea he would arrive unannounced and friendless. Perhaps it would be better to take the overland route through Central Asia in order to cultivate useful contacts along the way. Therefore he sailed north to the Persian Gulf – he and al-Tuzri very nearly losing their lives when they took an overland trip through the Yemen and were misled by an avaricious guide who hoped to steal their belongings once they had died in the desert – before recrossing the Arabian Peninsula to the Red Sea, and from Egypt making his way to Anatolia and the Crimea. The Crimea, like Persia, was ruled by a Mongol – in this case the Kipchak Khan, or the Khan of the Golden Horde.* A less prosperous relative of the Ilkhan, Khan Ozbeg of the Golden Horde had also converted to Islam and, like his cousin, he welcomed men of learning. He was a hard man to find, constantly shifting from one border to another, but in May 1332 Ibn Battuta caught up with him. Camped on a low hill to the north of the Azov Sea, he saw a massive convoy of horse-drawn wagons carrying houses, bazaars, mosques and kitchens, the smoke from its fires drifting into the air to give the impression of nothing less than 'a vast city on the move'. This was the Khan and his personal escort.

As soon as he made himself known, Ibn Battuta was given the freedom of the caravan. He found some of the Khan's practices offensive, such as his habit of greeting a wife (of which he had many) in the presence of his court and inviting her to sit down before he did. 'All this is done in full view of those present,' he wrote, 'and without any use of veils.' His sense of decorum, however, did not prevent him investigating the circumstances in which the chief wife, or *khatun*, lived. Marco Polo, whose book Ibn Battuta had not read, had been criticized for overstating the grandeur of Kubilai Khan's court

* The name had nothing to do with the number of his men, but came from the Turkish word *ordu*, meaning tent.

in China. Ibn Battuta's description of a *khatun's* entourage suggests that Polo was not exaggerating in the slightest. Although one of the minor Mongol khans, Ozbeg put on a show only slightly less splendid that that of Kubilai himself. The *khatun's* wagon was drawn by horses draped in gilt silk, and preceded by 10 or 15 slaves clad similarly in gold tunics encrusted with jewels, and bearing maces wrapped in golf leaf. Behind came another 100 wagons, each of them carrying four slave girls, followed in turn by a further 300 wagons containing the *khatun's* clothes, food and jewels. When added to the trains of the Khan's other wives, the Khan's officers and the Khan himself, not to mention the stream of servants and vehicles required to support them, the sight was spectacular.

Ibn Battuta and al-Tuzri (who soon faded from Ibn Battuta's journal and whose fate is unknown) accompanied this fantastical procession as far as Astrakhan, where he learned that Ozbeg's third wife, a daughter of the Emperor of Byzantium, wished to give birth at her father's home. With another 'good plan' in the offing, Ibn Battuta asked if he could accompany her. Ozbeg gave him his permission, 1,500 dinars, a valuable robe and several horses. Each of Ozbeg's wives donated several silver ingots, his daughter gave even more, and by the time Ibn Battuta left on 5 July 1332 he was weighed down with a large amount of bullion as well as a 'collection of horses, robes, and furs of miniver and sable'. They were accompanied by 5,000 Mongol horsemen, 500 soldiers of the *khatun's* personal escort, 200 slave girls, 20 pages, 400 wagons, 2,000 horses and 500 oxen. Like Kubilai, Ozbeg did nothing by halves.

At the border with Byzantium Ozbeg's wife proclaimed herself a Christian and sent the Khan's troops home, keeping only her own escort and Ibn Battuta. Stoically, he mentioned that 'Inner sentiments . . . suffered a change through our entry into the land of infidelity'. But he was happy that the Byzantine commander had one of his men beaten for laughing at the Muslims at prayer and was overjoyed when the Emperor of Byzantium gave him yet more robes and money. The Emperor's daughter said she would like to remain in Byzantium, so Ibn Battuta made a brief journey into Thrace before returning to the Golden Horde at the end of autumn 1332. He did not go far before he met the cold winter of the lower Ukrainian steppe. It was so icy, he said, that 'I used to perform my ablutions with hot water close to the fire, but not a drop of water fell without being frozen on the instant'. When he washed his face the water froze on his beard, and when he shook his head the ice fell in showers like dandruff. He hid within three fur coats, two pairs of trousers, two layers of socks and a pair of boots lined with bearskin. But, as he lamented, this did not ease matters: 'I was unable to mount a horse because of the quantity of clothes I had on, so that my associates had to help me into the saddle.' Accompanying the Golden Horde as far as the Volga, he then went south, skirting the Aral Sea, to Bukhara and Samarkand, in the direction of India. He crossed the Hindu Kush with a caravan of horse merchants, laying a trail of felt cloths to prevent the camels sinking into the snow, and reached the Indus on 12 September 1333.

The Sultan, Mohammed Tughluq, was subduing a provincial rebellion when Ibn Battuta arrived in Delhi, but he soon returned, announcing his presence in prodigiously extravagant fashion. His elephants were fitted with military catapults that hurled parcels of gold and silver coins before them, causing a scramble that continued right up to the doors of the palace. Summoning Ibn Battuta to the throne, he immediately made him a *qadi*, or judge, and gave him four villages producing 12,000 dinars a year, plus a 12,000-dinar bonus and other gifts. (To put this generosity in perspective, the average family had an income of 60 dinars a year.) When Ibn Battuta protested, feebly, that he specialized in a different kind of Islamic law from the one operating in Delhi, had no experience as a judge and did not speak Persian, the language in which all legal business was conducted, the Sultan swept his objections aside. He could have two Persian-speaking secretaries to do the work, and all he need do was sign the papers.

Ibn Battuta soon found that his sinecure was not the godsend it appeared. Mohammed Tughluq's rule was precarious, frenzied and arbitrary. Officials were expected to spend vast sums in imitation of the Sultan, and were dismissed if they failed to do so. Ibn Battuta swiftly ran up a debt of 55,000 dinars just trying to keep pace with the others. Moreover, Mohammed Tughluq was as violent as he was generous. An alien in a predominantly Hindu country, he bolstered his authority with terror. 'The sultan was far too free in shedding blood,' Ibn Battuta recorded, '[and] used to punish small faults and great, without respect of persons, whether men of learning or noble descent. Every day there [were] brought to the audience-hall hundreds of people, chained, pinioned, and fettered.' Most were lucky if they escaped with a beating; torture and execution were the other options. To the paranoid Sultan his whole court was a nest of potential traitors, as Ibn Battuta discovered when he visited a Sufi ascetic who openly disdained Mohammed Tughluq's worldly attitude. He was interested less in the man's opinions than in the curious underground home he had built for himself, complete with reception rooms, storerooms, an oven and a bath. Nevertheless, Mohammed Tughluq had the Sufi executed and Ibn Battuta put under house arrest on a charge of conspiracy. Then, after ten days or so, he released him on a whim. Ibn Battuta had had enough. Abandoning his house, his horses, his robes, slaves and dinars, he fled to a cave outside Delhi, where he practised fasting until he had trained himself to go without food for a period of 40 days. Having seen what Mohammed Tughluq was capabale of, he preferred a life of austerity to the extravagances of court. But he had not been forgotten: five months later, his penitence was interrupted by a summons from Delhi. Given his 'love of travel and sightseeing', he was to become the Sultan's ambassador to the Mongol Emperor of China. Fifteen Chinese envoys had recently arrived in Delhi bearing gifts. Ibn Battuta's job was to see them home with gifts of an even costlier nature. Having very little choice in the matter, he left the capital on 2 August 1341 with several hundred slaves, singers and dancers, 100 horses and numerous bales of textiles, ceramics and swords. At Calicut, on the south-western coast of India, three large junks awaited him. Supremely well constructed of overlapping strakes that were nailed rather than sewn together, with labour-saving, square-rigged sails of bamboo slats that could be raised and lowered like a Venetian blind, these were the most advanced vessels in the world. Every comfort was included – stewards, room-service, passenger saloons – and no safety measure was forgotten, from lifeboats and firefighting equipment to bulk-heads that enabled the vessels to survive several punctures to the hull. They were safe, spacious and private: as Ibn Battuta enthused, a man might lock himself in a cabin with his wives and not be seen again until the end of the journey. Compared to these behemoths, with their crews of 700 sailors and marines, the Arabian dhows that crossed the Indian Ocean were little more than cockleshells.

The envoys sailed first, leaving the Indian delegation to follow in the remaining two junks. The slaves and horses were taken aboard, as were all the other gifts, as well as Ibn Battuta's money and his entourage of slaves and concubines. When the loading was complete, however, there was no room for Ibn Battuta himself. Instead, he was invited to sail on a smaller junk, to which, with some resentment, he agreed. It was as well he did because, while waiting for transport to his humbler vessel, a storm blew up. The two large junks sank, their contents being washed up on the beach, where they were looted by the inhabitants of Calicut, and everyone on board was drowned. Meanwhile, the small junk fled to sea and did not return. Destitute and friendless, Ibn Battuta was saved by the arrival of a small fleet under Mohammed Tughluq's flag. Offering his services, he sailed up and down the west coast of India on campaigns of conquest until he had earned enough money to pay his passage to China. But when he returned to Calicut in January 1343 the first ship he met was bound for the Maldives. So he went there instead.

In every Asian kingdom he had visited Ibn Battuta had been welcomed as a representative of the Old Islamic World, a figure of authority and a repository of wisdom. In the Maldives, an isolated and backward realm of atolls which sat so low in the water that they would have been invisible were it not for their palm trees, he was revered almost as a god. Within a few months he had become one of the most important personages in the kingdom and had married the daughters of four of its most influential officials. 'After I had become connected by marriage with the above-mentioned people,' he explained, 'the viziers and islanders feared me for they felt themselves to be weak.' He later divorced two of these wives, and married another pair, as the political fancy took him.* By the time he sailed for Sri Lanka in August 1344

* His other wives were either dead or had been divorced. The concupiscent Ibn Battuta maintained a loose attitude to marriage, as he explained when extolling the virtues of the Maldives: 'It is easy to marry

he was so sure of his standing in Maldivian society that he hatched a plot with the Singhalese sultan to overthrow its ruler. Eventually, however, he abandoned his coup in favour of continuing to China.

His route, via Bengal, was beset with calamity. On the crossing to India his ship sank – 'Death stared us in the face and the passengers jettisoned all that they possessed and bade adieu to each other' – and after being rescued he found himself in a plague zone – 'whoever caught infection died on the morrow, or the day after, and if not on the third day, then on the fourth'. After that he was robbed – 'They left nothing on my body save my trousers' – and in the fertile but noisome plains of Bengal, which he described as 'a hell crammed with good things', he caught a fever. Yet, despite these setbacks, he took a ship to Sumatra and then sailed to China, in dogged pursuit of the envoys he had last seen in Calicut.

Among Ibn Battuta's many remarkable qualities was his capacity for self-preservation. Again and again he bounced from disaster to success, from poverty to riches, at every opportunity finding help and funds from the potentates he encountered. In some degree this was due to the close-knit Muslim fraternity and its tradition of helping fellow believers, particularly those with a smattering of religious authority. But largely it was down to Ibn Battuta himself: he was a chancer who had charm, resilience and, above all, luck on his side. After the destruction of his junks off Calicut, for example, he had been a penniless nobody. But by the time his next ship sank he had already acquired several slaves and concubines. When they drowned, he found a sponsor to buy him more. And when he was robbed it took no time at all before he had a pocketful of rubies and diamonds to cover the cost of a journey to China. A *qadi* of Delhi, one-time hermit, would-be ruler of the Maldives, shipwrecked mariner, friend to the Mongol khans, twice a pilgrim to Mecca, he was a man who seemed destined to see and do everything.

In sailing for China he took perhaps the biggest risk of his career. Although the Great Khan tolerated all religions, and had allowed Arab traders to establish colonies in his kingdom, he was the only Mongol ruler not to have accepted Islam. Ibn Battuta was entering a world where the cultural givens no longer applied and where, without letters of introduction or any certainty of encountering fellow Muslims, he would be lost. His luck held. Not only did he meet the envoys from Calicut, but – miraculously – he stumbled upon a fellow Moroccan. The man was expressive on the subject of China's wealth. When Ibn Battuta mentioned the magnificence of India his compatriot laughed and said that it was nothing compared to China. He had not been there long, but in that time he had 'prospered exceedingly and acquired

in these islands because of the smallness of the dowry ... When the ships put in, the crew marry; when they intend to leave they divorce.' Throughout his travels he married numerous women, usually because they were well-connected, then discarded them, with or without child, when it was time to seize the next opportunity.

enormous wealth. He told me that he had about fifty white slaves and as many slave-girls, and presented me with two of each.' How far Ibn Battuta travelled into China is uncertain. He probably did go to Canton and may, by his own account, have visited Beijing. But he may also have invented a great deal, or relied on reports from merchants he met in the south. Either way, he had reached his limits. He returned to India in January 1347, and within the year was back in Syria.

Damascus was all but empty. A new disease had emerged in China, travelling along the trade routes until it hit the Middle East. The Black Death, as Europeans called it, was a combination of bubonic plague, spread by rats' fleas, and pneumonic plague, spread by airborne droplets. There was no cure, and the end was swift. From first contact, a victim of the pneumonic strain had only 12 hours to live – just long enough to infect those around him. The crowded cities of medieval Europe and the Middle East were perfect incubators for the disease. There was the horrible tale of a ship that sailed from the Black Sea, trying to escape the epidemic: when it left it had 332 healthy passengers and crew; by the time it reached Alexandria only 45 were still alive. The survivors died shortly after arrival, but not before they had passed on their sickness. From Alexandria the plague spread to Cairo, where within weeks 2,000 people were dying every day. From more than half a million, the city's population shrank to 200,000 in a matter of months. Nowhere was left untouched, the most virulent and prolonged outbreaks occurring, naturally, in those places that attracted travellers – ports, capitals and religious centres. With sublime lack of concern, Ibn Battuta decided it would be a good plan to make another pilgrimage to Mecca.

He left Damascus in the summer of 1348, taking in the devastated cities of Alexandria and Cairo before crossing the Red Sea to Mecca, where the annual caravans of pilgrims had unleashed a fresh surge of pestilence. He stayed there for four months while the plague raged around him, then returned to Cairo, where the funeral processions were at last beginning to abate, and came home to Morocco in November 1349, having not even caught a cold. After 24 years away from his homeland it might have been expected that he would settle down. But Ibn Battuta remained irrepressibly inquisitive. Now in his late forties, he went north to examine the Mediterranean port of Ceuta, and was then struck by another good plan. Why not go to Mali?

The West African kingdom of Mali was far removed from the interconnected Islamic nations that occupied North Africa, the Middle East and India. But it was a realm that traders ignored at their peril, being so rich in gold that when its ruler, Mansa Musa, went on the *hajj* to Mecca in 1324 his spending devalued Cairo's currency for several years thereafter. The moneylenders were still talking about it when Ibn Battuta first visited the city in 1326. Mali was the most remote part of the Dar al-Islam, separated from North Africa by 1,000 miles of desert. But as he had made his living on the fringes of the Islamic world, Ibn Battuta saw no reason why he should not visit it. In the autumn of 1351 he joined a trans-Saharan caravan for the long journey to Mali.

His first stop in the desert was the salt mine of Taghaza. 'This is a village with nothing good about it,' he wrote. The slave miners worked in filthy conditions, suffering from the heat and the south-east winds that brought blinding sandstorms. Their only natural resource was salt, from which they built their houses and mosques. There were no trees and no wells, and it was 20 days to the nearest source of supplies. Other than the sacks of dates deposited by passing caravans, they had nothing to eat but their own camels. If a caravan failed they died; whereupon a new batch of slaves was brought out to replace them. It was not the worst place of its kind – the salt mines of Taoudeni, to the south, were even more remote and hideous – but it was nasty enough. 'We stayed in it but ten days,' Ibn Battuta wrote, 'in miserable condition because its water is bitter and it is of all places the most full of flies.' As soon as the salt had been loaded – the slabs being hung either side of the camels like thick paving stones – he left.

The rains had been heavy that year, with the result that the wells were full and the journey to Mali passed with the loss of only one man. (Typically, the Sahara claimed hundreds, if not thousands, of lives every year.) Ibn Battuta exhibited his customary fascination for minutiae. 'In that desert truffles are abundant,' he announced. 'There are also so many lice in it that people put strings around their necks in which there is mercury which kills [them].' On the other side of the Sahara, whose traverse took a good three weeks, he remarked upon the appearance of baobabs, the upside-down trees of Africa, which were so tall and so wide that 'a caravan can find shade in the shadow of one tree ... Some of these trees have rotted inside and rainwater collects in them ... Bees and honey are in some and people extract the honey from the trees.' Some of the trunks were so spacious that they had become homes: 'I have passed by one of these trees and found inside it a weaver with his loom set up in it – he was weaving. I was amazed by him.' Further on there were trees that bore plums, apricots, apples and peaches, but of a species he had never met before. There was also a tree that bore a cucumber-like fruit – 'when it ripens it bursts, uncovering something like flour' – which the natives cooked and ate. They also dug from the ground a crop like beans – 'and they fry it and eat it. Its taste is like fried peas. Sometimes they grind it and make from it something like a sponge cake.' The oil from these beans, maybe peanuts, was also used as ointment, lamp fuel, cooking fat and, mixed with earth, as plaster for their houses.

Ibn Battuta did not like the region very much. The natives were too morally relaxed for his taste and the food was awful. Of one town he wrote dismissively that it was 'a big place with black merchants living in it'. He reached Mali on 28 June 1353 and was gone by 27 February of the following year. Travelling south, he met the Niger, which he confusingly mistook for the Nile, but dared go no further: of the territories to the south he had been told, 'A white man cannot go there because they would kill him.' He did, however, visit Timbuctoo, from which he ventured a short distance along the river. He saw a crocodile that looked 'like a small canoe' and a herd of hippopotamuses 'with enormous bodies'. He thought they were elephants until they sank beneath the surface. 'They are more thickset than horses and they have manes and tails, their heads are like the heads of horses and their legs like the legs of elephants,' he wrote. 'The boatmen feared them and came in close to the shore so as not to be drowned by them.' He visited, too, many towns which were short on splendour but rich in hospitality. He remarked of one sultan that 'He was a gentle person, fond of making jokes, a man of merit. He died there after I left.'

Ibn Battuta left the Niger at Gao and went north-east to the Hoggar, the strange, mountainous plateau at the heart of the Sahara, so high that sometimes it snowed. He had very little to say about it other than that 'it has a scarcity of plants and an abundance of stones; the road, too, is rough'. He went north, again through the desert, until he reached the Tuat, a string of oases that led him eventually to the Atlas Mountains on 29 December 1353. The hills were covered with snow and the passes were icy. 'I have seen many rough roads and much snow in Bukhara and Samarkand and in Khurasan and in the land of the Turks,' he wrote, 'but I have never seen anything more difficult than the road of Umm Janaiba.' After many difficulties, he reached Fez later that winter.

This was Ibn Battuta's last journey. He had spent almost 30 years away from home, during which time his mother and father had died and he had become almost a stranger in his own land. He adapted to the situation with his usual panache. He was appointed *qadi* of Fez, and instructed by the Sultan of Morocco to produce an account of his exploits. Like Marco Polo, he did not write it himself but dictated it to a scribe. It was an incredible story, flawed in parts but mostly true, that circulated widely in the Islamic world. By the time of his death, in 1368 or 1369, Ibn Battuta had become the most famous traveller of his age. His fame, however, was restricted to the Dar al-Islam, and when his journal was finally translated into French in the 19th century nobody paid it much attention. Countless Europeans had since retraced his steps through Africa, Arabia, India and China: in terms of discovery Ibn Battuta's travelogue was an interesting but outdated curiosity. What they failed to appreciate was that it had taken them several hundred years to explore the known world, and they had succeeded with the aid of guns, swords, artillery and fleets of ships. Ibn Battuta had done the same thing in little more than a quarter of a century armed only with a Koran.

Christopher Columbus (1492–1506)

Resourceful, ambitious and possessed of an insatiable urge to prove himself, Christopher Columbus was the archetypal adventurer. Born in Genoa in 1451, the son of a weaver, he joined the Genoese fleet* and spent several years sailing the Mediterranean until, at last, he got his break. It came in an unconventional manner: in 1476 his ship was attacked and sunk off the Portuguese coast; paddling ashore on a piece of wreckage, Columbus made his way to Lisbon where he found employment in the city's large colony of expatriate Genoese merchants. Within a few years he had made several voyages – one, in 1477, which may have gone as far as Iceland, and at least one other to West Africa – had set up a small mapmaking business with his younger brother Bartholomew and had secured a wealthy and well-connected wife. For a shipwrecked mariner, it was a meteoric rise. But Columbus wanted more; and the place he thought he might find it was Cathay, China or, as it was generically known, the 'Indies'.

The spices, ivory, gems, silks and other exotic goods that trickled overland from the Far East showed that the region was wealthy. The journal of Marco Polo (which Columbus read and revered) proved it was possible for foreigners not only to enter Cathay but to thrive there. Since Polo's time, however, the Mongol Empire had disintegrated, and although trans-Asian trade continued it did so with more difficulty and at greater expense. Moreover, such goods as reached Europe had to pass through the Middle East, whose resurgent Muslim nations applied extortionate taxes. Therefore, if a man could find a direct sea route between west and east, one that would bypass the Muslim bottle-neck, his fortune would be assured. Columbus saw no reason why he should not be that person. Moreover, a successful voyage would reap spiritual as well as financial dividends. Of the few descriptions that remain of Columbus, all agree that he was a devout man. 'In religion he was so strict in fasting and prayer that one could easily have taken him to be a member of a religious order,' wrote his son Ferdinand. 'He hated swearing and blasphemy; the only oath I ever heard him say was, "By St.

---

* The details of Columbus's early life are obscure. By his own account, he went to sea at the age of 14. Later his son Ferdinand would claim that he attended university, where he studied astronomy, geography and cosmography.

Ferdinand!'" Unaware that several missionaries had already travelled over-land to China – and maybe not having read Polo's book very thoroughly – he dreamed of bringing Christianity to the Far East. As he later wrote, 'In the New Heaven and Earth which our Lord made He made me Cristoval Colon the messenger and showed me where to go'.

During his voyages to Africa he had estimated (incorrectly) that the earth's circumference at the equator was 20,400 miles. Given the distance that ships already covered between Portugal and Africa, he saw no reason why they should not sail that little bit further to China. True, there were several problems. The current state of navigation meant that most voyages were coastal, with ships rarely being out of sight of land for more than a few days. To sail halfway round the world in the open ocean with no certainty of finding an island along the way, with no idea whether the winds that took one there would carry one back, and with no guarantee that even if the winds *were* fair one would be able to find the port one had left, was a daunting prospect. On the other hand, the Portuguese had already probed into the Atlantic, discovering the Azores and the Canary Islands, so there were at least two revictualling points before one entered the unknown. And if the world was as small as Columbus thought it was, then maybe the journey was not so far-fetched. Indeed, by his calculations – which were short by more than 300 per cent – China was just 3,550 miles beyond the Canaries.

Columbus was not on his own. A map made 25 years earlier by the respected Florentine scientist Paolo da Toscanelli agreed precisely with his views. All contemporary charts of the Atlantic carried rumours of islands just beyond the horizon. Mostly imaginary, these bodies of land had a persuasive feel to them. There was, for instance, St Brendan's Land, report-edly sighted in the 6th century by an Irish monk who had sailed west for 40 days before discovering a series of islands, one of which was exceptionally lush and pleasant and may or may not – probably not – have been Barbados. There was also Antilia, a large island surrounded by other smaller ones, that 15th-century mapmakers consistently placed in the approximate position of the West Indies. And then there was Brazil, which lay off the west coast of Ireland – a position that appears less silly when one considers that St Bren-dan's Land, the putative Barbados, was supposed to be west of Iceland. By the muddled cartographic standards of the time, it was reasonable to assume that a ship sailing across the Atlantic should at least meet something, if not Cathay itself.

All of this Columbus put to King John of Portugal. But a royal committee refused to accept his abbreviated distances – besides, they were already pondering a route to the Indies via the southern tip of Africa. Undaunted, Columbus turned elsewhere. Neither the English nor the French were inter-ested. King Ferdinand and Queen Isabella of Spain considered his project in 1489, but eventually they too rejected it. They were not worried by his inaccurate calculations, and Isabella, who was as devout a Catholic as

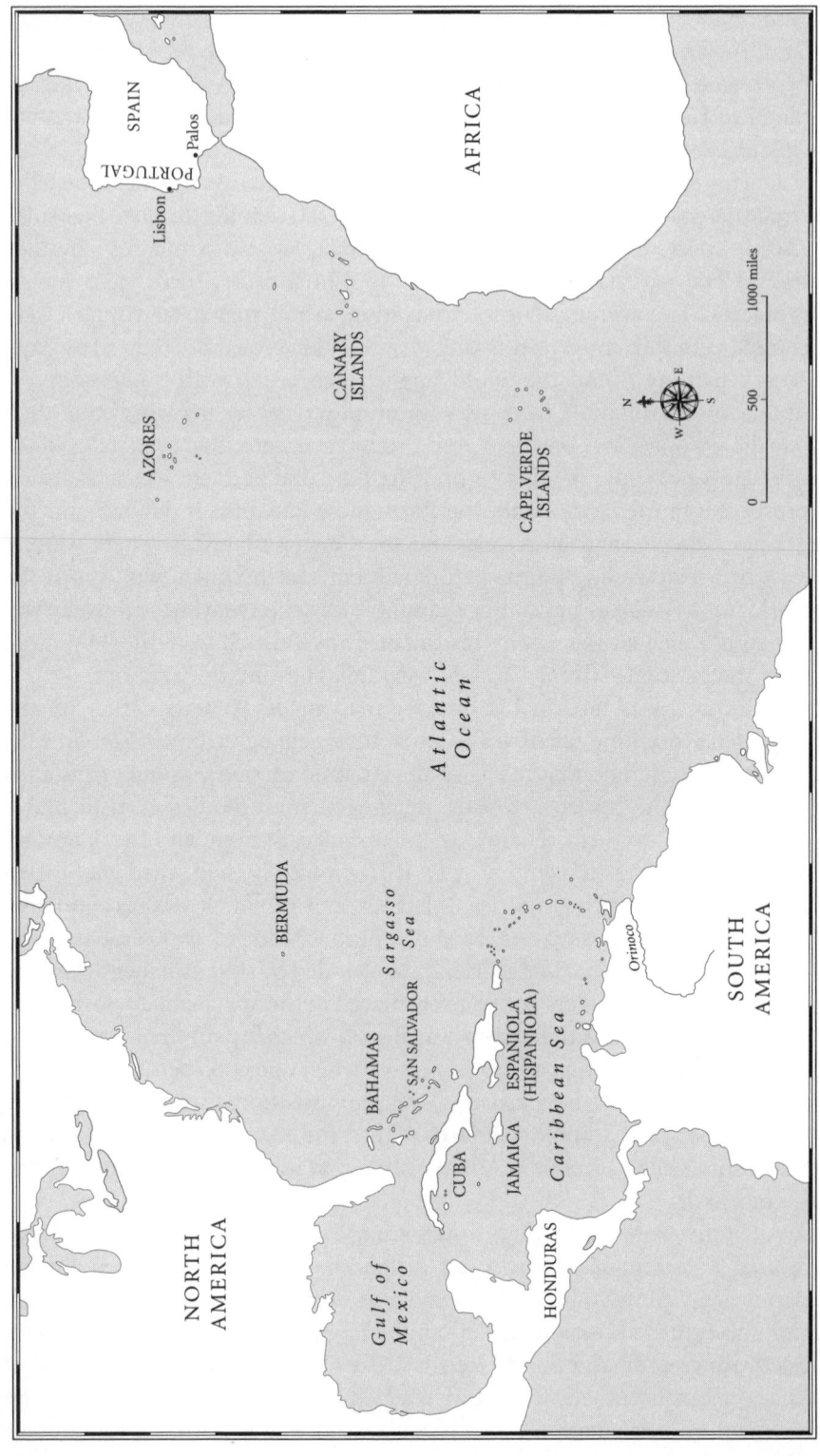

Columbus, particularly liked his idea of converting the Chinese. It was simply that they could not afford it, being engaged in an expensive campaign to expel the Moors from Granada. By this time Columbus was 38. He had been peddling his scheme for a decade, during which his money had run out, his wife had died and he had become *persona non grata* in Portugal. Nevertheless, he persevered in his quest, accompanied by his brother, his mistress and his two young sons.

His persistence was rewarded in 1492. In that year Granada fell to Spain and the whole of Iberia came under Christian rule, thereby giving Ferdinand and Isabella the time and the money to contemplate an expedition to the Indies. After a wrangle over terms – Columbus wanted the rank of admiral and to be appointed viceroy and governor-general of all lands he discovered with a 10 per cent cut of any profit – the Spanish Crown supported the project wholeheartedly. It directed carpenters, ships' chandlers, bakers and provisioners to supply Columbus with all he needed at reasonable rates. It exempted him from taxes on whatever he purchased. It promised to drop any outstanding civil or criminal actions against those who wished to sail with him. And it ordered the port of Palos, on the Gulf of Cádiz, to provide him with two ships free of charge. With this assistance, it took Columbus little more than two months to assemble his expedition. He left Palos for the Indies on 3 August 1492.

His fleet comprised three vessels: the caravels, *Pinta* and *Niña*, commanded respectively by the brothers Martín and Vicente Pinzón; and Columbus's flagship the *Santa Maria*. Small, agile and shallow-draughted, the caravels were ideal for coastal exploration. The *Santa Maria*, on the other hand, was a nao, a heavier, slower vessel that usually plied the Mediterranean routes. A nao was not what Columbus had wanted – he had asked for three caravels – but it did have the advantage of a large hold, which was useful for the vast quantity of food, fuel, spare equipment, weapons, ammunition and trade goods he was taking with him. All three ships were heavily manned: the *Santa Maria* carried 40 men, the *Pinta* 26 and the *Niña* 24, which was far more than was needed to sail them, but which probably included several supernumeraries. The owner of each vessel came on the voyage, as did scientific observers from the Spanish court, and many people were sailors only in name: one man, for example, although listed as an ordinary seaman, was a silversmith hired to assay any precious metals they might find.

The cramped flotilla sailed south-west to the Canaries, where they repaired their ships – the *Pinta* was already leaking and its rudder had broken – took aboard water, wood and meat, before leaving on 6 September for China. They made such good progress, averaging some 110 nautical miles per day, that Columbus feared they might outstrip his projected distances. 'I have decided to log less than our true run,' he recorded on the 9th, 'so that if the voyage is long the crew will not be afraid and lose heart.' It did not work. By the 19th he was writing, 'The men are beginning to complain about the length of the journey and about me for involving them in it ... [They are] impatient and outspoken in their complaints against me.' That day they met patches of bright green weed, which soon coalesced into great clumps covering the whole ocean. They assumed this was a sign of land but, despite several false alarms, none was to be seen. (In fact, they were in the Sargasso Sea.) This puzzling phenomenon, linked to the sudden disappearance of the prevailing south-east winds, alarmed the men. Rather than become becalmed in this mass of weed, they wondered if they shouldn't throw their admiral overboard and return to Spain. Even when the wind picked up it made them no happier. On 10 October there was a tentative mutiny aboard the *Santa Maria*. 'Sixty-two and a half leagues in the twenty-four hours; I told the men only forty-six and a half,' Columbus wrote in his journal. 'They could contain themselves no longer.' At first he tried to cajole them, painting glorious pictures of the wealth that would be theirs. And when that did not work he promised that he would consider turning back if they did not sight land in the next two or three days. In his journal, however, he revealed that this was just a sop: 'Having set out for the Indies I shall continue this voyage until, with God's grace, I reach them.'

At 2.00 a.m. on Friday 12 October, just before his deadline, he saw a light in the darkness ahead. It moved about, as if it was a candle or a flare. He pointed it out to one of the royal observers, but to Columbus's irritation the man did not see it. 'He was standing in the wrong place,' he wrote, 'but I was sure we were close to a landfall.' Whatever the cause of the light, Columbus was correct: come daylight there was an island before them. Clad in a scarlet doublet, and carrying the royal standard, Columbus stepped ashore to claim it for Spain. Having covered 3,066 miles in 33 days, he was at last in the Far East. He named his discovery San Salvador. It is a name that it bears to this day – except that it is to be found not in the Far East but in the Bahamas.

The island was flat, luxuriant and well watered, with a large lake in the middle. The inhabitants, however, were not quite what he had expected. 'They appeared to me to be a very poor people in all respects. They go about as naked as the day they were born, even the women, though I saw only one, who was quite young ... Their hair is coarse, almost like a horse's tail and short; they wear it short, cut over the brow, except a few strands of hair hanging down uncut at the back. Some paint themselves black, some with the colour of the Canary Islanders [red], neither black nor white, others with whatever they can find. Some have only their face painted, others their whole body, others just their eyes or nose. They carry no weapons and are ignorant of them; when I showed them some swords they took them by the blade and cut themselves.' They were very friendly – servile almost – giving him the impression that they were a race of slaves in thrall to the Great Khan. He had brought with him an interpreter who spoke both Aramaic and Hebrew, but the people of San Salvador understood neither language. All he could ascertain, by sign language, was that they had gold and that to the south or south-west 'there is a king with great jars full of it, enormous amounts. I tried to persuade them to go there but I saw the idea was not to their liking.' Columbus took several of the men prisoner, both as curiosities and guides, then headed south-west.

Stopping at several small islets, he was impressed by what he saw. The trees were 'as different from our own as night is from day, as is everything else, the fruits, the plants and the stones'. The fish were breathtaking: 'Some are like cocks, with the handsomest colouring in the world: blue, yellow, red, all colours; others are marked in a thousand different ways. No man could look at them without amazement and delight, the colours are so beautiful.' The inhabitants were universally friendly and peaceful, and 'exchanged their possessions for whatever one gave them'. At one point he recorded that they appeared to think him some kind of god. The rumours of gold increased, with reports of a king who wore copious amounts of the stuff – but as Columbus remarked, it was so difficult understanding the natives that they could have been telling him anything; 'also they have so little gold themselves that whatever small amount the king has will seem a lot to them'. Indeed, by 23 October he was certain that these tiny islands had no gold at all. Far more tempting was a body of land that he judged must be Japan. 'They call it Colba [Cuba], and say that there are many big ships there, and seafarers, and that it is very large. From there I shall go to another island called Bohio [modern Hispaniola, comprising Haiti and the Dominican Republic], also very large, according to them. The ones in between I shall observe in passing, and depending on what store of gold or spices I find I shall decide what to do. But I am still determined to continue to the mainland.'

Cuba did not live up to expectations. He studied its northern coast, reported on the state of the sea, the excellence of its harbours, the nature of its flora and fauna, the customs of its inhabitants and the hospitality of its rulers. The natives were as friendly as before, but his opinion of them now took an arrogant turn: 'Ten men could put ten thousand of them to flight,' he mocked. 'They are so cowardly and timid that they do not even carry real weapons, just staffs with a little sharp stick burned to a point on the end.' They did, however, believe in a god and were quite willing to repeat the prayers he taught them, from which he concluded they would happily accept Christianity. 'A host of peoples will soon be converted to our Holy Faith,' he exulted, 'and great domains and their wealth and all their peoples will be won for Spain, for there is no doubt that these lands hold enormous quantities of gold.' Behind his enthusiasm there was doubt. From both the Cubans and his captives (who had now learned a smattering of Spanish) came reports of gold, of pearls and of endless riches somewhere to the south. To the south, always to the south. They had been saying this ever since San Salvador. Yet no matter how far south he went, the gold was always one horizon ahead of him. That it existed he was sure, because he had purchased the occasional piece of jewellery and small amounts of gold dust. But he was no longer confident that it existed in the quantity he desired – or that if it did he would be able to find it on this expedition.

The same thought occurred to the captain of the *Pinta*, who had long since lost patience with his admiral. On 21 November he took matters into his own hands. 'Today,' Columbus wrote angrily, 'Martín Alonso Pinzón has sailed away on his own in the Pinta without my permission, moved by greed. He believes that an Indian I ordered him to take aboard his ship will give him a lot of gold. He went without waiting, not through stress of weather but because he chose to. He has gone against me in word and deed many times before.' What with Pinzón's departure, the continued absence of gold, and a general restlessness on the *Santa Maria* and the *Niña*, Columbus decided it was time to turn back. Before he did so he would visit the island of Bohio, partly in case it contained the longed-for gold, but also to cover as much new land as possible – because, if he did not find the wealth he sought, he could at least return with a map of his discoveries. 'I intend to make a new chart in which I will set out the whole of the Ocean Sea, with sea and land properly laid out with true positions and courses,' he declared. 'I also intend to compose a book including a true description of everything, giving its latitude from the Equator and its western longitude. Above all, I must have no regard for sleep, but must concentrate on the demands of navigation; all of which will be no small task.'

His resolution had an inauspicious start: on the day that Pinzón deserted Columbus calculated his position at 42° N – roughly the latitude of Cape Cod. He admitted, privately, that he must be wrong: 'I have hung up my quadrant until we reach port where I can have it adjusted, we cannot be so far north.' Then, wistfully: 'The heat makes me think that these islands and the area through which I am sailing must contain a lot of gold.'

Bohio, which he christened Espaniola, was no more profitable than Cuba, but the welcome was magnificent. A chief named Guacanagari treated them royally. 'He and his tutor and counsellor are very distressed that they do not understand me, nor I them, but nevertheless I understood him to tell me that if we needed anything the whole island was mine to command.' On 18 December – 'as I was eating under the sterncastle' – Guacanagari came aboard with his entourage to visit the strangers. 'I thought I should offer him food, and ordered some of what I was eating myself to be brought to him,' wrote Columbus. 'Whatever I put before him he took just enough of it to taste, sending the rest out to his people, who all took some. He did the same with the drink, scarcely touching it with his lips before giving it to others. All this was done with marvellous gravity and very few words, and what words he did utter, as far as I could judge, were full of sound good sense.' What he said was that if the foreigners wanted gold he knew where it could be found: not south this time, but north on the island of Babeque. It was just a day's journey away. 'I believe I am now very close to the source of the gold and that Our Lord God will reveal it to me,' Columbus all but wept into his journal. He left for Babeque on 24 December.

The next day, with palpable weariness, he took up his pen again. 'Last night,' began the entry for the 25th, 'around eleven o'clock, I decided to lie down to sleep, for I had not slept for two days and a night. Seeing it was calm, the helmsman gave the helm to an apprentice seaman and went off to sleep.' An hour later the *Santa Maria* struck a reef. The damage was not serious and, with a few hefty tugs to the stern, the ship would be afloat and seaworthy. Columbus therefore ordered the master – in this case the ship's owner, Juan La Cosa – to place an anchor so that it could be hauled free. But La Cosa and his men assumed the *Santa Maria* was lost, and rowed instead to the *Niña*. In the time it took to persuade La Cosa to return, the *Santa Maria* had swung beam on to the waves and was lost indeed. Columbus managed to transfer his crew to the *Niña*, ferry his supplies ashore and send word to Guacanagari, who despatched a flotilla of canoes to their rescue.

Badly shaken, Columbus retracted his derogatory remarks concerning the Indians. 'Nowhere in Castile could everything have been looked after better; not a thing from the ship has been lost; not a lace point, not a single plank or nail was missing ... They are of such a loving disposition, free from greed, friendly and willing to do anything ... I believe there can be no better people, nor a better land, anywhere on earth ... Men and women, it is true, go about as naked as they were born, but ... their behaviour among themselves is beyond reproach.' His admiration for them increased when Guacanagari – who had the measure of his guest – gave him more news about gold: in Japan they had so much gold they didn't know what to do with it, he said; there was gold on Espaniola too, buckets of it; in fact the interior was bursting with gold; and to obtain it one had to do nothing more than defeat the warlike Carib tribesmen who regularly attacked his people. Columbus ignored Guacanagari's hints that the white men help him eradicate his enemies, congratulating himself instead on the discovery of the source he had sought for so long: 'My misery at losing the ship has been somewhat tempered. I can see that Our Lord caused her to go aground with the purpose of establishing us here, for various things have come together so handily that it has been a piece of good fortune rather than a disaster.' At present he did not have the capacity to carry the gold, but he promised Guacanagari that he would return soon.

Because it was impossible to squeeze the crews of both remaining ships on the *Niña*, he ordered 39 men to stay behind. They acquiesced readily: given the superiority of their weapons, the balminess of the climate, the placidity of the population, and the squalor of life in Europe, they had no reason to object. Indeed, faced with the horrors of a return journey across the Atlantic, many of them *asked* to be left behind. The remains of the *Santa Maria* were dragged ashore to construct a fort, at a place called Navidad. It was a fine structure, with 'a tower, all good and sound, and a large moat', and on the evening of 26 December, just one day after the shipwreck, Columbus could contemplate his departure with serenity: 'So, they are finishing planks to use in building the fortifications, and I shall leave supplies of bread and wine for over a year, and seeds to sow, and the ship's boat, and a caulker, a carpenter, [a canoneer], a cooper and many other men who are eager ... to discover the mine which is the source of this gold.' He also left a doctor, a tailor, a secretary and an engineer, who would not be needed on the way back and, perhaps as a punishment for what Columbus described as his 'treachery', Juan La Cosa, the agent of the *Santa Maria*'s misfortune.

The *Niña* did not leave immediately. Columbus had first to be shown 'some vegetables and trees', accompanied by 1,000 natives, for which he rewarded Guacanagari with a shirt and a pair of gloves. Later he fired one of the *Santa Maria*'s cannons, whereupon he was given a wooden mask pierced with gold. On 28 December the chief invited him to a ceremony where a plaque of gold was apparently hung around his neck. On the 29th he was sent a 'great mask of gold'. On the 30th he was given yet another 'great plaque of gold'. On 1 January he dug up a patch of something he described as rhubarb – a renowned laxative, and one of China's most profitable exports, this confirmed his belief that he had reached the Far East – and on 2 January Guacanagari said he was having a lifesize gold statue made in the image of his new friend: it could be ready in as little as ten days.

The Espaniolan chief was exaggerating. And so, probably, was Columbus, when he spoke of great gold masks and solid plaques. Nevertheless, he had enough proof to show that he had discovered new lands and that even if he had not found Cathay – though he was sure he was close to it – there were regions to the south whose exploration would more than repay the Crown's investment. Columbus sailed on 2 January 1493, having enjoined the garrison to 'consider the mercies which God has granted them and me so far', and to conduct themselves in a decent manner.

Four days later, while attempting to enlarge his chart, he met the *Pinta*, which had been scouring the islands for gold. 'Martín Alonso Pinzón came aboard the Nina to make his excuses, saying that he had left me without meaning to and giving me his reasons, all false, for he left me that night through his own greed and pride,' Columbus wrote: 'I do not know how he acquired the arrogance and dishonesty with which he has behaved towards me during this voyage. I have tried to ignore it, not wishing to assist Satan in his evil work and his desire to hinder this voyage as he has done hitherto ... In order to escape from such evil company, with whom I must dissemble despite their rebelliousness, though I do have many decent men with me, I have decided to make no further stops, but to make all speed for home, this not being the time to speak of punishment.'

Contrary to his intentions, Columbus did make several more stops, on one of which he encountered the Caribs. They were better armed than the other tribes and extremely aggressive, attacking a shore party with no apparent provocation. The white men, who numbered only seven as opposed to the Carib's 50, killed two of their attackers, whereupon the rest fled. Columbus was saddened by this 'unpleasantness', but thought on the whole that a good example had been made. 'The people here are clearly evilly disposed; I believe ... that they eat human flesh. It is as well to leave them in fear, so that they will think twice before harming the crew of the boat which I have left with the thirty-nine men in the town and fort of Navidad.' Nevertheless, he was impressed by the contrast they made with the 'ridiculously cowardly and defenceless' people of the other islands. 'I should like to capture a few of them,' he added thoughtfully.

The crossing of the Atlantic was unpleasant. Both caravels leaked badly, the *Pinta*'s mast was faulty, and on the night of 13 February they were hit by a ferocious storm. The two ships became separated, and as he drifted helplessly before the wind Columbus put his trust entirely in God. Producing a bag of chickpeas, he cut a cross in one and ordered the crew to draw lots: if they were saved, whoever drew the marked pea would make a pilgrimage with a five-pound wax candle to the shrine of Santa María de Guadalupe. When the weather worsened, they drew again to send a pilgrim to Santa Maria de Loreto in Italy. Then, upping the stakes, they made a third draw for a pilgrim not only to spend a night's vigil in Santa Clara de Moguer but to pay for a mass. Finally, they swore together that if they landed safely they would put on their best clothes and make a procession to the first church they could find. 'As well as these communal vows, each man made his own personal ones, for none of us expected to survive,' Columbus wrote, 'we had all given ourselves up for lost, so terrible was the storm.' The crew's resentment, never far from the surface, now became vocal: 'Seeing themselves so beset, they cursed not only the fact that they had come but also the fear, or the restraint, which in the face of my persuasion had prevented them from turning back, as they were often resolved to do.' While the men raged, Columbus took steps to ensure that at least some record of his voyage would be preserved. He made two (very) abbreviated copies of his journal, wrapped them in waxcloth and placed them in barrels. One he threw overboard – 'everyone thought it was some kind of devotional offering' – the other he placed on the sterncastle so that if the *Niña* foundered the package would float free.

Their prayers were answered on the 15th when the storm finally blew itself out. With little idea where they were, they sailed north-east for three days until, by luck, they reached the Azores. Even here, however, they were not safe. Suspicious at the arrival of a Spanish ship, the Portuguese governor seized several of Columbus's men and sent armed boats to arrest their leader. Having come so far, and endured so much, Columbus's temper snapped. Unveiling the cannon that had hardly been used in the last six months, he explained that he had a letter of safe passage from the Spanish Crown, and 'gave them my solemn personal promise not to disembark from this vessel until I had taken a hundred Portuguese to Castile and laid waste the entire island'. The threat worked – as did a judicious distribution of gifts – and on the 24th, revictualled, repaired and with its full complement, the *Niña* resumed its journey.

Their trials were not over. On 3 March they were hit by another storm, as fierce as the first, which tore away their sails and left them running under bare poles. '[We] thought that we were sure to founder, with heavy conflicting seas and winds which seemed to pick the caravel out of the water,' Columbus wrote. 'There was heavy rain, with lightning on all sides.' Again they drew lots for a pilgrimage – this time the loser was to go in his shirt to Santa Maria de la Cinta in Huelva – after which 'we all vowed to eat only bread and water on the first Saturday after we make port'. And again their prayers worked. The next day they reached Lisbon, where Columbus had the great satisfaction of informing the king that he had completed for Spain the project that Portugal had turned down. They then continued to Palos, ending their extraordinary voyage on 15 March 1493.

They were beaten narrowly by the *Pinta*, whose captain was so ill that he died within a week, leaving the victorious Columbus to present his case before Ferdinand and Isabella. He did so persuasively, presenting them with gold, new plants, seven Indians and a journal that oozed promise. 'Rest assured, Your Majesties, that this land is the finest, most fertile, level, rich and temperate on the face of the earth,' ran one sentence. 'Do not be surprised, Your Majesties, that I am so lavish in my praise; I assure you that I do not think I am telling you a hundredth part of it all,' went another. Again, 'I assure your Majesties that there can be no finer lands under the sun for their fertility, their freedom from extremes of heat and cold, and their abundance of healthy water; not like the rivers of Guinea, which are full of disease, for praise be to God not a single member of my company has had so much as a headache or taken to his bed ill, except one old man with the stone, which he has suffered from all his life, and he recovered in a couple of days. I am writing here of all three ships. So it will please God, Your Majesties, to see learned men come here or be sent by you, for they will then see the truth of it all.'

Their Majesties did more than send learned men. In 1494 they ordered the despatch of 17 ships containing 1,500 sailors, soldiers, courtiers, nobles and priests, who were to invest the new territories, convert the natives, seize all available gold and find the Chinese mainland. Admiral Columbus was to be their leader. The fleet reached Navidad on 27 November to discover an empty, ruined fort. From Guacanagari they learned that the garrison had gone wild, stealing gold and molesting women, until they met the Caribs, who promptly slaughtered them. Of the original 39, the Spanish found only 11 bodies. Constructing two new forts, Isabella and Santo Tomás, in which he left sizeable garrisons, Columbus left for Cuba to establish whether it was joined to the mainland. He charted its southern coast within 100 miles of its western tip, then, feverish, exhausted, his eyes failing, and depressed by a battle with the natives, he gave up. He announced that it *was* part of the mainland, forced his men to sign a statement to that effect – the penalties were dire: according to one record he threatened to cut out the tongue of anyone who later recanted – and returned to Espaniola, where he spent most of 1495 in a coma. When he recovered in December it was to the news that one of his commanders had run amok, had repeated the crimes of the Navidad garrison and, convinced that there was nothing worth finding, had left for Spain with a party of like-minded malcontents.

Columbus was not the same man who had left Palos in 1492. Then he had been an energetic and forceful explorer with a reasonably open mind. Now he was a white-haired, vengeful despot. The goldmines having proved mythical, he turned to slavery. He corralled 1,600 Caribs, of whom he selected 350 men and women for transportation to Spain. The rest were let free, the women so terrified that they 'left their infants anywhere on the ground and started to flee like desperate people; and some fled so far they were removed from our settlement of Isabella 7 or 8 days beyond mountains and across huge rivers'. When he was finished with the Caribs, he enslaved Guacanagari's people. Then he instituted taxes. Every month, on pain of death, every male over 14 had to pay a certain amount of gold dust, or cotton to an equivalent value. It was an impossible demand, but one that he enforced rigorously. Those who fled were hunted down with dogs; those who stayed often took poison. When word reached Spain, he was recalled in 1496 to stand trial – though on the grounds of incompetence rather than brutality.

He not only acquitted himself but was awarded a new commission, eight more ships and an increased share of the profits. He returned to Espaniola in 1498, this time making a sweep past South America, where he sighted, but failed to investigate, the mouth of the Orinoco River. Two years later, however, reports of his tyranny became so constant that Spain sent a commissioner to investigate. Columbus was brought home in irons to face charges. Astoundingly, he was again acquitted. He sailed once more for the Far East on 9 May 1502 with four caravels and 150 men. He discovered Honduras and a few small islands before losing most of his fleet; the last ship fell apart on Jamaica. It was another year before he caught a passage home to Spain, where he died on 19 May 1506.

He went to his grave still clinging to the belief that he had found Cathay. Of course, he had not. In fact, he had failed in almost every task he set himself. Moreover, he had instigated the annihilation of the indigenous Caribbean population: in 1492 Espaniola had 300,000 inhabitants; after 15 years of Spanish rule there were only 40,000; soon there would be none, a pattern that was followed throughout the Caribbean. However, in terms of European exploration his failure had been very successful. Within a few decades Spanish and Portuguese navigators would complete his journey to the mainland, and in doing so would discover not China but a continent of even greater wealth, America.

Vasco da Gama (1497–9)

While Columbus was sailing west to America, the Portuguese were advancing on the Indies via Africa. In the belief that the continent might be round – or at least might not extend far south – King John II of Portugal despatched a number of expeditions to chart its coast. Equipped with caravels, commanded by extremely capable navigators, and carrying stone columns that they were to erect at prominent positions along the way, these were voyages of pure discovery. The first, under Diogo Cão, left in 1483, depositing its first column at the mouth of the Congo before continuing to Cape Santa Maria, at 13° S. It returned the following year with a number of Congolese natives as proof of its success. Cao made a second journey between 1485 and 1487, this time crossing the Tropic of Capricorn to place a third column at Cape Cross, just north of Walfisch Bay in modern Namibia. On the voyage back, he returned the Africans to their homes and explored the Congo, travelling some 200 miles upstream before his way was blocked by the Yellalla rapids. With 1,450 miles of newly explored coastline to his credit Cao had done well; but his successor, Bartolomeu Dias would do even better.

Dias departed in 1487, the year of Cão's return, with orders to 'sail southwards and on to the place where the sun rises, and to continue as long as it [is] possible to do so'. This time, given the expected length of the voyage and the uncertainty of finding food along the way, Dias took not only two of the standard caravels but a larger supply ship whose hold contained food as well as three more stone columns. Depositing the supply ship at a place where the natives seemed friendly and the fishing was good – possibly Luderitz Bay (Namibia) – he reprovisioned the caravels and sailed south. For a short while he followed the coast, then, bravely, struck out into the Atlantic. The water grew colder and at 40° S, where Dias turned east, the gales were so fierce that the crew were in 'mortal fear'. After a few days they sailed north, and after 500 miles landed at present-day Mossel Bay on the South African coast. Dias already suspected he had rounded the tip of Africa, but he could not yet be sure. So, having taken aboard food and water – and having, too, had an unpleasant confrontation with the natives, during which he shot a man with his crossbow – he sailed east again. The caravels landed at Algoa Bay, the site of modern Port Elizabeth, where they erected a huge wooden cross and then,

despite the crews' growing discontent, continued to the Great Fish River. Here, where the sea was warmer than before, and with every indication that the coast ran north – and, in Dias's mind, with India almost within sight – he at last agreed to turn back. During the return journey they landed at the Cape, which they had missed on the way out and where they erected another stone pillar, and after nine months were reunited with the supply ship. Of the nine men Dias had left as caretakers six had been killed in disputes with Africans, and the remaining three were so ill that one of them died – reportedly from joy at seeing his commander again – shortly after the caravels landed. Burning the supply ship to recover its nails, they stopped at West Africa to take aboard gold and slaves 'so as not to return home empty-handed', and reached Lisbon in December 1488.

They had been away for sixteen and a half months and had made tremendous inroads into the unknown. Dias apologized profusely for not having found the Indies, but the king was delighted with his efforts. Dias's map of his discoveries was incorporated into the official chart of the world, with the words: 'This is the true shape of modern Africa, according to the description of the Portuguese.' And, as a further mark of approval, the king added his own personal touch: crossing out the name Dias had given the tip of Africa – Cape of Storms, after the frightful conditions he had encountered – he rechristened it Cape of Good Hope.

With such long and hazardous distances yet to be traversed, King John's alteration might have seemed optimistic. However, much of the uncertainty and danger was dispelled by an ingenious man named Pedro de Covilhan. A 40-year-old professional spy, Covilhan had worked in France, Spain, Algeria and Morocco. He had a near-photographic memory, could speak Arabic and could pass as a Muslim, and was ordered in 1487 to work his way overland through the Middle East to India. He was to report on the wealth and nature of the regions through which he passed – paying particular attention to the availability of spices – and above all he was to make contact with the kingdom of Prester John. This mythical Christian monarch, of whom little was known save that he had written to the Pope offering his help against the Muslims, was supposed to reign somewhere to the east of the Tigris. If that was the case – and there was no reason to believe it was not: Marco Polo, informed by the same rumour, had written extensively about Prester John's battles with the Mongols – and if his descendants still wielded power, the kingdom could help break the Muslim stranglehold on the spice trade. Covilhan was given a brass medallion to present to the king when he found him: it was inscribed, 'King Dom John of Portugal, brother of the Christian monarchs'.

Accompanied by a lesser spy, Alfonso de Paiva, Covilhan left Portugal on 7 May 1487, travelling via Spain, Italy and Rhodes before entering Egypt disguised as an Arab merchant. The two Portuguese then travelled from Alexandria to Cairo – where Paiva was sent to investigate rumours that Christianity flourished in Ethiopia – and Covilhan proceeded to Arabia, where he caught a dhow to India, landing at the southern port of Calicut. Here, he reported, Muslim traders met ships from the spice islands to the east and, despite the town being predominantly Hindu, they formed a powerful and influential group. He sailed north, investigating the ports along the Malabar coast, amongst which was Goa, the centre of the horse trade with Arabia. From Goa he returned to the Persian Gulf, where he went down the east coast of Africa, describing Arab trading stations – Mombasa, Zanzibar and Sofala – that had been established as far south as the Island of the Moon (Madagascar). On reaching Cairo in 1490, he learned that Paiva had died, but he also met two Jewish travellers in the pay of King John, to whom he delivered a full account of his discoveries. The good news was that he had crossed the Indian Ocean and had learned that the east coast of Africa not only existed but had settlements where ships could reprovision. In case Dias was still within contact, he wrote: 'If you keep southward, the continent must come to an end. When your ships have reached the Indian ocean, let your men enquire for Sofala and the Island of the Moon. There they will find pilots to take them to India.' The bad news was that he had not yet found the kingdom of Prester John. It was not in Asia, of that he was certain, but it might be in Africa – probably Ethiopia. He would go there next.

Travelling via Aden, Mecca and Medina, he finally reached Ethiopia in

1492 or 1493. It was more primitive than he had expected, but it was Christian and therefore must be the lost realm of Prester John. In the mountains around the Blue Nile he presented the king with the medallion he had concealed in his luggage for the last six years. The king accepted it with pleasure, and pressed Covilhan to stay awhile as a member of his court. When Covilhan refused, the invitation became an order. Placed for many years under virtual house arrest, he eventually accepted his fate and became a trusted advisor to the king of Ethiopia, married a local woman and settled down with his new family. He sent letters home at regular intervals with Jewish traders, some of which must have reached Lisbon because in 1520 a Portuguese ambassador arrived in Ethiopia. By now in his seventies, Covilhan was too old to uproot himself, but he sent his 23-year-old son home to collect the reward he had been promised and to carry a supply of gold to his Portuguese wife. Covilhan died shortly after the party set out, to be followed four years later by his son.

It took a long time for the Portuguese to act on the discoveries made by Dias and Covilhan. For five years the Cape of Good Hope remained just that – a hope. Then, in March 1493, Christopher Columbus arrived in Lisbon with news that he had found the Indies in the west and had claimed them for Spain.* King John's fury was intense – and not just because he had earlier rejected Columbus's scheme. A treaty had already been signed in 1479 giving Portugal dominion over all lands, discovered or not, to the south of the Canary Islands. Its purpose had been to protect Portugal's interests in West Africa, but theoretically it could be argued that it included America as well. War between the two nations was prevented only by the intervention of the Pope. With divine insouciance he divided the world in two, the split running north-to-south 370 leagues west of the Canaries. By the 1494 Treaty of Tordesillas it was decreed that everything to the west of the line was Spain's, while everything to the east belonged to Portugal.** Unfettered, the Spanish began to colonize the islands Columbus had discovered. Portugal, however, was slower to respond. King John II died in 1495, and it was not until 1496 that his successor, Manoel, authorized a new expedition to the east. The man he chose to lead it was a nobleman named Vasco da Gama.

Gama would not have been everybody's choice. A diplomat and soldier by trade, he was not a professional seaman, and although he had considerable navigational knowledge he had never travelled far. The most obvious commander would have been Dias. But Dias was an explorer, and this was not to be a journey of exploration. In anticipation that the Indies – or more precisely India – were within easy sailing distance of South Africa, King

---

* Columbus had been present when Bartholomeu Dias returned from his voyage. According to some accounts, Dias's achievement spurred him to find the Indies. Ironically, the grand captain of Lisbon harbour to whom Columbus delivered his news in 1493 was none other than Dias himself.

** The easternmost bulge of Brazil was just within the limit, allowing Portugal later to claim both the coast and, by sleight of geographical hand, its vast hinterland.

Manoel determined that this would be a voyage of trade and diplomacy. For such matters it was necessary to send a man of culture and learning.

Gama's fleet, which left on 8 July 1497, comprised one caravel, the *Berrio*, commanded by a man named Nicolau Coelho, and two larger naos, the *São Gabriel* and the *São Rafael*, under Gama and his brother Paulo respectively. Heavily armed, carrying the by now traditional three stone columns, with a combined roster of maybe 180 men, including three interpreters and 36 *delgradados* – pardoned prisoners, who were to be used for tricky onshore operations – it had been equipped with the aid of Dias, who accompanied them for a while in a caravel bound for West Africa. (He also advised Gama on the selection of his crew, many of whom had previously sailed with him to South Africa.) On 27 July they arrived at the Cape Verde Islands, from where, in an act of great daring, Gama led his ships briefly towards Africa, then swooped out into the Atlantic, following a westward curve that brought them, on 7 November, to St Helena Bay, 100 miles north of the Cape. In the course of more than three months he had travelled 3,370 miles without seeing land, yet had brought his ships to almost precisely the place he wished to be. For the time it was an outstanding piece of navigation, unequalled even by Columbus's crossing of the Atlantic.

Gama received much the same welcome as had Dias when he first landed in South Africa. The natives were initially friendly, but then turned on them. In an unexpected ambush several of Gama's men were injured – Gama himself received an arrow in the leg – before a force of crossbowmen was sent ashore to exact retribution. There are no records of how many Africans were killed in this encounter, but the Portuguese learned a lesson from it. The expedition's chronicler, an anonymous member who later published *Roteiro da primeira viagem de Vasco da Gama* (Journal of the first voyage of Vasco da Gama), wrote that 'all this happened because we looked upon these people as men of little spirit, quite incapable of violence, and had therefore landed without first arming ourselves'. It was a mistake they would not make again.

Rounding the Cape, they took on food and water at Mossel Bay, where Dias had landed in 1487. They spent 13 days there, during which they purchased from the natives an ox whose meat they declared as fine as any to be found in Europe. But, as always, there were disagreements and misunderstandings. This time Gama settled matters with cannon-fire, and when the natives fled he took the opportunity to raise the first of the stone columns he carried. No sooner had the fleet left, on 6 December, than the Africans tore down both the column and the wooden cross Gama had placed on top of it.

By Christmas Day they were in new waters, passing a body of land to which Gama gave the name Natal, and by 11 January they were off Mozambique. Almost all of them now displayed the first signs of scurvy. Following standard practice, they used knives to trim their swollen gums and rubbed the wounds with urine. Fortunately, salvation was at hand. On Mozambique Island they met the southernmost Arab trading station. Initially they were welcomed with warmth, the Arabs mistaking them for Muslims and Gama doing nothing to dispel the impression. But they were soon uncovered, and as the Arabs became antagonistic Gama was forced to unleash his artillery.

The Muslims of the African coast were skilled navigators, but they were at a disadvantage when it came to naval warfare. Their vessels were not nailed together but held in place by wooden dowels and coconut fibre.* If they fired more than the smallest cannon their ships would unravel from the shock. Gama's naos, by contrast, carried 20 cannon apiece, plus numerous lesser pieces of artillery; the crew were protected by leather jerkins, iron breast-plates, armour and helmets, and were armed with crossbows, axes, spears, javelins and pikes. The Portuguese may have been few in number, but they were by far the most technologically advanced force in the Indian Ocean. Gama used his advantage to full effect. Knowing that he would be followed by others, and that he needed to show an example – knowing too that the Arabs planned to overwhelm him if he came close enough – he bombarded the port at random. Then, having kidnapped a couple of pilots and taken aboard food and water, he made his way up the coast.

Rumours of their barbarity travelled before them. Everywhere they went, the Portuguese met – and provoked – hostility, to which they responded in kind. When they could not get food they resorted to piracy; and when they could not get information they dripped boiling oil and resin onto their prisoners to make them talk. At the port of Mombasa they were attacked first by a force of 100 well-armed men and then by saboteurs who swam alongside one night and attempted to cut their anchors. 'These and other wicked tricks were practised upon us by these dogs,' wrote the author of *Roteiro*, 'but our Lord did not allow them to succeed, because they were unbelievers.' Only at Malindi, which was in competition with Mombasa, and whose ruler saw an advantage in befriending a potential new trading partner, did they receive a welcome. Here Gama obtained the fruit he needed to cure his men's scurvy and, invaluably, the services of a competent pilot whom he called the Good Moor. It has been speculated that the man was none other than Ahmad ibn Majid, one of the most famous astronomers of the age whose 12-part treatise, the *Fawa'id*, was one of the Islamic world's great navigational works. Whether or not this was the case, he proved himself a loyal and exceptionally able guide, being acquainted with the Indian Ocean and possessing charts of the African and Indian coasts.

Gama left Malindi on 24 April 1498, and a month later, thanks entirely to the Good Moor, his ships were off Calicut. Outwardly it was not an imposing place, extending only a short distance inland along seven miles of muddy, crocodile-infested shore. Its houses were single-storey and the city wall was

---

* According to some sources, this was due to a belief that iron nails might drag the ships towards underwater magnetic rocks.

scarcely 12 feet high. It was heavily populated and, to the surprise of the Portuguese, most of its citizens, although 'well-disposed and apparently of mild temper', were wretchedly poor. However, there was no doubt as to its importance as a trading centre. Warehouses along the waterfront were crammed with spices, ivory, cotton and sandalwood. Gold coins from Egypt and Venice were in common usage. Up to 700 ships waited offshore to take on goods. And Gama was astounded to be greeted in his own language by an Arab merchant who came aboard with the words, 'A lucky venture, a lucky venture! Plenty of rubies, plenty of emeralds! You owe great thanks to God, for having brought you to a country holding such riches!' He was further heartened on 28 May when he met the Zamorin, or ruler of the port. Carried inland on a palanquin, Gama was treated with more respect 'than is shown in Spain to a king' before being introduced to a man bedecked with gold, diamonds and pearls. The Zamorin listened to Gama's account of his voyage, and nodded sagely when it was explained, via interpreters, that the King of Portugal wished to form an alliance with him. He replied that he considered the king his friend and brother and would like to send ambassadors to his court.

From this promising start, their relationship deteriorated rapidly. The Zamorin had been led to believe that Gama's ships were forerunners of a mighty Portuguese fleet. When the ships did not materialize, Gama's stock diminished considerably. Also, after the manner in which Gama had described the wealth and power of his nation, the Zamorin was very disappointed with the gifts he received: a few lengths of striped cloth, some scarlet hoods, the odd case of sugar, oil and honey, plus a quantity of hand basins. At the same time, reports filtered across the Indian Ocean of Gama's actions in Africa. While these were of no concern to the Zamorin, they were deeply offensive to the Muslims who were his regular trading partners and who comprised a sizeable element of the port's population. The Zamorin was reluctant to compromise any future commercial arrangement with the Portuguese – as could be seen from their ships, they were certainly powerful; and the very fact they had come to Calicut meant that others would follow – but he was unwilling to jeopardize his current situation. He therefore gave the Arabs tacit permission to take matters into their own hands. Before long Gama and several of his men were effectively under house arrest, and the stock of goods that they had brought ashore had been impounded. The Portuguese responded by taking six of the Zamorin's subjects hostage. Complicated negotiations ensued, during which Gama managed by bluff, deception and force to obtain his freedom and to exchange some of his goods for a small quantity of spices. The Zamorin – protesting his complete innocence the while – also promised to erect one of Gama's stone columns and wrote a letter for the King of Portugal, demonstrating his willingness to trade. However, he retained one of Gama's officers and the rest of his merchandise as surety against the hostages' release. Furthermore, he reminded the

Portuguese that it was customary for all vessels to pay harbour taxes.

In delivering his terms, the Zamorin made a foolish mistake: he used the captive officer as an emissary. Taking him aboard Gama weighed anchor and on 29 August 1498 the Portuguese fled, 'greatly rejoicing at our good fortune in having made so great a discovery'. They were pursued by a fleet of about 70 ships, which they soon saw off. Then, remembering that he was a diplomat, and as they were still in the vicinity of Calicut, Gama put one of the hostages ashore with a message for the Zamorin. In it he made his excuses for an abrupt departure and looked forward to a long and profitable collaboration.

The Good Moor guided them up the west coast of India, where they alternately attacked, and were attacked by, local navies, before reprovisioning not far south of Goa. Then, against his advice, they insisted on sailing across the Indian Ocean – unwisely because, as the Moor explained, one could only cross the ocean with the aid of the monsoons. In spring they blew west to east, and in autumn they blew in the opposite direction. Typically the east–west winds did not arrive until November. But Gama was impatient. He sailed on 5 October for Portugal.

Considering the pressures of the journey, and his understandable eagerness to get home, Gama can be forgiven for his decision. But it might have been better to listen to the Good Moor. Tacking doggedly against the wind, they made such slow progress that scurvy once more took a grip. 'Our people again suffered from their gums,' wrote the author of *Roteiro*, 'which drew over their teeth so that they could not eat. Their legs also swelled, and other parts of the body, and these swellings spread until the sufferers died, without exhibiting symptoms of any other disease. Thirty of our men died in this manner.' At least 30 had died on the journey out, and with this extra loss Gama's ships were seriously undermanned. 'Those able to navigate each ship were only seven or eight,' the *Roteiro* continued, 'and even these were not as well as they ought to have been ... We had come to such a pass that all bonds of discipline had gone.'

It was almost three months before they reached Africa, on 2 January 1499. The port of Mogadishu was not far off but, too exhausted to face the inevitably hostile reception, they merely bombarded it from a distance before continuing to Malindi. Here, on 5 January, with the aid of huge sacks of oranges, they began their slow recovery. Even so, several more men died on arrival. Once again remembering, belatedly, that his was a diplomatic mission, and realizing the importance to future expeditions of having at least one friendly port in East Africa, Gama concocted a rudimentary alliance with the ruler of Malindi. The tokens they exchanged were somewhat uneven: the ruler gave Gama a large ivory tusk for the King of Portugal; in return, Gama gave the ruler permission to erect one of his stone columns on a nearby hill. If the ruler thought this a one-sided bargain he politely did not mention it. Five days later the Portuguese were on their way.

Wisely, Gama avoided the ports he had previously visited, stopping instead at isolated towns and villages. The death toll, however, continued to rise, and without enough men to manage the fleet he burned the *São Rafael*, transferring its crew and contents to the other two ships. The *São Gabriel* and the *São Miguel* landed on a small island off Mozambique, where they placed another of their columns, before proceeding to Mossel Bay, which they reached on 3 March 1499. By now the survivors were in better health, but after the heat of India and Malindi they were 'nearly dead' from cold. They spent nine days salting anchovies, seals and penguins, then sailed for the Cape and for home. On 16 April they were off the Cape Verde Islands, the ships so worm-eaten from the tropics that their crews worked the pumps around the clock. Then, with safety just a day or two away, they were hit by a storm that blew them north. The two ships lost sight of each other and, despite searching for more than 24 hours, Gama could not find the *Berrio*. (Coelho had, in fact, headed for Lisbon, where he arrived on 10 July 1499.) Sailing north to the Azores, where his brother Paulo died of tuberculosis, he then turned east. The *São Gabriel* docked in Lisbon just a few weeks after the *Berrio*.

The ordeal Gama and his men had undergone was reflected in their casualties. According to some accounts only 44 men out of an original 180 survived the journey. Their achievement, however, had been momentous: in the course of their 23,000-mile journey they had spent periods of up to 90 days without seeing land; and they had successfully navigated the Indian Ocean. Moreover, they had forged a link between east and west, breaking forever the Muslim stranglehold. The spices Gama brought with him were small in quantity – apparently no more than could fit in a biscuit barrel – but they proved the value of his discoveries. Within six months another, more powerful expedition was on its way east.

By 1510 the Portuguese had established their supremacy in the Indian Ocean, conquering all the major ports in Africa, Arabia and India – including Goa, which would remain theirs until 1961 – and annexing the Moluccas, the very heart of the spice trade. In Angola and Mozambique they created colonies to ease their passage around Africa. For a while Portugal was the wealthiest nation in Europe. As for Gama, he was given so many titles and estates that he could have spent the rest of his life in ease. But he chose not to, sailing on two further expeditions to the Far East as Admiral of India. He died in Cochin, in 1525. His remains were later brought back to Lisbon, to lie in the country he had set on the road to empire.

Ferdinand Magellan (1519–22)

When Vasco da Gama returned in 1499 from his epic voyage to India there was scarcely a man in Portugal who did not wish to sail east to make his fortune in the spice trade. Nineteen-year-old Ferdinand Magellan, third son of a provincial noble, and a lowly member of King Manoel I's court, was no different from the rest of his countrymen. Unfortunately, he had neither the wealth nor the political influence to become involved in an expedition – which was maybe as well, because the passage was so arduous that half those who left never returned. In 1504, however, Francisco d'Almeida was appointed Viceroy of India and given instructions to establish a series of fortified bases along the African coast, which it was hoped would make the passage easier, and to find, if possible, the islands from which the spices came. To this end he was allotted 22 ships and 1,980 men. Tired of waiting, Magellan resigned his appointment at court, offered his services as an unpaid seaman and thus, in 1505, became part of the largest fleet ever to have left Lisbon.

Magellan served in the Orient for eight years, taking part in the series of battles, massacres and invasions that established Portugal's presence in Africa, Arabia and India. The plunder was staggering: from the capture of Goa alone King Manoel received the equivalent in modern terms of 7 million US dollars; even the average seaman grabbed two years' worth of pay. And the brutality was on a similar scale: wherever they went, the Portuguese made an example of Arabs, cutting off the men's right hands and the ears and noses of the women. At Goa they forsook such niceties and simply slaughtered every Muslim they met: it took them three days to hack their way through 8,000 people. As the fleet pushed eastward it reached Malacca, the capital of the spice trade on the Malay Peninsula. Again the riches were magnificent. 'Truly,' wrote one captain, 'there are more ships in this harbour than in any place on earth. More riches too: for its warehouses are crammed with spice from the Moluccas, rubies from Ceylon, ivory from Thailand, silk and jade from China.' There were also slaves with sticks through their noses who came from 'the great island in the east' (probably New Guinea). A few bombardments later Malacca, like Goa, submitted to Portuguese rule. By this time, in a meteoric rise through the ranks, Magellan had been given

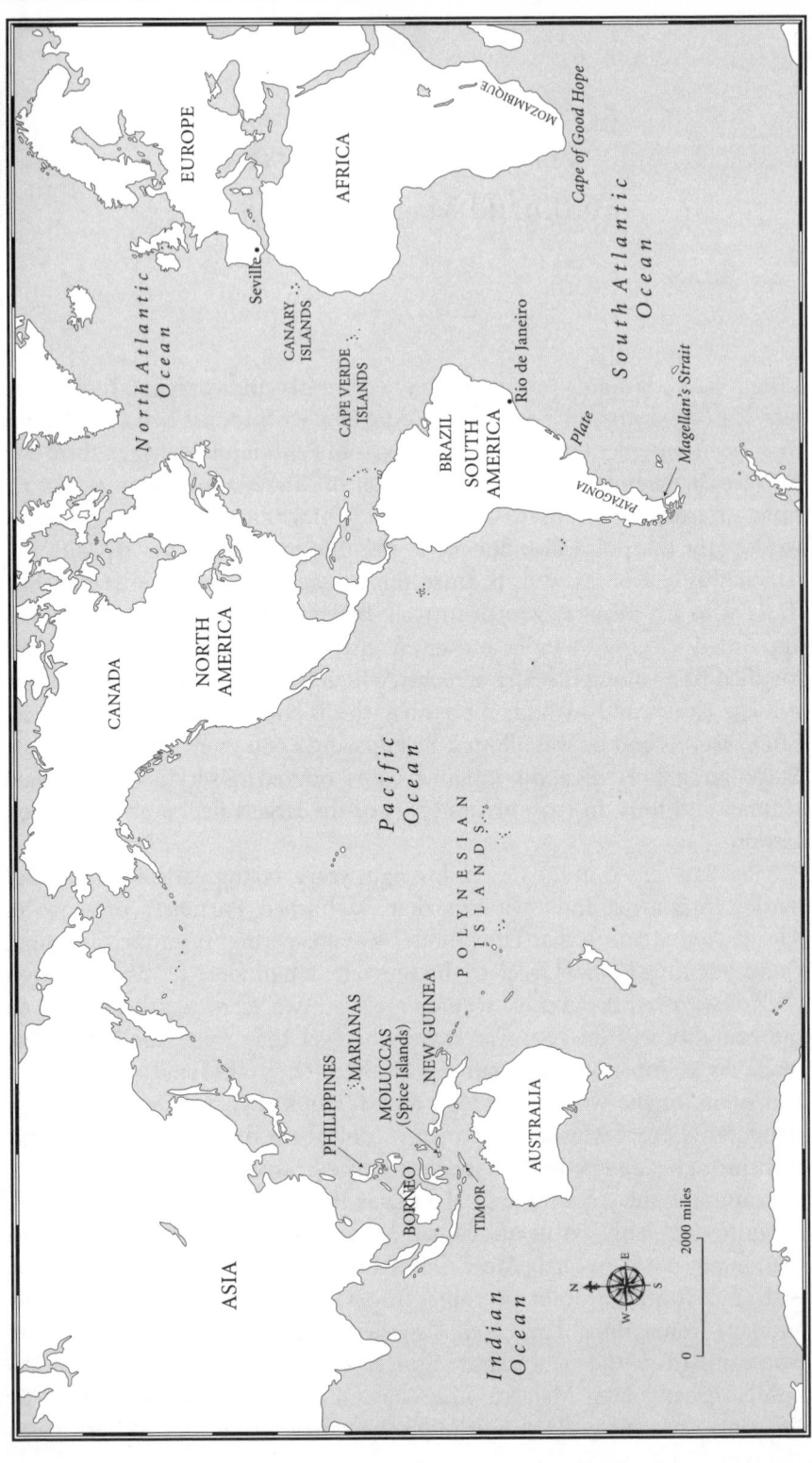

command of his own caravel. He sought, and received, permission to take his new command east. His exact destination remains a mystery. It might have been the Moluccas, or Spice Islands, which Portugal had already reached and where his cousin Serrano was ensconced as advisor to the local ruler, writing that 'I have found a New World, richer, greater and more beautiful than that of Vasco da Gama.' More probably he sailed to the Philippines. Wherever he went, he reported that it lay outside Portugal's sphere of influence. By the Tordesillas Treaty of 1494 Portuguese and Spanish interests had been separated by a line drawn through the Atlantic. Following Vasco da Gama's voyage, that line had been extended across the Poles to include the Indies. Magellan's report was not what the authorities wanted to hear. In 1513 he was sent back to Lisbon.

The former courtier cut an unimpressive figure in royal circles. He was considerably older than when he had left and, limping from a wound received at Malacca, was given the nickname 'Clubfoot'. Above all, he attracted opprobrium for his attempts to raise money for a new expedition to the Indies. It was not the goal itself that caused people to sneer but the manner in which he sought it, for what Magellan proposed was ridiculous: a voyage to the East Indies via the west. By now it was common knowledge that Columbus had found, not the Indies, but a collection of islands in what was called the Sea of Attilia. Several explorers had already reached South America, one of whom, Pedro Alvares Cabral, had raised the Portuguese flag on Brazil. Yet there was no certainty that South America did not continue to the bottom of the world and, with a passage already operating via the Cape of Good Hope, Magellan's project appeared both expensive and unnecessary. When Magellan put his plan to Manoel he was told, brusquely, that he could take his dreams elsewhere. Which he did. Using connections he had gathered during his stay in the east, he married the daughter of a Spanish noble, inveigled his way into the court of Madrid and persuaded King Charles of Spain to sponsor his expedition. Having learned from its experience with Columbus, who had suffered a similar rejection, Spain was eager to support any navigators who escaped Portugal's clutches. Thus, Magellan sailed under the Spanish flag with five vessels: the *San Antonio*, the *Trinidad*, the *Victoria*, the *Concepción* and the *Santiago*. Heavily armed and heavily provisioned, they were laden with trade goods – bars of copper, flasks of mercury, combs, knives, mirrors, bells, bracelets, scissors, crystals and cloth – and carried a total of 277 men, of whom a sizeable minority, including the captain of the *Santiago*, were Portuguese. They carried, too, a slave, Enrique, whom Magellan had purchased in the Indies, as well as a Venetian nobleman named Antonio Pigafetta, who at the last moment had expressed an urgent desire to 'see the wonders of the world' (he was probably a spy) and who became the expedition's unofficial chronicler.

Magellan's fleet departed on 20 September 1519, and within a week, while anchored at the Canaries, an argument broke out as to their course. Magellan wanted to sail south-east, but his three Spanish captains, Juan de Cartagena, Gaspar de Quesada and Luis de Mendoza, who had never been happy at sailing under a foreigner and suspected he was leading them to captivity in Portuguese West Africa, favoured a more westerly course. (According to one account, they had boasted before leaving Spain that they would kill Magellan if he displeased them.) Magellan held firm – and did indeed lead them towards Africa before striking west – but in mid-Atlantic Cartagena openly contested Magellan's right to command. He was arrested at swordpoint, stripped of his rank and only saved from chains by Mendoza's promise to keep him under open arrest on his ship.

Having asserted his authority, Magellan continued on his way, evading en route a Portuguese fleet that had been sent to intercept them and sailing through storms that produced the electrical phenomenon known as St Elmo's Fire, believed to be the embodiment of St Elmo, patron saint of seamen, and a sign of divine protection. Pigafetta, who had never experienced a storm at sea, let alone an electrical one, was awed and terrified. '[It] appeared to us many times,' he wrote, 'among other times on a very dark night, in such splendour, like a blazing torch, at the top of the mainmast, and stood there some two hours or more with us, consoling us in our lamentations. When that blessed light wished to leave us, so dazzling was its brightness in our eyes, that we all remained for more than an eighth of an hour quite blinded and crying out for mercy, truly believing that we were dead. Suddenly, the sea became calm.'

They sighted Brazil on 29 November, but did not land until 13 December when they were at modern Rio de Janeiro. One of Magellan's Portuguese officers, João de Carvalho, had already spent four years in Brazil on a previous voyage, so was well acquainted with the region. (Indeed, he had left there a half-Indian son, whom he now signed on as a member of the crew.) To the untravelled Pigafetta, however, Rio was a new and marvellous paradise. They could purchase ten parrots for the price of a mirror, and for a single needle 'a whole basket of sweet potatoes, which taste like chestnuts and are as long as turnips'. The natives slept in hammocks and travelled in canoes – two words that Pigafetta has been credited with introducing to Europe – and painted their bodies 'in a wonderful manner with fire in various designs'. He recorded that the women could be bought for the smallest piece of iron and that the men went mostly naked but when they dressed wore clothes made of parrot feathers that they fashioned into great wheels around their buttocks. He was worried, though, by reports of cannibalism and could not understand why it was so warm because, by his calculations, they were only twenty-three and a half degrees north of the South Pole.

Having careened and scraped his ships, and taken aboard the fruit and vegetables in which the region abounded, Magellan continued south, heading for a cape where previous navigators had reported nothing but empty sea to the south and west. It was the furthest any European had sailed along the coast, and was believed to be the point where South America either ended or was bisected by a passage leading to the Indies. Magellan proved the reports false: the cape was merely the upper lip of the River Plate estuary. In the face of a second tentative mutiny, he led his ships into unknown waters. During the next eight weeks the sea became colder and storms more frequent. Pigafetta noted the appearance of strange creatures he had never seen before: the penguin and the fur seal. 'These goslings,' he wrote, 'are black and white and have feathers over their whole body of the same size and fashion, and they do not fly, and live on fish. They were so fat that we did not pluck them but skinned them, and they have a beak like a crow's.' As for the 'sea wolves', they had no feet but something resembling a human hand: 'And if they could have run they would have been truly fierce and cruel; but they do not leave the water, where they swim wondrously and live on fish.' The fleet was scattered three times before, in late March, Magellan took his ships into a bay on the Patagonian coast where he said they would spend the rest of the southern winter.

St Julian Bay, as he named it, was a wretched, bleak spot. But not until Magellan ordered the crew to build huts and simultaneously cut their rations did they realize just how wretched and bleak it was. As Pigafetta put it, 'The captains and crew objected to both these orders, and the dissatisfied demanded to return home.' Magellan refused to discuss the matter, and when some of the crew persisted, he had them arrested and punished. This exasperated the men still further. On 1 April Cartagena, Mendoza and Quesada seized three of the ships and tried to escape. Magellan, however, 'by a cunning ruse', recaptured one of the ships – killing Mendoza in the process – and blocked the mouth of the bay. Outnumbered and unable to break free, Cartagena surrendered. Magellan's revenge was harsh. The ringleaders among the crew were chained and sentenced to careen the ships. Cartagena and his chaplain were ordered to be marooned. Quesada was executed – by his secretary, who was spared death on condition that he behead his master – and then the corpses of Quesada and Mendoza were dismembered and hung on gibbets. After this the hut-building proceeded smoothly and nobody complained about the rations.

Magellan still believed that there was a passage to the other side of South America, and that winter he sent the *Santiago* on reconnaissance missions to find it. On one of these voyages the ship was driven ashore and damaged beyond repair. The crew, luckily, were able to row ashore and send a party overland to fetch help from St Julian Bay. For several weeks rescue vessels plied to and fro until the contents of the *Santiago* had been retrieved. During this time Pigafetta recorded the arrival of a giant in St Julian Bay. He had thin hair, a stentorian voice and was so tall 'that we reached only up to his waist', but he was friendly and was soon followed by other giants, dressed in skins of a strange animal (later identified as the guanaco), carrying bows and arrows which were feathered like those in Europe. Whether these giants actually existed or were an adornment to Pigafetta's journal is unknown. His assertion that the Europeans only came up to their waist, for example, was an obvious exaggeration because he also claimed, more plausibly, that the giants were just a head taller than the white men. They did, however, feature so prominently in Pigafetta's account that they may have had some basis in reality. He even compiled a 100-word vocabulary of their language – some of the words are still used in the region – and Magellan named the land Patagonia in their honour, the word being Portuguese slang for Big Foot. They were so exotic that Magellan captured a couple,* whereupon they became so angry that he had to find a new harbour to the south.

The fleet sailed again on 18 October, and within three days met a cape that, according to the religious calendar, he named the Cape of Eleven Thousand Virgins. On the other side of it lay what at first appeared to be an estuary but on investigation turned out to be the strait Magellan had been waiting for. The relief of his men can only be imagined, for 'if we had not discovered this passage, the captain-general was determined to go as far south as seventy-five degrees towards the Antarctic Pole'. Surrounded by high, snow-capped mountains, it was not an easy passage – a series of bays linked by narrow channels through which flowed treacherous currents. But it was navigable, and at the last bay they encountered two openings. Magellan sent the *San Antonio* and *Concepción* to reconnoitre one, while he led the *Trinidad* and *Victoria* down the other. Seven days later Magellan found the sea. According to Pigafetta, the normally emotionless captain broke down and cried. (He called his discovery the Strait of Patagonia. Later it would be named after Magellan himself.) Returning to bring the good news to the others, however, he learned that the *San Antonio* was lost. The captain of the *Concepción* said they had separated to explore the coast of a large island, and on rounding the island the *San Antonio* had vanished. The three remaining ships scoured the bay; Magellan even sent the *Victoria* to the eastern opening of the strait. But the *San Antonio* was nowhere to be seen. Either it had sunk or, as seemed more likely, its commander Estevão Gomes had mutinied and sailed back to Spain. Whatever the cause, the loss of the *San Antonio* was a blow: it had been their largest ship and its hold contained much of the expedition's food.

On 28 November 1520 the fleet sailed into the unknown ocean. Before they left, Magellan ordered his priest to bless the ships, and called his crew on deck for prayers. The seas, he noted, were auspiciously calm. 'May we always find them as peaceful as this morning,' he said. 'In this hope, I shall name this Sea the Pacific.' It was not the nature of the ocean that would give them trouble so much as its scale. Prevailing wisdom held the world's circumference to be much smaller than it really was. By all accepted calculations Magellan should reach land within a matter of weeks. And had he

---

* It was common practice for Iberian travellers to bring back unusual specimens. The courts of Lisbon and Castile were awash with novelty humans of every shape and colour.

steered north-west he would have done so, hitting the chain of Polynesian islands that would eventually lead him to larger landmasses. But without the means to calculate longitude precisely he considered such a course too risky. Instead, adhering to standard navigational procedure, he sailed north for a predetermined latitude that he could follow until he met charted waters. This roundabout approach cost time, as did the unexpected size of the Pacific. Soon they were on the brink of starvation.

Pigafetta gave a vivid account of their plight: 'We were three months and twenty days without obtaining any kind of fresh supplies. We ate ship's biscuit that was no longer biscuit, but crumbs swarming with worms, for these had already devoured whatever was good. Besides, it stank powerfully of the urine of rats. The water we drank was yellow and had long been putrid. We were reduced even to eating certain pieces of leather that had been placed on top of the mainyard to prevent it from chafing the ropes. From exposure to sun, rain and wind, this leather had become very hard, so that we let it macerate for four or five days in the sea then placed it for a while on the embers and thus ate it. Often, too, we ate sawdust from the ships' timbers. Rats were sold for half a ducat a piece if we could catch any. But the worst of all our misfortunes was the following: the gums of both the lower and upper jaws of some of our men began to swell so much that they could no longer eat and consequently died. Nineteen of them died of this disease, as well as the ... Patagonian giant and one Indian from Brazil. In addition, some twenty-five or thirty more men fell ill of other diseases, in their arms, legs, or parts, so that very few remained well. I myself, by the grace of God, suffered however no sickness.' Pigafetta escaped scurvy because he caught and ate fish on a daily basis. Why the rest of the crew did not follow his example is a mystery.

On 6 March 1521 the fleet finally berthed at a small island – possibly Guam, in the Marianas – whose inhabitants swarmed aboard and, brushing the enfeebled Westerners aside, began to steal everything they could find. They did not leave until Magellan ordered his crossbowmen to shoot. Even then, they escaped with the *Trinidad*'s longboat. Vengefully, Magellan went ashore with 50 men to retrieve the boat and find supplies, in the process burning an entire village and all its canoes and killing seven men. For good measure, he then shelled the coast. He did not, however, bring back the entrails of those he had killed, despite his invalids' belief that this would cure them. Pigafetta accompanied the raiders and took notes on the natives' appearance: 'They wear hats woven of palm fronds, like the Albanians, and they are as tall as we and well built. They worship no God and have an olive-coloured complexion, though they are all born white. Their teeth are red and black.' He was interested, too, in their catamarans, which had sails made of palm leaves and which he compared to a Venetian gondola: 'For rudders they use a wooden blade like the shovel of a baker's oven with a wooden handle. They can change stern and prow at will, and their craft leap in the water like dolphins from wave to wave.' When the fleet left it was pursued by a regatta of these vessels, whose occupants tore their hair in grief and pelted the ships with stones.

By 18 March the fleet was anchored off Leyte in the Philippines, where the inhabitants were accustomed to foreigners – Magellan's pilot judged that several of the people who greeted them were either Mongolian or Chinese – and were willing to trade. With Magellan's slave Enrique acting as an interpreter, they soon established friendly relations. The sick men were taken ashore, where Magellan personally fed them coconut milk to cure their scurvy. Then the two sides bartered energetically, the Filipinos exchanging porcelain and gold for the Europeans' trinkets. The king of Leyte was so impressed by Magellan that he attended mass and accepted Christianity. It was the same on every island Magellan visited, until he came to Cebú on 7 April. Here too, at first, things went well: the king was converted, and was baptized with hundreds of his subjects. As a sign of friendship he invited Magellan to become his blood-brother, allowed him to erect a large cross in the marketplace and swore loyalty to the King of Spain. According to Pigafetta the baptism was so successful that a paralysed man was cured: 'This was a most manifest miracle accomplished in our times.' The trade was even busier here than it had been on Leyte, the people of Cebú offering 10 pounds of gold for 14 of iron. His material and spiritual success filled Magellan with evangelical zeal. When he heard that the king's vassal, Si Lapulapu, ruler of the island of Mactan, refused to accept the King of Spain as his overlord, he decided to teach him a lesson. The three Spanish ships, accompanied by a fleet of Cebú warriors, sailed at midnight on Friday 27 April. The following morning – he had always fought best on a Saturday and considered it a lucky day – Magellan led 50 men on to the beaches of Mactan.

Si Lapulapu was waiting for them. He had dug parallel lines of deep trenches in the sand, through which the armoured invaders clambered with difficulty. Then, as they approached Si Lapulapu's village, they were charged by 1,500 warriors. Even though they were vastly outnumbered, their armour saved them from the spears, stones and arrows that came their way. For a while they kept the Filipinos at a distance with crossbows and muskets. Hoping to demoralize his enemy, Magellan sent a group to burn the village. Two of the men were brought down, but the others completed the job. The sight of the flames served only to enrage the warriors. They now began to fire at the Spaniards' unprotected legs. Magellan, wounded in the thigh by an arrow, ordered a withdrawal. At first it went smoothly, the men retreating in orderly waves across the trenches, each party giving covering fire to the next. But once they were on the beach their nerve broke. They fled for the boats – one of which overturned beneath their weight – and rowed to safety, leaving the rearguard to fend for themselves.

Knee-deep in water, Magellan and his six remaining sailors put up a valiant defence. Their armour gave them an advantage, and although Magellan's helmet was twice knocked from his head they kept the Filipinos at bay for an hour. Extraordinarily, the ships made no attempt to rescue them, and when the king of Cebú tried to intervene they blew his canoe out of the water, killing four men. The end came when Magellan stabbed an attacker with his lance and, on drawing his sword for the *coup de grace*, was hit in the arm by a bamboo spear. Seizing their moment, Si Lupalupa's men closed in. One of them slashed Magellan's hamstring, and as he fell into the water the others belaboured him with clubs. The survivors discarded their armour and swam to the boats. Pigafetta, who had stayed with his captain-general to the last, and had been hit in the face by an arrow, recorded that even as he was being bludgeoned Magellan turned constantly to make sure that his men were safe (more likely, he was looking to see if they would rescue him). 'Had it not been for our poor captain, not a single one of us would have been saved in the boats,' Pigafetta mourned, 'for the others were able to withdraw to them while he was still fighting. I hope ... that the fame of so noble a captain will never be effaced in our times.'*

In Pigafetta's words, Magellan had been 'our mirror, our light, our comfort and our true leader'. In his absence nobody knew what to do. They tried to recover his bones but, according to Pigafetta, '[The Filipinos] would not give up such a man ... for all the greatest riches in the world, but they wished to keep him in order to remember him.' The expedition lost all purpose. Leadership was given to two men, Duarte Barbosa of the *Victoria* and Juan Serrano, erstwhile captain of the *Santiago*, who between them tried to restore amicable relations. Using Magellan's slave Enrique as a go-between, they arranged a dinner with the king of Cebú. The king no longer trusted them, neither did the slave, and the dinner was a trap. Serrano led 24 officers ashore, tempted by the king's offer of a set of jewellery that he had long coveted. Two of the officers, João de Carvalho and Gonzalo Gómez de Espinosa, suspected something was wrong and left early. They had only just returned to the ships when a riot broke out on land. Strafing the shore with their artillery, they moved closer. Serrano appeared on the beach. From a shouted conversation it became clear that everyone had been murdered save Enrique and Serrano. The captain begged them to ransom him, but Carvalho and Espinosa guessed it was a trick and, unwilling to lose more men, they raised sail and left Serrano to his plight.

Carvalho, now the expedition leader, sailed through the Philippines to Borneo, then south in search of the Moluccas. For six months he was, in effect, a pirate, pillaging without qualm and looting every ship he met. At one port he was asked to leave a hostage for goodwill: he gave them his son and sailed on. Eventually, the crew tired of his behaviour. They mutinied, tried him for his misdeeds, and replaced him with a Spanish officer, Juan del Cano. At the next demand for hostages it was Carvalho they handed over.

* Magellan's last stand would be replicated, almost action for action, by that of Captain James Cook in 1778.

Del Cano swiftly brought order to the voyage, and under his leadership they reached the Moluccas on 6 November 1521. Almost 27 months after leaving Seville, the Spanish fleet had finally arrived at its destination. They were pleased to find that the local rulers were not well disposed towards the Portuguese. They disliked their antagonism towards Islam, resented the manner in which they had monopolized trade for the last ten years, and were offended by the behaviour of their sailors. Knowing nothing about Spain save that it was Portugal's rival, and impressed by del Cano's insistence that his men behave with scrupulous decorum, they saw a chance to improve their bargaining position. The king of one island, Tidore, announced that his people were 'the most loyal friends and vassals to the King of Spain ... [and] wished us to give him a seal of the King of Spain and a royal banner, because he had decided that henceforth his own island and that which is named Ternate ... would both come under the dependency of the King of Castile. For the honour of his Suzerain, he was ready to fight to the death, and should he no longer be able to resist or defend himself, he would sail off to Spain, aboard a junk, with all his retinue.' To prove their good intentions, they offered the Spaniards as much spice as they wanted, at favourable rates, and promised to reserve all future crops against their next visit. Furthermore, they allowed del Cano to place a small garrison on one of the islands.

Del Cano and Espinosa stuffed their holds with spices. Their men, meanwhile, traded privately, selling everything they had to procure their own personal supplies. Spare clothes, food, weapons and equipment were bartered until nothing remained save the bare essentials for the passage home. On the point of departure, however, the *Trinidad* sprang a leak. The king of Tidore sent divers to investigate – Pigafetta reported how they swam around the ship for an hour, using their long hair to detect any signs of suction from the hull – and when they resurfaced it became apparent that the ship needed extensive repairs. Leaving Espinosa to oversee the work, del Cano sailed aboard the *Victoria* for the Cape of Good Hope on 21 December. In case he should be intercepted by the Portuguese, he ordered Espinosa to take the *Trinidad* in the opposite direction, to Spain's newly conquered territories in Central America. That way, at least one of them would return home.

For two months del Cano dodged in and out of the Indies, braving starvation, shipwreck and mutiny – several men deserted on the island of Timor – before heading into open seas. He did not follow the habitual route along the coasts of India, Arabia and Africa, but struck south-west across the Indian Ocean, trusting in his seamanship to bring them to the Cape. His navigation was perfect: by mid-May they had rounded the Cape and were in the Atlantic. But it had not been an easy trip. Having crammed their hold so full of spices, they had left little space for food, and what meat they had was unsalted and soon became putrid. By the time they approached Africa they were on a diet of rice and water, and some of the men begged to be landed at Mozambique even though it meant becoming prisoners of the Portuguese.

On consideration, however, they changed their minds (according to Pigafetta, because they were 'more anxious for their honour than their lives'). It was no better in the Atlantic. Del Cano dared not land lest the ship be captured, but continued north up the coast of Africa, his crew dying from starvation and disease. It was almost as bad as crossing the Pacific. Fifteen people had already died crossing the Indian Ocean. During the course of the next eight weeks another 22 corpses were thrown overboard. 'When we cast [them] into the ocean,' Pigafetta recorded sanctimoniously, 'the Christians sank to the bottom with their face turned upward, while the Indians always sank with their face turned downward. If God had not granted us favourable weather, we would all have died of hunger.'

By 9 July 1522 things were so dire that del Cano was forced, against his wishes, to dock at Santiago in the Cape Verde Islands. Explaining to the Portuguese governor that he had lost his way while returning from America, he was allowed to purchase rice and water. But when the last boatload of food had left, one of the crew foolishly offered to pay with spices instead of money. Realizing that del Cano had come not from America but from the Indies, the Portuguese arrested all 13 members of the shore party and ordered the *Victoria* ashore. With food aboard, home so near, and his cargo so valuable, del Cano abandoned his men, raised sail and headed for Spain. On Monday 8 September the *Victoria* docked at Seville, firing all its guns in celebration.

Its reception was less rapturous than expected. The *San Antonio* had, as Magellan suspected, returned home, and its captain Estevão Gomes had already lodged complaints against the way the expedition had been run. For a short while del Cano was imprisoned until, when the facts became clear, Gomes took his place in gaol. Thereupon, he and his crew were allowed to enjoy their success. Although the smallest of Magellan's ships, displacing only 85 tons, the *Victoria* carried a cargo of spices so valuable that it sold for ten thousand times the purchase price and raised enough money to cover the entire cost of the expedition. Even after the king had taken his cut, there was enough for del Cano and his men to live in comfort for the rest of their lives. They could claim, too, the privilege of having been the first people to circumnavigate the globe, en route charting a westward passage to the Indies, crossing the Pacific Ocean and revealing the true size of the world's oceans. They had also discovered an apparent hole in time. While supplies were being loaded at Cape Verde, Pigafetta had noticed a remarkable thing. According to his journal and the pilot's logbook, the date was 9 July. But at Santiago it was 10 July. 'We could not understand how we had made a mistake,' he wrote, 'as I, who had never been ill, had never ceased to keep a journal every day, without interruption.' Two centuries earlier Arab astronomers had theorized that if one travelled around the world against the passage of the sun one would gain a day on the calendar. Here, now, was the proof.

The expedition had a sad ending. The *Trinidad* was captured by the

Portuguese and its men imprisoned. The garrison del Cano left in the Moluc-cas held out for a few years before they, too, were taken prisoner. The climate, and Portuguese gaols, killed all but four, who eventually straggled back to Spain. Of the 277 people who had left Seville in 1519 only 69 survived, and 35 of those were the *San Antonio* mutineers. The strait that Magellan had discovered through South America was forgotten, and by 1560 had been expunged from the map: in that year a report stated (arbitrarily and with no proof) that 'the Strait of Magellan no longer exists; either a landslide has blocked it or else an island has risen out of the sea to dam up its channel'. Moreover, after much studying of the atlas, it was decided that the Spice Islands lay on the Portuguese side of the Tordesillas line and that Magellan had wasted his time.

Francisco de Orellana (1541–6)

On the face of it, the east was a far more profitable avenue of discovery than the west. Since Columbus's annexation of the West Indies, however, a stream of explorers had left Europe to probe the rumours of gold that Columbus had reported. They included the Spaniard Vicente Pinzón, one of Columbus's shipmates, who found the mouth of the Amazon (he called it Saint Mary of the Sweet Water) in 1500; Pedro Alvares Cabral, who discovered Brazil in the same year; John the Navigator, who went as far south as the River Plate; and an Italian, Amerigo Vespucci, who travelled on a number of expeditions to South America between 1497 and 1505, working variously for Spain and Portugal. Of all these voyages of discovery, Vespucci's had the greatest significance. A Florentine chandler, whose hobby was the study of navigation and geography, he never personally commanded an expedition and was an interpreter of discovery rather than an instigator. But he was the first to realize that Europe was divided from the Indies by a separate continent, and for this he was rewarded in 1507 by a cartographer who suggested the New World be christened in his honour – America.

By the time Vespucci returned, the West Indies had already attracted a number of settlers who had imported slaves, horses and cattle and set themselves up as ranchers. But they were an unreliable crowd, adventurers and ex-soldiers for the most part, who had left Spain in search of excitement rather than a settled agricultural life. After a short while they usually abandoned their holdings, either because they were bored or because they found the work too hard, or because they had heard rumours of a gold strike elsewhere. This population of restless desperadoes proved a perfect recruiting ground for Spain's designs on the New World. In a series of private ventures, licensed but not funded by the Crown, they probed west towards America, planting colonies on the Panamanian, Colombian and Ecuadorean coasts, where they flourished despite sickness, hunger and attacks by local Indians. By 1513 Vasco Núñez de Balboa had crossed the isthmus to the Pacific Ocean, founded the town of Darién, and explored both the Caribbean and Pacific coasts in boats built locally for the purpose. In 1519 Hernán Cortés left Cuba with a force of 600 volunteers to conquer the Maya civilization of Yucatan

and the Aztec of Mexico.* New Spain (Mexico) was just the beginning. The conquistadores, as they called themselves, moved simultaneously north and south, their armour, firearms and horses – never before seen in Central or South America – allowing them to conquer most of the lands around the Gulf of Mexico and a large portion of the Andes. For the latter, Spain could thank Francisco Pizarro.

A not very successful settler at Darién, Pizarro had been tempted, like others, by reports of a wealthy civilization to the south. After several abortive attempts, he reached Peru in 1530 where, with his four brothers and a few hundred soldiers, he conquered the vast, sophisticated empire of the Incas. The rumours of wealth were true – so true, in fact, as to surpass fable. When Pizarro captured the Inca himself, Atahuallpa, he demanded as ransom that the cell in which was kept be filled with gold as high as he could reach his hand. The request was honoured. Encouraged, Pizarro asked a further price for Atahuallpa's release: the right for his men to strip the gold from Inca temples. This too was done. Then, having melted down the gold, Pizarro ordered Atahuallpa to be executed on spurious charges of treason.

---

* In one of the famous moments of military history, he burned his ships on landing at Vera Cruz. Intended as a political gesture to prove his independence from Cuba (he successfully legalized his position as representative of the Spanish Crown), it was also a powerful declaration of intent: the Spaniards were there to stay – as Cortes soon showed.

Balking at the prospect of being burned at the stake, Atahuallpa accepted Christianity in return for an easier death. He was publicly garrotted on 26 July 1533.

Atahuallpa's murder did not complete the conquest, but when Pizarro finished the job in 1534 his men were still eager for gold. From Inca prisoners (who by now were willing to tell the victors anything they wanted to hear so long as they did not have to be burned or garrotted) Pizarro learned of a land whose ruler was so wealthy that he was dusted with a mixture of resin and gold dust in the morning, before washing it off in a nearby lake at night, to re-anoint himself the following day. 'He feels it would be less beautiful to wear any other ornament,' wrote one chronicler. 'It would be crude and common to put on armour plates or wear hammered or stamped gold, for other rich lords wear these when they wish ... I would rather have the sweepings of the chamber of this prince, than the great meltings of gold which have taken place in Peru.' He was called El Dorado, 'The Golden One'. In 1541 Pizarro's brother Gonzalo left the Andean city of Quito to find him.

A burly, coarsely spoken and highly effective soldier, Gonzalo Pizarro was attracted by tales not only of gold but of spices: La Canela, the Land of Cinnamon, was supposed to exist to the east of the Andes. To this was added the prospect of colonizing new territory. As Pizarro explained to the King of Spain, 'I became fascinated, and I decided to go and conquer and explore it ... In my zeal and eagerness to do this, I spent more than fifty thousand castellanos, which I paid out in advance to the men whom I took with me, both on foot and horse.'

The expedition that left Quito in March 1541 comprised 280 men, 260 horses, 4,000 Indian porters, a herd of 2,000 pigs (in addition to the usual stores of grain, biscuits and wine), plus a pack of several hundred dogs to harry any opposition they might meet. It was described as 'a very magnificent body of men and one well prepared for any adventure which might lie ahead'. Magnificent it may have been, but it was not prepared for the Andes. The mountains were steep, thickly forested and riven by streams and rivers. The passes were cold, cloudy and more than 14,000 feet high. For two months it rained incessantly – 'it never stopped long enough to dry the shirts on our backs'. They hacked their way through the jungle with machetes, built countless bridges, and when they emerged in the foothills, 90 miles later, were at the end of their strength. 'We were exhausted simply getting over the other side,' Pizarro wrote. 'The expeditionary force ... were quite worn out in consequence of the great hardships which they had gone through in climbing up and down the great mountains.' After recuperating in the fertile valley of Sumaco – where they were joined by a rearguard of 23 men led by the one-eyed conquistador Francisco de Orellana – Pizarro took 70 men in search of the Land of Cinnamon. His precise route is unknown, but it probably led south-east to the Napo River. He did find cinnamon, but the trees were too scattered, too few and too far distant to be harvested profitably. 'It is a land and a commodity by which Your Majesty cannot be rendered any service,' he wrote disconsolately. He tortured his Indian guides repeatedly (sometimes they were burned at the stake, sometimes thrown to the dogs, in both cases while still alive), but after several weeks' travel he had still not found what he wanted. According to one contemporary, he was 'much distressed at finding he could not reach any fertile and abundant province … and deplored many times that he had undertaken the expedition. Although he did not let his followers understand this, on the contrary giving them every encouragement.' When he reached the Napo's tributary, the Coca, however, he met a local chief, Delicola, who not only showed him the best place to build a bridge – above the frighteningly steep San Rafael Falls – but, having obviously heard of the Spaniards' methods, assured him that El Dorado lay to the east. Seizing him to act as a guide, Pizarro sent word for de Orellana to follow with the rest of the men.

Reunited, the Spanish force continued down the Coca, Delicola leading the way in chains. The ground was marshy, the forest nigh impenetrable, the climate stiflingly humid and fever rampant. By October most of the porters were dead from disease, mistreatment and exhaustion. Delicola had slipped his chains and fled into the jungle. In addition, the column was being attacked sporadically by local tribesmen. With insufficient porters to carry either his supplies or the 25 men who were now too ill to move, Pizarro ordered the construction of a boat. His men responded with ingenuity, felling trees, sawing planks, making charcoal, constructing furnaces, forging nails from horseshoes and shredding old clothes which, combined with tree sap, they used to seal the gaps between the planks. After several weeks they had produced a 26-foot-long watertight vessel that they named *San Pedro*. Pizarro loaded it with his food and his invalids, then on 9 November continued down the Coca. Delicola had spoken vaguely of El Dorado being at a point where two rivers met. They did not reach the junction – presumably that between the Coca and the Napo – and by Christmas Pizarro was in despair. Already in October they had finished the last of their pigs and had been reduced to scavenging for roots. Now they started on the dogs and horses. The Indians they captured told them that the road ahead was hard and barren, with no food for miles. With his men on the brink of mutiny, Pizarro considered a retreat to the Andes. But then Francisco de Orellana stepped forward.

A distant relation of Pizarro, and five years his junior, the 30-year-old Orellana proposed that he go ahead in the boat to find food, which he believed was only one day's journey away. According to Father Carvajal, a priest who accompanied him, he was sacrificing himself for the good of the expedition: 'If he, Pizarro, should find that Orellana was delayed, he should not be concerned about him, and in the meantime he should turn back to where food was to be had, and wait for Orellana there for three or four days, or for as long as he should see fit. And in case Orellana did not come back, he should not be concerned about him. Thereupon [Pizarro] told him to do whatever he thought best.' Pizarro told it slightly differently: 'I was pleased at the idea and [said] that he should see to it that he got back within twelve days, and in no case to go beyond the junction of the rivers, but bring the food and give attention to nothing else.' Orellana departed on 26 December 1541 with 57 men and most of the expedition's weapons.

Twelve days passed, then another 12, during which Pizarro's party ate more of their horses and all of their dogs. 'They wasted nothing, neither the viscera nor the hides nor any other parts,' wrote one contemporary. Starving, Pizarro sent an advance party down the Coca to its junction with the Napo. It found neither El Dorado nor Orellana but, travelling up the Napo, it did find an abandoned cassava plantation. When they returned 27 days later with their booty, Pizarro's conquistadores were starving. They had eaten 'nothing but saddles and stirrup leather, sliced, boiled and toasted over embers, with palm shoots and fruit stems fallen from the trees, together with toads and snakes. For we had by now eaten in this wild country over one thousand dogs and more than one hundred horses, and many of us were sick, and others weak, while some had actually died there of hunger.' Devouring the cassava, they set out for the plantation. It took a week just to cross the river, and then another ten days before they hacked their way to the grove. When they got there they were so ravenous that they barely bothered to cook the cassava roots before gorging themselves. Unfortunately, raw cassava is poisonous. Two men died as a result of their excesses, and most of the others were incapacitated. More disheartening still, a lone conquistador stumbled out of the jungle to announce himself as the last survivor of Orellana's group. His story was that Orellana had reached the junction between the Coca and the Napo but, the current being too strong for him to sail upriver, had gone east into uncharted territory. He, Hernán Sanchez de Varga, had objected, whereupon he had been left to fend for himself.

Outraged by what he saw as an example of abject cowardice and treachery, Pizarro put his sick men on the few remaining horses, tying their legs round the girths to stop them falling off, and led the party towards the Andes. A small advance guard blazed the trail, lighting a huge signal fire every evening, while the remainder waded after them, waist-deep in swamps. After 320 miles Pizarro was 'very depressed ... for he did not know in what land he was, nor what direction to take to reach Peru, or any other part where Christians might be'. Following now this river, now that, they toiled on, growing hungrier by the day. At first they drank their horses' blood; then they cut steaks from them while they were still alive, filling the holes in their flesh with clay. Finally they slaughtered them. After that they boiled vegetable soup in their helmets, collected wild berries and, occasionally, managed to shoot a jungle animal whose skins they used to replace their disintegrating clothes. 'In these conditions they pushed forward,' wrote one chronicler, 'half-starving, naked and barefoot, covered with sores, cutting a path with their swords, as it rained endlessly, so that for days on end the sun was obscured and they could not dry themselves. They cursed themselves repeatedly for having placed themselves in this situation, [exposing] themselves to these privations and hardships, which they could so easily have avoided.'

Having fought a fierce battle with Indians, they finally saw on the horizon the familiar peaks of Quito on the horizon. Not long afterwards they came to a set of rapids, which confirmed that they were on track for the foothills. It also meant they had a hard climb ahead of them, but after so long in the bogs and marshes of the forest they did not care. The prospect of being on firm ground was exhilarating: the stones in the rapids were the first they had seen in a thousand miles. Following the river as far as it went, and then striking towards the nearest pass, they crossed the Andes in a state of hallucinatory weakness. Pizarro was disturbed by dreams, in one of which his heart was ripped out by a vulture. The expedition's astrologer, Jerónimo de Villegas, interpreted it as a sign that someone close to him would die. Thus disheartened, they also saw a comet that they took to be an omen – but whether good or bad they could not tell. In June 1542 they limped down the steep gorge towards Quito. According to one account, horses were sent to carry them home but Pizarro refused to accept any assistance and covered the last miles, as he had the previous hundreds, on foot.

It had been 16 months since the expedition left Quito. Of the 4,280 who set out only 80 or so returned – half the number who had bade farewell to Orellana the previous November – and those 80 'were all so weak and gaunt that no one would have recognised them'. In practical terms the expedition had been a failure: it had discovered neither gold nor spices, and the region was worthless as a colony. Pizarro had also suffered a personal loss. On their return he learned that his brother Francisco had been murdered, fulfilling the prediction of his dream, and that Peru had been taken over by one of his confederates (a situation Gonzalo soon corrected, albeit briefly). In defence of the enterprise all that could be said – as one man immediately did – was that it had shown how tough the conquistadores were: 'No other race or nation,' wrote Pedro de Cieza de León, historian and conquistador himself, 'has with such resolution passed through such labours, or such long periods of starvation or traversed such long distances as [the Spanish] have. And in this expedition of Gonzalo Pizarro assuredly very great hardships were endured, for this exploration and conquest ... I am bound to say, was the most laborious expedition that has ever been undertaken in these Indies, and in it the Spanish endured hardships, famine and miseries, which truly tried the virtues of their nation.'

Forgotten, save for a few denigratory despatches to Spain, was Orellana. From the point where they had either deserted or, maybe, found the current too powerful to return to Pizarro's camp, Orellana and his men had sailed downriver on the *San Pedro*. According to a priest who accompanied him,

Gaspar de Carvajal, he had offered 1,000 gold pieces to anyone willing to walk back to Pizarro's camp and tell him of their predicament. But nobody was willing. (Carvajal made no mention of the abandoned man, Varga.) In fact, 49 of the 57 petitioned him not to return. Thus, putting the reasons for his decision in writing, Orellana sailed down the Napo to a world of terrifying excess. He passed a sediment-rich tributary whose water was 'black as ink ... The current so big and strong that for sixty miles it forms a black streak through the other river and the waters do not mix.' They called it the Río Negro. At another river which they called the Madeira, they were astonished by the quantity of logs that poured from its mouth. They found, too, settlements that made beautiful ceramics: 'the finest porcelain that was ever seen in this world, enamelled and embellished with all colours, so shiny and gleaming as to astonish the viewer'. The Napo led eventually to a bigger river, so vast that it was almost a flowing sea. Here the countryside was heavily populated* and although they kept to the middle of the stream they were attacked by warlike tribes who fired at them from both banks for more than 200 miles. 'What hardships, what bodily suffering, what extraordinary dangers we passed through,' wrote Carvajal, who lost an eye in one battle.

When they reached less hostile territory, Orellana landed the *San Pedro*, rebuilt its rotting hull and at the same time constructed a new vessel, the *Victoria*. The *Victoria* was 24 feet long, with seats for 18 oarsmen and a full set of sails. It was deep and wide and was intended not as a river boat but as a proper ocean-going vessel, for Orellana had no doubt that this river would sooner or later reach the sea. He had his destination very clearly in mind: once they hit salt water they would sail north-west to the conquistador colonies. But before they did so he and his men had to endure the ritual of the female warriors.

Ever since Marco Polo had reported the existence of Male and Female Islands off the coast of Africa it had become an *idée fixe* that there existed a domineering race of female warriors called the Amazons. Columbus had mentioned them, as had Vasco da Gama, and now Orellana elaborated the theme. According to Carvajal, they were attacked by an army led by a wild race of women, 'fighting as if they were in command'. Carvajal was specific as to their appearance and martial ability. They were white and tall, with long braided hair that they wound round their heads, and went naked '[but] with their privy parts covered'. One woman fought as hard as ten men, and together they peppered the boats with arrows so that they looked like porcupines. But they weren't strictly Amazons, he warned, because they did not cut their right breasts off to make it easier to fire their bows. When he interrogated a (male) prisoner he learned that they lived in stone-built houses whose furnishings were made – unsurprisingly – of gold and silver. Like Magellan's Patagonian giants, Carvajal's strange Nordic fantasy was

---

* It has been estimated that the central Amazon population was, in 1541, about two or three million. Carvajal recorded a town that stretched 18 miles along the riverbank.

immortalized on the atlas. So impressed was Orellana by these women that he named the river in their honour – Río de las Amazonas, the Amazon.

The *San Pedro* and the *Victoria* reached the mouth of the Amazon in early August, after a 'long and winding voyage' of, by their own calculation, approximately 5,000 miles. For nearly three weeks Orellana prepared them for the sea journey ahead. Dismantling both boats, he reforged their nails, replaced their planks and sailed for a place where he could give them a comprehensive overhaul. He landed on an island whose beaches were shallow enough for him to tip the vessels on their sides and scrape their hulls. Within a few weeks he re-rigged them with ropes made of vines and palm-fibre, provided them with bilge pumps made of hollowed tree trunks, and fashioned anchors from lumps of wood studded with rocks. Meanwhile, his men were reduced to grubbing snails and crabs from the beach. They called the place Starvation Island.

When they sailed again on 26 August it was one of the most preposterously optimistic departures in the history of exploration. According to Carvajal, they lacked everything: pilots, sailors and even compasses – all of which, he noted sardonically, 'are necessary things'. They had only the smallest amount of food. Their boats were homemade. They had little experience either of the sea or of navigation. And yet Orellana hoped that they could travel the 1,200-odd miles to Colombia. Creeping along the coast, they were blown out to sea by a storm so violent that the two ships became separated. The *San Pedro* survived the gales and by dint of good fortune and lucky navigation reached Colombia on 9 September. Assuming the others had been lost, the crew were lamenting the deaths of their compatriots when, two days later, the *Victoria* straggled into harbour. The combined companies of both vessels came to 47. During the whole journey Orellana had lost ten men – almost a fifth of his original muster. Proportionately, this was a terrible cost; but it was as nothing when set against Pizarro's losses on his overland trek. Indeed, given the distance they had covered, the company had emerged surprisingly intact. Even so, as one man remarked, it had been, 'Less a journey than a miracle.'

Orellana did not linger in South America – Pizarro had already marked him as a traitor – but sailed for Iberia, where he first tried to interest the King of Portugal in his discoveries and, when that failed, approached the King of Spain. His reports were passed to an ecclesiastical council to determine whether he had overstepped the Tordesillas line separating Spanish and Portuguese spheres of interest. The verdict was that although the mouth of the Amazon fell on the Portuguese side of the line its upper reaches were open to Spain. Orellana was given the title of Governor of Nueva Andalusia and sent to colonize the Amazon Basin.

He left in May 1545, with four ships, his new teenage wife and hundreds of would-be conquistadores. One ship foundered in the crossing and the others became lost in the Amazon delta. Orellana and most of his men died there. His teenage wife, however, escaped to Trinidad and reported that for 11 months they had wandered through a maze of rivers, where her husband and the others died one by one from fever. They had not even found the main body of the Amazon.

William Barents (1594–7)

While the Dutch and Portuguese squabbled over their possessions in the Indies, northern European nations were wondering how they, too, might lay their hands on the wealth of Cathay. The accepted sea route via the Cape of Good Hope was under Iberian control and therefore out of the question. Magellan's route through South America and the Pacific was similarly impossible, being too hazardous in terms of weather and enemy patrols. This did not mean, however, that the Orient was unattainable. For a long while Europeans had speculated on the nature of the Arctic. Ever since the fourth century BC, when Pytheas of Massilia had sailed to Britain and continued north for six days, sighting land – possibly Iceland – in a latitude where the sun shone constantly and the temperature was cold, conflicting legends had arisen about the polar region. Some said it was inhabited by dog-headed savages, others that it was home to a long-lived, peaceful and civilized race called the Hyperboreans, who lived in contempt of their neighbours, the one-eyed, gold-hungry Arimaspians. Whatever the physiognomy and morals of the inhabitants, it was generally agreed that the Pole was not as frigid as its surrounding ice would suggest. Somewhere to the north there must be a temperate zone – perhaps sheltered by mountains – where life was possible, or at least where ships could travel. This ran against all current geographical wisdom. The routes west to Iceland and Greenland were well known, and nobody had seen anything to suggest that the Pole was habitable. It was the same to the east: from Vardø and Kola, the northernmost ports in Scandinavia, where Dutch and English traders did business with the merchants of Novgorod, came tales of a bleak and dismal coast intersected by vast rivers whose outflow scarcely disturbed the year-round ice. Nevertheless, the belief in a temperate Pole persisted (encouraged by the report in 1360 of one Nicholas of Lynn that the earth's axis was topped by a black magnetic rock surrounded by whirlpools and mountainous islands), and by 1569 the influential Flemish mapmaker Gerardus Mercator had established it as a solid landmass. To those who mattered, Mercator's map was far more encouraging than the reports of sailors who said they had seen nothing but ice.

Following Mercator's projection, there existed three potential avenues to

Cathay. One could go straight north; one could go to Greenland, where a North-West Passage was believed to exist; or one could sail beyond Vardø in search of the North-East Passage. Of these three, a group of English merchants decided the North-East Passage was the most accessible. In 1551 they founded 'The Mysterie and Companie of the Merchants Adventurers for the Discoverie of Regions, Dominions, Islands and Places unknowen'. Two years later three ships, under Sir Hugh Willoughby and Richard Chancellor, sailed for Vardø and beyond. The fleet became separated off Norway, Willoughby sailing east with the *Bona Esperanza* and the *Bona Confidentia* until on 14 August he sighted land. Possibly it was Novaya Zemlya, but there was no mention of such a place on his maps. Confused, he wrote that it 'lay not as the Globe made mention'. Turning back, he followed the coast until he became trapped by ice not far from Kola.

Of what happened to Willoughby and his 70 men during the winter of 1553–4 little is known. They searched the coast for habitation, then, finding none, they returned to their ships. Food was short, as was fuel, and their clothing was inadequate. Most of them were still alive in January 1554, as recorded by Willoughby. But by the end of the winter they were all dead, either from scurvy or starvation, or possibly poisoned by fumes from the sea-coal they shovelled into their stoves. Their floating graves were discovered the following year. That at least some of them may have been killed by fumes would account for a curious tale reported by the Venetian ambassador: 'The mariners now returned . . . narrate strange things about the mode in which they were frozen, having found some of them seated in the act of writing, pen in hand, and the papers before them, others at table, platter in hand and spoon in mouth; others opening a locker, and others in various postures, like statues, as if they had been adjusted and placed in those attitudes.'

Chancellor was more fortunate. On the *Edward Bonaventure* he entered the White Sea, and at the Bay of St Nicholas, near modern Archangel, found a village that had contact with Moscow. Leaving his men, he travelled overland and established a trading agreement with the Tsar of Russia. Returning to England with news of his success, he sailed again in 1556 for the White Sea, this time promising to retrieve Willoughby's ships. His luck did not last. Having located and manned the *Bona Esperanza* and *Bona Confidentia*, he lost both ships off the Norwegian coast. Then, after a four-month homeward journey, the *Edward Bonaventure* sank off Scotland, and Chancellor was drowned while trying to rescue the Russian diplomats he was carrying.

Despite the loss of so many men and ships, the 'Mysterie and Companie' – renamed the Muscovy Company – continued to investigate the North-East Passage. Shortly after Chancellor's death his sailing master Stephen Burrough took the tiny *Searchthrift* to the southern tip of Novaya Zemlya and discovered the strait between it and Vaigach Island that led to the Kara Sea. In 1580 another two Englishmen, Arthur Pet and Charles Jackman, followed in Burrough's tracks aboard the *George* and *William*. Their instructions were

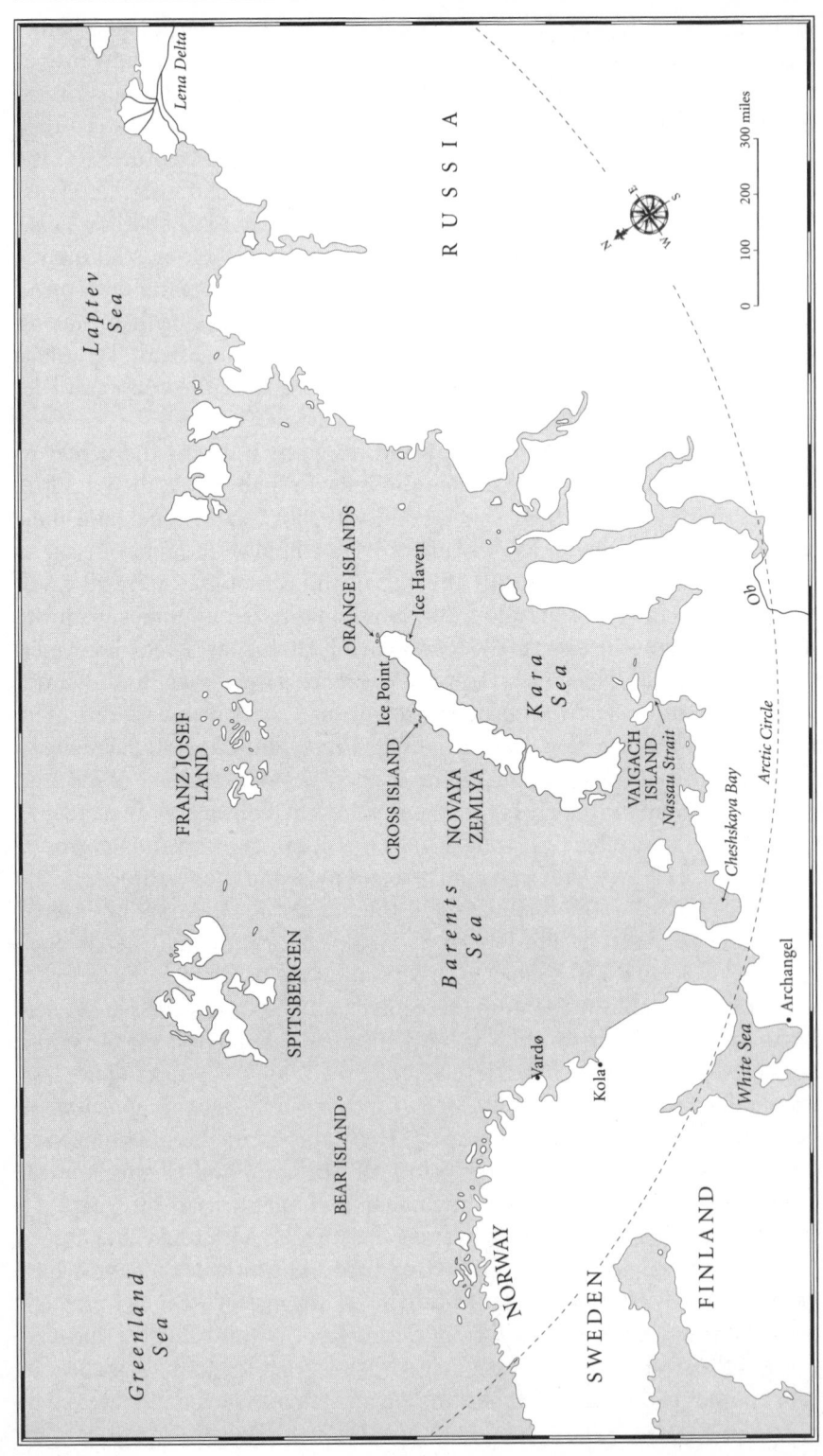

optimistic: the two captains and their small ships were to sail to Cathay, present the emperor with gifts and letters from Queen Elizabeth, and return home, having spent a winter either in Cathay or the north and having charted as much of the Siberian coast as was possible. They went no further than Vaigach Island, where they were driven back by storms and ice. On the return journey they became separated, and Jackman's ship was lost. Once again, nobody seemed to be deterred by this disaster. Over the next ten years Russian, Flemish and Dutch explorers travelled overland and by sea as far as the mouth of the Ob, in the Kara Sea. The usual exaggerated rumours seeped back to Europe. One said: 'this sea beyond Ob ... [is] so warme, that all kinde of Sea Fowles live there as well in the Winter as in the Summer, which report argueth that this Sea pierseth farre into the South parts of Asia'. Another said that beyond the Ob was a mighty river on which sailed 'great vessels, laden with rich and precious merchandize'. The people to whom these ships belonged were 'none other than the [inhabitants] of Cathay'. The prospect of the Orient being just around the corner was irresistible. And nobody, in the 1590s, found it more appealing than the Dutch.

For the last 30 years the Netherlands – or more precisely the United Provinces of the north – had been in revolt against Spain's Habsburg Empire, to which, by a dynastic quirk, they were deemed to belong. A loose coalition of city states rather than a single nation, the Provinces nevertheless operated under one flag, had strong mercantile ties and together owned the largest navy in Europe. They, more than anyone, had both the means and the motive to intrude upon Spain's trade with the Far East. Accordingly, in 1594, the cities of Middelburg, Enkhuisen and Amsterdam jointly funded a fleet of three ships to push back the frontiers of the North-East Passage. In charge of the Amsterdam vessel was a skilled navigator named William Barents.

It was a warm summer, with little ice to be seen, and the Middelburg and Enkhuisen ships managed to probe 150 miles into the Kara Sea. Barents, however, took a different route, following the west coast of Novaya Zemlya until he reached a spot – Ice Point – where the land fell away to the south. At a position of 77° N he was not only further north than any north-east explorer yet but, thanks to the eastward curve of Novaya Zemlya, he was also closer to China – although he did not have the instruments to calculate longitude accurately, Ice Point is almost at 70° E. When the fleet returned that year, Barents brought home a quantity of fool's gold, a polar bear skin, a stuffed walrus and, importantly, the news that a passage might be found to the north of Novaya Zemlya.

The success of this reconnaissance encouraged the United Provinces to despatch a second fleet in 1595. Its seven ships carried trade goods, 18 months' food, a Russian interpreter, an official chronicler named Gerrit de Veer, and a mixed company of merchants, factors and seamen. Rather than allow the fleet to separate, as had happened on the last expedition, the captains were given specific instructions: they were not to sail for Ice Point, but were to go through Nassau Strait, to the south of Vaigach Island. Barents, in command of the 200-ton *Greyhound*, was disappointed. But in the end it would not have mattered which route they took, because the ice that year was exceptionally thick. For weeks they hovered at the mouth of the Nassau Strait, waiting for a favourable wind. When it did not come Barents took matters into his own hands on 1 September and sailed anyway. Reluctantly the others followed him. They came to a halt at States Island, only a few miles into the Kara Sea. Here, with the ice stretching impenetrably to the east – 'so that it had the appearance of a continent, which was most frightful to behold' – Barents insisted they either carry on or, at the very least, leave two ships to overwinter before proceeding to Cathay the following summer. The senior three captains favoured an immediate retreat, but were unwilling to order it without unanimous agreement from the others. For almost a week the opposing factions squabbled over the state of the ice ahead, the likelihood of reaching Cathay, and the perils of overwintering so far north. While the captains deliberated, their men went ashore in search of crystals.

On 6 September, during one of these forays, an event occurred that helped make up the leaders' minds. Two men were grubbing through the rocks when, in de Veer's words, 'a great leane white beare came sodainly stealing out, and caught one of them fast by the necke, who not knowing what it was that tooke him by the necke, cried out and said, "Who is that that pulles me so by the necke?" Wherwith the other, that lay not farre from him, lifted up his head to see who it was, and perceiving it to be a monstrous beare, cryed and sayd, "Oh mate, it is a beare!" and therewith presently rose up and ran away.' A group of 20 men, armed with muskets, came to their companion's aid, but the polar bear had already started to eat him. It then ran at the rescuers, killing one and scattering the rest. Three valiant souls from the *Greyhound* mounted a counterattack, but it took four volleys to make any impression, and even when they shot it between the eyes the bear still did not die but reared up, its latest victim hanging from its jaws. They broke two cutlasses on it before a man darted in and cut the bear's throat. If this was what they could look forward to during a winter on States Island then they would rather leave while it was still possible.

Barents was recalcitrant. On 14 September he tried to sail into the ice, as he had done successfully in Nassau Strait. But this time his trick failed. Nobody followed him, and he was forced to join the others in a withdrawal to Holland. The United Provinces were less welcoming than they had been the year before. Two expeditions had now failed, and the most recent had involved a considerable amount of public money. Throwing the North-East Passage open to private enterprise, they placed a bounty on its head: 25,000 florins for its traverse, with lesser sums for discoveries that might lead to its completion. A consortium of Amsterdam merchants accepted the challenge. Barents was given two ships – their names are unknown – one of which was commanded by himself, with Jan Corneliszoon Rijp being given charge of the other. Rijp had sailed under Barents during his second voyage, as had another officer, Jacob van Heemskerck, who was appointed nominal commander of Barents's ship. And de Veer came with them too. They carried all the food, water and wine they would need during their absence, as well as a selection of trade goods for the Chinese: bales of velvet, mugs made of silver and pewter, plus a selection of engravings by the popular artist Goltzius. And just in case, they took chests of gold and silver coins – some Dutch, some Portuguese. The two ships were in the sea by 18 May 1596. By the 22nd they were off the Shetlands and sailing due north.

Barents had decided to take a new and riskier course, hoping that he might discover the open polar sea or that, if it did not exist, he would be able to follow the ice east until he hit Novaya Zemlya. His course took him to undiscovered lands – first Bear Island and then the archipelago of Spitsbergen – around which he dodged in a futile search for a gap in the ice. At 80° 10', the furthest north any European had ever sailed, Barents admitted defeat and turned for the North-East Passage. So did Rijp. But they did not sail together. Rijp believed they were in the region of Novaya Zemlya and insisted on staying where he was. Barents, who knew better, argued only for a short while before leaving for the east. In the end, Barents was proved right. Rijp endured a horrible period in the ice off Spitsbergen, discovered nothing, and finally went home. Barents, meanwhile, sailed blind across the ocean, evading pack ice, until he reached Novaya Zemlya on 17 July.

Continuing north along its coast, he reached Cross Island – so called because of the two wooden crosses that marked the graves of Russian mariners – where, on the 19th, his path was blocked by a mass of ice. He waited patiently for almost three weeks until, on 5 August, the sea cleared. He enjoyed open seas for only two days before the wind changed and the ice closed in again. Mooring the ship to one of the larger bergs in order to protect it from at least some of the jostling floes, he drifted with the current, battered all the while by a ferocious blizzard. It was a brave decision, for although the inside of the ship had been cross-braced to resist a squeeze by the ice, its unreinforced hull was vulnerable to the slightest knock. However, by luck, and by towing the ship from berg to berg, he emerged unscathed. By 15 August he had passed Ice Point and was within sight of the Orange Islands, the furthest he had sailed on his voyage of 1594. The Orange Islands were not much to speak of: rough, slatey and barren, they were so desolate that even seabirds seemed to avoid them. Their only value, as far as Barents was concerned, was that they offered a vantage point for spying the seas ahead. But, on climbing a small hill, he found the view was almost as disappointing as the islands themselves. To the north and east lay nothing but ice, confounding any hopes he may have had of a swift and trouble-free journey to Cathay. But there was one possible avenue: to the south, along the east coast of Novaya Zemlya, the sea was open for as far as he could see;

it was a narrow channel, but it might lead to a warmer, ice-free part of the ocean. He went down it.

The next few weeks were trying. Against all expectations, the coast of Novaya Zemlya led west, in exactly the direction they did not want to go, and although Barents tried repeatedly to break free of the channel he was driven back, again and again, by gales and ice. Their rudder was shattered and one of their three boats was crushed between a floe and the side of the ship. By 25 August – when the carpenter had repaired the rudder – it was obvious that they would never be able to cross the Kara Sea that season. Rather than retrace his route, Barents decided to continue south-west to Vaigach Island. If he could not reach Cathay he could at least circumnavigate Novaya Zemlya. A day later even that consolation was denied him. The coastal channel narrowed into a mess of sludgy ice, through which he could make no headway. Retreating north, Barents was caught by the early onset of winter. He anchored his ship in a nearby bay and, as the sea froze round it, prepared to overwinter. He called the place Ice Haven.

Within 24 hours the Arctic pack was pressing against their anchorage. The first the crew knew of it was a grinding, booming noise that seemed to come from all directions. They did not understand what it could be. It was, in fact, the sound of ice grating against ice, as winds and currents compressed the pack into pressure ridges. The ridges zigzagged into Ice Haven and eventually reached the ship, lifting its bow four feet out of the water. It could have been worse: some of the pressure ridges were 20 feet high. But it was bad enough for Barents to have their two remaining boats dragged onto a solid piece of ice and stocked with provisions. The pressure ridges continued to snake forward, and at the same time a gale blew up. The cracking of the ice, combined with the buffets of the wind, terrified de Veer: '[It was] most frightful both to see and heare, and made all ye haire of our heads to rise upright with feare.'

On 16 September, with the ship tilted at a crazy angle thanks to a second pressure ridge,* Barents ordered his men to build a hut for the winter. Although Novaya Zemlya was treeless, there was a bay, four miles to the north of Ice Haven, that contained massive amounts of driftwood – not the usual collection of gnarled stumps, but whole trees that had been carried down Siberia's rivers by the spring thaw and had ended up on this remote beach. They cut the logs into one-and-a-half-inch planks and dragged them to Ice Haven. Four corner posts were sunk into the ground – with difficulty, because even in summer the permafrost was only a foot or so beneath the surface – and were then boarded up to create a rough cabin. The driftwood being too unwieldy to make a roof, they raided the ship, ripping up its deck

---

* It did not sink, thanks to its rounded hull, popular amongst Dutch shipbuilders of the time, which gave the ice no grip and allowed the ice to rise to the surface. Four centuries later Fridtjof Nansen deployed the same technique on the *Fram*, which drifted on the pack for four years before being deposited safely in open water.

but taking care not to make it unseaworthy. Meanwhile, separate teams were deployed to cut and haul firewood for the winter. By the time they finished they had constructed a windowless shed, 50 feet by 30, with a single door protected by a porch. The roof was pyramidal, culminating in a chimney that vented the smoke from a central open fire. Logs were piled along the outside of one wall. Two tiers of bunks faced each other across the fire. Casks of wine, beer, flour, hard tack and salted meat were stacked nearby. They even built a one-person steam bath from empty barrels. When it was finished they called it *het behouden huis*, 'The House of Safety' or 'The House of the Unharmed'.

They were neither safe nor unharmed. During the building process one man died of an unknown ailment, and when they finally transferred from the ship to the hut two men were so incapacitated that they had to be carried ashore in their bedding. As winter closed in, and the sun disappeared, it became apparent that they were all suffering from scurvy. Their gums swelled, their teeth loosened, their joints ached, and unaccountable bruises broke out across their bodies. In the worst cases their hamstrings contracted so that they could no longer walk upright, but crept crabwise in an awkward crouch. They did not know what caused the disease, having only a vague notion that it might be cured by eating fresh vegetables, but none at all that it was the result of Vitamin C deficiency, nor that the same vitamin could be found in raw meat. Throughout the winter they trapped and shot Arctic foxes, whose semi-roasted meat tasted somewhat like rabbit and temporarily alleviated their complaint. They refused stubbornly, however, to eat polar bear meat, killing and skinning the creatures, but throwing the carcasses into the sea. As their supplies diminished, however, they tried eating one of them. They made the mistake of cooking the liver. The liver of a polar bear is a toxic source of Vitamin A, and the stew into which they threw it gave them indigestion and diarrhoea and made their skin peel. For several days they feared they would die. They did not repeat the experiment in a hurry – which was a pity, because the bears, whose constant encroachments made it necessary for the men to go in armed groups whenever they left the hut, would have provided a health-giving and plentiful source of meat. Still, once they had recovered from their food-poisoning they found that the bear's fat (all 100 pounds of it) made a splendid fuel for their lamps. Hungry they may have been, but at least they now had light.

Their worst enemy was the cold. Heemskerck broached the trade goods and issued them with cloth to make winter suits. They used fox pelts, too, to make hats. But with no sods or tussocks to plug the gaps between the planks, the wind whistled through the hut. Their bunks were frigid pallets, which they tried unsuccessfully to warm with heated stones and cannonballs. The men huddled round the fire, which was kept burning day and night, but its heat extended such a short distance from the flames that they felt cold even while their socks smouldered. Moreover, the wind blew the smoke around the room so that everyone was red-eyed and coughing. As the months wore on, the condensation from their cooking and their breath froze, covering roof, walls and bunks with an inch-thick sheet of ice. Although this had the benefit of keeping the wind out, it also deprived them of ventilation, as they discovered when they brought some sea-coal from the ship and piled it on the fire. They did not dare take too much, because they would need it when – or if – they made their escape. But it was a magnificent transformation: the coal burned longer and hotter than the driftwood, its heat reaching so far that the ice on the walls began to melt. To enjoy it to its fullest they closed the chimney, stopped up the door and 'went into our cabans to sleepe, well comforted with the heat, and so lay a great while talking together'. They were only saved from carbon monoxide poisoning by a man who flung open the door and let in draughts of icy air. Even so, they had 'great swounding and daseling in our heads'.

It became colder and colder. One day they hoisted a rag on a pikestaff up the chimney to see which way the wind was blowing. It froze almost before it could flutter. In January 1597 snow fell so heavily that it covered the hut to the eaves. They dug a tunnel in the snow for their slops, but even so conditions became increasingly squalid, the pervading stench of bear fat being augmented by that of excrement. Worse still, they could no longer reach the log pile. Every superfluous piece of wood was burned, including the door to the porch and even their chopping board. Above them, meanwhile, they could hear the pattering of foxes, interspersed with the heavier tread of polar bears. Once, a bear tried to tear open the roof and was driven off only with difficulty. After a few weeks they were able to dig their way free, but almost their first act in the open was to conduct a burial service. The carpenter had died of scurvy on 27 January. Unable to find open ground, they buried him seven feet deep in the snow.

A fortnight later the sun had reappeared and the wind had blown the snow from the log pile. As they stoked the fire, however, it became apparent that the driftwood could not last. Exhausted and bruised from scurvy, they set out for the beach where they had found the Siberian tree trunks. It took 11 men a whole day to saw the wood, load it onto sledges and drag it back to the hut. Their efforts produced only enough to last a week. Through February and March the wood-gathering trips became a dreaded ordeal – and one they had to undergo with increasing frequency. By now Barents and three others were so scorbutic that they were unable to move. The rest were in slightly better health, but as their legs contracted fewer and fewer could manage the journey to the beach and the amount of wood they brought back diminished proportionately.

By May the weather was warm enough for firewood to be less of a concern. And as the ice began to melt they turned their minds to escape. Heemskerck, now no longer nominally but actually in charge, hoped they would be able to use the ship. But just in case, they prepared the two boats for a sea journey, raising their sides, rigging them with sails and packing them with the last, paltry casks of food and wine. It was a wise precaution, for by the second week of June the ship was still trapped. Heemskerck transferred the money, velvet and other valuables from its hold, loaded the sick into the boats, and set sail. Behind them, hanging from the chimney in a powder-horn, they left an abbreviated account of their ordeal. It was not discovered until 1876. Still legible in places, the note ended: 'Our God will grant us safe voyage and bring us with good health in our fatherland.' The signatory was Barents.

Within three days they were at Ice Point, but Barents was now so ill that he had to ask de Veer to lift him up so that he could see it. He died on 20 June 1597, followed a few hours later by another man, Claes Andriesz. They were all sick now, but as they continued down the west coast of Novaya Zemlya they were able to kill seabirds that nested in astonishing numbers on the cliffs, and this small supply of meat prevented them deteriorating further. As well as eating the birds, they collected their eggs, hundreds at a time, and scrambled them in bear fat.* But they never killed enough birds or collected enough eggs to satisfy their appetites for long. Most of the time they lived on a thin porridge of ship's biscuit. On 5 July Jan Fransz, the nephew of Claes Andriesz, died of starvation and scurvy.

They were cheered by the sight of familiar features such as Cross Island, but disheartened by the state of the sea. They were imprisoned repeatedly by floes, and one day when camped on the ice they lost all their clothes, their chest of coins, their bales of velvet and most of their food when the ice split beneath them. On 18 July the wind changed, trapping them in a bay halfway down Novaya Zemlya where, with progress impossible, Heemskerck ordered the men ashore. They stayed there for more than a week, feasting off a colony of seabirds, before the wind changed again. On 28 July they rounded a headland and met two Russian fishing boats. For some time they had seen signs of life – huts, graves, stacks of firewood – but now they saw people. With sign language and the odd phrase he had picked up on his travels, Heemskerck explained that their ship had sunk. The Russians, whose boats were little larger than Heemskerck's and who were themselves short of food, could do little to help. They gave the Dutchmen a meal, wished them good luck – as far as Heemskerck could make out – and left the following morning for Vaigach Island. The two Dutch boats wallowed slowly in the same direction. On the last day of July they were again stranded by a change in the wind, this time on an island that at first sight seemed as barren and unpleasant as the rest of Novaya Zemlya. Yet when they looked closely they found small clumps of bright green vegetation. It was *Cochlearia groenlandica*, or

* Along the way they made a discovery that shed new light on an old mystery. A certain species of goose visited Europe every year, but nobody had ever found their nests or their eggs, which gave rise to the belief that they grew on a tree in tiny shells that then fell into the sea before maturing into birds. In medieval bestiaries they were known as barnacle geese. Heemskerck's men found the nests of the barnacle geese, thereby correcting a centuries-old misconception. That done, they ate the eggs.

scurvy grass. They picked the leaves and ate them. The cure was miraculous. When they continued, three days later, their gums had sunk back to normal size, their legs had straightened and their bruising had vanished.

Although Heemskerck was a leader of men and an experienced sailor, he was not, like Barents, a navigator, so the two boats fumbled their way through the ice, past Vaigach Island to the Russian coast, steering by compass and guesswork until they crossed a body of water they assumed was the White Sea. Landing on its westernmost promontory on 15 August, they congratulated themselves on being, at most, two days from the ports of Kola and Vardø. They were wrong. The captain of a passing Russian ship explained that they were not in the White Sea, but in Cheshskaya Bay to the east. He gave them as much food as he could spare and, having ensured that they would not starve, and with business pressing, he sailed eastwards. Wearily, Heemskerck led his boats in the opposite direction. He reached the White Sea, crossed it and sailed into a bay where two Russian ships were anchored. The Russians had food – which they shared willingly – and most importantly they had stoves. After 11 months cramped either in the *behouden huis* or on their boats, the Dutchmen experienced the unfamiliar sensation of warmth.

Living alongside the Russians was a small group of impoverished and diminutive Laplanders, one of whom Heemskerck hired to guide the fittest member of his crew overland to Kola. It was several weeks before a lone figure sprang over the hills and ran back towards them. Although he had jogged most of the way, the Lapp was not out of breath and informed them that he had reached Kola; that he had left his companion there because he was too weak to travel; but that the man had written a note for Heemskerck. When Heemskerck read the note he learned that a Dutch ship was at Kola and that its captain, none other than Jan Corneliszoon Rijp, was sending a boat to rescue them. Rijp came, gave them food, spent a night in their camp, then took them to Kola, on to Vardø and finally to Amsterdam, which they reached at noon on 1 November. In a civic version of a court-martial, the city elders called Heemskerck to account for losing the ship and its cargo of valuables. He responded in style. Dressing his men in the fox-skin hats and the greasy rags that they had worn for more than 12 months, he paraded them before his inquisitors. He was acquitted by smell alone.

Barents's failure did not disrupt the quest for the North-East Passage. In 1580 Mercator was still optimistic. 'The voyage to Catheio by the East', he wrote, 'is doutlesse verie easie and short.' Many people tried it, battling through the sea – now called the Barents Sea – that led to Novaya Zemlya, but their attacks were fruitless and in the end they gave up. In the 18th century a series of Russian expeditions took boats down the great Siberian rivers to chart most of the Arctic coastline. Not until 1878, however, was the North-East Passage finally completed.

Henry Hudson (1610–11)

According to the papally sanctioned Tordesillas Treaty of 1494 the undiscovered world belonged to Spain and Portugal. To the east of a certain line everything was Portugal's; to the west everything was Spain's. The nations of northern Europe – England and Holland in particular – refused to accept the Pope's edict. They too wanted a share of the pie and, calculating that the earth's circumference was shorter across the Poles than it was at the equator, they decided they were in an advantageous position to reach the Indies. While some sought Cathay via the North-East Passage, others suggested a more practicable route might be found to the west. One of the earliest advocates was a Venetian named John Cabot, born in 1455, who at the age of 30 settled in Bristol with the idea of finding the 'Island of Brasil', which rumour placed somewhere to the west of Ireland. But as reports seeped in of Columbus's discoveries in the Caribbean, it became clear that 'Brasil' did not exist – or that if it did it was not where everyone said it was supposed to be. In 1496, therefore, Cabot persuaded King Henry VII of England to sponsor a voyage in search of the North-West Passage. He sailed in May 1497 on the *Matthew*, with 20 men and instructions to investigate 'whatsoever islands, countries, regions or provinces of heathens and infidels, in whatsoever part of the world placed, which before this time were unknown to all Christians'. Anticipating a lucrative trade, Henry told Cabot that he could dock in Bristol free of charge, but that the Crown would take 20 per cent of the profit. Cabot discovered neither the North-West Passage nor anything that even remotely resembled profit. He did, however, discover Newfoundland in June 1497 and claimed it for England. When he returned that same year he was given £20 for his trouble. Convinced that he had found the north coast of Asia, he sailed again in 1498 with five ships. They encountered stormy weather, and only two of the ships survived. The others – with Cabot aboard – vanished without trace.

For some reason, the North-West Passage exerted a particular fascination for navigators. No matter that the North-East Passage was more convenient and its approaches better charted; they insisted on sailing across the Atlantic. In 1502 the 'Company of Adventurers to the New Found Land', was formed with the object of pursuing Cabot's discoveries. Two years later a pair of

GREENLAND

Baffin Bay

BAFFIN ISLAND

Davis Strait

Arctic Circle

Cumberland Sound

Frobisher Bay

Furious Overfall/Mistaken Straits
(Hudson Strait)

DIGGES ISLAND

Cape Wolstenholme

Hudson Bay

LABRADOR

NEWFOUNDLAND

Bottom of the Bay
(James Bay)

Atlantic
Ocean

Hudson

New Amsterdam
(New York)

0   100   200   300   400   500 miles

English ships returned from Newfoundland, carrying not gold or gems but a cargo of fish, mostly cod, which were so plentiful that even the dullest fisherman could fill his hold. From Spain, Britain and Portugal ships sailed for North America. They were interested solely in the fishing, but John Cabot's son Sebastian left Bristol in 1508 to continue his father's work. He went as far as Labrador before skirting down the coast and returning to Bristol in 1509. After a disastrous period in the employ of Spain he returned older and wiser to England, where he helped outfit Chancellor's voyages to the North-East Passage in 1553 and 1556.

By 1576 interest in the North-West Passage was riding high: as one Englishman pointed out, its discovery would be 'a great advancement to our Countrie, wonderfull inriching to our Prince, and [offering] unspeakable commodities to all the inhabitants of Europe'. In that year his fellow countryman Martin Frobisher seemed to prove him right. A man of immense physical strength, warlike disposition and rudimentary education (he seems to have written little save his name, which he spelled in a variety of ways), Frobisher was by nature a privateer rather than an explorer. Nevertheless, armed with an outdated and inaccurate map dating from the 14th century, he sailed with the *Gabriel* and *Michael* up the Labrador coast and crossed to what is now Baffin Island, where he found and named (after himself) a strait that appeared to be the door to the North-West Passage. He penetrated 180 miles before being blocked by ice, whereupon he sent his men ashore to gather souvenirs. The local Inuit were at first friendly, but then turned hostile. Five of the *Gabriel*'s crew were kidnapped, never to be seen again, and in one encounter Frobisher received an arrow in the buttocks.* Returning to England, he presented his sponsors with his findings. Apart from the discovery of Frobisher Strait – which was later found to be a bay – they did not amount to much: a few Inuit artefacts, one Inuit, and a small but strangely heavy lump of rock that two assayers declared was iron pyrites but that a third said was gold. Naturally, Frobisher accepted the last man's judgement as the most accurate. With its help, he was able to raise the money for two more journeys, in 1577 and 1578, on both occasions returning with his hold stuffed with ore.

The belated realization that it was, indeed, fool's gold brought an end to Frobisher's Arctic career. However, he did leave an important navigational legacy. On his 1578 expedition – in which he was given the title High Admiral, in charge of a fleet of 15 ships – he lost his way in a storm, and instead of hitting Frobisher Strait found himself in a seaway on the Labrador coast to the south of Baffin Island. It was broader and more promising than Frobisher Strait, but had remarkably powerful tides. 'Truly it was wonderful to heare and see the rushing and noise that the tides do make in this place,' wrote one

---

* He got his revenge: when an Inuit paddled out to the ship Frobisher grabbed his arm and hoisted him, kayak and all, over the gunwales. The unfortunate man was taken as a trophy back to England, where he died from a cold.

of his more literate companions, 'with so violent a force that our ships lying a hull were turned sometimes round about even in the manner of a whirlpoole, and the noise of the streame no lesse to be heard afarre off than the waterfall of London Bridge.' He went down it for 200 miles before returning to the south coast of Baffin Island – Meta Incognita – where he began gathering rocks again. His turbulent discovery, which he named Mistaken Straits, would play an important role in the quest for the North-West Passage.

The episode of Frobisher's gold having bankrupted most of his investors – or 'adventurers', as they were called – silence fell on the North-West Passage. For several years nobody was willing to touch it, but eventually new money was found and new expeditions were despatched. The first was that of John Davis, a gentler, more inquisitive character than Frobisher, who in 1585 took the *Sunshine* and *Moonshine* to the southern tip of Greenland. All he saw was 'mightie mountains all covered with snowe, no views of wood, grasse or earth to be seen, and the shore two leagues off into the sea so full of yce as that no shipping could by any meanes come near the same. The lothsome view of the shore, and irksome noise of the yce was such that it bred strange conceits among us, so that we supposed the place to be wast and voyd of any sensible or vegetable creatures, whereupon I called the same Desolation.' Entering the strait between Greenland and Baffin Island that now bears his name, he sailed up Greenland's west coast before crossing to Baffin Island, which he followed as far north as Cumberland Sound. It looked a likely opening for the North-West Passage, but the winds were not in his favour. He returned that year with the news that 'The North West Passage is a matter nothing doubtful, but at any tyme almost to be passed, the sea navigable, voyd of yce, the ayre tolerable, and the waters deepe'. In 1586 he made a second trip to Greenland, discovered nothing new, and returned via Labrador, where he encountered Frobisher's Mistaken Straits. He gave it a new name: Furious Overfall. Yet again English investors were disappointed. So was Davis. He did not return to the Arctic, preferring instead to find an easier route to Cathay via South America. His efforts led, in 1592, to the discovery of the Falkland Islands.

The journeys of Frobisher and Davis dampened slightly England's ambitions for the North-West Passage, but they did not quench its desire to find a passage of some sort. Authorities were beginning to question Mercator's view that there was a body of land at the North Pole. Although they knew no more about the Pole than Mercator, they hazarded that it might not be a continent but an open sea. Samuel Purchas, one of England's most prolific travel writers, described it – very accurately – as 'a Pointe, but Nothing but Vanitie'. Purchas and others, however, subscribed to the theory that the Pole sat in temperate waters. If a ship could break through the Pole's protective tonsure of ice, whose lower fringes reached to 70 N, it would be rewarded by fair seas all the way to the Pacific. In 1607, therefore, the Muscovy Company

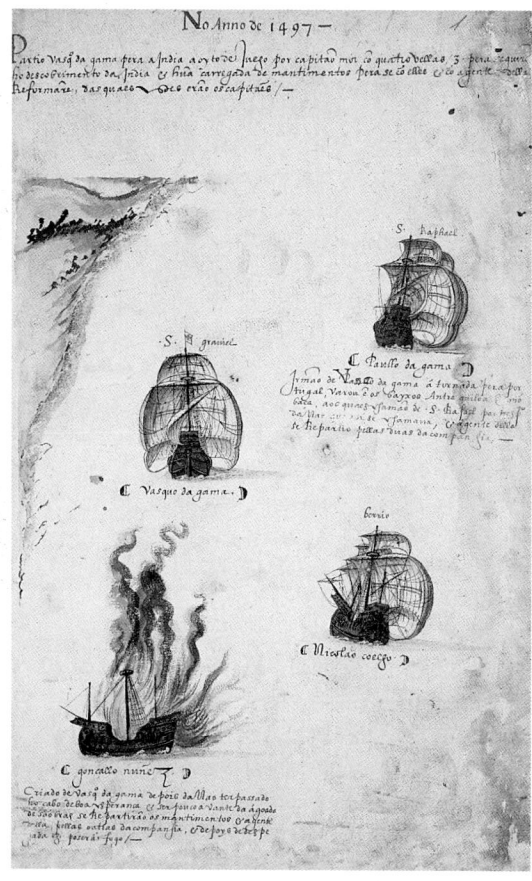

TOP Marco Polo arrives at Hormuz en route from China to Italy, *c.*1291.

ABOVE Christopher Columbus lands on Hispaniola, 1492.

RIGHT The departure of Vasco da Gama's fleet in 1497.

INSVLA MATHAN.

Victoria.

Ferdinand Magellan's assault on Mactan Island, 1521.

OPPOSITE
ABOVE A polar bear attacks William Barents's men, 1595.
BELOW Barents's hut at Ice Haven during the winter of 1596–7.

Charles-Marie de la Condamine's descent of the Amazon, 1743.

TOP Captain James Cook's death in Hawaii, 1779.
ABOVE The ascent of Mont Blanc by Horace-Bénédict de Saussure, 1787.

Alexander von Humboldt's sketch of a Mexican river. (1799–1804).

TOP Escaping a grizzly bear: Lewis and Clark's 1803–6 traverse of North America.
ABOVE W. E. Parry's *Hecla* being sawn into an ice harbour, 1824.

TOP A canoe strikes a tree and overturns: Lewis and Clark's 1803–6 traverse of North America.
ABOVE One of John Franklin's camps during his retreat through the Badlands, 1821.

sent Henry Hudson 'to discover a passage by the North Pole to Japan and China'.

Little is known of Hudson's background – not even the date of his birth – but by 1607 he must have been in his late thirties or forties because he had three sons, the eldest of whom made him a grandfather the following year. He was, however, an experienced navigator, obstinate and determined, somewhat in the same mould as Barents. He sailed for the Pole in April 1607 aboard the *Hopewell*, a small ship whose ten-strong crew included his son John – 'a boy'. The *Hopewell* went up the east coast of Greenland, possibly reaching a record north of 80° N before being driven back by ice, then spent a month probing the pack off Spitsbergen, where Hudson noted the presence of many whales and walruses, before returning to London. The Muscovy Company was not downcast. In 1608 it sent Hudson and the *Hopewell* on a second voyage, this time to the North-East Passage.

Hudson left on 22 April with a crew of 14 (including again his son John) for the north cape of Novaya Zemlya. He failed in the attempt and recorded little of worth save the sighting by two crewmen of a mermaid. She poked her head out of the water to peer at them before 'a sea came and overturned her: from the navill upward, her back and breasts were like a woman's ... Her skin very white; and longe haire hanging downe behinde, of colour blacke: in her going downe they saw her tayle, which was like the tayle of a porposse, and speckled like a mackrell.'* He also found on Novaya Zemlya 'a good store of wilde goose quills, a piece of an old oare and some flowers', which he took aboard as evidence that he had been there. He did not linger. 'I thought it my duty to save victuals, wages and tackle by my speedy return,' he wrote, 'and not by foolish rashness, the time being wasted, to lay more charge upon the action.' On the way home the *Hopewell* was caught in ice and was saved only 'by the mercie of God and his mightie help'.

The Muscovy Company wanted the 'action'. It did not want goose quills, old oars and flowers. Neither did it appreciate Hudson's methods. There was a suspicion that he had driven his men too hard. Having found the North-East Passage impassable, Hudson had apparently decided to take the *Hopewell* across the Atlantic to the North-West Passage, '[resolving] to use all means I could to sail to the north-west ... and to make trial of that place called ... the furious overfall, by Captain Davis, hoping to run into it an hundred leagues'. When the men threatened to mutiny, he was forced to sign an embarrassing affidavit: 'I gave my company a certificate under my hand, of my free and willing return, without persuasion or force of any one of them.' Disappointed in their choice of commander, the Muscovy Company did not send Hudson north again the following year.

---

* Mermaids featured prominently in histories of the time. One was captured in Belfast Lough and baptized. Another was found on the Dutch coast and taken to Haarlem, where she learned how to spin. A third was caught off Borneo where she was imprisoned in a vat, refused all food and died after a week, leaving droppings that were likened to those of a cat.

Turning to the Dutch, Hudson was given command of the *Half Moon*, in which he sailed on 25 March 1609 for the North-East Passage. Again his crew mutinied, but this time they allowed him to take the ship across the Atlantic. Perhaps fearing a second mutiny, Hudson did not head for Davis's Furious Overfall, but investigated reports of a transcontinental waterway further south. He explored the mouth of what is now the Hudson River, but soon realized that it was not the channel he sought. He returned to England on 7 November, having discovered little of interest save an island in the Hudson River that would later become the Dutch colony of New Amsterdam – and later still New York. He immediately despatched his log to Holland, with the request that they send him on a second attempt at the North-West Passage.

Hudson was by now one of the most experienced ice captains in Europe – a fact to which the English suddenly awoke. He was forbidden to go to Holland and was instead offered employment by a consortium of merchants – Sir Thomas Smythe, Sir Dudley Digges and Sir John Wolstenholme – who sent him, as he desired, to the North-West Passage. He left the Thames on 17 April 1610 aboard the *Discovery*. His 23-strong crew had varying qualifications. Five of them had served under him before: his son John, the carpenter Philip Staffe, the mate Robert Juet and two seamen, Arnold Lodlo and Michael Perse. Among the newcomers were John King the quartermaster; Robert Bylot, an experienced navigator who came aboard as an ordinary seaman; Thomas Woodehouse, 'a student in the mathematics'; Francis Clements, bosun; Bennet Mathews, cook and trumpeter; plus Abacuck Pricket, Dudley Digges's footman, who was there to safeguard the investors' interests and who became the expedition's chronicler. There was also Henry Greene, a powerful and hot-tempered wastrel who had ingratiated himself with Hudson (indeed, lived in his home) and who arrived unexpectedly at Gravesend to replace a man named Coleburne who had been appointed as an 'assistant' to help Pricket keep an eye on proceedings.

Hudson's goal was the Furious Overfall, or Mistaken Straits, which both Davis and Frobisher had marked as a potential avenue to the Pacific. By the time he reached it, via southern Greenland – Davis's 'Desolation' – the crew were in disarray. Greene picked a fight with one man before they were even clear of England, and came to blows with another when they stopped at Iceland. Juet had begun to prepare the men for a mutiny, telling them that the mission was a waste of time, that they should keep their weapons by their beds, and that Greene had been put in their midst as the captain's spy. When Hudson entered the Furious Overfall, and became temporarily trapped by the ice, matters came to a head. Juet and his supporters rebelled at being taken through such a 'great and whurling sea'.

Mutinies of the time were not as criminal as they would later become. It was understood that a captain relied on the goodwill of his men. They sailed of their own free will; if they did not wish to continue they said so; and their words were generally listened to. In this case they had every reason to turn back. The ice was terrifying, and 'the more he [the captain] strove, the worse he was, and the more enclosed, till we could go no further'. Hudson, therefore, asked them openly if they wished to carry on or not. 'He brought forth his card [chart], and showed all the company that he was entered above an hundred leagues further than any Englishman ever was; and left it to their choice whether they would proceed any further, yea or nay,' Pricket wrote. 'Whereupon some were of one mind and some of another, some wishing themselves at home, and some not caring where, so they were out of the ice. But there were some who then spake words which were remembered a great while after. There was one who told the master that if he had an hundred pounds, he would give fourscore and ten to be at home. But the carpenter made answer that if he had an hundred he would not give ten upon any such condition, but would think it to be as good money as ever he had any, and to bring it as well home, by the leave of God.' The carpenter, Staffe, won the day and, after 'much labour and time spent', the *Discovery* emerged on the western side of the Furious Overfall.

He was in a sour mood. He had been shaken by the mutiny and by the icy conditions. According to Pricket, 'Our master was in despair, and, as he told me after, he thought he should never have got out of this ice, but there perished.' His 'card' reflected the measure of his anxiety. Hitherto he had bestowed names of unexpected beauty – one island was called Paiva, a headland became Hold with Hope, a group of rocks was named The Isles of God's Mercies. Now his charting became less optimistic. A bleak, 1,000-foot cliff was called Cape Digges and a 2,000-foot, guano-smeared headland became Cape Wolstenholme. He had hoped to 'see Bantam [an island in the East Indies] by Candlemasse', but this now seemed an impossible deadline. On the other hand, he was confident that he was on the right track, for once he cleared the Furious Overfall he was met by a sea so vast that it could only be the Pacific. It was, in fact, a bay, and if Hudson had sailed west he would have discovered this in a couple of days. But he had neither the time nor the inclination – nor, in his mind, any reason – to do so. He sailed south as fast as he could for Bantam.

Before long Hudson was boxing about in a small bay – later known as James Bay, but which he called Bottom of the Bay – at the southern extremity of the larger one that he had mistaken for the Pacific. As he went north, west and south, probing for a channel, Juet and the bosun again became mutinous. On 10 September Hudson dealt with them summarily. After a trial in which several men testified to their past and present incitements, they were stripped of their rank. Robert Bylot was promoted to mate, and Francis Clements was replaced as bosun by 'a savage, foul-mouthed' man named Bill Wilson. Conceding their right to state their opinions, Hudson promised Juet and Clements that they would be reinstated if they behaved themselves. He was probably right to exert his authority, but he was wrong to pursue the course he then did. By October winter was coming in and James Bay was full of ice.

The *Discovery* had embarked with no more than eight months' food, and it was six months since it had left London. Nevertheless, Hudson decided they should overwinter before continuing to the Indies.

He had no luck at all. Every inlet was either blocked by ice or too shallow to offer protection. Once, when raising anchor, the current turned the ship, and three men were injured by the revolving capstan. He ran aground on a rock – irritatingly the carpenter had warned him to look out for rocks – and when the *Discovery* was freed he stopped looking for a safe anchorage and simply drove it into the shallows and let the ice freeze round it. Almost immediately, discord broke out.

It began with the most trivial of matters. In mid-November the gunner, John Williams, died and, following traditional practice, his belongings were put up for auction. Among the items was a much-coveted grey woollen smock. To the fury of all, Hudson said that his favourite, Henry Greene, should have it. The crew made their resentment clear. When Hudson asked Staffe to build them a hut, Staffe replied that it was too cold – 'Which when our master heard, he ferreted him out of his cabin to strike him, calling him by many foul names and threatening to hang him.' Coolly, Staffe told him he knew his job better than Hudson, that he was a ship's carpenter not a housebuilder, and that if Hudson did not like it then that was his problem. The next day Staffe went hunting and, per Hudson's instructions that nobody leave the ship unarmed or unaccompanied in case they met a polar bear, took Greene with him. Forgetting that Staffe had once been his supporter, Hudson assumed that he was now his enemy and, further, that Greene was consorting with him. In what can only be described as a fit of jealous rage, he told Greene that he could no longer have the smock and that it now belonged to Bylot. When Greene protested, 'the master did so rail on Greene, with so many words of disgrace, telling him that all his friends would not trust him with twenty shillings, and therefore why should he? As for wages, he had none, nor none should have, if he did not please him well.' Hudson's volatile behaviour continued. They shot enough ptarmigan and caught enough fish to keep them alive through the winter, but when Indians appeared who might have been able to help them find more solid supplies Hudson refused to trade evenly with them. They gave him four valuable furs, he gave them a knife and a few glass beads. They did not return.

By now Staffe had forgotten the matter of Greene's smock and had constructed a basic hut between which and the ship they divided their time. It was the first time an English vessel had wintered by choice in the Arctic, but the months passed without trouble. It was in spring that the arguments started afresh. As the ice began to melt, the crew asked if they could take the boat with a net to catch some fish. Hudson said no. Instead he took the boat and the net to find Indians with whom he could barter fish for meat – and also to find the North-West Passage. He gave no specific date for his return, merely instructing the crew to take aboard fuel, food and water while he was away. He did not find the Passage, and as the Indians avoided him (taunting him with their fires, whose smoke rose tantalizingly close to the shore) he returned with neither fish nor meat nor news of a route to the Indies. Hudson was on the verge of a breakdown. He did not know where to go or how to get out. The men netted 'fourscore small fish, a poore relief for so many hungrey bellies'. As their captain distributed a portion of bread to accompany their little fishes, the biblical comparison became obvious. Dividing the loaves, he wept.

By June the *Discovery* was free of the ice, and many, including Pricket, were suffering from scurvy. (Greene, one of the healthiest, had not scurvy but indigestion, Hudson having passed him a slice of rotten cheese.) Their one consolation was that they would soon be through the Furious Overfall and on their way home. But instead of heading north Hudson sailed northwest. Perhaps he was taking a circuitous route to the Furious Overfall, but it did not look that way to the men. Earlier he had emptied the bread locker and given everyone their allowance for the return journey; now he asked for it back again. A search of their sea chests revealed 30 small loaves, which he took for safekeeping into his own cabin to be redistributed at a later date. It was a rash move: apart from making him seem indecisive, it reinforced the crew's fear that he planned to extend the voyage; it also created the suspicion that he might be eating their bread on the sly; and, given that some had eaten their allowance within a fortnight (one man bolted his in a single day, and was sick for the following three), it was unfair to those who had rationed themselves more sensibly. This direct threat to their survival, from a captain who appeared to have no intention of abandoning his quest for the North-West Passage, was the catalyst for what happened next.

On the night of 23 June Greene and Wilson told Pricket they planned to take charge of the *Discovery* and put Hudson, his officers and his supporters into the ship's boat. 'For there was not fourteen days victuals left for all the company, at that poor allowance they were at, and that there they lay, the master not caring to go one way or other, and that they had not eaten anything these three days, and therefore were resolute either to mend or end, and what they had begun they would go through with it or die ... And for the good will they bare me, they would have me stay in the ship.' It was not so much goodwill as a hope that if the company man supported their cause the repercussions would be less on their return: disagreeing with the captain was one thing; killing him was quite another.

Lying on his sickbed, Pricket prevaricated: he told Greene that if he waited for three days, or two, or even one, he could persuade Hudson to go home. 'I did not join this ship to forsake her,' he said, 'nor to damage myself and others by such a deed.' He pointed out that they were married men and that if they went ahead with their plan they could never see their wives again and would be brought to trial if they entered English territory. Greene replied that he could not wait even a day and if Pricket felt so strongly about it he could take his chances in the boat. With little other choice, and after a visit from Juet, 'who sware plainly that he would justify this deed when he came home', Pricket sided with the mutineers. But, by his own (possibly self-serving) account, he persuaded them to keep the carpenter aboard, hoping that when Staffe was alerted he would warn Hudson. He also made them take an oath that 'You shall do no nothing but to the glory of God, and the good of the action in hand, and harm no man.' Greene, Wilson and Juet swore on the Bible that they would do so. Four other men came to Pricket's bedside to take the same oath. He asked them to sleep on it and make their decision in the morning, but 'It was dark, and they in readiness to put their deed of darkness in execution ... [W]ickedness sleepeth not.'

Greene saw through Pricket's ploy. Staffe was one of the first to be detained. Hudson was persuaded out of his cabin, whereupon his hands were tied and he was put in the boat, still wearing a multicoloured dressing-gown. His son followed him. John King the quartermaster was chased into the hold, where he defended himself bravely with a cutlass, but he too ended up in the boat. The sick were thrown after them. So too was Thomas Woodehouse, the student of mathematics, on the grounds that he was an intellectual and therefore untrustworthy. It was such a disorganized affair that two of the mutineers were also bound and put in the boat. They were only released when two of Greene's accomplices complained that they were personal friends. Greene agreed that they should be set free, but replaced them with another pair of mutineers. Staffe then came forward with his chest of tools and said that he would rather go with Hudson than with Greene. The *Discovery*'s new commander had no problem with that.

On the morning of the 24th, with ten men in the boat, Greene gave them a gun, powder and shot, a few pikes, an iron pot and a bit of flour, then cut the rope. When Hudson made to follow him, 'they let fall the mainsails and out with their topsails, and fly as from an enemy'. Once the boat had vanished, the mutineers ransacked the *Discovery*. In the hold they found one and a half barrels of flour, two firkins of butter, 27 joints of pork and half a bushel of peas. 'But in the master's cabin,' Pricket wrote, 'we found two hundred of biscuit cakes, a peck of meal, of beer to the quantity of a butt.' To the mutineers, the discovery of this secret hoard vindicated their actions.

Bylot was the only one of Hudson's appointees to escape retribution. He had hidden during the night of the 23rd, and when he emerged he was given the helm. By common assent, he was deemed a better navigator than Juet. The ex-mate protested – curiously, he wanted to sail north-west, as Hudson had; Bylot, on the other hand, favoured the north-east – but the decision was justified when Bylot led them safely to Digges Island, at the western mouth of the Furious Overfall. On the way in, they had found the Inuit of Digges Island welcoming and the game plentiful. Now, on the way out, they expected to find the same. Confidently, Greene led a boat party ashore to get food. Pricket, who was one of the group but remained in the boat, gave a graphic description of events. Greene and two others, John Thomas and Bill Wilson, stood by the boat showing the Inuit mirrors, bells and Jew's harps which they hoped to trade for meat. Meanwhile, another two men, Michael Perse and Andrew Moter, were gathering sorrel not far away. Everything seemed to be proceeding in a friendly fashion until, without warning, the Inuit attacked. One of them slipped onto the boat and stabbed Pricket from behind, reaching over his shoulder to strike at the heart. 'I cast up my right arm to save my breast,' Pricket wrote; 'he wounded my arm and struck me into the body under my right pap. He struck me a second blow, which I met with my left hand, and then he struck me into the right thigh, and had like to have cut off my little finger of the left hand. Now I had got hold of the string of the knife, and had wound it about my left hand, he striving with both hands to make an end of that he had begun. I found him but weak in the grip (God enabling me), and getting hold of the sleeve of his left arm, so bare him from me. His left side lay bare to me, which when I saw, I put his sleeve of his left arm into my left hand, holding the string of the knife fast in the same hand, and having got my right hand at liberty, I sought for somewhat wherewith to strike him, not remembering my dagger at my side; but looking down I saw it, and therewith struck him into the body and the throat.'

Meanwhile, John Thomas and Bill Wilson had been eviscerated, and Henry Greene and Michael Perse 'being mortally wounded came tumbling into the boat together'. Wilson and Thomas, too, managed somehow to make it aboard. Moter, unharmed, jumped into the sea and hung on to the edge, shouting for help. Despite being partially disembowelled, Greene and Perse put up a heroic defence. With a yell of '*Coragio!*' Greene laid about with a truncheon and Perse wielded a hatchet to deadly effect. Pricket described a scene of panic and confusion: 'I cried to them to clear the boat, and Andrew Moter cried to be taken in.' In his shock, vivid details imprinted themselves on his mind – one of them being the image of an Inuit bobbing dead in the water, the victim of Perse's hatchet. When they turned the boat, and Perse had dragged Moter aboard, the Inuit unleashed a hail of arrows. Greene was killed outright, Pricket was hit in the back, and they were all wounded to a greater or lesser degree. As Perse and Moter rowed away – how Perse did it is beyond comprehension for, apart from having his belly slit, he had been hit by several arrows – the Inuit ran to their kayaks. But for some reason they did not press their advantage and the white men escaped.

During the incident the *Discovery* had been lying offshore, its crew unable to see what was happening. The first they knew of the disaster was when the boat hove into view and, Perse having fainted, Moter waved for assistance. 'They could not tell what to make of us,' Pricket wrote, 'but in the end they stood for us, and so took us up.' Greene's body was thrown into the sea, and the survivors, including the Inuit Pricket had stabbed, were hauled aboard. Only Moter and Pricket survived. The Inuit never recovered consciousness and died the same day, as did all the others – Bill Wilson 'swearing and cursing in most fearful manner' – except for Perse, who lingered in agony for another 48 hours.

There were now nine men on the *Discovery*, only five of whom knew how to handle a ship, and their food was running out. In the manner of all mutinies, the mutineers had no clear idea what to do once they had taken charge of the ship. But in this case they were lucky to have Bylot. He took them successfully through the Furious Overfall, despatching parties along the way to ransack nesting colonies, from which they gathered 300 birds. Apart from a meagre amount of flour, this was all they had to see them across the Atlantic. Previously they had skinned the birds they shot, finding that this reduced the rank, fishy taste of the meat. But now, on Juet's recommendation, they just burned the feathers and ate everything – which alleviated their scurvy. In Pricket's words, they 'began to make trial of all whatsoever . . . and as for the garbage, it was not thrown away'.

By general agreement, Bylot was now their captain. Juet tried to assert his authority with a proposal that they sail for Newfoundland where, if they did not meet the fishing fleet, they would find huts and stores of food that had been left on the coast. Bylot overrode him and headed east for home. The journey was hard. As their stock of fat ran out they were reduced to cooking the birds in candle fat. When the birds ran out they were left with the candles, which were shared out, a pound a week, as a 'great dainty'. By the time the *Discovery* reached Ireland, Juet was dead and the others were starving. They tried to deal with the Irish, 'but found no relief, for in this place there was neither bread, drink, nor money to be had amongst them. Wherefore they advised us to deal with our countrymen who were there a-fishing; which we did, but found them so cold in kindness that they would do nothing without present money, whereof we had none in the ship.' One of England's first colonies, Ireland was even more impoverished than the Arctic. They pawned their anchor and their best cable to the local garrison commander, who then indentured several Irish seamen – on pain of death – to man the *Discovery* as far as Plymouth.

When the *Discovery*'s crew reached London in September 1611 they were brought before the Admiralty. Statements were taken, the ship was examined and so was the boat, particular attention being paid to the bloodstains that still marked both vessels. Bennet Mathews, the cook and trumpeter, gave a straightforward, if grisly, explanation: they 'became bloody by reason the Cannibals cut up [the men's] bellies and . . . they presently died, one in the boat and three in the ship'. The questioning continued for three months, but it was another seven years before the crew were finally brought to trial on the charge of 'feloniously pinioning and putting of Henry Hudson, master of the Discovery, out of the same ship with eight or more of his company . . . without meat, drink, clothes or other provisions, whereby they died'. By this time the majority had fled, leaving Mathews, Clements, Pricket and Edward

Wilson to face the judge. For unknown reasons, the case against Mathews and Clements was dropped. Pricket and Wilson were acquitted by jury. The only man to escape all censure was Bylot. This was not because he was thought any more innocent than the others. It was for the hard-headed reason that he was the only navigator alive who had sailed this newly dis-covered inland sea. To the many influential people who still hoped to find the North-West Passage, he was too valuable to lose. Scarcely had the questioning finished than he was once again in the Arctic, searching for a route to China.

Luke Foxe and Thomas James (1631–2)

The discoveries of Henry Hudson quickened the pulses of English financiers. After more than a hundred years of searching, Hudson Strait (as the Furious Overfall was rather drably named) and the 'sea' into which it led (later to be called Hudson Bay) seemed at last to be the door to the North-West Passage. The scramble to open it began as soon as the mutineers returned. On 26 July 1612 the 'Company of the Merchants Discoverers of the North-West Passage' was formed by Royal Charter. Its members included not only the men who had sponsored Hudson's last expedition, but a string of luminaries – Prince Henry, the Archbishop of Canterbury, Francis Bacon and Robert Hakluyt. Towards the bottom of the list was Richard Bylot, the man who had brought Hudson's ship, the *Discovery*, back to London. Even before the company was formed, one Thomas Button had been sent to Hudson Bay with the *Discovery* and the *Resolution*, taking Bylot as an advisor. The two ships explored the southern and western coasts of the bay, overwintered and returned in 1613, having found no exit and with their crews suffering from scurvy. In 1614 Bylot sailed again in the *Discovery* under William Gibbons, but they did not even reach Hudson Bay, becoming stuck in a bay on the Labrador Coast, where they stayed so long, because of either the weather or the captain's indifference, that the crew called it Gibbons His Hole. Bylot was subsequently given sole charge of the *Discovery* and resumed the attack in March 1615. Before the ship left London one of the expedition's sponsors, John Wolstenholme, came aboard to promise everyone triple wages if they discovered the Passage. But even with this inducement, Bylot managed only to chart the northern coast of the Bay. There was a channel to the north-west that looked hopeful, but his exceptionally capable pilot, a man named William Baffin, concluded that it was too shallow to be the seaway they sought. In Baffin's opinion, the seas to the west of Greenland offered a better chance of success. Bylot took his advice, and in March 1616 sailed with him for Davis Strait.

Baffin was an indefatigable observer. As the *Discovery* went north into what would later be called Baffin Bay, he recorded the plants and animals they found, the nature of the Inuit, the manner in which they lived and how they constructed their kayaks. He noted, too, the strange way in which his compass contradicted the star sightings that gave him true north. At the top of Baffin Bay the needle pointed to the south-west, a deviation of 56° and 'a thing almost incredible and matchless in the world beside'. Baffin and Bylot returned to London on 30 August 1616, having discovered at least three inlets that might be of interest: Smith Sound and Jones Sound to the north of Baffin Bay and Lancaster Sound to the west. They warned, however, that any future expeditions in this direction would have to battle an expanse of ice – the Middle Pack – that occupied the northern part of the bay and was extremely dangerous.

The warning was so severe that nobody bothered Baffin Bay for two centuries. Instead, they concentrated on Hudson Bay. In May 1631 two ships left England to explore the channel that Baffin had disparaged. The *Charles* was led by Luke Foxe, a colourful adventurer from London who had spent the last 25 years trying to obtain an Arctic command and had such a high opinion both of himself and his chances of success that he called himself 'North-West' Foxe. A strait-laced Bristol man, Captain Thomas James, commanded the *Henrietta Maria*. It had been suggested that they travel together, but the rivalry between England's two largest commercial ports was too intense for such a display of cooperation. Accordingly, when they sailed in May 1631 (within a few days of each other) they departed from opposite sides of the country. In his journal, James described the equipment and supplies aboard the *Henrietta Maria*, dutifully complimenting the abilities of all the men aboard. Foxe's account was not only more robust but gave an illuminating picture of what a Carolean expedition deemed necessary for a stay in the ice. 'I was victualled compleatly for 18 Moneths,' he wrote, 'but whether the Baker, Brewer, Butcher, and others were Masters of their Arts, or profession, or no, I know not; but this I am sure of: I had excellent fat Beefe, strong Beere, good wheaten Breade, good Iceland Ling, Butter and Cheese of the best, admirable Aquae vitae, Pease, Oat-meale, Wheat-meale, Oyle, Spice, Sugar, Fruit and rice; with chyrurgerie, as Sirrups, Iulips, condits, trechissis, antidotes, balsoms, gummes, unguents, implaisters, oyles, potions, suppositors, and purging Pils; and if I had wanted Instruments my Chirurgion had enough.' Not everything was to his liking, however. Although he had chosen most of his crew, the master and mate had been foisted upon him. He was dismissive of both. The mate, whose name he never quite gathered, shrivelled into obscurity as either Yurin or Hurin. As for the master, Foxe didn't even bother with his name, referring to him simply as 'the most arrogant bull calf that ever went or came as Master and the most fainteheartedest man'.

Foxe went through Hudson Strait and into the Bay, whose north coast he followed until he came to Southampton Island, which Bylot and Baffin had discovered in 1615. Here he found, not the shallow waters Baffin had mentioned, but a deep channel that he christened Sir Thomas Roe's Welcome. He didn't go far up it, instead sailing south to fill the gaps in Bylot's map of Hudson Bay. As he went, he crammed his journal with overblown

GREENLAND

Smith Sound

Jones Sound

Lancaster Sound

Baffin Bay

Arctic Circle

BAFFIN ISLAND

Davis Strait

Foxe Basin

Foxe Channel

Roe's Welcome

SOUTHAMPTON ISLAND

Hudson Strait

Hudson Bay

Cape Henrietta Maria

Bottom of the Bay (James Bay)

LABRADOR

NEWFOUNDLAND

CHARLTON ISLAND

Atlantic Ocean

Hudson

0   100   200   300   400   500 miles

descriptions of the kind he hoped his readers might enjoy. The Northern Lights were 'Pettiedancers' and 'most fearful to behold'. Of an Arctic dawn he wrote, 'This morning Aurora blusht, as though shee had ushered her Master from some unchast lodging, and the ayre so silent as though all those handmaides had promised secrecy'. But now and then he vented his true feelings: of another dawn he wrote, 'This fulsome ugly morning presented the foulest chilhe that the whole voyage brought forth.' (Conversely, he also said that one July day was as warm as any to be had in England.)

'North-West' Foxe was becoming tired of the North-West Passage. It was not as easy as he had hoped, and the charting of Hudson Bay was boring. Entertainment, however, presented itself at the Bottom of the Bay (later christened James Bay), where Thomas James of Bristol was searching for an outlet, as Hudson had done. The *Charles* and the *Henrietta Maria* met at the end of August. Politely, James sent a lieutenant to ask Foxe to lunch. Foxe took the officer into his cabin and quizzed him remorselessly for several hours about James's achievements – which weren't many – before accepting the invitation. The 'lunch' started in the afternoon and continued until the following morning, James treating his guest 'with variete of such cheere as his sea provisions could afford'. To Foxe, 'This 17 houres was the worst spent of any time of my discoverie'. It wasn't just that James was a bit prissy, nor that the *Henrietta Maria* leaked – '[it] threw in so much water as wee could not have wanted sause if we had had roast Mutton' – but that the ship stank. No doubt the *Charles* stank too, but Foxe was particular when it came to a rival. The smell was so bad that he wondered 'whether it were better for James's company to be impounded amongst ice, where they might be kept from putrefaction by piercing air, or in the open sea to be kept sweet by being thus pickled'. Foxe's irritation peaked when he saw that the *Henrietta Maria* was flying an English flag, as if it was a royal emissary. When James told him that he flew the flag because he carried letters from the King of England to the Emperor of Japan, Foxe retorted, 'Keepe it up then, but you are out of the way to Iapon, for this is not it'.

They stayed together long enough to chart the promontory marking the north-western tip of Bottom of the Bay. James named it Cape Henrietta Maria after his ship. Foxe called it Wolstenholmes Ultimum Vale because 'I do beleeve Sir John Wolstenholme will not lay out any monies in search of this Bay'. (James's name stuck.) After this they parted company, James examining the Bottom of the Bay, while Foxe returned for another stab at Roe's Welcome. The seas were clear, and he reached a latitude of 66° 47' N, discovering a new channel (Foxe Channel) and a new bay (Foxe Basin). If he had gone further he would have discovered a strait that, had it been navigable, would have led in a roundabout way to the North-West Passage.* But he did not. He turned back at a place he called, with suitable bravado, Foxe His

* Fury and Hecla Strait was discovered in 1822 by W. E. Parry and George Lyon. It was as impassable then as it was in Foxe's time.

Furthest. For all his 18 months' supplies and the excellence of his beef, beer and bread, his men were already suffering from scurvy. He went home at once, and at the end of October was able to write: 'The 31, blessed be Almighty God, I came into the Downes with all my men recovered and sound, not having lost one Man, nor Boy, nor any manner of Tackling, having beene forth neere 6 moneths, all Glory be to God.' This was an exceptionally good record: it was very rare for any ship to return from the Arctic with its full complement. But lives were not what Foxe's sponsors were interested in. Having failed to discover the Passage and returned sooner than expected, he was given a cool welcome. He received £160 14s 6d for his expenses, and for his time and trouble, nothing.

When Foxe reached his furthest north he announced that it would be a waste of money to spend a winter in the Arctic. Dutiful James had no such qualms. He had already decided to overwinter, and for the rest of the summer he doggedly explored the Bottom of the Bay. Although he did not know it, he was covering much the same ground as Hudson had done in 1611. And the events that followed were very similar to those that had befallen Hudson. The *Henrietta Maria*'s anchor slipped and the revolving capstan injured several people, one of whom, the gunner, had to have his leg amputated below the knee. Unable to find a sheltered cove, James, like Hudson, put his ship into the shallows – off Charlton Island. Hardly had he done so when on 19 November the gunner said that he was going to die and would like to spend the rest of his time drunk. With James's permission he enjoyed three days of oblivion before expiring on the 22nd. They rowed a good distance from the ship before tipping his body into the sea. James was now becoming worried by the ferocity of Arctic conditions. The wine, oil, vinegar and every other liquid 'was frozen as hard as a piece of wood, and we must cut it with a hatchet'. Most alarming were the conditions in which the gunner had died: despite being in the ship's smallest, warmest cabin, with as many clothes as could be fitted on him and a pan of hot coals burning around the clock, it was so cold that 'his plaister would freeze at his wound, and his bottle of Sacke at his head'.

Before winter set in for good they were hit by a storm that threw jagged clumps of ice at the ship, tearing off its rudder. Fearing that if he left the ship at anchor it would either be carried away or crushed, James took the drastic precaution of going below with the carpenter's auger and drilling a hole in its hull. In this manner, he hoped, the ship would not only remain where it was but, as the water froze within, would be protected from the ice without. Lined along the shore, the crew watched the *Henrietta Maria* sink. James rowed back and gave them a dispiriting speech of encouragement: they should not be dismayed, he said, because 'if it be our fortunes to end our dayes here, we are as neere heaven as in England; and we are much bound to God Almighty for giving us so large a time of repentance'.

Hudson may have been the first Englishman to survive a winter in the

Arctic. James, however, was the first to describe what it was like. On Charlton Island they constructed a hut, 20 feet square, which they roofed with canvas, insulating the walls with stacks of firewood. It was still bitterly cold, ice forming within a yard of the fire. They had plenty of wood, but water was more of a problem. They were suspicious of melted snow, which they found 'very unwholesome either to drinke or dresse our victualls. It made us so short-breathed that we were scarce able to speake.' Instead they dug a well, whose ice they broke laboriously on a daily basis. In a surprisingly modern touch, James recognized that facial hair became clumped with ice and offered only an illusory protection against the cold. He refused to let the men grow beards or moustaches but had the surgeon shave them regularly.

Christmas found them well. They 'solomnised [it] in the joyfullest fashion we could'. But the coming months were uncomfortable. Being incompetent hunters, they had not laid up a store of fresh meat and their diet consisted solely of flour and salt beef. Nor had they gathered enough firewood to fight the terrifying cold. 'They must worke daily,' James wrote, 'and goe abroad to fetch wood and timber, notwithstanding that most of them had no shooes to put on. Their shooes, upon coming to the fire, out of the snow, were burnt and schorcht upon their feete.' By February 1632 two-thirds of the crew were sick from either scurvy or frostbite. To illness was added anxiety. If the ice did not melt, and the *Henrietta Maria* remained where it was, how were they going to escape?

The carpenter asked – and the crew asked too – for permission to build a boat. James agreed. Throughout March, April and May the carpenter toiled away. As he did so, the supplies they had taken ashore in November began to run out. James had not expected the winter to last so long. On 9 May he led a party over the ice to chip at the *Henrietta Maria*'s frozen hold, uncovering five barrels of beef and pork, four of beer and one of cider. 'It has layne under water all winter, yet we could not perceive that it was anything the worse,' James recorded. But the barrels' contents were of no use against scurvy. James cleared a patch of earth and sowed it with peas in the hope of growing some 'greene thing to comfort us', but the peas did not sprout and the men began to die. Among them was the carpenter, who had yet to complete their boat. On the same day they buried the carpenter, the gunner's corpse bobbed up alongside the ship. James was astonished at the manner in which he was preserved – 'as free from noysomeness as when he was first committed to the sea' – and at the curious nature of his flesh, 'which would slip up and downe upon his bones like a glove on a man's hand'. He was laid in the soil of Charlton Island alongside the others.

By June the *Henrietta Maria* was still ice-bound, but the land had come to life. Patches of vegetation appeared, among them a plant that James called 'vetch' but which might have been scurvy grass. They fed on it avidly, twice a day gathering clumps which they boiled with oil and vinegar, crushed into their beer or just ate raw. The benefit soon showed: 'For now our feeble sicke men, that could not for their lives stirre these two or three months, can indure the ayre and walke about the house; our other sicke men gather strength also, and it is wonderful to see how soon they were recovered.' Their renewed strength, combined with the gradual disappearance of the ice, gave them hope that they might be able to salvage the *Henrietta Maria*. They plugged the holes, pumped it dry and, to their wonder, it floated. On 24 June they erected a cross bearing pictures of the King and Queen of England, then lit a celebratory beacon. The fire got out of control, engulfed their camp, spread across the island, and by 1 July had burned its way through 16 square miles of forest. James left, hurriedly, on the 2nd.

As he went, he stopped at a nearby island to gather fuel. A stone's throw from the waterline he discovered the remains of a fireplace and two stakes set about 18 inches into the ground. The stakes seemed to have been driven in with the head of a hatchet, and when he uprooted them he found they had been sharpened by an iron blade. Clearly this was not the work of Indians or Inuit. 'I could not conceive to what purpose they had been there set,' James wrote. 'This did augment my desire to speake with the Savages; for without doubt, they could have given notice of some Christians with whom they had some commerce.' What he may have found was the 20-year-old campsite of Hudson's marooned company.

Before going home James chose to complete his mission. He went up the west coast of Hudson Bay, poked his nose into Foxe Channel and sailed north of Southampton Island before retreating. On 26 August, with the sea freezing around the ship, he asked his crew what they wanted to do. Without hesitation they said that they very much wanted to go home. The *Henrietta Maria* docked at Bristol on 23 October 1632.

James became a hero, his journal being published in 1633 to great acclaim. But his winter in the Arctic had ruined his health. He spent two years fighting pirates in the Bristol Channel before dying on 4 May 1635. Foxe, who had not spent a winter in the ice, survived little longer. His own account, written in typically breezy style, came out in the year of James's death and was widely ignored. He died soon after its publication.

Foxe and James had not discovered much, but between them they had demolished the myth of the North-West Passage – or at least that any navigable passage might be found through Hudson Bay. In James's words, it would never be passed 'without extraordinary dangers'. A century later Christopher Middleton caused a brief stir when he took the *Furnace* and *Discovery* through Roe's Welcome, but all he found was a couple of inlets that led nowhere. It would be many decades before Britain reignited the question of the North-West Passage.

René La Salle (1669–87)

Less than 100 years after Columbus landed in the West Indies, northern Europe was firmly entrenched in the New World. In a surge of activity, men such as Walter Raleigh, Samuel de Champlain and Henry Hudson planted the flags of England, France and Holland along the coast of North America. Small bands of colonists followed, and by the mid-17th century they had established themselves on the eastern seaboard. Predominantly agricultural, with little in the way of centralized government, these settlements were more a statement of intent than a source of profit. Their wealth did not even begin to approach that of the Iberian colonies in South and Central America. To the west, however, lay a land of limitless promise. The French, from their territories along the St Lawrence River, were the first to exploit it.

Nouvelle France, as the first Canadian colony was called, was a rough and ready place. Theoretically under the jurisdiction of the French Crown, its royal overseer, or intendant, had little control over either the frontiersmen or the missionaries who probed constantly westwards. Its winters were harsh and its harvests unreliable. Nevertheless, it was the most profitable colony in North America. Indian trappers from the Great Lakes and beyond brought furs – predominantly beaver – that the traders of Nouvelle France purchased for a few trinkets, then sold at astronomical prices in Europe. Even after the intendant and his favourites had taken their percentages, it was still possible to make a decent living. All one had to do was put up with the rudimentary conditions. The allure of its open frontier drew a steady dribble of adventurers. Among them was René Robert Cavelier, Sieur de La Salle, who landed at Montreal in 1667.

The younger son of a landed gentleman, La Salle had trained as a Jesuit before deciding he detested the order. At the age of 24, therefore, he sailed for Nouvelle France, where his older brother was an influential priest. Almost as soon as La Salle arrived in Montreal he was given a stretch of land eight miles out of town and told to settle it. He did so efficiently and thoroughly, clearing an area of wilderness, constructing houses and populating them with tenant farmers. But he had not come to the New World merely to be a semi-feudal landlord. According to one description, he was 'A man of iron, if ever there was one – a man austere and cold in manner, and endowed with

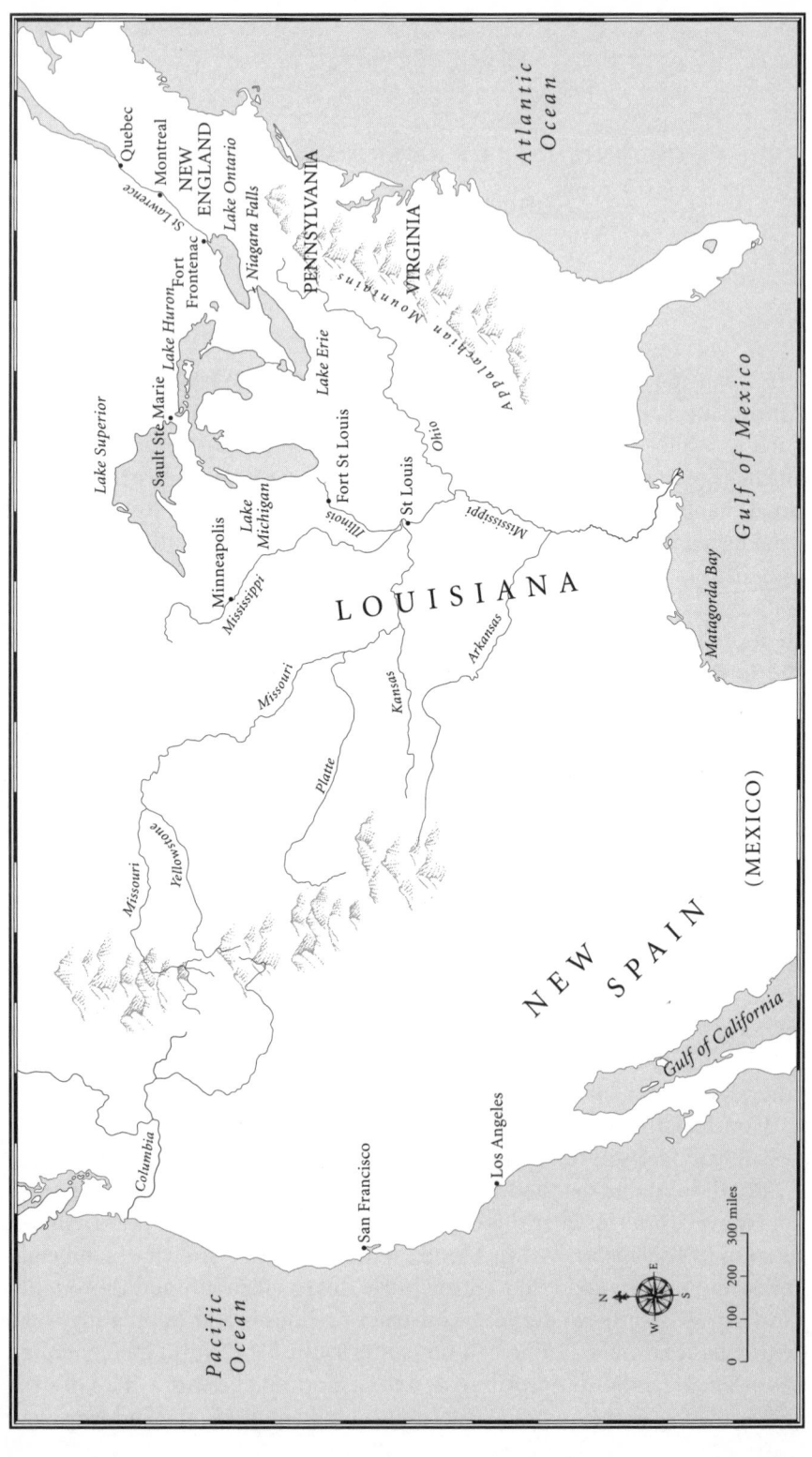

indomitable pluck and perseverance'. He was also calculating and ambitious. While developing his estate, he became fluent in several Indian languages, his object being to obtain first-hand knowledge of the country's trade potential. In this he was successful. After two years' inquiry he learned of a freshwater route that began somewhere to the south of the Great Lakes and emptied in the 'Vermilion Sea', or the Gulf of California. He promptly sold his land and, in conjunction with two priests, outfitted a party to search for what could only be a southern version of the North-West Passage. The joint expedition left Montreal on 6 July 1669 with nine canoes and 24 men, 15 of whom had been suborned from La Salle's estate.

At Lake Ontario they encountered the explorer and fur-trader Louis Joliet, who helpfully gave them a map he had made of the region. At the same time, however, he informed the priests that several Indian tribes around Lake Superior had never heard of Christianity. It was too great a temptation: the clerics set out immediately for the west. La Salle, feigning sickness, said he would be unable to accompany them. The priests held a brief mass, then went in search of souls. (They did not search long: having lost their altar trappings in a stream, they abandoned the quest and went home.) Once they were out of sight La Salle rose from his sickbed and continued south. For two years he and his men traipsed across the wilderness, by his own account discovering the rivers Ohio and Illinois, neither of which was the channel he sought. He returned penniless to Montreal in 1671, many of his men having already deserted. In derision they named his holding La Chine, 'China' – by which name it is still known today.

La Salle was unrepentant. Changing tack, he addressed the problem of imperialism. The British and Dutch were hemmed in by the Appalachian Mountains, but the French had already reached the Great Lakes, and between the Appalachians and the Pacific was an enormous tract of land. In June 1671 one Simon François de Saint-Lusson had reached Sault Ste. Marie on Lake Superior, and in the name of King Louis XIV had taken possession of 'all countries, rivers, lakes and streams ... bounded on one side by the seas of the North and West, and on the other side by the South Sea'. His claim (which took in most of North America) was as meaningless as it was sweeping. La Salle, however, proposed a more concrete assertion of sovereignty. To the west and south of the Great Lakes flowed a river that had various names but was commonly called the Mississippi. In standard colonial practice the conquest of a river conferred ownership of its entire watershed. It had yet to be determined whether the Mississippi emptied into the Gulf of California or the Gulf of Mexico (the latter was favoured by most), but wherever it went it would be a huge addition to France's possessions. With the support of Nouvelle France's intendant, Jean Talon – as well as its newly appointed governor, Count Louis Frontenac – La Salle sailed for France to petition the king for funds.

The Royal Court was interested. Louis XIV's minister for commerce had already heard of La Salle, writing to Talon in 1671, 'Your action in sending Sieur de la Salle to the southward and Sieur de Saint-Lusson to the northward to discover the passage to the South Sea is very good; but the principal thing to which you must look in these kinds of discoveries is to find copper mines.' Clearheadedly, the court was concerned less with the chimerical North-West Passage than with the tangible riches – whether mineral or fur – that North America might contain. When La Salle offered to chart the Mississippi to its mouth, erecting forts as he went, the king listened to him. The expedition would cost little, its potential was great, and if La Salle – who was grimmer and more abrupt than the usual supplicants – happened to die along the way with all his men, then who cared? And it wasn't as if they had to spend any money. They gave him a title, a patent to explore the Mississippi, 'through which, to all appearances a way may be found to Mexico', and a five-year monopoly on the trade in buffalo hides. With this he was expected to pay his way to the south. They imposed also the condition that he build and garrison a fort on the shores of Lake Ontario, and that he erect and maintain similar forts along the Mississippi. La Salle returned to Nouvelle France in 1675, built his first fort – Fort Frontenac, on Lake Ontario – using the royal approval to borrow money for the venture, and by 1678, after a second visit to France to collect men and materials, was ready to go.

La Salle's plan was to build a ship at Fort Frontenac, on which he would sail to a suitable spot on the Great Lakes, from where, a new fort and a new ship having been constructed, he would travel down the Mississippi. For his officers he had Father Louis Hennepin, an adventurous missionary whom he did not particularly like but who had been in Nouvelle France for three years, plus two friends from Paris: Dominique La Motte de Lucière, and Captain Henri Tonty, an Italian soldier who had lost a hand to a grenade while fighting in Sicily and wore a sinister iron replacement that he covered with a glove. Beneath him he had selection of about 40 men, mostly French sailors and shipwrights, with a sprinkling of Flemish, German and Italian adventurers. An advance party left Fort Frontenac on 18 November 1678 under Hennepin and La Motte. By 6 December they had discovered the Niagara Falls, and at a site six miles upriver they constructed the first of the expedition's forts. They also built a shipyard from which, despite cold, hunger and the distrust of the Indians, a small ship gradually emerged. Displacing about 45 tons, it took its name and its figurehead from the griffin that adorned La Salle's coat of arms. Having been delayed in Quebec, La Salle and Tonty followed later with the rest of the men and a shipload of supplies. A few hours from their destination they left the ship in charge of its pilot and went ahead on foot. When they reached the Niagara they found that La Motte had gone home, his health broken, and that the different nationalities were bickering among themselves. On top of this, news arrived that the pilot had crashed the ship. All the food and all the merchandise for the Mississippi trip were lost, the only articles saved being the anchors and cables for the *Griffin*. While detained at Quebec, La Salle had already encountered difficulties, including the hostility of the Jesuits – to which he responded in like measure – and an attempted poisoning by a rival explorer. These new setbacks were unwelcoming. As Hennepin wrote, it 'would have made anybody but himself give up the enterprise'.

La Salle did not give up. He walked through the snow to Fort Frontenac, accompanied by two men and a sledgeload of food pulled by a single dog, to fetch more provisions. Here, however, he learned that his creditors considered him a bad risk and had begun to seize his property. It took months to sort his affairs, and he did not return to Niagara until August 1679. By September the *Griffin* was in Lake Michigan, and already six men had deserted. La Salle and Tonty hunted them down, retrieved the property they had stolen, and continued south to the Mississippi.

La Salle was not a likeable person. 'By nature cold, reserved and reticent,' according to one of his more admiring biographers, 'he was not a genial man; and possessed little or none of that magnetism which wins men's hearts. Even the few most faithful and trusted companions of his labours could hardly be considered as on terms of intimacy with him.' He was not a natural leader, and his attitude towards his employees, 'who comprehended him not, but were simply compelled by the force of his will, certainly did not tend to establish that community of interest which should have existed between them. It was, in fact, this lacking quality in an otherwise magnificent character, which was ever thwarting his plans and which rendered his brief career of eight years in exploration work an almost uninterrupted record of disaster.'

He had assumed that a waterway existed between Lake Michigan and the Mississippi. When he found it did not, and had to make a portage to the Illinois, the expedition became even more fragile. 'It was to the last degree difficult to hold the men to their duty,' wrote one chronicler. 'Discipline had no resources and no guarantee.' Repeatedly La Salle went north to fetch supplies, leaving Hennepin to scout the Illinois while Tonty maintained order with his iron fist. The *Griffin* vanished, either sunk in a storm or destroyed by its discontented crew. Hennepin reached the confluence of the Illinois and the Mississippi, but was captured by Indians in the region of present-day Minneapolis; although later released, he never rejoined the expedition and caught the next ship home, refusing ever to set foot in America again. More and more men deserted. Those who remained did so mainly for the opportunity to poison La Salle – in which they nearly succeeded. By 7 December 1681 the party was at the junction of the Illinois and the Mississippi, where they were delayed by further desertions, the theft of supplies, a war between the Iroquois and Illinois Indians, and the wholesale plundering of their most recent fort by the garrison they had left to man it.

Back La Salle went to Fort Frontenac – a distance of several hundred miles – where he enlisted 23 Frenchmen and 18 Indians to drag canoes and food through the snow to the Mississippi. They reached the river in February 1682, waited a while for the ice to clear, then began their journey. They passed, one by one, the mouths of the Missouri, the Ohio and the Arkansas rivers, and after 62 days, on 6 April, reached the delta. It had three channels. La Salle took the western, Tonty the eastern and a new recruit, Jean Bourdon Dautray, the middle. They reconvened on the shores of the Gulf of Mexico on 9 April, where they raised a stone pillar carrying the royal coat of arms and La Salle officially claimed the new territory for France, naming it La Louisiane (Louisiana) in honour of his monarch. By territory he did not mean a small piece of land on the delta, nor even the area currently occupied by the US state of Louisiana, but a vast domain extending from the Gulf to the Great Lakes. Eleven years after Saint-Lusson had stood on the shores of Lake Superior and announced that the whole continent belonged to France, his excitable declaration now had some meaning.

The return journey up the Mississippi was little better than the one down. As their supplies dwindled they were forced to live off the land, sometimes surviving on nothing but acorns. They all suffered from fever, La Salle in particular. But at least there were no more desertions. Apart from the fact that there would have been no point in abandoning an expedition that was going home, the most unreliable members had already been winnowed out, leaving a solid core of loyal men. And at least, too, they were travelling over familiar ground. On the upper reaches of the Illinois, at a confluence of three tributaries, they paused for the winter. Clearing an acre of land on the top of a 125-foot high prominence called Starved Rock, La Salle built a stockade to which he gave the name Fort St Louis. It was an ideal defensive position, surrounded on three sides by perpendicular cliffs and approachable only by a steep track up the fourth. The surrounding forests contained game, the river was rich in fish and the ground was cultivable.

As part of his grand scheme to extend France's influence, La Salle had envisaged the creation of colonies. They were not to be colonies in the accepted imperial sense, but confederations of friendly Indian tribes protected by white overseers. By this means he hoped to eradicate the threat from warlike tribes such as the Iroquois and the Sioux, and to safeguard the uninterrupted flow of commodities from the interior. By the spring of 1683, with 20 Frenchmen living in Fort St Louis and approximately 20,000 Indians gathered beneath them for protection, Starved Rock had become the centre of his first colony. La Salle distributed land (which he did not own) to his men who, it was understood, would repay him with arms and a share of their profits. As the buffalo skins began to come in – La Salle had promised not to interfere with the fur trade – the two sides colluded in a feudal arrangement that seemed to benefit everyone. It was the same system, albeit in a wilder environment, by which La Salle had obtained his first holding in Nouvelle France. Starved Rock became the centre of a little kingdom with

La Salle at its head, a fact that was recognized in 1684 by a mapmaker who produced a detailed picture of the settlements south of the Great Lakes, labelling them as 'COLONIE DU SR. DE LA SALLE'.

Unfortunately, during La Salle's absence Frontenac had been replaced by a new governor, Le Fèvre de La Barre. No less corrupt than his predecessors, La Barre saw the colony as a threat to his own trading interests, and when a group of La Salle's men returned to civilization to obtain supplies La Barre had them arrested. At the same time he occupied Fort Frontenac, sold its contents and put his own cattle on La Salle's crops. Further, he sent to France denigratory reports of La Salle's behaviour, which reached such a high level that on 5 August 1683 the king himself intervened. 'I am convinced', he wrote, 'that the discovery of the Sieur de la Salle is very useless, and that such enterprises ought to be prevented in future.' La Salle, meanwhile, was becoming desperate. 'I have only twenty men, with scarcely a hundred pounds of powder; and I cannot long hold the country without more. The Illinois are very capricious and uncertain.' When pleading failed, he gave Tonty command of the colony and left for Quebec – passing en route an officer whom La Barre had sent to take control of Starved Rock – from where he sailed to France, accompanied by two Indian servants, to clear his name.

La Salle's petition to the king was impressive. Speaking of himself in the third person, he pointed out that 'he has omitted nothing that was needful to [the expedition's] success, notwithstanding dangerous illness, heavy losses and all the other evils he has suffered, which would have overcome the courage of any one who had not the same zeal and devotion for the accomplishment of this purpose. During five years he has made five journeys, of more, in all, than five thousand leagues, for the most part on foot, with extreme fatigue, through snow and through water, without escort, without provisions, without bread, without wine, without recreation, and without repose. He has traversed more than six hundred leagues of country hitherto unknown among savage and cannibal nations, against whom he must daily make fight.' And he had done it because he thought it 'would be agreeable to His Majesty'.

As the king weakened, La Salle asked permission to lead a second expedition to the Gulf of Mexico to safeguard the new territory. He proposed the creation of a fortified outpost at the mouth of the Mississippi and another about 180 miles upriver, where he reckoned he could raise an army of more than 15,000 Indians. 'Should foreigners anticipate us,' he warned, 'they will complete the ruin of Nouvelle France, which they already hem in by their establishments of Virginia, Pennsylvania, New England, and Hudson's Bay.' The establishments to which he referred were English, but he had other foreigners in mind too. France was currently at war with Spain, and he foresaw a time when the conflict might spread to the Americas. His Indian army could be used to invade Spain's Mexican colonies – the Spaniards were widely detested, he said, and it would be no trouble to overrun the nearest settlement, whose 400 or so white inhabitants were 'more fit to work the mines than fight'. All he asked was a single ship with 30 cannon and 200 men. He would collect a further 50 men from French settlements on Haiti. If need be, he could also summon several thousand warriors from his colony. And if the war stopped, within a year he would either repay the Crown or cede it his settlements. In practice, his proposals were ridiculous: he could not possibly persuade 15,000 Indians to join him, let alone form them into an army; he did not know precisely where he was going, having taken only a rough latitude of the Mississippi delta, which was meaningless without longitude; and the idea of the Illinois marching south to join a war in Mexico was laughable. On paper, however, his scheme looked very plausible.

The king was so impressed that he cancelled La Salle's debts, ordered La Barre to return his property, and gave him not a 30-gun ship but the 36-gun *Jolie*, complete with an experienced captain in the French navy named Beaujeu. In addition he supplied a six-gun frigate, *Belle*, a store-ship, *Aimable*, and a ketch, *St François*. He also gave him 100 soldiers, 100 sailors and artificers, plus an extensive library of gold-tooled books – on top of which several volunteers enlisted to join the new colony, including La Salle's brother, Jean Cavelier, and two nephews. With a thought to the future, a number of women and children were also put aboard. When La Salle sailed in 24 July 1684 he had not 200 but 280 people under his command. By the time they reached the Gulf of Mexico he had alienated almost every one of them and was barely on speaking terms with Beaujeu.

Everything started to go wrong at Haiti. The ketch, with its irreplaceable cargo of tools and building materials, was captured by the Spanish. La Salle fell ill and, as they waited for him to recover, so did everyone else. 'Now everyone is sick,' Beaujeu wrote home, 'and he himself has a violent fever, as dangerous, the surgeon tells me, to the mind as to the body.' Beaujeu also reported that those Frenchmen in Haiti who knew the Mississippi delta said it was too dangerous at this time of year and refused to accompany them. La Salle did not recover until the end of November, and when they finally reached the mainland in January they couldn't find the Mississippi. Convinced that they were to the east of the delta, La Salle led the ships westwards. With the land trending to the south, however, he realized he had gone too far. Retracing his course, he discovered a bay, which he named the Bay of St Louis, and from here, reconnoitring inland, he sighted a broad river that could only be a western branch of the Mississippi. He would have liked to take the ships further east, but Beaujeu balked at the suggestion: not only did he think the whole enterprise muddleheaded and its commander an arrogant fool, but he had barely enough food to see the *Jolie* back to France. He refused to be swayed, even when offered some of the colonists' provisions. La Salle, who disliked Beaujeu almost as much as Beaujeu disliked him, agreed that he could leave as soon as the colonists had landed. On 20 February 1685 the *Aimable* foundered on a sandbar at the mouth of the bay, with the loss of most of its cargo. A few days later two volunteers were killed and two more wounded by Indians. Having seen the group ashore, as agreed, Beaujeu told La Salle that he couldn't unload any more supplies because they were buried too deep in the hold. Then he departed, taking several of the more discontented volunteers with him. (According to some accounts, he later mapped the mouth of the Mississippi before sailing for France.)

From driftwood and the remains of the *Aimable* the 130 colonists erected a stockade, constructed pens for their pigs and geese, and raised three huts, one for the women and children, another for La Salle, his 'gentlemen' and an extravagant library that King Louis had bestowed on them, and a third for the enlisted men. They assumed the lodgings were temporary and that soon they would be moving up the Mississippi. But as La Salle discovered, the land to the north comprised not a network of rivers, but endless prairies: they were not in the delta at all, but far to its west.* Precisely how far he could not tell, but it was clearly too great a distance for the colonists to walk, and the *Belle* was too small to contain them all. He also found that most of his soldiers had joined the expedition only because it gave them a chance to escape prison, and that none of the artisans knew their business. The only people upon whom he could rely were his brother Jean Cavelier; Cavelier's son, who was little more than a schoolboy; La Salle's hot-headed and objectionable nephew Moranget; two friars, Zenobe Membré and Anastase Douay; the son of a Parisian friend's gardener, Henri Joutel; plus the Marquis de Sablonnière, a feeble aristocrat who was already beginning to show signs of the venereal diseases he had contracted in Haiti. They were in unfamiliar country, surrounded by hostile Indians – one of the first things La Salle built was a punishment cell for men who fell asleep on watch – with little food other than the buffalo they shot on the prairies that should not have been there and the fish they speared in the river that wasn't the Mississippi. Their nearest source of fuel was six miles away. Within the first week two men deserted and a volunteer was bitten in the foot by a snake. He lingered until Easter Sunday when he died following the amputation of his leg. The master carpenter went hunting and never returned. Their crops were hit by drought. By autumn another 30 people had died of the fever they had caught in Haiti.

La Salle sent the *Belle* to find the Mississippi, but it returned without success. In November, therefore, he put Joutel in charge of the fort – like almost everything he discovered or built, La Salle named it St Louis – and took 30 men and the *Belle* in search of what Joutel now called 'the fatal river'. He and 15 others returned in March, the *Belle* having sunk and the rest of the men having either deserted or been killed by Indians. He led a second expedition in April, this time with a team of 20. On 22 October he brought eight of them back: four had deserted, one had been eaten by an alligator

---

* They were in modern Matagorda Bay, approximately 500 miles west of the Mississippi.

and the others had got lost along the way. On 7 January 1687, after a prolonged bout of fever, he went out again. Previously, he had left Fort St Louis on the understanding that he would return with news of the Mississippi, but this time he was leaving for good, taking every able-bodied man with him. Fort St Louis, manned by a rump of 20 settlers – mostly women and children – was left in the hands of Friar Membré and the Marquis de Sablonnière, now so crippled by disease that he could not walk. La Salle gave them stores and ammunition and told them they were on their own: if he reached the Illinois they could expect a French rescue ship in two years. Until then they would have to fend for themselves.

By March 1687 La Salle was no nearer the Mississippi than he had been on his previous journey, and the party had become separated. While he trudged forward with his relatives, his Indian servants, plus Joutel and the two friars, five men lagged behind to shoot buffalo. Their leader, a gentleman volunteer named Duhaut, was becoming tired of La Salle's personality and his methods. He had a financial grudge, too, having invested heavily in the expedition. When La Salle sent two Indian servants, accompanied by his nephew Moranget, to hurry them along, Duhaut took umbrage. Moranget was no less objectionable than his uncle, and while the three men slept Duhaut ordered them to be killed. The lot fell to one Liotot (conveniently a surgeon), who crushed their heads with an axe. The Indians died at once, but Moranget 'started spasmodically into a sitting position, gasping and unable to speak'. Duhaut ordered another man to finish him off. After a few days La Salle rode back to see what had happened to Moranget. Duhaut shot him in the head, shouting, 'There you go, great Pasha, there you go!'

The shock was so great that Duhaut slid easily into the role of expedition commander. Even Joutel, one of La Salle's most capable and trustworthy employees, thought it prudent to obey his orders. 'We were all of us oblig'd to stifle our Resentment, that it might not appear,' he wrote, 'for our Lives depended on it.' Yet Duhaut had no real idea what he wanted to do. He suggested now that they go back to Fort St Louis, now that they continue looking for the Mississippi, looking constantly to Joutel for guidance. In the end, they went north.

As they proceeded towards the Mississippi they were reminded constantly of La Salle's heavy-handedness. From every Indian tribe they met there emerged a man – sometimes two – who had deserted from one or other of La Salle's expeditions. Naked, long-haired and tattooed, they had taken Indian wives and in some cases had forgotten how to speak French. They all showed a marked reluctance to identify themselves, and did so only when assured that La Salle was dead. By May the group had still not found the Mississippi and the mutineers were in disarray. Duhaut suggested they turn back for Fort St Louis, then after they had gone a few miles changed his mind and said they should carry on to the Mississippi. At this, one of his fellow conspirators, 'English Jem' Hiens, became angry. After a brief quarrel over how to divide the remaining trade goods, Hiens shot Duhaut. Then, as Liotot was to hand, he shot him as well.

'These Murders committed before us, put me into a terrible Consternation,' Joutel wrote, 'for believing the same was design'd for me, I laid hold of my Fire-Lock to defend my self.' Hiens, however, assured him that he and the others would be safe, and that he had merely been avenging the death of La Salle. Timidly, Joutel suggested they continue the journey north. Hiens merely laughed, saying 'that for his own Part, he would not hazard his Life to return into France, only to have his Head chopp'd off'. Magnanimously, however, he gave Joutel a fair share of the trade goods, in return for a document written in Latin by Jean Cavelier that exonerated him from any part in La Salle's murder – 'which was given him, because there was no refusing of it'. Then, in early June 1688, the Mississippi party departed. Two of the group decided to stay with the Indians, leaving only seven men – Joutel, Jean Cavelier and his son, Father Douay, and three others named Bartholomew, De Marle and Teissier – plus three Indian guides and six horses. 'A very small Number for so great an Enterprize,' Joutel wrote, 'but we put ourselves entirely into the Hands of Divine Providence, confiding in God's Mercy, which did not forsake us.'

For the first week or so it rained without cease, and the ground turned into a quagmire – 'which very much fatigued us, because we were oblig'd to unload our Horses for them to pass, and prevent their sticking in the Mire and fat Soil, whence we could not have drawn them out, and consequently we were fain to carry all our Luggage on our own Backs'. On 23 June De Marle drowned. They went on, following a 'pleasant and navigable' river that they hoped was the Mississippi, marvelling all the while at the Indians' hospitality and friendliness. In late July they came over a hill and saw a large cross beside a building that had clearly been built by Europeans. It contained two men, the remainder of a six-strong party that Tonty had sent from Starved Rock to rescue La Salle.

'It is hard to express the Joy conceiv'd on both Sides,' Joutel wrote. 'Ours was unspeakable ... [but] the Account we gave them of Monsr. La Sale's unfortunate Death was so afflicting, that it drew Tears from them, and the dismal History of his Troubles and Disasters render'd them almost inconsolable.' Whether they cried for La Salle is debatable. More likely they were concerned for their own fortunes: should the Indians learn that the founder of the colony was dead it might be difficult 'to keep them still in Awe and under Submission'. It was agreed, therefore, to say nothing of the matter, but to get Joutel and the survivors to France as swiftly as possible 'to give an Account at Court of what had happen'd, and to procure Succours'. They were wise to maintain the pretence that La Salle was still alive, for at every stop the Indians asked nervously after him. The Iroquois were on the rampage, and although Tonty was currently fighting them he did not command the same prestige as La Salle. Even when they reached Starved

Rock on 14 September they did not reveal the truth. Choosing their words carefully, they said La Salle had left them halfway into the journey and that the last time Joutel and Jean Cavelier had spoken to him he was in good health – none of which was strictly untrue. The news was received with jubilation. But as the Indians and French settlers fired their muskets into the air, Joutel wrote that '[it] refresh'd our Sorrow for his misfortune; perceiving that his Presence would have settled all Things advantageously'. Their one satisfaction was that a Jesuit priest who had been sent by La Barre to keep an eye on the colony's spiritual health became extremely nervous at the prospect of La Salle's return. Although sick, the man was so frightened that he left shortly afterwards. When Tonty returned in October Jean Cavelier drew a quantity of furs in his dead brother's name and, accompanied Joutel and the rest, used them to pay their way to Quebec. For a short while they hid in the town's seminaries to avoid detection, then scurried aboard a ship in August 1688. They arrived two months later in France.

Their story was greeted with indifference. The king issued a slightly pointless edict that La Salle's murderers were to be arrested if they set foot in Nouvelle France. (By this time Hiens had been shot by one of the Indianized deserters.) Jean Cavelier continued defiantly to pretend that his brother was still alive until he had secured the property that would otherwise have been seized by his creditors. The only person who seemed to care about La Salle was Tonty who, still under the illusion that he was somewhere in the interior, left Starved Rock in late 1688 to find him. For two years he ranged unsuccessfully through the territory where Jean Cavelier and Joutel had suggested they last saw their leader. Most of his party deserted in the early stages, leaving him with just one Frenchman and one Indian. The three explorers tramped west and south, and although they explored large sections of modern Arkansas they found no sign of La Salle. They returned to Starved Rock in September 1690, after a fatiguing passage through 150 miles of Mississippi floodwater.

There remained only the settlers at Fort St Louis on the Gulf of Mexico. Ever since La Salle's ketch had been captured, and its crew interrogated, the Spanish had searched for his other ships. They found the wrecks of the *Aimable* and *Belle*, discovered too some of La Salle's deserters; but Fort St Louis eluded them. In April 1689, however, a captain named Alonzo de Leon stumbled across it. His men blew trumpets to announce their presence, but there was no reply. De Leon rode on horseback through the gates. Nobody met him: 'Doors were torn from their hinges; broken boxes, staved barrels, and rusty kettles, mingled with a great number of stocks of arquebuses and muskets, were scattered about in confusion.' Everything was a mess. More than 200 books were trampled into the mud – 'many of which still retained the traces of costly bindings'. There was no sign of the inhabitants, but Leon discovered three skeletons, one of which, still wearing the remains of a dress, belonged to a woman. He could extract no information from the local

Indians, but eventually two of La Salle's deserters (one of whom, a man named L'Archevêque, had been part of the murder conspiracy) emerged from the bush and, having secured a promise of clemency, told how three months earlier the settlers had first been hit by smallpox and then attacked by a tribe of warlike Indians. Everyone had been killed except an Italian, a Frenchman and a group of five children, who had been taken captive. They themselves had buried 14 of the bodies. De Leon managed to retrieve all the prisoners, save for the Frenchman, whose fate was never ascertained. Reneging on his promise, he sent the two deserters to Spain, where they were imprisoned along with the Italian, whose only crime was his nationality. The youngest children – two boys and a girl – were also taken back to Spain, but the two oldest spent seven years in the Spanish navy before being captured by a French ship and taken to the family of their dead father. De Leon then razed Fort St Louis so comprehensively that it was more than 300 years before archaeologists located its site.

The enigmatic, iron-handed Tonty later helped secure possession of Louisiana, before dying of yellow fever in 1704. For some 50 years it looked as if France might yet fulfil its imperial ambitions in North America, but in the second half of the 18th century the territory became a colonial football, passing now to Spain, now to England and then back to Spain before reverting to France in 1800. Three years later Napoleon Bonaparte sold it to the United States, bringing to an end a dream that might have changed the face, and the language, of modern America.

· PART 2 ·

THE AGE OF INQUIRY

THE AGE OF INQUIRY

'Dare to know!' These words, written by the philosopher Immanuel Kant, encapsulated the spirit of the 18th century, a period of such unprecedented intellectual upheaval that it became known as the Enlightenment. Rejecting the preconceptions under which they laboured, scholars strove to explain the nature of the world – and in explaining it to alter it for the better. (Both the French and American revolutions were a product of Enlightenment thinking.) Science, which had been largely subservient to religion, took on a life of its own, and by 1750 every European nation boasted at least one learned body dedicated exclusively to the pursuit of knowledge. These societies, of which the French Academy of Sciences was one of the earliest and most influential, were haunted in equal measure by wise men, quacks, eccentrics and aristocratic amateurs. Ludicrous theories were floated, to be met by equally far-fetched counterproposals. On occasion tempers ran so high that academicians settled their disputes not by debate but by duel. Amidst the arguments, however, all parties accepted one obvious truth: to understand properly the world's workings, they had first to learn more about its undiscovered regions.

Unlike their predecessors, who had performed the rudimentary task of finding what was out there (and then, if it contained gold, silver or spices, conquering it), Enlightenment explorers were driven by a spirit of scientific inquiry. Evangelism, which had played such an important part in Renaissance discovery, was replaced by empirical fervour. They sought to investigate the unknown, to place it in context and, if necessary, to redefine that context: Leibniz, for example, having read travellers' journals, suggested China send missionaries to civilize Europe. The old anxieties of wealth and trade were never far away, as witnessed by the ongoing search for a short-cut to the Far East, but science, in some form or other, underpinned most expeditions. The leaders' instructions were specific: in exploring the globe they were to take meteorological, astronomical, magnetic and gravitational observations; they were to study the geological composition of the lands they visited, to chart their coastlines and to investigate the nature of the populations they contained.

So blurred were the boundaries between art, science and literature that few explorers considered themselves scientists. Indeed, many branches of science did not even have a name, falling under the catch-all description of 'natural philosophy', a term that captured admirably the Enlightenment desire to compress man and his surroundings into a seamless construct. Some people could be slotted into a recognizable category: the horde of adventurers, mostly French, who struggled over the globe, from India to Hudson Bay, in order to record the 1769 transit of Venus, were clearly astronomers; men like Jean de Luc and Horace de Saussure who investigated the Alps were geologists; Alexander von Humboldt and Aimé Bonpland, who travelled to South America, were everything from zoologists to marine biologists; Louis Antoine de Bougainville, who made his name in the Pacific, was a botanist. But at the time, if you had asked them what they were, they would probably have replied that they were natural philosophers.

Perhaps the most versatile natural philosopher was Britain's Sir Joseph Banks. Wealthy, well-connected and adventurous, he circumnavigated the globe between 1768 and 1771 with the century's outstanding explorer, Captain James Cook, botanized South America, Australia and New Zealand, and collected such a wealth of information that, two centuries later, his findings were still being examined. On his return, he founded the African Association, whose declared aim was to unravel the mysteries of the dark continent – and, unscientifically, to seize its gold-bearing territories. His home, 21 Soho Square, London, was for several decades the most exciting place to be for anyone interested in discovery. He sponsored several expeditions, both to Africa and to the Arctic. None of them were particularly successful, with the exception of that led by Mungo Park in 1805 to discover the River Niger – even then, Park and his entire party perished – but Banks did not seem to mind. Cheerfully, casually even, he let matters take their course. He was observant to the end: shortly before his death in 1820 he passed a kidney stone that, he remarked, bore an uncanny resemblance to a piece of coral he had encountered in the Pacific.

A major development during Banks's lifetime was the solution of what was known as the 'longitude problem'. For centuries seafarers had tried to find an accurate way of plotting their east-west progress. North-south was simple enough: with the aid of the stars and latitudinal tables they could plot their whereabouts fairly easily. Longitude, however, was more difficult. To find one's position one needed to compare local time with the time at a place whose longitude had been previously ascertained – the home port, say, or the nearest observatory. To do this, however, required a clock that kept perfect time. Such a thing did not exist on land, let alone at sea. Its lack caused so many deaths, either through shipwreck or scurvy, that in 1714 the British Parliament announced a prize of £20,000 for the first person to create an accurate timepiece. The English clockmaker John Harrison took the offer to heart. Between 1737 and 1759 he produced a series of machines whose array of springs and pendulums fitted Parliament's specifications. Later distilled into a watch, and later still into a chronometer, his device transformed the art of navigation. When Cook gave it a trial on his second great voyage of 1772 he was impressed. 'Our error can never be great,' he wrote, 'so long as we have so good a guide as [the] watch.' Harrison's chronometers were set to the time at Greenwich, a London suburb that was home to both the headquarters of the Royal Navy and the nation's foremost observatory. Other nations set their watches to their own meridians – French navigators, for example, used Paris time – but it was Greenwich Mean Time that eventually became the world standard. Harrison's invention gave sailors the technological competence to chart the globe. It was men like Cook, however, who proved that they could, and men like Banks who encouraged them to do so.

Banks was spiritual mentor to many explorers, but his most eager pupil was a bureaucrat named John Barrow. As Second Secretary of the Admiralty – a post he occupied almost without interruption from 1804 to 1847 – Barrow was the most influential man in the Royal Navy. Born the son of a tenant farmer in Ulverston, Lancashire, he had worked his way to power by dint of keen intelligence and unflagging use of the patronage system. He fancied himself as a geographer, having travelled to China and mapped portions of South Africa, but he was not, alas, a very good one. Opinionated and inflexible, he had definite ideas about how the blank areas of the atlas should look. He believed fervently in the existence of an open polar sea and was an even firmer advocate of the existence of a North-West Passage. He believed, too, that the Niger might be part of either the Congo or the Nile; and he was certain that the north coast of Australia was ripe for development as one of the world's great trading centres. All that can be said to his geographical credit is that he was unsure if Antarctica really did contain seams of gold and marble, and he doubted it was home to a race of aliens. (Both theories were popular in some quarters.) Had he merely been a wealthy enthusiast, like Banks, his views might have had little impact. As it was, he controlled the world's most professional navy and was funded by the world's richest industrial nation. This, combined with an absolute refusal to admit that he was wrong, produced the most comprehensive programme of exploration the world had seen.

When the Napoleonic Wars ended in 1816 Barrow had a glut of unemployed naval officers on his hands. Rather than pay them to do nothing, he sent them exploring. For almost half a century he fired handpicked bands of men across the globe. Year on year, expeditions left the Thames in pursuit of Barrow's dreams. They went singly, jointly and severally. In a single year there might be a sloop taking one man to the coast of Africa, a couple of frigates heading for the North-West Passage, and a transport dropping men in Hudson's Bay. Sometimes they attacked a single objective, sometimes they were dispersed to different points of the globe. It was a haphazard system, undermined by Barrow's harsh attitude towards those who failed to achieve the goals he set them and his misunderstanding of the conditions they faced – whether in the Arctic or the Sahara, officers were expected to wear appropriate regalia when dealing with the natives – but it was one that worked. In 1819 W. E. Parry went further west than anyone yet through the North-West Passage. In 1826 Major Gordon Laing became the first white man to reach Timbuctoo (but never came back), and in 1831 Richard Lander traced the Niger to its mouth. In 1827 Parry made a remarkable attempt at the North Pole, dragging his boats over the pack ice to 82° 45' 42" N, a record that would not be bettered for almost 50 years. And in the early 1830s John Ross and his nephew James Clark Ross found the Magnetic North Pole – a feat that involved being marooned in the ice for five years. In 1839 James Ross left for Antarctica, where he discovered the massive ice shelf that now bears his name and also Antarctica's active volcano, Mount Erebus.

Barrow's men were not the only explorers active during this period. Spain and Portugal, which had previously led the field, had neither the need nor the energy to increase their overseas possessions; but other countries were eager to catch up. The governments of France, Russia and, increasingly, the United States played a prominent role in mapping the globe, despatching expeditions to Africa, Siberia, Antarctica, the Pacific and the west coast of North America. Similarly a host of whaling and sealing companies made their own independent contributions to polar discovery. But, by sheer perseverance, Barrow set the standard that everyone wanted to match. His reign came to an end in 1845 when he sent Sir John Franklin into the North-West Passage. Franklin was never seen again; neither were his two ships or the couple of hundred men aboard them. To date, nobody has successfully unravelled the mystery of their deaths. Nor, in fairness to the Second Secretary who sent them to their doom, has any man in the history of exploration bettered Barrow in the cracking of barriers and the opening of new territories.

Barrow's programme was in tune with the times. Not only did his men bring back the required scientific information, but their deeds reflected a new vogue known as Romanticism. Superficially a rejection of Enlightenment ideals, Romanticism celebrated individual expression, the identity of nations and, particularly, the glory of what the French author Jean-Jacques Rousseau dubbed 'the noble savage'. Adherents of the craze delighted in wilderness and disorder, relished the unruliness of Nature (spelled always with a respectful capital), and sought in its crags and cliffs an expression of their own hidden nobility. Like their Enlightenment predecessors, the Romantics were obsessed with the workings of the world; but they sought less to change it than to find their place in it. The quest for identity – indeed, for many people, the realization that they *could* have an identity – had as much to do with money as with anything else. Thanks to innovations in agriculture and industry, Europe was by 1800 more prosperous than ever before and its wealth was distributed more widely across the social classes. Whereas power and influence had previously devolved from the Crown to a small circle of landowning aristocrats, they were now wielded by a growing number of bourgeois, whose commercial acumen was to define the coming century. Although far from being a paradise, the continent offered its citizens something they had rarely had before: opportunity. Ludwig van Beethoven spoke for many when he said, in 1802, 'I will seize fate by the throat.'

There was nothing new in the idea of glory – people had always tried to cheat death by means of reputation – but there were now more avenues whereby it could be attained and a larger audience to appreciate it. Not everyone could be a Beethoven: for every person who succeeded there were hundreds who failed and hundreds of thousands who did not even try. But even the most talentless individual participated vicariously in the pursuit of fame. Those who were literate bought the books; those who were not relied on interpreters who, for a few pennies, read newspapers aloud in their local hostelry. Poets, generals, admirals, inventors and even politicians acquired iconic status. It was the beginning of the age of celebrity.

The people who seemed most obviously to seize fate (to tempt it, too) were explorers. Travel books had always been popular – the newborn printing presses of the Middle Ages had produced little else, apart from religious screeds – but in the 18th and 19th centuries they became required reading. This was the high noon of exploration literature, writers, artists and armchair explorers feeding off the accounts that were published almost yearly. Cook was a favourite, but men like Alexander Mackenzie and Samuel Hearne, who had crossed North America, also thrilled people with their depictions of noble savagery (though in some cases, such as Hearne's gruesome images of warring Indian tribes, the savagery seemed to outweigh the nobility). Their exploits connected intimately with the Romantic ethos, informing many of the age's great creative works. Cook's voyage was the basis for Samuel Taylor Coleridge's *The Rime of the Ancient Mariner*; it inspired, too, Edgar Allan Poe's *Narrative of Arthur Gordon Pym*. Lord Byron, Percy Bysshe Shelley and John Keats produced some of their most famous poems when they followed the path of mountaineering pioneers to the Alps; Shelley's wife, Mary, drew on Arctic journals for her novel *Frankenstein*. Explorers were icons, as W. E. Parry discovered in 1820 after his return from the North-West Passage. 'Even strangers in the coffee-room introduce themselves, and beg to shake hands with me,' he wrote. Two years later, when Franklin published his journal of an expedition through Canada – a book which contained details of murder and starvation, and in which Franklin admitted to having eaten his boots – the first impression sold so rapidly that second-hand copies went for considerably more than the original asking price.

Above the Romantic gush, and the supposed scientific objectivity, rose the spectre of imperial conquest. Although not as pronounced or as objectionable as it would later become, the subjugation of foreign lands was an important element in every voyage of discovery. Already, France and Britain had established themselves in North America and India, and with every new land they reached there was a zealous unfurling of flags and firing of guns. No matter how barren or unprofitable the territory appeared, it still had to be claimed for the mother country. Britain was a major culprit in this respect, performing the same rites whether they were observed by a cluster of bemused natives or a rookery of penguins. Other nations sneered: in 1840, when Jules-Sébastien-César Dumont d'Urville became the first man to set foot on mainland Antarctica, he recorded that, 'following the venerable custom which the English have carefully maintained, we took possession in the name of France'. But he dared not do otherwise. In an increasingly competitive imperial age it was unwise to miss an opportunity.

The races who inhabited the lands on which Europeans raised their standards, and whom the intelligentsia lauded for their noble savagery, must have seen things very differently. From the Inuit of Etah and the Clatsops of Columbia to the Chukchis of eastern Siberia and the Aborigines of Australia, nobody was left in ignorance of the white man. There are few indigenous accounts to describe how they felt as the foreign ships approached with their guns and cargoes of trinkets. It is possible, however, to chart their reaction from statistics and the journals of their 'discoverers'. Take the island of Tahiti. When Cook visited it in 1769 two expeditions had been there before him, one British under Samuel Wallis, one French under Bougainville. Wallis, Bougainville and, in his turn, Cook, reported it a paradise where the weather was good, the food plentiful, the women easy and the men warlike but not unreasonable. In 1769 there were 40,000 Tahitians. Thirty years later, thanks to the introduction of western diseases and firearms, that number had dropped to 16,000. Christian missionaries cast a further pall: in 1820 a Russian navigator reported that no one danced, played music or wove traditional flower garlands and that moral guardians patrolled the island to prevent out-of-marriage sex. By 1850 the population of Tahiti stood at 6,000. It was the same throughout the South Pacific. In 1788, on the advice of Joseph Banks, Britain sent its first shipload of convicts to Australia. During succeeding decades Australia's estimated 300,000-strong population of Aborigines was halved and that of Tasmania was wiped out.

By the mid-19th century almost every corner of the world had been examined, conquered and described. The process had been arduous and, while producing the knowledge that Enlightenment scientists had anticipated, it had also redefined the nature of exploration. The tribulations of men like Caillié, Park, Parry and, most dramatically, Franklin had a profound effect on the public imagination. Some people condemned them for taking unnecessary risks, but many more saw them as heroes. Their example spawned hundreds of imitators, among them some of the great figures of the late 19th and early 20th centuries. Previously explorers had existed to perform a task; now exploration had become a task in itself.

Vitus Bering (1725–42)

I. – At Kamchatka or some other place you are to build one or two boats with decks.

II. – With these you are to sail along the land that goes to the north, and according to expectations (because its end is not known) that land, it appears, is part of America.

III. – You are to search for where it is joined to America, and to go to any city of European possessions, or if you see any European vessel, to find out from it what the coast is called and to write it down, and to go ashore yourself and obtain first-hand information, and placing it on a map, to return here.

In these magnificently sweeping terms Tsar Peter the Great ordered Captain Vitus Bering to go east on 23 December 1724.

It was not the first time Peter the Great had shown an interest in the extremities of his realm. During his reign he had despatched several expeditions to map the Siberian coast and to conquer outlying regions such as the Kamchatkan peninsula. In doing so he had acted mostly for selfish reasons: new additions to Russia's empire were always welcome, as were the minerals, furs and timber they contained. Lately, however, the French Academy of Sciences had advised him he would do the world a great service if he could ascertain whether the Asian and American landmasses were separate or whether, as some thought, they were linked. As a man who had spent his life trying to make Russia the cultural equal of Western Europe – Bering was part of that programme: born in Denmark in 1681, he had been employed in 1703 to bring much-needed expertise to Russia's infant navy – Peter was flattered by the Academy's approach.* The proposition was also economically attractive: if there was open water between the two continents this suggested the possibility of a navigable passage via the Arctic – the North-East Passage – linking his Siberian territories, and indeed the whole western

---

* The flattery was forced: the French had applied several times to do the job themselves and might have done so had not Peter forbidden foreigners to enter the northern territories. As for Peter's cultural pretensions, it was not until 1725 that he founded the Imperial Russian Academy of Sciences, and even then almost all of its members were foreigners.

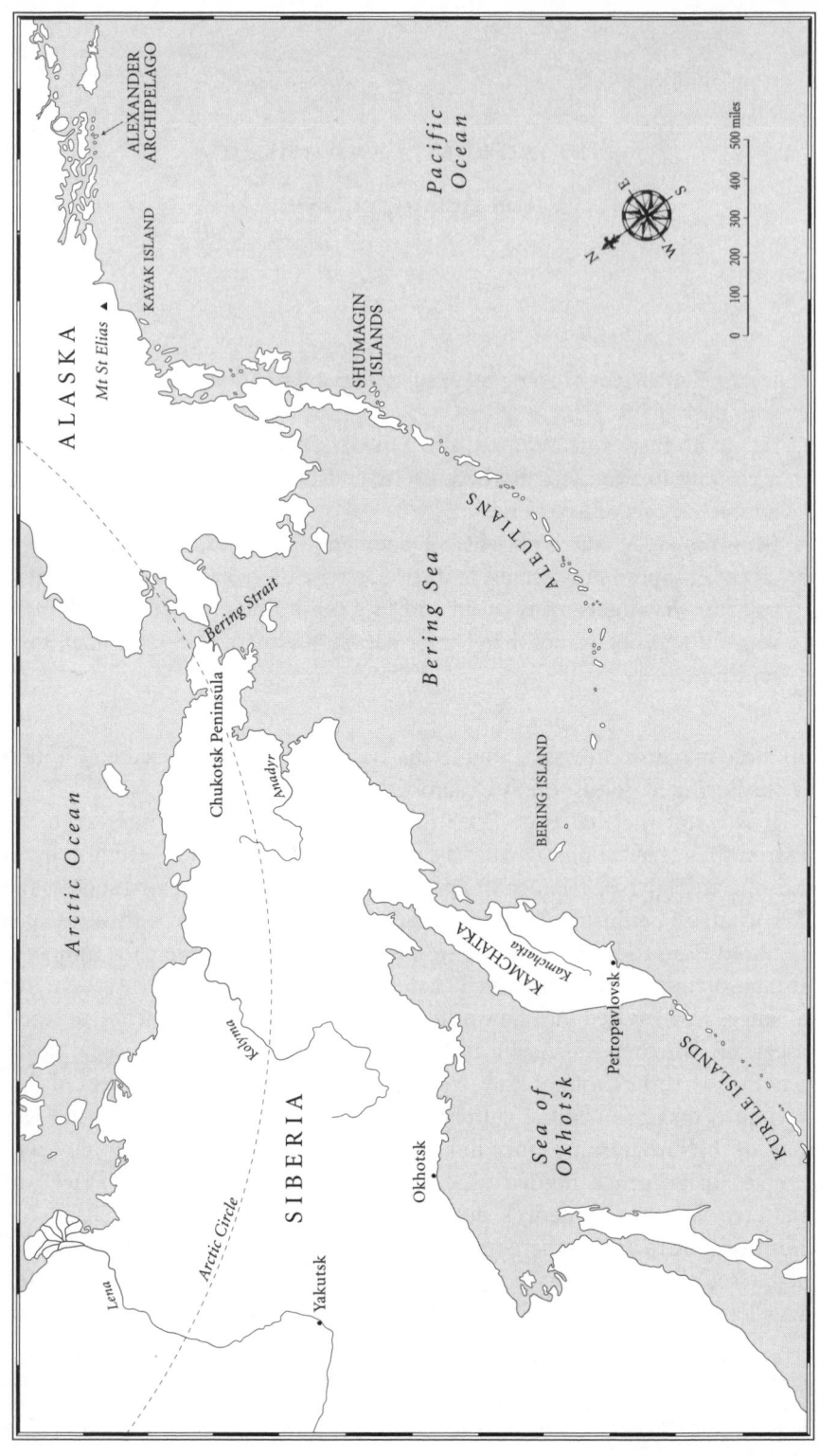

empire, to the markets of China; if there was not, and the two continents were joined, then his expansionary programme could continue unimpeded; and even if there was no North-East Passage, and no possibility of annexation, then profitable commerce could still be established with America, and possibly Japan too.

As far as the North-East Passage went, Peter the Great's expectations were the product of ignorance. In 1648 a Cossack named Semen Ivanovich Dezhnev had taken seven boats from Siberia's Kolyma River to the Anadyr River above Kamchatka. He rounded a mountainous promontory that he named the Chukotsk Peninsula, after the Chukchi tribe who lived there, and in doing so proved that a slender, fitful passage did exist between Siberia and the Far East. But Dezhnev's achievement was compromised by fatalities and poor communications. Of the 90 men with whom he sailed only 13 survived, and it was not until 1662 that he returned to Moscow. After 14 years the authorities had forgotten why he went to Siberia in the first place. His report vanished, leaving only a distant rumour of what he had done.

During the next 50 years, Russian expeditions probed the north-east corner of Asia. They explored most of Kamchatka and found no landmass connecting it to America. They tramped along the Siberian and Pacific coasts, discovering several rivers that might be useful to trade. But they never went to the Chukotsk Peninsula. Some mapmakers followed Dezhnev's example and portrayed it as a *finisterre*, on which they wrote 'Hostile Natives'. Others left an open-ended squiggle bearing the rubric: 'It is not known where this chain of mountains ends and whether it does not join some other continent.' Or, more promisingly: 'Mountain chain which is joined to what is believed to be the continent of America.' As for the North-East Passage, everyone declared it a chimera. The Dezhneviskis said it was too frigid to be a reliable trade route. Others said that it would be blocked by a chain of mountains – the so-called Shalatskii Promontory – that rose on the Chukotsk Peninsula and ended somewhere in North America.

If Bering's orders are anything to go by, Peter the Great favoured the Shalatskii theory, but whatever his thoughts, he died shortly after delivering them. By then, however, Bering and his second-in-command Aleksei Chirikov had already left St Petersburg, in January 1725, on the long journey through Siberia to the Sea of Okhotsk. From here, in the armpit between Kamchatka and mainland Asia, they intended to fulfil the late Tsar's instructions.

The crossing of Siberia was arduous. One party went by boat, to chart the region's rivers. Another, under Bering, struggled on horses across the tundra. Bering reached Okhotsk in mid-August 1726, having covered 685 miles of trackless terrain at terrible cost to his horses. While waiting for the boat party to arrive he erected a collection of huts and, as instructed, began to build a ship, the *Fortuna*. The boat party, however, did not appear until 6 January, having been forced to abandon their vessels at the onset of winter and having subsequently walked 250 miles overland. They were frostbitten and exhausted and had only avoided starvation by eating the dead horses that littered Bering's trail. Whatever comfort they felt at reaching Okhotsk was dispelled when they heard Bering's plan for the coming year: they were to finish the *Fortuna*, sail in it across the Sea of Okhotsk to the nearest part of Kamchatka, carry their boats, supplies and equipment overland to the River Kamchatka, travel down the river to its mouth on the north coast of the peninsula, and there build new ships to take them north to the land of the Chukchis.

The year 1727 was abominable. The completion of the *Fortuna* occupied most of the spring and summer, leaving them a very slender margin in which to cross Kamchatka. When they reached the Kamchatkan coast they found its waters were too shallow for the ship's draught, which necessitated the laborious and time-wasting task of landing their supplies by boat and barge. They then hauled everything into the interior – boats, fuel, food, not to mention the canvas, ropes and nails they needed to build their ships once they reached the other side. It was a harder, slower business than Bering had anticipated, and they had not gone halfway before winter overtook them. Their only option was to continue, which they did with remarkable fortitude and at the cost of several lives, until they reached their goal. The journey had taken six months. If Bering had simply sailed the *Fortuna* around the southern tip of Kamchatka he could have been there within 30 days or so.

They built their new ship, the *Gabriel*, in remarkably short time, and on 13 July 1728 they sailed north, leaving a shore party to await their return. By 7 August they were at the Chukotsk Peninsula and, with only one barrel of water remaining, went ashore to fill their 22 empties. A day later they met their first Chukchis. Or, more accurately, the Chukchis met them: eight natives came out in kayaks, and one man swam to the *Gabriel* where, with the promise of gifts, and through an interpreter, he told Bering all he knew of the region. He had little to say, and most of it was discouraging: he did not know of the Kolyma River, but had heard that reindeer herders went annually to a large river in the west; where he lived there were no forests nor any rivers of note; there was no promontory to the north; and as for the east, 'There is an island not far from the land, and if there were no fog, it could be seen. There are people on this island, and as for any more land there is only our Chukotsk land.' He was awarded a few metal toys, carrying which he swam back to his kayak.

The *Gabriel* rounded the Chukotsk Peninsula on 13 August 1728* where, at 65° 30' N, Bering convened a sea-council to determine their future course. Chirikov's written opinion gave an insight into both their situation and the formalities of Russian naval etiquette. 'On this date your excellency deigned

* Or perhaps it was the 14th. Not only was the Russian calendar 11 days ahead of the rest of Europe, but its days started and stopped at different hours. On land, a Russian day was measured from midnight to midnight. At sea, it was from noon to noon.

to summon us,' his report ran. 'I submit my humble opinion: since we have no information as to what degree of latitude in the Northern Sea along the eastern coast of Asia Europeans of known nations have been, we can not accordingly know with certainty about the separation of Asia and America … Because of this it is necessary for us without fail, by force of the *ukaz* [order] given your excellency by His Imperial Majesty, to proceed along the land to those places indicated in the aforesaid of His Imperial Majesty.'

To follow the coast, however, would have meant going west, when the expedition's goal lay in the opposite direction. Bering therefore sailed north. His decision was understandable: if there was a promontory – or *nos* in Russian – that arched from the Chukotsk Peninsula to America then he would meet it. If, instead, he found ice then it was likely that no such *nos* existed, and neither did a land passage between Asia and America. By 16 August, at 67° 18' N, with no sign of a *nos* and with less than a month before the sea froze, he dared go no further. He returned to Kamchatka, where the shore party and the crew of the *Gabriel* endured their fourth winter away from home.

During the winter and the following spring, Bering investigated the coast. Once an advocate of the *nos*, he was now certain that it did not exist, but everything he found on his walks suggested the presence of a large body of land to the east. The driftwood was not indigenous to Kamchatka, and the movement of the ice – slow to gather if the wind was from the north, quick if it was from the east – told him that America could not be far away. There was also a tale from the Chukchi describing how 'In the year 1715 a man had stranded there who said that his native land was far to the east and had large rivers and forests and many high trees'. Bering took the *Gabriel* on a brief foray towards America in 1729, but he discovered nothing. The expedition returned (this time by sea) to Okhotsk, where he mothballed the *Gabriel* and *Fortuna*, posting guards to protect them, and left for St Petersburg, where he arrived on 1 March 1730.

Bering's achievements had been noteworthy: he had led an expedition to the furthest corner of the Russian Empire, had discovered the strait between America and Asia that now bears his name, and had all but destroyed the myth of the Shalatskii Peninsula. The Imperial Academy of Sciences deliberated his findings for three years before concluding that he had not found America; therefore he had not fulfilled his instructions and would have to try again. Bering, who had proposed that very thing as soon as he returned, was back in Siberia by the spring of 1734, with an expedition that included not only his second-in-command Chirikov but a host of subsidiary officers, priests, doctors, their retainers, their families – Bering's own wife accompanied them for a while – and their porters, plus the men and boats for a separate expedition down the Lena River, the purpose of which was to chart the Arctic coast. In total, there were some 600 people under his command.

The wives and servants soon returned home, the river parties departed, and when Bering reached Okhotsk in the summer of 1737 his massive party had been reduced to less than 200. Rejecting the *Gabriel* and *Fortuna*, whose guards had long since fled, Bering began the construction of two new ships, the *St Peter* and the *St Paul*. The former was to be captained by himself, the latter by Chirikov, and they were both to be manned by 76 men. The building work, which had proceeded so swiftly on his first expedition, was now delayed by lack of food. Supplies were supposed to have been sent from the Siberian town of Yakutsk but, thanks to the sluggish manner in which the Russian Empire operated, they failed to arrive and Bering's men had to spend valuable time hunting. Progress was so slow that the *St Peter* and *St Paul* were not ready until June 1740.

The two ships, each of which displaced 80–100 tons, sailed for the east coast of Kamchatka on 4 September. Here, at a harbour he named Petropavlovsk, Bering overhauled his equipment and stores for the forthcoming trip. At the same time he sent for two scientists to join the expedition: one was a Frenchman, Louis Delisle de la Croyère, an astronomer from the Academy of Sciences, who was allotted to Chirikov; the other was a German named Georg Wilhelm Steller, naturalist and erstwhile physician to the Archbishop of Novgorod, who was placed with Bering.

The presence of these scientists in no way suggested that the expedition was a scientific one. To be sure, they could pursue scientific goals if they liked; but they were there primarily, in Delisle's case, to advise on the direction the ships should take; and in Steller's to assay any gold or silver they might discover. If Bering's first voyage had carried a gloss of scientific respectability, his second was purely one of conquest. As one of the expedition's organizers wrote, it was 'not only for great and immortal glory, but for the expansion of the empire and for inexhaustible wealth'. Its explicit objectives were 'to search for new lands and islands not yet conquered, as many as possible, and to bring them under subjection [and] to search for metals and minerals'. They were to extract tribute from any tribes they encountered, and in so doing to pave the way for Russia's ultimate annexation of the American coast as far south as Spain's colonies in California and Mexico – 'though I know that the Spanish will not be pleased'. In an unusual twist to the imperial ethos, they were to effect all this 'through kindness'.

Delisle and Steller arrived in March 1741, and on 4 May a council was held to determine their course. The surest and speediest way to America would have been to follow Bering's route of 1728. However, they suspected (rightly) that any land so far north would be cold, inhospitable and sparsely popu-lated. Moreover, the maps that Delisle possessed showed a large island or outcrop to the south-east. Gama Land, as it was known, had purportedly been sighted by a 15th-century navigator, Juan de Gama, on a journey from China to Mexico. As there was no reason to doubt its existence, and because it looked tantalizingly close on Delisle's map – also because Delisle was meant to be the expert in these matters – they decided to sail in that direction. The *St Peter* and *St Paul* left Petropavlovsk on 4 June.

Of what happened next Steller's journal provides the fullest record. Petulant, perpetually outraged that his advice was not followed, and indignant that the sailors treated him as an ignorant landlubber, he was by no means an objective narrator. But even if one ignores his rants and concentrates solely on the facts, this was a journey of astonishing incompetence. Bering, now in his sixties, was a tired and sick man – he may already have been suffering from scurvy – who 'lamented that his strength for enduring such a burden was often inadequate; that the expedition was much larger and more lengthy than he had projected; and also, that at his age, he wished for nothing better than the entire expedition might be taken from him and entrusted to a young, energetic, and determined man'. He remained constantly in his cabin, leaving the *St Peter* in the hands of two junior officers. These men, as Steller remarked, had lived nearly ten years in Siberia with 'the ignorant rabble', and had long since forgotten the meaning of discipline.

On 12 June Steller saw signs of land to the south-east. Thereupon the ships turned north. 'Just when it would have been most crucial to keep our objective most clearly in mind,' Steller fumed, 'the unreasonable behaviour of our officers began. They mocked, ridiculed and cast to the winds whatever was said by anyone not a seaman, as if all rules of navigation, all science and powers of reasoning were spontaneously acquired.' On this occasion they were right to do so. Steller had been wrong: there was no land to the south. But when the sailors thought they saw land to the north – and this time there *was* land – the officers ignored them and steered south. ('They, of course, have been in God's council chamber!' Steller sneered.) Meanwhile, on the morning of the 20th, the ships were hit by a 24-hour storm. When it passed there was no sign of the *St Paul*. Assuming it had either sunk or turned back for Kamchatka, Bering's officers arbitrarily forsook their southward course and sailed east.

The *St Paul* had neither foundered nor retreated. Chirikov continued towards America, where he discovered, on 15 July, the Alexander Archipelago off the coast of Alaska. In need of water, he sent an officer ashore with ten armed men. Three days later they had not returned, so he sent another armed party, led by the bosun, to chase up the first. The bosun's party did not return either. That night Chirikov saw campfires in the forest, and the next morning there was a pall of smoke along the shore. Assuming the men had been killed – and anyway, having lost both his boats, being unable to search for them – he sailed on 27 July for Kamchatka, arriving at Petro-pavlovsk on 12 October. Every man, including Chirikov, was scorbutic. Delisle, who had followed current medical wisdom by retiring to his cabin with a bottle, had alcohol poisoning as well. He expired on exposure to daylight.

The *St Peter*, whose crew was no healthier than that of the *St Paul*, reached an island – Kayak Island – within sight of the Alaskan coast at 10.30 a.m. on 20 July. It wasn't much of a place, a cold, pine-clad lump, visited by natives only in summer. Steller found an underground store containing bundles of smoked salmon and a number of artefacts, some of which he stole. They were later replaced by a pipe, a pound of tobacco, a kettle and a bolt of Chinese silk. The subsititution was considered fair trade by the officers, but Steller thought it an unsuitable exchange: 'If in the future we were to return to this place, the people would flee from us just as they did this time. Or, since we had shown them hostility [by opening the underground cache], they would be hostile in return, especially if they should use the tobacco for eating or drinking, since they might not know the true use of either the tobacco or the pipe, whereas at least a few knives or axes would have aroused greater insight since their use would have been quite obvious.' They collected other bits and pieces: a bark box, a whetstone, a canoe paddle, a fox-tail and, poignantly, 'A hollow ball of hard-burned clay two inches in diameter, enclosing a stone that rattles when shaken, which I regard as a toy for small children'. Steller gathered plants, made as many observations as he could, and took samples of the sand and coastal rock. But Bering did not allow him onto the Alaskan mainland – which was dominated by a peak that they named Mount St Elias – nor did he give him much time on Kayak Island.

Among the many symptoms of scurvy are depression and lethargy. According to Steller, Bering displayed them to the fullest. When they reached Kayak Island: 'It can easily be imagined how glad we all were when we finally caught sight of land. Everyone hastened to congratulate the Captain-Commander, to whom the fame of discovery would most redound. However, he not only reacted indifferently and without particular pleasure but in our very midst shrugged his shoulders.' Privately, he disparaged his officers: 'Now we think we have found everything,' he told Steller. 'But they do not consider where we have reached land, how far we are from home, and what accidents may yet happen. Who knows whether the trade winds may not come up and prevent our return? We do not know this country. We are not supplied with provisions to keep us through the winter.' He therefore turned back, having spent less than a day off the coast of Alaska.

'On the morning of July 21, two hours before daybreak,' Steller wrote, 'the Captain-Commander, contrary to his custom, got up, came on deck himself, and, without deliberating about it, gave orders to weigh anchor.' The decision was taken so abruptly that they could not complete their watering and departed having filled only 20 of their 46 barrels. When he thought about it Steller became irritable: 'The only reason for this is stupid obstinacy, a fear of a handful of natives, and pusillanimous homesickness.' Later he became angry: 'For ten years Bering had equipped himself for this great enterprise. The exploration lasted ten hours!' Bering, however, was too far gone to care.

The *St Peter* bounced back through the Aleutians – an archipelago that stretched west towards Kamchatka – and on 30 August they were in a cluster of islands, where they landed to fill their water barrels. To Steller's dismay, the crew insisted on using the nearest brackish pool rather than a fresh spring a little further inland. When he suggested they gather some scurvy grass, an edible plant that was known to alleviate the disease, they told him to do it himself. He did so angrily, resolving 'in the future, to look after the saving of myself alone, without the loss of one word more'. That day a man called Shumagin died. They named the islands in his honour, then left.

The scurvy grass went some way towards restoring the crew's health. After three days the sailors' teeth no longer wobbled in their gums, and in little more than a week the bedridden Bering was back on his feet. On 5 September, while attempting to replace their brackish water with fresh, they met their first Americans. A canoe came out to meet them, its two occupants wearing conical hats made of bark, painted red and green, with feathers and reeds protruding as an eyeshade. They dithered nervously, singing and shouting, then held out a stick on the end of which was a dead falcon. After several attempts to snatch the bird, the officers realized it was an intermediary, intended to accept trade goods on behalf of the canoeists. Steller exchanged some trifles for one of their hats, whereupon 'they headed for the shore without further ceremony, lighted a big fire, and shouted loudly for a time. Then, because it soon became dark, we did not see them any more.' On 6 September the Russians landed, giving Steller the chance to observe these new people at closer quarters. They had no facial hair and pierced their noses, foreheads and lips with bones and pieces of slate. They lived generally on the Alaskan mainland, but came to the Aleutians in search of birds' eggs, seals and beached whales. They were so similar to the Chukchi that he deduced that at some point in the past there must have been a strip of land joining Asia to America.

Steller was also fascinated by the zoology of the region. He saw whales puffing and splashing at close quarters, and recorded a mammal unknown to science – now extinct – that he called a sea ape. The creature had a dog-shaped head, pointy ears and long whiskers that 'made him look almost like a Chinaman'. It was about two yards long, had large eyes and a round body, red and white on the belly, with a long tail that tapered to a shark-like fin. It possessed neither forefeet nor flippers but showed great playfulness, raising itself from the water for minutes on end, staring all the while at the crew. For two hours it darted beneath the ship, pausing only to grab some seaweed that it carried to the Russians, 'and did such juggling tricks that one could not have asked for anything more comical from a monkey'. He tried, but failed, to shoot a specimen.

Their stay ended in an unsatisfactory manner. The natives became more fascinated with the foreigners than the foreigners were with them. When the Russians tried to leave, the natives pulled their boats back to shore and had to be discouraged by several volleys of musket-fire. Thus ended Russia's first, ignominious contact with the people it aimed to subjugate through kindness.

From that point the voyage deteriorated rapidly. Thanks to their imperfect ability to calculate longitude – it would be more than 30 years before an accurate chronometer was developed – they lost their way. The wind blew constantly from the west, their food and alcohol ran out, their water barrels began to leak, and scurvy resumed its grip. By the middle of October, with the weather worsening and with scarcely four able-bodied men to manage the ship, Bering abandoned hope of reaching Kamchatka. According to his calculations, they were somewhere near the coast of America, where they could spend the winter and hope for better conditions next summer. He could not have been more mistaken. They were, in fact, off the Kurile Islands, north of Japan. Had he continued east the ship would have been lost – as it was, the crew were already beginning to die – but fortunately his plans were thwarted by the weather. The *St Peter* was forced north by storms, and on 5 November they sighted land.

'How great and extraordinary was the joy of everyone over this sight is indescribable,' Steller wrote. 'The half-dead crawled out to see it. From our hearts we thanked God for his favour. The very sick Captain-Commander was himself not a little cheered, and everyone spoke about how he intended to take care of his health and to take a rest after suffering such terrible hardships.' Cups of brandy, which the crew had secreted before the barrel ran dry, were passed around to toast their safe arrival in Kamchatka. Only slowly did it dawn on them that it was not Kamchatka but an unknown island that they later named after Bering. Sailing for the mainland was out of the question: it was too late in the season, the crew were too ill, and the ship had taken too much of a battering. Their only choice was to stay for the winter. Luckily there was driftwood for fuel and the island teemed with game – predominantly foxes, but also sea otters and seals, all of which were so tame that killing them was an easy matter. Indeed, they were so plentiful that Steller spent the first few nights in a stone hut mortared with fox carcases.

It took ten days to unload the ship, bring the sick ashore and dig rudimentary shelters – Steller called them graves – that they covered with sticks and rags. The transition was too much for some: one man died when he was brought out of his cabin, another on the crossing and seven more as soon as they reached the shore. 'Even before they could be buried, the dead were mutilated by foxes that sniffed at and even dared to attack the sick ... who were lying everywhere without cover under the open sky,' Steller wrote. 'One screamed because he was cold, another from hunger and thirst, as the mouths of many were in such a wretched state from scurvy that they could not eat anything ... [their] gums were swollen up like a sponge, brown-black and grown high over the teeth and covering them.' In a vengeful madness the crew tortured the foxes, gouging out their eyes, cutting off their tails, roasting their paws and partially skinning them before letting them free as an example to the rest. But they kept coming and, as more and more men died, the foxes burrowed into the hospital trench. It was a hideous scene. As Steller put it, 'everywhere we looked on nothing but depressing and terrifying sights'.

Their one advantage was the supply of fresh meat, which Steller, long before his time, recognized as an effective anti-scorbutic. He tried to persuade the men to eat it, but they didn't like the flavour of seal meat and refused absolutely to touch the nutrient-rich blubber. Bering, who had been carried on a stretcher to Steller's trench on 11 November – 'we treated him, as well as the other officers who came to our "grave", to tea' – was particularly revolted by the suggestion: 'he declared a very great aversion for it and wondered at my taste'. He died on 8 December 1741, two hours before dawn, and was buried alongside several more of his men. Not until the depths of winter, when desperation drove them to eat the marine animals, did the crew begin to recover. For almost half of them it was too late: three months after they landed on Bering Island, 30 of the 76 were dead.

Steller penned a double-edged obituary to his late commander. Bering, he said, was 'by birth a Dane, by faith a righteous and godly Christian, by his conduct a well-mannered, friendly, quiet man, and for that reason always popular with the entire command, both high and low'. He was, however, 'not born to make quick decisions and conduct swift enterprises', and the men 'considered his esteem to be the result of fear and lack of ability to judge'. On arriving at Bering Island, 'He wished nothing more than our deliverance from this land and, from the bottom of his heart, his own complete deliverance from this misery. He might well not have found a better place to prepare himself for eternity than this deathbed under the open sky.' In short, he was pleasant, weak, unfit for command and, in Steller's opinion, deserved what he got.

The company's recovery was hampered by living in a sub-Arctic climate. Their 'graves' were frequently covered by snow, from which they had to dig themselves out every morning. The same snow fell on the beach, covering it so thickly that they were unable to collect driftwood. When their initial stockpile was consumed, they went further and further afield in search of fresh sources. By December they were already walking two and a half miles a day. By March they had to trudge ten miles to the other side of the island. The same applied to the game: on landing they had been able to shoot vast amounts; by the end of winter they were making daily journeys of more than 20 miles, returning with loads of up to 100 pounds strapped on their backs. It very nearly killed them. One group was caught in a storm and took refuge in a cave, where they starved for seven days. Another was similarly caught, but in the absence of a cave simply burrowed into crevices and let the drifts cover them. When they emerged the next morning they were senseless and speechless, so stiff from cold that they could hardly move their feet. The assistant surgeon, totally blind, fumbled his way behind them. Steller feared that one man would lose his hands and feet, 'since he had been lying in a creek the whole night and was hard as a stone and his clothes had frozen to his body, but God restored him without any injury whatsoever'. It was eight days before the assistant surgeon regained his sight.

With the coming of spring, life became easier. On their beach piles of driftwood emerged from the snow. Simultaneously there was an influx of sea-lions and manatees – Steller called them sea-cows – which meant they no longer had to tramp across the island for food and fuel. Scurvy grass appeared, as did cress and wild celery; and when a whale beached two miles down the coast their immediate survival was assured. But the winter's travelling had reduced their clothes to rags. Their shoes had been destroyed so comprehensively that they now wore clogs made from sea chests and leather food bags. The thaw, too, filled their underground 'graves' with water, driving them into overland shelters through whose walls the wind blew unremittingly. The new huts were so exposed that, some nights, the men crept back to their trenches, regardless of the seepage. It was important to devise a means of escape as soon as possible.

Winter storms had thrown the *St Peter* high on the beach, damaging it beyond use – not that they could have dragged it back to the sea anyway. Its timbers, however, were still solid, and with these they began to construct a new, smaller ship that they named after the first. After the back-breaking winter treks it was a relief to have a project close to hand and to work, moreover, to a positive end. They built furnaces, cut whetstones, dismantled the ship, made new water barrels and hauled driftwood from miles around to create a launch platform. 'There was not a one wanting to be idle, nor supposed to be, the closer and dearer to each was his hope of deliverance from this island to his homeland,' Steller wrote. They were so encouraged by their progress that for a while one or two men voted to remain another year on Bering Island to collect sea otter pelts, but 'they finally out of shame would not consider it'.

On 11 August, after a disappointment when the launch platform failed and the ship had to be winched back into position, the new *St Peter* was afloat. Measuring only 42 feet from stem to stern, it was too small to accommodate the whole party in any comfort. They came to a partial solution by dividing themselves into three watches, one of which was constantly on deck. But still the space was cramped, so, rather than jettison food or water, they threw out their pillows, blankets and mattresses. Uncomfortable, but exhilarated, they weighed anchor on 14 August. That afternoon, as Steller watched the coast of Bering Island slide past them, he could not conceal his delight. 'We knew all the mountains and valleys, whose paths we had climbed so many times with great effort to scout for food and for other reasons ... God's grace and mercy became manifested to all, the more brightly considering how miserably we had arrived there on November 6, had miraculously nourished ourselves on this barren land, and with amazing labour had become ever more healthy, hardened, and strengthened; and the more we gazed at the island on our farewell, the clearer appeared to us, as in a mirror, God's wonderful and loving guidance.'

He spoke too soon: that midnight, water began to pour into the ship. The pumps were choked with wood shavings and the hold was so tightly loaded it was impossible to find the leak. For a while there was pandemonium, everyone getting in each other's way as they simultaneously lowered the sails, bailed with cooking pots and threw baggage overboard. Fortunately, the leak was just below the waterline and as the ship became lighter they were able to plug the gap. (To their relief it was a minor repair: the hull had been twisted during the first, abortive launch and, being built with nails rather than wooden dowels, some of the strakes had sprung.) This was the last of their trials: on 17 August they sighted the Kamchatkan coast. They had spent ten months of deprivation on Bering Island, unaware that the mainland was just two days away.

Contrary winds, interspersed by periods of calm, meant that it was a further ten days, including a 24-hour stint at the oars, before they reached Petropavlovsk. Their homecoming was tainted by disappointment: 'Everyone had considered us dead or come to grief; our property left behind had fallen into other hands and mostly been carried off. Therefore, joy and sorrow often changed in a few moments, according to the nature of the news about general and special happenings.' But these were minor irritants set against their relief at returning to civilization. Expressing a sentiment that would be echoed by many other polar survivors, Steller wrote: 'We were all so accustomed to misery and wretched living that ... we considered the previous circumstances would always continue and thought we were dreaming.'

It was another eight months before they reached Okhotsk and the same time again before they returned to St Petersburg. Their journey had been successful, after a fashion: they had forged a link between Russia and America, and had returned with information about the new continent's flora, fauna and human population. They had also secured several hundred sea otter pelts that fetched a high price in St Petersburg and more than offset the cost of the goods they had lost while away. (Most of them were given to Steller in recognition of the part he had played in their survival on Bering Island.) But the price had been high and, thanks to Russia's fanatical secrecy about its eastern enterprises, the world knew little of what they had done. Not until the 20th century did Soviet archives divulge, reluctantly, the full extent of Peter the Great's programme. By then Bering's discoveries were old hat. Within 40 years of his death, the coast of Alaska and Bering Strait had been charted by Captain James Cook of Britain's Royal Navy.

Charles-Marie de la Condamine (1735–45)

Scientists had never really believed that the world was flat. In fact, at the dawn of the 18th century they agreed unanimously that it was round. But there was roundness and there was roundness. Some said the globe was a perfect sphere. Others maintained it was uneven. The English scientist Isaac Newton was of the opinion that it bulged slightly at the equator. Jacques Cassini, France's astronomer royal, held that it was a prolate spheroid, elongated at the poles and, if anything, pinched at the waist. But when Cassini sent a man to the South American colony of French Guiana to measure the equator's gravity with a pendulum, it was discovered that the gravitational pull was weaker there than in France, thus suggesting that the world did, indeed, bulge in the middle. Newton's supporters were delighted. Cassini, however, refused to accept the findings, denouncing his emissary as 'a hypocrite, a traitor … a sanctimonious, sneaking fabricator'. Thus one of the Enlightenment's many scientific squabbles bubbled into life.

In itself it was a petty controversy, centred less on facts than on patriotism and injured professional pride. But it did have an underlying seriousness, for the earth's curvature was important both to Europe's mapmakers and to its navigators. While it was impossible as yet to calculate longitude with any precision, latitude could be determined easily from the stars. However, without knowing how long a degree of latitude was, no chart could be guaranteed accurate. In 1670 the French scientist Jean Picard had triangulated a meridian of the arc between Corbeil and Amiens, to produce a length of 69.1 miles. An Englishman had responded with a measurement of 66.91 miles. Britain's Royal Navy, meanwhile, had made its own calculations according to ancient Mesopotamian mathematics and the clock: the *Seaman's Practice* decreed that a degree of latitude consisted of 60 minutes, subdivided into 60 seconds, each minute representing one nautical mile – which, to complicate matters further, was slightly longer than its land-based equivalent.

In December 1734 the French Academy of Sciences decided to settle the question of the earth's shape. Two expeditions would be despatched: one, under Pierre Louis de Maupertius, would go to Lapland; another, under Charles-Marie de la Condamine, would go to South America. Both parties would measure a degree of latitude and then compare their findings. If an

Arctic degree was shorter than an equatorial one, then Newton's theories were right and those of Cassini wrong. Alternatively, the globe might be spherical and the length of a degree could be standardized. Of the two expeditions the equatorial one was by far the most interesting: whereas Maupertius would be travelling through a dark and unprofitable region, Condamine's journey led to the secretive heart of Spain's overseas empire.

Condamine left France on 16 May 1735, bound for the port of Cartagena, in modern Colombia, carrying a royal passport that gave him unfettered access to Spain's vast American colonies and ordered every administrator and functionary to assist him in his project. He was accompanied by a sturdy array of scientists: Pierre Bouguer, astronomer; Louis Godin and his cousin Jean Godin des Odonais, mathematicians; Joseph de Jussieu, botanist; Jean Senièrgues, physician; M. Hugot, watchmaker and technician; M. de Morainville, draughtsman; M. Mabillon, traveller; Captain Verguin of the French navy; and M. Couplet, the nephew of an important Academy member. Lest the Frenchmen stray too far, they were to be joined at Cartagena by two captains from the Spanish navy: Jorge Juan y Santacilla and Antonio de Ulloa. From Cartagena, as Condamine explained to the French academicians, 'We shall make our way by the best means at hand to the province of Quito in the Viceroyalty of Peru. There we shall begin our work.'

Condamine was the man to undertake that work. Outwardly a pampered aristocrat whose natural habitat was the court of Louis XV, he was well travelled, a skilled geodesist and mathematician, and at the age of 34 he retained, as his childhood friend Voltaire put it, 'une curiosité ardente'. In the words of one writer, 'He was an ensemble of all the forces of that strange age in which religion, debauchery, intellect, fashion, and brutality seethed and bubbled together in such an extraordinary pot pourri'. Not every member of the expedition agreed with Condamine's appointment. Pierre Bouguer wrote that: 'M. Louis Godin had more pretension than anyone else to be placed at the head of our company ... For my own part, I had, at first, no intention of having anything to do with the enterprise.' Then again, Bouguer was resentful because he himself was not the Academy's first choice: 'When several of the mathematicians or astronomers on whom reliance was placed found themselves in a situation ... to be unable to give efficacy to their zeal,' he wrote sniffily, 'this determined me to conquer the repugnance which the weak state of my health had always given me to sea voyages.'

Condamine showed his worth almost as soon as they reached South America in November 1735. As their Spanish escorts explained, there were two ways to reach Quito from Cartagena: one was to make a detour via Panama, where they could catch a ship to the Ecuadorian coast; the other was to travel 400 miles up the Magdalena River, ascend the Andes by mule, and then follow the mountains for 500 miles. To a man, the party opted for the Panama route: it would be quicker and easier on both themselves and their instruments. But at Panama they found colonial life moved at a different

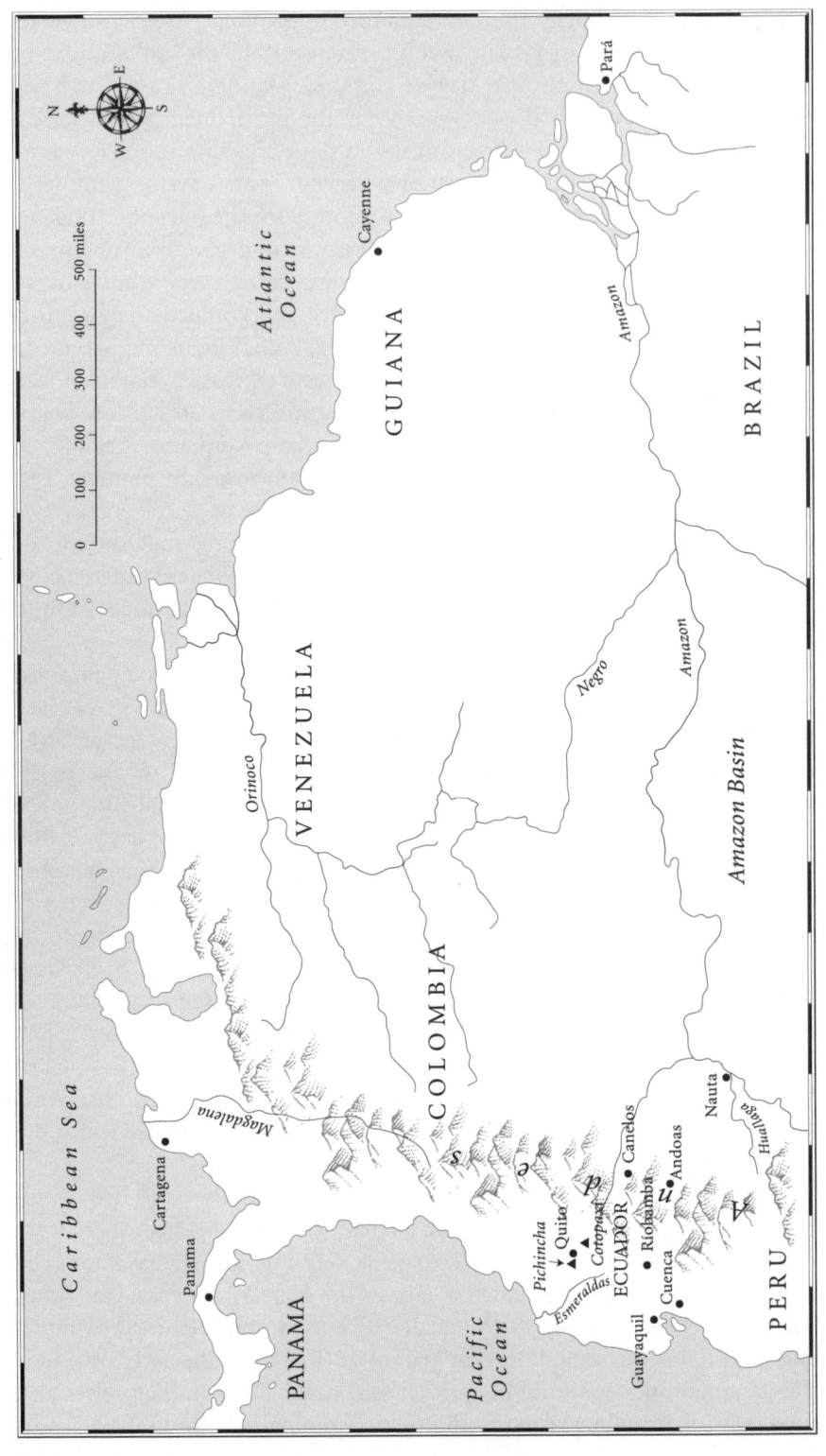

pace from their own. Spanish-American society was sluggish, and revolved around class distinction. The important posts were occupied by people from Spain. The indigenous Spaniards, the *creoles*, could not obtain rank and, although wealthy, resented their forced enfeeblement. The *creoles* despised newly arrived colonists, however hard they worked. And then there was the non-Spanish population – mixed blood, Indian and black – who were expected to work but were given no incentive to do so. The class system was reinforced by sumptuary rules dictating what clothes each social group was allowed to wear. As an aristocrat Condamine was acquainted with the niceties of court life; but those of Spanish-America left him flummoxed. As far as he could ascertain, the *creoles* spent most of the day lying in hammocks, smoking heavily. They smoked, moreover, in a manner that he had never encountered: 'They roll the tobacco into slender rolls and they put the lighted part of the roll into their mouths and there continue it a long time without its being quenched, or the fire incommoding them.'

Needless to say, the ship on which they had expected to sail had been delayed and would not leave until February. They occupied themselves by collecting botanical specimens, charting the coast, purchasing tents for their inland voyage and, in the case of Bouguer, replicating every observation independently of his leader. Condamine, who had been given two years to make his observations, wrote a letter to Paris: the survey might take longer than the Academy had anticipated.

The expedition moved slowly down the coast, landing at Bahía de Manta, in Ecuador, where the majority of the party went inland to the town of Guayaquil, where more comfortable accommodation could be found. Condamine, however, remained on the beach to begin his work. To his surprise and horror, Bouguer chose to stay with him. The shore was a desert, littered with the bones of whales and sea-lions, from which Condamine concluded he would have dry, clear conditions for observing the heavens. Unfortunately, the sky was obscured by mist, and only briefly on 26 March did they catch a glimpse of the moon (in the last stages of an eclipse) which enabled them to fix their position. Bouguer protested that they were wasting their time. Thereupon Condamine dragged him 70 miles north to the equator, where they spent another fortnight studying the heavens.

If before they had been plagued by fog, now they were beset by ants, mosquitoes and flying cockroaches. Condamine wrote with feeling of one particular parasite: 'They are shaped like a flea, but almost too small for sight ... They live mostly in the dust. They insinuate themselves into the soles of the feet, or toes, and pierce the skin with such subtlety that there is no being aware of them ... [The insect] forms a nest covered with a white integument, resembling a flat pearl, and there enlarges the nest in the toe. There is an absolute necessity of extracting them.' At the end of a fortnight Bouguer could stand it no longer and insisted they rejoin the other members of the expedition. Condamine concurred. Rather than follow the accepted overland route via Guayaquil to Quito, however, he decided to take a short-cut up the nearby River Esmeraldas. Not only might it be of scientific interest but it would also allow him, in the absence of their Spanish chaperones, Santacilla and Ulloa, to see a bit more of the country. His enthusiasm was boosted by the arrival in their camp of an unexpected visitor: the governor of Esmeraldas, Pedro Maldonado. Three years younger than Condamine, Maldonado was a Quito-born *creole* who had travelled up the river several times with a view to making it the city's main link with the outside world. He was highly intelligent, spoke the native language Quechua, as well as French and Spanish, and was one of the colony's most accomplished surveyors. When he asked to join Condamine's expedition the Frenchman accepted with delight. Notwithstanding Maldonado's expertise, Bouguer said he would rather go to Guayaquil like everyone else. The two men therefore left him to his devices and set out for the Esmeraldas.

The journey, in a 40-foot dugout, was as profitable as Condamine had expected. He travelled through his first jungle, taking notes on the trees and animals. He encountered numerous different peoples, including a population descended from a slave-ship that had foundered off the coast. He took mineral samples, one of which was an unfamilar ore later classified as platinum. He investigated a strange, stretchy substance called *caoutchouc*, drawn from the sap of a tree, from which he made a waterproof bag for his instruments.* He visited an emerald mine and studied Inca carvings. He acquired a taste for *masato*, a pungent beverage made of fermented plantains and, following Maldonado's example, abandoned his European finery for a straw hat, poncho and loose woollen trousers. As they left the Esmeraldas and climbed up the Andes, he recorded the enervating effects of altitude on the human frame – excusing his frequent pauses on the pretext of taking observations. On 4 June they stood at 12,000 feet above sea level, higher than Condamine had ever been in his life. That same day they entered Quito.

The main party was already established – Bouguer would take another six days to arrive – and together they 'began to deliberate on the best methods of performing our work'. The spot they chose as a baseline for their survey was the flat, desert-like plain of Yarqui, to the north-east of Quito. Before they even reached Yarqui, however, Couplet succumbed to fever and collapsed on 17 September. He died without regaining consciousness. This inauspicious start set the tone for the months to come. Unaccustomed to the searing daytime temperatures and freezing nights of the high Andes, the Frenchmen were constantly ill. Bouguer 'was in a fit of pique and knew no restraint'. Hugot developed such bad chilblains that he could not work. An Indian servant died, causing the entire contingent of porters to decamp. Only

---

* Although rubber had been described by previous explorers, Condamine was the first to give a scientific name to the tree that it came from and the first to bring samples back to Europe. It was of immediate interest to manufacturers. In the 19th century his discovery would create millionaires and alter the shape of empires.

Condamine and Maldonado had any energy for the task, but their efforts were thwarted by officials from Quito who, suspecting that they were looking for buried Inca treasure, interfered so intolerably that Condamine was forced to obtain a directive from the captain-general of Peru. To do that, he had to make a trip to Lima.

He did not mind the diversion: it would give him further opportunities to study the country. And his Spanish chaperones – one of whom accompanied him – did not seem to mind either. In fact, they were as interested as Condamine in the workings of South America, having been ordered secretly to write a report on the state of the colonies. It took Condamine and Santacilla eight months to make the 2,000-mile return journey to Lima. When they returned in July 1737, armed with the necessary paperwork, the team had become acclimatized and the survey began afresh.

Intrinsic to their project was the attainment of height: not only could one see the ground below but, by signalling to parties on a similar eminence, working from a prearranged baseline, one could calculate with accuracy the distance between two points. And from those two points one could extrapolate indefinitely. The scientists became, reluctantly, mountaineers. They scaled the 16,000-foot Pichincha volcano, and spent 23 days there, alternately baked and frozen, while they waited for signals from the surrounding mountains. They proceeded to the plains of Changalli and the Cotopaxi volcano, which shot flames 2,000 feet into the air. From peak to peak they covered most of the Ecuadorian Andes and, four years after they had left France, they were at the point of calculating the precise length of an equatorial degree of latitude. Their studies were halted by a message from Paris: Maupertius had completed his calculations; the world was thicker at the equator than at the Poles; Condamine and his associates could go home.

Condamine insisted they complete their survey. They did so reluctantly, coming to a halt in June 1739 at the town of Cuenca, slightly lower in altitude than Quito. According to Santacilla, the inhabitants 'were differing somewhat in their genius and manufacture from those of Quito; particularly in the most shameful indolence, which seems natural to them so that they have a strange aversion to all kinds of work. The vulgar are also rude, vindictive, and, in short, wicked in every sense.' In this provincial town, the surgeon Senièrgues made the mistake of adjudicating on a marital spat. He made the further mistake of attending a bullfight in the company of the wronged woman while the suitor was a member of the audience. He was called out. Leaping into the ring, he drew his sword and pistol. Thereupon, fearing that the bullfight would be cancelled, the audience jumped onto the sand and hacked him to death.

The tumult was so great, and Condamine's efforts to bring the culprits to justice so strenuous, that the expedition had to retreat to a nearby monastery in fear of their lives. Here Jussieu's servant accidentally destroyed the botanist's collection of specimens. The loss of four years' work affected him so strongly that he had a fit from which he never recovered, spending the rest of his life in a state of semi-derangement. Mabillon later went mad too. Condamine's expedition was rapidly falling apart. Two men were dead, two were insane, Louis Godin wanted to quit in order to take a post he had been offered by the University of San Marcos in Lima, his cousin Jean Godin des Odonais had fallen in love with a 13-year-old girl in the town of Ríobamba, and Hugot wanted to settle in Quito where he had found a wife. As a group, however, they still had one further task to perform: as instructed by the Academy of Sciences, they were to mark the baseline of their survey 'with monuments of a permanent nature'. The pyramids came naturally to Condamine's mind, so he drew designs for two such to be erected on the plain of Yarqui. When Hugot heard of the plan he was aghast: 'Pyramids here? It would be like erecting pyramids on the moon!'

The difficulties were, indeed, enormous. A kiln had to be built to fire the bricks. A six-mile canal had to be dug to provide water for the mortar. They had to sink wooden piles to reinforce the foundations. Slabs of rock had to be quarried from the Andes to provide a long-lasting surface on which could be inscribed the names of Condamine, Bouguer and Louis Godin, plus the dates of the expedition. When the pyramids were finished, each bearing a jaunty fleur-de-lys on its peak, they looked splendid. But Condamine had made a mistake: the inscriptions mentioned neither the King of Spain nor his two captains and the many colonists who had been instrumental in the survey. Furthermore, the fleur-de-lys was a symbol of the French crown and, although Condamine argued (correctly) that it was the emblem of the Bourbons and that the French and Spanish royals were branches of the same family, it appeared as if he was claiming Yarqui for France. Legal proceedings were instituted and for two years the expedition halted its work while the faintly ridiculous inquiry took its course. In 1742 it was decided that the pyramids could stay, provided that the fleur-de-lys were removed and the inscription altered.*

In the interim, Louis Godin left for Lima, Jean Godin des Odonais married his girl – the whole party, including the stricken Jussieu and Mabillon, attended the ceremony – Pedro Maldonado departed to explore the Amazon, and the draughtsman Morainville was crushed by scaffolding. As for Condamine, Bouguer and Verguin, they were already making preparations for their departure: Bouguer and Verguin were to return to Cartagena; Condamine intended to follow Maldonado down the Amazon. But Condamine refused to leave until he had made one further verification. It was agreed that, on his way to Cartagena, Bouger would take astronomical observations at the equator. Condamine, meanwhile, would take identical observations at Yarqui. Only when he had received the results, and compared them to those of the land surveys, would he consider his duty discharged. In March

---

* Six years later the authorities changed their minds and had the pyramids destroyed. They were restored in 1836 by the government of newly independent Ecuador.

1743, aided by Jean Godin des Odonais, who had ridden in from Ríobamba to help his leader on this final mission, Condamine took his readings, sighting his telescope on the same star that Bouguer was simultaneously plotting at the equator. The results of Bouguer's observations made their way slowly to Yarqui, where Condamine compared them to his own and those of the expedition. Between the astronomical and trigonometrical surveys there was a difference of less than two feet. 'The arc has been measured!' Condamine wrote. 'The intermediate between our two zeniths was effected by us both on the same night. By these simultaneous observations, we attained the singular advantage of being able to ascertain precisely and beyond dispute the real amplitude of an arc of the meridian of three degrees.' He left immediately for the Amazon, accompanied by two servants, several mules, and his 18-foot telescope.

After several months' travel he found himself in 'a new world, separated from all human intercourse, on a fresh-water sea, surrounded by a maze of lakes, rivers, and canals, and penetrating in every direction the gloom of an immense forest ... New plants, new animals, and new races of men were exhibited to my view. Accustomed during seven years to mountains lost in clouds, I was wrapped in admiration at the wide circle embraced by the eye, restricted here by no other boundary than the horizon.'

He worked his way east, assisted by Jesuit priests, whose scattered missions comprised the only European presence in the Amazon basin, and eventually caught up with Maldonado, who been waiting for the past six weeks at the mission of Nauta, on the Río Huallaga. The two scientists proceeded swiftly downriver, investigating and collecting plants unknown to science. One was *varvascu*, whose 'leaves or roots ... when thrown into the water have the faculty of intoxicating fish'. (Two centuries later it would be developed as an insecticide.) Another was the tree whose black resin, curare, the Indians used as a poison to tip their arrows. 'There is no danger in eating of the flesh killed by such means,' Condamine wrote, 'for the venom of this poison is only mortal when absorbed by the blood.' Learning that the antidote was salt or, preferably, sugar, he shot a chicken with a curare-coated arrow and then applied sugar to the wound to see what happened. He concluded that the antidote worked, for the chicken 'exhibited no signs of the least inconvenience'. They investigated, too, a supposed connection between the Amazon and the Orinoco: 'It has been generally suppressed in those maps by modern geographers as if by common consent,' Condamine wrote, 'and treated as chimerical by those who were supposed to have the best means of information.' He did not have a high opinion of the Indians, describing them as 'voracious gluttons ... pusillanimous and timid in the extreme unless transported by drunkenness ... [There] exist inland tribes of Americans who eat their prisoners.' But from their reports he concluded that: 'The positive certainty of an existing communication between the waters of the two rivers ... is a geographical fact.' Yet, as he admitted, he had no idea where it might be, nor did he have the resources to look for it. By 19 September the two scientists were at Para, at the mouth of the Amazon, from where they travelled to Cayenne, in French Guiana, and then to France, where they were reunited in spring 1745 with Bouguer and Verguin. The survey, which should have taken two years, had occupied a decade. And of the ten Frenchmen who had set out, only three had returned.

There was, however, one member still to come. Before Condamine had left the Andes, Jean Godin des Odonais had promised that he would follow him down the Amazon with his wife and four children. He left Ríobamba in March 1749, reaching French Guiana four months later. But, as he explained in a letter to Condamine, it had only been an exploratory journey to prepare the way for his family. The Amazon being under Portuguese control, might it be possible to approach Lisbon for a boat to take him back up again? Condamine forwarded his request to the appropriate authorities. Years passed while the paperwork ground through Lisbon's tortuous bureaucracy. Godin decided to speed matters by sending plans on how France might wrest the Amazon from Portuguese control. This extraordinarily foolish move backfired. The letter was never acknowledged, from which Godin deduced that it had been intercepted by the Portuguese. Thereafter, he dared not leave Cayenne for fear that he would be imprisoned. In fact, his letter had not been intercepted, and on 18 October 1765 a Portuguese vessel arrived at Cayenne with instructions to 'bring me to Para, thence transport me up the river as high as the first Spanish settlement to wait until I had returned with my family'. Godin, who had been waiting 15 years for this very thing, now thought it was a plot to lure him from Cayenne. He refused to accept the Portuguese offer, making excuse after transparent excuse, until the French governor lost patience and told the ship to sail without him. In his place would go a man called Tristan d'Oreasaval, who was charged with delivering a package of letters to Godin's wife, preparing canoes for her journey, and then bringing her reply back to Cayenne. Unfortunately, the letters went astray, and it was not until 1769, 20 years after her husband had reconnoitred the Amazon, that Isabella Godin finally learned it was safe to follow him.

Isabella Godin was a resilient woman. She had spent her entire life in a remote Andean town. She had not seen her husband for most of their marriage. During his absence she had lost all of her children. Now, in her forties, she was embarking on a 2,000-mile trip down the Amazon to catch a ship to a distant and foreign continent. She was preceded by her father Don Pedro Grandmaison y Bruno, who arranged palanquins and food depots as far as the village of Canelos where canoes were waiting to carry her to Para. Before proceeding downriver he sent her a warning note: 'The roads are bad. Keep down the amount of baggage and the members of your party. The canoes and space therein are limited.'

Isabella Godin's party was already large, comprising herself, her two broth-ers, her 12-year-old nephew, three women servants and a freed slave named

Joachim. At the last moment, ignoring her father's advice, she took three other men with her. Their names are unknown, but they were Frenchmen who had apparently made their way inland from the Pacific, and one of them claimed to be a doctor. The enlarged group left Ríobamba in late 1769, accompanied by 13 Indian porters. It took just seven days to reach Canelos, but when they arrived they found the village deserted and its houses burning. It had been hit by smallpox. That night the porters fled *en masse*, leaving the Andeans to their own devices. Isabella Godin took charge. She sent the men after Canelos's inhabitants, and when they returned with four terrified men she hired them to guide the party downriver.

Don Pedro had promised canoes, but there were only two craft: a 40-foot dugout and a raft for their food and equipment. With these they began their journey. The four Indians lasted only a day, vanishing as soon as darkness fell. Isabella thereupon ordered her two brothers to take charge of the raft, while one of the Frenchmen was given command of the dugout. It was a disastrous experiment: the Frenchman in charge of the dugout fell overboard and drowned; then, towards evening, it hit a log and its occupants were thrown into the water. Leaving Joachim to retrieve the canoe, the others constructed a makeshift cabin and ate a meal of boiled manioc garnished by two unfamiliar but turkey-like fowl that the Grandmaison brothers shot. Deserted by their guides, low on food, ignorant of jungle survival, and with no means of transport other than the canoe and the raft, neither of which they knew how to handle, the party was at a loss. The French doctor proposed a solution: he would take the dugout downriver, accompanied by Joachim, and return with help. It was less than four days to the nearest village, Andoas; they would be there and back within ten days. Isabella Godin agreed.

He did not return. For a week Isabella Godin, her family, servants and the remaining Frenchman stayed in their camp, not bothering to ration their supplies in the certainty that the doctor would soon be back. After the second week they cut down their consumption. After a month they were starving. Suspecting that the doctor and Joachim had drowned, Isabella Godin and her party followed them downstream on the raft. Again they were dogged by misfortune. The raft hit a half-submerged tree and broke apart, tipping its occupants and their remaining provisions into the water. They dragged themselves ashore, but it was already too late for Isabella Godin's nephew: Joaquin Grandmaison died that evening. In the morning they discovered that one of the maids had died in her sleep. Another wandered into the jungle and did not come back. The third also died. So did Isabella's two brothers and the remaining Frenchman. Isabella Godin was the sole survivor of her family and the expedition. She lay by the bodies for two days, then took a machete and hacked her way into the jungle, heading for Andoas.

The day she left, Joachim arrived at her camp. The French doctor had reneged on his promise and gone downriver as fast as he could. But Joachim had persuaded a team of Andoas canoeists to take him upstream to rescue his employer. He arrived shortly after Isabella Godin had departed. Seeing the corpses, which were now unrecognizable, he returned to Andoas with the news that she was dead.

Isabella Godin was not dead. For nine days she wandered through the jungle, eating grubs and fruit, before she met three Indians who led her, in January 1770, to a Jesuit mission. Word reached Don Pedro, who returned upriver to escort her to Cayenne where she was finally reunited with her husband. It took two years to arrange a ship to France, with the result that it was 1773 before the Godins finally came home. Thirty-eight years after it had set out, Condamine's expedition had officially terminated.

By this time Condamine was one of the most famous scientists in France, having made a name for himself not only as an expert on South America but as a champion of vaccination* and, in his determination for the world to adopt a standard unit of measurement, as the father of the metric system. He was in poor health, however. Deaf and paralysed, he died in 1774.

* He had seen it practised in South America and was vaccinated against smallpox five years before the birth of Edward Jenner, who is credited with its discovery.

James Cook (1768–79)

The world's astronomers calculated that in 1769 the planet Venus would pass across the face of the sun. This rare event was of considerable importance in that, if the transit was observed simultaneously from several points on the globe, it would be possible to determine the distances between the earth and its surrounding planets – measurements that were of interest both to scientists and to navigators. There had been one such transit in 1761, but its observation had been thwarted by bad weather. The next transit not being until 1874, it was vital that the 1769 readings be a success. As part of an international programme, involving Spain, France, Sweden, Denmark and Russia, Britain proposed the erection of observatories in three places: North Cape, Hudson's Bay and an undetermined spot in the Pacific – perhaps the newly discovered island of Otaheite (Tahiti) that had entered the charts as King George III Island. Of these three the last was the most promising, partly because the skies there were expected to be clear, partly too because the Pacific had yet to be properly explored. The man who led such an expedition would have to have a taste for discovery, be an expert navigator and surveyor, and be willing to sail halfway round the globe, if not to circumnavigate it. As it happened, just such a man was to hand, an officer who had recently returned from a survey of Newfoundland, who had proven himself in peace and war, and who had impressed the Admiralty as a level-headed, intelligent and humane leader of men. Thus, Lieutenant James Cook took command of the 368-ton Whitby barque *Endeavour* on 25 May 1768 for a voyage that would make him one of Britain's most famous explorers.

The *Endeavour* left Plymouth on 26 August 1768 carrying 18 months' stores, 22 cannon (ten carriage, 12 swivel), a crew of 85, and seven scientists: a botanist, Daniel Solander; two draughtsmen, Sydney Parkinson and Alexander Buchan; a secretary, Herman Spöring; a surgeon, William Monkhouse; an astronomer, William Green, who would be responsible along with Cook for the celestial observations; and, in charge of them all, a young botanist named Joseph Banks, who came aboard with four servants, two greyhounds and an unquenchable fount of enthusiasm. No greater contrast could be imagined than that between Banks and Cook. Banks was a wealthy, well-educated, irrepressibly inquisitive 25-year-old, whose charm and ability had

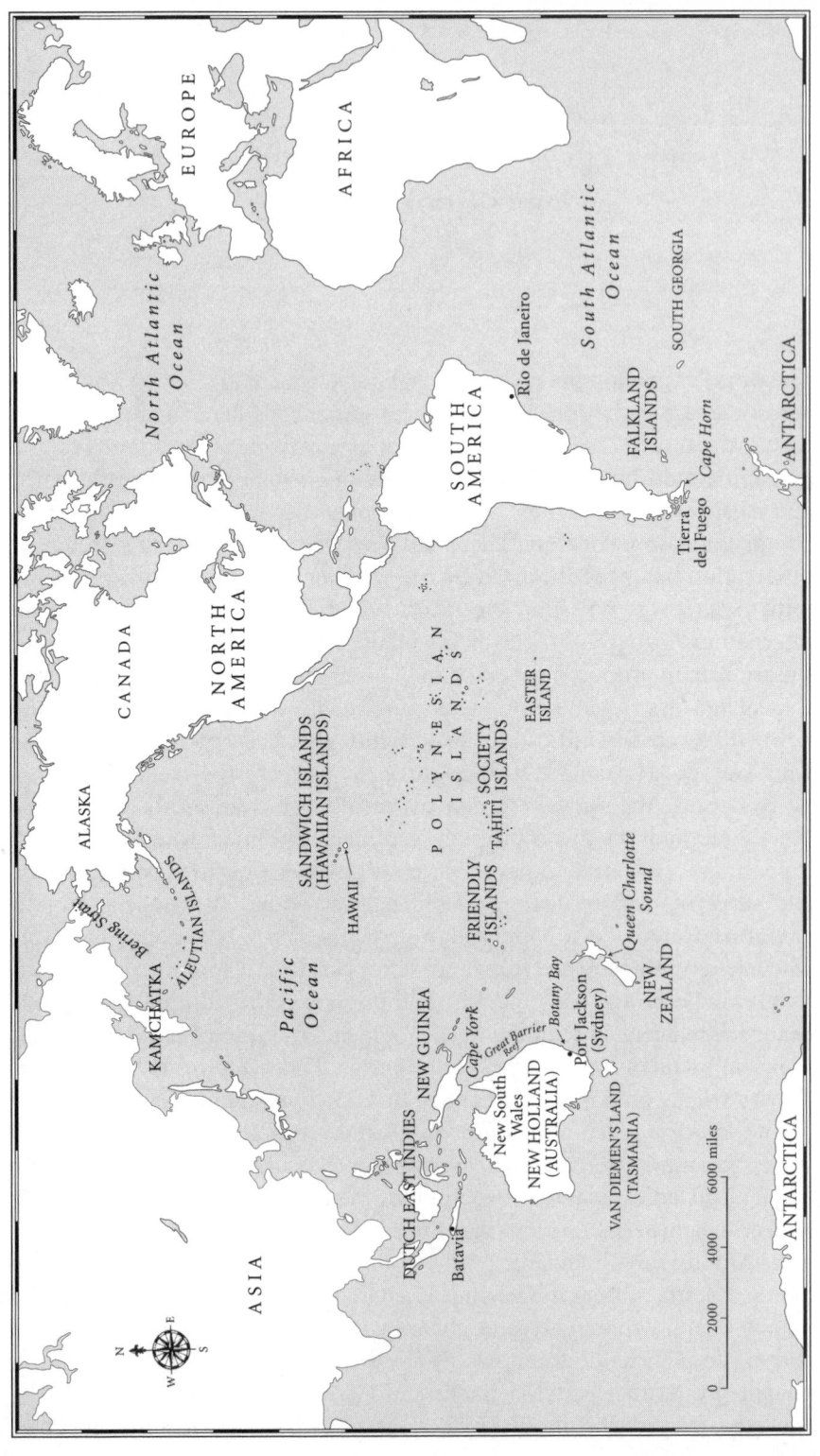

already secured him membership of Britain's Royal Society. By contrast, Cook was 40, the self-taught son of a labourer, who had worked his way through the ranks and had a steadfast, commonsensical approach to life. Whereas Banks had been once to Newfoundland, Cook was widely travelled, had seen danger and knew how to overcome it. He may not have enjoyed the same formal education as Banks, but he was by no means stupid, as his appointment to the expedition proved. Yet, despite the dissimilarities in their background and temperament, they made a surprisingly effective team.

The *Endeavour* sailed down the Atlantic, stopping at Madeira, where Banks and Solander dug up 700 plant specimens in the space of five days, and then Rio de Janeiro – again, the two botanists procured large quantities of plants, slipping ashore by night to confound the Portuguese guards placed around their ship – before entering the sub-Antarctic seas off the Falklands. By the second week in January 1769 they were in the Straits of Le Maire with Tierra del Fuego to the north and the Pacific beckoning enticingly to the west. Thus far, Cook had paid little attention to Banks's plant-gathering activities, being more concerned with keeping his ship sound and its crew healthy. Fresh meat had been taken aboard at every stop, along with quantities of sauerkraut to combat scurvy. But the sailors, accustomed to a diet of salt beef and hard tack, had refused the healthier provisions. It took constant supervision – and the occasional 12 lashes – before they accepted the regime. Once again, at Cape of Good Success on the north side of the Straits of Le Maire, Cook was too busy taking on water, wood and food to heed Banks's latest plan. When the eager botanist asked permission to explore Tierra del Fuego he gave him his vague blessing and continued with the business at hand.

On 16 January 1769 Banks led the entire scientific personnel of the *Endeavour* on a trip 'to penetrate into the countrey as far as we could'.* With two seamen and Banks's four servants to carry their equipment, the 12 men trudged through groves of evergreen Antarctic beech towards the mountains, from where they hoped to obtain an overview of the area. Previous explorers had warned that the Fuegan climate was treacherous, but Banks took no notice of this. The weather was 'vastly fine much like a sunshiny day in May,' he wrote, 'so that neither heat nor cold was troublesome to us nor were there any insects to molest us, which made me think the travelling much better than what I had before met with in Newfoundland'. It was such a nice day that he had no doubt they would be there and back before nightfall. In his confidence he packed neither a tent nor any provisions beyond a cold lunch and a bottle of rum. On they went, 'pressing through pathless thickets, always going up hill', until in the mid-afternoon they were greeted by a green plain, little more than a mile across, beyond which rose the mountains. But to their dismay the plain was not grass but a mass of waist-high dwarf birch set in glutinous moorland. The birch, Banks wrote, 'were so stubborn that they

* Despite his expensive education, Banks had managed somehow to avoid the basics. His disdain for grammar, spelling and punctuation give his writings a magnificent immediacy.

could not be bent out of the way, but at every step the leg must be lifted over them and on being plac'd again on the ground was almost sure to sink above the anckles in bog. No travelling could possibly be worse than this.'

They were two-thirds of the way through the birch bog when Buchan, the draughtsman, had an epileptic fit. Banks built a fire to comfort him and, leaving most of the party behind, continued with Solander, Green and Monkhouse. The mountains, he was pleased to find, had plants of an alpine nature. Less pleasingly, however, the climate was alpine too. Buffeted by strong winds, and with snow falling, they made their way back to the plateau, collected Buchan, and headed for the shelter of the beech woods. But the weather followed them and, halfway to safety, 'the cold seemd to have at once an effect infinitely beyond what I have ever experienced'. Solander collapsed and, saying he needed a few moments rest, fell asleep in the snow. A servant, Tom Richmond, did likewise. When Banks tried to rouse him, '[he] answerd that there he would lay and dye'. Banks split the party: his servant, George Dalton, accompanied by a seaman, was to remain with Richmond; the rest were to go ahead to build a fire; he, meanwhile, would drag Solander in their wake. As soon as the main group were safely in the woods, he ordered another two men to rescue the three who were still in the birch bog. They returned after half an hour, saying 'that they had been all round the place shouting and hallowing but could not get any answer'. Banks soon found why: the bottle of rum was missing; Richmond and his two guardians were too drunk to hear anything. The seaman did, eventually, stagger back to camp and was able to lead Banks to where Richmond and Dalton lay. But they were too comatose to walk, and in the bitter cold, unable to build a fire, Banks could only cover them with branches and hope they survived the night. He wrote: 'In these employments we had spent an hour and a half expos'd to the most penetrating cold I ever felt as well as continual snow. Peter Briscoe, another servant of mine, now began to complain and before we came to the fire became very ill but got there at last almost dead with cold. Now might our situation truely be calld terrible: of twelve our original number were 2 already past all hopes, one more was so ill that tho he was with us I had very little hopes of his being able to walk in the morning, and another very likely to relapse into his fitts either before we set out or in the course of our journey.'

The blizzard continued all night, and at dawn, Banks recorded, 'we had no hopes now but of staying here as long as the snow lasted and how long that would be God alone knew'. In fact, it lasted only a few hours more, and by 6.00 a.m. they were able to trek back for the invalids. Richmond and Dalton were dead. The remainder then cooked a vulture they had shot the previous day, which gave them three mouthfuls of meat apiece, and headed back to the ship. It took three hours to reach the *Endeavour*, which was considerably less than the journey out. This, they discovered to their chagrin, was because instead of marching directly inland they had trudged in a lengthy semicircle through the forest. Once aboard, they collapsed into bed – all that is, save Banks, who took the opportunity, 'considering our short Stay & the Uncertainty of the weather, to cast about with a seine net for marine specimens'. Only when the task was complete did he look back on the events of the last two days. 'With what pleasure ... did we congratulate each other on our safety no one can tell who has not been in such circumstances.'

The incident was not, in itself, particularly remarkable. Compared to the more extreme sufferings endured by others in the polar regions, the journey had been a bagatelle. That two people had died, however, was a salutary reminder that in unknown territory even a day trip could be hazardous. The experience did not check Banks's enthusiasm one jot; but in future he would act with more caution.

The *Endeavour* sailed on, Banks trawling the seas and scanning the skies for specimens. He caught a shark and was delighted to find it was pregnant: when its offspring were prised from the womb they swam energetically in a tub of water. He shot everything that flew overhead, including several albatross. In his journal he described how best to cook such a bird: 'The way of dressing them is thus: Skin them over night and soak their carcases in Salt water till morn, then parboil them and throw away the water, then stew them well with very little water and when sufficiently tender serve them up with a Savoury sauce.' They continued in this fashion until 13 April, when Banks wrote: 'This morn early came to anchor in Port Royal bay King George the third's Island.' They had arrived at Tahiti.

Cook was not the first European to visit the island. In 1767 Lieutenant Samuel Wallis of the *Dolphin* had spent time there, leaving a number of cannonballs, a goose and a turkey as mementos of his stay. And a year later he had been followed by Comte Louis Antoine de Bougainville* in the *Boudeuse* and *Etoile*, on a voyage that took him to the Falklands and then in a great loop through the Pacific to Tahiti, New Guinea and the north-east coast of New Holland (as Australia was then called). Cook was unaware of Bougainville's visit, but several of his crew had sailed with Wallis and they told extravagant tales of Tahiti's delights: it had a hierarchical society with kings and queens just like at home, the scenery was beautiful, there were fleets of impressive canoes, the houses were magnificent, the roast pork splendid and the natives exceptionally friendly. It was a perfect example of the Romantic dream as imagined by Jean-Jacques Rousseau: a realm of 'noble savages'.

As Cook sailed along the coast searching for a place to build an observatory, he found the island was not quite as described. Its hierarchy had been fragmented by recent wars, and a sense of uncertainty was prevalent. The grand houses had fallen into ruin, and there was little in the way of roast pork, there being only a few runty pigs. The natives, far from being noble,

* A national hero in France, this great explorer is immortalized in the name of a bright-flowered climber, native at that time only to Brazil. In fact it was Banks and Solander who found the plant and called it *Calyxsis ternaria*, but the name Bougainvillea stuck.

had a regrettable tendency to thieve. But they were, as reported, remarkably hospitable and would do anything for the price of a few nails. Banks wrote that 'the ladies ... shewed us all kind of civilities our situation could admit of, but as there were no places of retirement, the houses being entirely without walls, we had not the opportunity of putting their politeness to every test that maybe some of us would not have failed to have done had circumstances been more favourable'. Not everyone was so squeamish. The ladies being willing, the crew having been a long time at sea, and the *Endeavour* being a ship that carried a great many nails, Cook became a reluctant pimp. To ensure that his nails did not become debased he regulated their issue so that a man could only draw a certain number, rather than 'leave it to it to everyone's fancy which could not fail to bring on confusion'. Most men took 'wives', and Banks, after one ceremony, was entertained by a girl 'quickly unveiling all her charms'. Another girl soon appeared. 'I could not prevail upon them to stay more than an hour,' he wrote levelly.

In these libertine circumstances time passed quickly enough: the transit of Venus was observed successfully on 3 June; Banks and Solander gathered countless specimens; Cook became friendly with the local rulers; and if the pigs were not at their best, there was enough fish, breadfruit and vegetables to provide a healthy diet. The scientists did not delve into the Tahitians' intricate social and religious structure or the restrictions of taboo, but they recorded a few ethnological details. One of these was the practice of tattooing – Banks watched with fascination as a young girl's buttocks were pierced and inked; several of the crew underwent the same procedure, but on their arms. Another was a bizarre amusement whereby the 'Indians', as Banks called them, paddled into the sea and rode back on the waves, using broken canoes as a platform 'in a manner truly surprizing'. It was the first recorded example of surfing. 'We stood admiring this very wonderful scene for full half an hour,' Banks wrote, 'in which time none of these actors attempted to come ashore but all seemd most highly entertained with their strange diversion.' They also discovered a temple platform – the largest in Polynesia – that was built of, and paved with, stones cut to a perfect fit. 'Its size and workmanship almost exceeds belief, I shall set it down exactly,' Banks marvelled: '[It is] not smooth at the sides but formed into 11 steps, each of these 4 feet in hight making in all 44 feet, its length 267 its breadth 71. Every one of these steps were formd of one course of white coral stones most neatly squard and polishd ... The whole made part of one side of a spatious area which was walled in with stone, the size of this which seemd to be intended for a square was 118 by 110 paces ... It is almost beyond beleif that Indians could raise so large a structure without assistance of Iron tools to shape their stones or mortar to join them ... it is done tho, and almost as firmly as a European workman would have done it.' Beyond ascertaining that it was used for religious ceremonies, burials and sacrifice, they did not inquire further.

Against these gentlemanly peregrinations, their stay had its darker side. There were several contretemps involving theft, during one of which Cook's men shot and killed a Tahitian, and wounded several others. The Venusian observatory was less a scientific base than a fort, manned by armed patrols and equipped with cannon, both swivel and fixed. (The Tahitians still managed to steal several items, including one of the more vital pieces of equipment, later returned.) The draughtsman Buchan died of epilepsy, and John Reading, the bosun's mate, expired after swallowing three pints of rum.* There were arguments over women: at one point Banks and the surgeon Monkhouse were ready to fight a duel. The butcher got drunk and threatened to cut the throat of a chief's wife if she didn't give him the axe he wanted to kill her with. (He was thrashed on deck, to the dismay of the Tahitian women who were invited to witness his punishment.) An outbreak of syphilis – or perhaps the related disease yaws – did nothing to ease ship–shore relations. And two marines fled with their 'wives' into the mountains, upon which Cook felt it necessary to take several notables hostage until the deserters were returned. The Tahitians responded by kidnapping a midshipman and three marines. In turn, Cook sent an even stronger force of marines with the message that if every Briton, including the deserters, was not handed over forthwith, the consequences would be dire. His display of arms and the promise that 'the chiefs would suffer' did the trick. Things could have been handled more smoothly but, by the standards of the time, the *Endeavour*'s visitation had been relatively benign. When, at the end of his stay, Cook assured the Tahitians 'of our friendly disposition', he was not joking. And the Tahitians accepted his good wishes at face value. After all, the encounter could have been a lot worse.

The *Endeavour* sailed on 13 July, carrying with it a priest named Tupia and his servant Tiata. The two Tahitians came of their own accord, and Banks considered Tupia quite a catch. 'I do not know why I may not keep him as a curiosity,' he mused, 'as well as some of my neighbours do lions and tigers at a larger expense than he will ever put me to.' More practically, he would be useful as a guide and interpreter on the voyage, and his knowledge of the region would be most helpful to any navigators following in Cook's wake.

Cook's formal instructions had been simply to observe the transit of Venus. However, he had also been given a secret set of orders that he opened only when the *Endeavour* was on its way. These stated that, once he had finished with Venus, he was to proceed south in search of the great continent that was rumoured to lie at the bottom of the world. There was no reliable evidence that such a continent existed; but cartographers and natural philosophers were convinced that it did on the grounds that, in order to harmonize the globe, there must be a southern landmass to balance those that

---

* At 94 per cent proof, Royal Navy rum was not to be taken lightly. The daily issue was a pint per man, half a pint for boys. Most sailors swore by it, claiming that it kept disease at bay.

existed in the north.* Cook's orders, therefore, instructed him to sail as far as 40° S in search of this *Terra Australis Incognita*. He did not believe the continent existed (though Banks did) and, having gone as far south as his orders instructed without spying land, he examined those orders again. They read: 'If you should fail of discovering the Continent . . . you will upon falling in with New Zealand carefully observe the latitude and the longitude in which the land is situated.'

New Zealand had been discovered by the Dutch navigator Abel Janszoon Tasman in 1643. This intrepid explorer had circumnavigated Australia, had discovered a bushy prominence to the south that he named Van Diemen's Land (now Tasmania) and had touched on the coast of New Zealand. He had not, however, mapped either Van Diemen's Land or New Zealand in their entirety, and the latter might well have been a promontory of the fabled southern continent. Sailing east on a latitude of 38°, Cook hit New Zealand's North Island on 7 October. His relief was so great that he gave the surgeon's boy, Nicholas Young, a gallon of rum for being the first to spy land.

New Zealand was nothing like Tahiti. The landscape was rolling and green, and reminded Cook of the South Downs in England. Whenever he tried to land the Maoris were menacing, and even when given a display of the *Endeavour*'s might they seemed not to care. Eventually, Cook decided to demonstrate his good intentions by force: he would kidnap the first group of Maoris he met and take them aboard the *Endeavour*, whereupon, having fed them and given them gifts, he would release them again. This extraordinarily ill-conceived plan worked no better than might have been expected. On 10 October Cook sent three boats to surround a canoeful of Maori fishermen. Predictably, the canoe's seven occupants objected: they defended themselves with spears and sticks; when the spears ran out they used paddles; when the paddles were gone they threw stones; and finally, in desperation, they attacked their would-be kidnappers with fish. Their opposition was so fierce that Cook's men fired into the canoe, killing four of them instantly. The other three tried to swim to safety, but were captured and dragged on board. When they learned they were not going to be killed the captives cheered up slightly and, after consuming a gargantuan meal, allowed themselves to be sent to bed. Their acceptance of the ship's hospitality did nothing to ease the officers' embarrassment and remorse: to have killed four people in order to show how friendly the white men were was more than cack-handed; it was criminally incompetent. 'Thus ended the most disagreeable day my life has yet seen that such may never return to embitter future reflections,' Banks wrote in shame. To compound the disgrace, when Cook tried the following morning to return his three 'guests' he met such an angry reception that they refused to leave the ship and had to be sneaked

---

* Ironically, once Antarctica had been discovered, north polar explorers of the early 20th century went in search of a northern continent to balance that of the south.

ashore in the afternoon. However great and various his skills, the captain of the *Endeavour* could not count diplomacy among them.

When word spread that the captives had been treated well, and that the interlopers were not cannibals (which many of the Maoris were, according to Cook), a small degree of trust was established. As they sailed down the coast, Maoris came alongside in their canoes to trade for Tahitian cloth and, very occasionally, to stay the night. But, like the Tahitians, they were inveterate thieves and Cook's men were forced repeatedly to take punitive action. When one young midshipman was outwitted by a nimble-fingered native he cast a heavy-duty line and, hooking his quarry in the backside, proceeded to play him like a fish until the hook broke, leaving its barb in his flesh. More often, however, they just shot them – usually with bird pellets, but often with musket balls; on one occasion they fired a cannon into their midst. Even Banks, who was more tender-hearted than Cook, was driven to remark: 'this I am well convinced of, that till these warlike people have severely felt our superiority in the art of war they will never behave to us in a freindly manner'.

In this unsatisfactory fashion they all but circumnavigated North Island and on 7 February 1770 began their investigation of a landmass they saw to its south. Cook suspected it was yet another island – it was, indeed, South Island – and most people agreed with him. Banks, however, still hoped it might be a continent. In this he was supported by just 'one poor midshipman'. The inhabitants of South Island were no friendlier than those to the north and, apparently, also given to cannibalism. On the odd occasion when the two sides came together to trade, partially gnawed human bones were in strong demand as mementos. As Banks wrote, '[they] are now become a kind of article of trade among our people who constantly ask for and purchase them for whatever trifles they have'. He himself bought four heads, complete with flesh and hair but without brains – 'maybe they are a delicacy here,' he pondered.

On 10 February the *Endeavour* rounded the bottom of South Island – 'to the total demolition of our aerial fabrick calld continent', Banks wrote sadly – and by the end of March the entire coast of New Zealand had been charted. The season was now too windy for a comfortable return via Cape Horn, so Cook took his ship west for a partial exploration of New Holland, after which he intended to sail to the Dutch East Indies and then, via the Cape of Good Hope, to Britain. It took them a few weeks to reach Van Diemen's Land – which Cook did not investigate properly, and still thought was part of the mainland – whereupon they sailed up the east coast of New Holland. When Tasman made his epic voyage in the 17th century he touched Australia at many places but did not visit its east side, sailing instead to New Zealand before returning to the continent's north-east corner. Cook had some 2,000 miles of uncharted coastline before him. He approached it with determination and, after his experience with the Maoris, some caution.

On first inspection the Aborigines were 'exceedingly black', and in voice 'coarse and strong', but essentially harmless – though Cook could tell from the smoke of their fires that they were following him as he sailed up the coast. Having established that he was not going to spend his journey fighting the natives, Cook's next concern was to find a harbour where he could attend to his ship and take on food, water and fuel. After several disappointments he discovered, on 28 April 1770, a wide bay, fringed by promontories and inlets. Its shores were both geographically varied and rich in wildlife. Banks discovered so many new plants and animals, and did so with such enthusiasm, that what the *Endeavour*'s log called Sting Ray Harbour entered the charts as Botany Bay. So impressed was he by the spot that many years later, when asked where Britain should send its population of convicts, Botany Bay came immediately to mind. The ensuing settlement, at Cook's old anchorage, Port Jackson, grew into the modern city of Sydney.

North of Botany Bay, where Cook spent just over a week, the journey became more difficult. The ships were bedevilled by shoals and outcrops of coral, which became more numerous the further they went. They had reached the southern tip of the Great Barrier Reef, the world's largest animal structure, which stretched for 1,250 miles along the Australian coast. Working through an 'insane labyrinth' of islets, Cook had his men sound for depth night and day. Their efforts failed on the late evening of 10 June when, with a shudder, the *Endeavour* grounded on a lump of coral. 'Scarce were we in our beds,' wrote Banks, 'when we were called up with the alarming news of the ship being fast upon a rock, which she in a few moments convinced us by beating very violently against the rock. Our situation now became greatly alarming.' It was high tide – the worst possible level at which to hit a rock – and the *Endeavour* was shipping water fast. Cook used every means at his disposal to drag his ship off, but it was stuck fast. He could save it only by lightening it, and this he proceeded to do. Between 4.00 and 6.00 a.m. the crew flung overboard everything that was inessential to their purpose. Old food went out, as did iron ballast, stone ballast, barrels, spare barrels and the makings of new barrels. When this did not work they jettisoned six carriage guns and 50 tons of drinking water. Their efforts righted the ship but did not free it. By midday on the 11th the *Endeavour*'s four pumps could not clear the incoming water. Cook, who was not by nature a pessimist, wrote: 'This was an alarming and I may say terrible circumstance, and threatened immediate destruction to us as soon as we were afloat.' Riskily, he took his men off the pumps and ordered them to set anchors in the nearest lump of coral to stern. Then he swiftly wound his vessel free.

Against Cook's prognostications, the *Endeavour* was still afloat – but only just. Even with every man on the pumps the water in the hold was 3 feet 9 inches deep and rising. In desperation, Cook resorted to fothering. This involved lowering a sail stuffed with oakum and other fillers in front of the bow, then tightening it over the gaps. Cook had never used this technique before, but it worked. Within hours the water level had dropped and they were on their way again, the ship bandaged as if it had a sore tooth. Their ordeal was far from over: during the next two months they battled in and out of the reef, landed for food, water and repairs, and made a terrifying passage through a narrow channel separating the inner lagoon from the ocean. By the time they emerged in the last week of August, and were sailing west through Endeavour Strait, they were exhausted. But they were jubilant too. 'I may land no more upon this eastern coast of New Holland, and on the western side I can make no new discovery the honour of which belongs to the Dutch navigators,' Cook wrote in his journal. 'But the eastern coast from the latitude of 38° south to this place I am confident was never seen or visited by any European before us.' Landing at the continent's northernmost promontory, to which he gave the name Cape York, he raised the flag and claimed the entire territory for Britain under the name New South Wales. His party fired three volleys into the air, to which the ship replied in kind, then everyone gave three cheers, rowed back to the *Endeavour* and sailed for home.

Cook reached Batavia in the Dutch East Indies on 7 October 1770, and sent a jubilant message to London: he had done all that was required of him and more; moreover, he had not lost a single man to sickness in the process. This last boast was premature. True, he had done well to keep his men free of scurvy, but he was now in disease-ridden Batavia, one of the world's most notorious death-traps, where dysentery and malaria claimed the lives of some 50,000 people a year. It was reckoned a stroke of great fortune if a visiting captain left with more than half his crew alive. Could he have helped it, Cook would not have stayed there. But his ship was in wretched condition: apart from the coral damage, its hull had been eaten by worms and was in places just an eighth of an inch thick. The Dutch shipwrights did a professional job, for which Cook was grateful. While they worked, however, his men began to die. The surgeon Monkhouse was the first to go, on 5 November, followed by Tiata, Tupia and five others. Everyone fell ill, and when the *Endeavour* sailed on 26 December 40 men were too sick to move and only 20 were strong enough to man the ship. Escape from Batavia provided no relief. The pestilence raged throughout the ship, killing Green, Parkinson, Spöring and many more. By the time Cook reached Cape Town he had lost a total of 33 men, and another 29 needed urgent medical attention. One of the sick men died before he could be brought ashore, and another five expired in hospital. Having travelled so far, and dared so much, it was a horrible irony that the bulk of the *Endeavour*'s casualties should come from their first contact with 'civilization'.

The ship was beginning to show the strain of its voyage, and the journey north did nothing to improve its condition. In the English Channel its rigging, sails and masts were so bad that something was breaking every day. But it brought them home safely, and in the early hours of Sunday 14 July 1771, Banks, Cook and Solander found themselves in central London. Here, in the insalubrious byways of Piccadilly, they shook hands and went their separate ways, Cook to the Admiralty, Banks and Solander to Banks's London house. After almost three years aboard the *Endeavour* their partnership had come to a close.

Banks and Cook were both lionized by the establishment, but in different ways. The Admiralty congratulated Cook in a quiet but appreciative manner for having undertaken such a tremendous voyage, and promoted him to captain. The scientific community, meanwhile, were overwhelmed by the mass of information Banks had brought back and said he was 'the glory not only of England but the whole world'. In response, Banks did nothing to dispel the impression that he alone was responsible for the expedition's success. Soon it was accepted that he had been in charge of the whole undertaking. Considering Cook's achievement, the modesty with which he received his small reward, and his impoverished circumstances – he lived in a small house in Mile End, East London; during his absence he had lost two children, the first a daughter who had been crawling when he left, the second a son whom he had never seen – it was perhaps unjust that Banks used his social status to grab the glory for himself. Ultimately, however, it was to the benefit of Cook's career, for Banks's fame became so great that he persuaded the Admiralty – the First Lord was a personal friend – to send a second expedition to the South Seas. As Banks said, 'That a Southern Continent really exists, I firmly believe; but if ask'd why I beleive so, I confess my reasons are weak; yet I have a preposession in favour of the fact which I find it difficult to account for'. On these flimsy grounds Captain James Cook left England on 21 June 1772 aboard the *Resolution* – a converted collier – accompanied by the *Adventure* under Lieutenant Tobias Furneaux, bound again for *Terra Australis Incognita*. He did so without Banks, who decided at the last moment that the ships were too cramped for his liking and, when the Admiralty refused to alter them to his specification, flounced off to Iceland in a fit of pique.

Cook did not share Banks's certainty that there was a southern continent, and even if there was he didn't think he could reach it or, if he did, that it would be worth finding. But employment was employment, and it would be a pity if 'the object of many ages and nations should not now be wholly cleared up'. The question could be settled 'without either much trouble or danger or fear for it'. It would also allow him to explore the South Pacific and (a matter of navigational pride) to circumnavigate the globe in an anti-clockwise direction. He had also been instructed to test a new clock, developed by the watchmaker John Harrison, that promised to keep Greenwich Time without deviation, thereby solving the eternal problem of calculating longitude. To a navigator like Cook, this alone was worth the trip.

The *Resolution* and *Adventure* sailed through the Atlantic to the Cape of Good Hope, where they took aboard a quantity of livestock, and dipped south towards Antarctica. In late November, amidst high winds and cold so fearful that their sheep, pigs and chickens began to die, they met their first icebergs. They were astonished at their size: one was as high as St Paul's Cathedral, others were two miles wide. And they were appalled by the danger they presented: 'the mind is filled with horror, for was a ship to get against the weather side of one of these islands when the seas run high she would be dashed to pieces in a moment'. Weaving through the bergs, they attained 67° 15' S on 18 January 1773 to find their progress blocked by impenetrable sheets of ice. Cook therefore retreated a few degrees north and sailed east, following roughly the 60th meridian, towards New Zealand.

At Cape Town they had heard of a French expedition led by Yves-Joseph de Kerguelen-Trémairec that had, that very February, discovered land which its commander was convinced was part of the Great Southern Continent. To Cook's satisfaction, this land was nowhere to be seen. As one of his officers gloated, 'if my friend Monsieur found any land, he's been confoundedly out in the latitudes and longitudes of it for we've searched the spot he represented it in and its environs too pretty narrowly and the devil an inch of land is there'. This, however, was their only discovery in four months of sub-Antarctic travel, and when Cook anchored off New Zealand for reprovisioning they were all heartily glad. But the men were physically healthy and, as Cook wrote on 23 March, 'We've now arrived at a port with a ship's crew in the best order that I believe was heard of after such a long passage at sea'.

The *Adventure* had become separated from the *Resolution* on 7 February and did not reach the prearranged rendezvous of Queen Charlotte Sound, in the strait between North and South Island, until 11 May. To Cook's irritation, Furneaux had maintained neither the discipline nor the diet he expected of him. There had been several cases of insubordination and drunkenness, and scurvy had taken hold. Furneaux also seemed to have no sense of urgency, and gave every appearance of expecting to spend the winter in New Zealand. Cook told him that they would be leaving shortly for a further exploration of the seas east and south of the Society Islands, after which they would go north-west to refresh themselves at Tahiti before returning to New Zealand. Conditions were not ideal for such a job but, as Cook wrote, 'It nevertheless appeared to me necessary that something must be done'. They left on 7 June 1773.

The weather was not good. In heavy winds Cook's helmsman was thrown in a circle over the top of the wheel. When he ordered another man to help, it made no difference: the second man was whirled onto the first and then, when the rudder swirled again, the first flew back on top of the second. Nevertheless, they made reasonable progress through a large quadrant of unexplored ocean, the only drawback being that Furneaux yet again neglected to feed his men properly: six weeks into the journey one man had died from scurvy and 20 more were incapacitated. Cursing, Cook repeated the instructions he had given him three times already, and headed for Tahiti. By late August they were on the island and were being accorded a rapturous reception by the Tahitians, who seemed to have forgotten the unpleasantness that had occurred during Cook's last visit. They were soon reminded: the white men were accused of drunkenness and rape; in return, the Tahitians captured one man and stripped him of his clothes and possessions before sending him packing; an armed party was sent to retrieve the clothes; shortly afterwards the Tahitians resumed their petty theft. Thereafter relations settled into their normal pattern, save that both sides were now accustomed to the practices of the other and outbreaks of violence were less extreme. Tahiti was also more peaceful and more prosperous than on Cook's last visit, with the result that the white men were able to obtain all the stores they needed and the Tahitians were less persistent in their thieving.

In all, it was a harmonious stay, and when the ships left on 18 September Cook's lieutenant, Charles Clerke, wrote: 'I must own that 'tis with some reluctance I bid adieu to these happy isles where I've spent many very happy days, both in the years '69 and '73.' It was not just the bounteous provisions – the pork this time lived up to every promise that had been made of it; the vegetables were also abundant and luscious – nor that the women were 'very handsome and very kind, and the men very civil and to the last degree benevolent'. It was more that Tahiti's paradisiacal surroundings felt like home to those who had been there before and that, as Clerke wrote, 'we may with very great safety say we've got into a very good neighbourhood. In short, in my opinion, they are as pleasant and happy spots as this world contains.' It was not so pleasant, however, as to deter a Tahitian from sailing with the *Resolution*, like the ill-fated Tupai before him. The crew called him Odiddy.

The two ships made a sweep of the Friendly Islands, where they once again became separated, and the *Resolution* returned to Queen Charlotte Sound at the beginning of November to await the *Adventure*'s return. After three weeks, when Furneaux had not appeared, Cook departed for the Antarctic. He left a note for his second-in-command, informing him that he would investigate the ice below New Zealand and then, if he failed to find the Great Southern Continent, would sail north-east for Easter Island, the easternmost outpost of Polynesia, which had been visited only once by a European and whose precise position was a matter of guesswork.

Furneaux arrived a week after Cook had departed, and was relieved to find that Cook's letter mentioned nothing about any specific rendezvous; nor did it contain any instructions as to what the *Adventure* should do. He decided, therefore, that he was free to go home. By 17 December the ship was ready for its journey, and Furneaux sent Midshipman John Rowe with ten men to gather anti-scorbutic vegetables. The following morning they had yet to return, so Furneaux despatched a second boat, this time with a contingent of marines, to find them. Patrolling the coast, they at last came across evidence of Rowe's party. It consisted of a few shoes, a hand, some pieces of their boat, and 20 baskets of roast flesh. Continuing to the next bay, they met a large number of Maoris gathered round a fire. Dispersing them with musket volleys, they examined the beach. Burney, the officer in charge,* recorded the scene: 'On the beach were two bundles of celery, which had been gathered for loading into the cutter. A broken oar was stuck upright in the ground, to which the natives had tied their canoes; a proof that the attack had been made here. I then searched all along at the back of the beach to see if the cutter was there. We found no boat, but instead of her such a shocking scene of carnage and barbarity as can never be mentioned or thought of but with horror; for the heads, hearts and lungs of several of our people were seen lying on the beach, and, at a little distance, the dogs gnawing their intrails.'

The men's immediate instinct was to launch a retributive attack. But rain had begun to fall, dampening the powder in their muskets' firing pans. It was also the end of the day. Burney, therefore, thought it best to retreat to the ship. His decision was a wise one for, as they drew away, they could hear what sounded like thousands of Maoris cheering from the forests that lined the shore. Outnumbered, their weapons misfiring and darkness upon them, it would have been madness to make any aggressive move. Moreover, as Burney reasoned, it would not bring back the dead: 'we could expect to reap no other advantage than the poor satisfaction of killing some more of the savages'. Logic, however, did nothing to quell their rage as they watched sparks rise into the night sky from a celebratory bonfire the Maoris had lit on a nearby hill. The next morning the *Adventure*'s crew was all for bombarding every settlement in Queen Charlotte Sound. But Furneaux, like Burney, realized that wanton destruction was no solution. Why so many Maoris should have descended on the area, and why they should have attacked Rowe's men, were questions to which Furneaux had no answers. Nor did he seek them. Having lost more people in one day than on the whole of the voyage, he was not going to risk the lives of the others in an inquiry that would be dangerous and probably futile, and that, if more deaths occurred, might jeopardize his chances of getting home.

A man like Cook might have exercised his authority more forcibly and demanded retribution. But Furneaux was not Cook: he was a second-in-command, unused to dealing with the natives and unsuited to the responsibilities of exploration. He was alone in the South Pacific, almost as far from Britain as it was possible to be; he had no clear orders and had lost at one stroke such a large percentage of his crew that the ship was seriously undermanned. One can sympathize with his decision to abandon the quest. The *Adventure* left immediately for Cape Horn, from where it crossed to Cape Town and thence to England.

Cook, meanwhile, was proceeding south towards Antarctica, dodging icebergs and enduring such cold that his rigging became nigh unworkable from the weight of frozen spray. Towards the end of January he was halted by a massive sheet of pack ice. Here, at 71° 10' S, he decided his search for the

---

* James 'Jem' Burney, who had enlisted as an ordinary seaman, was the brother of the famous novelist and diarist, Fanny Burney.

Great Southern Continent was at an end. 'I will not say it was impossible anywhere to get farther to the south,' he wrote, 'but the attempting it would have been a dangerous and rash exercise, and what I believe no man in my situation would have thought of.' It was his opinion that the ice extended unbroken to the South Pole or 'to some land to which it has been fixed from the creation'. Apart from the occasional penguin, there were 'but few other birds or any other thing that could induce us to think any land was near'. In a telling passage, Cook described his conflicting frustration and relief: 'I who had ambitions not only to go farther than anyone had done before, but as far as it was possible for man to go, was not sorry at meeting with this interruption as it in some measure ... shortened the dangers and hardships inseparable with the navigation of the south polar regions.'

Retreating from the ice, Cook sailed first to Easter Island – despite its whereabouts being so doubtful that 'I have little hopes of finding it' – then to Tahiti, where Odiddy was returned to his people, and finally to Queen Charlotte Sound, where he learned of the calamity that had befallen Furneaux's men and of its cause: a typical combination of drunkenness on the part of the shore party and acquisitiveness on the part of the Maoris. Leaving New Zealand, he headed for Cape Horn and, as Christmas approached, was able to write: 'I have now done with the SOUTHERN PACIFIC OCEAN, and flatter myself that no one will think I have left it unexplored, or that more could have been done in one voyage towards obtaining that end than has been done in this.' He had not given up on the Antarctic: in February 1774 he discovered South Georgia, an island (or collection of islands) of such inhospitable and icy aspect that he did nothing more than name it and claim it, before turning north. He reached London in the first week of August 1775, to universal acclaim. He had charted almost every island in the Pacific, not to mention a few more off the Atlantic coast of South America while en route to Cape Town, and he had returned with not a single death from scurvy. His greatest achievement, however, was making the first circumnavigation of Antarctica and probing further south than any human had yet been.

Cook's assessment of the Antarctic dispelled every romantic notion that adhered to it and was so accurate that, long after the event, one cannot but admire his intuitive feel for the environment. He wrote: 'The greatest part of this Southern Continent (supposing there is one) must lie within the Polar Circle where the sea is so pestered with ice that the land is thereby inaccessible ... Thick fogs, snowstorms, intense cold and every other thing that can render navigation dangerous one has to encounter, and these difficulties are greatly heightened by the inexpressibly horrible aspect of the country, a country doomed by nature never once to feel the warmth of the sun's rays, but to lie for ever buried under everlasting snow and ice.' He was careful, however, not to deny the possibility of reaching Antarctica: he might, he said, have had a go himself had he not been carrying so much valuable information.

Cook's was the crispest, clearest analysis of the region to date, and one that would be confirmed by subsequent expeditions. In 1820 Fabien Gottlieb von Bellingshausen replicated Cook's journey. An American sealer, John Davis, landed on the Antarctic Peninsula, south of Cape Horn, in 1821. James Weddell, a Dutch-born English navigator, reached 74° 15' S in 1822–4. In 1831 a ship belonging to Enderby Brothers (a British whaling firm) sighted land. James Ross in 1839, and then men like Scott, Shackleton and Amundsen followed. Everything they found supported Cook's conclusion: Antarctica was, as he had predicted, a land of perpetual snow and ice.

For this, Cook was honoured less with medals and promotion than with a job that suited him perfectly. The Board of Longitude, who had commissioned the chronometer he had taken on his last journey – which, by the by, performed so well that he never sailed without it again – had set a bounty on the North-West Passage. It was understood that the passage, linking the Pacific and Atlantic Oceans, ran through the Arctic seas north of Canada. Many navigators had sought it in the past, but they had approached mostly from the east. Cook was therefore invited to try from the west, through Bering Strait.* If he succeeded – and everybody was certain that he would, for he was now the most outstanding explorer of the age – he and his crew could claim £20,000, more than £1 million today, of which the lion's share would fall to the captain. This, and the chance of once again going further than anyone before him, was Cook's reward.

He left on 12 July 1776 aboard his old ship, the *Resolution*, accompanied by Lieutenant Charles Clerke in the *Discovery*. The two ships sailed south to Cape Town and then headed east to the Pacific to reprovision for the journey north. They stopped, naturally, at Tahiti, where Cook repatriated a man named Omai, whom Furneaux had brought home on the *Adventure*, before proceeding north.** Along the way he made a new discovery: an archipelago whose inhabitants spoke a language similar to that of Tahiti, and whose islands were as bounteous as those to the south. He had stumbled on the northernmost outpost of Polynesian culture, now known as the Hawaiian Islands but which he named the Sandwich Islands after the 4th Earl of Sandwich, First Lord of the Admiralty (and inventor of the snack which bears his name). Unfortunately, he lacked the time to explore them fully: if he was to complete the North-West Passage he needed to reach Bering Strait before the brief Arctic summer closed. Five weeks was all he allowed himself, by the end of which he had charted three islands and still had not collected

* At first he was employed only as a consultant for the expedition but, faced with the Admiralty's lengthy deliberations as to who should be the leader, Cook lost patience and said he would accept the post. The deliberations, and the decision, apparently involved several bottles of wine.

** Omai had been the exotic highlight of London's season. Dressed in finery, he impressed everyone with his noble savagery. He was at ease with dukes, earls and admirals and, on being introduced to George III, addressed him as King Tosh. But when the novelty faded he was sent home. In a tawdry example of social engineering, he was given money, servants, muskets and fine clothes; Cook's men also built him a house and dug him a garden. Thus equipped, Omai was meant to show the savages an example of true nobility. He died of fever shortly after his homecoming.

as much water as he would have liked. He sailed up the west coast of America – cautiously, lest he offend the Spaniards who laid claim to it – and reached the Aleutian Islands in June 1777. Two months later he was moving from side to side of the Bering Strait, fraternizing now with the natives of America and now with those of Asia. When in harbour he sent boats on 30-mile rowing trips to explore neighbouring bays. One midshipman described these outings as hard work but a welcome diversion, because they were allowed to eat and drink as much as they liked.

This last was odd because, although Cook had always been a stickler for diet, he had never kept his men on short rations. Now rationing seemed to weigh heavily on his mind. Perhaps he was conserving food for the forthcoming voyage through the Passage. But many people noted that he was not the same leader to whom they had entrusted their lives in past years. At times he was querulous, hesitating at opportunities he would have seized before. At others he was rash, raising full sail in a fog and stopping only when the ship was 100 yards from the shore, having passed a nightmare of rocks that he admitted he must have navigated in a dream. He was brusque, impatient and applied shipboard rules more strictly than ever before. One officer, on returning from a 30-mile trip, wrote: 'Captain Cook ... on these occasions would sometimes relax from his almost constant severity of disposition and condescended now and then to converse familiarly with us. But it was only for a time: as soon as on board the ship he became again a despot.'

Cook's strange behaviour has been attributed to a parasitical disease contracted on his second voyage. It might also have been the result of nerves and an understandable fear of the North-West Passage, whose traverse, as he must have known, would be harder than anything he had faced to date. Or it could simply have been age and exhaustion – he had been exploring, almost without interruption, for a decade. Whatever the cause, he was definitely more quarrelsome and capricious than before. When he reached 70° 44' N above the Bering Strait and found his way blocked by a solid mass of ice, he informed the men that he was going west to find the North-East Passage above Siberia. Then after a few days he changed his mind and said they were going south to reprovision for a second try at the North-West Passage. His goal was the Hawaiian Islands, which were the nearest, most comfortable source of provender and also offered the chance of further discovery. Sure enough, on 30 November he met a volcanic island, larger than any other he had discovered in the Pacific. Its inhabitants called it Owhyhe (Hawaii). As Cook sailed round the island he found the natives to be astonishingly friendly, waving white banners when the ship approached and trading with gusto. Priests welcomed him ashore and gave him all the food and water he needed. He was invited to rituals on a stone platform similar to the one he had seen in Tahiti, and was greeted at every step by people who called him *Orono*. When they left on 4 February they were presented with a remarkable quantity of food, including a small herd of pigs.

Never, in anyone's recollection, had they met with such generosity in the Pacific.

The paradise was marred only by Cook, whose behaviour grew stranger and stranger. At one point he abolished the rum ration and told the crew they would have to drink beer instead. However ardently he advocated beer as an anti-scorbutic – which current thinking held it to be – the crew were not having it. Nor were they willing to accept another of their captain's peculiar orders: that no women were to be allowed on ship. In the face of mutiny Cook had, humiliatingly, to rescind both edicts. Matters improved once they left the island and resumed standard shipboard routine. But they had been at sea for only four days when a storm split the *Resolution*'s foremast. A safe anchorage was needed for the lengthy process of repairing it, and the nearest such place was the one they had just left – Kealakekua Bay on Hawaii. So back they went. This time their reception was noticeably cooler.

Cook had been aware that the Hawaiians considered him some kind of god, but paid little attention to it. Unfortunately, he did not appreciate the ramifications of his visit. In Hawaiian mythology, the island's prosperity depended upon the regular arrival and departure of a white-skinned god Lono, or Orono, who presided over the rainy season. His coming was celebrated by a four-month festival, Makihiki, during which his image was carried clockwise around the island, its progress punctuated by ceremonies and sacrifices. When the rains ended Lono was ritually killed in battle with Ku, the god of the dry season, and left for his home over the waves, to reappear the following year. The authority of Hawaii's rulers and priests rested on this routine, and the placatory rituals had been conducted for centuries without major incident. Lono came, he went; and this was how it was.

Cook's arrival in November had coincided with the festival of Makihiki. As he was white (a pale skin was associated throughout Polynesia with divinity), and as he had, by coincidence, sailed clockwise round the island, the islanders assumed that this year Lono had decided to join the celebrations in person rather than effigy. The assumption was reinforced when Cook accepted the offerings they gave him and participated in the rituals to ensure his departure. Moreover, his ships had anchored at, and then left, Kealakekua Bay, by chance the very place where Lono had for hundreds of years met his ritual demise. Normally, it would have been clear from the white men's drunkenness and womanizing that they were by no means gods. But Cook's uncharacteristic strictness had given them a gloss of respectability. And if he was very obviously human, this did not seem to bother the priests at all. After generations as an effigy, Lono had become a symbol, and so long as Cook obeyed the rules of Makihiki – which he did – then it did not really matter what he was, as long as he served his symbolic purpose. Cook's return so soon after his departure, however, disrupted the age-old routine. If Lono was not dead, Hawaii's hierarchy was in jeopardy and the island's crops might fail.

Oblivious to his mythical status, Cook sent his carpenters ashore and had them erect a workshop for repairing the foremast. The first sign he had of the islanders' discontent was their refusal to trade for anything but knives, and their inquiries as to how many warriors he had aboard. Then they began to steal, on an unprecedented scale. On Saturday 13 November the thieving became so blatant that Clerke ordered his men to open fire; they missed their target. Later, an unarmed shore party narrowly escaped annihilation when they were pelted with rocks. These incidents severely dented the foreigners' reputation for invincibility and drove Cook into one of his sudden rages. 'The behaviour of these Indians must at last oblige me to use force,' he told an officer. 'They must not imagine they have gained an advantage over us by what has occurred today.' But the 'Indians' very obviously did have the advantage: that night they swam alongside Clerke's *Discovery* and stole its cutter.

The theft of tools and small metal items was a tiresome but expected adjunct to any stay in Polynesia. To steal a boat, however, struck at the heart of Royal Naval pride. When Cook heard of the loss he demanded retribution. In a conference with Clerke, he outlined their plan of action. Boats from both ships would block the mouth of Kealakekua Bay and drive the Hawaiian canoes ashore; nobody was to escape, and the gunnery officers were ordered to fire their cannon if need be. The aim of the exercise, he stressed, was not to kill innocent people but to apprehend and punish the culprits who had stolen the cutter.

On Sunday 14 November the bay was full of canoes, and Cook put his plan to the test. At first it went well, the Hawaiians fleeing before the power of the Westerners' guns. But they did not flee in as much disarray as he would have liked: an ominous humming sound came from the forests, interspersed with the blare of conch shells. Ignoring the hidden presence of an army that must have been several thousand strong, Cook announced that he would advance on the village of Kealakekua and take the local ruler hostage. Why he thought this gambit would work, when it had failed so miserably in New Zealand, is a mystery. Nevertheless, with the ships' four-pounders lobbing shells into the canoes, and his boat parties firing musket volleys, he was in a strong position. When he landed with three boats and marched up the beach to the village, accompanied by one of the *Resolution*'s officers and nine marines, including a corporal and a sergeant – all fully armed – he was confident of success. Then everything went wrong.

A crowd of Hawaiians materialized, armed with clubs, spears and daggers. They did not come close, but threw stones from a distance, one of which knocked down a marine. Cook shot the stone-thrower; then, on being advised by his sergeant that he had shot the wrong man, he shot another one. The Hawaiians responded with more stones. The marines replied with a volley of lead, whereupon the Hawaiians retreated. Cook could still have faced them down, but his marines had other ideas. It would take at least half a minute to reload their muskets, in which time they might be rushed by a horde of infuriated warriors. Most of them therefore dropped their weapons and fled for the boats. Heartened by their enemy's retreat, the Hawaiians moved in. The marine corporal, who had just finished reloading his musket, was stabbed in the stomach. The officer, Lieutenant Molesworth Phillips, went down. And then, one by one, the remaining marines were despatched with spears and stones. Those who had fled were now scrambling into the nearest boat, which threatened to sink under their weight.

Amidst the carnage, Cook remained calm. Preserving his dignity, he strode slowly down the beach, one hand behind his head to protect him from stones, the other clutching a musket. For a while his bravado worked: the Hawaiians dashed towards him but halted at the last moment, apparently fearful that he would turn round. But when Cook reached the sea one man summoned the courage to club him. It was not a fatal blow, but it was strong enough to make him stumble and drop his musket. Another man stabbed him in the neck. This time Cook went down, in knee-deep water just four yards from the boat, and a horde of Hawaiians fell on him. He managed to fight them off, calling meanwhile to the boat for assistance; but, whether from shock, fear or incompetence, the marines did not come to his rescue. Still defiant, Cook struggled towards some nearby rocks. Here, however, the fight ended: the last his men saw as they rowed to safety was a frenzy of warriors stabbing and clubbing his corpse.

Aboard the ships, the Britons reacted with confusion and shock. Their first impulse was to shell the village – which they did – then, while the cannon blasted away, they began to argue over who was to blame for Cook's death and what they should do by way of more specific retaliation. Clerke, who now had command of the expedition, ordered the immediate evacuation of the carpenters, whose workshop was on the other side of the bay from the village. Next, he sent 40 men ashore to recover the bodies; but they had long since been dragged away, and all they got was a promise from a terrified chief that he would return Cook's corpse. The following day they received a small bundle containing a slab of partially roasted flesh from Cook's hip. The priest who delivered it to the *Discovery* apologized sincerely for the smallness of the parcel: Lono's remains, he explained, had been distributed across the island, but he would do his best to retrieve them. His apologies were undermined by the appearance of a man in a canoe, who hoisted Cook's hat on a stick then bared his buttocks. On shore, meanwhile, a group of jeering Hawaiians waved the marines' red jackets and likewise showed their buttocks. The British fury was uncontrollable. More cannon-fire ensued and an armed party wreaked further destruction on Kealakekua village, shooting everyone they saw, decapitating several men and hoisting their heads on poles. As a finale, they burned the entire village to the ground. In return, they were given Cook's hands, scalp, skull, shins and feet. The rest had been either eaten or destroyed.

Nothing more could be accomplished at Hawaii. Cook's remains were buried at sea, those of the marines were abandoned and, on 23 February 1779, the *Resolution* and *Discovery* left on a survey of the Sandwich Islands. That done, they sailed for Kamchatka and a second attempt at the North-West Passage. The surgeon died of tuberculosis, as did Clerke; they made no progress through the passage; and when they reached London on 2 October 1780 they were greeted with dismay. They had failed in their main purpose, had lost their captain, their second-in-command, their surgeon, a sergeant, a corporal and seven marines, and had taken four years and three months to do so. Cook, the perceived giant of exploration, had acquitted himself ignobly: any geographical advance had been made by Clerke's sailing master, William Bligh, who took meticulous observations of the Sandwich Islands, Alaska and every coast from Kamchatka to England.*

In a very English way, however, their failure became a national triumph. Cook was lauded as 'one of the greatest navigators our nation or any other nation ever had'. The *London Gazette* said his demise was 'an irreparable Loss to the Public ... for in him were united every successful and amiable quality that could adorn his Profession; nor was his singular Modesty less conspicuous than his other Virtues'. Encomiums were written – by Banks, among others – describing his manifold achievements. People squabbled over his possessions, and mementos changed hands at vastly inflated prices. Not until the death of Nelson in 1805 would the nation be seized again by such hysteria.

Whether Cook deserved the hero-worship is debatable. His navigation was not as impeccable as legend would have it: he failed, for example, to ascertain that Tasmania was an island. Many of his discoveries were mere gap-fillers in the broader sweep of Dutch and French exploration. Apart from the circumnavigation of Antarctica, his exploits were no more remarkable than those of his contemporaries and less important than those of his predecessors. He was also an inconsiderate, sometimes brutal, ambassador for European civilization. On the other hand, he was the most professional explorer the world had yet seen. For a decade he went wherever he was ordered, tackling the Antarctic, the Arctic and the Pacific with the same smooth efficiency. His anti-scorbutic diet, of which he was so proud, became a model for subsequent expeditions and for all long-distance sea-travel. If he made the odd mistake, his charts were generally accurate – nobody has bettered his maps of some sub-Antarctic islands. And his voyages, particularly the first, in association with Banks, were of outstanding benefit to science. For 80 years, until sail was ousted by steam, he was the example against which all sea explorers were compared.

* Bligh was to achieve his own fame in 1787 when Banks sent him to Tahiti on the *Bounty* to collect breadfruit plants for transplantation in the West Indies. Two years later, his crew became so demoralized by his disciplinarian attitude that they put him overboard in a small boat and sailed, as some of Cook's men would have liked to have done, for a paradisiacal existence with their Tahitian 'wives'. In a stupendous act of seamanship Bligh steered his boat, and the 12 loyal men aboard it, on a 3,900-mile voyage to safety.

Horace-Bénédict de Saussure (1760–88)

From childhood, the Swiss aristocrat Horace-Bénédict de Saussure was besotted by the Alps. They glimmered tantalizingly on the horizon, clearly visible from his home town of Geneva but, although so near, they remained a mystery. Nobody had explored their peaks, nobody knew what mysteries they contained. Rumour told of dragons, witches and demons who tumbled rocks onto the heads of unwary travellers. Saussure gave these tales little credence, but he wanted very much to visit the mountains that gave rise to them. It was not until 1760, however, when he was a 20-year-old student studying natural philosophy (with emphasis on geology), that he walked the 50 miles from Geneva to Chamonix to inspect the Alps at close quarters.

Set in a narrow valley, high in the Kingdom of Savoy, Chamonix charmed him with its clean air, its forests and its quaint hamlets. It seemed 'a new world, a sort of earthly paradise, enclosed by a kindly Deity in the circle of the mountains'. He was entranced by the needle-like peaks, or *aiguilles*, that sprouted like cathedral spires, and by the glaciers that flowed between them, presenting 'one of the noblest and most singular spectacles it is possible to imagine'. Led by a guide, he went on geological forays that rendered him almost speechless with excitement. Of all the area's wonders, however, none impressed him so much as the mountain that rose on the valley's south side: Mont Blanc. He had already gained a sense of its majesty from Geneva; but here, close to, it appeared overwhelming. At 15,771 feet it was not the highest mountain then known to Westerners – South America's Mount Chimborazo claimed that prize – but Saussure reckoned it was the highest in Europe, Africa and Asia. As such it had to be conquered, both for the glory and for the scientific benefits that would accrue from standing on top of the Old World. When he returned to Geneva he put a price on its head. The exact sum he offered is unknown, but it was probably princely, given that he also promised to recompense anybody who failed for the time they spent trying. To show that he meant it, he repeated the offer on a second visit in 1761 and had it posted around the valley.

Again and again Saussure returned to Chamonix, his adoration of Mont Blanc increasing with every summer to the extent that on the approach he chose his *auberges* less for their comfort than for their views of the mountain.

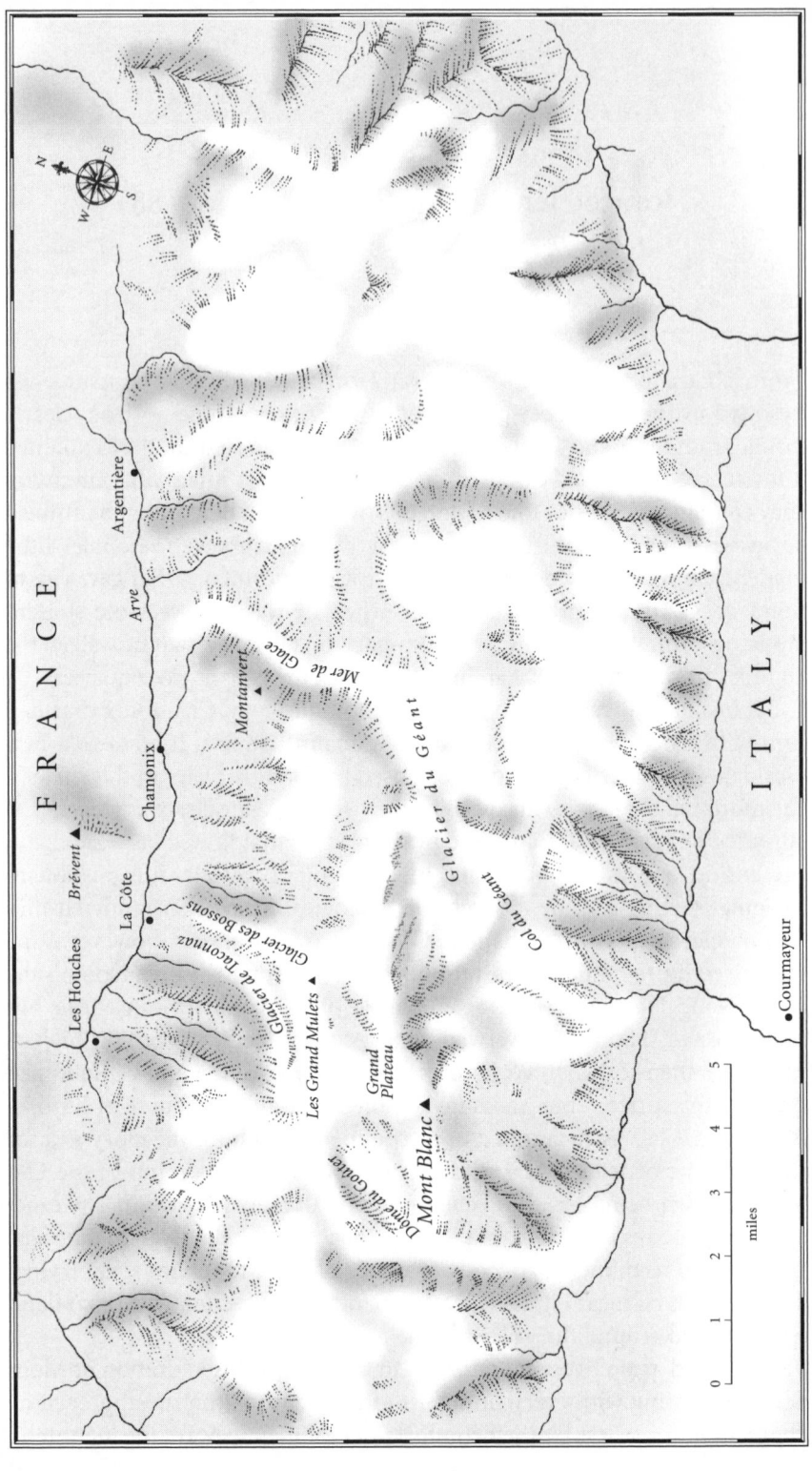

But he never received the news that he desired. It wasn't that his bounty was inadequate or that there was a shortage of people willing to tackle the mountain – several locals had a go; the Precentor of Geneva Cathedral made repeated attempts; Saussure himself gave it a try in 1785 – it was more that Mont Blanc was impenetrably rugged and horribly high. Apart from a few souls who earned a precarious income hunting chamois and gathering crystals, the locals did not go above the snowline if they could help it. Of those who did, none had ventured far up Mont Blanc for fear of its crevasses and avalanches. There was no known route to its summit; few people had the mountaineering skills to forge one; and the only available climbing aids consisted of a crude, two-pronged crampon and a six-foot stave, or alpenstock. Besides, it was unknown if humans could even survive at that altitude. By 1785, a quarter of a century after he had advertised his bounty, Saussure wondered gloomily if Mont Blanc would have to be conquered by balloon.

Not everyone shared his pessimism. In Chamonix there were two men – Michel-Gabriel Paccard and Jacques Balmat, one a local doctor, the other a farmer-cum-crystal-gatherer – who both thought they knew a way to the top. Paccard had the greater experience, having climbed the mountain several times before, reaching 11,400 feet with Saussure in 1785. But Balmat had the better physique – as he liked to boast, 'I had a famous calf and a stomach like cast-iron, and I could walk three days consecutively without eating' – and he had the more carefully planned route. After many months' reconnaissance, he thought it would be possible to ascend from the village of La Côte via the Glacier de Taconnaz to the rocky outcrops known as Les Grands Mulets. From there he would proceed to the snowy mound of the Dôme du Goûter and thence, if luck was with him, to the summit itself.

On 5 June 1786 Balmat put his plan to the test. He scrambled to Les Grands Mulets without mishap and then, finding his way blocked by cloud, decided to stay where he was until morning. This was unheard of: people had climbed to Les Grands Mulets before, but nobody had ever spent the night there. Moreover, Balmat's only sustenance was a loaf of bread and a bottle of brandy. Huddled on a small ledge, with an 800-foot drop below him, he sat on his knapsack, beating his hands and feet to keep warm. 'My breath was frozen,' he recalled, 'and my clothes were soaked ... soon I felt as if I was stark naked. I moved my hands and feet faster, and began to sing to drive away the thoughts that were seething in my brain ... Everything was dead in this ice-bound world and the sound of my voice almost terrified me. I became silent and afraid.'

He waited another day and night for the mist to clear before admitting defeat. On the way down, however, he was outraged to meet a party of three Chamoniards heading the way he had just come. He was not fooled when they said they were looking for lost goats: 'I felt that the men were trying to deceive, and at once surmised that they were about to attempt the journey which I had just failed to achieve.' When they invited him to join them he accepted at once. By 3.00 a.m. on 8 June all four men were standing on the Dôme du Goûter where, to Balmat's inexpressible disgust, they were joined by another two men. This time the excuse was that they had a wager to see who could climb the highest. Unwilling to share Saussure's prize with these interlopers, Balmat wandered off on his own, towards a narrow ridge that seemed to lead to the summit. His path was blocked by a clump of rocks but, sitting astride the ridge, he saw a field of ice below – the Grand Plateau – that looked promising. When he returned to the Dôme the others had gone home, so he took advantage of their absence to reconnoitre his new find. For the rest of the day he traversed the Grand Plateau and then spent his third consecutive night on Mont Blanc. It was no more comfortable than the previous two. Far below, he saw the lights of Chamonix extinguished one by one. For a while he was comforted by the sound of a dog barking in the village of Courmayeur, several miles away on the other side of the mountain. But the barking stopped at midnight, and thereafter all he heard was the crack of glaciers and the occasional rumble of an avalanche. 'No man is made of iron,' he confessed, 'and I felt far from cheerful.'

He started his descent at 2.00 a.m. on 9 June and reached home six hours later. It had been a record-breaking journey. He had climbed higher than anyone yet, had found a potential route to the summit and had survived three nights on the mountain with virtually no food. Little wonder that when he arrived, utterly exhausted, he threw himself onto a pile of hay and slept for 24 hours. When he woke he was so badly sunburned that he had to seek medical attention. The man to whom he turned was Dr Michel-Gabriel Paccard.

While Paccard applied the salve, Balmat explained his ambitions. He knew how to reach the top of Mont Blanc and was confident that he could do it. But he needed a companion, a man of learning, a man who could read barometers and thermometers, a man whose word the outside world would respect. Such a man might be an academic, a cleric, a lawyer or, perhaps, a doctor. Paccard had been climbing Mont Blanc for the last three years, and between ascents had been studying it through his telescope. He accepted immediately.

They would have left at once were it not for their work schedule and the weather. Paccard had patients, Balmat the harvest, and for weeks Mont Blanc was shrouded in fog. As Balmat knew, it was impossible to find one's way in poor visibility; more importantly, if nobody could see them on the summit they might as well not have been there. The clouds cleared on 6 August 1786 and the following day, with a clear sky beckoning, Balmat knocked on Paccard's door. They set out at 5.00 p.m., spent the first night above La Côte, between the glaciers of Bossons and Taconnaz, and at 2.00 a.m. began their assault on the mountain.

According to Balmat, whose boastful account of their journey is the only one that survives, Paccard was nervous and hesitant, 'but the sight of my alertness gave him confidence, and we went on safe and sound'. Above Les Grands Mulets they were hit by violent gusts of wind that carried Paccard's hat away and 'passed whistling over our heads, driving great balls of snow almost as big as houses before it ... At the first respite I rose, but the Doctor could only continue on all fours.' Apparently, Paccard did not regain his feet until the Dôme du Goûter where, Balmat having arranged for the villagers to be on the look-out for them, he was forced to stand up from 'considerations of self-respect'. If Balmat's violently partisan account is to be believed, the effort was too much for Paccard.

'Having used up all his strength in getting to his feet, neither the encouragement from below, nor my earnest entreaties could induce him to continue the ascent. My eloquence exhausted, I told him to keep moving so as not to get benumbed. He listened without seeming to understand ... I saw that he was suffering from the cold, while I also was nearly frozen. Leaving him the bottle, I went on alone, saying that I should very soon come back to find him. He answered, "Yes! Yes!" and telling him again to be sure not to stand still, I went off. I had hardly gone thirty paces when, on turning round, I saw him actually sitting down on the snow, with his back turned to the wind as some precaution.

'From that time onward the route presented no very great difficulty, but as I rose higher the air became much less easy to breathe, and I had to stop almost every ten steps and wheeze like one with consumption. I felt as if my lungs had gone, and my chest was quite empty. I folded my handkerchief over my mouth, which made me a little more comfortable as I breathed through it. The cold got worse and worse, and to go a quarter of a league took an hour. I kept walking upward, with my head bent down, but finding I was on a peak which was new to me, I lifted my head and saw that at last I had reached the summit of Mont Blanc!

'I had no longer any strength to go higher; the muscles of my legs seemed only held together by my trousers. But behold I was at the end of my journey ... Everything around belonged to me! I was the monarch of Mont Blanc! Ah, then I turned towards Chamonix and waved my hat on the end of my stick. I could see through my glass the response. My subjects in the valley perceived. The whole village was gathered together in the market place.'

Returning to fetch Paccard, he found the doctor curled on the snow 'just like a cat when she makes herself into a muff'. His only response when Balmat told him of his victory was, 'Where can I lie down and go to sleep?' Balmat pushed and cajoled him into continuing the ascent and finally, at 6.23 p.m. on 8 August 1786, they both stood on the summit. Paccard produced his instruments, and for half an hour took readings – though the ink froze in his pen when he tried to record them – while Balmat admired the view. Above them the sky was dark blue and, although the sun was shining brightly, it was possible to see the stars. 'Below, was nothing but gaunt peaks, ice, rocks, and snow. The great chain which crosses the Dauphine and stretches as far as the Tyrol was spread out before us, its four hundred glaciers shining in the sunlight. Could there be space for any green ground on earth? The lakes of Geneva and Neuchâtel were specks of blue on the horizon. To the left lay the mountains of my dear country all fleecy with snow, and rising from meadows of the richest green. To the right was all Piedmont, and Lombardy as far as Genoa, and Italy was opposite.'

Just before 7.00 p.m. they began the return journey, Paccard so helpless that Balmat had to carry him over the more difficult stretches. Repeatedly, the doctor said he wanted to do nothing but sleep. At 11.00 both men found their hands were suffering from frostbite, which they cured by rubbing them with snow. 'Soon sensation returned, but accompanied by pains as if every vein had been pricked by needles. I rolled my baby up in his rug and put him to bed under the shelter of a rock; we ate and drank a little; pressed as close to one another as possible, and fell fast asleep.' The next day they were back in Chamonix, where Balmat painted a dramatic portrait of his appearance: 'My eyes were red, my face black and my lips blue. Every time I laughed or yawned the blood spouted out from my lips and cheeks, and in addition I was half blind.' (He made less play of the fact that Paccard was completely snowblind and that he had left him behind at La Côte to feel his way home with a stick.) Within a week, he was in Geneva to claim Saussure's prize.

There was no doubt that the two men had reached the summit and little that Balmat had been first; but the way in which Balmat described the conquest caused controversy. He gave two versions of the climb, one as told to the Precentor of Geneva, Marc-Théodore Bourrit, while he 'still carried on his face the honourable marks of his intrepidity', the other 56 years later to the French author Alexandre Dumas (from which the above quotations have been taken). The Dumas version was riddled with fabrications and impossibilities: the two men had never been to the Dôme du Goûter, having crossed the Grand Plateau instead; Paccard was not as unfit as Balmat made him out to be, and he probably wasn't as faint-hearted either; and if the doctor had collapsed where he was supposed to have done, he would have frozen to death in the time it took Balmat to reach the summit, wave to his 'subjects' and return to collect him. The Bourrit version omitted many of these details, but its gist was the same: Paccard had been a useless piece of baggage whom Balmat had lugged heroically up and down the hill.

Saussure kept his distance from the squabbles: Mont Blanc had been taken and the prize had been claimed. But the manner of its conquest did not satisfy him. Paccard had taken the most paltry of observations, and none of the great scientific questions to which Saussure sought an answer had been addressed. Moreover, the letters of congratulation – including one from England's Lord Palmerston – read as if he himself had stood on the summit rather than acting as a mere sponsor; while this was flattering, it was an accolade he did not deserve. Therefore, for reasons of personal and professional pride, Saussure felt he had to climb Mont Blanc himself.

He did so in August 1787, accompanied by a retinue of 18 porters. The ascent was hard, and they suffered horribly from exhaustion, altitude sickness and fear. Camped on the Grand Plateau, Saussure had nothing but admiration for Balmat and Paccard. 'There were no living beings, no sign of vegetation; it was a realm of frigid silence. When I imagined [them] reaching this desert at the end of the day, without shelter, without the possibility of rescue, without even the knowledge that men could survive where they intended to go, but nevertheless carrying on, I could not help but admire their courage.' A little further on he was even more admiring. Where Balmat had spoken only of physical exertion, Saussure described the conditions he encountered. 'The slope is 39 degrees, the precipice below is frightful, and the snow, hard on the surface, was flour beneath. Steps were cut, but the legs insecurely placed in this flour rested on a lower crust which was often very thin, and then slipped.' But the view from the top was worth the effort. 'I could not believe my eyes,' he wrote. 'It seemed as if it was a dream when I saw beneath my feet these majestic peaks ... of which I had found even the bases so difficult and dangerous of approach.' The panorama, combined with the five and a half hours that he spent taking readings, told him more about the Alps than he had learned in a lifetime of study. When he returned to Chamonix he was suffused with joy. 'Congratulate me!' he said to a friend. 'I come from the conquest of Mont Blanc!'

For many, Saussure's was indeed the true conquest. He was a respectable man of science, whereas Balmat and Paccard – whose argument over who had done what, where, was beginning to heat up – were provincial nobodies. Still, Saussure was not satisfied. The climb had been too hard, had taken too long and had not given him as much time on the summit as he would have liked. 'The length of the struggle, the recollection and the still vivid impression of the exertion it had cost me, caused me a kind of irritation,' he wrote. 'At the moment that I trod the highest point of the snow that crowned the summit I trampled it with a feeling of anger rather than pleasure.' The experience had left him empty. He felt 'like an epicure invited to a splendid festival and prevented from enjoying it by violent nausea'.

In July 1788 he sated his appetite with an ascent of the Col du Géant. Situated on Mont Blanc, roughly midway between Chamonix and the Italian village of Courmayeur, the col, or shoulder, was not particularly high – approximately 11,000 feet – nor, apart from a tricky glacier on the Chamonix side, was it very hard to reach. It had already been climbed, and there was no glory in repeating the process. Saussure, however, wanted to do more than climb it: to gain a full appreciation of the geology and meteorology of the Alps he intended to camp there for at least a fortnight.

People were just adjusting to the fact that it was possible to breathe at the top of Mont Blanc. They conceded, reluctantly, that one might also be able to survive a few nights at high altitude. But to spend two weeks at 11,000 feet was unheard of. The cold, the storms, the avalanches, the altitude sickness, the stress: it was more than the human frame could bear. The weather and the gods had permitted a few mortals to climb Europe's highest mountain. To tempt providence further was rash. Saussure didn't care. Accompanied by his teenage son, his manservant, and four guides led by Jacques Balmat, he went up the glacier and onto the col. He erected tents for the guides and, on a small ledge, with a cliff above and a cliff below, he built a stone hut for himself and his son.

Their day began at 4.00 a.m. and did not stop until Saussure doused the lamps at 10.00 p.m. During that period they observed the progress of the clouds beneath them, measured the atmosphere's electricity, watched their thermometers, recorded every swing of the barometer, and marvelled at the butterflies, carried on thermals from Chamonix, that landed, bemused, on their blankets. Sleeping on the edge of a precipice did not bother Saussure – if anything he enjoyed it: 'on my little mattress which had been laid on the ground next to that of my son, I slept better than I did in my own bed at home'.

When the weather was good, as it generally was, their happiness was infinite. 'We have had the most magnificent evenings,' Saussure wrote, 'all these high peaks that surround us and the snows that separate them were coloured with the most beautiful shades of rose and carmine. The Italian horizon was girdled with a broad belt from which the full moon, of a rich vermillion tint, rose with the majesty of a queen ... These snows and rocks, of which the brilliancy is unsupportable by sunlight, present a wonderful and delightful spectacle by the soft radiance of the moon ... The soul is uplifted, the powers of the intelligence seem to widen and in the midst of this majestic silence, one seems to hear the voice of Nature and to become the confidant of her most secret workings.' One of these secrets, which Saussure and his son enjoyed, was seeing what happened when they tipped boulders down the hill: 'they produce really magnificent torrents of stones and snow'.

When the weather was not so good, however, life was bothersome. Between 5.00 and 10.00 p.m. they were often plagued by a cold wind that brought snow and hail. 'The warmest clothes – even furs – could not protect us,' Saussure wrote. 'We could scarcely light a fire in our tents; and the hut ... was hardly warmed at all by our little stoves; the coal only smouldered without the use of bellows and if, finally, we managed to warm our feet and calves our bodies remained constantly frozen thanks to the wind which blew through the hut.' Sometimes, too, they became more intimately acquainted with nature's workings than they would have liked. One night the camp was hit by a thunderstorm. It has been calculated that, with its lightning and its repetitive up-down cycles of wind, a single thunder-cloud contains as much energy as ten Hiroshima-sized nuclear bombs. Saussure was facing not one cloud but scores of them. And at 11,000 feet he was not just under the storm but *in* it.

He described the experience with a mixture of objectivity and awe. 'The gale had this peculiarity, that it was periodically interrupted by intervals of the most perfect calm. In these intervals we heard the wind howling below us . . . while the utmost tranquillity reigned around our cabin. But these calm moments were succeeded by blasts of an indescribable violence; double blows like discharges of artillery. We felt even the mountain shake under our mattresses.' At dawn, fearing that his hut would fall over the edge, he took refuge with the guides in one of their tents. But there it was no better: it took the weight of every man, hanging on the posts, to stop the tent being lifted into the sky; and when a guide crawled out to fetch food and water, he had to cling to the rocks lest he be blown over the edge. Even though the distance between their tent and their supplies was only 16 feet, it took more than ten minutes to make the return journey. At 7.00 a.m. the storm reached a peak. Hailstones battered the tent, and one flash of lightning struck so close that they distinctly heard a spark hiss down the wet canvas. 'The air was so full of electricity,' Saussure recorded, 'that directly I put only the point of my electrometer outside the tent the bubbles separated as far as the threads would allow them, and at almost every explosion of thunder the electricity changed from positive to negative or vice versa.'

The tempest died at midday, leaving him badly shaken. He had been one of the first people to survive the heart of a thunderstorm, and he had not liked it. As he said, it was 'the most terrible [thing] I have ever witnessed'. The guides felt the same. After 16 days, with Saussure rhapsodizing over a particularly beautiful sunset and looking as if he would stay there for ever, they took unilateral action. In a single night they ate the remaining supplies, leaving Saussure no option but to retreat. He chose the descent to Courmayeur rather than Chamonix, arriving weak with hunger but fizzing with excitement.

Saussure continued to explore the Alps until his death in 1798, but nothing matched the Mont Blanc years. It had been a unique, if not scientifically earth-shattering, time. And it had made him, in a way, one of the fathers of mountaineering. By the 1820s a visit to Chamonix was an accepted part of a wealthy young gentleman's education, while those of a sporting disposition actually climbed the hill itself. From the mid-19th century alpinism became a sport, a skill and, eventually, a mania. Every person who subsequently stood on the summit of an Alp appreciated, and was inspired by, Saussure's envoi to Mont Blanc. As he said, on descending the Col du Géant, he had been 'a neighbour to heaven'.

Alexander von Humboldt (1799–1804)

In 1796, at the age of 27, Alexander von Humboldt was a man of sorrow, acquainted with grief. His mother had just died of breast cancer, and the love of his life, Reinhard von Häften, an infantry subaltern in the Grevenitz Regiment stationed at Bayreuth, had decided to get married. His career as an inspector of Prussian mines was unexciting and although he had been offered promotion the prospect did not appeal. He was a forward-looking man, however, and the future still held promise: he came from an aristocratic family, was highly intelligent and very well connected, counting amongst his friends such luminaries of the European literary scene as Goethe and Schiller. He was a capable surveyor, an admirable organizer and an expert in practically every branch of science. As for love, he had decided he could do without it. 'A man should get used to standing alone early on in his life,' he wrote. 'Isolation has a lot in its favour.' Moreover, following his mother's death he commanded estates producing more than 3,000 thalers per annum, a sum that made him the equivalent of a modern millionaire. He therefore resigned his job in the mines and embarked on what he had always wanted to do: to make a thorough scientific examination of the world beyond Europe.

In 1797 he accepted an offer from Britain's eccentric Lord Bristol to join an expedition to Egypt, but the project collapsed the next year amidst rumours that Napoleon was about to invade the country. Undeterred, he took a post with the French explorer Bougainville, who was planning a five-year circumnavigation that would touch every major landmass on the globe, including the Great Southern Continent that the British had said was unreachable. 'I was busy with magnetic research at the time,' Humboldt wrote, 'so it seemed to me that an expedition to the South Pole might be a lot more use than a trip to Egypt.' Once again he was thwarted by Napoleon's ambitions, this time a war with Austria. Accordingly, he mounted his own expedition to North Africa, accompanied by a French botanist and draughtsman, Aimé Bonpland, who, like him, had been a disappointed member of Bougainville's party. As he explained, 'A man can't just sit down and cry, he's got to do something'. The trip would provide ample opportunity to test the dictum. At Marseilles, the Swedish ship on which he had booked passage to

Algiers failed to materialize. When he bought tickets to Tunis he learned that it was closed to French passengers. He therefore dragged Bonpland on foot over the Pyrenees to Madrid, in the hope of catching a ship to Smyrna. He was well received at the Spanish court and, on the spur of the moment, told the king that he was particularly interested in his American colonies. This was not exactly a lie: the Indies, East or West, had always tempted him. But he was unprepared for the response. Eager to have a Prussian professional increase the output of his gold and silver mines – and perhaps even find new ones – the king ordered him to go there at once.

In June 1799, three months after arriving in Madrid with the vague hope of catching a ride to Turkey, Bonpland and Humboldt were aboard the *Pizarro*, bound for the New World and carrying passports that gave them unfettered access to every corner of the king's domains. It was an extraordinary and unheard-of opportunity. Spain's American possessions stretched from California to Cape Horn; they covered most of South and Central America, a large chunk of North America and practically all the Caribbean islands. Within this area trade was forbidden with any country other than Spain, and foreigners were rarely allowed entry. After 300 years of Spanish occupation only 12 or so expeditions had been dispatched and most of those had been to the coast. Charles-Marie de la Condamine, several decades earlier, had triangulated a small portion of the Andes and travelled down the Amazon, but otherwise the interior was a mystery, offering immense possibilities to a man with a touch of vim and the requisite instruments. Humboldt, who had no less than 40 of the latter, ranging from rain gauges and hygrometers to microscopes and a two-inch 'snuff-box' sextant, considered himself equal to the challenge. Aboard the *Pizarro*, he wrote a letter that amounted to a manifesto of Enlightenment thinking: 'I shall try to find out how the forces of nature interact upon one another and how the geographical environment influences plant and animal life. In other words, I must find out about the unity of nature.'

He and Bonpland were kept busy on the Atlantic crossing. They measured the sea's temperature, analysed its chemistry, and observed strange phenomena, such as a host of jellyfish drifting south at four times the speed of the current. Bonpland examined the specimens they retrieved from the waves, while Humboldt filled his journal with words and pictures. At Tenerife they explored a 12,300-foot, semi-dormant volcano. 'What a fantastic place! What a time we had!' Humboldt wrote. 'We climbed some way down into the crater, perhaps further than any previous scientific traveller. There isn't much danger in the ascent, you just get rather done up by the heat and cold; the sulphurous vapour in the crater burnt holes in our clothes while our hands were frozen numb.' Lower down they found a tree whose 45-foot girth had not, reportedly, altered in the last 400 years. Humboldt was entranced: 'I could almost weep at the prospect of leaving this place.' The *Pizarro* weighed anchor on 25 June, bound for Havana. By the time it was off the

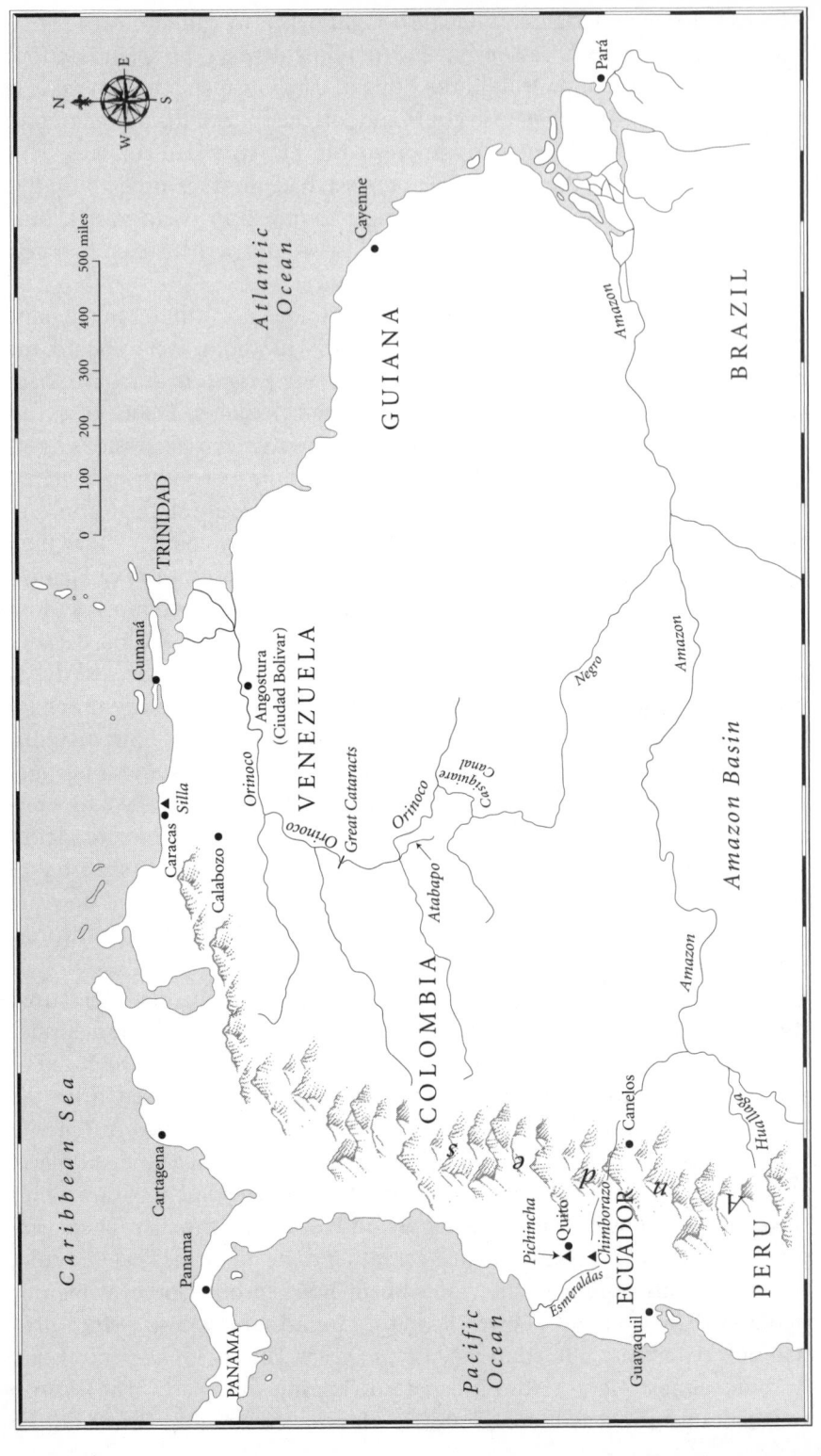

coast of South America, however, it was gripped by an epidemic of typhoid fever. On 14 July, with one man dead, another mad and several more in delirium, Humboldt decided to leave while he was still alive to do so. Two days later he and Bonpland disembarked at the Venezuelan port of Cumaná.

The two scientists were enraptured. 'What a fabulous and extravagant country we're in!' Humboldt wrote to his brother. 'Fantastic plants, electric eels, armadillos, monkeys, parrots: and many, many, real, half-savage Indians ... We've been running around like a couple of mad things; for the first three days we couldn't settle to anything: we'd find one thing, only to abandon it for the next. Bonpland keeps telling me he'll go out of his mind if the wonders don't cease.' For four months they indulged in an orgy of cataloguing and exploration. They measured the magnetic variations caused by an earth-quake; studied an eclipse of the sun; forayed into the rainforest; examined the astonishing guacharo bird, whose breast was equipped with a pad of fat that produced a fine cooking oil; and interviewed a father who had suckled his children with his own breast milk. They learned to dance the samba, listed the varieties of lice to be found in the local women's hair, noted with disapproval the iniquities of the slave system, and goggled at the brilliance of the stars: 'Venus plays the role of the moon here,' Humboldt enthused. 'She shows big, luminous haloes and the most beautiful rainbow colour, even when the air is quite clear and the sky is perfectly blue.' Now and then they suffered a setback – on 27 October Bonpland was concussed by a club-wielding madman, from which he did not fully recover for three months; on 28 October, a very hot day, Humboldt burned his face so badly while observing the heavens that he had to spend two days in bed (with typical thoroughness, he recorded that one of his instruments measured 124° F) – but generally it was a profitable and unforgettable time. When they left on 16 November for the Venezuelan capital, Caracas, they did so with regret.

At Caracas – where they accumulated yet more data and climbed the Silla, at 8,000 feet the highest of the city's surrounding peaks – Humboldt finally outlined their plan of action. They would travel over the *llanos*, the extensive plains of the interior, until they reached the Orinoco. From there they would go upriver to find its undiscovered source. At the same time they would investigate a strange phenomenon that Condamine had reported: a water-way, the Casiquiare, a channel that purportedly connected the Orinoco and the Amazon to produce a river that 'flowed both ways'. He did not enter the *llanos*, however, without making critical comments on the Spanish system of land management, particularly the wholesale destruction of forests to make way for indigo. 'By felling the trees that cover the tops and sides of the mountains,' he wrote, 'men in every climate prepare at once two calamities for future generations: the want of fuel and a scarcity of water.' He also noted that deforestation caused flash floods and eroded the soil. It would be almost 200 years before anyone took his warnings seriously.

Humboldt was impressed by the *llanos*: 'the plains seemed to reach to the sky, and this vast and profound solitude looked like an ocean covered with seaweed'. But he did not enjoy the traverse. The temperature reached 106° F, the mirages were so extreme that two suns rose at dawn and the flat plain swam with illusory mountains, lakes and trees. Once they came across a cattle ranch, whose half-naked peóns rode with lances across the plains to inspect their herds. 'Their food is meat dried in the air and a little salted,' Humboldt recorded, 'and of this even their horses sometimes eat. Always in the saddle, they fancy they cannot make the slightest excursion on foot.' The water was foul and 'we asked in vain for a bowl of milk'.

At the trading station of Calabozo, they found an unexpected source of intellectual refreshment. A local inventor, Señor del Pozo, had read Benjamin Franklin's *Memoirs* and had constructed an electrical apparatus to his own design that was almost as sophisticated as those to be found in Europe. He was delighted to meet men of his own ilk and acceded happily when the foreigners asked if he could help them catch an electric eel. Humboldt had long been fascinated by these creatures, whose bodies, up to nine feet long, contained an organ capable of delivering 650 volts that could paralyse and even kill a man from a distance. Understandably, he had not yet obtained a specimen and, despite offering large sums of money, had been unable to persuade anybody to help him. Señor del Pozo, however, had a solution: they would go fishing with horses.

This barbaric but effective procedure involved driving 30 horses and mules into a pool and keeping them there while the eels elecrocuted them. Humboldt watched in fascination: 'These yellowish and livid eels, resembling large aquatic serpents, swim on the surface of the water and crowd under the bellies of the horses and mules. A contest between animals of such different organisation furnishes a very striking spectacle ... Several horses sink beneath the violence of the invisible strokes, which they receive from all sides in organs the most essential to life, and, stunned by the force and frequency of the shocks, disappear under the water. Others, panting, with mane erect and haggard eyes expressing anguish, raise themselves and endeavour to flee from the storm by which they are overtaken. They are driven back by the Indians into the middle of the water ... In less than five minutes two horses were drowned.' The struggle seemed so unequal that he expected all 30 beasts would die. But the eels could not cope with such a mass of horseflesh. After a while they had discharged their batteries and were harmless. 'The mules and horses appear less frightened,' Humboldt wrote, 'their manes are no longer bristled, and their eyes express less dread. The gymnoti [eels] approach timidly the edge of the marsh, where they are taken by means of small harpoons fastened to long cords.'

At the end of it Humboldt and Bonpland had five eels which they poked, prodded, pulled and, occasionally, stepped upon. 'I do not remember having received from the discharge of a large Leyden jar a more dreadful shock than the one I experienced when I very stupidly placed both my feet on an electric eel that had just been taken out of the water,' Humboldt recorded. 'I was affected for the rest of the day with a violent pain in the knees and almost every joint.' However frequently they put them to the test, the eels did not register on the electrometer and made no impact at all on their magnetic equipment. Dishearteningly, they were later classified as a distant relative of the minnow.

On 5 April the explorers reached the Orinoco, where they hired canoes and crews for the trip upriver. Humboldt was awed by the scale of everything: the river was the size of a lake; the beaches were so extensive that they had their own mirages; the waves were several feet high, like those of the sea. On one island the turtles (today nearly extinct) were so prodigiously abundant that the Indians harvested some 33 million eggs per annum. Further up, they encountered the Great Cataracts, at 40 miles one of the longest rapids in the continent, where the flies were so thick it was hard to breathe and the locals swatted themselves automatically even in their sleep. Different varieties emerged at different times and, as Humboldt wrote wearily, 'we might guess blindfold the hour of the day or night by the hum of the insects, and by their stings'.

Above the Great Cataracts they were in virgin territory. Few white men had entered Venezuela's interior in the three centuries since Spain had claimed it as a colony. The only ones living there now were a handful of missionaries. Nobody had ever written about it, and wild rumours circulated of men with heads in the middle of their chests and eyes in their foreheads. Humboldt and Bonpland entered this *terra incognita* with excitement. Their plan, following the directions of a missionary who had previously made the journey, was to follow the Orinoco to the mouth of its tributary, the Atabapo. At the top of the Atabapo they would make a portage across the watershed to the Negro, tributary to the Amazon, and then take the Casiquiare back to the Orinoco.

The journey, in a 40-foot-long canoe hollowed out of a single tree trunk, was uncomfortable but not particularly dangerous. There was plenty for the scientists to record: trees more than 100 feet tall, a school of freshwater dolphins, a tribe of cannibals whose favourite cut was the palm of a man's hand, immense depths of untouched forest humus, and an extraordinary abundance of flora and fauna. 'The earth is loaded with plants,' Humboldt noted. 'The crocodiles and the boas are masters of the river; the jaguar, the peccary, the tapir, and the monkeys traverse the forest without fear and without danger; there they dwell as in an ancient inheritance.' By 10 May they were at the Casiquiare, where Humboldt was quietly complacent about their achievements. 'We had been confined thirty-six days in a narrow boat, so unstable that it would have been overset by any person rising imprudently from his seat . . . we had suffered severely from the sting of insects . . . we had withstood the insalubrity of the climate; we had passed without accident the great number of falls of water and bars that impede the navigation of the rivers and often render it more dangerous than long voyages by sea. After all we had endured, I may be permitted, perhaps, to speak of the satisfaction we felt in having reached the tributary systems of the Amazon.' There was satisfaction, too, in having reached the channel that everyone believed to be a chimera. Only a year before they had set out, a French geographer had remarked: 'The long supposed connection between the Orinoco and the Amazon is a monstrous error in geography.' Well, it wasn't any longer.

The 12-day journey through the Casiquiare was unpleasant. The humidity was so great that they could not light a fire, the water was foul, and food was so scarce that they were reduced to eating ants. In the overhanging jungle 'we could see the jaguars – large jaguars I may add – up in the trees, because the dense undergrowth prevented them walking along the ground'. Nor did their spirits improve markedly when they reached 'a remote and terrible place called Esmeralda', at the junction of the Casiquiare and the Orinoco. 'By now all of us had reached a stage of desperate hunger and exhaustion,' Humboldt wrote. 'Here the insects are still more cruel and voracious than elsewhere on the Orinoco – Esmeralda gives the traveller the impression of having arrived at the end of the world.'

The return journey down the Orinoco was uneventful – if one excluded their experimental quaffing of a cup of curare, and the discovery of a tribe that ate earth – and on 15 June they were at Angostura (now Ciudad Bolívar), in Guiana. Here they caught typhoid fever and, though Humboldt treated himself successfully with a bitter concoction for which Angostura would later become famous, Bonpland nearly died. It was a month before he was well enough to toil across the *llanos* to the coast. From there the two men caught a ship to Cumaná, where they landed at the end of August (en route being captured by a Nova Scotian privateer, then rescued by the Royal Navy). From Cumaná they sailed for Cuba, and on 19 December 1800 disembarked at Havana, having finally reached the destination for which they had embarked 18 months earlier aboard the *Pizarro*.

Their unplanned excursion had been exceptionally productive. They had covered 1,500 miles and collected 12,000 specimens, many of them new to science. They had mapped a large part of Venezuela's hinterland and had proved the existence of a natural canal linking two major river systems. They had provided Western science with its most thorough study to date of the wonders that South America contained. And, as they had hoped, they had made many observations on the unity of nature, their only depressing discovery being how insignificant a role humankind played in it. 'In that interior part of the New Continent,' Humboldt wrote, 'we almost accustomed ourselves to regard men as not being essential . . . This aspect of animated nature, in which man is nothing, has something in it strange and sad . . . Here in a fertile country adorned with eternal verdure, we seek in vain the traces of the power of man; we seem to be transported into a world different from that which gave us birth.'

Humboldt's new-found humility did not quench his desire for exploration. He filed as much information as he could in Cuba, and despatched it to Europe along with his records of Venezuela – to ensure his findings were not lost he made three copies: one for France, one for Germany and, in case the ships foundered, one that he left in Havana – then arranged a trip via Mexico to the Philippines. Before he departed, however, he learned that Bougainville's much-delayed expedition would at last be leaving France. Thereupon he cancelled his plans and hauled Bonpland on a journey over the Andes to Lima, the capital of Peru, where he hoped to meet members of the French squadron.

They stopped first at Trinidad, where Humboldt was immediately fascinated by the local practice of keeping fireflies in a hollowed-out gourd, pierced with holes, which, when shaken, acted as a lantern. From Trinidad they sailed to Cartagena in Colombia, and then travelled overland to the Ecuadorian capital of Quito. Here they saw a number of interesting peaks, mostly volcanic and by no means dormant. Despite having no mountaineering experience, they went up them. They climbed the 15,672-foot-high Pichincha, its summit a mile-wide crater that flickered ominously with blue flames. They also ascended Chimborazo to an altitude of 19,000 feet. They might even have reached the top had not the ridge they were following been bisected by a 400-foot-deep chasm. As it was, they had stood higher than anyone else on earth, a record that would not be beaten for 30 years.

At Quito they learned that Bougainville would not, after all, be passing by South America. Nevertheless, they continued to Peru, following ancient Inca highways through the Andes, now dipping east to make a quick map of the upper Amazon, now investigating a Peruvian silver mine, now visiting the cell in which the Spanish conquistadores had imprisoned the Inca Atahuallpa for nine months until his subjects had filled the room with gold (after which they had killed him). As they went, they amassed case upon case of botanical and geological specimens. 'The conveyance of these objects, and the minute care they required, occasioned us such embarrassments as would scarcely be conceived, even by those who have travelled the most uncultivated parts of Europe,' Humboldt later wrote. 'Our progress was often retarded by the three-fold necessity of dragging after us, during expeditions of five or six months, twelve, fifteen and sometimes twenty loaded mules, exchanging these animals every eight or ten days, and superintending the Indians who were employed in leading so numerous a caravan.'

On 22 October 1802 they reached Lima, where they spent two months preparing their specimens for shipment to Paris. In their spare time they measured the transit of Mercury and took samples of a bird manure that the Peruvians had long valued as a fertilizer but which was barely known outside South America, enclosing these findings with their others. (When the manure was analysed, and found to be 30 times richer than the standard farmyard variety, it prompted a guano rush by European entrepreneurs.) On

Christmas Eve they sailed via Guayaquil to Mexico,* where again they were indefatigable in their studies. They were drawn irresistibly to the volcano of Jorullo, which less than 50 years before had been a flat field of indigo and sugar cane. In June 1759, however, the area had been hit by 60 days of earthquakes; hardly had the tremors subsided than, on 28 September, four square miles of earth began to rise, producing hundreds of fuming cones, the largest of which was several thousand feet high. Humboldt scaled the world's youngest volcano, saw that it was still alight, and promptly climbed into the crater, descending 250 feet before the smoke and heat drove him back.

From Mexico they went to Havana and then to the United States where, their fame having preceded them, they were wined and dined by President Thomas Jefferson. By this time Humboldt had run through a third of his capital and felt it was time to go home. They landed at Bordeaux on 3 August 1804, and were soon in Paris where they unleashed their findings on the French intelligentsia. Over the course of five years and 6,000 miles they had collected 60,000 plants – at a stroke doubling the number of species known to European science – had calculated the position of hundreds of South American towns and mountains with greater precision than ever before, had gathered rocks from the highest altitude on record, had studied the insides of volcanoes, had taken magnetic, meteorological and oceanographic readings. In fact, they had done so much that it would be decades before the scientific community absorbed the impact of their extraordinary journey. They capped it all by an ancillary trip to the Alps, where Humboldt took further magnetic observations to augment those he had taken in the Andes. That done, the two men went their separate ways.

Humboldt parted sorrowfully with Bonpland, of whom he wrote, 'I could never have hoped to meet again with such a loyal and brave and hard-working friend'. The Frenchman stayed in Paris for ten years as a companion to Napoleon's wife, Josephine, married a young prostitute and, when the marriage failed, returned to South America where he was offered a professorship at Buenos Aires. He moved in with a Brazilian girl and never returned to Europe – thanks largely to nine years' imprisonment in Paraguay, on suspicion of espionage – becoming progressively enfeebled until he died in 1858 at the age of 85.

Humboldt did not abandon his research: between May 1806 and June 1807 he took 6,000 magnetic readings from a cottage outside Berlin and, thanks to a freak appearance of the Northern Lights, was the first person to describe a magnetic storm. In later years he devoted himself exclusively to the journals of his time in South and Central America. His three-volume *Personal Narrative of Travels to the Equinoctial Region* was a bestseller when it was pub-

---

* The journey allowed Humboldt to study the cold Pacific current that now bears his name. He did not seek the honour. In his journal he called it the Peruvian Current, by which name it had always been known.

lished in 1814. He became one of the most widely revered scientists of his time, inspiring many followers, among them a young Englishman named Charles Darwin. His *Political Essay on the Kingdom of New Spain* earned him lucrative directorships that he turned down in favour of writing *Voyage of Humboldt and Bonpland*, whose 35-volumes took him 30 years to perfect and which he self-published at the cost of his remaining inheritance. By 1829, aged 60, he was near destitute, but could not resist an invitation to explore the Urals, which he did within the year. He then began a new tome, *Cosmos, a Vision of the Nature of the World and the Forces of Earth*, in which he tried to unite his discoveries into a single philosophical creed. It followed exactly the same Enlightenment ethos that he had espoused when he first left Spain for South America, and which he had later tried in vain to explain to a missionary in the middle of the jungle: 'The most important result of all thoughtful exploration ... is to recognise in the apparent confusion and opulence of nature a quintessential unity – to study each detail thoroughly yet never be defeated by the contradictions of a mass of fact, to remember the elevated destiny of homo sapiens and thereby to grasp the spirit of nature, its essential meaning which lies concealed under a blanket of multifarious manifestations.'

The first volume came out in 1845 and the fourth in 1858, by which time he was receiving 3,000 letters per annum and answering, personally, 2,000 of them. Eventually he had to place a notice in the press, asking his fans to give him 'a little rest and spare time for my own work, at a time when my physical and intellectual powers are anyway decreasing'. He was 85 pages into the fifth volume when he died, aged 90, on 6 May 1859. Perhaps it was as well he did not finish it. In the very year of Humboldt's death Charles Darwin published his revolutionary *On the Origin of Species*, a work that would shatter the Enlightenment dream of uniting man and Nature within a perfectible, orderly system.

The Great Trigonometrical Survey (1800–66)

In 1800 Britain wanted to know two things about India. First, and rather basically, it wanted to know how big it was; second, and more abstrusely, it wanted to know if its north–south curvature differed from that of the northern hemisphere, a calculation that would allow scientists to determine the shape of the earth. It had already been confirmed by Newton, Condamine and others that the planet bulged outwards at the equator. But it was still a matter of conjecture whether the globe was a mirror-image either side of the equator or whether, as some suspected, it was flatter on the top than at the bottom. India, rather than Africa or America, was chosen because it was mostly under British rule. And William Lambton was selected for the job because he seemed to have nothing better to do.

An amiable, self-effacing man with a talent for mathematics, Lambton had one goal in life: to triangulate. The theory of triangulation is relatively simple: one measures a baseline, ascertains its position by the stars, then takes sightings with a theodolite from either end of the line to a third position, thus creating a triangle whose angles are known and allowing one to calculate the length of its sides by trigonometry. The first triangle having been established, it can be used to create second and third triangles without the need for a new baseline; and from these spring myriad further triangles. The resulting grid provides a framework from which cartographers can produce accurate maps. At the same time, if regular readings have been taken, the grid can also reveal the terrestrial length between astronomical degrees which, when compared with other surveys, can measure the curvature of the planet. With the necessary maths and a set of logarithmic tables, it is a time-consuming but reasonably straightforward business.

In practice, however, triangulation is beset with difficulties. The baseline has to be measured with impeccable precision, for the smallest error will be repeated and multiplied over succeeding triangles; the theodolite must be on firm, level ground and set to a true vertical; and there must be a clear view from either end of the baseline to the third point of the triangle. If, however, one is in a cold climate where the precalibrated steel chain used for measuring the baseline does not expand and contract, and if one is in a region with high mountains and clear skies, some of these difficulties are diminished. In 1800 Lambton was surveying just such a landscape – New Brunswick – when the call came for him to go to India.

Lambton arrived in 1802, with all the necessary gear. He had a zenith sector for astronomical observations (so large that it required 14 men to carry it); a precalibrated chain 100 feet long for measuring his baseline; trestles to support his chain, capstans to tension it, wooden boxes to contain it and brass wires to ensure that it remained level. He also had the Great Theodolite, a half-ton contraption of metal, glass and wood that was the largest portable example of its kind in the world. He employed a team of mathematicians to assist in the calculations, a herd of camels, elephants and oxen to carry the supplies, and a small army of porters to manhandle the instruments over the terrain. Thus equipped, Lambton measured two seven-mile baselines at Bangalore and Madras and began to triangulate the sub-continent.

From the start he was bedevilled by the climate, which caused his chain to expand and contract unpredictably. No sooner had he solved that problem than new ones arose. Working his way north, he battled through forests, jungles and plains, none of which gave him a clear view of his continually desired third point. Trees were felled and houses knocked down to give a path through which he could see the flagmen he sent ahead. All too often, though, it took weeks for the flagmen to reach their position and sometimes they did not reach it at all, having been eaten by tigers. Lambton and his fellow Europeans were crippled by malaria and nameless fevers that forced them repeatedly to cancel operations. And then there was the monsoon, which swelled rivers and sometimes stranded forward elements for weeks on little, foodless hillocks. Even when the weather was good, unforeseen disasters happened. In 1808, in the Kaveri delta, for example, Lambton chose the 217-foot-high Rajarajeshwara temple as a suitable vantage point from which to take his measurements. But as the Great Theodolite was being hauled into position, the pulley slipped and the carefully calibrated instrument smashed into the temple's 1,000-year-old sandstone flanks. The temple was unscathed, but the theodolite was ruined. Lambton retired to his tent where, over the course of six sweat-soaked weeks, he disassembled his precious instrument, pulled it back into shape and, with the aid of tiny wooden hammers, straightened its bent components. He was pleased with the result, but ordered a replacement nevertheless. It took a year and £650 of Lambton's own money before it arrived from England.

The Great Trigonometrical Survey (to give it its official name) ground slowly through India, sprouting branches of triangles as it did so. In the outside world great events came and went: the shelling of Washington, the introduction of gas lighting, Waterloo, the Luddite uprising, the Congress of Vienna, the Peterloo Massacre, the liberation of South America. Members of the Survey came and went too. In 1816 a Lieutenant James Garling took a party west through Hyderabad. One of his assistants died three years later,

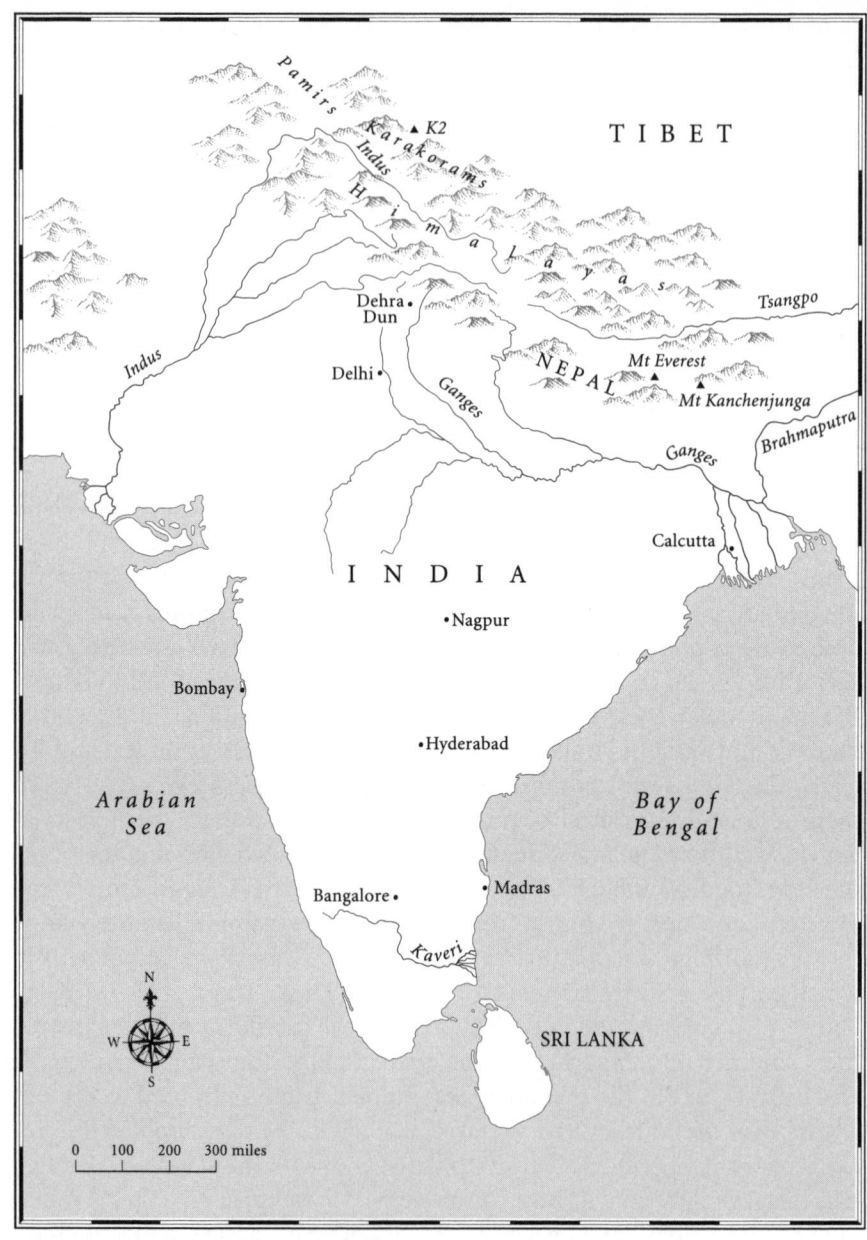

and Garling himself died in 1820. A man by the name of Conner was sent to replace him, but he had not been in Hyderabad a month before he too died. Conner was succeeded by Young, who lasted only two seasons, dying in July 1823. Crisp took over from Young and then, in 1827, the exhausted Crisp handed the job to Webb. In 1829 Webb returned to England on sick leave. And so it continued. Oblivious to it all, Lambton marched on until, in January 1823, when he was 40 miles south of Nagpur and had just sent a party to triangulate the territory west to Bombay, he too died, aged 70. The Great Trigonometrical Survey continued its juggernaut progress under the leadership of George Everest.

Lieutenant G. Everest (pronounced Eve-rest, as in Adam and Eve) was a strong-willed and irritable martinet. As Lambton's second-in-command, he had a full appreciation of the difficulties involved in triangulating India and had come up with several means whereby it could be made easier. He took advantage of the dusk hours, when refraction raised hidden highpoints above the horizon, and he used men with lamps to make those highpoints discernible. Unlike Lambton, who had 'gone native' (or at least semi-native), and whose many mixed-blood children had accompanied the survey, Everest intended to finish the job with true, scientific British grit. In the still problematical Hyderabad he lost 15 men in one season. Again and again he had to take a year off in Britain or South Africa to recover from malaria. But he always returned, crushing every impediment underfoot as he drove his mission onwards.

The Chartists, the 1848 Revolutions and the Crimean War all passed unnoticed as Everest hauled the Great Theodolite northwards. When no highpoints were available he built them – great towers of brick that dominated the Ganges plain. In Calcutta, teams of mathematicians were employed to elucidate his more difficult calculations. Eventually, in 1834, he reached the top of India. From his last vantage point, above the hill station of Dehra Dun, he saw a range of towering peaks – the Himalayas. He went no further, because the mountains lay in Nepal, which was then closed to Britain. And, his task being at an end, he didn't much care about them.

But other people did. Various hardy officers sighted a large mountain that they thought might be the highest in the world. They also sighted two other mountains which might be just as high. Uncertain how to name them, and learning that they were part of the Karakorams, they gave them the appellation K. K_1 was later discovered to have a name – Kanchenjunga – but K_2, which at 28,168 feet was slightly higher than K_1, remained just a letter and a number. As for the very highest peak (standing approximately 29,000 feet above sea level) they rejected the Nepali 'Sagarmatha', the Tibetan 'Chomolungma' and the Chinese 'Qomolangma'. Instead, one of Everest's surveyors decided to name it after his employer.

Everest did not complain. As leader of the 19th century's greatest cartographical expedition, he maybe felt it was his due. He grew a voluminous beard and moustache, posed grumpily for the photographers who sought to immortalize him and died in 1866, leaving a name that would become associated with some of mountaineering's greatest feats of endurance and that – perhaps appropriately for such a stickler to detail – has been mispronounced ever since.

Meriwether Lewis and William Clark (1803–6)

On 4 March 1801 Thomas Jefferson became the third president of the United States. The country he governed was not populous, containing some 5,300,000 inhabitants (a fifth of them slaves), but it was large, running down the Atlantic seaboard from the Great Lakes almost to the Gulf of Mexico, bounded on the west by the River Mississippi. Jefferson wanted to make it larger still – wanted, in fact, to create a nation that occupied as much of the continent as possible. To the north his plans were blocked by the British, whose Canadian territories already stretched from the Atlantic to the Pacific. To the south and west, however, there was scope for expansion. Acquiring the colony of Louisiana – an ill-defined territory stretching north from the Gulf of Mexico to the watersheds of the Mississippi and Missouri, owned theoretically by France – was a simple matter. Its distance from Europe, at a time when France was already planning further conquests, made its defence impracticable; and Napoleon had no qualms in selling it to the States, which he did in 1803 for the price of 60 million francs. A more difficult question was how to take the west.

With the exception of California, the region between the Pacific and the Mississippi was virtually unexplored. Nobody knew who lived there, what the terrain was like, or how one might best approach it. Had the States been a developed nation, the problem might have been simpler. As it was, communications were poor even within the settled areas. Many rivers had neither bridges nor ferries. Roads were appalling, limited in number – there were only four across the whole range of the Appalachian Mountains – and in many places nonexistent. It took six weeks for a letter to make its way from the Mississippi to the Atlantic; for anything larger the journey was two months or more. Just traversing the known territory was so troublesome that one can only admire Jefferson's foresight in insisting that the unknown areas west of the Mississippi be brought under US control.

Central to his ambition – as with so many grand geographic plans of the time – was the prospect of finding a short-cut to the Far East. For centuries Europe had sent explorers in search of the North-West Passage, a seaway that was supposed to run through the Arctic. Jefferson, however, envisaged a fresh-water solution. His inspiration came from the deeds of the Scottish explorer

Alexander Mackenzie, who had followed the river that now bears his name from Canada's Lake Athabasca to the Arctic Ocean, and in 1793 had found a pass through the Rockies that might serve as a trade route between east and west. Jefferson's hope was that a waterway could be discovered between the Mississippi and the Rockies south of Canada, from where, if a portage like Mackenzie's could be found, the US would have its own passage to the Pacific. In 1803 he sent his personal secretary, Meriwether Lewis, to find it.

For a president's secretary Lewis was remarkably untutored. Born in 1774, he knew nothing about most branches of science and had to endure an apprenticeship with the Philosophical Society of America before he learned how to handle a sextant or make a map. Scholarship, however, was not high on Jefferson's list of priorities. He needed a man with wilderness skills and the natural authority to take a party of adventurers safely to the coast and back. Lewis, who had military experience, possessed in Jefferson's opinion 'the firmness of constitution & character, prudence, habits adapted to the woods, & a familiarity with the Indian manners & character, requisite for this undertaking'. For his second-in-command Lewis chose an ex-army officer and friend named William Clark (accompanied by his black slave, York), and together the two men picked a select band of nine volunteers who were sworn into the army, two being given the rank of sergeant. The expedition would swell in number to 45, but these 12 men (including Lewis, Clark and York) were at its heart. The only ones considered worthy of trust, and the only ones allowed to carry firearms, they were dubbed the 'Corps of Discovery'.

The Corps left Clarksville on the Ohio River on 26 October 1803 aboard two pirogues, flat-bottomed but sturdy vessels that could sail into the wind, accompanied by a number of smaller canoes. They carried a swivel cannon, the latest US issue flintlock rifles – .54 calibre, muzzle-loading, with a 33-inch barrel, accurate to 100 yards, and capable of two shots per minute – plus numerous trade goods that included beads, knives, fishing gear and three dozen tomahawks made to Lewis's specification by blacksmiths at the military depot of Harper's Ferry. The same blacksmiths also constructed – again to Lewis's design – the iron frame of a collapsible boat, nicknamed the *Experiment*, that he intended for use should they encounter a portage that was too great for the pirogues. Food was limited, for they expected to be able to collect provisions during the early stages and then shoot game as they went, but they took a good stock of medicines and all the surveying equipment necessary for charting their position in the wilderness. They also carried a list of queries from the American Philosophical Society regarding the Indians beyond the Mississippi. Some were sensible, some were not. What time did they get up? How fast were their pulses in the morning, midday and evening? Did they bathe, did they drink and did they sacrifice animals? Were they the lost tribe of Israel? (Lewis thought this far-fetched, favouring with Jefferson the theory that they were a lost tribe of Welshmen.)

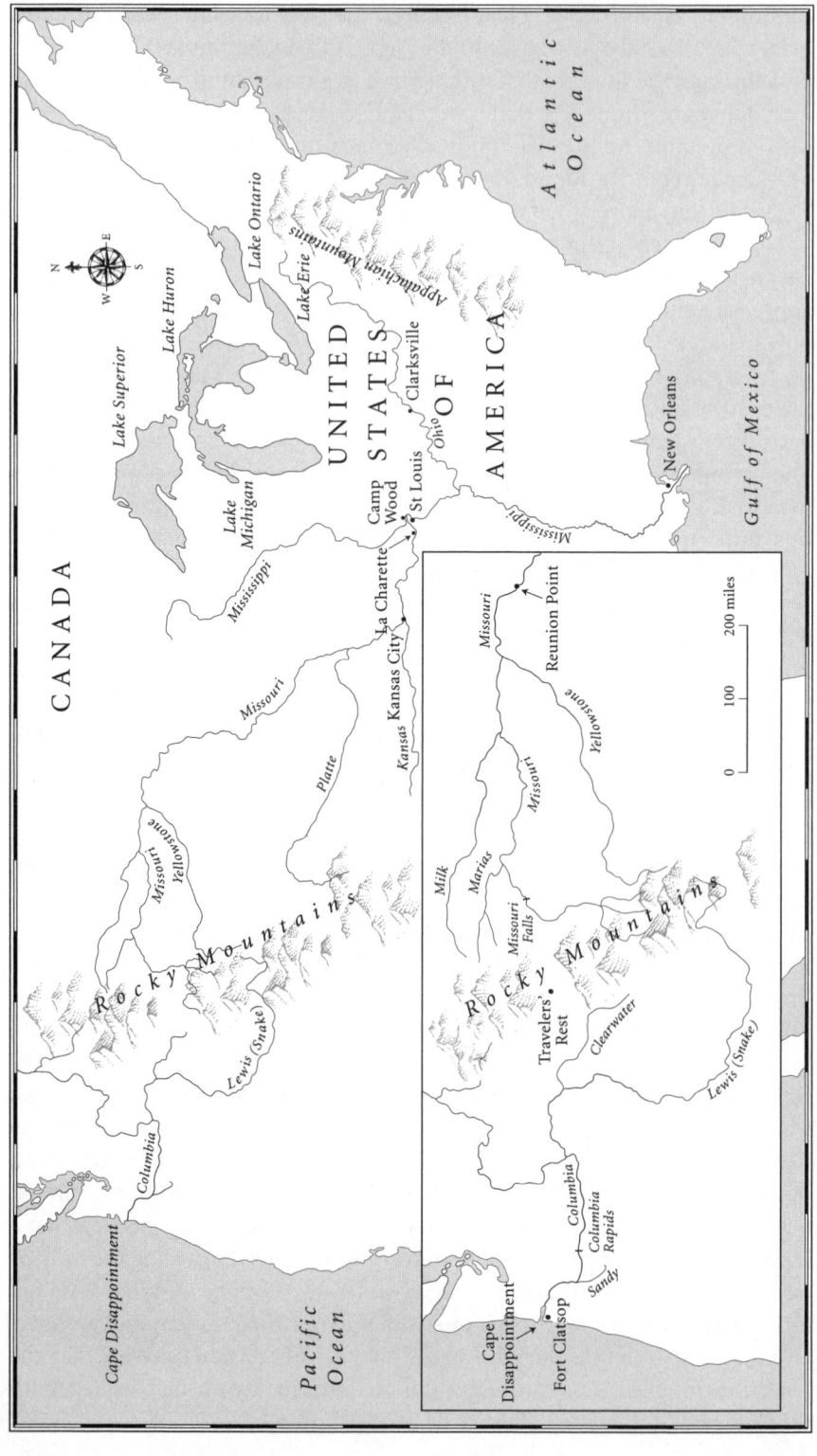

From Clarksville the expedition went down the Ohio to the Mississippi, where they travelled upstream and spent their first winter at Camp Wood, just north of St Louis at the confluence of the Mississippi and the Missouri. From here, when the weather improved the following spring, they intended to follow the Missouri west to its source in the Rockies. They began their long journey on 21 May, their vessels laden with men, equipment, food (mostly flour, salt pork and corn), 120 gallons of whisky and the skeleton of Lewis's boat, the *Experiment*. Four days later they passed La Charette, the last white settlement on the river, and thereafter they were on their own.

On 26 June they arrived at the mouth of the Kansas, where they spent four days on the site of present-day Kansas City. Clark, even less tutored than Lewis, described the area as 'verry fine', albeit 'the waters of the Kansas is verry disigreeably tasted to me'. Only 400 miles into their journey they were already suffering the effects of a poor, vegetable-free diet. On 17 June Clark had written, 'The party is much afflicted with Boils and Several have the Decissentary, which I contribute to the water which is muddy'. On the 18th he added that several more 'had the Disentary, and two thirds of them with ulsers or Boils, Some with 8 or 10 of those Tumers'. The party was also showing signs of indiscipline. Two men were accused of stealing whisky, and another committed the crime of falling asleep on night watch. Lewis and Clark responded with severity: the drunkards received 100 and 50 lashes respectively; the lax sentinel got 100 lashes each day for four days.

There was one overriding reason why keeping watch was so important: the expedition's arsenal. If it should fall into the hands of the Indians it would disrupt the local balance of power and hinder the States' future control of the region. But their precautions were wasted: the Indians were hunting buffalo on the plains, and it was not until 2 August that the expedition met the first of them. Lewis delivered a long speech, explaining that the French and the Spanish would soon be gone and that henceforth their 'only father' was the President of the United States. His harangue mixed promises of trade if they were good with threats of fire and brimstone if they were bad, and was followed by the distribution of one bottle of whisky, a few odds and ends, and medals bearing either the likeness of their new father or, more prosaically, the image of a comb. The gifts did not match Lewis's description of the bounties that his country had to offer; nevertheless, as Clark noted, 'These people express great Satisfaction at the Speech Delivered'.

Less satisfactory, during the following weeks, was the state of the Corps. One man deserted on 4 August and was only brought back after a fortnight, whereupon he was stripped of his right to hold a firearm and was demoted to the status of hired help. He was also given a punishment of some 500 lashes, being forced to run the gauntlet four times, each member of the company giving him nine blows as he passed. Hardly had the deserter received his dues than a sergeant died of what Clark called 'Bilose Chorlick' but was probably a ruptured appendix. In the democratic spirit of their new country, Lewis did not appoint a replacement but invited the Corps to elect one. This they did on 22 August. Four days later another man vanished on a hunting expedition, not to be found, near starving, until 11 September. He had walked up the Missouri in search of the boats that were, in fact, downriver. His ammunition exhausted, he had lived the last two weeks on a diet of grapes and plums.

On 2 August they saw their first coyote; on the 23rd they killed their first buffalo; and on the 27th they met their first Sioux, a powerful Indian tribe that controlled the river and were notorious for barring access to white traders. Despite their warlike reputation, Lewis and Clark found the Sioux to be a fine, well-built people who were very happy to accept their medals and be presented with a US flag. That they were a particularly peaceful branch of the Sioux they did not know; nor did the Sioux realize that their acceptance of the flag implied some fealty to the distant white father whose face appeared on the medals. The two sides parted, content in their ignorance.

By 16 September Lewis and Clark had discovered a number of animals new to science and were in an area of the plains where game abounded in quantities beyond their imagination. 'This scenery already rich and pleasing', Lewis wrote, 'was still farther hightened by immence herds of Buffaloe deer Elk an antelopes which we saw in every direction feeding on the hills and plains. I do not think I exaggerate when I estimated the number of Buffaloes which could be comprehended at one view to amount to 3000.' Further on, the idyll disintegrated when they met a new tribe of Sioux whose temperament was not as placid as the first. When the expedition's gifts proved insufficient they became threatening and tried to haul one of the pirogues ashore. Lewis loaded the cannon and was prepared to fire. The crisis was dispelled when the Sioux chieftain ordered his warriors away; but for the next two days relations between the two sides were uneasy. They parted on 29 September, after yet another stand-off involving the cannon and the pirogue, tempers hot but no blood having been shed.

In October, passing through North Dakota, they noted that the Indians were so impressed by the white men's power that they offered them their wives in the hope of gaining some of their magic.* They had, however, already gained an acquaintance with this dubious magic: from French traders they had contracted venereal disease (which they passed back to Lewis's men); whole villages were still empty after a smallpox epidemic in 1780; and they were unimpressed when it came to Lewis's whisky, being 'surprised that their father should present to them a liquor which would make them act like fools'.

---

* It was Clark's black slave, York, who was deemed to possess the greatest power. One husband went so far as to guard the door while York was inside with his wife. Throughout the journey he was considered a far greater marvel than the white men with their meagre gifts.

On the 13th yet another man was arraigned for mutiny (or perhaps just discontent). He was dropped from the Corps and given 75 lashes. In a telling example of noble savagery, the Indians protested – as the South Pacific Islanders did when Cook ordered his men to be flogged – explaining to Clark that while they understood the need to make an example, they preferred death to humiliation: as a nation they did not even strike their children. Lewis paid them little attention. He and his men – who sat in jury on every offender's trial and decided the penalty – seem to have been by nature floggers.

They spent that winter with the Mandan tribe, some 100 miles from the Canadian border. The Mandans were friendly and seemed delighted to have the white men stay with them. They were disappointed at the scale of Lewis's gifts, but proved receptive to his speech, one of their leaders going so far as to say he might visit Washington in the spring to meet the 'great father'. Soon, however, Lewis was lost in the intricacies of Indian diplomacy. On visiting a nearby tribe, the Hidatsas, his attempts to persuade them to live peaceably with their neighbours produced only puzzlement. They didn't like his claim that he belonged to a nation of great warriors, and they didn't like the meagreness of his presents. When two other neighbours, a tribe of Sioux and a tribe of Arikaras, joined forces to raid the Mandans, Lewis's reaction confused the Indians still further. He advocated a counterstrike in which his men would join the Mandans to chase down the raiders. The Mandans were baffled. At one moment he preached peace, at the next he was advocating war. They did not support his move and let it be understood that in the future they would rather he did not meddle in their affairs.

Despite his firepower, Lewis had yet to gain influence: for all his speeches and flag-waving, the Indians beyond the Missouri were loyal to those who produced the goods. Lewis, who had been charged with travelling to the Pacific and back, had been niggardly with his gifts – understandably, given the distance he expected to cover and the small budget he had been allotted. But it had not helped his cause. Why should the Indians bother with the US when they could deal with Canadians, whose reputation was well established and who attached no moral qualifications to their commerce? Lewis met two of these traders in October 1804. Their names were François-Antoine Larocque and Charles Mackenzie, who had come 150 miles to do business with the Missouri Indians. The officers greeted them with as much warmth as their position allowed – which is to say that Lewis spent a whole day mending the French-speaking Larocque's compass, but was distant towards his companion, Mackenzie, a Scot. As Mackenzie wrote, 'Mr. Larocque and I ... lived contentedly and became intimate with the gentlemen of the American expedition, who on all occasions seemed happy to see us, and always treated us with civility and kindness ... It is true, Captain Lewis could not make himself agreeable to us. He could speak fluently and learnedly on all subjects, but his inveterate disposition against the British stained, at least in our eyes, all his eloquence.' More profitable from Lewis's point of view was the arrival of a French hunter named Toussaint Charbonneau, who offered his services as interpreter. Hitherto the expedition had got by with sign language, and Charbonneau, who could not speak English, was not an obvious asset. However, his 15-year-old wife Sacagawea was. Born near the source of the Missouri, she had been captured by marauding Hidatsas before being acquired by Charbonneau as the result of a bet. She and Charbonneau shared Hidatsa; Charbonneau and a member of the Corps shared French; and in this tortuous way communication could be established. That she was a Shoshone, a tribe whose friendship and services Lewis would need if he were to cross the Rockies, clinched the deal. They were hired at once.

That winter, the two captains prepared for Jefferson a summary of their discoveries. They waxed lyrical on the fertility of the land, which had topsoil up to 20 feet deep. They described 72 different tribes, from the warlike Sioux ('the vilest miscreants of the savage race ... the pirates of the Missouri'), to the Mandans ('the most friendly, well-disposed Indians'). They recommended the installation of garrisons, both to maintain peace and to dissuade British traders. They drew maps of the regions they had traversed. And, to give the expedition a scientific gloss, they sent home 108 botanical specimens, numerous animal skins and skeletons (including five live birds and a prairie dog), plus an eclectic assortment of 64 mineral samples ranging from a handful of Missouri pebbles, and a pint of its water, to lead ore, pumice and fossils. They also appended an outline of the country ahead, as gleaned from descriptions given by the Indians: it was rich in furs, watered by numerous rivers and, some 540 miles from their present position, the Missouri split into three branches, the northernmost of which was navigable 'to the foot of a chain of high mountains, being the ridge that divides the waters of the Atlantic from those of the Pacific Ocean'. Apparently, it was but half a day's journey to cross the ridge; and on the other side lay a navigable river (the Columbia) that flowed west. Moreover, the land to the west of the mountains was said to be as fertile as that to the east. Lewis was excited – and even more so was Jefferson when he received the report – to think that a transcontinental passage really did exist.

The expedition continued upriver, finding everything as the Indians had described, until on 26 May they caught their first glimpse of the Rockies. The triumph was offset by weariness. They had encountered no great natural hazard, had not crossed a desert or an ice-cap, had never been far from human contact and had rarely been short of food. By the standards of global exploration they had an easy time. Indeed, they were explorers mostly on paper, for the areas they visited were already known to Canadian traders. But the journey had been hard, and the crossing of new ground had been a strain. Since leaving the Mandans they had been attacked by grizzly bears, had nearly lost one of their pirogues in a storm, and could never be sure that their guns could hold off a serious attack in numbers. Moreover, they were in poor health, suffering from dysentery, mild scurvy and, in many cases, syphilis.

A week later, the Missouri was joined from the north by another river of almost equal size and depth. The Indians had made no mention of this fork. Which of the two should they follow? Most of the men were convinced that the northernmost river was the Missouri, but Lewis and Clark were uncertain. There was one way to tell. When describing the Missouri the Indians had mentioned a mighty cascade, not far from their present position. Lewis therefore set out on foot to scout the southern branch. On 13 June he was proved correct when he sighted rising above the plains a column of spray from which came 'a roaring too termendious to be mistaken for any cause short of the great falls of the Missouri'. He took 700 words to describe what he summarized as 'the grandest sight I ever beheld ... *sublimely grand*', and even then felt he had not done it justice. Which was just as well, for the next day he met a second fall that produced further rhapsodies. '[I] was again presented by one of the most beautifull objects in nature', a perpendicular cascade 50 feet high that stretched a quarter of a mile from side to side of the river. 'I now thought that if a skillfull painter had been asked to make a beautifull cascade that he would most probably have presented the precise immage of this one.' There were more falls, five in total, interspersed with rapids that covered a stretch of 12 miles. Hurrying back to camp, Lewis led the others to this natural marvel.

Leaving the pirogues at the bottom of the falls with a cache of supplies for the return journey, they dragged the smaller canoes overland to the top of the cascade. This was precisely the point where Lewis had anticipated his *Experiment* would come in handy. Sure enough, the frame fitted together perfectly, and once it had been covered with hides Lewis declared that his design 'in every rispect completely answers my most sanguine expectation'. But it was impossible to make the boat watertight. They had no pitch, and the makeshift substitute, created by mixing charcoal with tallow and beeswax, did not adhere to the hides. Lewis thought he knew how to fix it – by sewing the hides together with a different needle and by leaving the hair on to provide a key for the beeswax 'pitch' – but they had already spent a fortnight on the boat and could not spare the time. 'Mortifyed', Lewis left his pet project on the bank, and turned instead to a nearby stand of cottonwoods, from which they fashioned two dugouts, three feet wide and about 30 feet long. They were neither as light nor as capacious as the *Experiment*, but they served the purpose.

That autumn they encountered the Shoshone, from whom, thanks to Sacagawea (who, it transpired, was the long-lost sister of the Shoshone chief), they bought horses to carry them over the mountains. It was a longer journey than they had anticipated: the western rivers were too tumultuous for canoes and passed through hills too steep for overland travel, so they were forced to make a 160-mile detour to the south. The weather was freezing, there was little game to be had, the horses stumbled and slipped, and their food began to run out. On 22 September 1805, after not the half-day journey they had expected but ten days' hard slog during which they 'suffered everything Cold, Hunger & Fatigue could impart . . . [and felt] the Keenest Anxiety . . . for the fate of [our] Expedition in which our whole Souls were embarked', they reached the villages of the Nez Percé, or Pierced Nose, Indians. 'The pleasure I now felt in having triumphed over the rocky Mountains and descending once more to a level and fertile country where there was every rational hope of finding a comfortable subsistence for myself and party can be more readily conceived than expressed,' Lewis wrote.

The Nez Percé were welcoming, but their food – consisting mainly of fish and roots – upset the Americans' stomachs. For several days the party was gripped by dysentery. Clark reported vividly that on 4 October 'Capt. Lewis & my Self eate a supper of roots boiled, which filled us So full of wind, that we were Scercely able to Breathe all night felt the effects of it'. As they continued west, to the limits of Nez Percé territory, the effort of staying on their horses was more than several members of the Corps could manage. They dismounted and lay on the ground, clutching their stomachs until the crisis had passed. Lewis himself spent the best part of a fortnight 'sick feeble & emaciated' before he regained his strength. Nevertheless, by 13 October they had fashioned some dugouts and, having secured the promise of the Nez Percé to look after their horses until they returned, were travelling down the River Clearwater, which soon led to the Columbia itself.

For some time Lewis had been aware that the Columbia would be trouble-some. He knew the position of the Pacific thanks to previous explorers, among them Britain's Captain George Vancouver who in 1762 had charted much of the north-west coast, including the mouth of the Columbia. He also knew, thanks to his own observations, the position of the Rockies. Between the two, there was not space for a slow-moving river such as the Missouri. The Columbia, therefore, had to be steep and hazardous, at least in its early stages. This was proved on 23 October when they encountered a series of violent rapids, 55 miles long and in places flanked by cliffs 3,000 feet high. They were so hazardous that even the local Indians, who were expert canoeists, did not dare attempt them. The Americans were too tired to care. While Lewis took the rifles, ammunition, trade goods and other valuables over dry ground, the rest of the Corps tried the rapids. The Indians lined the banks, expecting the white men to drown, but to their astonishment the dugouts emerged intact on the other side. On 2 November the expedition reached the Sandy River, the furthest Vancouver's men had penetrated upstream, and four days later Clark was able to write in his journal, 'Ocian in view! O! the joy.' By his calculations they had travelled 4,142 miles from the mouth of the Missouri. Their travails were not quite at an end: for more than a week they were pinned by bad weather on the shores of the Columbia estuary, and it was not until 18 November that they were able to put a full-stop to their transcontinental odyssey. They did so on a tree. At their westernmost point, with the Pacific Ocean slapping against the rocks, Lewis and Clark carved their names, followed by the immortal words, 'By Land from the U. States in 1804 & 1805'.

The tree stood on the coast of what Lewis dubbed Cape Disappointment, a name that reflected less a sense of failure than one of foreboding. Lewis had hoped to find a trading station near the Columbia – or if not a station then at least white traders – where he and his men could buy food and gifts for the return journey. In anticipation, Jefferson had given him a letter of credit, redeemable on the US Government. But there was nobody to take his credit. Although the Columbia was visited by traders, they stayed only from April to October and did not establish a land presence, preferring to conduct business aboard ship. The Corps of Discovery had therefore to rely on their diminishing supply of trade goods to see them home.

They spent that winter at Fort Clatsop, named after the Indians who lived in the vicinity and who seemed reasonably friendly, if tough bargainers and occasional pilferers. The dark months were easy but dull. Their diet consisted entirely of elk, and they spent their time sewing moccasins, sleeping with Indian women – syphilis again manifested itself – and keeping half-hearted guard against the Clatsops. The main diversion came in January when they heard that a whale was stranded on a beach to the south. Clark went with 11 men to examine it, taking also Sacagawea, who insisted forcefully that she be included because, as she explained, it was not only the whites who were interested in exploration. 'The Indian woman was very impotunate to be permited to go, and was therefore indulged,' Lewis wrote. 'She observed that she had traveled a long way with us to see the great waters, and now that monstrous fish was also to be seen, she thought it very hard that she could not be permitted to see either.' The carcase had already been stripped by the time they got there, but Clark was able to buy 300 pounds of blubber and several gallons of oil: 'We prize it highly, and thank the hand of providence for directing the whale to us, and think him much more kind to us than he was to jona.'

The Corps left Fort Clatsop on 23 March 1806. Their trade goods were near exhausted, consisting of 11 'robes' (five of which were made out of a flag), an artillery officer's coat and hat, plus a length of ribbon. As for their trinkets, 'Two handkercheifs would not contain all the small articles of merchandize which we possess.' They were too impoverished to buy a canoe for the return trip up the Columbia so, reluctantly, they stole one. It carried them as far as the rapids, whereupon they bought horses – at an extortionate price – and made their way to the Nez Percé settlements. Here they found themselves financially embarrassed. Without the means to pay for their food, Clark set up surgery, accepting payment in kind for medical treatment. He had very few drugs, and those he dispensed were usually placebos. He did, however, have a doctor's authority, and his patients seemed on the whole to appreciate his ministrations. He scored a notable success when he constructed a steam bath with which he cured a chief who was paralysed from the neck down. His medical fees, coupled with the sale of the brass buttons from their jackets, kept the Corps fed for several months.

However impressive Clark's doctoring, the expedition could not stay with the Nez Percé indefinitely. They wanted to get home that year, and to do so they had to cross the Rockies and reach the Missouri before it froze. But it had been a hard winter, and by June, when the pass would normally have been clear, the Rockies were still covered with snow. The Nez Percé told the white men to wait a bit – and then a bit longer, until Lewis's patience snapped. They all dreaded 'the Rocky Mountain, where hungar and cold in their most rigorous forms assail the waried traveller; not any of us have yet forgotten our sufferings in those mountains in September last, and I think it probable we never shall.' Regardless, Lewis attempted the crossing, first unassisted and then, having been driven back by the snow, with Nez Percé guides. They reached the other side, at a point they called Travelers' Rest, on 30 June. The traverse was shorter than the one out – 156 miles in six days – and the men and horses were in considerably better condition, a fact that Lewis credited entirely to the skill of his guides.

At this point Lewis could have led his men safely and swiftly to the Missouri. But he chose to do a bit more exploring. Following a plan they had hatched at Fort Clatsop, he and Clark divided the Corps. Lewis would take nine men overland on a short-cut to the head of the Missouri Falls; thereupon three of his party would retrieve the cache beneath the *Experiment* and carry the supplies to the bottom of the falls. Lewis, meanwhile, would lead the others on another overland trek to investigate the Marias River – that mysterious northern offshoot of the Missouri they had encountered the previous May – before returning to the base of the falls. As for Clark, he would take a party overland to the head of the Missouri. Here one segment would proceed downriver to the falls to meet Lewis's men, while he himself would cross the watershed to the Yellowstone River and follow it as far as the Missouri where, it was agreed, all parties would meet.

It was a complicated and dangerous plan, and an unnecessary one too: they had fulfilled their instructions to cross the continent; they were not required to undertake additional journeys; and the smaller groups were at far greater risk from hostile Indians than if the Corps had stayed together. But Lewis and Clark were convinced it was worthwhile. If Clark went down the Yellowstone he would open whole new areas to American commerce. And if Lewis went north up the Marias he might dissuade a tribe of Indians, the Blackfeet, from trading with the British and bring them within the fatherly fold of Washington. Clark's expedition was a success. Lewis's was not. He did meet the Blackfeet, but they were too numerous and too well-armed for his liking. A group of outriders stole his horses and, for the first time, the white men's temper got the better of them. One of Lewis's men stabbed an Indian in the heart, and Lewis shot another in the stomach –

which did not stop the injured Blackfoot levelling his musket. 'I felt the wind of his bullet very distinctly,' Lewis recorded. In the knowledge that there were several hundred Blackfeet hunting buffalo beyond the horizon, Lewis and his men ran for the Missouri falls.

They rejoined their own men and those of Clark, resurrected the pirogues at the bottom of the falls, and sped down the Missouri, where they rejoined Clark's Yellowstone expedition on 12 August. (The circumstances were uncomfortable: while hunting, one of Lewis's men mistook him for a deer and shot him through the buttocks.) Two days later they were with the Mandans, who were as friendly as before but gave them the depressing news that the region was in a state of war. All Lewis's talk of peace had come to nothing. He did, however, with exceptional difficulty, persuade one chief to accompany them to St Louis, from where he would be escorted to Washington and then returned to his home.

Their journey was near its end. As they continued downriver, they encountered small parties of trappers heading north in search of furs. And finally, on 20 September, they reached the settlement of La Charette. Overjoyed, they fired three volleys into the air and were answered in kind by a group of five trading boats tied up on the bank. The villagers greeted them effusively but, as Clark recorded, 'acknowledged them selves much astonished in Seeing us return. they informed us that we were Supposed to have been lost long Since.' Two days later the Corps of Discovery paddled into St Louis. After 8,000 miles and 28 months they had reached their journey's end.

The expedition had been a success, even if its findings did not always make happy reading. There was no transcontinental waterway, or at least not one that could be put to commercial use: the Missouri's upper stretches were barely navigable, those of the Columbia not at all, and the Rockies presented a formidable barrier. As for the Indians, the idea of their accepting peace and prosperity under the US flag seemed to be a pipedream: not only were the Sioux and the Blackfeet determinedly aggressive but, as Lewis's last stay with the Mandans had shown, even the more accommodating tribes were unwilling to abandon a pattern of war. These disappointments were offset by the scale and multiplicity of the expedition's achievements. Lewis and Clark had described the habits and physiognomy of tribes unknown to white men. They had discovered 178 new plants and 122 species of animals. They had produced the first authoritative charts of the Missouri river system and had mapped immense swathes of territory from the Mississippi to the Pacific. They had encountered regions of incalculable natural wealth, rich in land, furs, timber and buffalo. They had laid the geographical foundations of what would, within a century, become the world's most powerful nation. And they had lost only one man in the process – and then to natural causes. As Lewis wrote to Jefferson: 'The whole of the party who accompanyed me from the Mandans have returned in good health, which is not, I assure you, to me one of the least pleasing considerations of the Voyage.'

What *was* one of the least pleasing considerations was the effect Lewis and Clark's expedition had on the Indians. Spurred by their reports of limitless riches, and supported by an expansionist administration that was willing to grant land to those who extended America's frontiers, US settlers swarmed west. Jefferson excused the invasion on economic grounds: the Indians had land but lacked manufactured goods; the Americans had goods but lacked land. Both sides would therefore be obeying the natural laws of supply and demand. That it was a forcible exchange did not disturb him – he had, anyway, neither the army nor the money to prevent it. Within a few decades the Indians were displaced – in some cases eradicated by disease – and by the middle of the century the herds of buffalo, which in Lewis's time had roamed the prairies in their hundreds of thousands, had been all but exterminated.

The Corps of Discovery, who had set the process in motion, did not live to see its end. Several of them died early of syphilis – one of the expedition's more controversial assessments was that the disease originated in America – and Lewis succumbed to alcohol and depression. On 1 October 1809, at the age of 35, he committed suicide.

W. E. Parry (1818–27)

At the end of the Napoleonic Wars Britain's naval officers were mostly redundant. They had no enemy to fight, no ships to command and nothing much to do except draw their half-pay. To these men, who had no particular purpose, Sir John Barrow was a godsend. Second Secretary to the Admiralty, Barrow had no great interest in warfare, but was very keen on exploration. The North-West Passage, especially, piqued his interest. Did it exist, and if so why was Britain doing so little to find it? It wasn't every day that the world's most powerful navy had surplus gold braid to hand; and the passage, if it could be found, had such commercial value as to outweigh the cost of sending a couple of ships to find it. In 1818 the *Isabella* and the *Alexander* left Deptford for the Arctic. Their task was to chart Baffin Bay and to ascertain whether an open waterway led to the west – or, indeed, to the north.

At the helm of the *Isabella* was a veteran, Commander John Ross: a Scot, brave, undoubtedly capable, but tempestuous, irritable and defiant. The *Alexander* was commanded by Lieutenant William Edward Parry, a calm, bluff-faced, equally capable Englishman, whose social connections endeared him to Barrow. The *Isabella* was faster than the *Alexander* and surged around Baffin Bay, Ross ticking off the various outlets as he went. The existing maps, which were ancient and in Barrow's opinion made up, showed three potential exits to the North-West Passage: Smith Sound and Jones Sound at the north of Baffin Bay and, further south and to the west, Lancaster Sound. Of the first two Ross was blithely dismissive: they did exist, he said, the maps had not lied; but Smith Sound was blocked by a range of mountains and Jones Sound was a bay. The northern regions of Baffin Bay were not wholly without interest, however. On the coast of Greenland, to the east of Smith Sound, he discovered the world's most northerly inhabitants.

The Inuit of Etah, or the Arctic Highlanders as Ross called them, had migrated north in the 16th century, since when they had adapted so absolutely to life in the snow and ice that they had forgotten the traditional skills of their southern cousins. They did not know how to use a kayak, net fish, hunt caribou or shoot a bow and arrow. They were, however, masters of their particular environment, surviving in their igloos on a diet of birds, seals, walruses and polar bears, from whose carcases they also extracted the

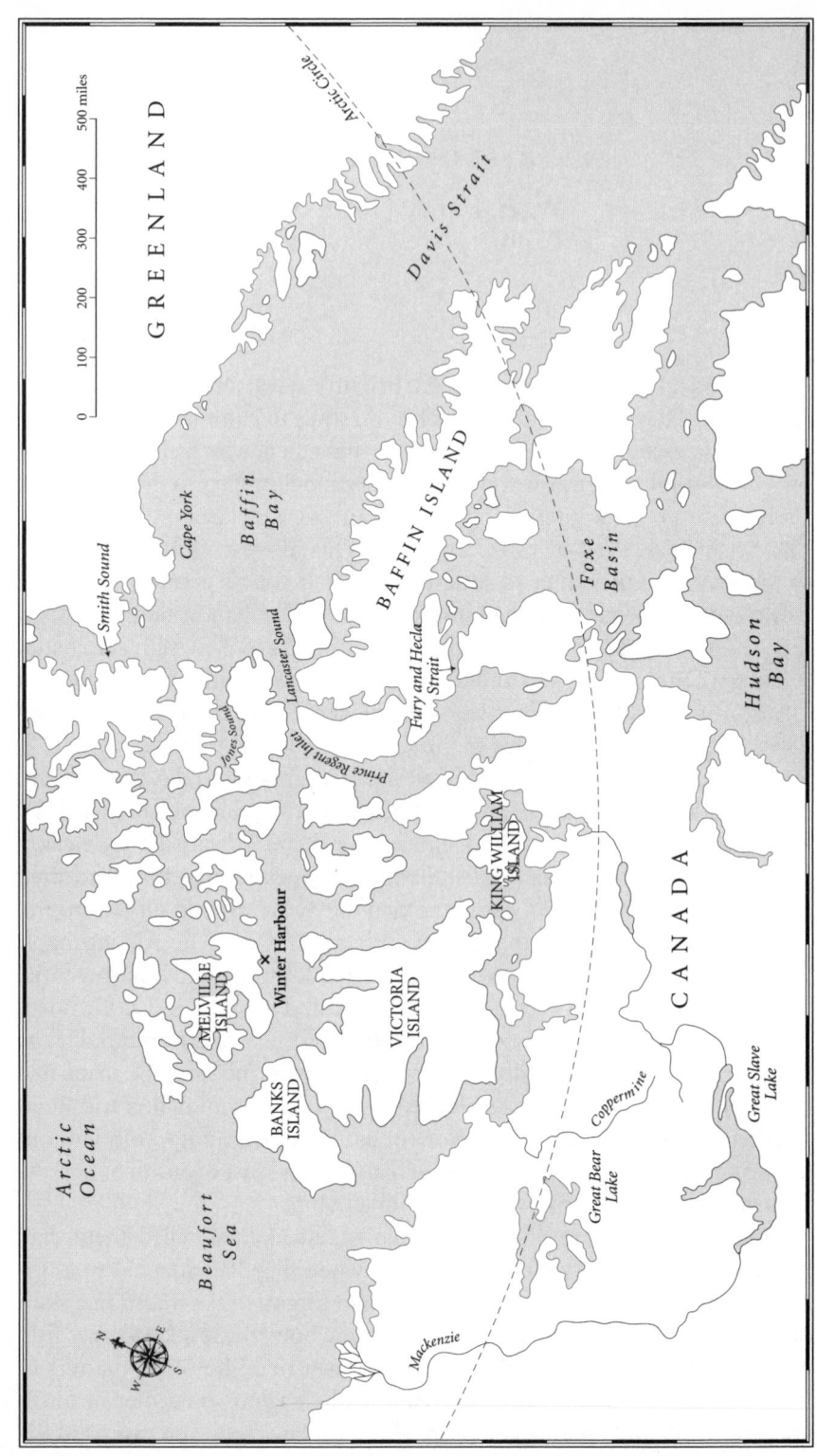

basics for survival: fuel, clothing, tools and transport, the latter taking the form of bone sledges hauled by their one domesticated animal, the husky. Their isolation was such that they believed themselves the only people on the earth. It must therefore have been something of a shock when Ross and Parry stepped out of their ships on 8 August 1818 and advanced over the ice towards them, clad in cocked hats and full naval regalia.

The Inuit's bewilderment was complete. Communicating through a South Greenland interpreter whom Ross had brought from London, they pestered the strangers with questions. Were the ships a species of giant bird? Were the sails their wings? Were they truly made of wood? (The only tree they had ever seen was a dwarf willow whose trunk was no thicker than a finger.) And what were all these things they contained? Was one meant to eat a watch? Did anyone live on the other side of a mirror? From what kind of animal did they make their ropes and clothes? They were puzzled, too, by the lack of women: did the newcomers belong to a race composed solely of men? Ross and Parry were similarly amazed by the pristine innocence of the Etah Inuit. They could count no higher than five, and anything beyond 'two fives' was simply 'a lot'. They did not believe in an afterlife. They had no concept of ownership, simply using things as they felt like it. For entertainment they played either football or a form of ice hockey using walrus flippers as balls and pucks. They did not know the meaning of warfare because they had nobody to fight. And they had iron. How this could be was a mystery to the British, for the Inuit were clearly incapable of mining. In a flash of insight, Ross wondered if there might be a meteorite nearby from which they had managed to hack small slivers of metal. He took one of their knives and had it analysed on his return. Sure enough, it was of extra-terrestrial origin. The Etah Inuit had no laws, no religion, no army, no king, yet possessed everything that was needed for life and happiness: they were the epitome of noble savagery.

Ross and Parry spent less than a week with the Arctic Highlanders. On the 16th, rounding a promontory that Ross named Cape York, they made another bizarre discovery: a 600-foot-high slope that was coloured crimson from top to bottom. Suspecting it might be a surface coating of dust or seeds from the vegetation above, they dug down; but no, the snow was red to the rock. In fact, though they did not know it, they were right to think it might have vegetable origins: now a well-attested Arctic phenomenon, red snow is caused by a microscopic, unicellular plant called *Protococcus nivalis*.

The voyage so far had been successful: Ross had charted the east coast of Baffin Bay, had scotched the rumours that Smith and Jones Sound were navigable, and had found the Arctic Highlanders and the red snow of Cape York. All that remained was to see if Lancaster Sound might be the door to the North-West Passage. He entered it on 1 September and found an ice-choked bay at the end of which rose a range of steep mountains. He noted the fact in his log and took the *Isabella* and *Alexander* back to London, where he delivered his findings to the Admiralty on 16 November, doubtless expecting to be congratulated on the completion of his mission. Barrow, however, was outraged that he had failed to find the Passage and was not in the slightest impressed by his tales of red snow and 'Arctic Highlanders'. Seizing on a small detail, he noted that the *Alexander* had been a good eight miles behind the *Isabella* when Ross entered Lancaster Sound, and that Parry had not been able to confirm the existence of these mountains. In these circumstances, he concluded, Ross had very likely been wrong, and a new expedition would have to be despatched. Naturally, it would not be led by Ross – whom he had never liked and now detested – but by his favourite, Parry.

It was very slight grounds for justifying the expense of another Arctic expedition, particularly as Barrow would have accepted the same evidence had it come from any other officer. But as time would prove, Barrow was right. Ross had been mistaken: Smith Sound did not end in mountains but was a viable sea route up the west coast of Greenland; Jones Sound was not a bay but another passage into the Arctic; and the range he had reported at the end of Lancaster Sound was a mirage. His reports on Smith and Jones Sounds were the result of carelessness; but in the case of Lancaster Sound he could be excused. The range of mountains he had seen were produced by Arctic refraction, whereby light bounces off the ice and is then moulded by turbulence and warm air currents to create an aerial reflection that takes the shape of jagged, grey peaks outlined by dark ridges. However, nobody knew this then. In Barrow's opinion Ross was an incompetent fool, and he made it his job to ensure that the Royal Navy never employed him in any capacity for the rest of his life.

In 1819 Parry sailed aboard the *Hecla* for Baffin Bay, accompanied by the much smaller *Griper* commanded by Lieutenant Matthew Lidden. As they approached Lancaster Sound they were assailed by doubts. Had Ross been right after all? Would they, too, see the same mountains and impenetrable ice? 'It is more easy to imagine than describe the oppressive anxiety which was visible in every countenance while, as the breeze increased to a fresh gale, we ran quickly to the Westward,' Parry wrote. When, on 4 August, they entered the Sound and found it free of both ice and mountains, their doubts were replaced by exhilaration. Here was the North-West Passage! One of Parry's fellow officers described the pride and wonder of discovery: 'We had arrived in a sea which had never before been navigated, we were gazing on land that European eyes had never before beheld ... and before us was the prospect of realizing all our wishes, and of exalting the honour of our country.'

Westward they sailed through Lancaster Sound, which was in places 80 miles wide, passing low, sandy islands, dramatic rock buttresses and 'noble' channels that led north and south. It was clear that they were on a main road to the west and, should ice block their path, any one of the channels on either side might be an alternative route to the Passage. On 4 September they crossed the 110th meridian and the next day they dropped anchor for the first time since leaving Britain, off the coast of an island to which Parry gave the name Melville. Since the days of Banks's early voyages, Parliament – more exactly the Board of Longitude – had offered prizes to stimulate the search for the North-West Passage. There was £5,000 for reaching 110° W, with an additional £5,000 for every ten degrees' longitude towards the Pacific. The victors could expect £20,000 – a vast sum by modern standards – for reaching the Pacific. In less than a month of easy sailing, Parry had earned the first instalment – more than £250,000 today – to be shared between officers and crew, and the sea was still open before him. He continued westward until a honey-like sludge of ice brought him to a halt at 112° 51' W. Retreating to Melville Island, Parry announced they would try again in the summer of 1820 when the ice had melted. But they were not going to return to London in the interim: instead they would spend the winter in the Arctic.

Unlike previous explorers, Parry was prepared for the ordeal. He ordered his men to cut a channel through the ice surrounding Melville Island and, once the ships were berthed, had the sails made into canvas tents above the upper decks. The crew shovelled snow against the hulls to insulate them from the wind. They erected huts in which they could take meteorological and astronomical observations. They dug holes in the ice against the seaman's ever-present fear of fire. They shot a quantity of wildlife. And then they battened down for the winter. 'We had plenty of provisions,' Parry wrote, 'crew in high health and spirits; a sea if not open then at least navigable; and a zealous and unanimous determination in both officers and men to accomplish, by all possible means, the grand object on which we had the happiness to be employed.' Furthermore, 'I had little doubt of our accomplishing the object of our enterprise before the close of the next season'. He called their anchorage Winter Harbour.

When the long Arctic night descended, Parry's immediate task was to distract their minds from the gloom in which they dwelt. He kept them busy, either scrubbing the deck, exercising on the ice or working in the *Hecla*'s onboard brewery and bakery. Anything, he reckoned, was better than inactivity. He printed a ship's newspaper, the *North Georgia Gazette and Winter Chronicle* – all contributions were welcome – and instituted the Royal Arctic Theatre, in which he and his fellow officers performed skits for the delectation of the crew. The image of midshipmen dressing up as shepherdesses and scantily clad nymphs while trapped in the depths of the North-West Passage has to be one of the most surreal in the history of exploration. To those on stage it was a torment – the theatre was on the upper deck, heated by nothing more than a pile of heated shot; one actor became frostbitten in two fingers – but Parry was pleased at its success: 'The good effect of these performances is more and more perceived by us,' he wrote. 'And we shall certainly go on with them, till we can have a nobler employment.'

As the winter progressed, the temperature fell and fell. Normally, the ships' living quarters were kept comfortable by a variety of strategically placed stoves, but in February the cold became intense. With the thermometer showing –55° F, they huddled in their greatcoats, while about them chronometers stopped and the lime juice they had packed to counteract scurvy froze and burst its bottles. Every time they opened a hatch a miasma of cold fog sank into the ship, clotting their clothes and blankets with ice. On 24 February their observatory hut caught light; they extinguished the blaze, but it took three-quarters of an hour and every firefighter was frostbitten to some degree: 16 of them had to be put on the sick list, some of them for three weeks. The worst affected was the hut's occupant, who had bravely dragged the instruments to safety but had forgotten to wear his gloves: within 30 minutes his hands were the colour and consistency of marble, and when they were placed in a bowl of cold water the water froze. He lost seven fingers. Throughout, Parry kept an optimistic face. But as their coal began to run low he secretly drew up a plan of evacuation to Canada.

Cold was not their only worry. That month the *Hecla*'s gunnery officer, Mr Scallon, showed the first signs of scurvy. How he could have contracted the disease was a mystery to Parry, for a daily tot of lime juice was part of the crew's morning routine. He comforted himself that it was caused by Scallon's age and by decades of eating the Navy's standard issue salt beef. In fact, it was more likely the product of Parry's own anti-scorbutic regime, in which beer and exercise played a prominent part. As would later be discovered, alcohol and exertion exacerbated the condition. Parry responded with ingenuity: he placed several seedbeds of mustard-and-cress on the ship's hot water pipes and, when they sprouted, fed the resulting salad to Scallon. Within nine days the gunnery officer boasted he could 'run a mile'. This was a new development in the treatment of scurvy and one that caused Parry a moment of contemplation. 'I shall be most thankful, should it prove that we can cure, or even check, this disease by our own resources,' he wrote thoughtfully, 'for I cannot help feeling that, under Providence, our making the North-West Passage depends upon it.'

By the end of April the temperature was the same as it had been on 9 September when they had sawed their way into Winter Harbour. On 6 May Parry ordered his men to saw their way out again. The ice that had been a seven-inch skin in September was now seven feet deep, and although the ships were released – jumping 18 inches into the air as they did so, thanks to the weight of food and fuel consumed over the winter – they had no chance of breaking free. They could only wait for a thaw. Taking advantage of their entrapment, Parry led an overland party to explore Melville Island. They set off on 1 June, dragging a cart laden with 800 pounds of food and equipment, and returned 15 days later, the cart having broken – its wheels were found in the last decade of the 20th century – and having discovered nothing but a lumpy, desolate land bisected by ravines and covered with rocks that, when broken, emitted a stench of decay. Parry had hoped that Winter Harbour might have cleared while he was away. But it was just as he had left it.

Throughout June and July Parry waited impatiently for the ice to melt. The ships were floating on water by mid-July, but still the bay was blocked by a barrier of ice that stretched across its mouth. On the last day of the month a wind blew the ice apart, and the *Hecla* and *Griper* sailed to freedom. They had been trapped for 11 months, there were only a few weeks left of the navigable season and neither ship had coal or provisions to last a second winter. In these circumstances most captains would have fled for home, but Parry was so certain of success that he continued where he had left off. At the western end of Melville Island he sent an officer to climb one of its hills and see what he could see. The report was encouraging: there was land to the south-west, which might be the north coast of Canada – it was in fact an island, Banks Island – and the intervening seaway was a potential North-West Passage but one so crammed with bergs that no ship had a chance this late in the season and it would probably be unnavigable at any time of the year. Still Parry did not give up. He went south, to examine the inlets he had passed on his way to Melville Island, but they were blocked by ice. It was too late to explore further. With the sea coagulating behind him, he fled down Lancaster Sound, reached Baffin Bay in mid-August and was back home by 31 October.

For his record-breaking voyage Parry was promoted to commander and showered with honours. The adulation was justified: no Arctic captain in recent years had done half as well or shown a smidgen of his resource, let alone brought off the feat of wintering at such cold latitudes. Above all, he had brought every single one of his men home alive.

As a reward, Parry was put in charge of two further expeditions in search of the North-West Passage. Bearing in mind the difficulties he had faced at Melville Island, he thought it prudent to try a different avenue. Thus, his first voyage, between 1821 and 1823, was to Foxe Basin, north of Hudson Bay. For his command ship Parry chose the *Fury*, while his old vessel, the *Hecla*, was given to a boisterous young lieutenant named George Lyon. Having proved how easy it was to winter in the Arctic, Parry had no qualms about spending two years in the ice: it was just a matter of taking extra food and fuel, piping the heat more efficiently round the ships and taking care not to become trapped in the ice – which would be far less of a hazard in the warmer, more southerly waters of Foxe Basin.

Their first winter passed uneventfully, and in the summer of 1822 they found what they were looking for almost immediately. That August they discovered a strait leading from the north-west corner of Foxe Basin. Unfortunately it was frozen, but beyond lay an expanse of open sea from which came a strong, eastward-flowing current. Parry waited optimistically for the ice to clear, but it remained solid. As they settled in for a second winter, he became despondent. 'Whatever the last summer's navigation had added to our geographical knowledge of the eastern coast of America, and its adjacent lands, very little had in reality been effected in furtherance of the North-West Passage. Even the actual discovery of the desired outlet into the Polar Sea, had been of no practical benefit in the prosecution of our enterprise; for we had only discovered this channel to find it impassable, and to see the barriers of nature closed against us, to the utmost limit of the navigable season.' Nevertheless, it was possible that next season might be better; and if it was, the newly named Fury and Hecla Strait was certainly worth investigating.

The summer of 1823, however, was no better than the previous one. Fury and Hecla Strait was still iced up and, worryingly, some of the crew were beginning to show signs of scurvy despite being fed the hothouse salads of mustard-and-cress. Parry did not understand how this could be, but when the first man died on 9 August 1823 he gave up trying to understand and sailed home before there were any more casualties.

As far as the North-West Passage went, the voyage was, in Parry's words, 'a matter of extreme disappointment'. In other ways, however, it had been a success. A group of local Inuit had camped by the ships for several months, enabling the officers to learn much about their lifestyle. Parry was slightly standoffish, appreciating their mapmaking skills, disliking their dog sledges, and remarking that on a basic level they were almost as good as white folk. Lyon, on the other hand, was an enthusiastic researcher. He ate their unfamiliar food – the half-digested contents of a deer's stomach, he recorded manfully, tasted 'as near as I could judge a mixture of sorrel and radish leaves' – he played with their children, slept in their huts, allowed himself to be tattooed, witnessed a shaman's festival, attended their parties and participated diligently in their day-to-day activities. When the Hecla raised anchor, two pregnant women waved him goodbye.

Usually when an Arctic expedition published its scientific appendices people could expect long and tedious tables of temperatures, tides, the motion of a pendulum and the appearance of the sky. In this case, unintentionally, Parry and Lyon had compiled a small gem of anthropological research. The manner in which the material had been gathered left a lot to be desired – and a lot more to the imagination; the words 'misbehaviour' and 'disgrace' were bruited in public – but it remained a genuine, first-hand account of the Inuit that would not be bettered for 40 years. John Barrow, however, was not concerned with the Inuit: his business was the North-West Passage. This time he welcomed Parry with palpable coolness.

Following his failure at Foxe Basin, Parry returned with the Fury and the Hecla to Lancaster Sound in 1824. After his first voyage he had warned Barrow that the chances of success in this direction were slim: 'I knew the difficulties of the whole accomplishment of the North-West Passage too well to make light of them ... The success we met with is to be attributed, under Providence, to the concurrence of many favourable circumstances.' But, not

TOP Richard and John Lander travel in rare style down the Niger, 1830.
ABOVE Timbuctoo, as drawn by René Caillié, 1828.

TOP An Inuit settlement: John Ross's Arctic voyage of 1829–33.
ABOVE James Clark Ross claims Antarctica's Possession Island for Britain, 1841.

OPPOSITE The note found at Victory Point by Franklin searchers in 1859.

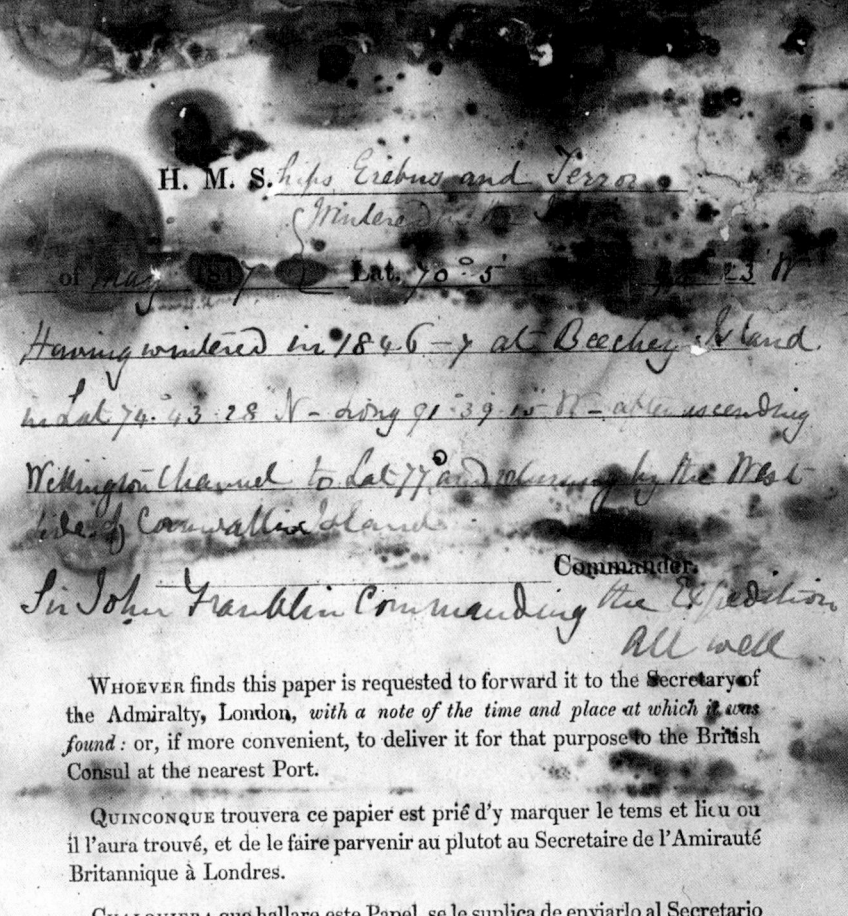

H. M. S.hips _Erebus and Terror_
(Wintered)

of May 1847 Lat. 70°5 . . . 23 W

Having wintered in 1846-7 at Beechey Island
in Lat 74.43.28 N — Long 91.39.15 W — after ascending
Wellington Channel to Lat 77 and returning by the West
side of Cornwallis Island

Commander

Sir John Franklin Commanding the Expedition
All well

WHOEVER finds this paper is requested to forward it to the Secretary of
the Admiralty, London, *with a note of the time and place at which it was
found :* or, if more convenient, to deliver it for that purpose to the British
Consul at the nearest Port.

QUINCONQUE trouvera ce papier est prié d'y marquer le tems et lieu ou
il l'aura trouvé, et de le faire parvenir au plutot au Secretaire de l'Amirauté
Britannique à Londres.

CUALQUIERA que hallare este Papel, se le suplica de enviarlo al Secretario
del Almirantazgo, en Londrés, con una nota del tiempo y del lugar en
donde se halló.

EEN ieder die dit Papier mogt vinden, wordt hiermede verzogt, om het
zelve, ten spoedigste, te willen zenden aan den Heer Minister van de
Marine der Nederlanden in 's Gravenhage, of wel aan den Secretaris der
Britsche Admiraliteit, te London, en daar by te voegen eene Nota,
inhoudende de tyd en de plaats alwaar dit Papier is gevonden geworden.

FINDEREN af dette Papiir ombedes, naar Leilighed gives, at sende
samme til Admiralitets Secretairen i London, eller nœrmeste Embedsmand
i Danmark, Norge, eller Sverrig. Tiden og Stœdit hvor dette er fundet
önskes venskabeligt paategnet.

WER diesen Zettel findet, wird hier-durch ersucht denselben an den
Secretair des Admiralitets in London einzusenden, mit gefälliger angabe
an welchen ort und zu welcher zeit er gefunden worden ist.

Left the Ships Monday 24th May 1847 — the party
consisting of 2 officers and 6 men —

Gm Gore   Lieut
Chas F Des Voeux Mate —

ABOVE Robert O'Hara Burke and William Wills after their 1860–1 crossing of Australia.

OPPOSITE Samuel Baker, big-game hunter and explorer of the Nile. (1864–5).

OPPOSITE The apparition that greeted Edward Whymper following the Matterhorn disaster, 1865.

TOP Charles Francis Hall's winter funeral, 1872.
ABOVE George Tyson's separation from the *Polaris*, 1872.

TOP The wreck of the Hansa, 1869.
ABOVE David Livingstone surprised by a lion. (1858–64).

wishing to disappoint his employer, he made a half-hearted stab at Prince Regent Inlet, one of the southern channels he had passed en route to Melville Island. It was a failure. After a few score miles the *Fury* was caught by the ice and very nearly sank. Parry had to abandon the ship and most of its stores at a spot he named Fury Beach before limping home in the *Hecla*. 'The only real cause for wonder is our long exemption from such a catastrophe,' he wrote. Barrow's welcome was frostier than the last time. He let Parry stew for three years before calling on his services again. This time a less delicate task was to hand: Parry was to reach the North Pole.

The idea was Parry's, but the more Barrow thought about it the more attractive it seemed. The Arctic pack was as flat as a billiard table, if one was to go by the 1773 report of Lieutenant Constantine Phipps, who had sailed to its edge and seen 'one continued plain of smooth unbroken ice, broken only by the horizon'. Compared to the North-West Passage, the Pole was a relatively simple affair, well within Parry's capabilities. All he had to do was reach the pack and walk north. Just in case the North Pole should be water instead of ice, he was instructed to take a couple of boats with him.

Parry reached Spitsbergen aboard the *Hecla* on 14 May, and ten days later the ship was nudging the pack. The boats were offloaded, along with Parry's secret weapon: eight reindeer that he had collected from Norway on the way north. The two boats were equipped with a removable framework of wheels, four reindeers were harnessed to each, and the order was given to go. Axle-deep in snow, the boats went nowhere. 'Picturesque in the extreme,' chortled one officer. Parry slid east to Spitsbergen, charted a bit of unknown coast, then came back to the pack, this time with heavy sledges from whose prows hung leather traces. By these means his boats would be man-hauled to the Pole.

The pack was nothing like Phipps had described it. Five men to a boat, dragging 260 pounds per person, they traversed ridges, hummocks and pans of water, Parry and two other officers leading the way. Sometimes the snow was so deep that they sank to their knees, and often the sun was so bright that they became snowblind. Usually it was hot – so much so that the tar oozed from their boats – but frequently it rained. At night they turned the boats upside down and sheltered beneath them, smoking heavily to raise the temperature. When the rain fell, they waded hip-deep through basins of water; when it did not, they hopped uncomfortably over dried lakes covered in sharp, green shards that they nicknamed 'penknives' for the ease with which they cut through their boots. Worst of all were the leads, strips of open water that necessitated unloading the sledges, launching the boats, rowing a few strokes, then reassembling everything for a haul that might last only a few minutes before they reached another lead and had to repeat the performance all over again.

All this they might have withstood, believing that the North Pole was within their grasp, were it not for Parry's chronometer and sextant. These two instruments were their bane and downfall: on 20 July they showed that they were five miles further north than they had been on the 17th. Yet the men had travelled a good 12 miles over the last three days. On 26 July the instruments told a worse tale: they were only one mile further north than on the 21st and had lost three miles in the last four days. The pack was drifting south and, no matter how hard they tried, Parry's men could not beat it. That day they came to a halt. Parry ordered a 24-hour rest, then took them back to the *Hecla*.

When Parry presented his journal to the Admiralty, Barrow's disappointment could not have been more complete. His favourite son had failed to find the Pole and had produced an appendix so meagre that it had to be bulked out with a section labelled 'INSECT' (one fly, dead when found). Parry's reputation was too great for him to be sacked, but he was never sent on another Arctic voyage. Instead he was shunted sideways to the position of Hydrographer to the Royal Navy, a post for which he had no qualifications whatsoever.

He left behind him an exemplary record of Arctic exploration. No other man of his generation had done as much. His furthest west in 1819 via Melville Island would not be beaten for decades, and it was 1875 before George Nares outstripped his furthest north. What he had done was outstanding, given the equipment available to him. When he died on 8 July 1855, *The Times* lauded him in heroic terms: 'No successor on the path of Arctic exploration has yet snatched the chaplet from the brow of this great navigator. Parry is still the champion of the North!'

John Franklin (1818–25)

When Edward Parry sailed in 1821 on his second attempt at the North-West Passage, he was not the only Briton in the field. Determined to crack this irritating geographical nut, Sir John Barrow had sent another expedition, under Lieutenant John Franklin, to investigate Canada's northern coastline. The region was virtually *terra incognita*: Western explorers had visited the mouths of the Mackenzie River and the Coppermine River, 500 miles to the east, but everything between these two points was a mystery. What was known, however, was that both the Mackenzie and the Coppermine flowed into open seas. It was reasonable to suppose that these seas were connected; and if that was the case, they might well extend on either side to form a channel running from Bering Strait in the west to an as yet undiscovered point in the east. Here, in other words, was the underbelly of the North-West Passage. Franklin's orders were to drag a couple of sturdy boats overland to the Coppermine and thence sail west from its mouth to the Mackenzie or – should he so desire – sail east. If he went west, he could chart the coast for unexpected promontories and peninsulas; if he went east, and if Parry's voyage to Foxe Basin was as successful as Barrow expected it to be, there was a good chance that the two expeditions might meet. Either way, Franklin would provide vital information as to the Passage's viability.

Barrow's plan could not be faulted in geographical terms. When it came to personnel and organization, however, it left a lot to be desired. Franklin was a brave, extremely charming officer with much naval experience: he had circumnavigated Australia with Matthew Flinders in 1800, had fought in the battles of Trafalgar and New Orleans and had, when Ross and Parry went into Baffin Bay, been second-in-command of a failed, ancillary expedition to the North Pole, from whose gale-ridden pack he had returned with tales of his ship being heeled over so hard that its bell rang. He was religious, carrying a 12-point checklist whose first catechism was, 'Have I this day walked with God?' Against this, he was overweight and unfit, with a weak heart and poor circulation. He could not hunt, canoe or trek, nor did he know anything about overland travel. Three meals a day were a must; he could not move without tea; and, in the words of one contemporary, he could not cover more than eight miles a day without being carried. By the

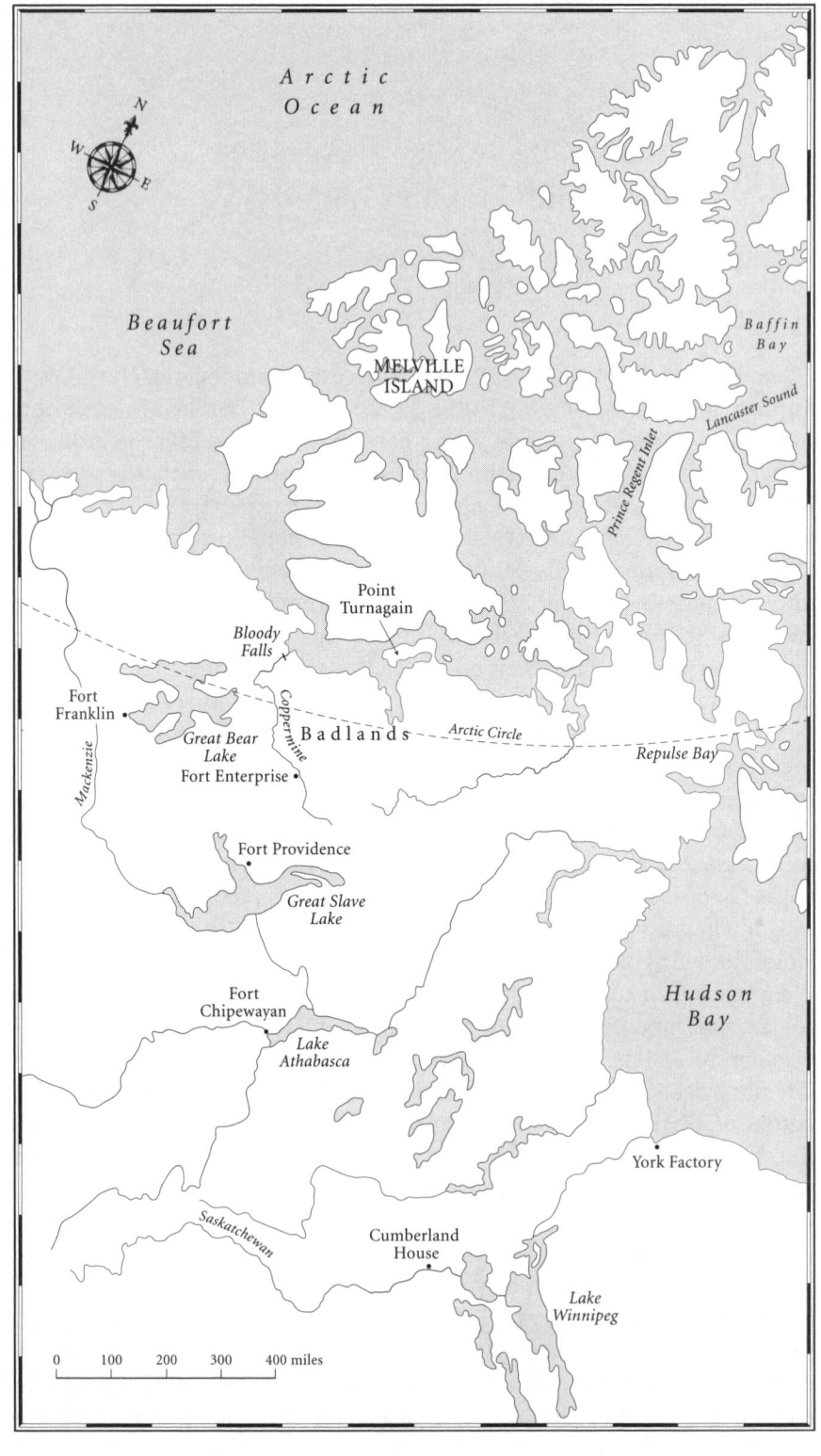

standards of his time and calling he was peculiarly sensitive: he trembled whenever a man had to be flogged, and disliked bloodshed to the point of not killing mosquitoes – he waved them away, saying that there was room enough in the world for him and them. In short, a very pleasant man but a puzzling choice of leader for what would undoubtedly be a long and tiring journey. Accompanying him were two midshipmen, George Back and Robert Hood, who had sailed on the abortive 1818 North Pole expedition; a Royal Marine surgeon, Dr John Richardson, who came as second-in-command and naturalist despite never having been on an expedition before and having, as he confessed, very little knowledge of natural history; and, finally, an ordinary seaman named John Hepburn.

Barrow's idea was that Franklin's party would sail to the Orkney Islands, where they would collect a group of hardy boatmen before proceeding to Hudson Bay. From there they would row and carry two boats (to be acquired in Canada) many hundreds of miles to the mouth of the Coppermine, travelling via Cumberland House (a depot on the Saskatchewan River), Fort Chipewayan on Lake Athabasca, and the Great Slave Lake. It would be a strong party but a small one, capable of living off the area's resources. Whatever food they needed could be supplied by either the Hudson's Bay Company or the North-West Company – two fur-trading concerns whose reach extended across northern Canada – and to assist them in the long haul they could hire local voyageurs, the mixed-race guides-cum-porters who were the backbone of all journeys into the hinterland. The flaws in the plan soon became apparent. When Franklin reached the Orkneys only four men were willing to enlist, and then for only as far as Fort Chipewayan. On landing at York Factory in Hudson's Bay, he found the two fur companies in a state of such mutual antipathy – they had recently been at war – that he had great difficulty obtaining the boats and provisions he needed even for the first stages of the journey. The best voyageurs did not want to join the expedition – they didn't know the country, were frightened of the Indians, didn't like the sea, and thought the prospect too hazardous – so he had to hire whatever left-overs were available, along with their wives and dependants. The lean group of fast-moving men that Barrow had envisaged was soon a cumbersome rabble of more than 20. Even in a good year it would have been difficult to feed such a swollen party without prior arrangement, but 1820 was a lean one. The deer on which the region's inhabitants depended had been scarce, and there was insufficient game to keep the Britons alive, let alone to make the pemmican (a mixture of ground meat and fat) that they required. The best Franklin could elicit was the promise of Indian hunters to shoot whatever wildlife was foolish enough to show itself.

For the British tenderfoots, the journey through Canada's pine forests from York Factory to Cumberland House and then to Fort Chipewayan was a nightmare. Their one supply-laden boat (a second had been promised) was too heavy and half of its contents had to be dumped. The weather was so cold that mercury in their thermometers froze, as did their tea seconds after it had been poured. They had no tents, so slept in the open, counting themselves lucky if an insulating layer of snow covered their fur blankets. When they donned snowshoes Midshipman Hood – a shy, romantic type, who painted their surroundings with near-photographic clarity – found the journey agonizing: 'The sufferer feels his frame crushed by unaccountable pressure; he drags a galling and stubborn weight at his feet, and his track is marked with blood . . . When he arises from sleep, half his body seems dead, till quickened into feeling by the irritation of his sores.'

They left Fort Chipewayan on 18 July 1820 and were at Fort Providence on the Great Slave Lake ten days later. Here they met an Indian chief named Akaitcho, who understood perfectly the idea of the North-West Passage (perspicaciously he asked why, if it was so important, it had not already been discovered) and promised to supply Franklin for as long as he could. However, his men would not venture into Inuit territory because they had recently fought a battle on the Coppermine at a place called Bloody Falls, an experience so horrible to both sides that neither wished to revisit the spot. Franklin tried to charm his way through the impasse, but Akaitcho was adamant: his men would see them to within a few miles of Bloody Falls, but thereafter they would be on their own; he would wait at Fort Providence until they returned.

Off Franklin went, each step being marked by disaster and disappointment. At their first stop the campfire got out of hand and burned down a large section of forest. Then Back nearly killed himself when his sleeping fur caught light. Akaitcho's hunters were hardly to be seen, and when they did make an appearance had little to show for their troubles. The squabbling fur companies could not agree who was to provide the party with food, with the result that supplies became so short that the voyageurs mutinied, forcing Franklin to send Back to fetch pemmican from Cumberland House. Donning snowshoes, Back made the 1,200-mile round journey in a matter of months, and returned 'having succeeded in the procuration of supplies beyond [their] most sanguine expectations'. But Back's efforts were not enough to quell the voyageurs' pessimism. When Franklin warned the ringleader, a man called St Germain, of the penalty he might face if brought to trial in England, he was greeted with hollow laughter. 'It is immaterial to me where I lose my life,' said St Germain, 'for the whole party will perish.' The only positive aspect of the trip was that they no longer had to lug the weighty wooden boat behind them. Seeing the impracticability of hauling it to the Coppermine, Franklin had opted instead for three, lightweight bark canoes that could be either sailed or paddled and were seaworthy enough for the coastal reconnaissance he had in mind.

That winter they built a camp comprising two log huts, one of five rooms for the four officers and a slightly smaller one for the 16 voyageurs – the Indians were left to find what shelter they could – to which they gave the name Fort Enterprise. Here, nursing their grievances and discontents (Back and Hood had fallen in love with an Indian girl named Greenstockings and at one point were ready to fight a duel over her), they festered until June 1821, when they resumed their march for the mouth of the Coppermine. By 18 July they were approaching Bloody Falls, where it had been agreed the Indians would turn back. Franklin felt no great sadness at their departure: besides being lacklustre hunters, they had also proved incompetent guides, knowing the terrain no better than he himself. In some ways, too, it was as well they should leave, for there was much preparation to be done for the expedition's return. Franklin had already decided to go east when he reached the sea, and he was aware that in order to chart the maximum amount of coastline he ran the risk of being cut off by the ice, in which case he would have to return overland to the Coppermine, relying for sustenance on what-ever wildlife he could trap or shoot. His party would be near-starving when they arrived and would have no time to lay down stores for the winter. It was imperative, therefore, that the Indians leave caches of food at certain prearranged points and, above all, that they stock Fort Enterprise with dried meat. He drummed it into them: if they did not stock Fort Enterprise he and his men would die. A few days later he ordered his party into the canoes and, with 14 days' food, paddled down the Coppermine.

The sea was open, the canoes handled well and the voyageurs managed to subdue their terror at being afloat on the waves. (None of them had ever seen the sea before.) Franklin steered his little fleet through the North-West Passage, charting every creek and bay for 555 miles until, on 18 August, he called a halt. He would have gone further had there been enough food, but game had generally been scarce and even when it was plentiful, as for instance at the mouth of a river that he named after Hood, the voyageurs had shot little. In Franklin's mind this was yet another sign of their untrustworthiness: 'we now strongly suspected that their recent want of success in hunting had proceeded from an intentional relaxation in their efforts to kill deer in order that the want of provisions might compel us to put a period to our voyage'. Walking along the shore, he marked his furthest east – a promontory that he called Point Turnagain – then readied his group for the journey home.

The season was too far advanced for them to reach the mouth of the Coppermine, so they sailed back to Hood River where they could shoot enough game to last them during the march to Fort Enterprise. The canoes having been badly damaged by storms, they dismantled all three and reassembled them to create two smaller models for crossing the many rivers that blocked their path. Unfortunately, they had left it too late: the deer had already fled south before the coming winter, and Hood River, once so bountiful, was now devoid of wildlife. As the Arctic winter came down, bringing snowstorms and gales, they struggled to control their cut-down canoes, which blew about in the wind and snagged against rocks. The going was slippery and, in Richardson's words, 'If anyone had broken a limb here, his fate would have been melancholy indeed, we could neither have remained with him, nor carried him on with us'. They ate their last pemmican on 4 September. On the same day Franklin fainted from hunger and exposure, and the voyageurs dropped one of the canoes, breaking its fragile hull beyond repair. Franklin suspected it had been done on purpose; but, turning adversity to advantage, he used the remains to build a fire, on which they boiled the last of their provisions: a tin of soup. From that date they had nothing to eat save what they could scavenge.

The region through which they were travelling was known as the Badlands. They soon learned why. The terrain was difficult, comprising a mess of rocks, bog and rivers, and game was in short supply. They managed to shoot a few deer in the early stages, but as the weather harshened they were reduced to foraging the rocks for *tripes de roche*, a barely nutritious lichen that gave them diarrhoea and whose embedded crumbs of stone broke their teeth. On 14 September their remaining canoe was lost when it overturned in a river, nearly killing a voyageur who was plunged into sub-zero water.

The voyageurs were now almost uncontrollable. 'The men had become desperate and were perfectly regardless of the commands of the officers,' Richardson wrote. The only thing that stopped them running for Fort Enterprise was the fact that they didn't know where it was. Neither, come to that, did Franklin for most of the time. In weather that ranged from heavy rain to dense mist and occasionally light snow, it was impossible to take a reading from the sun. By chance, however, on 26 September they stumbled on a river whose size and speed meant that it could only be the Coppermine. When the sun made a brief appearance Franklin calculated they were just 40 miles from Fort Enterprise. To this cheery news was added the discovery of a putrid deer carcase that they devoured to its intestines before grazing on a grove of cranberry and blueberry bushes. Unfortunately, the Coppermine was 120 yards wide at this point and they had no means of crossing it. 'They bitterly execrated their folly and impatience in breaking the canoe,' Richardson wrote of the voyageurs, 'and the remainder of the day was spent in wandering slowly along the river, looking in vain for a fordable place and inventing schemes for crossing, no sooner devised than abandoned.'

They constructed a raft from green willows that grew along the bank, but it was unsteady, could only carry one man at a time and sank on its first trial. Richardson stepped into the breach. He offered to swim to the other bank with a line on which they could then manhandle their way across, balancing on the raft. The water was so cold that after a few strokes he lost the use of his arms; turning on his back, he continued with his legs, but they too became paralysed. The men dragged him back by the line he was carrying, stripped off his wet clothes and placed him by the fire to recover. Gradually he regained feeling, but it was another five months before he regained full strength in his left arm and leg. As he lay there, in their single tent, they realized how horribly they had all declined. 'I cannot describe,' Franklin wrote, 'what everyone felt at beholding the skeleton which the doctor's debilitated frame exhibited.'

It was St Germain, the most obstructive of the voyageurs, who came to their rescue. Volunteering to make a canoe from willow branches and the canvas that contained their bedding, he disappeared into a small grove of willows and emerged two days later with a frail but watertight vessel capable of holding a single man. It was too late for one voyageur, who wandered into the wilderness, never to be seen again. And it was very nearly too late for the rest of the party: the voyageurs refused to collect *tripes de roche*, and the officers were so enfeebled that they had to rely on the able seaman John Hepburn to gather the lichen for them. As a measure of their weakness, Franklin tried one day to visit St Germain at his grove, three-quarters of a mile away: he returned after three hours without having attained his goal.

On 4 October they crossed the Coppermine one by one, the canoe becoming more and more waterlogged with each passage. The last package, containing their spare clothes and bedding, was soaked through when it arrived. Still, they were only 40 miles from Fort Enterprise and if they covered just six miles per day they would be there in a week. But a week was too long. Barely had they started than two voyageurs, far to the rear, collapsed. When Richardson went back to find them one man was nearly dead from exhaustion – he died in Richardson's arms – and the other had vanished. The officers were in little better condition: Hood, who had been unable to stomach the *tripes de roche*, was a walking shadow; Richardson was lame; Franklin was woefully diminished; and even Back could not move without the aid of a stick. A page from Franklin's journal revealed how desperate they were. On 5 October he wrote that a voyageur had uncovered the backbone and antlers of a long-dead deer: 'The wolves and birds of prey had picked them clean, but there still remained a quantity of the spinal marrow which they had not been able to extract. This, although putrid, was esteemed a valuable prize, and the spine being divided into portions, was distributed equally. After eating the marrow, which was so acrid as to excoriate the lips, we rendered the bones friable by burning, and ate them also.' Almost casually, he related that their hideous dinner was *haute cuisine* compared to their breakfast: 'Previous to setting out, the whole party ate the remains of their old shoes, and whatever scraps of leather they had, to strengthen their stomachs for the fatigue of the day's journey.'

Realizing that they would not go far in their present state, Franklin sent Back ahead with St Germain and two other voyageurs, Gabriel Beauparlant and Solomon Belanger, to alert the Indians at Fort Enterprise to their plight. No sooner had Back set out, however, than Richardson proposed a second split in the party: Hood was too weak to move, he himself was almost crippled, so why didn't Franklin leave them in the care of Hepburn and intercept the supplies that would surely be on their way within the next few days? Against his inclinations, but persuaded by hunger and by Richardson's pleading, Franklin agreed that the plan made sense. He gave his compatriots a tent and hobbled south after Back with the remaining voyageurs.

On 7 October two of Franklin's voyageurs – Jean Baptiste Belanger and Michel Teroahauté – said they were weary and would like to return to Richardson's camp. Franklin assented. Then two others, Perrault and Fontano, asked if they could follow. Wearily, Franklin agreed, and having bade them farewell, continued south. 'There was no tripes de roche,' he recorded, so 'we drank tea and ate some of our shoes for supper.' He reached Fort Enterprise on 12 October. There were no Indians, no food and no sign of Back, apart from a note saying he had been there two days earlier and was going in search of Akaitcho, who had taken his men hunting. Franklin and his men nestled painfully into Fort Enterprise, where they took up the floorboards and lit a fire to roast the previous season's left-overs: a few bones from the rubbish heap and some deer skins that the Indians had used for bedding. While they lay there, Solomon Belanger burst through the door. He was covered in ice and incapable of speech. When he thawed, he said that Back had not located Akaitcho and awaited instructions.

Franklin sent Belanger to tell Back to make for Fort Providence, and even accompanied him part of the way with two voyageurs before his snowshoes disintegrated. Returning alone to Fort Enterprise, he tried to comfort the remaining three voyageurs: Adam, Peltier and Samandré. It was a difficult task, for they had not tasted meat in a month and lay weeping on the floor. 'We perceived our strength decline every day, and every exertion began to be irksome. When we were once seated the greatest effort was necessary in order to rise, and we frequently had to lift each other from our seats.'

Richardson's party was in even worse shape. Of the four voyageurs whom Franklin had sent back only one, Michel, arrived – he had become separated from the others, he said – and although he was a capable hunter, his presence around the campfire was unnerving. He seemed on edge and refused to sleep with the Europeans. One evening he returned with the news that he had found a wolf carcase; the slices of meat which he distributed were eaten gratefully. But as the days passed his behaviour became odder and odder: he refused to gather *tripes de roche*; he spent the days on his own somewhere in the wilderness, and brought back no more meat; on 16 October he threatened to leave them. When Richardson said he could go ahead to Fort Enterprise with Hepburn, provided he spend another four days hunting, he replied, 'It is no use, there are no animals, you had better kill and eat me.' The mystification of Richardson and Hood soon turned to suspicion. They concluded that Michel had killed the other voyageurs and that his 'hunting' forays were an excuse to devour their corpses. The 'wolf' they had been eating was human flesh.

On the 20th, while Hepburn and Richardson were gathering firewood and *tripes de roche*, they heard a gunshot. Returning to the tent, they found Hood dead, shot through the back of the head at such close range that his nightcap was still smouldering. Michel greeted them, a gun in his hand, and gave the extraordinary explanation that Hood had been cleaning his gun when it went off – either that or he had committed suicide. It didn't take much detective work to see what had happened. The weapon was too long for a man to be able to shoot himself in the head, let alone in the back of the head while reading a copy of Bickersteth's *Scripture Helps* (it was still in Hood's hand when they found him). Clearly, Michel had killed him. However, as Michel protested his innocence so vehemently – and because he was armed – they listened to his story.

Richardson and Hepburn were in an unenviable position. They were too weak for a fight and, although they had a gun and a pistol in the tent, Michel – carrying a gun, two pistols, a bayonet and a knife – refused to let them out of his sight. For two days they cowered as Michel raved, daring them to accuse him of Hood's murder. Eventually, Richardson persuaded the deranged voyageur to accompany them to Fort Enterprise, and on the 23rd, when Michel left them alone for a few minutes – ostensibly to gather *tripes de roche* – Richardson loaded his pistol. When Michel returned Richardson shot him in the head.

On 29 October, having eaten nothing but lichen and Hood's fur blanket, they climbed a small hill and at last saw Fort Enterprise, smoke drifting cheerily from its chimney. Elated, they didn't stop to wonder why Franklin had sent them no assistance, but staggered towards safety. Richardson was now so weak that he collapsed 20 times covering a distance of 100 yards, but the prospect of food and warmth drove him on. Their tribulations were at an end. That evening they flung open the door of Fort Enterprise.

'No words can convey an idea of the filth and wretchedness that met our eyes,' Richardson wrote. The partitions had been taken down to feed the stove, the floorboards had been lifted, and four corpse-like figures lay on the bare earth. He did not have to be told that Akaitcho's Indians had failed to stock Fort Enterprise. The evidence was there before him: 'the ghastly countenances, dilated eye-balls, and sepulchral voices of Captain Franklin and those with him were more than we could at first bear'.

Exhausted as they were, Richardson and Hepburn were far stronger than the inmates of Fort Enterprise. They chopped wood for the stove and tried also to shoot some deer. But on the rare occasions when they saw an animal their hands shook so badly that they could not draw a bead, leaving the party dependent on a few bones and a pile of 26 deer skins that had been discarded the previous winter. The hides were rotten and riddled with warble-fly grubs, but they dragged them inside and ate them, squeezing the grubs into their mouths. Richardson said they tasted as sweet as gooseberries.

Franklin and the voyageurs were swollen with pre-starvation oedema, which Richardson drained with his scalpel, but he could not save Peltier and Samandré, both of whom died on the night of 1 November. Six days later, with the last of the bones gone and the hides coming to an end, they heard a shot. Back had located Akaitcho two days earlier – at a cost: one of his voyageurs had died en route and the whole group was in appalling shape – and three Indians now stood outside the door bearing emergency supplies of fat and dried meat. When they saw the state of the occupants, one man went back for more food while the other two swept the hut clean, stoked the fire to a crackling blaze, carefully spooned food into the starving men's mouths, and washed and shaved them as if they were babies. The ease with which they performed these simple tasks was a revelation to Richardson: 'We could scarcely, by any effort of reasoning, efface from our minds the idea that they possessed a supernatural degree of strength.'

Franklin and his men left Fort Enterprise on 16 November and were reunited with Back at Fort Providence on 11 December. By 14 July 1822 they were at York Factory, where rumours and recriminations were already mounting. The expedition had been impressive in terms of hardship and distance covered – 5,500 miles across land and water – but it had done nothing more than map a small strip of coastline, the existence of which had never seriously been in doubt, and establish that a portion of open sea, which might or might not be part of the North-West Passage, lay to the north of Canada. Franklin had not forged a link with Parry's expedition and had not investigated the coast between the Coppermine and the Mackenzie. At great expense and effort he had contributed very little to geography, had lost 11 of his 20-strong party in the process and had become involved, vicariously, in a case of murder that was already attracting attention. No wonder that Governor George Simpson of the Hudson's Bay Company wrote: 'They do not feel themselves at liberty to enter into the particulars of their disastrous enterprize, and I fear they have not fully achieved the object of their mission.' Franklin left York Factory on the first available ship for England.

In London nobody bothered about Franklin's failings. When his journal was published the public was far too interested in his ordeal to bother with passages north, west, east or south. They wanted sensation, and Franklin supplied it. He became known as the man who ate his boots – actually they were soft moccasins, but who cared – and, like Parry, he became a hero of such stature that complete strangers crossed the street to shake his hand. It was hard to move without meeting someone willing to relate a second-hand story of his fortitude.

Despite his failure in the field, Franklin's renown at home ensured that he was not forgotten by Sir John Barrow, and in 1824 he became part of the most ambitious assault on the North-West Passage yet. That year Barrow dispatched four expeditions to various quarters of the Arctic: one ship, under Lieutenant George Lyon, was to sail to Repulse Bay, in Foxe Basin, and from there walk overland to Point Turnagain; another, under Parry, was to sail through Lancaster Sound and then south down Prince Regent Inlet; a third, under Lieutenant Frederick Beechey, was to sail through Bering Strait and attempt to break into the Passage from the west; Franklin, meanwhile, was to make a second overland journey with Richardson, this time to the Mackenzie

River, from where the two men were to chart the coastline between the Mackenzie and the Coppermine, as well as to probe west towards Bering Strait. With luck, this torrential onslaught of men and matériel would sweep away the North-West Passage's last defences and, if perhaps it was too much to hope that all four parties would meet in the middle, then it was not at all fanciful to expect that some contact would be made.

This time Franklin was not going to make the mistakes he had made on his previous journey: to rely on the fur companies for support; and to take low-grade voyageurs as companions. Accordingly, he sent vast amounts of food to Canada during 1824, and placed an order for pemmican so large that the entire region could not meet it until the following spring. He had canoes built to his own specifications – strong but portable – and packed a novel collapsible boat against any repetition of his difficulties crossing the Coppermine. As to the composition of the group, Back and Richardson were once again present, along with one other midshipman, N. E. Kendall, and a professional naturalist named Drummond. The bulk of the party, however, was composed of British seamen: while recognizing that he would have to use Indian hunters once he was in the wild, Franklin wanted men beneath him who could be depended upon.

Franklin's party reached North America in April 1825, and by 16 August he was at the mouth of the Mackenzie. Having ascertained that it was ice-free, he retreated to a camp on the Great Bear Lake – Fort Franklin – where he settled down for a comfortable winter surrounded by all the food he could desire. The following June they returned to the delta and split into two groups: Franklin sailed west with Back and 14 men; Richardson, meanwhile, headed east to the Coppermine with Kendall and ten seamen. They were effortlessly successful. Richardson reached the Coppermine on 7 August, from where he walked overland to Fort Franklin. On the same date Franklin reached his furthest west, Foggy Island, where bad weather and lack of food forced him to turn back. He arrived at Fort Franklin three weeks after Richardson. It was a triumph. Between them they had covered 5,000 miles, of which 1,610 was virgin territory; they had charted practically the whole northern Canadian coast, proving that a navigable passage did exist, in summer at least; and they had done so without a single casualty.

When they returned to Britain in September 1827 they were showered with honours and promotions. The other two expeditions from the east, those under Parry and Lyon, had been less successful, but Beechey had attained a new furthest east from Bering Strait, coming to within 160 miles of Franklin's Foggy Island. The North-West Passage was all but in the bag. The channel between Beechey's and Franklin's furthest was a formality. All that remained was to find the section leading from Point Turnagain to Lancaster Sound. In 1845, after a brief hiatus during which the Admiralty's attentions were diverted elsewhere, Franklin returned to the fray with a ground-breaking voyage that established him as one of the most famous explorers of his age.

Hugh Clapperton and Richard Lander (1821–31)

In the first quarter of the 19th century the Niger River was a headache for Europe's geographers. They knew it existed because everyone, including the Phoenicians, the Ancient Greeks and, not least, the West Africans who lived on it, had told them it did. But they were exercised as to where it went. Conflicting reports placed it in every corner of Africa: it was part of the Nile; it was linked to the Congo; it emanated from a series of lakes near the eastern coast; it vanished into a great sinkhole in the desert; it ran sometimes overground, sometimes underground, emerging who knew where to surprise the traveller with a sudden gush of water. It flowed north, south, east and, according to some theorists, west. Of the continent's many mysteries, the Niger was one of the greatest.

Where the Niger started was of little concern – somewhere in Senegal, most authorities agreed – but its end was a matter of dispute. In 1795 the Scottish explorer Mungo Park found its middle, describing a river 'glittering to the morning sun, as wide as the Thames at Westminster, and flowing slowly to the eastward'. But *where* to the east? On a second journey in 1805 Park tried to answer that question, but he vanished along the way, together with his 44 redcoats. By all accounts he was attacked by natives in a narrow stretch of the river, his canoe overturned and he, his companions and his belongings were lost in the tumult. To the problem of finding the mouth of the Niger was added that of discovering what had happened to Park and, particularly, what had become of his journal. In 1816, therefore, Britain sent an expedition to the mouth of the Congo. The authorities – that is, Sir John Barrow of the Admiralty – saw nothing silly in this: there was no reason why the Niger (if that really *was* its name) should not curl from Senegal through west and central Africa to join the Congo. As the Congo was also called the Zaïre, why should it not, at some point, also be called the Niger? And, as both rivers were sometimes called the Nile, maybe they were both linked to the Egyptian river that bore the same name.

The 1816 expedition, under Captain James Hingston Tuckey, was not successful. It went a few hundred miles upriver before being halted by a series of rapids, whereupon Tuckey and a small group staggered overland for a few weeks before dying of yellow fever. None of the officers, and very few of the crew, returned alive. This terrible start did not deter Barrow, however. In 1818 he sent another expedition under Dr Joseph Ritchie and Lieutenant George Lyon to Tripoli, expecting they would be able to catch one of the many caravans that he knew for a fact ran like clockwork up and down the Sahara. Once at the other side, they would be able to investigate another of Barrow's theories: that the Niger emptied into Lake Chad. Lyon returned in 1820 with the news that Ritchie was dead, they had got nowhere, the caravans didn't operate as Barrow thought they did, and that North Africa was an unwholesome, disease-ridden place whose inhabitants were ill-disposed towards Christians. Again, Barrow was unperturbed. In 1821 he learned that for just £6,000 the Pasha of Tripoli was willing to provide an escort to Lake Chad. So another small group was despatched, comprising two Scots: a serious-minded scientist named Walter Oudney and the tall, red-bearded, pipe-smoking figure of Lieutenant Hugh Clapperton; to these was attached an English artillery officer, Major Dixon Denham. Oudney was nominally in charge, but owing to an administrative oversight Denham had been given the impression that the expedition was his. The ensuing disputes were predictably virulent.

The two Scots resented Denham's high-handed manner. Oudney complained that had he known the man he would never have accepted the job. Clapperton was equally scathing, protesting that Denham's ignorance of the most basic surveying skills was so profound as to render him a useless and expensive deadweight. For his part, Denham described them as the 'most tiresome companions imaginable'. Of Clapperton he wrote: 'so vulgar, conceited and quarrelsome a person I scarcely ever met with'. As for Oudney, he noted tartly that he spoke no foreign languages, could not ride a horse and had never in his life travelled further overland than 30 miles from Edinburgh. But despite this lack of qualifications, 'this son of War, or rather Bluster, completely rules; therefore any proposition coming from me is generally negatived by a majority'.

The situation was so little to Denham's taste that he left Oudney and Clapperton to travel on their own to Murzouk, one of the gateways to the Sahara, following them on 5 March 1822 with a shipwright named William Hillman, who had agreed to accompany him as the expedition's carpenter. When he reached Murzouk, however, Denham was disgusted to find that the local sultan – supposedly a vassal of the Pasha of Tripoli – had refused to supply the promised escort across the Sahara. Already disillusioned by the expedition, and irritated by the discomfort of his month-long journey from Tripoli, during which he had gone several days without water and had endured blinding sandstorms, Denham announced his immediate return to Tripoli. To Oudney, Clapperton and Hillman, none of whom was in good health, he promised that he would speak urgently to the Pasha and would return shortly with the escort. In fact, when he reached Tripoli all he did was book a passage to London via France. He had been promised a

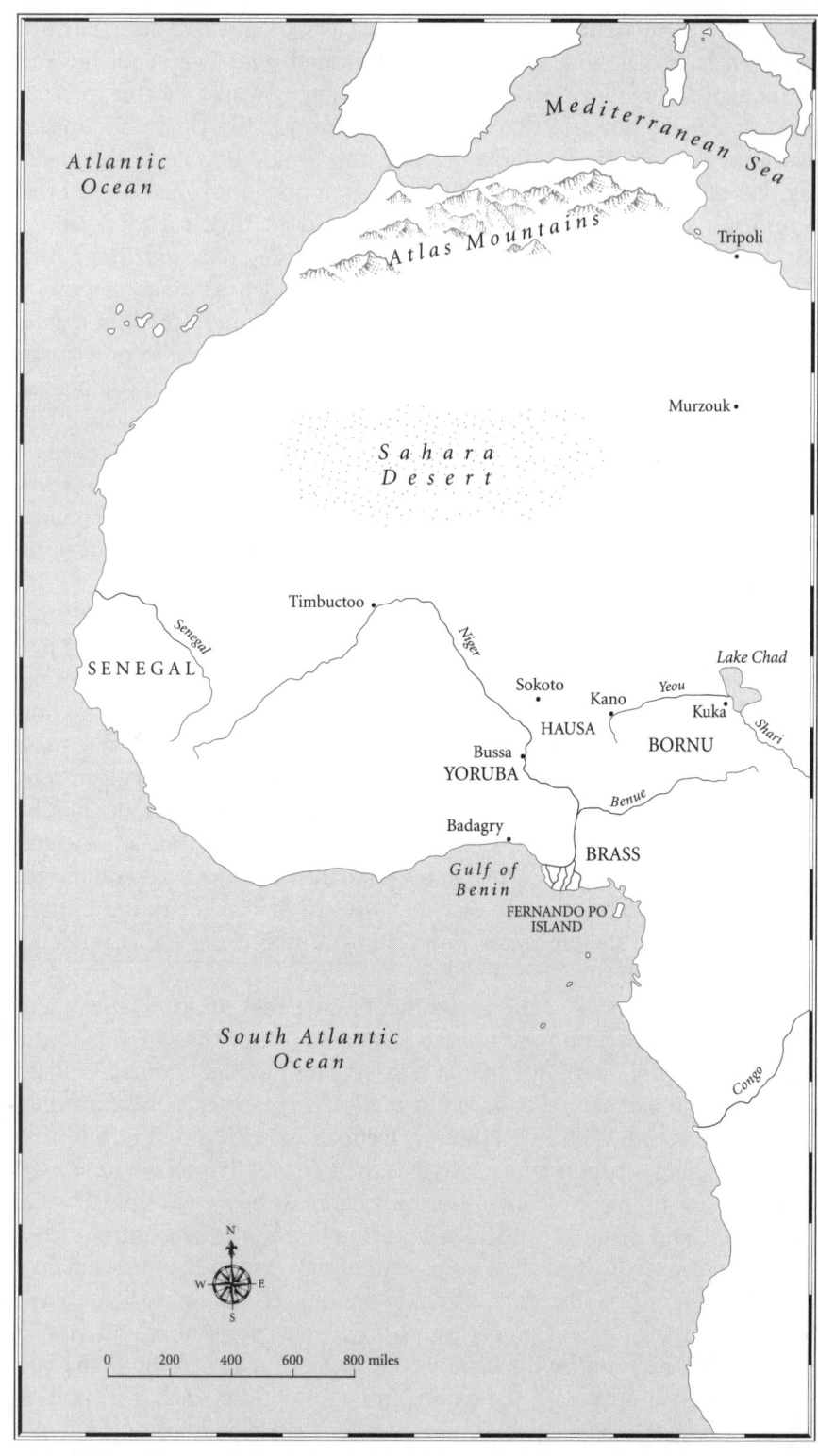

Atlantic
Ocean

Mediterranean Sea

Atlas Mountains

Tripoli

Murzouk •

Sahara
Desert

Timbuctoo •

SENEGAL

Senegal

Niger

Sokoto •

Kano •

Yeou

Lake Chad

Shari

HAUSA

Kuka •

BORNU

Bussa •

YORUBA

Benue

Badagry •

BRASS

Gulf of
Benin

FERNANDO PO
ISLAND

South Atlantic
Ocean

Congo

N

W   E

S

0   200   400   600   800 miles

lieutenant-colonelcy for joining the expedition and, since it was impossible to cross the Sahara without the protection of arms and no such protection was forthcoming, he felt it was time to claim his reward. Far better, he reasoned, to press his case in person than by letter from some distant spot in the desert. Oudney and Clapperton did not learn of his change of heart until September. Their outrage was cut short by a fever that confined them to their beds for a fortnight and reappeared at intervals in the following weeks.

If Denham had lost interest in the expedition, the British consul at Tripoli, Hanmer Warrington, had not. A man of force, charm and intelligence, who had occupied his post since 1814, he had inveigled himself so successfully into the Pasha's confidence that he was, in all but name, his foreign secretary. It was he who pressed the Pasha to have an escort ready for the explorers and he who sent a message to Denham – currently in Marseilles – informing him of his success. Reluctantly, Denham returned to Africa, and on 30 October he galloped into Murzouk bearing the good, if untruthful, news that he alone had organized the escort they needed. Nobody came out to welcome him, which he thought odd until he peered into the white men's quarters. Oudney and Clapperton lay on their beds, wracked by fever, while Hillman hobbled around weakly as their manservant. 'Nothing could be more disheartening than their appearance,' Denham remarked.

They left Murzouk on 19 November for Bornu, a kingdom situated to the west of Lake Chad, from where they hoped to gain access to the Niger. The road to Bornu was 700 miles long and strewn with the bones of those who had fallen by the wayside. The cost of a Saharan passage was high: even if the wells were full, slave caravans expected to lose much of their human cargo; and whole caravans, larger in population than some towns, were known to have perished in the crossing. It was not just a matter of meeting the occasional skeleton, but of crunching over mats of them. At one point Denham was dozing on his camel when he was woken by the sound of breaking bones; he watched in horror as a skull, disturbed by the camel's pads, bounced over the rocks. 'This event,' he wrote, 'gave me a sensation which it took some time to remove.' Occasionally, the bodies lay in piles a hundred deep, their limbs torn apart, a sight that troubled Oudney: 'here a leg, there an arm, fixed with their ligaments at considerable distances from the trunk. What could have done this? ... Man forced by hunger, or the camels?' And they weren't always old dead, as Denham recorded: 'One of the skeletons we passed today had a very fresh appearance; the beard was still hanging to the skin of the face and the features were still discernible.'

The going was hard, through featureless pavements of black rock and precipitous dunes so high and convoluted that it was easy to imagine a caravan being swallowed in their depths. The few wells they met required heavy digging before they yielded a small flow of brackish fluid. By January 1823 four camels were dead from exhaustion, and the Europeans weren't in much better shape. Oudney was so weak that he could not walk a hundred yards without a pause, Hillman could not walk at all – could not, in fact, even get off his mule without assistance – and Clapperton was still groggy from fever. However, they still had enough strength to squabble with Denham, who remained in good health and reciprocated energetically. They kept it up until 4 February when they saw a vision that temporarily dispelled their animosity. Before them, 'glowing with the golden rays of the sun', lay Lake Chad.

After the nightmare of the desert, Lake Chad was an Eden. Pink forests of flamingos stood in its shallows, alongside thousands of pelicans. Fish were so numerous that they could be taken by hand. The shore was covered with trees, from whose branches hung monkeys and snakes. Buffalo, antelope, elephants, wild boar and guinea fowl roamed the countryside. The wildlife – so Denham said – was so tame that it was theirs for the asking: when he waded into the lake the flamingos shuffled aside to make space for him. The humans, too, seemed very amenable: after an initial flight, fearing that the caravan was a band of Tuareg, they welcomed the newcomers. His companions being under the weather, Denham was alone in recording the appearance of 'good looking, laughing negresses, all but naked', one of whom he purchased. The ruler of Bornu, Sultan El Kanemi, was no less hospitable than his subjects. Escorting them to his capital, Kuka,* he provided them with food, ordered houses to be built for them and offered to take them wherever they wished to go.

By December Oudney and Clapperton were marching west, following the course of the River Yeou (Yobe) that flowed into Lake Chad. It was far too small to be the Niger, but it might be some secondary branch, perhaps proceeding from another lake into which the main river flowed. Denham, meanwhile, continued south around Lake Chad and discovered the River Shari. The Shari seemed the right size, but its upper stretches were in a war zone and Denham was unable to ascertain whether it was the Niger. He returned with little solid information other than that the natives inoculated themselves 'by inserting into the flesh the sharp point of a dagger charged with the disease'. (In this they were apparently far ahead of Europeans, who had only recently taken to vaccination.) The Shari was not the river he sought, but it very nearly was; for if Denham had followed it to its source and then crossed the watershed he would have found the Benue, a river that *did* connect with the Niger. He returned to Kuka, where he waited to see what Oudney and Clapperton had found.

The two Scots had aimed initially for Kano, a large town 300 miles from Lake Chad on the upper stretches of the Yeou. From there, if the river was not the Niger, they intended to strike west for Sokoto, capital of the Hausa nation. Oudney, alas, never saw either town. He died halfway to Kano on

---

* The Europeans were taken aback by the men El Kanemi sent to fetch them. Anticipating a primitive rabble, they saw a disciplined body of cavalry whose swords, shields and chainmail gave them the appearance of a crusader army lost in time.

12 January 1824. Collecting the doctor's notes and journals, Clapperton continued on his own, reaching Kano on 20 January. Hoping to make an imposing entrance, he donned his naval uniform and strode into town but, to his surprise, nobody turned a hair. This was an important trading centre where one could buy a diverse array of goods – French writing paper, Egyptian cotton, Maltese swords, English umbrellas – and the sight of strangers in unusual costumes was nothing new to its inhabitants. Belatedly, Clapperton realized that these supposedly dark and ignorant regions of Africa were, in fact, highly sophisticated. The impression was reinforced when, after a fever-ridden month in Kano, he entered Sokoto on 16 March. Its ruler, Sultan Bello, was quite up to date with proceedings in the wider world, knew all about Britain's military machinations, inquired penetratingly about its ambitions in India, and showed a remarkable familiarity with its press. Clapperton having brought a few newspapers with him to impress uneducated natives with the West's mastery of the written word, Bello asked him to read them aloud so he could catch up with things.

When Clapperton inquired about the Niger and, on the offchance, Timbuctoo, Bello's response was guarded. Yes, there was a river to the south that his people called the Quorra; yes, he had heard of a white man who had been killed on it, his possessions having been taken by a local potentate, the Sultan of Yauri. And yes, he did know of Timbuctoo: it lay 600 miles to the west; but the way there was difficult and the tribes dangerous. He could not advise Clapperton to go there. Nor, for the same reasons, would it be wise to seek the Quorra. He said this in such menacing tones that Clapperton thought it prudent not to try his luck. To assuage his visitor's curiosity, however, Bello drew a map in the sand to show the Quorra's course. From its source the river curled northwards, then, at Park's furthest recorded point, shot east to terminate in Egypt – as so many British geographers, whose opinions were reported in the papers that Bello read, thought it might. Clapperton thanked him and left for Bornu. Before departing, he recorded of the people of Sokoto that: 'It is commonly believed among them that strangers would come and take their country from them, if they knew the course of the Quorra.' Given the subsequent colonization of West Africa, one cannot but admire Bello for his sagacity and foresight.

Clapperton was back in Kuka by 8 July, so wracked by his journey that he collapsed in his hut. Not having seen the man for eight months, Denham came to investigate. 'So satisfied was I,' he wrote, 'that the sunburnt, sickly person that lay extended on the floor, rolled in a dark-blue shirt, was not my companion, that I was about to leave the place when he convinced me of my error by calling me by name.' When Denham heard Clapperton's news he immediately proposed an expedition across the desert to Egypt. But good sense prevailed, and the three Europeans – Hillman was now much better and had passed his spare hours making a throne and ceremonial carriage for El Kanemi – crossed the Sahara once again, reaching London in May 1825.

They received a mixed welcome. The *Edinburgh Review* said they had covered more ground and opened more expanses of uncharted desert than any other African expedition to date – in which there was some truth. But Barrow was dissatisfied: for all the information the explorers had brought home, they had not solved the riddle of the Niger. As he wrote: 'The information obtained by Clapperton has entangled the question more than before.' Another expedition was therefore necessary. Having secured his promotion, Denham wanted nothing more to do with the desert, so the job fell to Clapperton. A repeat journey through the Sahara was deemed too expensive and troublesome, so he was ordered to take his chances in the tropics. His task, as outlined by Barrow, was monumental: he was to cross the Niger, ascertain what had happened to Park, retrieve his journal, then travel via Sokoto to Timbuctoo* before returning down the Niger. He left London on 27 August 1825 with three officers and a manservant named Richard Lemon Lander.

Lander was a 20-year-old Cornishman who had grown up in the West Indies. He was poorly educated but intelligent and displayed what he described as 'rambling inclinations'. Remembering the black women who had nursed him as a child, these inclinations led him to Africa. 'There was always a charm in the very sound of [its name], that always made my heart flutter on hearing it mentioned,' he wrote, 'whilst its boundless deserts of sand, the awful obscurity in which many of the interior regions were enveloped; the strange and wild aspect of countries that had never been trodden by the foot of a European, and even the very failure of all former undertakings to explore its hidden wonder, united to strengthen the determination I had come to.' He had visited South Africa in 1823 as servant to a colonial administrator, and when he heard that Clapperton was departing to 'ascertain the source, progress and termination of the mysterious Niger', he volunteered his services at once. He was accepted because he seemed straightforward, dependable, honest and obedient.

On 30 November Clapperton's men landed at the port of Badagry, not far west of modern Lagos. To cheer their transport on its way Lander pulled a small bugle from his pocket and played 'Over the hills and far away'. The party then set off inland, enticing so many expatriate adventurers that it eventually swelled to nine (not including the small column of porters who carried the white men's goods and, often, the white men themselves). But disease took its usual toll, and by January the group had shrunk to three: Clapperton, Lander and an African interpreter named Pasko, of whom only Lander and Pasko were able to walk. (The boots Clapperton had purchased in London did not fit; so, after experimenting with slippers, he was carried

---

* Major Gordon Laing, who was currently heading for Timbuctoo via the Sahara, was outraged when he heard of Clapperton's departure. 'I smile at the idea of his reaching Timbuctoo before me. How can he expect it? Has he not already had the power? Has he not already thrown away the chance ... It is destined for me. It is due me, and [no] Clapperton can interfere with me.'

in a hammock for the rest of the journey.) They encountered the Yoruba, whose state seemed near heavenly. According to Clapperton they were a kind people, at ease with each other and their rulers. Their government was 'conducted with the greatest mildness' and their carvings, of which they were justly proud, were in Lander's words '[the] rival, in point of delicacy, [to] any of a similar kind I have seen in Europe'. To the north, however, the land was tyrannized either by Sultan Bello from Sokoto or Sheikh El Kanemi from Kuka.

Clapperton, Lander and Pasko pressed on, buying their way north with trinkets and trade goods, brandishing documents that proved their friendship with both Bello and El Kanemi. They reached the town of Bussa, near the Niger, where people told them how Mungo Park had met his death at the hands of bowmen who had fired on him from both banks and how his canoe had overturned in the rapids. They even pointed out the spot where it had happened. But when questioned about Park's belongings they became 'very uneasy' and muttered contradictorily. They had been destroyed, they said; they had been taken away by 'learned men'; they had no idea what had happened to them; they had been children at the time; but if they were anywhere they were upstream with the Sultan of Yauri. When Clapperton wrote to the sultan to inquire, a message came back to the effect that he did, indeed, have some of Park's books and would sell them for the price of a rifle. But the white men would have to collect the goods themselves.

Clapperton did not have the time. The rains were at hand and he wanted to be in the healthier climate of Sokoto before they arrived. He was already suffering from malaria and dysentery, neither of which would improve if he stayed where he was. Park's belongings could be collected on the way back. He reached Sokoto on 19 October 1825, only to find that Sultan Bello of the Hausa was now at war with El Kanemi of Bornu and that he, Clapperton, was regarded as a spy for the opposite camp. Bello, his usual well-informed self, told Clapperton that he had been warned the English had designs on his nation and, given a chance, would 'seize on the country and dispossess him, as they had done with regard to India'. As for Timbuctoo, he could not possibly go there: it was too dangerous. Meanwhile, if Clapperton did not mind, he would relieve him of his weapons. But he was welcome to stay in Sokoto. Indeed, there was no question but that he *must* stay in Sokoto. And lest he be concerned about his baggage and trade goods, Bello would take care of them on his behalf. Stripped of his possessions and placed under virtual house arrest, Clapperton became angry. 'At no time am I possessed of a sweet and passive temper,' he wrote, 'and when the ague is coming on me it is a little worse.' But there was nothing he could do. He and Lander were allotted a hut that resembled an 'immense bee hive', in which Clapperton paced to and fro, clad in dressing-gown and slippers, and smoking cigars. Of an evening Lander played cheery tunes on his bugle. On Christmas Day Clapperton gave him one of his six remaining gold sovereigns in recognition of his efforts – 'for he is well deserving, and has never once shown want of courage or enterprise unworthy of an Englishman'.

Festering in his beehive, Clapperton lost all strength. 'It is most violently hot here,' he wrote. 'I fancy the weather has already made some impression on my health, for I feel now and then a little feverish and unwell. I sincerely wish it may not increase upon me. Heaven knows I have had enough of sickness since I first set my foot on African soil.' As for Timbuctoo, it was impossible. A group had just arrived from the place, and 'had with the greatest difficulty been allowed to come here with nothing but a staff and a shirt, and had been twelve months on the road owing to the war'. In these conditions, 'were I to go, all the country would hear of me, and his enemies would have me and all my baggage before I had been two months on the road'. They spent six months as unwilling guests in Sokoto until, on 12 March, Bello scored a crushing victory over El Kanemi and announced they were free to leave. But that same evening Clapperton was struck by such a fierce bout of dysentery that he could go nowhere. 'I believe I shall never recover,' he told Lander. For a month he drifted in and out of consciousness, in his waking moments instructing Lander how to proceed without him. Then on 10 April he said, 'Richard, I shall shortly be no more. I feel myself dying.' Surprisingly, he improved. By the 12th he was eating well and was convinced he would pull through. On the 13th he sat up unaided for the first time in weeks – only to shudder in Lander's arms and fall dead.

For a man who was in theory just a servant, who did not really know where he was, and who had no authority, Lander showed great resource. First, he forced Bello to provide a suitable funeral for Clapperton, complete with camel cortège and an array of slaves to dig the grave. 'I read the impressive funeral service of the Church of England over the remains of my valued master,' he wrote, 'the English flag waving slowly and mournfully over them at the same moment. Not a single soul listened to this distressing ceremony, for the slaves were quarrelling with each other the whole of the time it lasted.' Then he demanded Bello repay him for the goods he had seized from the expedition. Surprisingly, Bello did so – not to the full value, but enough for Lander to make his way home. But how would he get there? 'I could not help but be deeply affected with my lonesome and dangerous position,' he wrote, 'a hundred and fifteen days journey from the nearest sea-coast, surrounded by a selfish and cruel race of strangers, my only friend and master mouldering in his grave, and myself suffering dreadfully from fever.' Clapperton had suggested he catch a caravan to Tripoli, but Lander had other ideas. He would complete the expedition's task and follow the Niger to its mouth, accompanied by a couple of slaves and the interpreter Pasko, who had hitherto lurked unobtrusively in Sokoto's suburbs.

So great was Lander's new-found confidence that he might well have made it. But when he reached Bussa he found that the middle reaches of the Niger were once again involved in a war. He therefore travelled overland through

Yoruba territory, relying on the generosity of its inhabitants to supplement his dwindling supply of trade goods. He was very lucky to reach the coast – but unlucky to reach it when he did. He arrived while King Adele, the ruler of Badagry, was transferring a large – and illegal – consignment of slaves to Brazilian and Portuguese vessels. Persuaded by the slavers that Lander was a spy, Adele arrested him and sentenced him to trial by poison. If he drank it and survived, all would be well; but if he died, it was proof of his guilt. Having endured so much, and being now so close to salvation, Lander was infuriated 'that my life should be destroyed; that my skull should be preserved as a trophy by heartless savages, and my body devoured ... by birds of prey'. Before an audience of 500 to 600 people, he drank the bowl of poison. It *was* poison, of that Lander was sure, but it was a slow-acting one. Feeling dizzy, he pushed through the crowds to his hut and took an emetic. When he had finished vomiting he was congratulated by Adele: nobody had survived a trial by poison in years; in recompense for the inconvenience to which he had been put he was to consider himself a guest of the town. For obvious reasons neither the Brazilians nor the Portuguese were willing to have him aboard, so Lander had to wait for a British ship to take him home. He arrived in Portsmouth on 30 April 1828, dishevelled, sunburned and weary, but still carrying Clapperton's chest of papers.

When the trunk was opened the authorities were disappointed. Clapperton seemed to have fulfilled none of his primary goals, and although he had learned a little about Park's death had not retrieved his journal. In fact, the only physical trace of anything to do with Park was a shirt labelled 'Thomas Park' that Lander had purchased in the last stages of his journey. Thomas, the son of Mungo, had taken three years' leave from the navy to search for his father. He had never been in Africa before, but it seemed to him obvious that to survive in the tropics one should act as he had heard Africans did. He therefore smeared himself with oil and clay and strode inland from Badagry carrying little food, fewer clothes and no medicine. He died two days after leaving the coast.

Clapperton's failure – for that was how it was seen, despite the fact that in the course of his two expeditions he had become the first European to find a route from the Mediterranean to the Gulf of Benin – necessitated a third expedition. Timbuctoo had already been found by Gordon Laing, so that was out of the way; but it was imperative to find Park's journal and trace the Niger to its mouth. Forward stepped Richard Lander. He would complete the business, he told Barrow, for the sum of £100 in travelling expenses, £356 for trade goods and equipment, plus a pension of £100 for himself and his wife while he was away. And, if it was acceptable, he would take his brother John with him – free of charge. Of all the strange proposals advanced in the history of African exploration this seemed the most far-fetched. How could two untrained men, of lowly social status, be expected to succeed where their betters had fared so disastrously? Why, Lander didn't even know how to use a sextant. It was laughable. On the other hand, Lander was an intelligent young man who had already travelled in West Africa, and his expedition was outstandingly inexpensive. If he succeeded, well and fine. If he and his brother perished a few miles inland, like so many others, it would not matter a jot for, as Lander was the first to admit, 'the gap we may make in society will be hardly noticed at all'. Barrow took a chance. The two Landers left Portsmouth on 9 January 1830, and on 22 March coasted through the Badagrian surf to be 'flung with violence on the burning sands'.

Hitherto, all Niger expeditions had been bedevilled by a very British question of propriety. What clothes should one wear in front of the natives? One faction supported the adoption of regional fashions. George Lyon had stated: 'I am confident that it would never be possible for any man to pass through Africa unless in every respect he qualified himself to appear as a Mohammedan; and should I myself return to that country, I would not be accompanied by anyone who would refuse to observe these precautions.' Others said this was an insult to the flag and that Westerners should wear the garb of civilized men. Thus, on Clapperton's first expedition to Africa he, Denham and Oudney wore thick serge, with waistcoats and brass buttons – sometimes also dress uniform. It was uncomfortable but, Oudney wrote, 'I have not once experienced any opposition on account of being a Christian and a Briton. It is much easier for us to support our own character than one that must not but be hard even after several years of experience.' The Landers supported Lyon and arrived at Badagry in the clothes they thought Arab traders might wear. Emerging from the sea in baggy trousers, long gowns and wide-brimmed straw hats, they were greeted with hilarity.

Ignoring the mockery, Richard Lander employed his old slave Pasko, plus a couple of 'wives' he had acquired on his last trip, and then set off with his brother John for the Niger. On 17 June they reached Bussa, whose ruler forgot that he had no knowledge of Park's belongings and happily showed them a book that had been taken from the scene of the murder. As he unwrapped the volume their hearts 'beat high with expectation'. But it was not Park's journal, merely a book of logarithms, containing a tailor's bill and an invitation to dine with Mr and Mrs Watson of the Strand. The king of Bussa refused to sell the book, claiming that it was revered as a household god, so they paddled upriver to Yauri to collect the journals that the sultan had promised Clapperton. Their optimism was boosted by the scenery. 'Beautiful, spreading trees adorned the country on each side of the river, like a park,' Richard Lander wrote, 'corn, nearly ripe, waved over the water's edge; large, open villages appeared every half-hour; and herds of spotted cattle were observed grazing and enjoying the cool of the shade ... The river was as smooth as a lake; canoes laden with sheep and goats, were paddled by women down its almost imperceptible current.' At Yauri, however, their hopes were confounded. It was a miserable village, swamped by pools of sewage-filled water. Everyone was poor and unhealthy, and the sultan reigned from a dingy courtyard covered in swallows' droppings. Worse still, he said he did not have Park's journal and was affronted by the very suggestion. 'How do you think I could have the books of a person that was lost at Bussa?' he sneered. Then he refused to let the Landers leave until they paid a large enough bribe. It took a letter from the king of Bussa before they were at last permitted to quit their cockroach-ridden quarters and paddle down the Niger.

At Bussa, however, they were given similar treatment. A canoe was on its way from the Sultan of Wawa downriver, the king explained. A small payment would secure it. The payment was made, but the canoe did not materialize. They waited and waited, using their limited trade goods to buy food – typically, rancid hippo meat – and by 6 September they were becoming anxious. 'Our resources . . . are diminishing rapidly,' John Lander wrote, 'and when they are gone, we know not what we shall do.' They managed to procure various items of Park memorabilia – a gown, a gun, a sword, a sprung seat from his canoe and other oddments – but while this fulfilled one of their objectives, the Niger seemed daily more impossible. A canoe did finally appear, but it was patently inadequate for their needs, despite having cost almost all they had. Richard Lander lost his temper. 'There is infinitely more difficulty and greater bustle and discussion in simply purchasing a canoe here,' he raged, 'than there would be in Europe in drawing up a treaty of peace, or in determining the boundaries of an Empire.' He told the king that if they couldn't buy another vessel they would leave without it. Miraculously, a second canoe appeared. It was not much bigger than the first, and in no better condition, but it would do. They paid for it and left.

Their journey down the Niger was as frustrating as their stay at Bussa, only longer. The canoes leaked so badly that they had to find new ones. But wherever they stopped it was the same story: a good, big canoe was nearby; all they had to do was wait. As they waited, they spent their ever-dwindling resources. 'They have played with us as if we were great dolls,' wrote John Lander. 'We have been driven about like shuttlecocks . . . Why this double-dealing, this deceit, this chicanery?' Tired of dickering and waiting, they eventually stole the canoes they needed and pressed on. They met the mouth of the Benue – the river Denham might have discovered had he been able to – but finding its current too strong for their canoes, they continued with the flow. On 22 October the sight of a seagull told them they were near the coast. The river became busier, the banks lusher. Grey parrots whistled from palm trees and bits of Western detritus could be found on the shore. The villages appeared daily more prosperous. They anticipated at any moment the sight of friendly traders who could escort them for the rest of their journey, and on 5 November their hopes were realized. Plying upriver came a flotilla of vessels, bedecked with flags. They were unusual flags, some of them displaying bottles and glasses, others chairs and tables, one of them a leg; but above the motley fluttered the Union Jack. Their certainty that they had reached civilization was underlined when they noticed that the rowers wore shirts and coats – it was as quickly dashed, however, when the flotilla unveiled its cannons and began to fire at them.

The boats were not those of friendly traders but of pirates. A short tussle ensued, during which they lost their clothes, their guns, Richard's journal, all Park's memorabilia and everything of value that they possessed, before being hauled to meet the pirate chief, King Obie, at his palace. John Lander, who had somehow retained his notebook, scribbled a description of the outlandish figure before them. 'His head was graced with a cap shaped like a sugar loaf, and thickly covered with strings of coral and pieces of broken looking glass ... his neck, or rather his throat, was encircled with several strings of the same kind of bead, which were fastened so tightly, as in some degree to affect his circulation, and to give his throat and cheeks an inflamed appearance ... He wore a short Spanish surtout of red cloth, which fitted close to his person, being much too small ... Thirteen or fourteen bracelets (we had the curiosity to count them) decorated each wrist, and to give them full effect, the sleeves of the coat had been cut off ... The king's trousers ... reached no further than his legs, the lower parts ... being ornamented like the wrists and with precisely the same number of strings of beads; besides which, a string of little brass bells encircled each leg above the ankles.' King Obie shook his legs to make the bells tinkle, then informed the Landers that they were now his property. They need not worry, though, because there was an English ship at the river mouth, the *Thomas of Liverpool*, whose captain would undoubtedly pay the 20-slaves'-worth he had set as the price of their release. There was one proviso: all negotiations were to be conducted inland; under no circumstances could the Landers go to the coast.

The Landers knew very well that the type of captain to be found in these waters – the *Thomas* was ostensibly trading for palm oil – would be unwilling to spend that amount, and would certainly not do so if he couldn't see what he was buying. They had all but resigned themselves to being 'classed with the most degraded and despicable of mankind, [to] become slaves in a land of ignorance and barbarism', when a saviour emerged from downriver. King Boy, who ruled the coastal region of Brass, was willing to sell them on Obie's behalf for 15 extra slaves and a cask of rum. They left in Boy's canoe on 12 November to complete the remaining 60 miles to the river mouth. In his mind, Richard Lander was already standing on the brig, freshly washed and relating the details of his triumphant journey to a sympathetic captain. At Brass, however, King Boy decided that, while Richard could visit the *Thomas*, John, Pasko and the others must stay where they were. Richard Lander was not happy about these conditions, but was certain that the captain of the *Thomas* would honour the deal.

The captain, a man named Lake, was not in a good mood. Four of his eight crew were dead and the remainder were bedridden. He was stuck behind a sandbar at the mouth of the Niger and his only way out was to pay a notoriously treacherous pilot to see him through the shallows. As Lander approached the *Thomas*, 'the emotions of delight ... quite beyond my powers of description', Lake watched with a sullen eye. When the stranger climbed aboard, presented Barrow's orders and asked if he could draw a bill to pay his captors, Lake exploded. 'If you think you have a —— fool to deal with you are mistaken; I'll not give you a b——y flint for your bill, I would not give you a —— for it.' But then his tone changed. Among King Boy's captives were men who could replace his lost crew. He told Boy to have the men on board within three days or he would sail without them and Boy would never get a penny for his so-called slaves. Heartened by the prospect of action, he hauled his mate, Spittle, from his sickbed and sent him to reconnoitre the sandbar. When Lander protested at Lake's language and callous attitude Lake told him to —— off. When the pilot captured Spittle and asked £50 for his return Lake said the same to him too. Against all wisdom, King Boy ferried John Lander and the remnants of the Niger expedition to the *Thomas*. Lake accepted the 'goods' and told Boy that he wasn't to expect a penny out of the deal; moreover, if Spittle wasn't returned forthwith he would summon 1,000 men-of-war and blast Brass to pieces. Spittle was duly returned.

How right Sultan Bello had been to reject the approaches of men like Clapperton and Lander: they might have seemed helpless at the time, but they were harbingers of a power that would eventually swallow scores of West African nations similar to his own. At the same time, one cannot but admire Lake's audacity. He did not have 1,000 men-of-war – he barely had a crew – and his single weapon was a small cannon. He was far weaker than the men of Brass whose powerful artillery was ranged on his ship. The winds, too, were against him: as soon as he raised anchor he would be blown ashore, where small groups of armed warriors awaited his arrival, cheerfully pointing out places where he could land. All he had was a foul-mouthed strength of purpose and one vital bit of luck. At 8.00 a.m. on 27 November the prevailing northerly winds switched to a tiny sea breeze, and with the use of boats Lake dragged the *Thomas* over the sandbar in three fathoms of water. He deposited the Landers on Fernando Po, a small island to the east of the mouth of the Niger, before going about his undefined and shady business. The last they saw of their crude but effective saviour was his ship rounding a headland, pursued by pirates. There came the sound of cannon-fire and then darkness fell. The next day the sea was clear. Lake and his ship were never heard of again.

On 10 June 1831 Richard Lander was in London, presenting his findings to the Admiralty. Despite a few misgivings as to the paucity of facts and figures, his report was received warmly. It was, according to the *Edinburgh Review*, 'perhaps the most important discovery of the age'. The scale of the achievement was not reflected in the reward. The Landers received precisely what they had asked at the outset: in Richard's case £100 and in John's nothing. In 1832 Richard Lander received the Royal Geographical Society's first gold medal, but he was not there to collect it. In that year he had sailed for the Gulf of Benin to lead a commercial expedition up the Niger. Near Bussa his party was attacked by 10,000 angry Africans, one of whom aimed his musket at Lander. A copper bolt struck him near the anus. Gangrene ensued and he died on 2 February 1834. Ravaged by disease, the expedition hastily retired. When it reached Britain only eight of its 48 members were still alive.

The quest for the Niger had taken 40 years and had killed practically every man who joined it. Geographers such as Barrow could perhaps take pride in having filled another small blank on the atlas. But their pride was bought at huge financial and human cost. Moreover, as Lander's final, fatal mission showed, while the Niger may have been 'found', it had very obviously not been conquered.

Gordon Laing and René Caillié (1824–8)

Timbuctoo! Here was a word that quickened the spirit of every red-blooded explorer. What were Atlantis and Eldorado against these three sing-song syllables? Timbuctoo was the end of the world and its beginning. In an age that knew nothing of the Olduvai Gorge and the Rift Valley, Timbuctoo was the ancient heart of Africa. It was so distant as to be a byword for distance and so wealthy as to stagger the imagination. In Timbuctoo people could hardly stand from the weight of gold they wore; their doors had gold locks and gold bolts; the streets were literally paved with the stuff; the climate was healthy and invigorating; and the inhabitants' libidos were so inflamed that it was hard to move without tripping over an act of copulation. At the same time Timbuctoo was a city of culture and sophistication, a repository of learning whose universities and libraries contained rich and marvellous secrets.

So, at least, the story went in the 18th century. In fact no Westerner had ever visited the place, and everything about it was the product of wishful thinking. The legend had arisen in the 14th century when the Arab traveller Ibn Battuta returned from the gold-rich Empire of Mali and mentioned in his journal that one of Mali's trade centres went by the name of Timbuctoo. Mali's gold soon ran out, but the connection between Timbuctoo and extravagant wealth refused to die. Indeed, the rumours swelled with every passing century until Timbuctoo was fixed in the European mind as *the* source of Africa's riches. 'Its treasures [surpassed] those of Mexico and Peru,' read one 17th-century report. 'The roofs of the houses were represented to be covered with plates of gold . . . and the mountains had only to be excavated to yield a profusion of the metallic treasure.' Scholars as well as merchants lusted after it, for it was said that: 'We shall one day correct the texts of our Greek and Latin classics by the manuscripts which are preserved there.' In 1809 an English trader in Morocco named James G. Jackson published *An Accurate and Interesting Account of Timbuctoo, the Great Emporium of Central Africa*, in which he wrote that Timbuctoo (which he had never seen) was situated so prosperously on the Niger that its outlying villages were 'as populous as those of any river in China' and that its rulers moved from palace to lustrous mosque accompanied by retinues of slaves. His book

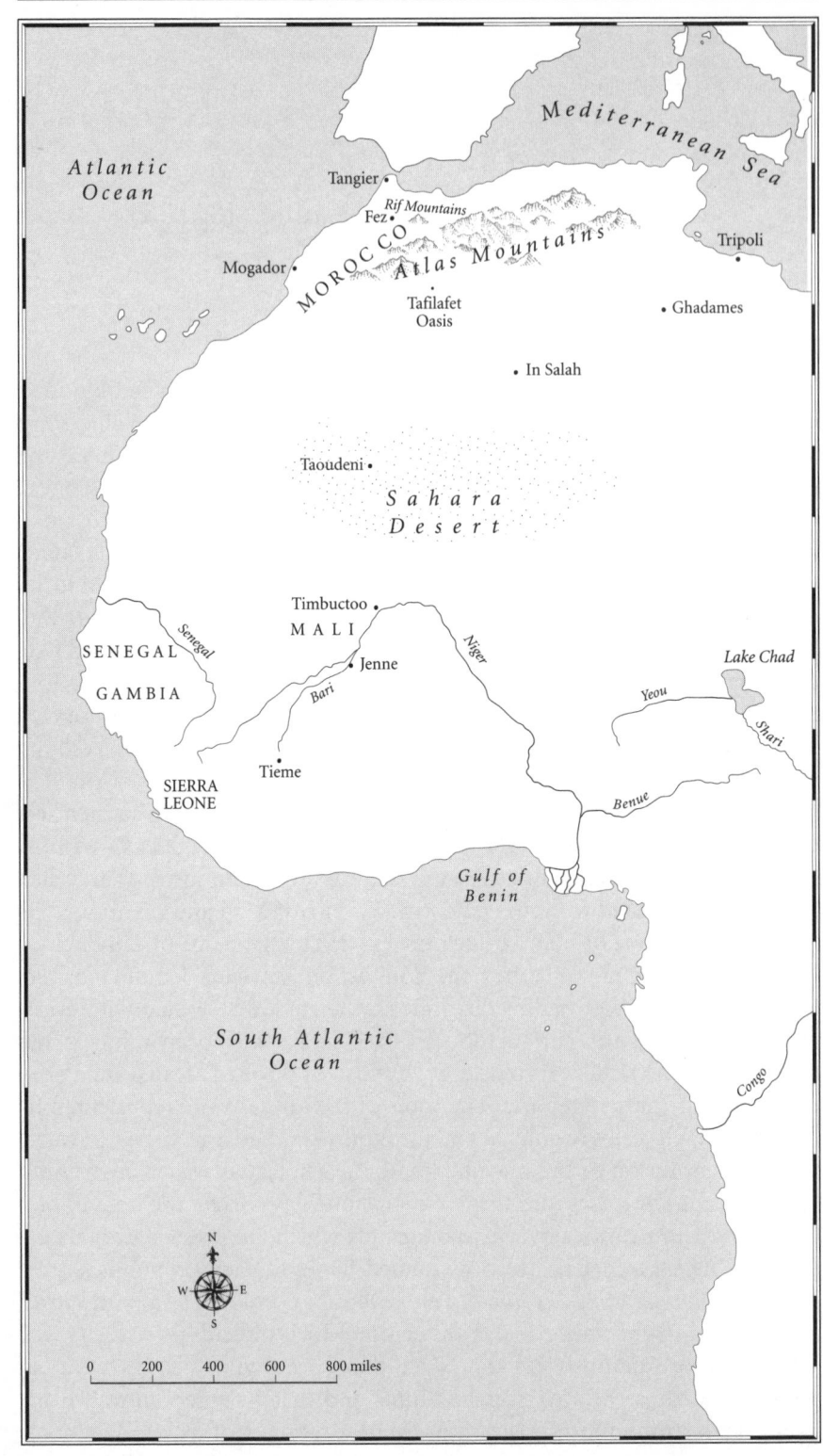

proved so popular that it was still in print eleven years later.

What made the legend so tantalizing was the fact that, although Timbuctoo did exist and was indeed one of the main embarkation points for trans-Saharan caravans, no white man seemed able to reach it. Situated on the Niger's uppermost bulge, it could only be approached via the bandit-ridden desert to the north or the pestilential tropics of West Africa. Both routes had been tried and both had been found too unhealthy for a Westerner's liking. In 1618, for example, an English company had been formed expressly for the purpose of trading with Timbuctoo. First one, then the other, of its two expeditions were lost in the Gambia, setting a precedent that soon began to look inviolable. Whether Europeans came from the north, east, west or south, whether they travelled singly or in groups, they could not break the cordon of inaccessibility that surrounded Timbuctoo. In the late 18th century Sir Joseph Banks, President of the African Association, turned his mind to the problem, despatching in rapid succession the American John Ledyard, the Irishman Daniel Houghton and the 'Moor' Ben Ali. The first two died in the attempt and the third didn't even bother, vanishing somewhere in London. In 1795 Banks sent the Scottish explorer Mungo Park, who survived imprisonment and near-starvation to reach the Niger, but still failed to find Timbuctoo. He went back again in 1805, this time with an escort of 44 redcoats. The soldiers died of disease, and at some unknown date Park was attacked and killed while navigating a stretch of rapids.

While Banks pondered his next move, an American sailor materialized at the British consulate in Mogador (then an important port on Morocco's western seaboard) with the news that he had reached the city they had all been trying to find. He was taken to London, where he related his story to the Committee of the Company of Merchants Trading to Africa, a body affliated to the African Association. Calling himself variously Benjamin Rose and Robert Adams, he claimed to have been shipwrecked off the North African coast in 1810 and subsequently enslaved by Moroccan traders who forced him to join a caravan to Timbuctoo. In hindsight, his description of desert travel was very accurate – the steady progress of 15 to 20 miles per day, the unreliability of the wells, the callous treatment accorded to those who failed to keep pace – but what he had to say about Timbuctoo struck the Committee as ludicrous. He portrayed it as a 'dull, filthy and exceedingly unattractive town', where not a speck of gold was to be seen but whose inhabitants were reasonably hospitable. Occasionally it was visited by Arab merchants in the tobacco trade. Considering 'how widely his account of Timbuctoo differed from the notions generally entertained of the magnificence of that city, and of its civilisation and of its inhabitants', the Committee felt justified in dismissing his tale. In doing so, it noted that the Mogador consul had portrayed him as 'exceedingly stupid and insensible'. Accordingly, more expeditions were sent forth, each larger and more expensive than the last, but just as unsuccessful.

Banks died in 1820, but his programme was perpetuated by his acolyte, John Barrow, Second Secretary to the Admiralty. Barrow had as little luck as Banks until, in 1824, one Captain Gordon Laing put his name forward for the task. Born in 1794, Laing was an impulsive and energetic, if opinionated, Scot who had served in Senegal, had discovered what he believed to be the source of the Niger and was willing not only to travel from Tripoli to Timbuctoo but to trace the course of the Niger to its mouth, a project that had long exercised Europe's geographers. Normally, Barrow rejected such crackpot notions – he had already sponsored several expeditions to the Niger, all of which had failed – but Laing's proposal was financially irresistible. He was willing to go without salary at an initial outlay of £640 10s. plus annual costs of £173 7s. 6d. This was incomparably cheaper than anything to date. To put it in context, one previous expedition, that led by Major Peddie, which returned from West Africa in 1821 with most of its members dead, had cost £13,000 and the bills yet to be presented would push the figure to £40,000. How could Laing's offer be refused?

Barrow gave his approval, and in May 1825 Laing – newly promoted to major – arrived in Tripoli, where the crews of two British ships scaled the rigging to give him three cheers. 'There are moments in a man's life,' wrote Laing, 'which he would not exchange for living years.' He then met the British consul, Hanmer Warrington, fell in love with his daughter Emma and proposed to her. Warrington was taken aback: he was not at all sure that he wanted this strange, impulsive adventurer as a son-in-law; moreover he had doubts as to his physical and mental stability. 'I much fear the delicate state of his health will not carry him through this arduous task,' he wrote. The wedding went ahead, but Warrington imposed a condition that the union not be consummated until Laing had returned from Timbuctoo. Laing accepted without demur. Emma was his love, but Timbuctoo was his goal: 'I am so wrapt up in the success of this enterprise that I think of nothing else all day and dream of nothing else all night.' Blithely, he ordered Warrington to pay the Pasha of Tripoli £4,000 for permission to pass unhindered through his territory. That he had at a stroke increased the cost of his expedition sixfold bothered him not at all. 'I shall do more than has ever been done before,' he boasted, 'and shall show myself to be what I have ever considered myself, a man of enterprise and genius.'

He left Tripoli in July 1825 with several camels, a quantity of food, three guides, an interpreter and a few servants. 'Please God,' he wrote to Emma Warrington, '[I] shall sleep in the long-looked-after city in forty-two days more.' His estimate was characteristically over-optimistic. Travelling via the Tripolitanian town of Ghadames, he reached the central Saharan oasis of In Salah on 2 December, by which time his self-imposed deadline had long expired. The journey had not been easy – food and water ran short; continual detours had to be made to avoid bandits – and at In Salah he found himself the object of intense and less than welcome curiosity. Few of the oasis-dwellers had ever seen a white man, with the result that at one point he had to stand on a roof while a hundred-strong crowd gathered to stare at him. Eventually, he had to nail his door shut to keep the hordes at bay.

Alone as he was, uncertain as to what lay ahead and fearful as to his safety – Christians were treated with suspicion in the predominantly Muslim Sahara – Laing's confidence waxed and waned but, if his correspondence is anything to go by, was never eclipsed. In a letter to his sister, he bragged: 'I am already possessed of much curious and valuable information, and feel confident that I shall realize the most sanguine expectations of my numerous friends.' A few sentences later: 'My father used often to accuse me of want of common sense ... 'Tis true, I never possessed any, nor ever shall ... I admit that common sense is more necessary for conducting the petty affairs of life than genius or enterprise, but the man who soars into the regions of speculation should never be hampered by it.' To Warrington: 'I am still the African traveller, and as eager as ever for discovery.' But then, 'I am now almost afraid to trust myself with the full swing of thought, and for the first time in my life I express a wish that I had with me a *companion de voyage* ... who would have united with me in saying, "I have not travelled to Timbuctoo for the sake of any other reward than that which I shall derive from the consciousness of having achieved an enterprise which will rescue my name from oblivion."' This last piece of false modesty came hard on the heel of several missives inquiring about the colonelcy he felt his achievements merited. On 25 December he wrote to a minion of the colonial secretary, Lord Bathurst (who awarded such promotions), assuring him 'with how much sincerity I wish His Lordship all the compliments and many happy returns of the season'. It was certainly the first, and probably the most unlikely, greeting ever to be sent from the middle of the Sahara.

Laing stayed in In Salah for more than a month while Tuareg tribesmen – notorious predators of the trans-Saharan trade routes – roamed hungrily to the south. As the oasis became choked with other caravans waiting, like his own, for a chance to reach Timbuctoo, he became more uncertain. His state of mind was not helped by the arrival of a portrait of Emma Warrington he had commissioned in Tripoli, which showed her to be a trifle peaky. 'My Emma is ill, is melancholy, is unhappy – her sunken eye, her pale cheek and colourless lips,' he wrote. 'Should anything happen to my Emma, which God forbid, I no longer wish to see the face of man; my course will be run – a few short days and I shall follow her to heaven ... I must lay down my pen awhile – oh that picture.'

On 9 January 1826 the road was deemed safe, and his spirits rose. Two weeks into the journey he wrote that: 'I have little ... to say more than my prospects are bright and expectations sanguine. I do not calculate upon the most trifling future difficulty between me and my return to England.' Not long afterwards his caravan was attacked by Tuareg, who killed as many men as they could before ransacking the convoy's valuables. They sliced open Laing's tent and shot, stabbed and hacked him before leaving him for dead. The following day, very much to his own surprise, Laing resurfaced. He wrote a graphic report to Warrington. 'To begin from the top: I have five sabre cuts on the crown of the head and three on the left temple, all fractures from which much bone has come away; one on my left cheek which fractured the jaw bone and has divided the ear, forming a very unsightly wound; one over the right temple and a dreadful gash on the back of the neck, which slightly grazed the windpipe; a musket ball in the hip, which made its way through my back, slightly grazing the backbone; five sabre cuts on my right arm and hand, three of the fingers broken, the hand cut three-fourths across, and the wrist bones cut through; three cuts on the left arm, the bone of which has been broken but is again uniting; one slight wound on the right leg and two with one dreadful gash on the left, to say nothing of a cut across the fingers of my left hand, now healed up.'

With the aid of a similarly wounded camel driver he continued south for 400 miles, strapped like baggage over a camel's hump, until he reached the oasis of Sidi el Muktar, where he caught plague and, while recuperating, had his pistol stolen. He was by now the only survivor of the party that had left Tripoli, his assistants having died either from disease or at the hands of the Tuareg. He had no money, no weapons and, according to the later testimony of one Arab, no right hand. Everyone at Sidi el Muktar beseeched him to return from whence he came. Writing with the thumb and middle finger of his left hand – he had practised left-handed writing before he set out, against just such an emergency – Laing assured the world that 'I am nevertheless doing well and hope yet to return to England with much important geographical information'.

Attaching himself to a new caravan, Laing covered the remaining 200 miles to Timbuctoo in approximately a fortnight, entering the fabled city on 13 August 1826. He had completed the 2,650-mile journey from Tripoli in 13 months, had become the first European to cross the central Sahara from north to south, and had done so in the face of tribulations that would have undone a lesser (and perhaps saner) man. It had been, to quote his own words, a display of considerable enterprise and genius. Unfortunately, Timbuctoo did not repay the trouble he had taken to find it. An impoverished settlement of mud houses, it did not resemble in the slightest anything he had been led to expect. It did have mosques and a ruler, but the mosques were nothing to write home about and the ruler was a powerless figure, theoretically a vassal of the Niger kingdoms to the east but dominated in reality by the Tuareg, possessing neither palaces nor retinues of slaves. There were no libraries, no universities and not a trace of the 'elegance and suavity' that Westerners had anticipated so longingly. Everything that had been written about it was wrong.

With the help of his caravan leader, Laing found a billet and began to investigate the town. Accounts tell of him galloping at night into the surrounding countryside, returning at dawn to stride through the streets, in uniform, waving a letter of credit from the Pasha of Tripoli and announcing himself as the personal representative of the King of England. In his rooms he wrote a deranged letter to Warrington, stating that Timbuctoo, 'has completely met my expectations . . . I have been busily employed during my stay searching the records in the town, which are abundant, and in acquiring information of every kind.' At the same time, however, he admitted that the ruler 'trembles for my safety and strongly urges my immediate departure'. He had envisaged a stay of at least six months, but with nothing to do, and having had it drummed into his head that he would certainly be killed if he tried to follow the Niger to its mouth, he left within six weeks.

On 22 September he caught a caravan north to Morocco. Three days later the Tuareg attacked, finishing what they had left undone in January. Two of them wrapped Laing's turban round his neck and hauled on either end until he was dead. To make sure, they then decapitated him. A black servant, who feigned death, made his way back to Ghadames, from where the news of Laing's death reached Warrington in March 1827. There was immediate uproar. Warrington, who could be violent when aroused, accused the consuls of every other country, particularly France, of having ordered Laing's assassination. He demanded the immediate retrieval of Laing's journal, which was believed to be hidden somewhere in Timbuctoo, and when it did not appear accused the Pasha's chief minister of having sold it to the French. The French consul promptly took refuge in the American consulate before fleeing to Spain.

Warrington thrashed in vain. There was no proof that Laing had even written a journal, let alone that the French had stolen it. Eventually he reverted to his time-honoured pastime of insulting the consul of Sardinia. Meanwhile, a letter from his daughter wandered on camel across the Sahara to Timbuctoo before being returned to Tripoli. 'Alas, Laing, how cruel, how sad, has been our fate,' it read. 'Will you, my own idolized husband, return to your Emma's fond arms? Will you come and repose on her faithful bosom? Will you restore happiness to her torn heart?' On 13 April 1829 Warrington married her to one of his vice-consuls, and she died six months later from tuberculosis, whose telltale signs Laing had seen in her portrait at In Salah.

Warrington's squabbles were of no interest to London – he would eventually be sacked for them in 1847 – but his allegations against the French touched a nerve. It was known that France, for reasons undisclosed but obviously pernicious, wanted to beat Britain to Timbuctoo. When Laing had first presented his case John Barrow and the Colonial Office had approved it because it was so cheap, but also because, if a Briton did not do it – God forbid – a Frenchman might. Competitors were already in the field, and the British would be left behind if they did not move swiftly. They had moved and they had discovered Timbuctoo, but their man had not returned alive and the few letters he had sent had given very little information about the town. Meanwhile, the French were closing in.

René Caillié was six years younger than Laing and very much a single-issue man, that issue being the exploration of Africa. '[Even as a youth] I already felt an ambition to signalize myself by some important discovery,' he later wrote. 'The map of Africa, in which I scarcely saw any but countries marked as desert or unknown, excited my attention more than any other.' Of all the unknown spots in those desert spaces, it was Timbuctoo that attracted him most. By the age of 16 he was in Senegal, where he successfully wangled his way on to one of Britain's many expeditions. Its failure and the discomfort he endured – 'I have since been told that my eyes were hollow, that I panted for breath, and that my tongue hung out of my mouth. For my own part I recollect that at every halt, I fell to the ground from weakness, and had not even the strength to eat ... I was not, however, the worst off, for I saw several drink their urine' – did not deter him a jot and, after a spell working in France, he had raised enough money for the passage back to Africa. Unlike the British, who refused to insult their civilization by travelling in anything other than Western clothes, Caillié decided that the key to successful exploration was to adopt local garb and manners. Thus in 1824, while Laing was promoting himself in London, Caillié was back in West Africa acclimatizing himself to life as an Arab trader, the disguise in which he intended to reach Timbuctoo. After nine months learning Arabic and studying Islam (he pretended to his tutors that he was an eager convert) he was confident he could hold his own in caravan society. Returning to the coast, he found work supervising an indigo factory in the British colony of Sierra Leone where he soon amassed savings of 2,000 francs, 'and this treasure seemed to me to be sufficient to carry me all over the world'.

While at the indigo works he received heartening news: the Geographical Society of Paris had announced in December 1824 an award of 10,000 francs for the first person to reach Timbuctoo. In theory, it did not care about the explorer's nationality – though exceptions could be made for Britons: Laing did not receive the prize – nor did it support heavily-manned expeditions, 'which would require the concurrence of several observers and many years' peaceable residence in the country'. All it wanted was 'precise information, such as may be expected from a man provided with instruments, and who is no stranger either to natural or mathematical science'. And the proof was to be presented in 'a manuscript narrative, with a geographical map, founded upon celestial observations'.

It took 18 months for the news to reach Sierra Leone, and when Caillié heard it he was overjoyed. 'Dead or alive, it will be mine,' he proclaimed. Like Laing he was spurred by an attachment to the opposite sex – in this case his sister, who needed expensive medical attention – but unlike Laing he had no governmental support and, despite the transfer of several thousand francs left over from a recent (failed) attempt via Senegal, he expected none. He would, instead, undertake it at his own expense. Presenting himself as an Egyptian who had been carried in infancy to France and, newly released in West Africa, was trying to regain his homeland, he caught a caravan to the interior on 19 April 1827. He carried a Koran, a small chest of trinkets and an umbrella.

Caillié's disguise held up, and he was able to keep reasonable track of his whereabouts, having earlier trained himself in the course of many long and laborious treks to estimate distances without using instruments. He committed to memory the name of every town they passed, and when he had the chance he scribbled surreptitious notes under the cover of reading the Koran. His travelling companions were pleasant enough and the locals were almost unanimously friendly. Indeed, apart from the physical diffi-culties of travelling on foot in the tropics, and the intermittent bouts of fever that were the curse of the region, the only thing to complain of was that the caravan's tortuous progress was to the east rather than north. Wherever he stopped he was admired for his generosity, his unassuming attitude and his umbrella, which he furled and unfurled to repeated hurrahs.

In August they reached the little village of Tieme, having covered approxi-mately 530 miles, and it was here that Caillié's health gave way. A parasitical worm had infected his foot, producing a sore that refused to heal. As the rains were heavy, and he was suffering another attack of fever, he decided to take a short break. By the end of August the sore had abated and he felt able to resume his journey. Unfortunately, 'another sore much larger than the first broke out on the same foot. I suffered considerable pain, and my foot was so swelled that I could not walk.' When the rains ceased at the end of October he was still bedridden, and his hosts' hospitality faltered as his supply of trade goods began to diminish. The village women, he recorded, were a torment: 'I was at once an object of curiosity and aversion to them. They ridiculed my gestures and my words, and went about the village mim-icking me and repeating what I had said ... the difficulty I experienced in walking excited their immoderate laughter.' On 10 November his sore had healed and he could once again contemplate the journey ahead. His intention was to join a caravan that would take him to the town of Jenne, 600-odd miles to the north, from where it was a matter of just 200 miles to Timbuctoo. But even as he looked forward, his health held him back. 'At that very time,' he wrote, 'violent pains in my jaw informed me that I was attacked with scurvy.'

It was a measure of Westerners' dietary ignorance that Caillié should succumb to the disease so swiftly. And to do so in the tropics, where fruit and vegetables were so freely available, was a terrible indictment. But scurvy was considered a scourge of the sea, so perhaps Caillié could be forgiven for not anticipating its appearance on land. For a while he suffered agonies: 'The roof of my mouth became quite bare, part of the bones exfoliated and fell away, and my teeth seemed ready to drop out of their sockets. I feared that my brain would be affected by the agonising pains I felt in my head, and I was more than a fortnight without sleep.' A kindly African woman served him twice-daily doses of rice water, which seemed to help. But then his sores broke out afresh and 'all hope of departure vanished'. He was 'soon reduced to a skeleton ... One thought alone absorbed my mind – that of Death. I wished for it and prayed for it to God.'

After 'six weeks of indescribable suffering' he felt a bit better, and by 9 January was on the move to Jenne, accompanying a caravan that had arrived in Tieme with a cargo of kola nuts. He was still scorbutic, unable to join campfire meals because his wobbly teeth made eating an embarrassment and because his palate tended to shed onto his tongue. But he persevered: 'I never for a moment reproached myself for the resolution which had brought me to these deserts, where I had suffered so much misery.' His misery increased, to the point where he found himself shivering with fever at the bottom of a canoe as it plied down the Bari, one of the Niger's tributaries. He was so destitute that its occupants 'were emboldened ... to insult me in the grossest manner ... and the slaves, following this example, behaved with grossest insolence towards me.' A year after his departure from the coast, Caillié reached Jenne. The local ruler gave him permission to stay in town until the next departure for Timbuctoo and, in exchange for Caillié's umbrella, promised him a trouble-free trip to the Niger.

The following month, on 20 April, Caillié arrived in Timbuctoo. 'On entering this mysterious city, which is an object of curiosity and research to the civilised nations of Europe, I experienced an indescribable satisfaction. How many grateful thanksgivings did I pour forth for the protection which God had vouchsafed me, amidst obstacles and dangers which appeared insurmountable. This duty being ended, I looked around.' It was not what he had hoped for: 'I had formed a totally different idea of the wealth and grandeur of Timbuctoo.' The houses were dull – he was shown the one in which Laing had stayed – and the countryside was monotonous. 'Nothing was to be seen in all directions but immense plains of quicksand of a yellowish-white colour. The sky was pale and red as far as the horizon: all nature wore a dreary aspect, and the most profound silence prevailed; not even the warbling of a bird was to be heard ... Timbuctoo and its environs present the most monotonous and barren scene I ever beheld.' All he could say in its praise was that 'the difficulties surmounted by its founders cannot fail to excite the admiration'.

The people, however, of whom he judged there were between 10,000 and 12,000, were 'of a gentle and cheerful disposition' and showed him great kindness during his stay. Admiring of his apparent devoutness and of his determination to reach Egypt, they provided him with food, lodging and even a few slaves. Less attractive were the Tuareg who controlled the surrounding countryside and who sauntered regularly into town to receive 'gifts' – followed by demands for more 'gifts' for going away again. Occasionally the chief of the Tuareg honoured the town with his presence, a privilege so expensive that 'it is a general calamity'. Caillié described how the inhabitants lived in fear of the Tuareg denying them access to the Niger, and kept their warehouses full in anticipation of a siege that might descend at any moment. He noted, however, that a steady dribble of caravans passed through Timbuctoo, bound for the north with cargoes of slaves, a little bit of gold, ivory, gum and ostrich feathers. Despite its outwardly wretched situation – there was no cultivable land, the main source of fuel was camel dung, except for water everything necessary to human survival had to be imported – he had to admit to a sneaking admiration for the way Timbuctoo struggled on, destitute of every resource, but surviving, as it had done for centuries, on trade alone.

With regular meals Caillié regained some of his strength, but he could not recommend the desert climate. The nights were oppressively calm, and when a wind did blow 'it is felt like a burning vapour and seems almost to scorch the lungs. I was continually ill at Timbuctoo.' He was afflicted, too, by the mental strain of maintaining his disguise: one day while taking notes in his Koran he was approached by an Arab; fearing he had been found out, he was delighted when the man simply slid some cowrie shells (the region's currency) into his pocket. It was yet another example of the town's hospitality, but the incident reminded him how dangerous a path he trod. After a fortnight he had seen all he wanted to and was ready to leave. He could have retraced his steps to the West African coast, but he decided instead to catch a caravan to Morocco, on the grounds that nobody would believe he had visited Timbuctoo if he did not continue to the Mediterranean – or, as he put it, 'returning via the Barbary States ... would impose conviction on the envious'. In the first week of May a 1,400-camel caravan left for the north-west. Caillié's hosts were so reluctant to let him go that he missed its departure and had to run for a mile through the sand. When he caught up he was too weak to walk and had to be thrown onto a baggage camel.

Caillié remained on the camel for the rest of the trip, his charm having affected the caravan leader as much as it had the people of Timbuctoo. But even in such comfort he found the journey appalling. The caravan moved from oasis to oasis, where the water was brackish at best and at times so contaminated as to be undrinkable. They reached the salt mines of Taoudeni, a place in which slaves, and the occasional free man working to pay off debts, toiled in abominable conditions. Caillié, the first European to see the place, was appalled: there were no women, no means of sustenance other than what was brought by caravans, and the wells were so chlorinated as to poison anybody who drank from them regularly. Leaving this dismal spot, they entered a desert of total hostility. Their water was dispensed once a day from the communal tanks that the camels carried, and Caillié's attempts to purchase a private supply were rejected with contempt. The rules of trans-Saharan travel were straightforward: everyone, even the slaves, was allotted the same amount every 24 hours.* To the oppressive heat and the lack of water was added the bleakness of the environment. Caillié's caravan plodded through plains of sand and rock so featureless that he could only liken it to the sea. Like mariners, they endured gales, one of which Caillié described as so vicious that the men were thrown about like toys and lay on the ground, their heads covered, praying to Allah. 'Through the shouts and prayers and the roaring of the wind I could distinguish the plaintive moans of the camels who were as much alarmed as their masters, and more to be pitied for they had not tasted food for four days.' When the storm abated they continued as before, but more thirstily. 'The heat was stifling,' Caillié wrote. 'The allowance of water was every time more and more scanty. We suffered beyond all expression.' In the dry heat the soles of their feet cracked; they sewed them together with needle and thread. To Caillié the journey was a torment, and his relief on reaching the oasis of Tafilafet on 23 July was indescribable. There were melons, dates and apples in abundance, though the latter were hard going because his teeth were still loose from scurvy. He found it hard to believe that people put themselves through such torture on a regular basis – but some obviously did, because he was given the chance to buy Laing's compass and sextant.

With his last pieces of gold and silver, which he had concealed in a money belt, he bought an ass and crossed the Atlas Mountains into Morocco. Still he was not safe, for the southern reaches of Morocco were as lawless as the Sahara, and even in the north a Christian ventured at his peril. He bluffed his way forward as a healer, dispensing magic charms wherever he stopped. (Prudently, he warned the recipients that his tokens would not become effective for 20 days, which he guessed would give him time to get out of range.) He reached Fez on 12 August and, on being informed that the French consul was in Tangiers, trudged the extra 100 miles to the Mediterranean.

On 7 September, penniless, filthy, bedraggled and sunburned, he knocked on the consul's door. 'I am a Frenchman,' he said. 'I have been to Timbuctoo.' He was told that the consul was dead. So limited at that time was France's influence in the Maghreb (it would become greater very shortly) that it took three days of sleeping in doorways, skulking outside the consulate and being hounded as a beggar before Caillié was finally permitted access. He slunk in under cover of darkness, and for two weeks luxuriated in comforts he had not seen for three years: sheets, pillows and a mattress. 'After returning thanks to Almighty God,' he wrote, 'I lay down upon a good bed, rejoicing in my escape from the society of men debased by ignorance and fanaticism.' (An ungrateful return for those he had duped into helping him.) 'It would be difficult to describe my sensations on casting off for ever my Arab costume.' On 27 September he donned a new disguise, that of a sailor, and was

---

* Eighty years later, France's General Henri Lapperine travelled north from Taoudeni with a column of experienced camel warriors. The wells were so caustic as to bleach his men's clothes and render some of them insane. When his column reached safety its members were horribly bloated and near starvation.

collected by a French sloop from Cadiz. Ten days later he was at Toulon, from where a short train journey took him to the capital.

The Geographical Society of Paris honoured its commitment to the cent. Caillée was awarded the promised 10,000 francs for finding Timbuctoo and was given a 6,000-franc pension as well. King Charles X of France, soon to be deposed, made him a Chevalier of the Légion d'Honneur. With these awards, Caillié looked forward to many years of prosperity, fame and comfort. His retirement, however, was marred by virulent attacks from the British, who didn't believe he had been to Timbuctoo and that even if he had, had done so in an undignified manner with possibly fraudulent intent. How demeaning to go dressed as an Arab! How dishonourable to pretend to be a Muslim! How were they to know that he hadn't somehow acquired Laing's journal and used it to fabricate his own? Sir John Barrow said his report was 'an obvious imposture ... unworthy of notice' and that 'the ostentatious display which the French attach to the most trifling things is strongly manifested'. On thinking about it, he added that their self-congratulation displayed 'a constantly recurring consciousness of the intellectual and physical superiority of our countrymen over theirs'. And even if Timbuctoo had been found, what did it matter, a Briton having got there first? 'The French have contributed so little, of late years, to the improvement of geography,' he wrote, 'that when the mountain has brought forth the mouse, the tiny animal is so fondled and dandled, and crammed, that it swells out to the unwieldy size of an elephant.' In a final blast of rudeness, he remarked that Caillié had done nothing to trace the course of the Niger, and for all the geographical information he had gathered he might as well have stayed at home.

It was overstepping the mark to attack Caillée for not tracing the Niger, since it had never been his goal. Moreover, he had produced considerably more information on the region than Laing, and had, indeed, made a number of inquiries from which it appeared that the Niger flowed, as it did, into the Gulf of Benin. 'I must confess,' wrote the poor man, 'that these unjust attacks have affected me more deeply than all the hardships, fatigues and privations which I have encountered in the interior of Africa.' On the proceeds of his fame he married, bought a farm in his hometown of Mauze – from where he was able to give his disabled sister the attention she needed – and was elected mayor. He still hankered after Africa, and was promised the consulship of Bambara, a gold-mining area near Timbuctoo, should the position by some miracle become available. He never got his wish: the area lay undisturbed by Europeans for almost a quarter of a century, the next white man to visit it being the German explorer Heinrich Barth who, between 1850 and 1855, made an epic 10,000-mile return journey across the Sahara from Tripoli to Timbuctoo. By that time, however, Caillié had long been a stranger to news from Africa. On 17 May 1838 he had died of tuberculosis.

John Ross (1829–33)

The cantankerous John Ross was not a man to forgive and forget. Foremost on his list of unforgettables was the embarrassing fiasco of 1818 when he had failed to identify Lancaster Sound as the door to the North-West Passage. In the same position on his list of unforgivables was the state of Barrow-inspired pariahdom into which he had been thrown. Throughout the 1820s he waited and plotted for a chance to reestablish his name. With his knowledge of Arctic conditions, and having examined the journals of subsequent expeditions, he came to two conclusions: first, that the ice was always weakest near the coast and that explorers should therefore be equipped with ships of shallow draft; secondly, that the ships most capable of exploiting cracks in the Arctic's natural defences were those powered by steam. As a corollary, it was pointless sending heavily manned expeditions in large vessels when the job could be done more effectively by a small but sturdy steamer whose reduced crew could live off the region's resources without recourse to the endless barrels of salt beef carried by ships hitherto.

He said all this to the Admiralty, but was dismissed as a crackpot. Steamships had already been experimented with and had proved useless. Besides, the very idea of steam ran counter to everything the Royal Navy prided itself upon, and in the opinion of one Admiralty lord 'was calculated to strike a fatal blow to the naval supremacy of the Empire'. As for taking small ships instead of large, the proposition was ridiculous: it had been proved that large crews were indispensable in the Arctic because they had sometimes to drag ships through the ice and always to saw them into a harbour; these men had to be fed somehow, and only the hold of a large ship could contain the provisions they needed. With this circular argument, the Admiralty invited Ross to take his ideas elsewhere.

Ross did so. Approaching a number of would-be sponsors, he found satisfaction in Felix Booth, a gin magnate who opened his wallet in 1829 for an expedition to the North-West Passage. Eighteen thousand pounds later – Booth had contemplated something in the order of ten – Ross owned the *Victory*, a 150-ton, paddle-driven steam packet that had once delivered mail between Liverpool and the Isle of Man but was now strengthened for Arctic service and given an experimental engine by the firm of Braithwaite and

Erickson, amongst whose novelties was a set of bellows to replace the conventional funnel. He had, too, an ex-whaler, the *John*, that was to follow the *Victory* to Baffin Bay carrying coal and food, plus a tender, the *Kreusenstern*, donated by a reluctant Admiralty. He had a crew of nine – one of them being his nephew, James Clark Ross – and food and fuel to keep them alive for 1,000 days. He also had a small library of reference books, plus an arsenal of scientific instruments that would have put a larger ship to shame – 12 thermometers, six chronometers, five sextants, four barometers, two dipping needles and numerous telescopes, theodolites and compasses.

So colourful was Ross's publicity that a visit to Deptford became a part of the London season. Among the tourists was Ross's old second-in-command, W. E. Parry, who was impressed by what he called 'a bold, public-spirited undertaking'. He had doubts, though, about the gadgetry: 'There is, in the whole thing, rather too much that is new and untried; and this is certainly not the kind of service on which novelties of that sort first ought to be tried.'

When the *Victory* left on 23 May 1829 it immediately broke down: the boilers leaked, Braithwaite and Erickson's patented bellows did not work, nuts and bolts flew off in all directions. Cursing his 'wretched and discreditable machinery', Ross steamed north at the pitiful rate of three knots to Galloway, where they took aboard a bullock, a man fell into the cogs – Ross had to amputate his arm – and the crew of the *John* mutinied. The *Victory* limped westward, with the *Kreusenstern* in tow and the steam apparatus proving so useless that they crossed the Atlantic mostly under sail.

The *Victory* entered Lancaster Sound on 6 August, and four days later was sailing down Prince Regent Inlet. At Fury Beach they plundered the mounds of food and equipment that Parry had offloaded in 1824 – wine, anchors, lime juice, bread, flour, sugar, sails, masts, coal: everything was still there and in perfect condition – and on 16 August were in uncharted waters. Ross named the mountainous land to their west Boothia Felix, after his sponsor, and its various capes and promontories were christened after members of either Ross's or Booth's family. By the end of September the *Victory* was anchored off Andrew Ross Island and its captain was feeling justifiably pleased with himself. He had travelled 300 miles further south than Parry, and it was only 280 miles to Franklin's Point Turnagain on Canada's northern coast. The weather had been mild, the sea had been clear, game had been plentiful, and if conditions were the same next year he was confident of success. The only thing that could stop him was Boothia Felix: if it was an island he would be able to skirt its southern tip and sail west to Point Turnagain; if it was a peninsula, however, he would be in a cul de sac. Still, if it was a cul de sac it had so far been a very profitable one in terms of geographical discovery, and if his way was blocked all he had to do was retrace his course to Lancaster Sound and thence to London, where he would

receive the applause and recognition that (in his own mind) he so richly deserved.

In early October, when winter arrived, and with it the ice, Ross snugged the *Victory* into a bay he called Felix Harbour, prepared it for winter, and contemplated his coming glory. He did so with the satisfaction of having dumped Braithwaite and Erickson's machinery on Andrew Ross Island. The thing took up two-thirds of the ship's tonnage, occupied the constant attention of four men, and performed so badly – even when it worked, the *Victory* would have moved faster had it been towed by two rowing boats – that every one agreed it was a waste of time and space. 'I believe there was now not one present who ever again wished to see its minutest fragment,' Ross wrote.

He congratulated himself too soon. There would come a time when the steam engine – although he never admitted it – could have been useful. For Boothia Felix *was* a peninsula, and Ross's optimism as to the conditions was misplaced. Perhaps one year in six the Arctic enjoyed a warm, relatively ice-free spell during which passages that were normally closed became open. Eighteen twenty-nine had been one of those years. Ross did not know it yet, but he had entered a meteorological trap from which he would find it hard to extricate himself without the aid of steam.

That first winter Ross followed the routines perfected by Parry, with the emphasis on constant activity. Alongside the usual tedious chores of cleaning, polishing, exercising and keeping watch, there were evening classes in reading, writing, navigation and maths. But Ross was a martial man at heart – he forswore anything so frivolous as plays – and the atmosphere, as his steward complained, was more like that of a man-of-war than a civilian expedition. The captain's anger became increasingly evident as the months passed. He was by nature impatient and, while capable of keeping the crew alive and healthy over the winter, he did not like being trapped in Prince Regent Inlet. 'The prison door was shut upon us,' he wrote, as the sea froze around them. 'It was indeed a dull prospect. Amid all its brilliancy, this land, the land of ice and snow, has been, and ever will be a dull, dreary, heart-sinking, monotonous waste, under the influence of which the very mind is paralysed, ceasing to care or think ... it is but the view of uniformity and silence and death ... where nothing moves and nothing changes, but all is for ever the same, cheerless, cold and still.'

If a relic in some ways, Ross was ahead of his time in others. Nobody knew what caused scurvy: it had been established that vegetables and lime juice kept it at bay, but the reason they did so remained a mystery. Decades before anyone else, Ross concluded that whatever magic ingredient was inside a lime must also be in a slab of fish or meat. His reasoning was that the Arctic diet was predominantly vegetable-free, yet the Inuit had existed for centuries without catching scurvy. It was his opinion that 'the large use of oil and fats is the true secret of life in these frozen countries, and that the natives cannot subsist without it, becoming diseased and dying under a more meagre diet'. Here he was truly far-sighted: the idea that if one wished to survive in the Arctic one should eat as the Inuit did was logical (though it was not accepted for a long while); but the pinpointing of oils and fats was revolutionary. It would take more than a century for scientists to discover the three simple truths of scurvy: first, that it was caused by lack of Vitamin C; second, that while humans required a daily intake of Vitamin C to remain healthy, most other creatures produced it without need of supplement; and third, that it was stored at highest concentrations in fats and oils. By process of evolution, every Arctic fish or mammal was insulated against the cold by layers of fat or oily blubber. All one had to do, therefore, was to eat the wildlife. This Ross ordered his men to do, bidding them shoot the caribou that ranged over Boothia Felix and net the salmon that ran though Prince Regent Inlet.

The big event of that winter was the arrival of Inuit on 9 January. The two groups got on well, Ross presenting the Inuit with pieces of iron and ordering the ship's carpenter to make a wooden leg for a man who had lost a limb to a polar bear. In return, the Inuit showed the white men the best fishing spots and where musk-oxen could be found. They also provided them with dog teams and sledges, and gave them instructions on their use. The Britons marvelled at the sledges, which ranged from the elaborate (lengths of bone cunningly bound with sinews) to the basic (a simple bowl of ice) to the edible (two frozen salmon wrapped in hides and joined by crosspieces of bone); but they found the dogs hard to handle. James Clark Ross picked up the theory fast enough, but frequently fell off, while the dogs disappeared over the snow, necessitating a bothersome slog of several miles to retrieve them. His uncle had no success at all, and after one occasion in which the dogs ran in separate directions, twirling him round and round like a top, he decided that man-hauled sledges were preferable.

The Inuit drew maps to aid Ross in his exploration. He was not grateful for their assistance: '[they] gave us no encouragement, assuring us that the land here was continuous from north to south within the whole range of their knowledge, and affirming positively that there was no passage where we fancied that one might possibly exist. But we did not think ourselves at all justified in taking this on their showing: they might not be correct.' Unfortunately they *were* correct, as James Clark Ross realized that April when he took a number of sledge trips with Inuit guides and proved that Boothia Felix was most likely a peninsula. During his explorations he made a very important discovery. Crossing to the other side of Boothia, he surveyed a bleak, low-lying lump of terrain that bulged from the peninsula's western coast and to which he gave the name King William Land. At Victory Point, his furthest west, he judged it was only 200 miles to Point Turnagain: in the distance he could see open water. The intervening channel was choked with ice – indeed, there were huge chunks of the stuff piled on the shore of King William Land, well above the high-tide mark, which puzzled him – but if a way could be found to that open water from either Prince Regent Inlet or the seas around Melville Island, then the quest for the North-West Passage was over.

By June 1830 preparations were underway for the *Victory*'s retreat, and in August the ship – still with the *Kreusenstern* – broke out of Felix Harbour. On the first day Ross sailed three miles before the ice brought him to a halt. By the end of September he had made another 300 yards, and on 2 November he was cutting his way into new winter quarters, Sheriff Harbour – which was at most two hours' walk from Felix Harbour. That season was bad: Ross drank heavily and became more irritable and heavy-handed than usual. No Inuit appeared, and in temperatures of −43° F they amused themselves by firing balls of frozen mercury through a one-inch plank. The one bright spot came when James Clark Ross sledged over Boothia and found the North Magnetic Pole – the place, as he put it, which 'Nature ... had chosen as the centre of one of her great and dark powers'. At 70° 5' 17" N, 96° 46' 45" W, he raised the Union Jack and took possession of it and its surrounding territories 'in the name of Great Britain and King William the Fourth'.

With the North Magnetic Pole under their belts, and the North-West Passage nearly so, the Rosses had made enormous contributions to geography. All they had to do now was sail home with their findings. But the summer of 1831 was as cold as that of 1830, and by October they were cutting a new harbour little more than four miles north of their old one. Ross cursed the monotony: 'On no occasion, even when all was new, had there been much to interest; far less was there, now that we had been imprisoned to almost one spot.' Again there were no Inuit, and the temperature was even colder than the previous winter – for a record 136 days the thermometer stuck below zero. They were unable to explore, to hunt or to fish. The dogs perished from licking a corrosive fluid that dribbled from the disconnected steam pipes, and the crew fell ill. One man died of tuberculosis, and Ross's wounds, sustained in the Napoleonic Wars, opened up and began to bleed – one of the first signs of scurvy.

Ross calculated that they had one year's supply of food in their hold. Unless the Inuit returned with supplies of fresh meat, and unless 1832 was warmer than 1831 – neither of which seemed likely – they were doomed. He therefore decided to abandon ship and drag three boats overland to Fury Beach, where they could replenish their supplies and where, come summer, conditions allowing, they would be able to sail for the whaling grounds of Baffin Bay. He put his plan into effect that April, stripping the *Victory* and *Kreusenstern* of anything that might be useful and sending sledge parties to lay a trail of depots in the direction of Fury Beach. The last group left on 29 May.

By 1 July, after a semi-mutiny that Ross quelled in forceful and peremptory fashion, they were safely at Fury Beach. The amount of food they had been able to carry from the *Victory* had been of necessity limited, and by mid-June they had passed the last of their caches. Reduced to what they could carry, they had cut their rations again and again, and when they reached Fury Beach they were on the point of starvation. Parry's piles of provisions loomed as bounteously as they had in 1829; against Ross's orders, the men gorged themselves and suffered accordingly. When their stomachs recovered they used a set of the *Fury*'s discarded sails to erect a temporary shelter, Somerset House, in which they waited for the summer to come. The ice broke on 31 July, and they sailed joyfully to salvation.

They went only eight miles before the shifting floes drove them ashore. They lingered in the hope that the ice would clear, but the winter seemed to come even earlier this year than the last. Leaving the boats where they were, they retreated overland to Somerset House. 'There could be no recourse for us,' Ross wrote, 'but another winter, another year, I should say, on Fury Beach; if indeed it should be the fortune of any one to survive after another such year as the three last.' They barricaded Somerset House with blocks of snow, fired their two portable stoves, and entered their fourth winter's confinement. In the early months they shot the odd fox, but this prevented for only a short while the encroachment of scurvy. Soon, they were all experiencing the telltale lassitude and joint pains. The carpenter died on 16 February. Meanwhile it snowed and snowed, until only the top of Somerset House was visible. Ross made them build a raised floor for the tent, had them dig an enclosure in the snow, and ordered them to exercise in it. Raging and cursing at their entrapment and at his own deteriorating health, he did everything to keep them busy. 'Better was it,' he wrote, 'that they should work themselves into utter weariness, that they should so hunger as to think only of their stomachs, fall asleep and dream of nothing but a better dinner, as they awoke to hope and labour for it.'

Ross had sailed north in 1829 to prove his worth and to show that his methodology was superior to the Admiralty's. He had failed in the last but succeeded beyond all expectation in the first: he was now in his fourth Arctic winter – not for 70 years would his record be beaten – and had kept his company more or less intact into the bargain. What was more, he had done it with minimal help from the Admiralty and on a shoestring budget. Recalling the popularity of Parry's and Franklin's journals, he fired a caustic volley at his predecessors: 'Let him who reads to condemn what is so meagre, have some compassion on the writer who had nothing better than this meagreness, this repetition, this reiteration of the ever-resembling, every day dullness to record, and what was infinitely worse, to endure. I might have seen more, it has been said: it may be; but I saw only ice and snow, cloud and drift and storm. Still, I might have seen what I did not; seen as a painter, and felt like a poet; and then like the painter and poet have written. That also may be, but let painter and poet come hither and try; try how far cold and hunger, misery and depression, aid those faculties which seem always best developed under the comforts of life ... Our "*faecundi calices*" were cold snow water; and though, according to Persius, it is hunger that which makes poets write as it makes parrots speak, I suspect that neither poet nor parrot would have gained much under a "fox" diet, and that an insufficient one, in the blessed regions of Boothia Felix.'

In the spring of 1833, while the snow was still firm around Somerset House, Ross ordered his men to lay a string of food caches along the coast. On 8 July they began the trek to the abandoned boats. This time there could be no turning back: they had eaten the last of the *Fury*'s salted meat a week before.

The carpenter having died, they could only hope that the boats were still in one piece. Luckily, they were; but the sea was still frozen. They waited for weeks, their supplies diminishing, until at 4.00 a.m. on 14 August the ice opened. They fled up Prince Regent Inlet and east to Baffin Bay. When the wind failed they took to their oars, rowing for now 12 and now 20 hours at a stretch. On 25 August, while camped at the mouth of Navy Board Inlet on the southern coast of Lancaster Sound, they were aroused by the look-out's cry that he had seen a sail. They lit smoke signals with wet gunpowder, and when that failed they rowed out to sea. But the ship sailed away, leaving them bobbing on the waves. Six hours later, at 10.00 a.m., they saw another sail and once again rowed towards it. This time they were spotted. By strange coincidence their rescuer was the *Isabella*, the same ship that Ross had commanded in 1818. When he said as much to the crew they laughed uneasily: no, that could not be, for Captain Ross was long since dead in the North-West Passage. Ross assured them that he wasn't.

That night the survivors were bewildered. 'All, everything, too, was to be done at once; it was washing, dressing, shaving, eating, all intermingled, it was the materials of each jumbled together.' The transition was physically overwhelming: when Ross was offered a bed he found the mattress too soft after months on the ice and took instead to a chair.

On Ross's return he was knighted, granted an audience with the king, given the keys to cities across Britain, and awarded countless gold medals. He became the man of the moment, his journal sold in thousands, and panoramas of the voyage were projected on the rotunda at Leicester Square. His nephew was merely promoted from lieutenant to commander – a less than satisfactory reward for a man who had done the lion's share of the discovery. But James Clark Ross would soon vindicate himself.

James Clark Ross (1839–43)

Since Antarctica had been circumnavigated, first by James Cook in 1773 and then by Thaddeus Bellingshausen in 1820, naval and scientific circles had shown little interest in the bottom of the world. A number of fantasists insisted there was a continent inside all that ice, conjecturing variously that it contained a portal to the inside of the globe, was home to a race of undiscovered humans, and was the site of either Atlantis or the Garden of Eden. But the general view, as propounded by Cook, held that there was nothing down there and that, even if there was, it was too difficult to reach and not worth finding anyway. During the 1820s and 1830s, however, as whalers and sealers explored the region in search of new and profitable killing grounds, it became clear that there was land and that it could be reached. In 1820 the American John Davis landed on the Antarctic Peninsula; and in 1830–2 a captain from the British firm of Enderby Brothers sighted a portion of the continent that would later be called Enderby Land. As these and other reports came in, European and American governments took a renewed interest in Antarctica. In 1837 Captain Jules Sébastien-César Dumont d'Urville sailed south with orders to find the South Pole. He came nowhere near the Pole, but he did very creditably nonetheless, becoming the first man to land on the main continent and naming the territory Adélie Land after his wife. In 1838 a US expedition under Lieutenant Charles Wilkes charted 1,500 miles of Antarctic coastline – or said it did; the findings were later proved false – that duly entered the charts as Wilkes Land. Then, not wanting to be left behind, Britain launched its own expedition in 1839. The man chosen to lead it was Commander James Clark Ross.

James Ross was, in 1838, the Admiralty's most experienced polar officer. Of the last 20 years he had spent 17 in the Arctic and had overwintered for six; he had reached, with Parry, the furthest north over the Arctic pack; and he had discovered the North Magnetic Pole. He had received little kudos for his trouble, never having been the leader of an expedition; but now he seemed the obvious choice, not just because of long service but because, as the discoverer of the North Magnetic Pole, he was considered a magnetist of distinction. This was an important qualification, for the first British Antarctic Expedition of the 19th century was to be a scientific one. This did not mean that it was driven any less by a desire for national prestige than its Arctic predecessors, just that unlike them it did have a genuinely worthwhile purpose. In 1838 it had been proposed that Europe's leading maritime powers should take simultaneous readings across the world with the aim of creating a geomagnetic map of the globe. Ross's expedition was part of that project, and so he was instructed to erect and maintain observatories through-out the known lands of the southern hemisphere. After that, however, Antarctica – and particularly the South Magnetic Pole – was his to conquer and claim for Great Britain.

Ross and his second-in command, Lieutenant Francis Crozier, an Irish-man who had sailed on all of Parry's voyages and who was almost as experi-enced as Ross himself, were given two bomb-ships, *Erebus* and *Terror*, for their journey into the ice. Designed for coastal mortar bombardments, bomb-ships were ideal for the conditions he expected to meet. They didn't sail particularly well, but they were strong and had a shallow draught, and their capacious holds, once used to store ammunition, had ample space for the supplies he intended to take. Once the two ships had undergone the by now standard process of reinforcement – double-planking the hulls, insulating the decks, copper-sheathing the keels and prows, fitting triple-strength canvas – the food and equipment was loaded. It was the best outfitted expedition in British history, thanks to Ross's insistence that every-thing be done to keep the crews both healthy and comfortable. Ice-saws, portable forges and piles of good winter clothing came aboard, as did a phenomenal amount of food, comprising not just the everyday salt beef and preserved meat, but a comprehensive array of anti-scorbutics – 2,618 pints of vegetable soup, 2,398 pounds of pickled cabbage, 10,782 pounds of carrots, plus a small flock of sheep.

Ross and Crozier left London in the autumn of 1839, and by 31 January were building their first observatory on the island of St Helena. They repeated the process at Cape Town on 17 March and again at Kerguelen Island on 15 May, where the winds were sometimes so strong that the men had to lie flat lest they be blown into the sea. On 16 August they reached the penal colony of Van Diemen's Land – modern Tasmania – where they received a warm welcome from its governor, none other than the veteran explorer Sir John Franklin. After three months' recuperation, during which Franklin had his convicts build an observatory for them, they sailed down the 180th meridian. Crossing the Antarctic Circle on New Year's Day 1841, they headed into the unknown. Everyone was excited, particularly Crozier's surgeon-cum-naturalist, Robert McCormick, who predicted they would enter 'a region of our globe as fresh and new as at creation's first dawn'.

It was understood that the Antarctic pack would be hard, and that the weather would be bad. To their delight, gales were few, and the ice, after skilful, repetitive ramming, broke before them. On 9 January they broke through the pack and floated in a new world. Within Antarctica's protective

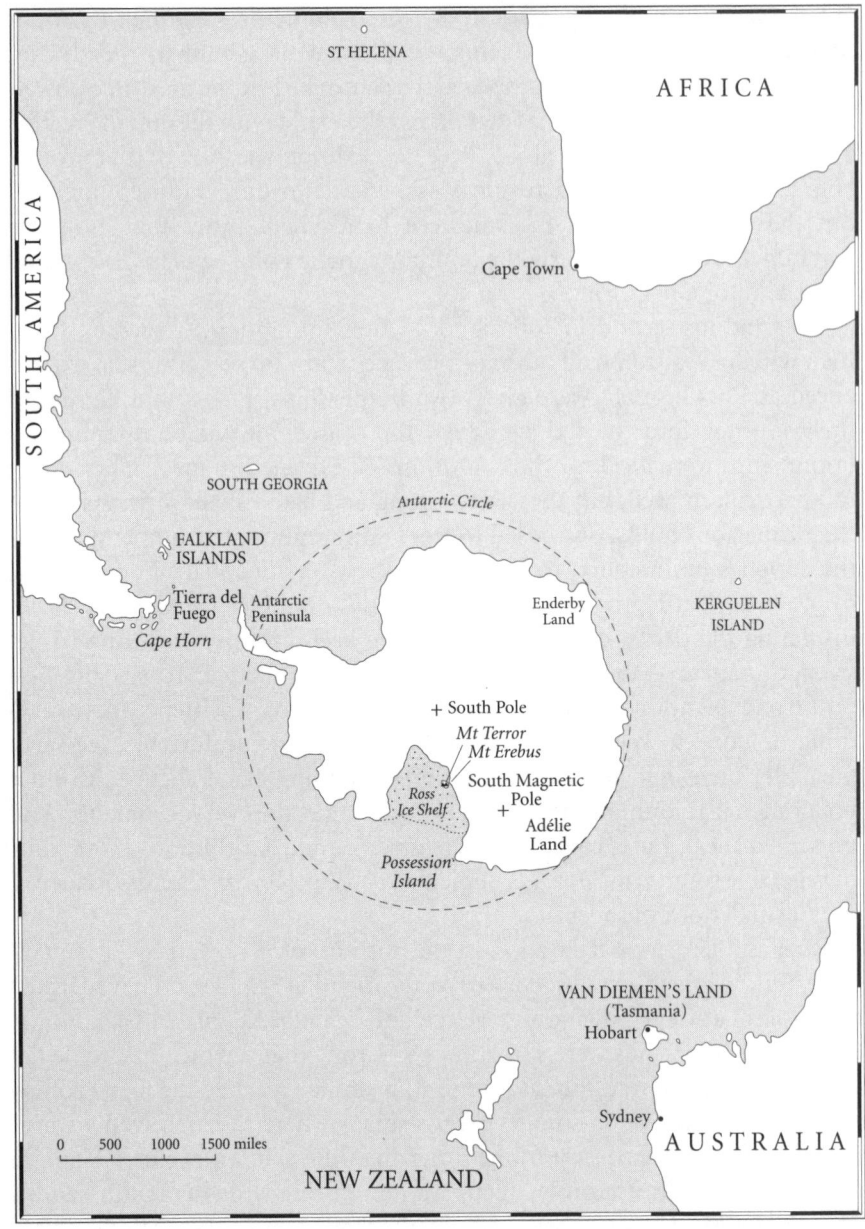

ring of ice the sea was calm, the air hazy and the weather, as McCormick wrote, was like 'the finest May day in England'. The rumours of an undiscovered Arcadia seemed suddenly plausible as they sailed beneath a sky of indigo, in their little wooden ships, towards a white horizon. They knew that the white was caused by the sun's reflection off a large body of ice – it was known as ice sky, or ice blink, as opposed to water sky, which was black – but Ross and Crozier had both seen ice blink before and were not worried.

Two days later they sighted land 'of so extensive a coastline and attaining such altitude as to justify the appellation of a Great new Southern Continent', wrote McCormick. It was 100 miles distant, but they soon met its outlying islands, one of which, Possession Island, they claimed as the first territorial conquest made in the name of Queen Victoria. Further south than any human had travelled before, they named and claimed with abandon. On 29 January they saw a mountain, 12,400 feet high, above whose peak hung a cloud of snow. As they approached, they realized that the snow was in fact smoke and that it was split by jets of flame. Amidst a realm of snow and ice they had discovered a live volcano.

Christening it Mount Erebus after Ross's command ship (a dormant neighbour of 10,900 feet was named Mount Terror), they sailed east to be greeted by yet another wonder: a cliff of ice, 300 feet high, that stretched as far as the eye could see. It was the Ross Ice Shelf, the largest of its kind in the world, and a phenomenon the like of which neither Ross nor Crozier had seen in the whole of their polar careers. As Ross said: 'It was ... an obstruction of such a character as to leave no doubt upon my mind as to our future proceedings, for we might as well sail through the cliffs of Dover as penetrate such a mass ... It would be impossible to conceive a more solid-looking mass of ice; not the smallest appearance of any rent or fissure could we discover throughout its whole extent, and the intensely bright sky beyond it but too plainly indicated the great distance to which it reached to the southward.' Two weeks and 250 miles later they had still not reached its end – although at one point it sank to a height of 50 feet, allowing Ross a glimpse from his mast of 'an immense plain of frosted silver' – and with the austral summer coming to an end they dared not risk being trapped. On 9 February they turned for Tasmania.

The journey out was considerably harder than the one in, but, after a close shave with a flotilla of bergs, they escaped the pack on 8 March and were on their way. Ross took a short detour to investigate Wilkes's coordinates and found, to his satisfaction, that Wilkes Land was in fact a stretch of ocean so deep that their 600-fathom sounding line did not touch bottom. On the morning of 10 April 1841 they were in Tasmania's Derwent River, where Franklin rowed out to greet them in his governor's barge. They were welcomed with bands and parties and galas; every member of Hobart's tiny 'society' came out to cheer their accomplishments; they would have been given the freedom of the city had such a thing not been incongruous in a penal colony. They deserved it all, for theirs had been a remarkable voyage. They had penetrated the pack; they had discovered new land and new and astounding ice features; they had not reached the South Magnetic Pole, but their compasses had shown it was nearby; and (a matter of national rather than scientific pride) they had debunked America's claim to have sighted the continent. Furthermore, they were not going to sit on their laurels: Ross intended to complete his survey. He lingered awhile in Hobart to erect a new observatory alongside the old, and then dashed to Sydney in New South Wales to take magnetic readings on Garden Island. Scientific obligations completed, he and Crozier left Hobart on 5 August 1841, their holds replete with three years' fresh provisions.

Approaching Antarctica via the 146th meridian, they were in the pack by Christmas and celebrated New Year by mooring the two ships against a floe on which they constructed an ice ballroom, complete with dance-floor, a bar, two thrones for the captains, and a statue of the Venus de Medici. Their festivities, however, were premature. The pack was obdurate this season: it froze around them; then, on 19 January 1842, it gave them hell. A storm broke, of such fury that it ripped the pack to shreds. 'Our ships were involved in an ocean of rolling fragments of ice,' Ross wrote, 'hard as floating rocks of granite, which were dashed against them by the waves with so much violence that their masts quivered as if they would fall at any given moment and the destruction of the ships seemed inevitable ... Each of us could only secure a hold, waiting the issue with resignation to the will of Him who alone could bring us through such extreme danger.' For 28 hours they were knocked to and fro. Their hawsers snapped, their sails blew away and the *Erebus* lost its copper sheathing. Both ships lost their rudders. Crozier had to flood the *Terror*'s hold to extinguish a fire. And by the end of it they were still surrounded by mile after mile of wave-tossed ice. Seeking refuge behind a row of bergs so enormous as to protect them from the wind, they made repairs and emerged from the pack on 2 February. Twenty days later they met the Ross Ice Shelf, which they followed eastwards for two days until it veered north to reconnect with the pack.

It had been a hard voyage and, after his recent experiences, Ross was in no mood to battle round the continent. He ordered his ships north to the nearest refuge – the Falkland Islands. By 7.00 on the evening of 24 February they were free of the pack and sailing towards Cape Horn. In the small hours of 13 March, however, the Antarctic came after them. Out of the darkness a berg materialized in front of the *Erebus*. Ross turned to avoid it, and in doing so ran directly before the *Terror*. The two ships collided with a crash that woke everybody aboard. According to Ross, 'The concussion when she struck us was such as to throw almost every one off his feet; our bowsprit, foretopmast, and other smaller spars, were carried away.' McCormick wrote: 'So sudden was the collision that there was scant time for dressing, and an officer might have been seen clinging to the capstan in his nightshirt only.' For a while the two ships broached to in a horrible entanglement, the *Terror* rising so high with each wave that it threatened to fall on the *Erebus*.

When they cut themselves free the *Erebus* was helpless, its deck buried under a mass of spars and fallen sails. Normally, the crew would have been able to repair the damage, but these were not normal circumstances. The berg that Ross had swerved to avoid was the forerunner of a chain of similar behemoths that wallowed towards them, separated by only a few yards.

Unable to sail out of danger, Ross turned his rudder so that the *Erebus* began, slowly, to rotate. The procedure, known as a sternboard, was difficult at the best of times, but was even more so now, for when the *Erebus* turned full circle its prow had to enter a gap between one of the bergs. There was no second chance: the ship had to go through on its first attempt. They made the gap, but then came the dreaded passage to the other side. While the ice-master shouted directions, Ross stood on deck, arms folded, awaiting the outcome. 'His whole bearing,' McCormick wrote, 'whilst lacking nothing in firmness, yet betrayed both in the expression of his countenance and attitude, the all-but despair with which he anxiously watched the result of this last and only expedient left to us in the awful position we were placed in … But for the howling of the winds, and the turmoil of the roaring waters, the falling of a pin might have been heard on the *Erebus*'s deck.'

They slid between 'two perpendicular walls of ice' into a calm sea where the *Terror* was waiting for them. Thanks to Ross's superb seamanship, the *Erebus* was intact – but only just: its sails and masts were wrecked; the bow anchor had driven through wood and copper sheathing to puncture the hull – and if nobody had been physically injured they were psychologically at their limits. When they reached Port Louis on the Falkland Islands on 6 April it was not a day too soon.

The Falklands were not the nicest place for a furlough. The weather was bad, accommodation was basic, company was restricted to the military garrison plus a few missionaries en route to South America, and food was so limited that for a while the entire island survived off the stores in Ross's ships. The crews of *Erebus* and *Terror* agreed that Ross had only chosen such a vile spot to stop them jumping ship. Ignoring their ill-temper, Ross had them build an observatory for magnetic readings. After that he told them to build a warehouse and a pier. Then, with time on his hands, he surveyed the island for a better harbour than Port Louis. His eventual choice was a spot now known as Port Stanley, the capital of the Falklands.

When not surveying and building they hunted the feral cattle that roamed the interior – the skin on one bull's neck was two inches thick – and when tired of that they sailed to Tierra del Fuego for more magnetic observations, then back to the Falklands where, supplies having newly arrived, they filled their holds and departed on 17 December for another stab at Antarctica.

Their third try, down the 55th meridian, was less successful than their second. They barely penetrated the Antarctic Circle, reaching 71° 30' S as against 78° 11' in 1840. But they found new islands off South Georgia and had the enviable experience of travelling though a pod of whales so dense that they had to nudge them aside. On 5 March Ross considered his task was done and signalled to Crozier that they should go north. They docked at Simon's Bay, South Africa, on 4 April. As at Hobart, colonialists prepared a grand welcome. But Ross and Crozier did not have the heart for it: they had been away too long and were incapable of polite chit-chat. When an admiral's daughter approached Ross – who had once been considered the handsomest man in the Navy – he said, 'You see how our hands shake? One night in the Antarctic did this for both of us.' They returned to Britain on 5 September, after four and half years in the southern ice.

Ross was rewarded handsomely. He was knighted, promoted and awarded gold medals, married the woman of his dreams, and earned enough money to buy a modest estate in Buckinghamshire. Crozier received less – a promotion from lieutenant to commander. He continued in naval service, becoming second-in-command to Franklin on his 1845 expedition to the North-West Passage. Ross, however, sank into retirement, too blasted by his Antarctic ordeal to contemplate further polar exploits. He died in 1862.

His achievements outlived him. What he had done was without compare. In two wooden ships – the last expedition ever to be conducted solely by sail – he had broken a record that would not be bettered for 50 years, and then with difficulty, by steam power. Maybe Dumont d'Urville had been the first to stand on Antarctica, but Ross had gone further south and had prepared the ground for others to come. In the 1900s, when Shackleton, Scott and Amundsen vied to reach the South Pole, they did so via the Ross Ice Shelf. Ross was the best Antarctic navigator of the century and, incidentally, one of the first charters of global warming. After Robert Falcon Scott's conquest of the South Pole in 1912 the naturalist Joseph Hooker, last surviving crew member of the *Terror*, looked at Scott's maps of the Ross Ice Shelf and said: 'the only serious omission ... is that of the marvellous retrocession of the Barrier since Ross mapped it. To me this seems the most momentous change to be brought about in little more than half a century. I have seen doubts cast upon Ross's demarcation of the sea front of the Barrier – but that is ridiculous, he was a first-rate naval surveyor.' The clean white world envisaged by Ross's men had shrunk by approximately a mile every year since they discovered it.

The search for Franklin (1845–59)

Sir John Franklin, the man who had done so much to chart the North-West Passage and whose boot-eating odyssey had thrilled the world during the 1820s, was, in 1844, at a loose end. Newly returned from the penal colony of Tasmania, where his governorship had not been a success, he was keen to find employment and, as it happened, there was a project in the Admiralty pipeline for which he felt himself perfectly suited: the North-West Passage. In what would be one of his last acts in office, Second Secretary Sir John Barrow was launching yet another expedition to find the troublesome seaway.

It did not matter to Barrow that the North-West Passage had already been proved commercially unviable, or that, as many people had told him many times, Arctic weather conditions were such that it could be traversed only on rare occasions. These considerations had long since ceased to bother him. No, the North-West Passage was now a badge of honour, and Barrow was determined that Britain should pin it to the national lapel. 'If the completion of the passage be left to be performed by some other power,' he admonished, 'England, by her neglect of it, after having opened both the East and West doors, would be laughed at by all the world for having hesitated to cross the threshold.' There were only 300 miles or so between the seas around Melville Island and the Canadian coast; there were two ships, the *Erebus* and *Terror*, ready primed for polar service after their return from Antarctica in 1843; and there was an experienced and well-trained squad of officers at hand to lead the expedition. After a brief period of bullying and blustering, Barrow received parliamentary approval for the final conquest of the North-West Passage.

Then came an embarrassing hiatus: who, from the Royal Navy's elite band of Arctic explorers, was to lead the expedition? James Ross refused, as did Parry; Crozier said he would go, but not as overall commander; Barrow had a favourite in mind, an eager if untried lieutenant named James Fitzjames; but then Franklin raised his head. Old, overweight and unfit, he was clearly beyond his prime; he was, however, the Royal Navy's senior Arctic officer, and as such his application could not be refused. Frantic politicking ensued, wiser officers doing their best to coax Parry or James Ross out of retirement,

but they succeeded merely in strengthening Franklin's hand. The higher Arctic echelons thought it only right that Franklin be given the post – what were a few hundred miles to a man such as he – and his physical incapacity was immaterial, given that he had to do nothing but sit in his ship. 'If you don't let him go,' Parry warned Lord Haddington, First Lord of the Admiralty, 'he will die of disappointment.' Haddington summoned Franklin for an interview in which he tried tactfully to dissuade him. To his every objection

Franklin had an answer. At a loss, Haddington resorted to blunt facts. 'You are sixty,' he accused. 'No, my Lord,' Franklin replied, 'I am fifty-nine.' On 7 February 1845 Franklin was given his command.

His orders were straightforward: he was to proceed to Lancaster Sound, sail as far west as he could, then go south to Point Turnagain – perhaps down Peel Sound, the next passage west after Prince Regent Inlet, to King William Island – and thence west to Bering Strait along the coast he had mapped in the 1820s. Should his path south be blocked, he was instructed to go north in search of the open polar sea, an entity that, despite every indication to the contrary, Barrow still believed was lurking somewhere above Greenland.

Erebus and *Terror* were given a thorough overhaul and, somewhat against Barrow's instincts, were equipped with steam engines – in the case of the *Erebus* a second-hand model from the Greenwich Railway. Canned food to last three years was packed into their holds. They were supplied with every comfort known to Victorian man, from soap and slippers to silver cutlery and silk handkerchiefs. Against the possibility of a long winter, a 1,700-volume library was installed, including bound editions of *Punch* to keep them laughing in the darkness. Nobody, however, expected them to be away for very long. They would be revictualling at the Sandwich Islands within a season.

Franklin left the Thames on 19 May 1845, the whole company in good spirits. He and his second-in-command, Fitzjames, were happy aboard *Erebus*. Crozier, on *Terror*, had a few reservations, fearing that they had left too late in the season and that Franklin, in whose judgement he did not have complete confidence, would 'blunder into the ice and make a second 1824 out of it'. But he concealed his worries so effectively that Franklin was able to write to Parry: 'It would do your heart good to see how zealously officers and men in both ships are working and how amicably we all work together.' On 26 July they reached Lancaster Sound, where they met two whalers. The explorers seemed confident, and announced that if they did not make the Passage this year then they would do it the next; it was just a matter of waiting, for they could make their supplies last another five years if they had to – perhaps even seven if they killed enough wildlife. Neither Franklin nor Crozier, nor the 133 men under their command, were ever seen alive again.

The years passed. By 1848 the Admiralty was worried by Franklin's non-appearance in the Pacific. There was, they told themselves, no *real* cause for concern: John Ross had survived longer than this with less food and feebler ships; besides, Franklin had intimated he could last until at least 1850, perhaps 1852. But the more experienced officers knew how perilous the North-West Passage could be and were unwilling to take chances. In that year three expeditions went in search of Franklin: one via Lancaster Sound under James Ross (he had grown tired of retirement); another via Bering Strait under one Captain Henry Kellett; and a third overland to the Mackenzie under John Richardson. When all three returned empty-handed a new sense of urgency prevailed. John Barrow, so long the grand master of polar exploration, had died on 23 November 1848, and his successors were at a loss. They therefore instituted a prize for Franklin's rescue – £20,000 for the man himself, £10,000 for his ships and £10,000 for the North-West Passage – then turned the business over to the Arctic Council. A nebulous group comprising every big name in Britain's exploring community, the Council had been in existence since the 1830s, mainly as an advisory body. Now, however, it showed that it was capable of action as well as advice. By 1850 there were 13 vessels in Lancaster Sound: two Admiralty fleets under Captains Horatio Austin and William Penny, two US ships financed by the New York philanthropist Henry Grinnell,* a ship sent by Franklin's widow, Lady Jane, plus a small schooner and a yacht commanded by Sir John Ross.

With only Franklin's orders to go by, the rescuers were searching blind. They looked into Peel Sound but found it blocked by ice, so they turned their attention north, assuming he must have gone in that direction. Here, at a spot called Beechey Island, they discovered signs of his presence: a mound of empty food cans and three graves dated 1845. They did not stop to wonder if Peel Sound had been open when Franklin met it, nor why Beechey Island had such a large cemetery. On their own, three graves were nothing to write home about, but in the Arctic they represented an unheard-of casualty rate: no North-West Passager had ever lost so many men to illness in a whole voyage, let alone during the first season. That winter the rescuers cast about, the most energetic searcher being one of Austin's lieutenants, an Irishman named Francis Leopold McClintock, who led man-hauled sledge parties over remarkable distances across the ice. They came home in 1851, with nothing to show for their efforts beyond a rumour from John Ross's interpreter that Franklin and his men had been killed by Inuit.

This was good enough for the Admiralty, who were reluctant to spend more money on a lost cause – these Arctic expeditions were very expensive. But it was not good enough for Lady Jane Franklin; neither was it good enough for the Arctic Council or the British public. Nobody cared any longer about the North-West Passage, but '[It impinges] most emphatically on our national honour that we should ascertain the fate of our missing countrymen and redeem them, if living, from the dangers to which they had been consigned,' *The Times* wrote sternly. Franklin, who was at best only a reasonably capable explorer and at worst one of the most ill-starred commanders to set foot in the Arctic, was elevated to the rank of national hero. 'The blooming child lisps Franklin's name, as with glittering eye and greedy ear it hears of the wonders of the North, and the brave deeds done there,' glowed one writer. The Admiralty capitulated. In 1852 a fleet of five ships left for Lancaster Sound, commanded by the odious Captain Sir Edward Belcher.

A bad-tempered, chancrous martinet, who had sailed as a lieutenant with

---

* Aboard one of them was Dr Elisha Kent Kane, who would later become America's foremost Arctic explorer of the 1850s.

Beechey aboard the *Blossom*, Belcher was roundly detested by all who served under him. According to his entry in the *Dictionary of National Biography*, 'Perhaps no officer of equal ability has ever succeeded in inspiring so much personal dislike', and his spell in the Arctic did nothing to diminish that reputation. Wintering at Cornwallis Island, to the north of Prince Regent Inlet and Peel Sound, he took little direct part in operations, leaving his officers – Kellett, McClintock and a newcomer, Lieutenant Sherard Osborn – to scour the landscape for traces of Franklin while he sat in his cabin and drank, writing vituperative reports on his underlings, occasionally breaking his diatribe to inspect the ice and, if it looked threatening, to move to a safer ship.

Only too pleased to escape Belcher's regime, the search parties roamed the ice. They advertised their presence and position in every conceivable way: by painting directions on cliffs, by distributing medals to the Inuit, by strapping collars to Arctic foxes and by sending up balloons with timed fuses that released messages in their wake. The Arctic was so big – and they were looking in the wrong place anyway – that there was little chance of Franklin seeing their notes. But it was an optimistic venture whose chances of producing a result were reinforced by the fact that they were no longer looking for Franklin alone. When the Arctic Council sent the first band of rescuers to Lancaster Sound in 1850 it had not ignored the possibility that Franklin might be stranded at the western end of the North-West Passage. So it had ordered two ships, the *Investigator* and the *Enterprise*, to approach via Bering Strait. Nothing had been heard of them since, and Belcher was instructed to rescue them as well.

If Belcher was bad, so too were Captain Robert McClure of the *Investigator* and Captain Richard Collinson of the *Enterprise*. These two men were unflinching disciplinarians who liked receiving orders almost as much as they liked to give them. They were also extremely competitive. They became separated when rounding Cape Horn – the *Investigator* lost a mast: 'The fury of the captain was terrible, positively inhuman' – and when McClure reached Hawaii he heard that Collinson, who was in overall command of the expedition, had stolen a lead. Dragging his men out of the bars – two had already drunk so much that they were on the sick list for a month – he took a perilous short-cut through the Aleutian Islands and darted into the North-West Passage, ignoring strict orders that no ship should be on its own in the Arctic. By the first week of September he had passed the Mackenzie delta, had charted the southern coast of Banks Island, which Parry had spotted from Melville Island 30 years before, and was at the top of a narrow passage that separated it from an as yet undiscovered landmass to the south that he christened Prince Albert Land. On 9 September, at the top of what he called Prince of Wales Strait, his readings showed that he was just 60 miles from Melville Island. It was so near that he could see it. 'Can it be that so humble a creature as I am will be permitted to perform what has baffled the talented and wise for hundreds of years?' he wondered.

It was not to be. The *Investigator* was hurled back by a gale that lasted for a week, peaking with 17 hours of uninterrupted fury. Convinced they were going to die, the 66 crew ignored their officers' orders and broached the rum barrels. When the storm abated the ship was stuck in the ice 30 miles south of its 9 September position. The hungover men lined up wretchedly on deck as McClure read them the Articles of War. The *Investigator* stayed where it was for the rest of the winter, its position making it a perfect base for the man-hauled sledge parties that McClure despatched over Banks Island and Prince Albert Land. The latter was, in fact, a peninsula of the much larger Victoria Island that stretched south-east towards King William Island, and bordered the channel Richardson had discovered in 1826 between the Mackenzie and Coppermine Rivers. McClure and his men would have discovered this had they sledged far enough. Their efforts at overland exploration, however, were so ham-fisted as almost to kill them. McClure, who for all his faults was not one to stand by while others did the work, led many of the expeditions, at one point driving himself so hard that he had to spend a month in bed. He expected the same sacrifice from his officers, forcing them into harness even when badly frostbitten. Ill-prepared and poorly fed, it was no wonder that the crew broke ranks to wander over the ice on impromptu game shoots from which, as they inevitably became lost in the snow and fog, they had to be rescued.

The ice broke in Prince of Wales Strait in June 1851, and by August McClure was back where he had been the previous September, staring across the ice to Melville Island. At this point he had three options: to stay where he was and hope the ice broke in 1852; to retrace his route and search for a passage across the north of Banks Island; or to go home. He chose the second without hesitation. Seventeen days later he was at 73° 55' N, with Banks Island to starboard, the Arctic pack to port, and ahead of him a sliver of open water barely wider than the ship itself. If he entered that channel he was committed: he would be unable to reverse or turn around; he could only continue until he reached a dead end or open seas. In he went.

One has to admire McClure. He was so stubborn, so determined not to be defeated by the Arctic, that he was willing to stake his life on this slender chance of success. On the other hand, he was risking not just his life but the lives of everyone aboard, and he was doing so for the worst of reasons: fame. It was remotely conceivable that Franklin might have sailed to Banks Island, but had he done so it would have been against orders and in the face of every report since 1820 stating that the ice was impassable west of Melville Island. Of course, 1845 might have been one of those freak years when the ice was open; but in that case it would have been open in Peel Sound too and Franklin, whose primary directive was to sail south-west, would not have bothered with Banks Island. But McClure no longer cared much about Franklin. Since the moment in September 1850 when he came within an ace of reaching Melville Island his goal had been to claim the £10,000 bounty for being first through the North-West Passage.

He applied himself to the task with vigour: when the wind failed he ordered his men to tow the ship; when ice blocked the channel he blew it apart with gunpowder. By the end of September he was at Mercy Bay on the north-east shore of Banks Island, even closer to Melville Island than he had been the previous year; and, miraculously, the sea was clear. Here was the opportunity he had been waiting for. But at the last moment his nerve failed. The season was far advanced and, rather than risk an entrapment in the pack, he decided to stay where he was. Completion of the Passage would have to wait until the following year.

Collinson, meanwhile, had entered the ice a year behind McClure, and had followed almost exactly the same route up Prince of Wales Strait and then round the western coast of Banks Island to a point named Cape Kellett. Here, discovering that McClure had sailed that way only 13 days before, he turned south for the open waters of the North American mainland and put the *Enterprise* into a harbour on Victoria Island – Cambridge Bay, north-east of Franklin's Point Turnagain. From there he sledged to Melville Island, only to find that, once again, McClure had beaten him to it. 'We had passed within sixty miles of the *Investigator* and had fallen upon the traces of her exploring parties [but] we again missed the opportunity of communication,' he recorded with asperity. Returning to winter quarters, he put his ice-master, Francis Skead, under arrest for insubordination. What he might have done was go east to King William Island, the one part of the Arctic that had yet to be searched, and in which Franklin might yet be found. But he did not, instead sending his sledgers to chart the west coast of Victoria Island, a relatively unimportant mission that had little to do with the matter at hand. From his cabin Skead sneered at Collinson, who he claimed was not only a drunk but an overcautious, hidebound bully. In his opinion, the only thing stopping them going east as well as west was that two perfectly sound officers had, like himself, been placed under arrest 'on trifling charges'. Collinson ignored Skead's fulminations. 'Discipline,' he intoned, 'is essential to comfort.'

Collinson's disappointment at Melville Island was nothing compared with McClure's. When the *Investigator*'s sledgers reached the spot 20 days before, they found a cairn containing a message from McClintock dated the previous summer. McClure fell to his knees and wept. If only he had risked that last stretch of open water – or if he had crossed the ice earlier in the season – he might have met Austin's western division. Still, he would have a chance this coming summer. Placing a note of his own in the cairn, he retreated to the ship to await warmer weather. But there *was* no summer for McClure and his men – at least not in the accepted meaning of the word. In August, a month by which they could have expected to be afloat, they were able to skate on Mercy Bay; and by September new ice was forming. Obviously, they would have to wait until the summer of 1853 to complete the Passage.

The medical officer Alexander Armstrong did not share his captain's confidence: his concern was not whether a crossing would be feasible but whether they would be alive to make it. McClure had put his men on two-thirds rations when the *Investigator* reached Mercy Bay; the next winter he had cut that to half-rations; now their allowance was reduced still further, to six ounces of meat and two of vegetables per diem. There was game to be shot on Banks Island, but their inexperience and incompetence meant that they rarely hit anything. As Armstrong pointed out, their supplies were 'Quite inadequate ... to sustain life for any lengthened period'. Maybe, though, it did not matter if food was scarce, because it looked as if scurvy would get them long before starvation did. By July, 16 men had the disease, and as McClure halved the crew's daily measure of lemon juice – it was running out like everything else – the numbers multiplied. Come New Year almost everybody was showing signs of scurvy, and 20 men were sick, two of them near death.

McClure ignored the growing casualty list. To him, the only thing that mattered was the completion of the North-West Passage. He spent most of the winter alone in his cabin, emerging only to refuse the crews' petitions for extra rations, to have people flogged for stealing food, and to order the company to reduce its consumption of coal. As the temperature dropped to −99° F, the coldest ever recorded on an Arctic expedition, one man slipped and broke his leg, another lost his mind and a third became so demented that he started howling at night. Reading McClure's journal, one gets the impression that he too had taken leave of his senses. 'The winter found us ready to combat its rigours as cheerfully as on previous occasions,' he wrote. 'Dancing, skylarking and singing were kept up on the lower deck with unflagging spirit, good humour and vitality.' All they had to do to survive the winter was maintain a regime of 'cheerfulness, energetic exercise and regularity of habits'. This was news to his crew. They gnawed their meat raw (it lasted longer that way) while beneath them the ship's bolts cracked in the cold.

For all his insouciance, McClure knew that he could make the North-West Passage only if he found more food or reduced the number of mouths he had to feed. He therefore drew up a plan of evacuation. One team would sledge to Melville Island, where they might meet a rescue ship. (Belcher's fleet was now in the vicinity, but they did not know that.) Another was to travel south to the mainland in the hope of finding assistance from an outpost of the Hudson's Bay Company. He, meanwhile, would remain on the *Investigator* to forge the Passage with a skeleton crew. When Armstrong saw the sledging roster he was dismayed: it included the sickest, least essential men on the expedition. (McClure had actually sought his advice as to who was most dispensable.) He thought they would be lucky if they covered half the distance before keeling over, and advised McClure 'of the absolute unfitness of the men for the performance of this journey'. McClure noted his comments and proceeded with the cull of useless mouths.

In the first week of April 1853 the sledge parties were ready – eager even, for they would at least be doing something, and however slim their chances they could be no worse than if they stayed on the *Investigator*. Then, after long months of inaction and boredom, time suddenly contracted. One of the stronger men, who had been in charge of the sick bay, fell ill. He went to bed on 5 April and died on the 6th from scurvy. While gravediggers hacked at the frozen ground, McClure took a stroll with one of his lieutenants. Pondering the wasteland of ice that lay before them, they noticed a figure at the mouth of Mercy Bay. It was one of the sledgers practising, McClure said. When the man ran towards them, waving his arms, they assumed he was being chased by a polar bear. Too far off to help, they waited for the kill. But there was no polar bear. The man came nearer and nearer, gesticulating wildly. From his soot-blackened face and clothes McClure wondered if he was an Inuit. But if that was the case, why was he behaving so oddly? 'In the name of God, who are you?' he shouted. The man replied: 'I'm Lieutenant Pim of the *Resolute*, and I've come to relieve Captain McClure and the Investigators.' Behind him, a sledge party emerged at the mouth of Mercy Bay.

As Pim and his team doled out food to the starving men, McClure questioned them about the *Resolute*. It was part of Belcher's fleet, he learned, and was anchored off Melville Island under the command of Henry Kellett. Alongside was the *Intrepid*, under Frank McClintock, whose long-distance sledgers had discovered the note McClure had left the summer before. Belcher's other three ships, meanwhile, were safely moored in Wellington Channel, off Cornwallis Island. McClure was overjoyed, but not at the prospect of salvation: in his madness, he saw his rescuers as a means whereby he could complete the North-West Pasage. If he could offload the weaker half of his crew onto the *Resolute*, then he and the remainder would have enough food to sail the *Investigator* to freedom in the summer. On 8 April he sledged with Pim to the *Resolute* and very nearly succeeded in persuading Kellett to accept his plan. Unfortunately, he had ordered Armstrong to bring the invalids in his wake. When Kellett saw the horrible company of insane, lame, blind, frostbitten and scorbutic scarecrows staggering over the ice, and when Armstrong informed him that another two men had died shortly after McClure's departure, he realized the *Investigator* was in far worse shape than McClure had been willing to admit. His doctors confirmed his suspicion. Returning with McClure to Mercy Bay, they reported that of the 20 'healthy' men on board, none was fit for service and only four were willing to spend another season in the ice. On Kellett's orders McClure mothballed the *Investigator*, and by 17 June he was aboard the *Resolute* with the rest of his crew.

Safety did not mean escape. The *Resolute* could not sail without the *Intrepid*, whose commander was still sledging west in search of Franklin.

When McClintock returned a few weeks later he had been away 106 days, during which he had man-hauled 1,328 miles without seeing a trace of his quarry. The journey, moreover, had been so arduous that one man had died in harness, two others were on the point of death and the rest did not recover fully for another 12 months. When the two ships eventually sailed in August they were trapped by the ice before they had gone 100 miles. Clad only in the one set of clothes they had worn on the journey from the *Investigator*, McClure's men shivered the winter away in cramped and uncomfortable conditions. More men died and the sick list grew longer. It was now their fourth winter in the Arctic.

By April 1854 McClintock had undertaken several more mammoth sledge journeys and had, finally, come to the conclusion that they ought to look south, in the direction of Peel Sound and King William Island. But, ready as he was to make the attempt, he found himself unable to do so. This was not because the men were unavailable (though they might have been unwilling: McClintock's man-hauling took a terrible toll; another two of his sledgers had died in January) but because Kellett needed them for his own purposes. An extraordinary message had come in from Belcher, ordering him to abandon both ships and bring the crews to Beechey Island. In Kellett's opinion, anyone who left their ships – particularly when they were sound and had every expectation of being able to escape in the summer – 'would deserve to have their jackets taken off their backs'. He therefore ordered McClintock to sledge to Beechey Island and persuade Belcher of his folly. Belcher didn't care what Kellett thought. He had already decided to abandon not only Kellett's two ships but another two of his own. The crews of all four would escape on the remaining vessel, *North Star*, which was anchored in the open waters off Beechey Island. This they did, to the disgust of every officer, cramming the crews of six ships – Kellett's two, Belcher's two, McClure's one, plus the survivors of the *Breadalbane*, a transport that had been nipped the year before – onto the *North Star* before sailing ignominiously to Lancaster Sound where, luckily, they were able to transfer excess personnel onto a couple of supply ships that were sailing north with extra provisions. The severity of Belcher's regime shocked even McClure who, after a taste of life on the *North Star*, wrote that the Arctic was a place 'which I hope to have done with forever'.

When they arrived in London, Belcher was court-martialled for the loss of his fleet* and was acquitted of any culpable wrongdoing. But the board handed back his sword in stony silence, thereby signalling their disapproval of his failure to find Franklin and his abandonment not only of his own ships but of Collinson's *Enterprise*. They were appreciative, however, of

---

* To the Royal Navy's embarrassment, the *Resolute*, one of the ships Belcher had deserted in Wellington Channel, floated free and made its way through Lancaster Sound to Davis Strait where it was seized by an American whaler. Polished, buffed and restored to working condition, it was presented to Queen Victoria as a friendly gesture to allay the current diplomatic tension between the two countries. Britain responded in the same spirit: the *Resolute*'s timbers were made into a desk that was presented to the President. It remains in the Oval Office today.

McClure's exploits. In taking his ship to Banks Island, and then crossing the ice to Melville Island, he had become the first man to traverse the North-West Passage. He was given a gold medal and was awarded the £10,000 prize he had longed for. That he had completed the last stretch on foot instead of by sail was a technicality the Admiralty hadn't the strength to argue. After so much expense and loss of life it just wanted the thing done with.

The last loose end (apart from Franklin himself) was Collinson, who returned in 1855 with every single officer under arrest save the surgeon, his assistant and the mate – Skead had been kept in his cabin for 32 months – and having attracted such intense hostility that every man aboard was willing to sacrifice his pension to bring him to justice. 'Never was there such an expedition set sail under such auspicious auspices; had such golden opportunities which were thrown away; and made such signal failures,' wrote one critic. His personal failings aside, Collinson could perhaps be condemned on professional grounds for failing to explore King William Island. On the other hand, had the *Investigator* not sailed ahead he would have had the extra manpower he needed for such an expedition. As it was, his voyage to Victoria Island had proved that the Canadian coast could be navigated in a large ship; and if he had not found Franklin, he had come closer than anyone yet to forging the missing link in the North-West Passage. Roald Amundsen would later describe him as 'one of the most capable and enterprising sailors the world has ever produced'. Justifiably, he was irritated that McClure should receive £10,000 for what amounted to disobeying orders. He let this be known, at the same time responding to his officers' demands for legal action with an application to have the whole lot court-martialled. Again, though, the affair was swept under the carpet.

In the same year, the Admiralty informed Lady Jane Franklin that her husband was dead and that they would no longer be looking for him. They did so on evidence supplied not by Her Majesty's Navy but by a Hudsons's Bay employee named John Rae who, while Belcher, Collinson, McClure and co. were frozen in their various bays and channels, had sledged overland from Repulse Bay towards King William Island. En route he had met a group of Inuit who told of an event that had occurred four winters before, in 1849–50. They had met a party of white men dragging a boat down King William Island, led by a tall, middle-aged officer (perhaps Crozier), and had sold them a seal. They said the strangers fell down and died as they walked. Later, they had found the remains of the same party on an island off the Canadian mainland. There were 35 corpses, the officer among them, and from the contents of their cooking pots they had resorted to cannibalism before they died. But some must have survived because the Inuit heard gunshots to the south in May 1850. As proof of their encounter they produced a quantity of silver cutlery bearing the initials of Franklin's officers, plus one of Franklin's medals. For Rae, and the Admiralty, this was enough.

When another man from the Hudson's Bay Company went to investigate the scene, however, he couldn't find a single body. At one spot there were signs that a boat had been repaired – one piece of wood bore the word *Erebus* – but other than that, nothing. Encouraged, Lady Jane Franklin raised money to continue the search, and in 1857 sent McClintock to the Arctic on a tiny steamer, the *Fox*. McClintock pushed down Prince Regent Inlet, as John Ross had done 20 years before, and began a comprehensive survey of King William Island. On 25 May 1859 he found his first skeleton – a steward, as far as he could make out. The Inuit had not been lying after all – the men *had* fallen as they walked. A little later he discovered two more skeletons lying in a boat. One, an officer, was still wrapped in his fur overcoat; the other was larger, less well protected, and had been gnawed by wild animals. Two guns were propped against the boat, and inside were slippers, boots, handkerchiefs, sealing-wax, silver cutlery, towels, soap, toothbrushes and countless other inessentials. There were also 40 pounds of chocolate and a 22-pound tin of meat – empty. A number of books bearing the initials 'G.G.' suggested that the skeleton in the fur coat might have been Graham Gore, one of Franklin's officers. Gore and his companion could not have pulled the boat by themselves – with its sledge it weighed a good 1,500 pounds – so the likeliest scenario was that they had fallen ill and been left to fend for themselves while their fellow haulers went ahead in search of food and assistance. Where then were those men? The only clue was the direction in which the boat faced: north.

To the north lay Victory Point, and it was here that McClintock found the remains of the Franklin expedition. The *Erebus* and *Terror* were nowhere to be seen, but discarded equipment lay everywhere: stoves, lightning conductors, curtain rods, medicine chests, scientific instruments, bibles, boot polish, bits of rigging, all sorts of rubbish, and a pile of winter clothing that came up to his shoulders. It was as if some giant hand had emptied the ships of their contents before throwing them away. From a cairn he uncovered a note whose contents went a long way to explaining the mystery. It was dated 28 May 1847 and described how the *Erebus* and *Terror* had spent the previous winter at Beechey Island – this would explain the graves and detritus that Austin had found – and had circled Cornwallis Island before sailing down Peel Sound. Around the margin was scrawled a second message that read:

> April 25th, 1848. H.M. Ships 'Erebus' and 'Terror' were deserted on the 22nd April, 5 leagues N.N.W. of this, having been beset since 12th September 1846. The officers and crews, consisting of 105 souls, under the command of F. R. M. Crozier, landed here, in lat. 69° 37' 42" N, long. 98° 41' W. Sir John Franklin died on the 11th June 1847; and the total loss by deaths in this expedition has been, to this date, 9 officers and 15 men.
>
> And start on to-morrow, 26th, for Backs's Fish River.
>
> F.R.M. CROZIER, Captain and Senior Officer. JAMES FITZJAMES, Captain, H.M.S 'Erebus'.

Backs's Fish River to which the note referred was the Great Fish River, which had been discovered in the 1830s by George Back, Franklin's erstwhile travelling companion, and lay due south of King William Island. Now Rae's reports made sense: Crozier had taken his men to the nearest point of escape but had been defeated by the climate and terrain. But if that was the case, why had Gore's boat been pointing north? Had a group turned back for Victory Point, perhaps with the idea of crossing overland to Prince Regent Inlet and escaping as John Ross had done in 1833? North of Victory Point McClintock found tantalizing suggestions that this might have been the case: cairns, campsites, some pieces of clothing and three small tents. One of the cairns contained a piece of white paper, but its message had long since faded, and although they dug a ten-foot-wide trench around it they found no new clues. Most importantly, neither at Victory Point, nor at the campsites to the north, nor at any point on his journey over King William Island, did McClintock find more than the barest trace of the countless tins of food that Franklin had confidently expected would see him through five years in the Arctic. Understandably, the survivors would have hoarded them to the last minute; but one would expect a trail of empties to have been dropped on the way. Where had they gone? McClintock and his men did not have the time for further detective work. By August they were back on the *Fox*, two men suffering from scurvy and the rest exhausted. They reached Britain on the 20th with their unwelcome news.

That Franklin was dead could no longer be disputed, to the relief of all save his widow. Seven hundred thousand pounds sterling and 250 US dollars of public and private money had been spent looking for him, and now a line could be drawn under the accounts. How he had died, and what had happened to the survivors (if any) and the two ships, was a mystery that the Admiralty did not wish to pursue. Privately funded American expeditions would later go in search of him – those led in the 1860s by Charles Francis Hall unearthed (possibly unreliable) Inuit testimony regarding the fate of the last survivors – but too often their real goal was the North Pole. For more than a century the world had to be content with the findings of Rae, McClintock and Hall, a rumour that the tinned meat had been bad, and the extraordinary sighting in 1851 of two ships floating down Baffin Bay on an ice floe. The latter was not a mirage but solid fact, reported by a navy brig: furthermore, the ships had been painted the Admiralty's distinctive black with a yellow stripe, and the only naval vessels missing in the Arctic at that date were the *Erebus* and *Terror*. It seems odd that they could have drifted from Peel Sound to Baffin Bay, especially as part of the journey was against prevailing currents; but Belcher's *Resolute* would do something similar, so the possibility cannot be discounted. On the other hand, Collinson had found wreckage near Cambridge Bay that included a fragment of doorframe. He thought nothing of it at the time but, unless the North-West Passage had ingested some hapless whaler from the seas above Bering Strait, he had probably stumbled on the remains of one of Franklin's ships. The findings of Collinson in 1854, and the navy brig in 1851, have yet to be reconciled.

In the late 20th century forensic science was applied to the problem. During the 1980s a pair of US researchers exhumed the three graves on Beechey Island (the bodies were nightmarishly well preserved) and gave them a proper autopsy. The corpses had already been examined by the Franklin searchers, who had concluded that they had died of pneumonia-related illnesses. A more detailed analysis, however, revealed that they contained toxic quantities of lead, probably from the solder used to seal the seams of their food cans. Lead poisoning causes lethargy, irrationality and debilitation, all of which could have contributed to the expedition's downfall. But lead poisoning is a slow, accumulative illness and it is hard to believe it could have been responsible for the sudden rash of deaths that had hit the ships. The first message, written in May 1847, had ended 'All well'. By the time Crozier wrote his marginal addendum in April 1848, 24 men were dead. One imagines Franklin suffered the heart attack that was, by all accounts, long overdue. But what of the others? Whatever malady hit the *Erebus* and *Terror*, it was something swifter and more virulent than lead poisoning. In the 1990s new evidence suggested that, as the Victorians suspected, the canned meat had been tainted. This was a more likely proposition. Their immune systems weakened by two Arctic winters on standard naval provisions, officers and men would have been devastated by botulism. Scurvy might also have worked its malign influence. But if their provisions ran out, as Franklin had said and John Ross had proved, they could have lived off the land: there were deer, there were salmon, there were birds, bears, seals and prawns. Why Franklin's men were unable to kill game – or perhaps to find it? – is, like so much else surrounding his expedition, a mystery.

Where some of the men went after they abandoned ship has been plotted with a degree of accuracy: investigators have found a trail of skulls and skeletons leading down the west coast of King William Island and the shores of mainland America. None of the remains have been identified, but from their distribution it appears that some men were killed and that their meatier parts were eaten on the spot, while the torsos – lighter than thighs and arms – were carried for some while before the ribs were carved up. Knife marks on the finger bones have been given as evidence that the men were jointed before being shared out. Some, however, claim that the same marks are typical of a man defending himself against a foe armed with a knife, and that Crozier's party was attacked and massacred by Inuit. The scenario is not far-fetched, but if the victims were defending themselves against anybody, it may well have been against the cannibals in their midst rather than the Inuit.

The questions that hang over the Franklin expedition can only be settled when its journals are discovered. These would certainly have been the last thing Crozier discarded, and would equally certainly have been placed where future searchers could find them. The Inuit spoke of a hole being dug on land and covered with a strange, soft stuff that later went hard (cement?). Perhaps this was Franklin's grave, perhaps it was a repository for the journals, or perhaps it was just a platform for the expedition's scientific instruments. When it can be ascertained whether Crozier went north or south, and when somebody has the time, money and luck to find his and Franklin's records, then all will be revealed. At the time of writing they have yet to be found, despite a burgeoning tourist industry dedicated to that very task.

If the fate of Britain's most notorious Arctic expedition remains uncertain, its legacy is precise. In geographical terms the search for Franklin filled every gap in the Arctic that earlier explorers had left untouched, the most poignant of which was that around King William Island. It was not a land but an island, and if Franklin had gone east instead of west at the bottom of Peel Sound he would have discovered a narrow strait between King William Island and Boothia that led to the softer waters of Point Turnagain. As it was, he had been trapped by the ice pouring in from the Arctic Ocean, whose pressure, in the form of stranded berglets on King William Island, had first been recorded by James Ross in 1832. More importantly, Franklin inspired a new generation of polar explorers. One of the officers involved in his non-rescue was a lieutenant named Clements Markham, who was so taken with the romance of it all that he later instigated Britain's doomed, man-hauled attempts at the North and South Poles. The thrill was not exclusive to Britain: Norway's Roald Amundsen, who would become the 20th century's most garlanded explorer, wrote: '[Franklin's story] thrilled me as nothing I had ever read before. What appealed to me most was the sufferings that Sir John and his men had to endure. A strange ambition burned inside me, to endure the same privations ... I decided to be an explorer.' Dead, Franklin became an even greater hero than when he was alive.

· PART 3 ·

THE AGE OF ENDEAVOUR

THE AGE OF ENDEAVOUR

On 1 May 1851 the Great Exhibition opened in London's Hyde Park. Here, canopied under a monumental edifice of cast-iron and glass, was a showcase of industrial prowess the like of which had never been seen before. In every field, from mining to manufacturing, from furniture to farming, the power of technology was laid bare – there were great engines and machines, locomotives, bridges, a knife with 300 blades, a glass fountain 27 feet high and weighing 11 tons, the largest sideboard known to humankind, and countless other marvels. Even the building bore the stamp of Victorian ingenuity. The 'Crystal Palace', as it was dubbed, was a revolutionary piece of architecture, whose statistics spoke for themselves: constructed in the course of seven months by 2,200 workers, it comprised 4,000 tons of iron, 400 tons of glass, 30 miles of guttering and 200 miles of wooden sash bars, was tall enough to contain three mature elm trees and was twice as long as St Paul's Cathedral. All in all, the Great Exhibition was a stupendous experience, a statement not only of present might but of future potential. By the time it closed on 15 October more than six million visitors from all over the globe had paid a total of £365,000 to pass through its gates. One 85-year-old woman walked all the way from Cornwall to see it. Another woman made the shorter journey from Windsor Castle and was so impressed that she came not once but 30 times, each visit filling her with deeper awe for the period over which she and her country presided: 'We are capable', Queen Victoria wrote in her diary, 'of doing anything.'

The certainty that one could do anything underpinned the Victorian Age. Although discovery was seen by some as a peripheral activity compared with the nitty-gritty of increasing output, building sewers, developing new medicines and generally getting on with business, it was intrinsic to many themes of the industrial world, particularly that of Empire. Missionaries and travellers who opened stretches of 'darkest' Africa were often precursors to armed invasion. Even in places it seemed pointless or impossible to conquer – the Poles, for instance, or the Himalayas – it was still important to plant the flag, because there was always the hope that they might be commercially valuable. The main reason France explored the Sahara during the last half of the 19th century was to build a railway connecting Algeria to its West

African colonies. (The rumour that a field of emeralds lay hidden in the dunes did nothing to put them off.) The discovery of coal on Greenland and Ellesmere Island caused a brief flurry of excitement. Similarly, the presence in the Arctic of seals, walruses and narwhals indicated that there was money to be made in the region – wildlife was considered as much a resource as minerals: pelts, oil and ivory all fetched good prices – and if they were insufficient in number to merit full-scale exploitation, they were a handy source of income for individuals who needed to offset the costs of private ventures. In 1909, when Robert Peary and Frederick Cook claimed simultaneously to have attained the North Pole, their dispute centred not just on priority but on possession of a cache of walrus ivory. Three years later Captain Robert Falcon Scott's sledge journey to the South Pole foundered partly because it was carrying unnecessary quantities of rock samples. In fairness, the rocks were collected for scientific purposes; but until they were analysed, who knew what they might not reveal about Antarctica's potential?

Alongside national prestige and commercial benefit came a third inducement to go exploring: the prospect of having one's name in the papers. Ever since printing began, people had always been interested in tales of far-off places. In the industrial age an increasingly literate population was informed by an efficient and technologically sophisticated press. As newspaper magnates soon realized, their readers liked sensation. Murder, scandal and gossip sold copies, but nothing increased circulation like a saga of harrowing tribulation amidst exotic surroundings. James Gordon Bennett, the innovatory proprietor of the *New York Herald*, who has been credited as the father of modern journalism, exploited the seam to its fullest. Too impatient to wait for news to happen, he decided to make it himself. In 1869, for example, it had been several years since anyone had heard of the British missionary and explorer David Livingstone; it was known that he was in southern Africa, but nobody knew precisely where, or if he was dead or alive. Bennett took one of his reporters aside and said: 'I will tell you what you will do. Draw a thousand pounds now and when you have gone through that, draw another thousand, and when that is spent, draw another, and when you have finished that, draw another and so on – BUT FIND LIVINGSTONE.' His reporter was a man named Henry Morton Stanley, who not only found Livingstone but became one of the most famous (and newsworthy) African explorers of the century.

There were others like Stanley. Bennett's 'Special Correspondents', as he called them, roamed the globe in increasingly daring, and circulation-boosting, fashion. The programme came to an end in 1879 when Bennett sent an expedition to the North Pole under a US Navy officer, George Washington De Long. Three years later De Long and half his crew were dead, a price that embarrassed even Bennett (though not enough to stop him making headlines out of the disaster). The *Herald*'s policy was copied by newspapers across the world. Britain's *Daily Telegraph* sponsored an African expedition, the *Daily Mail* an Arctic one, and the *Chicago Record Herald* made no less than three futile efforts to get an airship to the North Pole. In 1913 a Russian newspaper, the *Noyoe Vremya*, sent Grigoriy Yakovlevich Sedov to his death on an expedition to Franz Josef Land.

If the media used explorers, explorers also used the media. When governments refused to fund an expedition – as they increasingly did – it was to the press that explorers next appealed. And if the press did not provide the cash, advertisements placed in its pages often did. On an explorer's successful return he was guaranteed good money for an exclusive account of his deeds. And once again the small ads came to his aid: for among the hundreds of products whose advertising revenue provided newspapers with their income there was not a single one that did not benefit from having an explorer's name attached. When Karl Weyprecht and Julius von Payer returned to Vienna in 1874, following their discovery of Franz Josef Land, there was a craze for Payer coats and Weyprecht cravats. When the Norwegian neuroscientist Fridtjof Nansen completed the first traverse of Greenland in 1888 his name was attached to caps, cakes, cigars, pens and several pieces of music. There was even a Nansen fly-button. Dr Frederick Cook, who in 1909 claimed to have discovered the North Pole, franchised toy sledges, little figurines of himself in travelling furs, and a remarkable two-foot high pyramid of brown fuzz, adorned by a white plume on its left flank, that was sold to New Yorkers as the 'Dr Cook Hat'. Cook's polar rival, Robert Peary, lent his name to practically every manufactured article he had taken on his journey, and several he had not. A shaving brush was given his imprimatur, despite the fact that he was simultaneously selling photographs of himself in full moustaches. The makers of Shredded Wheat wanted it to be known that theirs was the cereal of choice at the Pole. 'The Underclothes Peary Wore Ninety Degrees North,' cried the Norfolk & New Brunswick Hosiery Co. There was nothing too low for Peary to franchise, and no price too high for him to accept for it. Even in strait-laced Britain, the Antarctic hero Ernest Shackleton wrote to Vilhjalmur Stefansson (Arctic explorer, also journalist) that the rewards could be great, 'particularly when you come home from an expedition with a big hurrah'. Roald Amundsen, who traversed the North-West Passage and the North-East Passage, skied to the South Pole, and flew a Zeppelin to the North Pole, was fully aware of the money-spinning potential of his trade. Exploration was not just something he did exceptionally well – it was his livelihood, his career.

To garner the big hurrahs one had, naturally, to do something big, and the biggest things were to be done at either end of the world's axis. This was the heyday of polar exploration, in which expedition after expedition went north and south, advancing by tiny increments and at great human cost towards the ends of the earth. The 'international steeple chase', as one Austrian dismissively called it, culminated in 1909 with Peary's supposed conquest of the North Pole (he probably got no further than 89° N) and Robert

Falcon Scott's tragic attainment in 1912 of the South Pole, where he not only discovered that Amundsen had beaten him by a few weeks but died with his entire party on the return journey. The towering egos and dramatic exploits of those who sought the Poles overshadowed the achievements of those who went after slightly smaller hurrahs. The Franz Josef Land surveys of Frederick Jackson and Benjamin Leigh-Smith, for example, were barely recognized at the time and are treasured today only by Arctic cognoscenti. The Marquess of Ava and Dufferin's bizarre tour of Iceland is likewise forgotten, as is the Prince of Monaco's charting of Spitsbergen's coast. So too are Walter Wellman's attempt to explore the Arctic in what amounted to a canoe slung beneath a balloon, and the extraordinarily incompetent antics of Evelyn Baldwin and Anthony Fiala in Franz Josef Land. The Danish Literary Expedition to Greenland, meanwhile, has vanished from all but the most abstruse records.

Those who sought the Poles were either wealthy in their own right, were financed by learned bodies and charitable bequests or had raised subscriptions through the press. Having burned their fingers in the past, governments had little enthusiasm for polar exploration (though they were quick to parade their citizens' success). Elsewhere, however, fame and fortune could be had relatively cheaply. These were heady days, in which a chap – and they were usually, though not exclusively, chaps; often also British – could buy a gun, catch a steamer to some distant port, hire a team of porters and stride off in search of undiscovered lands. If no new territory was to hand then the old would do, so long as one could have a bit of fun along the way. The fun might consist of shooting tigers, lions or elephants, climbing a new mountain, investigating ancient ruins or, in the case of Ewart Grogan, proving oneself worthy of a bride. In 1900 this enterprising man of Irish descent travelled from the Cape to Cairo, partly for the thrill of being the first to do so, but mainly because he wanted to impress his prospective father-in-law.

Africa, in particular, attracted a unique assortment of multi-national adventurers, who soon became objects of caricature: there was the obsessed, quinine-guzzling explorer, the yellow-fever-tinged conman, the big game hunter, the would-be farmer, the desperate prospector. Their paths crossed so frequently that one London publisher produced a guide to frontier etiquette: except in South Africa it was forbidden to touch a visitor's horse; an American camp would expect travellers to stay for dinner; with Britons or Germans one should wait for an invitation; and so forth. Some of these men – Richard Burton, John Hanning Speke, Samuel Baker and Pierre Savorgnan de Brazza – went to Africa to solve geographical conundrums such as the source of the Nile or the whereabouts of the River Congo. Others posed as scientists and the stereotypical photograph of a white man standing with rifle in hand on the carcase of a recently slain beast was not just a statement of sporting prowess but an accurate depiction of science at work: if you found a new species you shot it and, with a bit of luck, brought it home to the British Museum or the Smithsonian. Yet others came to Africa in search of wealth. Europeans were amazed at how big the continent was, how fertile its soil, how inexhaustible its mineral deposits. That it was not theirs for the taking bothered very few.

Africa was perhaps the most glamorous destination for an explorer, but it was far from the only one. All over the world teams of Europeans were crossing deserts, climbing mountains, charting new lands, investigating the habits of those who lived in them and discovering new species of flora and fauna. Their journeys took them to Kamchatka, Mongolia, New Guinea, the Australian interior and many other destinations. They could also be found in lands that were generally considered 'tamed': Europe itself, for example, the United States and Canada. Wherever the smallest blank existed on a map, someone was trying to fill it.

Explorers of the time described their adventures not only by charts and journals but by objects. This was an age of trophy, in which specimens and artefacts burgeoned throughout Western museums. Every traveller was an amateur curator and their collections – a rock, a buffalo head, a spear, a fetish, an album of photographs, a shrunken skull – were both a brag and a source of instruction. For those who had never encountered such things there was enlightenment, as well as vicarious excitement, to be had in seeing first-hand an Asanti stool, in touching a table made of hippo hide, in turning a Tibetan prayer-wheel, or gazing into the eyes of a stuffed tiger. Trophies also catered to the current fad for interior design: in Europe and America more homes were being built at a faster rate than ever before and their occupants needed to decorate them. As befitted the age, exoticism was the theme: Japanese-style furniture, Chinese carvings and Persian carpets were all the rage; so, in some circles, were zebra skins, a pair of gazelle horns, a walrus tusk and a cabinet of fossils.

The mania for collecting extended to human beings. In the past, explorers had brought natives home and tried to assimilate them into Western society. The experiments had always failed, but this did not stop them trying again. Robert Peary provided the most extreme example in 1895 when he collected several Etah Inuit, who he hoped would raise funds for another polar exped-ition. Mistreated, housed in dank basements and hired out to Barnum's Circus, they succumbed to Western diseases. Their skeletons were later exhibited in the Smithsonian Museum. Only two were returned to the Arctic, physically and psychologically scarred, with a profound detestation of their host nation.

There were other, less notorious, instances of colonial acquisitiveness. Between 1891 and 1893 the 15-strong African Choir from Cape Colony were paraded through Britain and America before being abandoned by their white agents and returning, ill and in debt, to their homes. A similar gimmick occurred in 1868 when a team of Aborigine cricketers was brought over for a tour against English county elevens: playing barefoot, they were derided as 'circus freaks' until they beat the MCC at Lords by 154 runs. They won a further 14 matches before retiring on grounds of homesickness. When they left they were asked to give a display of boomerang throwing; no doubt by accident, but very satisfactorily, they clipped a spectator on the head.

The concept of 'noble savagery', so much a part of Enlightenment thinking, was one of the first casualties of industrialism. To their credit, many explorers protested that the savages were best left alone, that the Western way of life was no better and often much worse than their own. But their words were frequently qualified by their actions. Livingstone, for example, admired Africans – if only they could be brought round to a Christian way of thinking. Likewise, Peary said the Inuit of northern Greenland had no need of the alcoholism, gambling and greed that would accrue from contact with Western civilization – he then stole two large meteorites that for centuries had been their only source of iron, and sold them to the Smithsonian (where they presently languish) on the grounds that the Inuit were now part of the Western trading system. Others saw nothing noble in any foreigner at all. British officer and journalist Colonel Frederick Burnaby, who spoke more than five languages but who was described as 'opaque in intelligence', travelled throughout Asia asking its Muslim inhabitants if the devil was the Grand Vizier of Allah. Despite standing six feet four inches in his socks, having a 45-inch chest and being able to carry a pony under one arm, he failed to impress his audience and was eventually killed in 1885.

For all its seamier aspects, the period 1850 to 1918 was the golden age of exploration. Golden in that there was so much to be discovered, so many willing to do it, and so many glad to see it done (with the notable exception of those who were 'discovered'). Golden, too, in that technology had not advanced sufficiently to obviate the need for personal endeavour. By the 1920s, however, everything had changed. The Poles had been taken, Africa was no longer dark, India had been triangulated to death, Asia, the Arctic and the Antarctic had been delimited if not yet fully investigated, and the world was no longer the limitless expanse it had been when Queen Victoria opened the Great Exhibition. There was less to be found, fewer people who wanted to find it, and fewer still who were willing to support their quest. The dark side of 'we can do anything' had become increasingly apparent during half a century of colonization, but not until the 1914–18 war did Europeans realize its true blackness. Against the horrors of Passchendaele and the Somme, explorers were seen as irrelevant, self-important triflers. When, for example, Ernest Shackleton returned in 1916 from a two-year sojourn in the Antarctic, public uninterest could not have been greater. It did not matter that three members of his expedition subsequently died in combat, nor that another five were injured, nor that he refused to accept royalties from his journal for the duration of the war. In 1913 he would have been a hero. In 1916 he was not.

Exploration did not stop with World War I, but it took a new direction. Thanks to the combustion engine, human endeavour became increasingly irrelevant. By the 1920s discovery involved as much skilful juggling of the fuel throttle as physical endurance. Caterpillar-tracked machines crawled through the Sahara, triple-engined Dorniers scoured the Arctic and, in 1926, a Zeppelin crossed the North Pole. Mechanized exploration had its own perils – if the machine broke, as it always might and sometimes did, the operator was doomed – but its practitioners did not inspire people as their predecessors had done. Even in the sphere of mountaineering, purists grumbled darkly about 'mechanization' (by which they meant the use of pitons, karabiner clips and other dastardly devices) and it was in the mountains that the golden age of exploration died.

Technology had already conquered the Alps, riddling them with funicular railways, one of which tunnelled through the very heart of the Eiger, peeping occasionally from the fabled North Face as if through the holes of a Swiss cheese, before emerging on the Jungfraujoch. The Himalayas, however, defied the combustion engine in all its forms. Higher than planes could fly, steeper than cars could climb, too rugged for locomotives, they and the associated ranges that curled over the top of India were nature's final bastion against the might of industry. One did not approach these hills at whim, with a sandwich and a flask of tea, as was possible in the Alps. One went, instead, with a full expedition of porters, support teams and supplies, as if on an Arctic voyage. Since the late 19th century teams from every nation had attacked the region, sometimes with success, sometimes to vanish beneath avalanches and rock slides. But whatever they achieved, they were always taunted by the presence of the highest mountain in the world: Everest, or the Third Pole as it was known. In 1924, after several unsuccessful attempts, Britain launched its most ambitious assault to date. On the morning of 8 June George Mallory and Sandy Irvine were seen less than 1,000 feet from the summit when the clouds covered them. They did not return. Mallory's body was discovered in 1999, Irvine's has yet to be found – as has the camera they took with them to capture their moment of triumph. Did they reach the summit? Most experts agree that they probably did not, but without proof it is impossible to say. It would be nice, if perhaps wishful, to think that they did. It would be the perfect culmination to an age that claimed so many other firsts.

Robert Burke and William Wills (1860–1)

Robert O'Hara Burke had a thick beard into which he dribbled copiously, was 'of very ordinary physique', and shambled about town in a low-slung pair of trousers with a slouch hat pulled over his eyes. Of an afternoon he might be found sitting in a pool in his garden, reading a book and wearing a pith helmet. When he had money he spent it liberally. At a loose end, he would ride 30 miles in order to infuriate a local magistrate by swinging on his gate. Acquaintances described him variously as 'a careless dare-devil', 'kind and generous to a fault', and 'not quite sane'. He was, in 1857, inspector of police in the mining town of Castlemaine, State of Victoria, Australia.

Beneath his tramp-like skin Burke was a man of many parts. He had travelled widely and seen many things: born in Ireland, educated in Belgium, he had served with an Austrian cavalry regiment – and had a duelling scar to prove it – had been a member of the Irish Constabulary and had earned distinction as one of the more humane police officers in Australia's gold-mines. He was a well-read and talented linguist who decorated his office walls with quotations, one of which (his own) read, 'Do not read anything on the walls'. According to one person, 'He had thorough discipline and no one dared to contradict him'. According to another, 'Either he did not realise danger or his mind was so unhinged that he revelled in it'. He was frequently absent from his post, having a tendency to disappear for days on end, but nobody blamed him for it. Charming, eccentric, hot-headed and sentimental, Inspector Burke was a respected member of Castlemaine's community, and if he was away now and then it was only because he had become lost. As everyone knew, and as one man stated, 'He was the worst bushman I ever met.'

Considering this well-meaning but shambolic character, it is a bit of a mystery why the Committee of the Royal Society of Victoria decided he should become the first man to cross the continent of Australia. Possibly it was because of his charm, his distinguished service record, and his official rank. Possibly (in fact, certainly) the Royal Society hoped his wayward nature would be tempered by the team of scientists they selected to accompany him. Possibly, too, it was because he had a measure of the come-what-may bravado on which Australians already prided themselves. But probably it was because, in a thinly populated province on the edge of a large and unexplored continent, there weren't that many people to choose from. In 1858 the Committee voted ten to five in favour of Burke leading a mission into the interior. He accepted the post in the vague, optimistic spirit in which it was offered.

The £9,000 that the Royal Society raised for Burke's mission was ridiculously small by contemporary standards – far less than the French government allocated to Saharan exploration and a drop in the ocean compared with Britain's Arctic budget in previous years – but it produced the largest and best funded expedition ever to have attempted a crossing of Australia. Twenty-five camels were purchased from India, along with three sepoys to handle them. There was a similar number of horses. Novel, amphibious wagons were constructed – minus the wheels they became punts – and a huge armoury was assembled in case Burke met opposition along the way: 19 revolvers, eight rifles, ten double-barrelled shotguns and 50 rockets. Burke was given fishing lines, tents, beds, boots, surgical equipment and 30 'cabbage-tree' hats whose high crowns and wide brims looked somewhat comical but cooled the head wonderfully. Against scurvy in men there were eight demi-johns of lime juice, and against the same complaint in camels there were 60 gallons of rum. (It was believed that they responded favourably to alcohol.) Like Arctic explorers, they also took pemmican, biscuit and preserved vegetables. With these provisions, and a hefty baggage of trade goods, Burke's cavalcade departed from Melbourne's Royal Park on the afternoon of 20 August 1860.

Burke's orders were hazy. He was to travel north to Menindie, on the Darling River, then proceed to Cooper's Creek, to the east of Lake Eyre, whose year-round supply of water and grazing made it a perfect base for future operations. What form these operations would take was left entirely up to Burke. He could travel to the west coast of Australia, he could travel to the Gulf of Carpentaria on the north coast, he could go to any point in between, and he could return to Melbourne by whatever route seemed best. The one thing the Committee did specifically request was that he blaze his trail 'as permanently as possible, by leaving records, sowing seeds, building cairns, and marking trees' – but even this was to be done only if 'consistent with your various other duties'. What those other duties were the orders did not state. Fortunately for the Committee, Burke had a pretty fair idea of what he wanted to do: go north to the Gulf of Carpentaria. He also wanted to get there as swiftly as possible, because he had learned that a rival expedition, led by the experienced explorer John Stuart, was soon to depart from Adelaide.

By the time they left Menindie on 19 October, Burke's desire for speed was already causing friction. When his hired drays proved too slow he abandoned them and auctioned their contents. When the men protested at their rate of progress he fired them. When officers took umbrage at his dictatorial manner he accepted their resignations with equanimity. When the people of

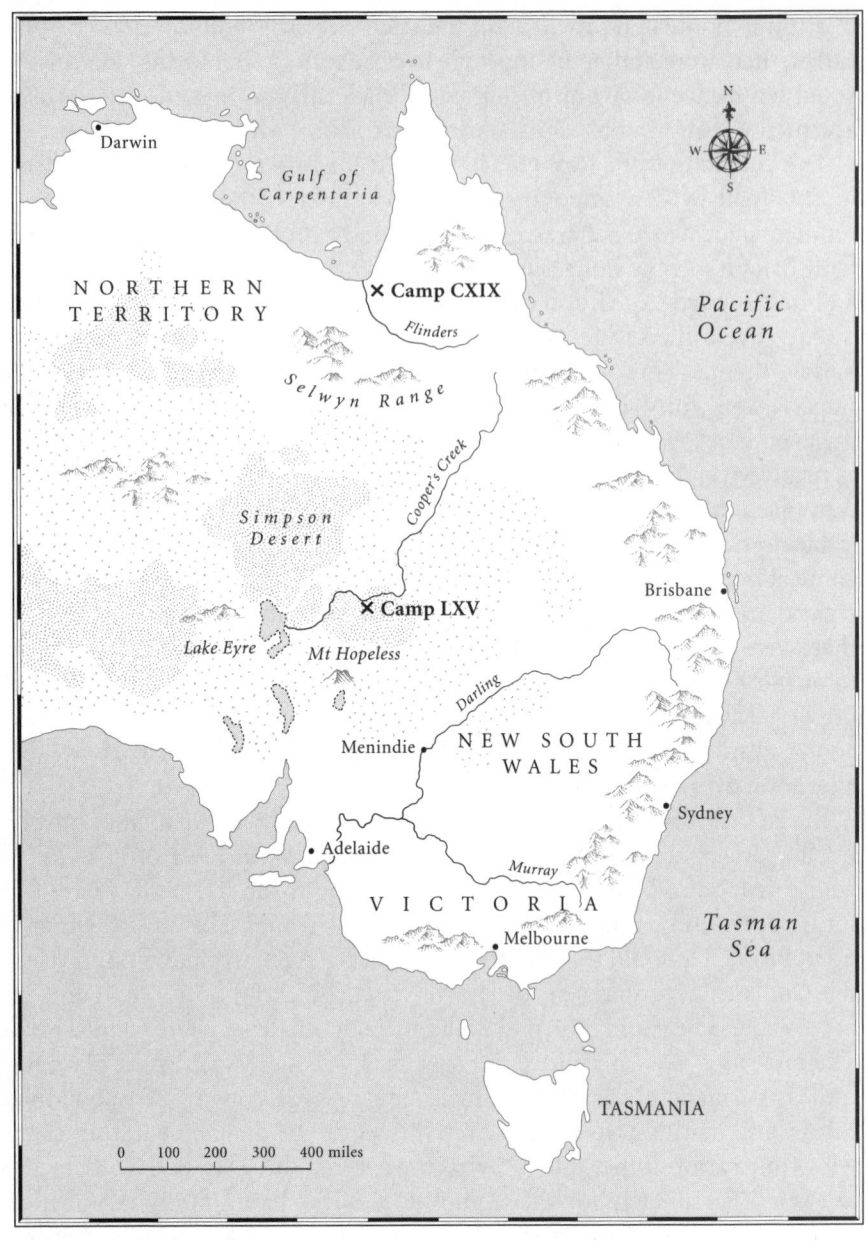

Menindie warned him that it would be dangerous to cross the 400, mostly waterless, miles to Cooper's Creek with summer just beginning he carried on regardless. When the expedition doctor and most of the scientists said they were too exhausted to continue he told them to catch up later. Thus, the party that left Menindie for Cooper's Creek comprised eight men, with 16 camels and 15 horses, the six other men to follow at leisure with the remainder of the animals and supplies.

Among the advance party were four men who would play an important part in the expedition's future. The first was a semi-literate but competent bushman named William Wright, whom Burke had hired as a guide. The second was the foreman, William Brahe, an educated German who had worked in the goldmines and on sheep stations and who had a smattering of surveying skills. The third was William Wills, a tough, serious-minded English scientist who had joined the expedition as surveyor and who had formed such a bond with Burke that he was appointed second-in-command. The fourth was John King, a mild-mannered Irishman of 21, who had recently discharged himself after several years in the army and had come from India with the camels.

As Burke's group pressed north for Cooper's Creek it crossed desolate plains, ancient ravines and stark, rocky hills. Despite the landscape's barren appearance, water was plentiful and they made good going, marking a tree at every campsite with a large B and allocating it a Roman numeral. Despite these route marks, Burke felt that the rest of the column would need assistance, so on 29 October, 200 miles into the journey, he sent Wright back to Menindie to escort the remaining men and camels. He was so impressed by Wright's bushmanship that he gave him a letter, to be forwarded to Melbourne, in which he promoted him to third-in-command. He might even have promoted him to second-in-command, had not Wills proved such an excellent man in the field. Wherever they went, Wills was always first to the next hill, first to spot the next waterhole, and first to record every discovery made. He was indispensable – as Burke wrote, 'Mr. Wills ... is a capital officer, zealous and untiring in the performance of his duties and I trust he will remain my second as long as I am in charge of the expedition.' In many ways, Wills *was* the expedition. It was he who kept a journal, Burke finding it either beneath or beyond himself to do so. It was he who turned their journey from a simple march over untrodden ground into a voyage of exploration. And it was he, following Wright's departure, who led the advance party safely to Cooper's Creek on 11 November. But he never once questioned Burke's authority, always seeking his approval for journal entries and acquiescing to every whim of his commander. By any standards, he was the perfect adjutant.

Cooper's Creek had already been visited by the famous explorer Charles Sturt in 1844 and it had not changed when Burke's entourage arrived in November 1860. Centuries ago it had been a river, flowing westwards into Lake Eyre; but now the rains came so infrequently that Lake Eyre had dried up and only once every decade did it and the Cooper revert to their original glory. For large stretches, however, the creek was never entirely dry, and at the point where Burke's party struck it there were a series of deep waterholes, some of them more than a mile long. It was surrounded by vegetation and teemed with fish and fowl. Admittedly, there were flies, mosquitoes and rats, and the temperature reached 109° F in the shade, but apart from these irritations it was a perfect base. Burke set up camp (on the trunk of a nearby coolabah tree he carved the numerals LXV) and waited for Wright to catch up with the rest of the men and supplies. In Wills's words the trip so far '[had] been but a picnic party'.

By mid-December Wright and the others had yet to arrive, and Burke decided he could wait no longer. There had been several bad thunderstorms in the past weeks, and all the signs suggested it had been raining to the north as well. It was too good an opportunity to let pass. Accordingly, he divided his party yet again and on 16 December set out for the Gulf of Carpentaria with Wills, King and an ex-sailor named Charles Gray, who had joined the expedition on the way to Menindie and was regarded as a dependable bushman. Brahe was left behind at Depot LXV with orders to follow Burke if Wright appeared within the next few days, but otherwise to stay put until the explorers returned from the north. How long would they be away? Burke estimated it might take three months to cover the 1,400-odd miles to the Gulf and back. But if the going was poor, or if they encountered some unforeseen disaster, they might well be gone for only a month. If they were not back in three months then Brahe was to remain at Cooper's Creek for as long as his supplies lasted before heading south. Burke, however, was confident this would never happen. When he divided the provisions with Brahe he took sufficient to last four men 12 weeks and, if eked out, the food might stretch a little longer; but he did not expect the need for serious rationing. Brahe thought Burke's estimate was optimistic. As the six camels moved out, he called to King, 'Goodbye, I do not expect to see you for at least four months.'

To begin with, everything seemed fine. True, the ground was rough underfoot, the landscape monotonous, the flies ubiquitous and the heat so great that they had to march by night. But they rarely went more than a few days without finding water and grazing for the camels. When on 22 December they reached the expanse of rock that Sturt had named Stony Desert, Wills was amazed by how little it resembled a desert. 'I do not know whether it arose from our exaggerated anticipation of horrors or not,' he wrote, 'but we thought it far from bad travelling ground, and as to pasture ... many a sheep run is, in fact, worse.' Four days later the Stony Desert was behind them, and on 9 January Wills was able to write: 'Traversed six miles of undulating plains, covered with vegetation richer than ever; several ducks rose from the little creeks as we passed, and flocks of pigeons were flying in all directions.' By 30 January they had climbed a series of sharp 1,000-feet peaks (the Selwyn Range) and were struggling through the boggy territory alongside the Flinders River. Only 30 miles separated them from the coast.

The route they were following was not unknown to Europeans. The explorers Augustus Charles Gregory and Ludwig Leichardt had previously probed south from the Gulf of Carpentaria. Burke had thus linked the furthest north of Sturt to the furthest south of Gregory and Leichardt and in doing so had effectively crossed the continent. Instead of the baking sands or boundless sea that some had told him to expect, he had found a relatively fertile land. The journey had never been hard, and now, with Aborigines materializing from every quarter to point out the best waterholes, with wild yams growing so freely that one could simply pluck them from the soil, and with flocks of geese, plover and pelican swooping over the marshes, it seemed positively easy. All that remained was to reach the Gulf, which they did on 10 February – or rather did not quite, tasting salt water in the river but not actually seeing the sea, which Burke decided was superfluous. On a tree at their northernmost camp they carved the numerals CXIX.

At this point Brahe's judgement looked more accurate than Burke's. It had taken them two months to cross Australia, and they now had one month's provisions for the return journey to Cooper's Creek. But all was not lost: for at least part of the way the terrain had water, vegetation and wildlife; and with careful rationing – 12 strips of dried meat plus a quarter-pound of flour per person per day – Burke reckoned they could reach Cooper's Creek before Brahe left for Menindie. As they retraced their steps, however, and the rains fell without cease, they made poor progress. By 7 March they had covered about 100 miles and were feeling ill. They had dysentery and were afflicted by what Wills described as 'a helpless feeling of lassitude that I have never before experienced to such an extent'. Gray was particularly badly affected, and often they had to stop for him to catch up. By 25 March they were through the Selwyn Ranges, but they were no more than halfway home and it had taken them 40 days to get that far. The wildlife that Wills had reported on the way north seemed to have disappeared, and all the land offered (apart from endless rain and mud) was the hardy desert plant portulac, with which they supplemented their rations. Gray, who was in charge of the stores, became weaker, and one day was caught stealing flour, an offence for which, according to Wills, he 'received a good thrashing. There is no knowing to what extent he has been robbing us. Many things have been found to run unaccountably short.'

They began to slaughter their animals, drying what meat they could carry and gorging themselves on the rest. They abandoned inessential equipment, hoping thereby to increase their pace. But the rain continued to hamper them. And the further south they went the more frequently they encountered another hazard: sandstorms whose red clouds of dust whipped their faces, reduced visibility to a matter of yards, and for days on end made progress impossible. On 10 April they re-encountered the Stony Desert, through which they struggled grimly, taking it in turns to ride their two remaining camels. Wills, who had written earlier about how fanciful its perils seemed, remarked only that they were very lucky to find water. Seven days later, with the desert behind them, Gray died of exhaustion and hunger. His companions were now so weak that it took them a whole day to dig his three-foot-deep grave. To mark the spot they slung a rifle from the branches of a nearby tree. They also discarded the last of their equipment, retaining only the bare minimum to see them the 70 miles to Depot LXV: a compass and barometer, two spades, their rifles, a small amount of dried meat, and some padding that had been meant for the camels but which they now used as bedding. (They did not have a tent, having slept in the open since their departure.) On Sunday 21 April Burke, King and Wills rose early for the last dash to Depot LXV. It was 30 miles, a hard day's work by any standard, but the prospect of food – and company – spurred them on. Wright would have arrived and the camp would be a cornucopia. In their debilitated condition the journey was a nightmare. Wills recorded that their legs 'were almost paralysed, so that each of us found it a most trying task only to walk a few yards. Such a leg-bound feeling I never before experienced and hope I never shall again. The exertion required to get up a slight piece of rising ground, even without any load, induces an incredible sensation of pain and help-lessness, and the general lassitude makes one unfit for anything.' But what did this matter when salvation was so close?

Brahe, meanwhile, was wondering what to do. Wright had not appeared, neither had Burke, and his food could not last much longer. During the past four months his party had been pestered by marauding Aborigines, who pilfered items of equipment and occasionally threatened them with spears. Brahe had seen the marauders off by firing his rifle in the air. Latterly, he had constructed a stockade to keep the natives at bay. More worrying to Brahe than the Aborigines or the uncertainty of his position, however, was a strange malady that had spread among them. His men's gums were sore, their legs hurt and their joints were swollen. They felt increasingly feeble. Puzzled, Brahe put it down to kicks they had received from the horses and camels. He did not know it, but they were in the first stages of scurvy. Among the many things Burke had sold on his way north, were the wagons of lime juice. Brahe and his company had been living off a Melbourne-sourced diet of salt port and beef, rice, flour, sugar and tea. Unlike Burke, Wills and King, who had eaten portulac, they had not bothered with vegetables. Nor had they bothered to shoot any game – they had plenty of food, so why go to the trouble of shooting more? By the middle of April, with one man on the point of death and two of his camels going lame, Brahe decided he had no option but to turn for home. He buried his excess provisions, enclosed with them a note saying where he was going, and left for Menindie.

When Burke, Wills and King staggered into Depot LXV on the evening of the 21st, the camp was empty. Engraved on a tree were the words:

DIG

3 FT. N.W.

APR. 21 1861

Digging as instructed, they uncovered a box of rations and Brahe's note. The most dispiriting thing was the date it bore: 21 April. They had missed him by a matter of hours. For a moment they contemplated chasing after him – he was probably camped only 20 miles away. But Burke pointed out the madness of such a scheme. In the note Brahe had specifically said: 'We have six camels and twelve horses in good working condition.' Their own two camels were so exhausted that they could not do more than five miles a day. They would never be able to catch up before he moved on. Moreover, the 400 miles between Cooper's Creek and Menindie was not the picnic that Wills had previously called it; large stretches were waterless and could only be crossed with beasts in prime condition. A more sensible course would be to follow Cooper's Creek to the west and then strike south to Mount Hopeless, in South Australia, where there was a police station and from where the country was hospitable all the way to Adelaide. Brahe's box contained food for a month; the distance to Mount Hopeless was 150 miles. At five miles per day they could just make it.

Burke wrote a note and buried it in the same spot where Brahe had buried his. In it he related their successful crossing of the continent and announced his intention to head for Mount Hopeless. They were infuriated by Brahe's departure – their rage exacerbated by his taking the spare clothes they had left in his care; their trousers were now so tattered that, as Wills delicately put it, they were 'in a very awkward position' – and they were equally cross at Wright's non-appearance. Burke had given him instructions to return at once with the support group – had expected him to do so in a couple of days – but four months had apparently passed without a sign of him. In his message Burke said nothing of their frustration and resentment. He remarked merely that events had left them 'greatly disappointed'. Then, finding a rake in the abandoned camp, he propped it against the tree to show that they had been there, his assumption being that it would draw any rescuer's attention to the words already carved into the trunk. On the morning of 23 April they left Depot LXV and moved down Cooper's Creek.

At the start all went well. They travelled slowly, but the water was good and Brahe's supplies had restored their flagging strength. Occasionally they met groups of Aborigines with whom they bartered small items such as fish hooks in exchange for food. 'I believe that in less than a week we shall be fit to undergo any fatigue whatsoever,' wrote the ever-optimistic Wills on 26 April. 'The camels are improving and seem capable of doing all that we are likely to require of them.' Two days later one of their camels sank to its neck in mud. Unable to extricate it, they shot it and dried as much of its flesh as they could reach. Shortly afterwards they came to the end of the Cooper's Creek waterholes. On 8 May their remaining camel collapsed. It was shot and butchered like the first. They were now reduced to living off the land, an experience for which, despite their epic journey to the Gulf, they were unprepared. Wills befriended a passing tribe of Aborigines, who gave him food and showed him how to prepare flour from seeds of the nardoo plant that grew wild in the region. He also trapped birds and rats. By 12 May, however, the Aborigines had moved on, leaving the white men to their own devices.

While Burke's party moved west, Brahe's was travelling south. Not far into his journey he met, at last, the laggardly Wright. Wright's excuse for not coming to their assistance sooner was lengthy and insubstantial. Some of Burke's cheques had bounced; nobody would give them credit; he had sent to Melbourne for confirmation that he would be paid as third-in-command but had received no reply; he had been unwilling to move without knowing that he would be paid; and in the absence of news from the organizing Committee he had left the Menindie group – who were completely disorganized – and had spent some time with his wife who lived 14 miles away. He had passed four months in this fashion, until one of his assistants, despairing of his idleness, rode to Melbourne, where an astonished Committee denied all knowledge of Wright's letter, gave him £400 in cash with which to purchase extra supplies, and instructed Wright to rejoin Burke without delay. He had set out immediately, he said, but had faced terrible difficulties along the way. The Aborigines had been antagonistic, and his group had fallen unaccountably sick. When he met Brahe on 28 April, three of his men were already dead (from scurvy) and he was packing his bags for the return journey.

Brahe suggested that he and Wright should send the invalids home and make a quick visit to Cooper's Creek, just to make sure Burke had not returned in his absence. Wright agreed. And so, on 8 May – the day on which Burke was slicing up his last camel – they rode into Depot LXV. They saw the remains of Burke's campfires, but assumed they had been lit by Aborigines. They saw camel tracks, but reckoned they had been made by Brahe's animals. They saw the rake leaning against the 'DIG' tree, but Brahe thought he must have put it there himself. They did not dig up the cache for fear that Aborigines would notice the disturbed earth and steal the food that Burke might yet – as they thought – find. In total they spent 15 minutes at the empty camp before rejoining the scorbutic casualties in their retreat to civilization. On 8 May Burke, King and Wills were just 30 miles from Depot LXV.

When, a few days later, the Aborigines moved on, leaving Burke's party to fend for themselves, the white men were not particularly downcast: they had a quantity of dried meat, there were extensive fields of nardoo in the vicinity and, although they no longer had camels, they were able to cover a fair distance every day. If they continued in this fashion they were sure to find a waterhole somewhere. But after travelling 45 miles south-west towards Mount Hopeless they had yet to find water, and the terrain stretched in a blank, dry expanse before them. So they turned back. On 24 May, while camped on a tendril of Cooper's Creek, they heard a gunshot. It could only mean one thing: a rescue party had arrived. Wills, the strongest, left on the 27th and reached Depot LXV three days later. Nobody was there. Although he did not know it, the explosion they had heard was not a gunshot but the sound of falling rock as, in the distance, a cliff disintegrated in the heat. Underneath the tree where it said 'DIG', Wills deposited his journals and a letter in which he wrote: 'Both camels are dead, and our provisions are done ... We are trying to live the best way we can, like the blacks, but find it hard work. Our clothes are going to pieces fast. Send provisions and clothes as soon as possible ... The depot party, having left contrary to instructions, has put us in this fix.' He returned to the others on 2 June.

By the third week of June Burke's party was fading fast. The Aborigines had returned and had welcomed them into their camp. But one morning, in their inexplicable fashion, they vanished. The white men did their best, but the diet was too poor and conditions too hard for a group that was already weakened by months in the outback. It took all their energy to gather and pound the nardoo seeds on which their survival depended. In addition, their tattered clothes offered no protection against the thunderstorms and cold nights that now beset them. On 21 June Wills wrote: 'Unless relief comes in some form or other, I cannot possibly last more than a fortnight. It is a great consolation, at least, in this position of ours, to know that we have done all we could, and that our deaths will rather be the result of mismanagement of others than any rash acts of our own.' It became apparent that their only hope lay in finding the Aborigines and throwing themselves on their mercy. But Wills, previously the strongest, was now the weakest of the group; he had not the energy even to gather nardoo, let alone trek through the bush. Accordingly, he came to a decision. Burke and King were to leave him behind, he said, while they went ahead to get help. They protested. But as Wills calmly pointed out, if they remained where they were they would surely perish. Splitting the party was their last, slender chance of survival. With a small amount of firewood and some nardoo cakes, he could last for the few days he expected them to be away. If they did not return he would die. But if they did not go he would die anyway. What difference would it make? On 27 June he wrote a final letter to his father: 'These are probably the last lines you will ever get from me. We are on the point of starvation ... I think to live about four or five days ... My spirits are excellent.'

Burke and King left on the 28th. Within two days, however, Burke was unable to continue. Like Wills, he wrote a last note for posterity: 'I hope we shall be done justice to. We have fulfilled our task, but we have been [abandoned].' He asked King to place his pistol in his right hand. Then, as an afterthought, knowing that King was too enfeebled to dig a grave, he ordered that on no account was he to be buried. Burke never pulled the trigger. He died of starvation on the morning of (probably) 30 June. King pressed on, alone. Two days later he found the remains of an Aborigine camp, which contained a fortnight's supply of nardoo and where he was able to shoot four crows. Pausing to rest for another couple of days, he took the food back to Wills. But when he arrived Wills was dead.

It was impossible to tell when the young scientist had died, but if one assumes that he showed the same accuracy when estimating the time left to him as he did when taking the expedition's readings, it would have been within 24 hours of Burke. For King the sense of solitude must have been overpowering. But there was worse to come. As he prepared to bury the Englishman, he noted that some of his clothes had gone missing. Between Wills's death and King's arrival the camp had been visited by natives. The people he had been chasing, the ones who might possibly have saved both Burke and Wills, had been there all the time.

For a while King stayed where he was, dazed by the position in which he found himself. Then, belatedly, he realized that the Aborigines could not be far away. Following their tracks, he traipsed into the bush, shooting crows as he went. It was the sound of his gunfire that attracted the Aborigines. They led King to their camp, nourished him back to health – even though their own food was scarce – and allowed him to accompany them when they moved on. 'They treated me with uniform kindness, and looked upon me as one of themselves,' King recorded. He was to stay with them for a period of almost two months.

Brahe, meanwhile, was back in the field. When he returned to Melbourne with his disquieting news of Wright's incompetence and of Burke's apparent non-return from the Gulf of Carpentaria, the Royal Society of Victoria at last realized that something must be done. It despatched no less than four rescue expeditions, by land and by sea, to find the missing men. It was assumed that if Burke's party was alive it must be either at the Gulf or stranded by a waterhole somewhere in the interior; it was to these goals, therefore, that the rescuers were directed. There was no evidence to suggest that Burke might have reached Cooper's Creek; nevertheless, it was thought best to send a small group to Depot LXV just in case. Led by a local businessman and geologist, Alfred Howitt, and guided by Brahe, the nine-man team left Melbourne on 9 July. By 13 September they were at the depot. Nothing had changed since Brahe's last visit. There were signs that Aborigines had passed through, but otherwise everything was as before. There were no blazes on the trees; nothing had been added to the 'DIG' message; the cache did not seem to have been disturbed. Had they opened it they would have found Burke's and Wills's letters. But they did not open it. As Howitt later explained, why should they? It contained nothing but food, and their supplies were quite adequate. Thus it was not until the 15th, by which time they had moved down the creek, that they learned of the disaster. It was not Brahe or Howitt, but a surveyor named Welch, who found King. Prompted by Aborigines who pointed north, crying, '*Gow!*', 'Go on!', he rode into their camp. The inhabitants scattered, leaving 'one solitary figure, apparently covered in scarecrow rags and part of a hat, and prominently alone on the sand ... [I]t tottered, threw up its hands in an attitude of prayer, and fell on the ground.' When summoned to the scene, Howitt was appalled. '[King] presented a melancholy appearance; wasted to a shadow, and hardly to be distinguished as a civilised being but for the remnants of clothes upon him. He seemed exceedingly weak, and found it occasionally difficult to follow what we said. The natives were all gathered round, seated on the ground, looking with a most gratified and delighted expression.' While King was fed spoonfuls of rice, butter and sugar, Howitt's doctor examined him. His diagnosis was that, in his current state, he could not have survived more than a few days.

Over the following weeks Howitt and Brahe visited each gravesite, returned to Depot LXV, and then departed for Melbourne with Wills's journals (the last section of which had been buried alongside him) and the damning letters from the 'DIG' cache. Their arrival caused such a furore that a Royal Commission was convened to investigate the circumstances surrounding the expedition's failure. Nobody – from Brahe to Wright to the members of the Royal Society of Victoria – emerged blameless. But nobody was judged guilty either. The conclusion was that Burke had done what he had been asked to do. He had opened a route from Victoria to the Gulf of Carpentaria and had therefore answered the question which had been posed on his outset: whether there 'really existed within [the] great continent, a Sahara . . . great lakes . . . or watered plains which might tempt men to build new cities'. Whether somebody else might have done it better, and without loss of life, was beyond the Commission's remit. Neither did it take into account the fact that Burke's rival, Stuart, had travelled much further across the truly inhospitable Northern Territory and in doing so had uncovered far more about the Sahara (yes, it did exist) that covered much of Australia. Whatever Stuart had done, Burke's foray was judged a success. In later years the territory he had covered would be colonized by ranchers, and his expedition would become one of the legendary moments of Australian history.

Richard Burton and John Speke (1857–65)

Of the many secrets which darkest Africa hid from early Victorians, the source of the Nile was the most penumbrous. Everyone knew that this great river had given rise to one of the earliest recorded civilizations; that its annual floods had produced the prosperity on which the pyramids were built; and that it was the economic, topographical and cultural given of North-East Africa. But they did not know where it came from. According to the Greek scholar Ptolemy, it originated in a region of vast, sub-equatorial lakes hemmed by a range of mountains that he called *Lunae Montes*, or Mountains of the Moon. (Which was not far off the mark.) However, Ptolemy's map of Africa dated from AD 140. It had already been found wanting in practically every respect and, 17 centuries later, geographers saw no reason to trust his assertions about the Nile.

In the 1840s, however, three German missionaries, Jacob Erhardt, Ludwig Krapf and Johannes Rebmann, reported some startling facts about the geography of East Africa. Probing west from Mombasa, they encountered a huge, snow-capped mountain; and according to the natives there existed in the vicinity a great inland sea that they judged to be approximately the size of the Caspian and to which Erhardt gave the name 'Sea of Ujiji' after a town on its coast. Did this mean that Ptolemy was right after all? Had Erhardt, Krapf and Rebmann discovered the Mountains of the Moon, whose rivers fed the lakes that ultimately fed the Nile? By 1857 Richard Burton was on the spot.

Tall, broad-shouldered, scar-faced and aggressive, Burton was the bad boy of British exploration. Sent to Oxford University at the age of 19 on the assumption that he would become a cleric, he had swiftly decamped to India and thence the Middle East, where he proved himself a talented linguist (during his lifetime he would master 29 languages) and an anthropologist of unique, if unorthodox bent, establishing himself as the foremost authority on sexual practices in the Orient. Tough, intelligent, and irrepressibly curious, he was exotically anti-establishment, protesting that England was the only place in the world where he did not feel at home. He was also extremely competitive: as he once remarked, having climbed a peak in Cameroon, 'to be first in such matters is everything, to be second nothing'.

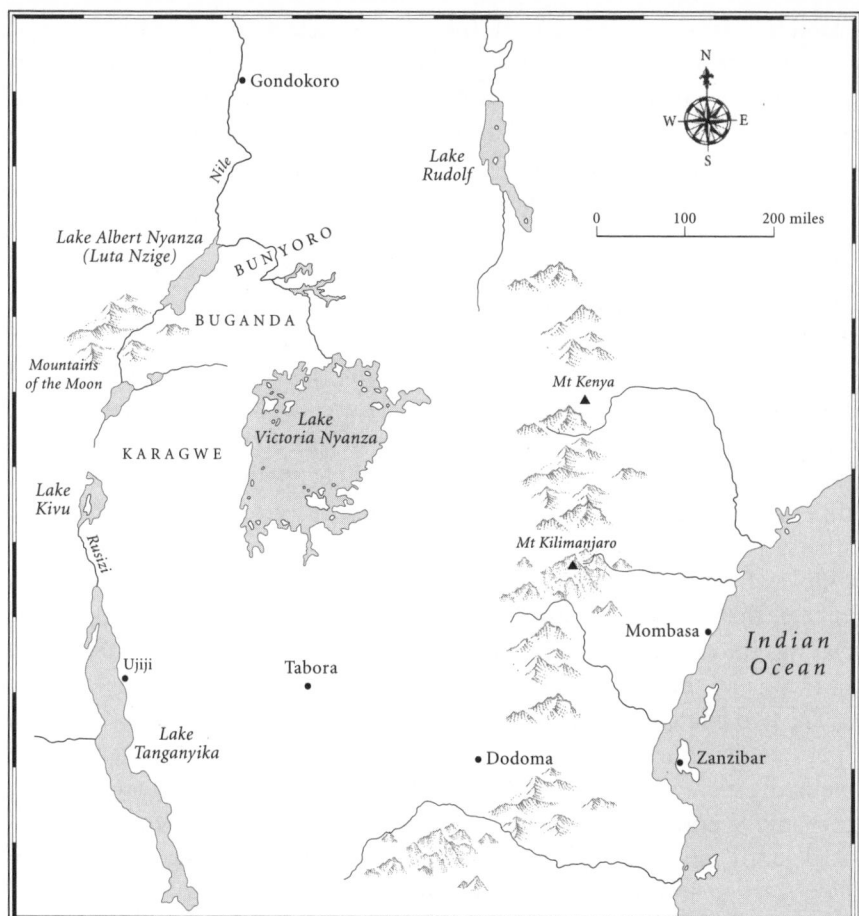

According to one contemporary, he prided himself on looking like Satan – which, in some lights, he did.

In 1857 Burton was 36 and had determined that he would be the first to discover the source of the Nile. Unfortunately, the various learned bodies and governmental departments that had sponsored his expedition had determined that the discovery could not be his alone. They had sent him to Africa in the company of one other Briton: John Hanning Speke. Ten years Burton's junior, a well-travelled, well-spoken army officer who had served in India, Speke was also excitable, touchy and somewhat naïve. But he was strong and brave, an indefatigable hunter of game and a capable outdoorsman. He had also accompanied Burton on an expedition to Somalia and had served with him in the Crimean War. Burton did not like him overmuch.

The two men landed at Zanzibar on 20 December 1856 and spent six months there, during which time they gathered a caravan of 130 men and 30 animals to carry them into the interior and Burton not only became fluent in Swahili but collated enough material to fill a two-volume account of the island (his vivid descriptions of filth-strewn streets, slave traders and disease caused quite a stir on publication). Then, in June 1857, they set out for the interior with a cargo of brandy, camp beds, books, rifles, bullets, moulds for making more bullets, trade goods, umbrellas, tables, chairs, plus a quantity of daggers, knives and swords.

Through forest, bog and open bush they tramped, attacked by insects and ants of every species, which bit them mercilessly. The Africans they met were, in Burton's words, 'a futile race of barbarians, drunken and immoral; cowardly and destructive; boisterous and loquacious; indolent, greedy and thriftless'. Speke linked their lack of fibre to spiritual poverty. Burton put it down to the sapping effects of sexual prowess – a judgement that illustrated perfectly the differences between the two. However barbaric the natives may or may not have been, they were sufficiently well informed to provide Burton and Speke with details about the topography to the west. Erhardt's 'Sea of Ujiji' was, in fact, a series of lakes, two of which were much larger than the others. It was on the largest and southernmost of these two that the town of Ujiji lay. Burton guessed that the two lakes might be joined by a river and, further, that the northernmost lake might eventually flow into the Nile. If that was the case, the southernmost one would be the river's ultimate source and Ujiji was the place for which they should aim.

The two white men were by now beginning to get on each other's nerves. Speke envied Burton's command of the language and his familiarity with the natives. He resented his refusal to halt the expedition so that he could go game-shooting. And he disliked his overbearing manner. He was 'a blackguard', he concluded; a man 'who never *can* be wrong, and will not acknowledge an error'. Burton, meanwhile, thought Speke was a boastful incompetent, a bearer of petty grudges, possessed of 'an immense and abnormal fund of self-esteem, who ever held, not only that he had done his best on all occasions, but also that no living man could do better'. The state of the two men's health did nothing to help matters. Burton was stricken so violently by malaria that he temporarily lost the use of his legs and had to be carried in a hammock. And Speke contracted an eye infection that all but blinded him. Still, they persevered in their quest and on 13 February 1858, from the peak of a hill so steep that Speke's ass collapsed and died during the ascent, they finally caught sight of their goal. Filled, in Burton's words, with 'admiration, wonder and delight', they became the first Europeans to set eyes on Lake Tanganyika.

They staggered into Ujiji where, after a brief rest, Speke's eyes began to improve. Burton, however, deteriorated to the point where he barely had the strength to talk, let alone move. Weakly, he instructed Speke to hire a dhow and explore the lake; in particular, he was to search for the river that connected it to its northern counterpart. Speke returned four weeks later with a badly infected ear – he had tried to extricate a burrowing parasite with his penknife – and the news that there was only one ship on the whole lake, that its owner demanded an extortionate price for its hire and that, in any case, it would not be free for another three months. Damning his compatriot's uselessness, Burton purchased a couple of leaky dugouts, had his bearers carry him to the largest and then, Union Jack fluttering in the breeze, set out with Speke on a tour of Lake Tanganyika.

Paddling northwards, Burton was relieved to hear that there was indeed a river – the Rusizi – linking Lake Tanganyika with the lake to its north (Lake Kivu). But he was less pleased when he learned that the Rusizi flowed *into* rather than out of Lake Tanganyika. His attempts to ascertain the truth were thwarted by the absolute refusal of his canoemen to go anywhere near the Rusizi: it was the home of cannibals, they said; they were also unwilling to go any further because the rainy season was upon them. So he and Speke returned to Ujiji a month later, sodden, surrounded by heaps of excrement which no one dared jettison for fear of attracting crocodiles, and little the wiser as to whether Lake Tanganyika was (as Burton still hoped) the source of the Nile.

By now their supplies were running out, and Ujiji did not have the resources to feed the vast caravan the white men had brought with them. Accordingly, Burton and Speke were forced to return to Mombasa. Speke found the trek intolerably boring: 'There is literally nothing to write about in this uninteresting country,' he wrote to a friend. 'Nothing could surpass these tracts, jungles, plains for same dullness, the people are the same. Everywhere in fact the country is one vast senseless map of sameness.' Halfway to the coast, at the town of Tabora, Burton had to halt because of his malaria. At a loose end, Speke proposed a little excursion on his own to the north: he might shoot something and, possibly, he might find a lake that was rumoured to be in the vicinity. Relieved to be rid of him, Burton waved him goodbye.

In less than three weeks Speke made a discovery that turned Burton's theories on their head. He found not just a lake but an expanse of water so vast as truly to merit the term 'inland sea'. Through an interpreter he questioned the shore dwellers as to its extent. They shrugged their shoulders: nobody had ever been to the other side; for all they knew it did not have one. Here, Speke was convinced, lay the true source of the Nile. He christened it Lake Victoria Nyanza and rushed back to tell Burton the news. Jealous of Speke's success and piqued at his unilateral naming of the lake, Burton feigned indifference. Perhaps, he conceded, Speke might have found a feeder lake, but Lake Tanganyika was more probably the source. When Speke urged him to see Victoria Nyanza for himself, Burton replied that he was too ill and their supplies were too low. Better to return to civilization and regroup for a new expedition. Speke reluctantly acquiesced.

The journey home was marked for both men by debilitating attacks of fever. Speke was seized by fits, during which he dwelled deliriously on the Nile and Burton's personal failings. Burton, himself sickly, acted as unwilling nursemaid through his illness (which he caustically described as hydrophobia). Then on the ship home Burton was crippled so severely by malaria that he had to convalesce in Aden, leaving a now healthy Speke to continue alone to Britain. Speke's parting words were a promise not to speak about the Nile – a subject on which they had agreed to disagree – until Burton returned to London: 'You may be quite sure I shall not go up to the Royal Geographical Society until you come to the fore and we appear together. Make your mind quite easy about that.'

When Burton reached London in May 1859 he found that Speke had not only discussed the matter with the Royal Geographical Society but had persuaded its president to fund a new expedition, led by himself, to Victoria Nyanza. His companion would be a Scot named James Augustus Grant. Tall, strong and, like Speke, an ex-Indian officer who was partial to a bit of shooting, Grant was also unassuming and happy to accept orders. It was these last qualities that Speke valued most: he did not want a repeat of his experience with Burton. In response, Burton prepared his journal for publication. In *Lake Regions of Central Africa* he waxed ungenerously on Speke's failings – 'unfit for anything other than a subordinate capacity' – and spoke proprietorially of the ground that Speke intended to cover, protesting that he had reneged on his promise and had 'lost no time in taking measures to secure for himself the right of working the field I had opened'. When the book came out in 1860 it was read with concern. But Burton was not there to enlarge on his criticisms: he had embarked with his wife on an investigation of West Africa; by that time Speke and Grant were already in East Africa.

Speke's plan was to march inland to Tabora and then strike north to Victoria Nyanza. Once there, he and Grant would skirt around its western coast in search of the outflow. If the lake emptied to the north, as seemed likely, then they would continue in that direction until they reached Gondokoro, a drab outpost, first attained from Cairo in 1839, that represented the *non plus ultra* of southwards exploration. Here, it had been arranged, the British consul John Petherick would furnish them with supplies and boats for their journey to Cairo.

After considerable delays the two men reached Tabora, and by the end of 1861 were in the kingdom of Karagwe, to the west of Victoria Nyanza. Grant had an infected leg wound, so Speke left him in Karagwe and continued on his own to the neighbouring kingdom of Buganda. Here he was excited to learn of a river that flowed from the lake's northern shore. On 7 July, Grant having finally caught up, Speke marched off to find what he was convinced could only be the Nile. Grant, however, was not allowed to accompany him; instead, he was instructed to proceed to the next kingdom up, Bunyoro. Both men later claimed that it was a joint decision; but in likelihood Speke wanted to have the discovery of the Nile to himself. Sure enough, on 21 July 1862, while Grant was toiling through Bunyoro, Speke became the first European to see what he described as 'a magnificent stream ... dotted with islets and rocks'. Travelling upriver for some 40 miles, he saw an even more magnificent sight: a series of waterfalls 12 feet high and 700 yards wide, over which Victoria Nyanza emptied into the Nile. 'The expedition,' Speke wrote, 'had now performed its functions.'

Or had it? When Speke rejoined Grant in Bunyoro he learned of another great lake ten days' march to the west called Luta Nzige that bisected a mighty river. If this river connected with the Nile – as Speke suspected it might – then it would mean the river had a secondary source. And if Luta Nzige was connected to Tanganyika then maybe Victoria Nyanza was not the main source of the Nile after all. Maybe, horribly, Burton was right. Speke ignored this possibility and marched north with Grant to Gondokoro, where they arrived, ragged and sunbaked, on 15 February 1863. Petherick was not there.

Having waited for almost two years in this godforsaken spot – little more than a tented entrepôt for the slave trade – Petherick had gone on safari. In case Speke turned up while he was away, he had left four boats and a pile of supplies. But Speke refused to use them. Petherick, in his opinion, was a deserter and backslider – possibly, too, a slave trader. Instead, he availed himself of the assistance proffered by a fellow Briton whom he had met once before in London and who was now in Gondokoro. His name was Sam Baker.

Baker was Speke with added caffeine. Bearded, hearty, and a dedicated big game hunter, he had fought a bit, farmed a bit (first in the English county of Gloucestershire, then on a desolate Sinhalese mountain), and had travelled copiously. In 1858, while passing through the Balkans, he had acquired a teenage Hungarian slave, Florence, who would in due course become his wife but for the moment was his ever-present paramour and companion. He had heard of Speke's expedition from the Royal Geographical Society and, being a man of independent means, had decided to strike south in the hope of being able to participate in the quest. And that was why, when Speke arrived at Gondokoro, he was greeted by a man whose basso profundo was loud enough to rattle window panes, who carried 14 guns in his personal baggage and who was accompanied by a tough, young, blonde-haired woman who spoke German.

When Baker heard of Speke's discovery he was disappointed. 'And does not one leaf of the laurel remain for me?' he inquired. Airily, Speke mentioned Luta Nzige. That was enough for Sam and Florence Baker. While Speke and Grant travelled victoriously north, the Bakers struck south for Luta Nzige with a team of porters, a large Union Jack, a quantity of supplies, their complement of firearms, a tin chest containing full Highland regalia, and a satin jacket that Sam Baker insisted on wearing for dinner in the bush.

Theirs was the usual tale of obstruction, demands for presents – at one point Sam Baker was only allowed to proceed once he had given the local chief his kilt – plus, inevitably, disease and other physical setbacks. On fording a river, Sam Baker wrote that he had waded barely a quarter of the way across when '[I] looked back to see if my wife followed close to me when I was horrified to see her standing in one spot, and sinking gradually through the weeds, while her face was distorted and perfectly purple'. Whatever kind of seizure she had suffered was so severe that Sam Baker ordered his men to dig a grave. No sooner had they started, however, than Florence recovered. As she later recounted, the sound of spade on soil was the first thing she heard on emerging from her coma.

On 14 March 1864 the Bakers surmounted a hill and saw, at last, Luta Nzige. 'There,' wrote Sam, 'like a sea of quicksilver, lay far beneath the grand expanse of water – a boundless sea horizon on the south and south west, glittering in the noonday sun: and on the west, at fifty or sixty miles distance, blue mountains rose from the bosom of the lake to a height of about 7,000 feet above its level.' Nothing could have fitted more perfectly Ptolemy's description. Sam Baker christened his find Lake Albert Nyanza, then, having attached a mast and a square of plaid to a dugout canoe, he and Florence sailed around its eastern coast until they discovered the point at which it emptied into the Nile.

By 5 May 1865 the Bakers were back in Khartoum, having spent a hideous journey on a dhow filled with plague victims. Among the mail waiting for them was a French translation of Speke's *Journal of the Discovery of the Source of the Nile*. Sam Baker read it with what must have been some satisfaction: if Albert Nyanza was connected to lakes further south, then Victoria Nyanza, not Albert, would be the supplementary feeder and he, Baker, could claim to have made an even greater discovery than Speke. But he would never be able to bring Speke the news. At the end of the book there was a depressing footnote: its author was dead.

In the months following his return to London Speke had made a fool of himself. He issued slanderous accusations against Petherick; he questioned the competence of the Royal Geographical Society; and he spread extraordinary rumours concerning Burton, the least offensive of which was that he was an ignoramus who had learned everything he knew at the knee of Speke. The irresponsibility and plain wrongness of these fulminations tarred his statement that 'the Nile is settled'. Neither did his published account of the expedition help much – as one reader pointed out, Speke's observations were so faulty that at one point he had the Nile flowing 90 miles uphill. By 1864, the year after his journal appeared in print, Speke was feeling less sure of himself. And then Burton came home.

Fresh from Dahomey, Burton disagreed both with Speke's assessment of his character and, more importantly, with his assertion that he had discovered the source of the Nile. He advanced the proposition that Lake Victoria was not a single body of water but a collection of smaller lakes, and that it had yet to be disproved that Lake Tanganyika was the ultimate source. Speke responded angrily. Burton counterattacked with vim. Eventually they agreed to debate the matter in public. The date was set for 6 September 1864; the venue was Bath, where the British Association for the Advancement of Science had arranged its annual meeting; and the adjudicator would be the renowned African explorer David Livingstone. Come the day, however, only Burton was on the platform. After a short delay, during which Burton shuffled his papers, a delegation came forward. It was led by Sir Roderick Murchison, President of the Royal Geographical Society. Climbing onstage, Murchison made a short announcement: at approximately 4.30 on the previous afternoon, while shooting partridges on his cousin's estate, Speke had shot himself. He had climbed a wall, armed with a double-barrelled, breech-loading Lancaster shotgun, set at half-cock, and in doing so had loosed a cartridge upwards into his ribcage.

The official verdict was that Speke had met an accidental death. Many, however, thought he had committed suicide rather than defend a theory he already knew to be flawed against a man whose intellectual and physical abilities were superior to his own. The manner of Speke's death would never be resolved. But his theory was settled in 1871, when David Livingstone and journalist-turned-explorer Henry Morton Stanley discovered that Lake Albert led nowhere and that Victoria Nyanza was the primary source of the Nile. Before his death in 1890 Burton admitted that he knew Speke had been right all along.

Speke's monument was a Cleopatra-like needle in London's Kensington Gardens. Burton's was the burning by his wife of both his diaries and the manuscript of his final book, *The Scented Garden*, whose contents she judged too risqué for publication.

Edward Whymper (1865)

In the mid-19th century the Alps were Europe's last undiscovered wilderness. It was incredible, in a way, that this should be so: Europe contained so many people, had such a long history and was so expansionist that it had already begun colonizing most of the world. Yet in its midst there was a chain of mountains – indeed, a completely different climate zone – about which little was known. True, the passes had been frequented since ancient times; Mont Blanc had been conquered as far back as 1786; and one or two intrepid climbers had attacked some of the more accessible peaks. On the whole, however, the Alps remained an uncharted blank on the map. From the 1850s Britain began to address this deplorable state of affairs.

Supported by a strong, stable economy, possessed of wealth and long summer holidays, Britain's professional middle class took to the hills with a vengeance. Thanks to the advent of steam locomotion, a London lawyer (say) could walk out of his courtroom, on to a train, and alight at Geneva a couple of days later. From there it was only a few connections and a hike or two before he was facing mountains that had never before been climbed by humankind, and valleys that might contain – well, anything. Alpine dwellers told of demons and witches who cackled from the glaciers and peaks; even for the less superstitious the Alps were so inaccessible that it was still possible for diligent explorers to discover isolated communities descended from Huns, Vandals and even Saracens. After a few weeks' exhilarating scramble the same lawyer could be back in his courtroom, shuffling his papers with hands that had recently grappled the Eiger.

The excitement of being able to go where no one had yet gone – and in one's holidays too – was irresistible. It was cheaper and more convenient than travelling to the Arctic, and almost as hazardous. Many papers likened the Alps to the North Pole and railed against those who risked their lives to conquer them. Many others, however, lauded their bravery: Englishmen, said one journal, were famed for their love of sport (defined as exercise combined with danger) and if they could not afford to hunt foxes or shoot tigers then mountaineering was a perfect outlet for their natural instincts. And so, throughout the 1850s, a growing number of part-time, budget explorers caught the ferry train from London Bridge to Geneva. Among the band were John Tyndall and Edward Whymper.

Tyndall was an Irish scientist, based in London, who specialized in the study of gases. He was renowned for the strength of his opinions and the remarkable physique with which he was prepared to defend them. Should someone deride his favourite writers he would at once offer to fight them – an offer that met with incredulity and then frustration, for Tyndall was so slight that it was hard to find a place to punch. Slope-shouldered and skinny, weighing no more than ten stone at the best of times, with a dis-proportionately large head whose chin was noosed by a 'Newgate fringe' beard, he was outwardly the feeblest of specimens. Wracked by constant intestinal complaints, he rarely ate or slept and was so nervous in company that he hesitated even to approach a woman for fear of rebuff. To assuage his indigestion he ran every morning in Kensington Gardens, which calmed him sufficiently to have a small bowl of soup for lunch. Then he went for another run to alleviate its disagreeable effects. Of an evening he might lecture at the Royal Society before retiring dinnerless, with his notes, for another dyspeptic bout of insomnia. In the Alps, however, Tyndall became a superman. His appetite returned, he was able to sleep and, thanks to his exercise programme, he could haul himself up the rockiest summit faster than any guide. His fitness and application were so prodigious that he soon dispensed with guides altogether. In 1858 he made the first solo ascent of Monte Rosa, carrying nothing more than a flask of tea and a ham sandwich. Wherever he went – Mont Blanc, the Bernese Oberland, the Valais – he climbed with a desperate ferocity.

No less ferocious was Whymper. A Southwark wood engraver and printer's apprentice, he first visited the Alps in 1860, at the age of twenty, on a commission from Longman's publishing house. Initially contemptuous of what he considered the mountains' over-touted attractions, he soon became as fervent a convert as anyone. As with Tyndall, there were two sides to his existence. In London he was a mere wood engraver, a solitary, humourless man who dropped his aitches and in the evenings went for long, lonely walks. In the Alps he was lord of all creation. Here it did not matter how he spoke or what he did for a living, only how well he acquitted himself on the peaks. And he acquitted himself superbly. He flung himself, quite literally, at the mountains, determined not so much to climb them as to conquer them. He had no time for summits that had already been done; his one desire was to break new ground, to go where nobody else had gone, to stand where no other had stood. If he saw a crag he did not pause to admire its beauty but planned how to defeat it. In many ways he was pursuing a form of personal imperialism, stamping his name on as much ground as he could in as short a time as possible. He was tougher than his guides – for most of whom he had profound contempt – and tougher than any of the other Britons who went to the Alps. In one remarkable burst of energy he climbed

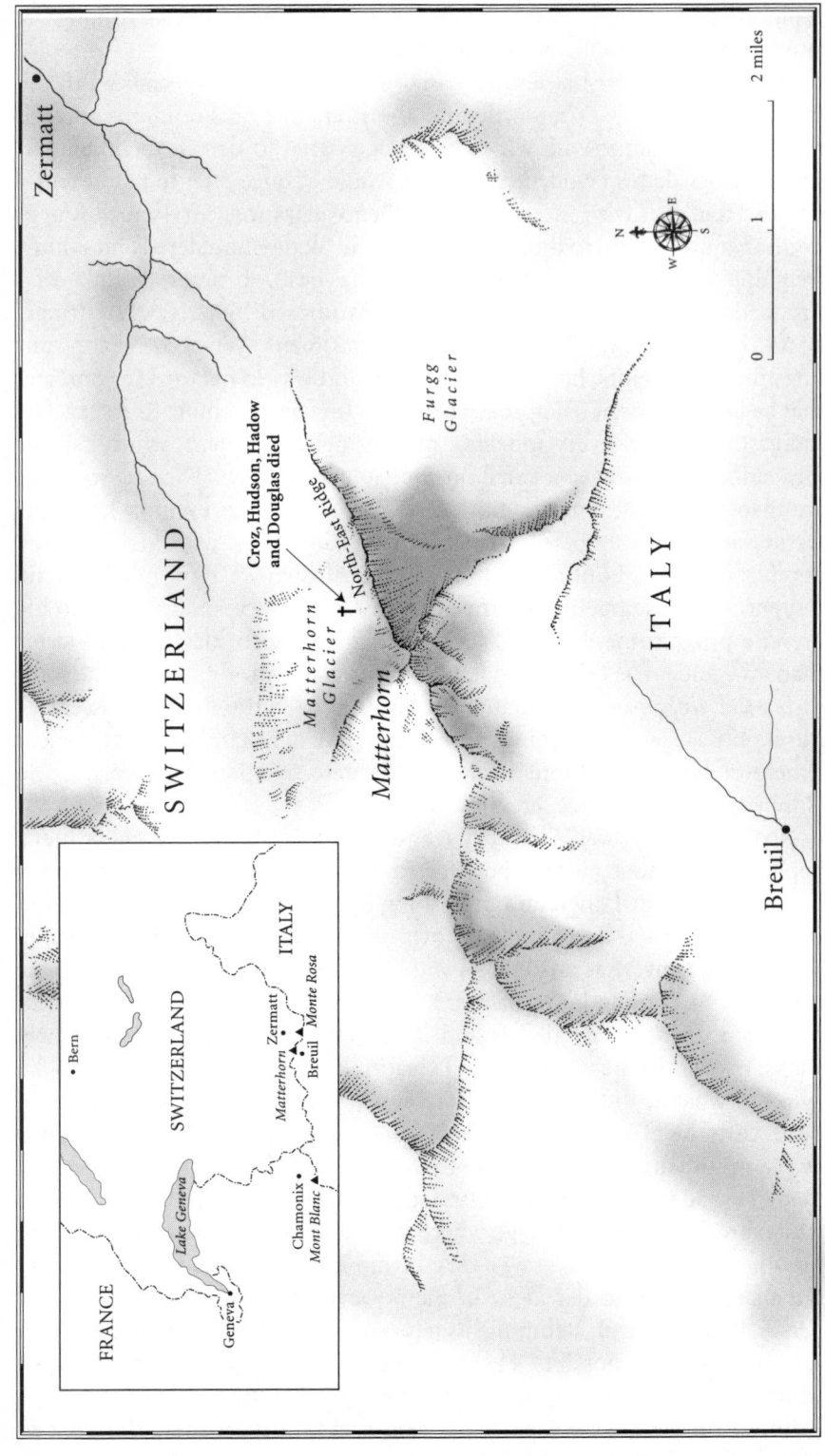

a total of 100,000 feet in a period of just 18 days. People regarded him with awe, disbelief and a certain amount of fear. One reluctant admirer would later write: 'To Mr. Whymper belongs the credit of having had no weak spot at all.'

Whymper and Tyndall were in the vanguard of a wave of British climbers who swept through the Alps during the early 1860s. Equipped with nothing more sophisticated than ropes (Tyndall was one of their earliest advocates), ice-axes and crampons (in both cases Whymper was an innovator), and clad in flannel suits and tackety boots, they raised a metaphorical Union Jack on peak after peak. By 1865, in what would later be dubbed the Golden Age of Mountaineering, British climbers had opened virtually the whole of the Swiss Alpine range. But there was one important mountain that still eluded them. It was not the highest in the Alps, nor the last to be climbed, but it was certainly the most dramatic and to all appearances the most inaccessible. It was called the Matterhorn.

A sheer-sided fang of rock rising 14,688 feet on the Swiss-Italian border, the Matterhorn was seen as the ultimate challenge. Rocks dribbled down its flanks 24 hours a day in all seasons. Even in summer its slopes were clad in treacherous black ice. Its weather system was unpredictable, localized storms descending with terrible swiftness on the sunniest day. Rarely was it cloud-free, and on a summer evening the summit smoked as if the very mountain was ablaze. Above all, there was no obvious way up it. On the Swiss side, above the village of Zermatt, the cliffs were so precipitous that local guides just laughed if anyone suggested climbing them. The pointlessness of such an exercise was reinforced when one Briton tried to do just that, only to be driven back by a storm that blew blocks of ice a foot wide *up* at him from the glaciers hundreds of feet below. On the Italian side, above the hamlet of Breuil, however, the Matterhorn's forbidding outline was broken by a few shoulders and plateaux. It was from this direction, therefore, that most attempts were made. But even here, at its most forgiving, the Matterhorn was still a terrible foe. Only Tyndall and Whymper could make any impression on it, but despite repeated attempts they were always defeated. Whymper wrote: 'There seemed to be a cordon drawn around it, up to which one might go but no further. Within that invisible line gins and effreets were supposed to exist – the Wandering Jew and the spirits of the damned. The superstitious natives spoke of a ruined city on its summit wherein the spirits dwelt; and if you laughed, they gravely shook their heads; told you to look yourself to see the castles and the walls, and warned one against rash approach, lest the infuriated demons from their impregnable heights might hurl down vengeance for one's derision.'

For both men the Matterhorn became an obsession. In 1860 Tyndall went up it, scrambling to a height of 13,000 feet along ledges one foot wide, through waterfalls, up rock chimneys, and over 'a wilderness of blocks, roofed and festooned with huge plates and stalactites of ice'. On his return he vowed to try again the following year. But in 1861 his guide informed him the weather was too bad. Tyndall ground his hobnailed boots into the soil with frustration. Not being able to climb the Matterhorn was 'like the removal of a pleasant drug, or the breaking down of a religious faith. I hardly knew what to do with myself.' He vented his fury on the surrounding peaks. Next year, though, the Matterhorn would be his.

Whymper thought exactly the same. Having already made two attempts from Breuil in previous years, he arrived for a third in 1862. Starting on 9 July, he pitched camp at 12,550 feet and was poised to go further, in perfect, cloudless weather, when one of his guides complained of illness. Reluctantly, Whymper agreed to retreat, but in such foul temper that he did not even bother to take his tent with him. After a restorative ascent of nearby Monte Rosa he returned to Breuil on 17 July for another try. But all the guides were booked, so Whymper stomped angrily up the Matterhorn on his own to collect the tent he had left behind the previous week. He had never made a solo climb before, and the experience agreed with him. When he reached the tent he decided it would be a shame not to climb a little bit further. And then a little bit further still. At every turn the mountain seemed more interesting than before. Soon he had surpassed his highest point and was in virgin territory, a surreal field of towers and turrets that valley-dwellers called The Coxcomb. 'The pinnacles ... were wagging in the wind. Without exaggeration, one could take hold of huge Egyptian-like blocks, ten or more feet high, and rock them backwards and forwards,' he wrote. 'Strangely fascinated, on I went.'

He came to within 1,400 feet of the summit before being blocked by precipices that were insurmountable without the assistance of other climbers. Exultantly he dashed down to Breuil, once again neglecting to take his tent with him. But, as he wrote, his 'exultation was a little premature'. At the head of a 200-foot gully he lost his footing. Tipped onto his back by the weight of his knapsack, he slid down the chute. Within seconds he was ricocheting from side to side, each bound longer than the last and each impact more violent. After a final leap of 60 feet he was hurled against a clump of rocks which halted his fall for a few seconds. Although knocked almost senseless, he scrabbled instinctively for survival. When he finally brought himself to a stop, he was only ten feet from the lip of the gully, beyond which fell an 800-foot cliff. His situation was terrifying. 'The rocks could not be left go for a moment,' he wrote, 'and the blood was spirting [sic] out of more than twenty cuts. The most serious ones were in the head, and I vainly tried to staunch them with one hand, while holding on with the other. It was useless; the blood jerking out in blinding jets at each pulsation. At last, in a moment of inspiration, I kicked out a big lump of snow and stuck it as a plaster on my head.' He crawled halfway up the 60-degree slope to the safety of another group of boulders, and there he fainted.

He came to as night was falling, and in the light of the setting sun he took stock of his injuries. He had lost the tips of both ears, every limb was grazed and bleeding, his head was gashed in a number of places, and a rock had taken a neat circular slice out of his boot, sock and ankle. Fortunately, however, no bones had been broken, and so he continued his crawl up the gully. Then, in darkness, he descended the remaining 4,800 feet to Breuil, where his hotelier rubbed salt and vinegar into the wounds.

Covered in scabs, he hired a guide and resumed the battle on 23 July. This time he reached 12,992 feet, but was forced to retreat because the weather was too foul. He submitted with bad grace. Privately, he suspected that his guide – the best in Breuil, Jean-Antoine Carrel – was keeping the Matterhorn for himself and for Italy, a suspicion reinforced when, Whymper having booked him for another ascent on the 25th, Carrel sent word that he was unavailable because he was hunting marmots. Not to be thwarted, Whymper hired a small, hunchbacked porter instead. Once again, though, he was blocked by the same precipices he had encountered on his solo climb. He would need not one helper but at least two if he was to overcome the obstacle. Returning to base, he sought out Carrel for another attempt on the 26th. But Tyndall had got to him first.

Marching over the mountains from Visp, in Switzerland, Tyndall was in jovial mood. 'The Matterhorn was our temple,' he wrote, 'and we approached it with feelings not unworthy of so great a shrine.' At Breuil he was appalled that Whymper had been attacking 'his' mountain, but pleased to discover that the enemy – as he now called him – had not reached the summit. When he left, with Carrel and another equally capable guide he had brought from Switzerland, he did so with confidence: he would conquer the Matterhorn this time; failing that, he would at least go further than anyone else. Whymper offered him the use of his tent, damned him privately, 'with envy and all uncharitableness', and then as soon as he had left remembered he needed one or two essentials that he had left behind at camp. For the fourth time that year he went up the Matterhorn, climbing skilfully and swiftly past the rival party, showering them with rocks in the process, then descended to congratulate Tyndall on his laggardly progress.

Tyndall went on. 'We worked up bit by bit, holding on almost by our eyelids.' Clambering ever upwards, they paused only for a second at Whymper's cliffs. 'It was these precipices that stopped Whymper,' Tyndall wrote. 'Well, we scaled them.' On they went until, with the summit in sight, and while edging their way along a ridge, they were blocked by a notch several hundred feet deep. If only they could cross this obstacle, Tyndall was certain, the Matterhorn would be theirs. But there was no way over. From whatever angle they looked at it the problem was insoluble. They descended the mountain, battered by an abrupt and vengeful shower of hail. The Matterhorn, Tyndall finally admitted, was inaccessible. 'This defeat has fallen upon us like the chill of age,' he wrote to a friend. 'Well ... goodbye to my climbing. For there is nothing else in the Alps that I should care to do.'

Whymper, too, was 'almost inclined' to believe the Matterhorn was unconquerable. That did not stop him returning to Breuil in 1863, when he was driven back by bad weather, and again in 1864, when hardly had he put his boots on than he was recalled to London by urgent business. He was back yet again in 1865, having taken the precaution of pre-booking Jean-Antoine Carrel the previous year. But this time Whymper was fighting not only the mountain but, unbeknown to him, the forces of nationalism. The Italian government had decided that as the Matterhorn lay half in Italy it was only right that an Italian should be the first to the top of it. A man named Felice Giordano was duly appointed as the Matterhorn's conqueror, and when Whymper arrived that season he found that Giordano had not only poached Carrel but had made sure that every other guide – every porter even – was unavailable for the duration of his stay. It had been arranged so skilfully that Whymper did not realize he had been 'bamboozled and humbugged' until Giordano and Carrel were well into their ascent.

Whymper had one chance: Giordano's party was large and unwieldy; it would take them at least three days to reach the summit; if he could find a guide he might yet be able to beat them. But there were no guides; Giordano had seen to that. Then, as if by divine providence, the 18-year-old Lord Francis Douglas arrived in Breuil. He remarked that his guides, a father-and-son team both named Peter Taugwalder, had scouted the Matterhorn's north-east ridge and were confident that the mountain could be climbed from the Swiss side. Casually, he said that he had hired them for an attempt in two days' time. Whymper took charge. The next day all four were in Zermatt preparing for the ascent.

No sooner had they arrived than Whymper encountered a new threat: an English vicar, the Revd Charles Hudson, was also planning an attack on the Matterhorn. Hudson was an experienced climber – perhaps not in the same class as Whymper, but good enough. He also had the services of a famous Chamonix guide, Michel Croz. By unspoken etiquette, two Englishmen did not climb the same mountain by the same route on the same day. In this case, Hudson had priority. Whymper suggested they combine parties. Hudson happily agreed, adding as an aside that there was a third member of his group, a youngster named Douglas Hadow, who was a decent chap but not quite as accomplished a mountaineer as himself or Croz. When Whymper questioned him as to Hadow's fitness Hudson replied that he had recently climbed Mont Blanc in record time and was quite competent for an assault on the Matterhorn. Hudson and Whymper shook hands.

The enlarged group of three guides and four Englishmen left Zermatt in the early hours of 13 July 1865. To their delight, the north-eastern ridge was perfectly feasible. It was not exactly easy, presenting difficult traverses and at points being unpleasantly exposed. But it was indescribably nicer than the ascent from Breuil – so much so that Hudson and Whymper overtook their guides and forged ahead on their own. Even when the going became hard, and Croz and Old Taugwalder took the lead, all they had to do was lend an occasional hand to their employers. The group spent one night on the ridge, and then on 14 July scrambled to the summit. 'At 1.40 pm the world was at our feet,' wrote Whymper, 'and the Matterhorn was conquered.'

There remained one thing to do. On the other side of the mountain, 1,250 feet below them, like a column of ants, the Italian party crawled slowly over the rocks. Whymper and Croz waved and shouted to get their attention. When that did not work they hurled boulders down the slope at them. 'There was no doubt about it this time,' Whymper jubilated. 'The Italians turned and fled.' Whymper's party spent an hour on the summit, then started on the descent. After their rapid, adrenalin-filled climb they were now exhausted. Moreover, their limbs were unaccustomed to the strange sensation of moving downhill. It was a mental and physical turnaround they had all experienced before, one that could lead to accidents, so they took every precaution as they left the summit. Croz went first, followed by Hadow. After Hadow came Hudson, with Douglas above him. Last in line were the two Taugwalders, with Whymper roped between them. They moved slowly, Croz helping Hadow, and Hudson helping Douglas, taking care that no more than one man moved at a time when they reached steep or icy patches. It was a perfectly planned and competently executed descent, save for one thing: from Croz to Douglas the party was linked by sturdy ropes; from Old Taugwalder to Young Taugwalder it was the same; yet, for some unfathomable reason, Douglas and Old Taugwalder were linked by a length of much weaker sashcord. To their knowledge there was nothing inherently wrong with this type of rope; they had used it before, and Whymper had employed it on some of his most perilous climbs. That it was called sashcord, however, gave a hint as to its limitations: in normal circumstances it was used to suspend the lead counterbalances in sash windows.

At 3.00 p.m. on 14 July Croz put aside his ice-axe to guide Hadow's feet into the notches he had just cut. Hadow slipped, knocking Croz over. The combined weight of their two bodies pulled first Hudson and then Douglas off their feet. As all four men fell, Old Taugwalder wound the rope around his arm and braced himself against a rock. Behind him, Whymper and Young Taugwalder also took the strain. Their combined strength might possibly have halted the fall, had the sashcord not snapped. For a moment the four men tried to find a grip in the ice, but slowly at first, then with gathering speed, they slid downhill. One after another they vanished from sight, to land on the glacier 4,000 feet below.

For half an hour Whymper and the two Taugwalders were transfixed by shock. When at last they continued the descent they did so like automata. Every now and then they would call for their companions, but no answer came back. By 6.30 p.m. they were on relatively easy ground when an arc of light illuminated the clouds. Within the arc three crosses became clearly visible. Whymper recognized it as a solar fogbow, a not unheard-of phenomenon but one which at that particular time filled him with superstitious dread. They spent a sleepless night on a small slab of rock, and the following morning ran for Zermatt.

Whymper's triumph was overwhelmed by the disaster. Never in alpine history had so many men died in a single accident. And never had they fallen so far and so horribly. When Whymper took a rescue party to find the bodies he was sickened. Croz, Hudson and Hadow had been stripped naked, various limbs were missing, their skulls had been broken and, in the case of Croz, the top of his head had been sliced off, leaving only a jawbone in which was embedded his rosary cross. Of Douglas there remained nothing whatsoever, save a pair of gloves, a belt and a boot. His body was never found. It was assumed that he had either caught on the rocks or, more likely, had been shredded during his mile-long plummet. Whymper oversaw their burial in the glacier on which they had met their end. Later the three bodies were disinterred and relocated to a churchyard in Zermatt.

The Matterhorn's conquest brought the Golden Age of Mountaineering to a lurid and very public climax. The British press seethed with speculation: a vicar and a peer of the realm had died. Why? And how? There was talk of Old Taugwalder having cut the rope to prevent himself being dragged after them, or having weakened it in anticipation of their fall. Whymper and Taugwalder denied the accusations, but nothing they said could halt the gossip. In France, Germany, Switzerland, Italy and, above all, Britain, the Matterhorn dominated the news. Men and women from all walks of life wrote to the papers, condemning every form of alpinism. Those who had the means flocked to Zermatt from where they could better condemn – and better relish – the tragedy. A subculture of 'penny-dreadful' novels flourished around the image of the cut rope: was the cutter or the cuttee to be pitied most? Whymper stood firm. He answered the questions put to him by an official inquiry, and by the blunt directness of his responses ensured that nobody was found responsible for the deaths. It had been an accident – appalling but unforeseeable. Amidst the furore it went almost unnoticed when later in the season Jean-Antoine Carrel succeeded in climbing the Matterhorn from Breuil, an ascent that was hailed by experts as one of the most accomplished feats of mountaineering on record.

Whymper fled to the obscurity of his print works in Southwark, where he sank into depression. He later went to the Andes and the Rockies, and led two expeditions to Greenland, but he rarely climbed in the Alps again. Never able to escape his double-edged fame, he lived for the rest of his life with the Matterhorn disaster, in whose shadow he grew grimmer by the year. As for Tyndall, he at last climbed the mountain in 1868 and was likewise disheartened. 'Hardly two things can be more different than the two aspects of the mountain from above and below,' he wrote. 'From above, it seems torn to pieces by the frosts of ages, while its vast facettes are so foreshortened as to stretch out into the distance like plains ... There is something chilling in the contemplation of those infinitesimal forces, whose integration through the ages pulls down even the Matterhorn. Hacked and hurt by time, the aspect of the mountain from its higher crags saddened me.' As with Whymper, the ascent marked the effective closure of his alpine career.

The conquest of the Matterhorn was one of the definitive events in 19th-century exploration. Like Sir John Franklin's disappearance in search of the North-West Passage, it shaped the mythology of an age – indeed, of an empire. It also brought to an end the glory days of alpine exploration. In the last ten or so years virtually every major peak in the Alps had been climbed and the last major blank on the map of Europe had been filled. People would continue to visit the mountains, to find new and ever harder routes to their summits, but they were no longer the mystery they had once been.

The Pundits (1865–1902)

The Great Survey of India, which had occupied British cartographers since 1800, was not restricted solely to mapping the subcontinent. Its secondary function was to provide the military with topographical intelligence on the surrounding countries of Afghanistan, Turkestan and Tibet, possession of which (or at least the neutrality of which) was considered vital to India's security. If Russia was to invade these border regions, or if Britain was to make a preemptive invasion, it was vital to have reliable maps. Unfortunately, these were not places where British surveyors could march about, as they had done in the past, with gigantic theodolites and teams of porters. Not only were they likely to be murdered by bandits, but their presence could possibly spark a war with Russia. Moreover, the country of Tibet, in which Britain was most interested, was fraught with hazards of every description: it was topographically hostile, being the highest, coldest, most mountainous nation in the world; its government (theoretically in thrall to China) had closed its borders to Westerners, threatening dire penalties for trespassers; and the border regions were lawless and insecure. With very good reason, therefore, the Viceroy of India had stated expressly that British officers were not to cross the frontier. Yet the maps had to be made.

It was Captain Thomas Montgomerie, currently triangulating Kashmir, who came up with a solution. Instead of sending British surveyors, why not send native ones? And, anticipating the response that mapmakers of any nationality would be killed, he suggested they go in disguise; even if they were uncovered, it would be a lot less embarrassing than if they had been British. Surprisingly, his bold and unconventional plan was taken up, and so, at Dehra Dun in the shadow of Sir George Everest's headquarters, Montgomerie began training his band of spies.

He chose the candidates carefully, selecting only hillmen of exceptional stamina and intelligence. Their first task was to measure the length of their pace and then practice taking the same stride whether walking uphill, downhill or on the flat. Next they were taught how to use a compass, how to measure altitude by means of a thermometer and how to take bearings with a sextant – a business that required advanced mathematical skills. Their agreed disguise was that of Buddhist pilgrims, not just because such pilgrims were common, but because they carried several items that were ideal for Montgomerie's purpose: a stick, a rosary, a trunk, a begging bowl and a cylindrical prayer-wheel whose top could be removed to give access to the prayer scrolls within. The stick was hollowed out to contain a thermometer, the rosaries were used to record paces (a bead would be slipped for every 100 paces) and at the end of the day the results could be recorded on the scrolls inside the prayer-wheel. The compass was hidden in the top of the prayer-wheel and a false bottom was built in to each trunk to conceal the sextant. Mercury was contained in cowrie shells and then poured into the begging bowl to make an artificial horizon for use with the sextant. The equipment was prepared at the Dehra Dun workshops in conditions of great secrecy. In fact, the whole operation was so clandestine that even within the Survey Montgomerie's men were known only by numbers or initials. As a group, they called themselves 'pundits', or teachers.

In 1865 pundit 'No. 1' (a.k.a. Nain Singh) travelled across the Himalayas to Tibet. He returned 18 months later, having taken the bearings of the capital, Lhasa, having mapped mountains, glaciers, rivers and valleys, and having covered in the process 1,250 miles. On his rosary he had recorded two and a half million paces of precisely 33 inches. 'No. 1' subsequently explored the region north of the Indus to chart, and to report on, Tibet's fabled goldmines. Once again he did his job splendidly, returning with a prayer-wheel full of fascinating information: the route had taken him over suspension bridges whose great iron chains were rust-proofed annually with yak butter; the mines, he said, were operated on an open-cast system by several thousand freelance prospectors who dug pits 20 feet deep and panned the spoil for gold dust in a nearby stream; the miners believed that nuggets were alive and gave birth to gold dust, so they reburied those they found, including one monster that Nain Singh reckoned at more than two pounds in weight; there were more miners in winter than in summer, because the pits tended to collapse without warning in the warmth; and the place was so cold, even in summer, that people dug their tents eight feet underground and slept under a mound of furs on their knees and elbows in order to minimize contact with the frozen soil. Off 'No. 1' went again in 1874, this time walking from Ladakh to Lhasa via the 16,500-foot-high Chang Thang plateau. This freezing, windblown, foodless expanse, dotted with lakes 50 miles long (unnavigable due to violent, unpredictable gales and too brackish for drinking), was truly desolate: it was possible for a traveller to go 80 days without meeting another human being. 'No. 1' paced through it insouciantly – he described it as easy enough, if a touch barren – sighting en route a new range of mountains whose highest peak he measured at 25,000 feet.

Again and again 'No. 1' went out, sometimes on his own, sometimes accompanied by others, including his cousin 'No. 2' (T. K. Singh). But by this time other pundits had graduated from Dehra Dun and were making their own methodical way into the unknown. In 1878, shortly after 'No. 1's'

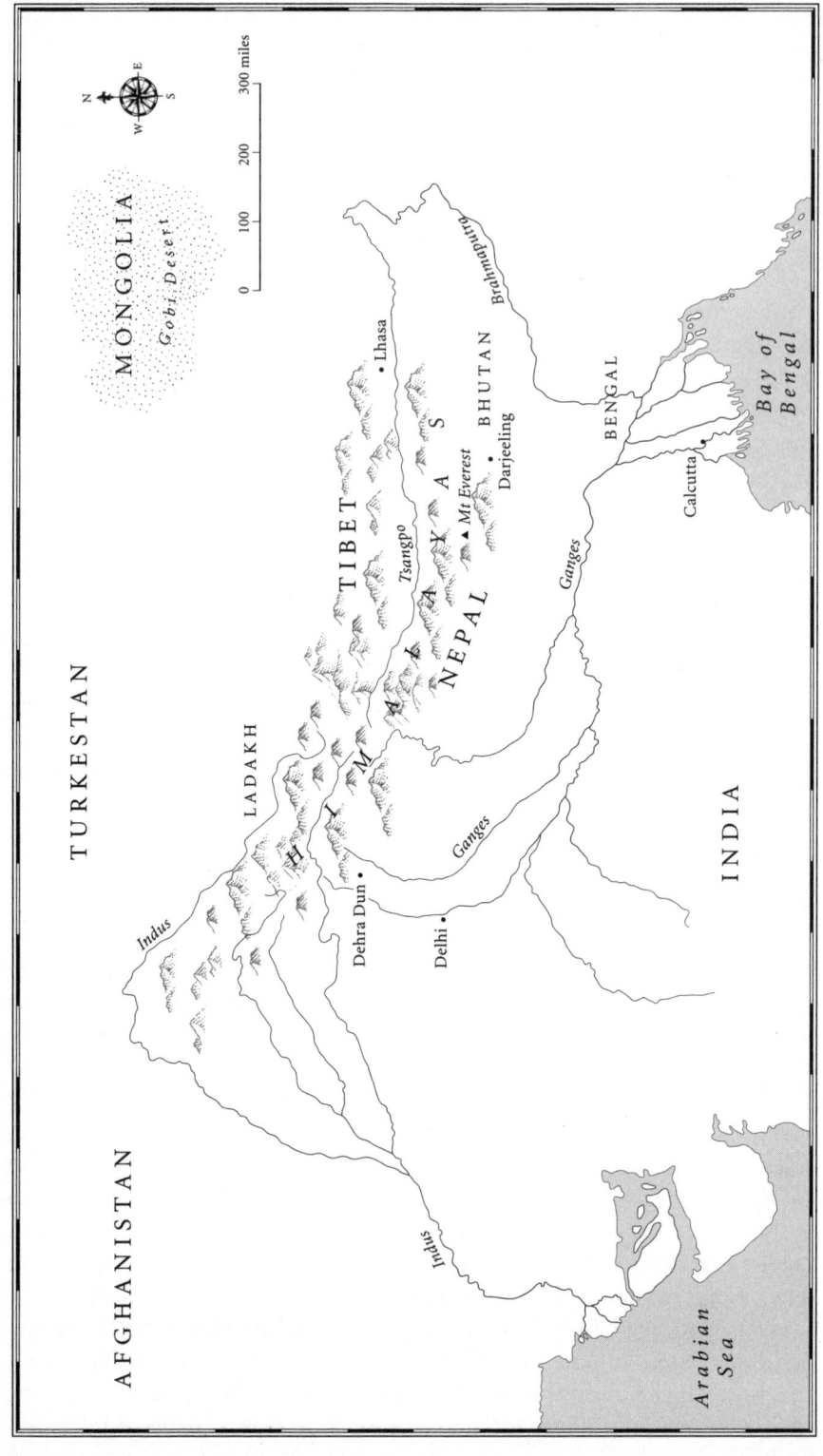

return, pundit 'A. K.' (Kishen Singh, no relation) struck north across Tibet for Mongolia. He was robbed, imprisoned and forced to work as a herdsman and a lama's servant, but managed nevertheless to cross the Gobi Desert and return to Tibet, where he was imprisoned yet again. In 1882, by which time his masters assumed he was dead, 'A. K.' staggered back to India with information on 4,750 miles of unknown territory.

The British treated 'No. 1', 'A. K.' and their companions in a remarkably cavalier manner. Although their programme was meant to be secret, every detail was published in the Royal Geographical Society's journal from 1865 onwards. Fortunately, Lhasa did not subscribe to the journal. But after a particularly successful pundit, Sarat Chandra Das, had made two journeys into Tibet, in 1879 and 1881, news of the subterfuge leaked out. As they had promised, the Tibetans visited a dire vengeance on those involved. The lama who had unwittingly allowed him into the country was flogged, bound and thrown into the Tsangpo River. The lama's servants had their eyes burned out, and their hands and feet cut off, before being left to die. The responsible border officials were imprisoned; 19 years later they were still chained in a Lhasa dungeon. Blithely, the British continued to send pundits into Tibet; and remarkably, the pundits agreed to go.

While 'A. K.' was still in the field, the Great Survey despatched its most bizarre agents yet – a Mongolian lama and his Sikkimese porter 'K. P.', or Kintup. The lama was not a pundit, just a hired hand, and 'K. P.', although capable and intelligent, could neither read nor write, so they were given a task that did not require mathematics or the use of abstruse instruments. What the Survey wanted to know was whether the Tsangpo River, which ran through the Himalayas, dropping 5,000 feet along the way, connected with the Brahmaputra in Bengal. To this end, the lama was paid to fell trees which would be cut into 500 one-foot-long logs that he would drop into the Tsangpo at the point where it entered the mountains. Fifty logs per day were to be thrown into the river, each one being tagged with the date and place it was deposited. Officers from the Survey would be waiting to record their exit. The lama proved an unreliable spy: he spent the money on women and drink, and sold 'K. P.' as a slave, before returning to Mongolia. But 'K. P.' managed to escape and, despite a period in jail, was felling the trees four months later. It took him a further three months to travel to Lhasa, where he dictated a letter to the Survey alerting them to be on the look-out at a specified date. Nine months later he released the 500 logs. Alas, the officer who had given him his instructions had since returned to England, and the messenger who was to carry 'K. P.'s letter died on the way, so the logs wallowed downriver to the Brahmaputra and floated unnoticed out to sea. When 'K. P.' made his way back to India, he found that the Tsangpo-Brahmaputra question had already been answered by 'A. K.' All his efforts had been in vain, and nobody believed his story. He sank into obscurity and died, some 30 years later, working as a tailor in Darjeeling.

By 1902, thanks largely to the pundits' efforts, Britain had annexed Tibet. The men who had made this territorial gain possible were appreciated by their employers and by the Royal Geographical Society, which awarded Nain Singh its gold medal, for adding 'a greater amount of positive knowledge to the map of Asia than any other individual in our time'. The RGS also gave Kishen Singh a gold watch (it was stolen during one of his many absences). But, as mere Indians, the pundits were never properly rewarded for their services. They were paid little for time in the field and received meagre pensions when they were no longer needed. William Rockhill, an American traveller, wrote in 1891: 'If any British explorer had done one third of what Nain Singh [or others] accomplished, medals and decorations, lucrative offices and professional promotion, freedom of cities, and every form of lionisation would have been his. As for those native explorers, a small pecuniary award and obscurity are all to which they can look forward.'

Kishen Singh was the longest-lived of this extraordinary band. He survived, in constant ill-health as a result of his ordeals, until 1921. The last Briton to have given the pundits their orders died in 1967. Neither man left any clue as to what motivated the pundits to do what they so bravely but thanklessly did.

Paul Hegemann and Karl Koldewey (1869–70)

Of all the theories as to how the North Pole could be attained, that of the German geographer August Petermann was perhaps the most radical. Looking at how effectively the Gulf Stream warmed the coasts of Western Europe and Scandinavia, he saw no reason why its influence should suddenly vanish when it reached the Arctic seas. It was surely wrong to imagine that such a great body of water should, in some vague fashion, just disappear once it had passed Norway. No, he said, it did not disappear but continued into the Arctic where, encountering a body of land (of whose existence he had no proof), it looped west to emerge above the east coast of Greenland. Along its course, which perhaps appropriately he envisaged as being in the shape of a vast aquatic question mark, the sea would be ice-free. Therefore, rather than struggle through Smith Sound to the west of Greenland as every navigator had done to date, it was more sensible to follow nature's own path to the Pole – to enter, as Petermann put it, the 'thermometric gateways'.

On 15 June 1869 that year two ships sailed from Bremerhaven to put his theory to the test. The larger, the *Germania*, was a sturdy, newly built, iron-sheathed steamer under the command of Karl Koldewey. The smaller, the *Hansa*, was an unreinforced sailing ship under Paul Hegemann. Their destination was the east coast of Greenland. It was not anticipated that they would reach the Pole – the voyage was more of an exploratory probe than an outright attempt – but they carried a heavy burden of expectation. This was Germany's first Arctic expedition and, as Koldewey wrote, '[we will] show that German sailors are as qualified, as bold, and as persevering as other nations'.

Koldewey's brave words belied an understandable nervousness. Few crew-members on either ship had experience of the ice. The scientists who accompanied the expedition had never been on a ship before, let alone been to the Arctic, and some of them had never even seen the sea. But by the time they reached Greenland in July their fear had been replaced by excitement. 'We stood and felt that we were at the entrance to a new world,' Koldewey wrote, 'whose whole enchantment had thus burst upon us.' His optimism was premature. On 19 July Koldewey flagged Hegemann to come aboard to discuss how they should proceed. Hegemann, however, misunderstood the

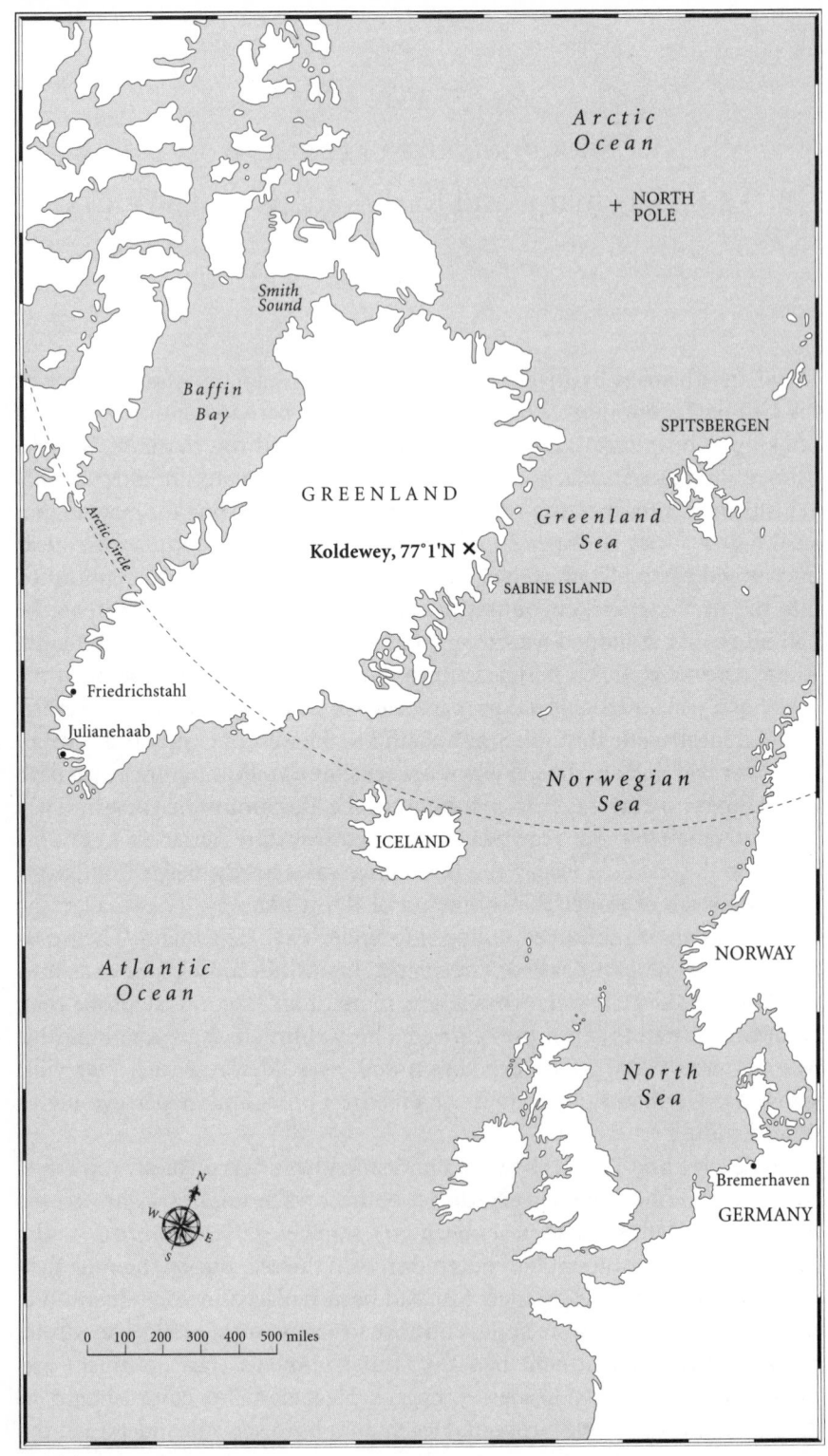

Arctic
Ocean

+ NORTH
POLE

Smith
Sound

Baffin
Bay

SPITSBERGEN

GREENLAND

Greenland
Sea

Koldewey, 77°1'N ✕

SABINE ISLAND

Arctic Circle

Friedrichstahl

Julianehaab

Norwegian
Sea

ICELAND

Atlantic
Ocean

NORWAY

North
Sea

Bremerhaven

GERMANY

N
W   E
S

0   100   200   300   400   500 miles

signal and sailed the *Hansa* straight for Greenland, where it was rapidly swallowed by fog. Koldewey stared in incredulity: both he and Hegemann knew the *Hansa* was not sturdy enough for a battle with the ice; it was intended merely as a supply ship, while the *Germania* was to do all the rough work. Still, it had been agreed that if the slower, weaker *Hansa* became separated from its partner the two vessels were to rendezvous at nearby Sabine Island, so Koldewey set up camp there and steamed for Greenland. He reached the coast on 5 August at a latitude of 74° 18' N.

For the next 12 months Koldewey's men investigated this unknown stretch of land. Under his second-in-command, Julius von Payer, they sledged as far north as 77° 1' N, discovering herds of musk-ox, seams of coal and the remains of Inuit settlements, all of which made East Greenland seem an eminently rewarding place in terms of polar exploration. Their equipment was not of the finest, and they were hampered by lack of experience. But their enthusiasm inured them to all discomforts: when one of the scientists, a Dr Borgen, was attacked by a polar bear, which sank its teeth into his head and dragged him for several hundred yards before being frightened off, he declared the experience to have been absolutely painless. Sailing for home on 22 July 1870, Koldewey congratulated himself on a successful mission. True, the *Hansa* had not reappeared, but he was not too worried: Hegemann was a capable officer and, after his first brush with the floes, would almost certainly have sailed back to Bremerhaven.

Nothing would have pleased Hegemann more. However, he had not just brushed the floes but become entangled in them. Realizing his mistake, he made valiant efforts to regain Sabine Island, but by 25 August 1869 the *Hansa* was imprisoned in the ice and being carried south. Without steam power, Hegemann was unable to break free. All he could do was watch as his ship drifted at the mercy of the current. That it was a southward flowing current, as Petermann had predicted, was not a great comfort.

Inexperienced the Germans may have been, but they knew that being 'nipped' was the worst hazard of Arctic navigation: once a ship was frozen in place it had a limited chance of survival. If, by a miracle, there were no storms, and the floes remained stable, the *Hansa* might – just might – be carried to the safety of warmer waters. If, however, a gale blew, the jostling ice would smash it. Standard procedure in these circumstances was to abandon ship, build a shelter on the ice and hope that, if the worst came to the worst, the crew could make an escape in their boats. Hegemann did just that.

Being a supply ship, the *Hansa* was replete with all the necessaries for survival. Using coal bricks intended for the *Germania*'s boilers, Hegemann's men constructed a miniature chalet (complete with stove, chimney and dormer windows) on the floe in which they were embedded. They decorated its walls with barometers and a gilt mirror from Hegemann's cabin. The boats were dragged alongside and a separate shed was erected for their stores.

Thus ensconced, they waited while the ice floated slowly south. For almost two months nothing happened, and then, on 19 October, they were hit by a storm. As the floes ground and squeezed against each other, the *Hansa* rose on its rudder, twisted around and then snapped. The crew just had time to remove its masts (for firewood), its galley ranges and a quantity of redundant scientific instruments before their ship disappeared beneath the waves. There was little to mark its passing, save a horde of rats who limped feebly over the floe and died. The temperature was −41° F.

Re-marooned, the castaways bumped down Greenland on their island of ice. As the weeks passed, Hegemann did his best to keep his men occupied, lest they succumb to Arctic winter madness. He had them maintain shipboard discipline and ordered them to perform countless meaningless tasks to prevent them dwelling on their circumstances. Come Christmas he opened two crates of presents that had been packed before they left Germany. Out fell a collection of gewgaws and tiny musical instruments. The trinkets kept them amused for a while, but they were not enough for one of Hegemann's scientists, Dr Bucholz, who went mad and had to be confined to quarters.

On 2 January they heard a strange noise – 'a scraping, blustering, crackling, sawing, grating and jarring sound, as if a ghost was wandering under the floe,' wrote Hegemann. It was a mystery until they pressed their ears (briefly) to the ice. The floe was grounding in shallow waters and breaking up from below. Then, on 3 January, came a second storm that raged for more than a week. As the ice buckled and heaved, their floe, which had been measured in thousands of yards at the outset, became steadily smaller. By 11 January their coal-brick hut sat on a piece of ice measuring only 150 feet in diameter. Three days later another eruption tore the floe in half, cutting through the middle of the hut and forcing its occupants into the open.

They rebuilt the hut and took stock of their supplies. The inventory was promising: they had adequate provisions and stacks of inessentials such as gunpowder and books. But their main worry was the floe, now so small that it would disintegrate as soon as it met the warmer waters of the Atlantic. They devoured the food with abandon and built bonfires out of the books. When the books ran low they threw Hegemann's gilt mirror onto the pyre. They lit a few piles of gunpowder to see what would happen. A few enterprising men detonated rudimentary fireworks that exploded with an unsatisfactory thud. As the months passed, the expedition's reserves were consumed in an orgy of despair.

On 6 May Hegemann took their position and discovered they were at 61° 4' N – they had travelled 840 nautical miles since being separated from the *Germania*. On the 7th, however, he found they had drifted to the north. The southward current had petered out. If they stayed where they were they would circle gently until their ever-decreasing chunk of ice finally melted and tipped them into the ocean. They could not sail to freedom because although their floe was shrinking it was still surrounded by a mass of similar floes that made navigation impossible. Their only recourse was to haul their boats from floe to floe in the hope of meeting open water. They left at 4.00 p.m. on 7 May and did not stop dragging until 6 June when at last they met a strip of clear sea. They launched the boats, raised sail, and by 13 June were being treated to buttered rusks, cigars and Greenland beer by Moravian missionaries at the outpost of Friedrichstahl.

From Friedrichstahl it was a mere 80 miles to the port of Julianehaab, where the Danish governor steadfastly refused to believe their story and where they were able to catch a lift home. They arrived at Bremerhaven in early August. Few people were there to greet them – France having declared war on Germany, the nation had lost interest in its first Arctic explorers – but Hegemann was proud of his achievement even if no one else was. While Koldewey spoke bombastically about patriotism, flags and the discovery of unknown regions, Hegemann remarked drily: 'We cannot flatter ourselves that we have greatly increased the knowledge of Greenland; but we have shown what man's strength and perseverance can accomplish.' Those same qualities would be in even greater demand three years later, when once again a Petermann-inspired expedition sailed for the so-called 'thermometric gateway' to the Pole.

Charles Hall, George Tyson and the *Polaris* (1871–3)

Charles Francis Hall, ex-blacksmith, ex-engraver, school drop-out and God-fearing editor of the *Cincinnati News*, had never been to the Arctic in his life. In fact, he had never been to sea. He could not tell an Eskimo from a Chinaman. He had never been on an expedition and knew very little about life in the wild. Nonetheless, he saw no reason why any this should disqualify him from becoming an explorer. He was certain that his faith would compensate for his lack of experience. And so, in 1860, he left his job and went to the Arctic in search of Sir John Franklin, whose disappearance in 1845 along with more than a hundred crewmen, remained one of the North's great mysteries.

Hall showed a remarkable aptitude for the task. Completely ill-equipped, he strode through the tundra in a broken-crowned hat, with a pair of opera glasses hung round his neck, relying for his survival solely on the goodwill of the Inuit. On his first expedition, to Baffin Island, he learned nothing about Franklin but unearthed several piles of coal left by Martin Frobisher, a discovery that had him somersaulting with joy. He also discovered that the Inuit's oral tradition was so strong that they still spoke of Frobisher's visit of the 1570s as if it had happened yesterday. It occurred to him that if the Inuit of Baffin Island could remember events four centuries in the past, those around King William Island would surely have something to say about any Franklin survivors. He returned to America in 1862 to show the world his findings – he had packed some of Frobisher's coal in a spare pair of socks – and to raise funds for a second voyage. In 1863 he was back in the Arctic, this time landing at Repulse Bay, to the north of Hudson Bay, from where he travelled inland and heard tales suggesting that Franklin's men had walked south from King William Island, dying one by one, the last to go being his second-in-command, Crozier, and one other, unnamed man. This problem solved, Hall arrived in New York in 1869 and said he was ready to tackle a second one: the North Pole. By dint of perseverance and an absolute refusal to admit that God would allow him to be thwarted, he raised the necessary dollars and in July 1871 sailed for Smith Sound on a reinforced steam tug, once called the *Periwinkle* but now more glamorously christened *Polaris*.

Hall was proud of the *Polaris*'s complement. No fewer than three experienced captains were on the roster: George Tyson, assistant navigator; Chester Hubbard, first mate; and Sidney Budington, sailing master. There was a three-man scientific team led by a German doctor named Emil Bessels. There were two Inuit from his previous expeditions, Tookolito and Ebierbing (later to be augmented by a third, Hans Hendrik, who came aboard at Etah with his wife). And there were eight hard-working German seamen. Hall ignored the potential for disputes implicit in having four separate captains (including himself) and a crew that was half German, half American. With God's help all would be well. 'Though we may be surrounded by innumerable icebergs,' he wrote, 'and though our vessel may be crushed like an egg-shell, I believe they will stand by me to the last.' They were, it was, and they didn't.

The *Polaris* steamed through Smith Sound, and by September had reached virgin territory. Beyond Kane Basin it entered a narrow stretch of sea that Hall called Robeson Channel, flanked to the east by a portion of Greenland that he named Hall Land after himself, and to the west by what he christened Grant Land (now part of Ellesmere Island). At 81° 38' N the *Polaris* made its winter anchorage in Hall Land, the furthest north any ship had penetrated via Smith Sound. In recognition of his debt to the Almighty, who had allowed him to proceed so far and so successfully, Hall named the bay Thank God Harbour.

Already, however, the crew had begun to fall apart. The Germans squabbled with the Americans; Bessels threatened to resign unless extra personnel were allocated to scientific duties; Budington, who had no interest in the North Pole, stole food and drink from the officers' mess; Hubbard and Tyson, meanwhile, chafed under his command, considering him incompetent and cowardly. Hall was helpless in the face of such divisions. All he could do was promise to care for them 'as a prudent father cares for his faithful children', and dissipate the personality clashes by sending sledge expeditions to the north. He himself led one of these expeditions, returning on 24 October with good news: 'I can go to the Pole, I think, on this shore.' He drank a cup of coffee and was immediately sick.

Nobody thought anything of it. They assumed it was a reaction to the stress of sledging and the sudden transition from cold to warmth. Hall was sent to bed. But the following morning he felt worse, and as the days passed he began to rave deliriously. When Bessels tried to medicate him Hall said he was a poisoner: he could see noxious blue fumes emanating from his body. It was agreed that he must have suffered a stroke. 'He begins a thing, and don't finish it,' Tyson wrote in dismay. 'He begins to talk about one thing then goes off on another.' Hall continued to protest that he was being poisoned. On the night of 8 November they found him sitting up, trying to spell the word 'murder'. He died at 3.30 the following morning.

With Hall's death, the expedition was leaderless. Nobody knew what to do or who to follow. Budington was nominally in charge, but he was often drunk and the crews' allegiance vacillated between Tyson, Hubbard, Bessels

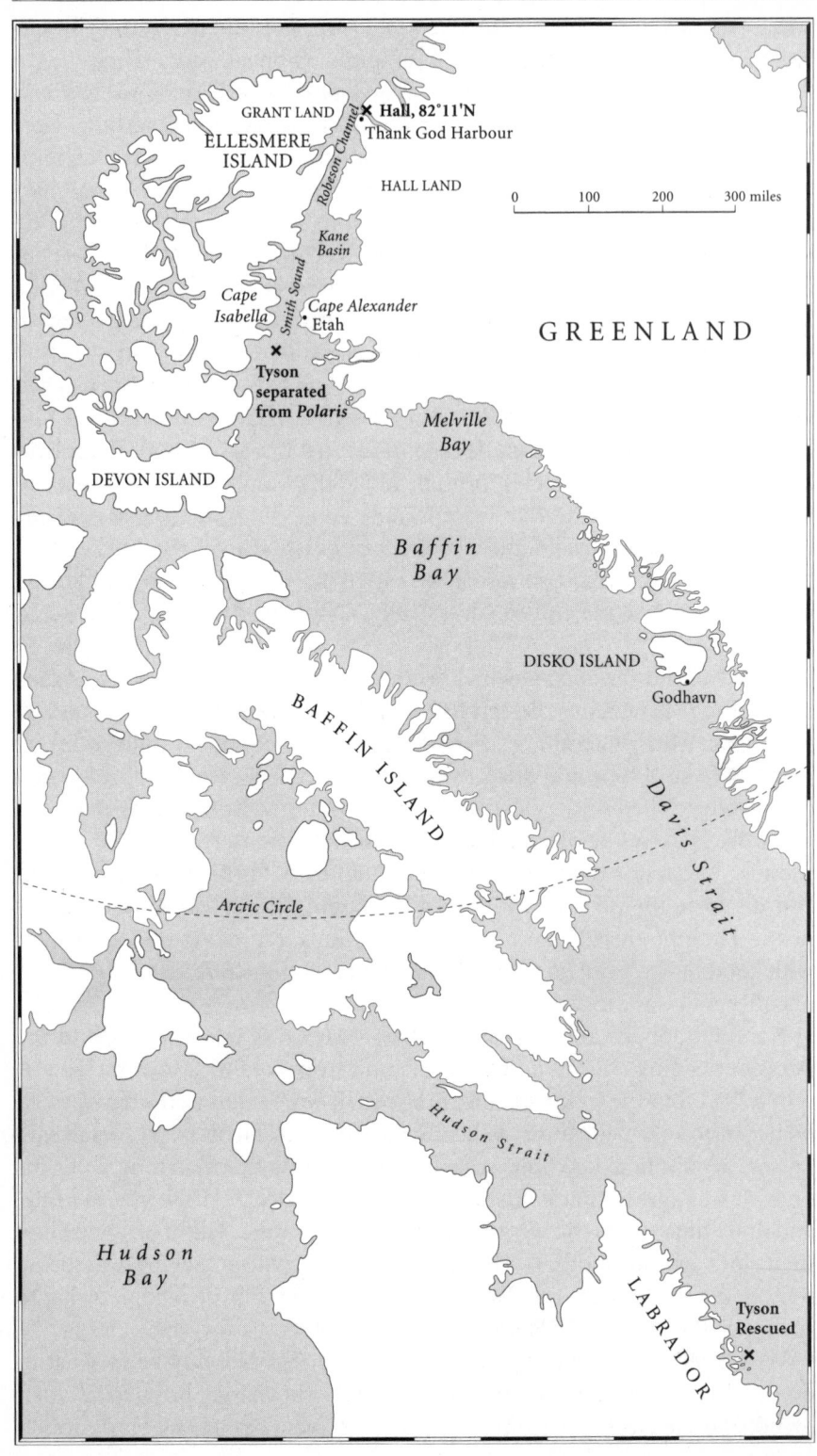

GRANT LAND ✕ **Hall, 82°11'N**
ELLESMERE
ISLAND Thank God Harbour

HALL LAND

Kane
Basin

Cape
Isabella • Cape Alexander
• Etah

✕
**Tyson
separated
from *Polaris***

GREENLAND

0   100   200   300 miles

Melville
Bay

DEVON ISLAND

*Baffin
Bay*

DISKO ISLAND
Godhavn

BAFFIN ISLAND

Davis Strait

Arctic Circle

Hudson Strait

*Hudson
Bay*

LABRADOR

**Tyson
Rescued**
✕

and one of Bessels's subordinates, a German scientist named Frederick Meyer. During the course of the winter discipline collapsed. Budington issued each man with a gun, prized open the medicine locker and allowed them free access to the spirits within. There was vague talk of sledge journeys in the spring, but nothing much came of it. 'Whoever wants to go North, let them go, but I won't,' Budington announced. All he wanted was to be free of the ice. On 12 August 1872 his wish came true: the ice broke and the *Polaris* escaped into Robeson Channel. On the same day, to everyone's surprise, Hans Hendrik's wife gave birth to a baby boy. Seeing his birth as a good omen, the crew christened him Charlie Polaris.

The ship was not free for long. Three days after leaving Thank God Harbour it was once again in the ice, drifting helplessly south at the centre of a large floe. The ship began to leak, necessitating constant use of steam pumps, but while this used up valuable coal, they were in no immediate danger. At the portal of Smith Sound, however, in the treacherous strait between Capes Isabella and Alexander, the floe began to fragment. Nuggets of ice began to jostle and crash against the *Polaris*, and then, at 6.00 p.m. on 15 October, it was struck by a massive berg. The ship was squeezed hard against a floe, and as it heeled over the engineer ran on deck, yelling that water was coming in fast. Budington ordered an immediate evacuation. The Inuit were among the first to be taken off. Then, in the teeth of a heavy storm, barrels and boxes were hurled over the side, where Tyson and a working party dragged them to the centre of the floe. For four hours the unloading continued, the men hauling food and fuel from the hold before it filled with water. But at 10.00 p.m. Tyson noticed that the *Polaris* was no lower in the water than it had been when they started. On investigation he discovered that it was not sinking at all and the whole business had been a false alarm. Irritated, he ordered his men to carry everything back to the ship. At that moment the floe cracked. The *Polaris* righted itself and vanished into the night, leaving Tyson and his men alone on the ice, drifting through one of the Arctic's most hazardous waterways.

Tyson spent the night rowing from fragment to fragment of the constantly splintering floe, rescuing what people and supplies he could. Come morning, when the blizzard died down, he spotted the *Polaris* at a distance of about ten miles, and flagged for it to come to his assistance. But Budington either did not see, or ignored, his signal. A sudden storm prevented Tyson from rowing for assistance, and when the weather cleared the *Polaris* had vanished. Their one consolation was that the storm had blown them past Capes Isabella and Alexander into the relative safety of Baffin Bay. Tyson took stock: he had under his command nine white men, predominantly Germans, led by Frederick Meyer; one black cook; four adult Inuit and their five children. To feed them he had 14 cans of pemmican, 14 hams, a can of apples and eleven and a half bags of ship's biscuit. The floe was four miles in circumference, dotted with hillocks and small lakes of fresh water. Everyone had a bag of spare clothes, plus a rifle and ammunition – except for Tyson, who had been too busy to grab any firearms for himself and possessed only the clothes he wore plus a few garments he had bagged up just in time. They had three boats and one compass, and were surrounded by thousands of other ice-blocks that, like their own, were floating placidly towards ultimate dis-integration in the Atlantic. This was Tyson's situation at the start of a journey that would continue for nine months and 2,000 miles.

Life on the floe was as anarchic as it had been aboard the *Polaris*. When a seal was shot (the Inuit showed them how) it was eaten on the spot. When rations fell low Meyer made a show of weighing out portions, but no sooner had he put his scales away than the men rifled the stores. One night they ate so much pemmican that they were sick. On another, feeling cold, they burned one of their boats. Grotesquely, they hoped that they would not be rescued too soon, on the grounds that they were still part of the expedition and would therefore be entitled to overtime. Tyson was unable to keep order: he couldn't speak German and didn't have a rifle. After a few months he found he no longer had any spare clothes either: they had been stolen. Clammy and dispirited, he sought refuge with the Inuit, their igloo being the only place he could be certain of hearing English. By Christmas they had con-sumed the last of their supplies. On New Year's Day Tyson recorded: 'I have dined today on about *two feet of frozen entrails* and a little blubber.' Throughout the winter they shot seals and the occasional bird, which was enough to keep the company alive but not to satisfy their appetites. Soon they began to eye the Inuit's children.

Cannibalism was averted by the advent of spring. Game multiplied and was theirs for the taking. But the Germans had started to strip and reassemble their rifles in the hope of improving them. As a result, few of the weapons now functioned, and the only effective hunters were the Inuit. Apart from fresh meat, spring also brought warm seas and bad weather. On 11 March 1873 an exceptionally fierce gale tore the floe to shreds. When the wind subsided their once substantial ice island had been reduced to a paltry strip measuring 75 by 100 yards. Two and a half weeks later, on 1 April, Tyson decided they were near enough to Greenland to risk an evacuation in their last remaining boat.

The embarkation was typically disorganized. Food, ammunition and other essentials were flung into the sea, as 19 people crammed themselves into a vessel that had been designed to hold eight. When they left, the boat was so low that water lapped over the edge and Hans Hendrik had to crawl between people's knees with a baling tin. The journey, through monstrous bergs and floes, was so frightful that the Germans cried aloud in terror – though they were not so terrified as to stop filching the stores when they felt hungry. Some days they rowed, others they dragged the boat onto floes so weak that they split under their weight and so small that there was standing room only. Their faces and bodies began to swell – not through scurvy but from another ailment that Tyson could not fathom. (It might have been kidney malfunction, due to lack of carbohydrates.)

On the night of the 19th, while resting on a floe, they were hit by yet another storm. Placing the children in the boat, they hung on as the waves knocked them to and fro and the wind battered them with lumps of ice. When they were ankle-deep in water, and it became apparent that the floe could no longer hold their weight, Tyson ordered them into the boat. 'This was the greatest fight for life we had had yet,' he wrote. 'How we held out I know not.' Twelve hours later, having hauled continually at the oars, they were in calm seas, exhausted, bruised, but alive. 'Man can never believe, nor pen describe, the scene we passed through,' Tyson marvelled. 'Surely we are saved by the will of God alone, and I suppose for some good purpose of his own ... Half-drowned we are, and cold enough in our wet clothes, without shelter, and not sun enough to dry us even on the outside. We have nothing to eat: everything is finished and gone. The prospect looks bad.' Fortunately, they were now in whaling waters and it could be only a question of time before they met a ship. Whether they could survive that long, however, was another matter. They rowed south from floe to floe until on the evening of 28 April they spotted a steamer flying the Stars and Stripes. But despite lighting their remaining seal blubber as a beacon, and discharging volleys of rifle-fire, they went unnoticed. It was another two days before they were finally rescued by the *Tigress*, a Newfoundland sealer, which brought them back to civilization on 9 May.

The men on the *Polaris*, meanwhile, had had almost as dreadful a time as those on the floe. Since the two parties separated, the ship had sprung a serious leak, and Budington had landed the crew on the west coast of Smith Sound. Taking to their boats, they had rowed south until they, like Tyson, reached the safety of the whaling grounds and were rescued by a Scottish whaler, the *Ravenscraig*. They were brought home not long after Tyson.

The American Arctic establishment was appalled by the disaster: but for luck, and the bravery of those involved, it might now be facing a tragedy as comprehensive and mysterious as Franklin's. True, Hall had been somewhat of an amateur, but even so there was no excuse for such a shambles. A Board of Inquiry was convened, whose members were ruthless in their examination of the expedition's failure: the incompetence, the drunkenness, the weakness of command, the insubordination, the ineffectualness of the sledge parties – every flaw, large or small, was brought to light. The Board was particularly rigorous when it came to the subject of Hall's death. It had the officers' verbal description of his demise and the conditions leading up to it, but there should also have been supporting paperwork. A ship had since visited the site of Budington's beaching in Smith Sound and had retrieved some of the officers' journals, but the relevant pages had been cut out. Where was the evidence to prove that he had not been poisoned, as he had claimed at the time? Where, in fact, was Hall's journal? Here there came a shuffling of feet.

Somebody recalled a sealed trunk that had been thrown overboard. Or had it had been left on the ice? No, it had been with them for some time but had been mislaid. Helpfully, one man remembered using some old papers to start a fire. In the absence of proof to the contrary, the Board concluded that Hall must have died of a stroke. But it was a reluctant conclusion, and although nobody was accused, neither were they completely exonerated.

The strange tale of the *Polaris* had an even stranger ending. In 1968 an American author named Chauncey Loomis was working on a biography of Hall and secured permission to exhume the body. On opening the grave he noted that Hall had decayed somewhat from water seepage, but the Arctic cold had mummified him so effectively that he was still recognizable from photographs taken in the 1860s. His hair and beard were intact; so (more or less) were his skin and his fingernails. Loomis snipped a few slivers of nail, reinterred the corpse, then brought the samples home for analysis. Laboratory tests showed that Hall's body contained toxic amounts of arsenic. Two possibilities could be inferred from this. The first was that Hall had dosed himself with arsenic, as many Victorians did to settle an uneven stomach. (Hall was prone to indigestion.) The second was that someone had poisoned him because they did not want to go further north. (From the many conflicting testimonies that the Inquiry heard there was one consistent theme: had Hall not died, he would have taken them to the Pole.) Several people had stated, on record, that they thought his voyage a delusion and the goal unattainable. But who among them could have given him the arsenic? Bessels? Budington? A rogue crewman? Maybe Tyson? No single person had both the motive and the opportunity. Hall's death, like the Pole itself, remained a mystery.

TOP   Life in the tent: Julius von Payer's exploration of Franz Josef Land, 1874.
ABOVE   The wintering of HMS *Alert* at Floeberg Beach, 1875.

TOP LEFT Adolphus Greely, leader of the US expedition to Ellesmere Island. (1881–4).
TOP RIGHT Fridtjof Nansen at Cape Flora, 1895.
ABOVE Salomon Andrée's *Eagle* fails to reach the North Pole, 1897.

OPPOSITE Fernand Foureau, conqueror of the Sahara. (1899–1900).

Le Petit Journal

ADMINISTRATION
61, RUE LAFAYETTE, 61

Les manuscrits ne sont pas rendus

On s'abonne sans frais dans tous les bureaux de poste

5 CENT.

SUPPLÉMENT ILLUSTRÉ

5 CENT.

20ᵐᵉ Année

Numéro 983

DIMANCHE 19 SEPTEMBRE 1909

ABONNEMENTS

	SIX MOIS	UN AN
SEINE et SEINE-ET-OISE..	2 fr.	3 fr. 50
DÉPARTEMENTS..........	2 fr.	4 fr. »
ÉTRANGER	2 50	5 fr. »

LA CONQUÉTE DU POLE NORD
Le docteur Cook et le commandant Peary s'en disputent la gloire

OPPOSITE The *Stella Polare* caught by an ice ridge, 1899.

ABOVE Robert Peary and Francis Cook dispute their right to the North Pole, 1909.

TOP Robert Falcon Scott (centre) and party at the South Pole, January 1912.
ABOVE LEFT Roald Amundsen, who reached the South Pole before Scott on 14 December 1911.
ABOVE RIGHT Douglas Mawson, leader of another expedition to Antartica, 1911–13.

TOP Ernest Shackleton's men hack a passage through the Weddell Sea, 1915.
ABOVE The *Italia* before the start to the North Pole, 23 May 1928.

OVERLEAF George Mallory and Edward Norton on Everest in 1922.

David Livingstone and H. M. Stanley (1871–7)

By the mid-1860s Britain's foremost African explorer was, without doubt, the Scottish missionary David Livingstone. A dogged man, studious if not scholarly, somewhat humourless and of a solitary bent, with little time for fools, Livingstone had been tramping through the continent for the past two decades. His avowed aim was to open its dark interior to the light of Christianity – in which he was successful to a certain degree – but it was for his discoveries rather than his proselytizing that he became famous. Studying his career it is hard not to conclude that he was as much interested in Africa's geographical mysteries as he was in the souls of its inhabitants. If there was a lake, river or mountain to be found, Livingstone was the one to find it – and he liked it to be known that he had done so for, despite having chosen such a lonely path, he coveted fame.

In June 1849, while stationed just over the border of South Africa's Cape Colony, Livingstone departed in search of a legendary Lake Ngami that was supposed to lie more than 500 miles to the north across the Kalahari Desert. Even the locals, with their experience of life in a semi-arid climate, had never been there. In July, after a month's journey through baked ground where the grass crumbled to dust between his fingers, Livingstone found the lake. Encouraged, he then decided he should also find a ruler who was rumoured to live some 200 miles further on and who might be receptive to Christianity. Two years later, in 1851, he succeeded in this too. And while finding the ruler (who died shortly after his arrival), he found the upper stretches of the Zambezi. He returned in 1853 and followed the river west until it petered out in a marsh that marked the watershed between it and the Congo, whereupon he marched more than 1,000 miles overland to the Portuguese-controlled port of Luanda. In 1855 he was back at the Zambezi, this time searching in an easterly direction. He followed the river to its mouth and found, as well as a number of warlike tribes, an astonishing natural feature that he named Victoria Falls.

On his return to London in December 1856 he was greeted as a hero. The President of the Royal Geographical Society announced that Livingstone had achieved 'The greatest triumph in geographical research . . . in our times'. He made countless appearances before learned bodies and gave lecture after

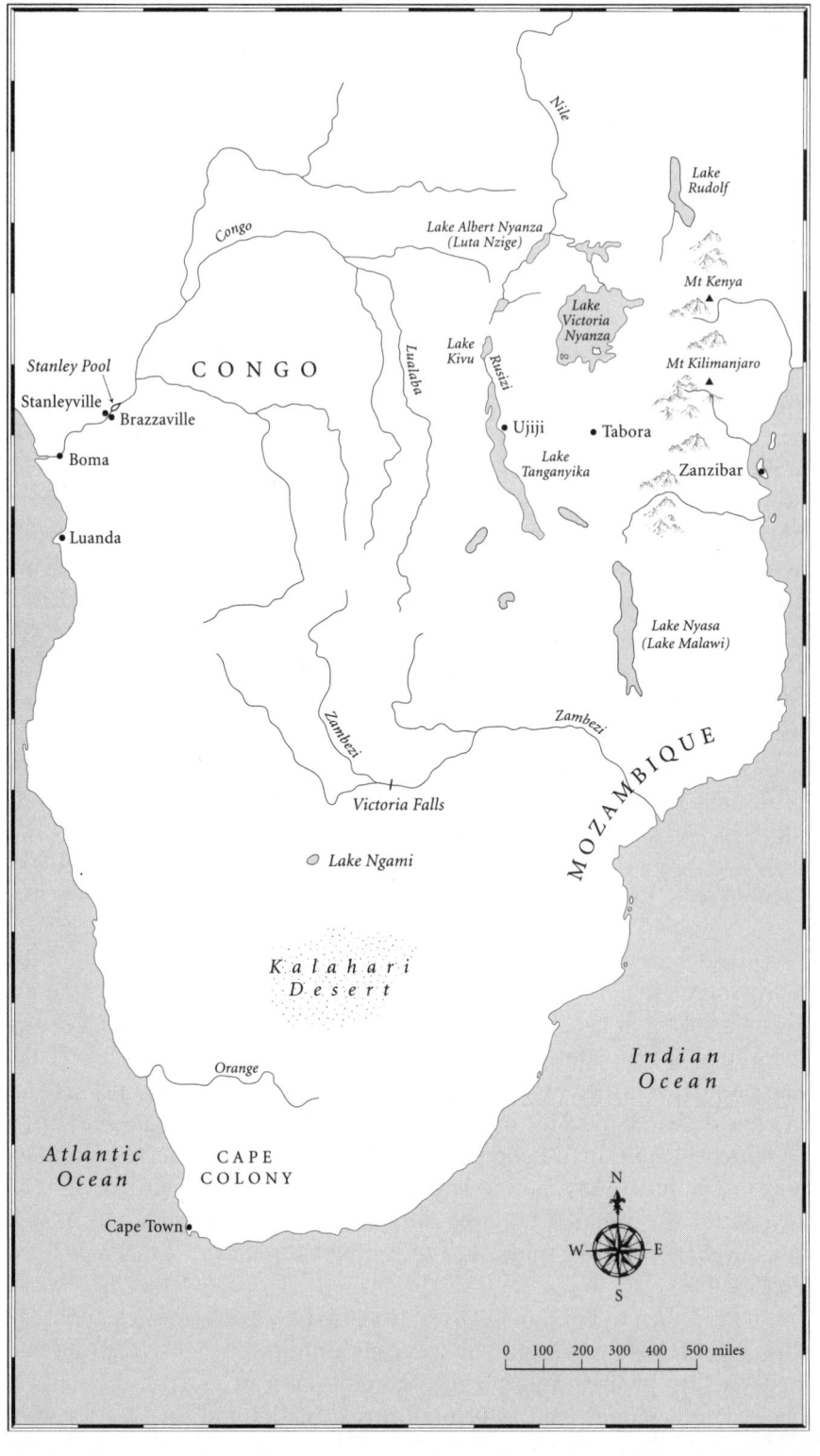

Nile

Congo

Lake
Rudolf

Lake Albert Nyanza
(*Luta Nzige*)

Mt Kenya ▲

Lualaba

Lake
Kivu

Lake
Victoria
Nyanza

Mt Kilimanjaro ▲

Stanley Pool

C O N G O

Rusizi

• Ujiji

• Tabora

Stanleyville ●
● Brazzaville

Lake
Tanganyika

Zanzibar ●

● Boma

● Luanda

Lake Nyasa
(*Lake Malawi*)

Zambezi

Zambezi

M O Z A M B I Q U E

Victoria Falls

Lake Ngami

*K a l a h a r i
D e s e r t*

*Indian
Ocean*

Orange

*Atlantic
Ocean*

CAPE
COLONY

N

Cape Town ●

W   E

S

0   100   200   300   400   500 miles

lecture, wearing always the squab, peaked hat that was his trademark. His journal was snapped up as soon as it left the press. (In 1857 the public had to make do with *Missionary Travels and Researches in South Africa*; they did not get *Narrative of an Expedition to the Zambezi and its Tributaries* until 1865.) So enormous was his fame that when the London Missionary Society complained that his travels were 'only remotely connected with the spread of the gospel', he did not bother to argue but simply resigned his membership. And when the British government offered him the post of Consul for the East Coast of Africa, with responsibility for extending Britain's knowledge of the interior and advancing thereby the dual causes of Christianity and commerce, Livingstone accepted without hesitation.

By 1858 he was back in Africa, accompanied by his brother and five other Europeans, among them the famous artist Thomas Baines. After a short time the party was swelled by a band of six missionaries who had such high hopes of Livingstone that their number included a full-blown bishop. And later on Livingstone's wife came out to join them. The expectations of the missionaries were soon dashed, however, for Livingstone seemed interested only in discovery – this time of a lake to the north of the Zambezi of which he had heard tell. By 1862 he had found and charted the lake – Lake Nyasa – but the discovery came at a cost. On the way north he and his white companions were attacked by hostile tribesmen and felt obliged to respond. Of the bloodshed Livingstone wrote in his diary: 'People will not approve of men coming out to convert people shooting them. I am sorry I am mixed up in it, as they will not care what view of my character is given at home.' His wife died of fever, as did the bishop, and the missionaries returned to Zanzibar. Livingstone continued to chart Lake Nyasa regardless, driving the column so harshly that one man wrote: 'the Doctor daily becomes more incapable of self-control. A catastrophe, or tragedy, I fear, is not far off.' Another Briton died and two others went home. Undeterred, Livingstone pressed on, uncovering as he did so instances of the slave trade that was still being plied by the Portuguese. However, reports of his mania had already filtered back to London, and in 1863 he received a letter demanding his immediate return. When he got home in 1864 it was to official coolness. It was felt that he had overstepped the mark; and although there was no absolute censure, it was noted that he had done little to promote British interests and, if anything, had left the region less stable than when he arrived. Moreover, his outspoken comments about Portugal's involvement in slavery did not please the royal family: Queen Victoria's husband, Prince Albert, was the cousin of King Pedro of Portugal.

Yet there were some who still saw Livingstone as the most capable explorer the nation possessed – the man best placed to answer a question that in 1864 burned brighter than ever: where was the source of the Nile? Livingstone thought little of Baker, Burton, Grant and Speke and scoffed at the idea of the Nile originating either in Victoria Nyanza or Lake Tanganyika. His own theory, far more Ptolemaic, was that an as yet undiscovered lake lay far to the south and was connected via Tanganyika to Albert Nyanza and thence to the Nile. The Royal Geographical Society and a well-to-do industrial chemist named James Young donated £1,500 to help him prove his point. In 1865 Livingstone left once again for Africa. It was, primarily, a journey of discovery, but he also stated his intention to uncover the truth about the slave trade.

For the next five years silence reigned, and by 1871 the world was wondering what had happened to him. Had he died of fever? Had he been murdered by some slave trader in the employ of the Portuguese? Or was he still alive, in need of rescue? The image of a brave missionary risking his life to save the heathen was irresistible – a fact that did not escape the attention of James Gordon Bennett, proprietor of the *New York Herald*. One of the most astute newspapermen of the age, Bennett knew very well what big news Livingstone's return or rescue would be. He decided, therefore, to make it happen. Summoning one of his correspondents, he told him to raise an expedition to East Africa. He could have as much money as he needed – one thousand, two thousand, three thousand, whatever it took – but he was not to return without having found Livingstone. The reporter's name was Henry Morton Stanley.

A moustachioed 27-year-old, Stanley had led an adventurous life. Born the illegitimate son of a Welshwoman, he had worked variously as teacher, shop assistant and errand boy before running away to sea. Jumping ship in America, he served on both sides in the American Civil War before joining the US Navy, from which he subsequently deserted to become a journalist. It was his successful reporting of a war in Abyssinia that drew him to the attention of Bennett, who saw in this socially insecure but undeniably tough and capable man the very person who might best find Livingstone.

Stanley arrived in Zanzibar on 7 January 1871 and set about organizing one of the best equipped caravans yet to enter the interior. Shotguns, rifles, muskets, pistols, ammunition, food, tents, medicine and trade goods were purchased in quantity and at great expense. There were also two boats for river travel which, when added to the other supplies, brought the expedition's baggage to a remarkable six tons. To carry this immense load Stanley hired 157 porters, and against the eventuality of hostile tribesmen he also hired a 20-strong escort under a man named Bombay, who had served with Speke and Burton (and who had a large gap in his teeth where Speke had struck him for insubordination). What with interpreters, hangers-on and two white assistants he had picked up in Zanzibar, the expedition that left for the interior on 6 February numbered almost 200 men.

Stanley's plan was to head for Ujiji on Lake Tanganyika, where he hoped, if not to find Livingstone, then at least to learn something of his whereabouts. The journey took him nine long months, during which his progress was hindered by rains, floods, disease and obstructive rulers. His two assistants died early on; he himself spent long periods in a feverish coma; and the porters deserted in dribs and drabs, taking their loads with them. But Stanley did not let such troubles deter him. He responded to any signs of disobedience or discontent with the lash. Deserters were chased, recaptured and flogged before being chained by the neck. If local rulers sought to impede him he attacked them. Rather than indulge in time-wasting haggling, he permitted his men to plunder villages. In this manner, Stanley hacked his way through both the landscape and its inhabitants until, in the first week of November, he was within a few days' march of Ujiji. Here, he learned from a number of sources, dwelled an old white man with a long beard. It could only be Livingstone. 'At last,' he wrote, 'the sublime hour has arrived!'

Arraying himself in his smartest outfit, he led his men into Ujiji, ordering them to fire their guns in greeting. Assuming they were under attack, the people of Ujiji prepared to flee, but were reassured by the sight of Stanley, in polished boots, white flannels and freshly chalked pith helmet, marching at the head of his column. In the main square Stanley saw a European walking towards him, dressed in grey tweed trousers, a red-sleeved waistcoat and a blue cap encircled by a gold band. All of a sudden the Stanley who had battled his way through Africa was unmanned by the niceties of etiquette. Uncertain how to behave, he extended his hand and said, 'Dr Livingstone, I presume?' To which Livingstone smiled, raised his cap very slightly, and replied, 'Yes.'

Reports differ as to what happened next. Stanley's account suggests that Livingstone was overjoyed to see him and declared, 'You have brought me new life.' Others say that Livingstone was in no need of rescue, that he gave Stanley the first good meal he had had in months, and on learning that he had been 'saved' by the *New York Herald* was openly contemptuous. (The *Herald*, under Bennett's ownership, had acquired a reputation for scandalmongering.) Whatever the truth, the two men got on well. Stanley hero-worshipped Livingstone, openly and without qualification. Livingstone, for his part, took to the newcomer – especially when Stanley offered to help explore Lake Tanganyika.

A week after Stanley's arrival the two were aboard a canoe with 20 men, paddling towards the lake's northern shore. Here, at last, they determined that the Rusizi flowed into the lake rather than out of it, finally settling the question of whether Tanganyika might be the source of the Nile. During their 28-day round trip they covered 300 miles. Back in Ujiji, Livingstone declared it had been 'a picnic'. However, he was no nearer finding an alternative source, which he suspected might be the River Lualaba, to the west of Lake Tanganyika. He asked Stanley if he would accompany him, but Stanley declined: he had to go home to file his report. On 27 December they left for the town of Tabora, Livingstone to obtain supplies for his new odyssey, Stanley to continue east to Zanzibar. When they parted Stanley took out his regrets on his men. 'No more weakness,' he wrote. 'I shall show them such marching as will make them remember me. In forty days I shall do what took me three months to perform before.' In fact, it took them 35 days. An observer who was present at Stanley's arrival was shocked by his appearance: he was emaciated, his hair had turned grey, and he looked more like a man in his forties than his twenties.

While Stanley basked in praise (albeit mixed with sneering from the Royal Geographical Society, who resented an American having 'discovered' a Briton), Livingstone proceeded on his quest for the Nile. It was to be his last journey. He crossed Lake Tanganyika, surmounted a range of hills beyond and then, weakened by dysentery, began to falter. By 22 April 1873 he could no longer walk, and had to be carried in a litter. 'I encourage myself in the Lord my God, and go forward,' he wrote. On the night of 30 April, just three days from the Lualaba, he knelt by his bed to pray. He was in the same position when his men discovered him the following morning, dead. They buried his heart and left the body to dry for two weeks in the sun. Then they wrapped it in canvas and bark, slung it on a pole, and began the long trek back to the coast. Almost a year after his death, Livingstone was given a state funeral in Westminster Abbey. Stanley, the principal pallbearer, swore to continue the struggle: 'Another sacrifice to Africa! His mission, however, must not be allowed to cease; others must go forward and fill the gap. "Close up, boys! Close up! Death must find us everywhere."'

In August 1874, backed by not only the *New York Herald* but also Britain's *Daily Telegraph*, Stanley sailed once again for Zanzibar. With 347 porters, guides and dependants, laden with rifles, the expedition that marched for the Lualaba on 17 November was even bigger and more extravagant than the one he had raised to rescue Livingstone, and it followed the same pattern. Two of the three Britons Stanley took with him died after a few months; he himself was stricken by fever (by Christmas he was 42 pounds lighter than when he had left Zanzibar); the porters deserted, and when recaptured were flogged and chained; the column pillaged indiscriminately; and battle after battle was fought when the way was blocked. Stanley forced his men (and himself) to ever greater endeavour. After 103 days in the field he consulted his pedometer and discovered the column had covered 720 miles – a distance that he reckoned would have taken a standard caravan between nine months and a year.

Among the porters' baggage were the five sections of the *Lady Alice*, a craft designed by Stanley, which was used to explore both Victoria Nyanza and Lake Tanganyika and which was reassembled in November 1876 when at last they reached the Lualaba. Anticipating trouble, Stanley acquired the support of a prominent Arab trader, whose 700 warriors turned the already well-armed expedition into a small army more than 1,000 strong. Thus reinforced, Stanley proceeded downriver to the Nile. Actually, he was uncertain whether the Lualaba led to the Nile or the Congo: from what he had seen and read, it seemed too powerful to be part of the Nile system. Nevertheless, having come so far, he was not going to turn back. In a morale-boosting speech he announced, 'I am not going to leave this river until I reach the sea.' His escort departed shortly thereafter.

Stanley's journey, through territory no European had ever seen, was hard. He was attacked by tribesmen who fired poisoned arrows from the riverbank. Sometimes they came at him, 2,000 strong, in canoes. After one night ashore, Stanley found his camp had been quietly encircled by nets and a carpet of cane splinters. The attacks continued for a distance of more than 1,000 miles. Always, his well-armed force managed to blow its way through human opposition; nevertheless, the spears and arrows took a gradual toll on his men – as did the river itself.

On 6 January 1877 the expedition met the first of a series of seven cataracts that extended, interspersed with rapids, for more than 50 miles. At every cataract the *Lady Alice* and its accompanying canoes – cumbersome, 50-foot lengths of hollowed-out tree trunk – had to be hauled overland using cables made of rattan creeper cut from the surrounding forest. By day they were tormented by ants; by night they toiled in the light of gum-soaked bundles of reeds. During the portages, and in the narrower stretches of rapids, they were attacked repeatedly; canoes overturned; men drowned, baggage and weapons were lost. After one particularly bad capsizing, three men were stranded on a rock on the very brink of a waterfall (one of them actually went over the edge, but at the last moment grabbed a rope thrown to him by his crewmates). Stanley described his predicament in dramatic terms: 'A Fall 50 yards in width separated the island from us, and to the right was a Fall about 300 yards wide, and below them was half a mile of Falls and Rapids and great whirlpools and waves rising like hills in the middle of the terrible stream, and below these were the cannibals of Mane-Mukwa.' It took a day and a night of failed attempts before Stanley finally flung the stranded men a line strong enough to bear their weight.

By the end of the month they were free of the cataracts (which Stanley felt justified in naming after himself) and on 7 February they enjoyed a day in which they did not have to kill someone. That same day Stanley noted that the river (rechristened by him the Livingstone River) had taken a decisive turn to the west. It could not, therefore, be the Nile, but was – as locals for the first time began to call it – the Congo. He continued downriver, in conditions that became ever more alarming. One day they fought a five-hour running battle against tribesmen who harried them from the banks and chased them in canoes. On another they strode through a deserted village strewn with skulls and bones that, to Stanley, displayed all the marks of cannibalism. Increasingly, their adversaries used muskets instead of bows – a good sign in that it meant they were within reach of European traders, but bad in that Stanley could no longer rely on the total superiority of his weapons. In mid-March, having survived a total of 32 major battles and countless minor skirmishes, the flotilla reached a pool 15 miles wide and 17 long where the locals, for once, seemed friendly. They had travelled 1,235 miles in 128 days, had lost half the 100 guns with which they had started, had used most of their ammunition and trade goods, and were reduced in number to less than 150. Pausing only to name their haven Stanley Pool (later to be the site of Stanleyville, capital of Belgian Congo and, across the river, Brazzaville, capital of French Congo), Stanley led his depleted force to the sea, as he had promised he would.

Stanley Pool flowed into a chain of gorges, rapids and waterfalls that ran for 155 miles before widening, at the town of Boma, into a placid, navigable waterway. The portages were worse even than Stanley Falls: at every cataract – all 32 of them – they had to hack a path for their vessels, using felled trunks to create a rolling tramway over which they dragged the canoes. They hauled in and out of jungle and up and down hills, were plagued by insects and disease, and suffered the usual calamities in the rapids. On 3 June a canoe containing Stanley's last white companion, a man named Pocock, overturned in a whirlpool. Pocock came to the surface, unconscious, but could not be rescued before he was carried downstream. Two African canoeists were also lost. By mid-July 12 canoes and 13 men had vanished into the Congo, along with most of the expedition's trade goods and weapons. 'Had I the least suspicion that such a terrible series of Falls were before us, I should never have risked so many lives and such amount of money,' Stanley wrote. Shortly afterwards, one of his most capable men went mad and wandered into the jungle, carrying nothing but a parrot on a stick. 'Poor Safeni, how will he fare now!' Stanley lamented. 'I cannot stay as my goods are terribly short. I must haste, haste away from this hateful region of death, terror and barbarism.'

Still, he was not blind to what he had achieved. Summarizing the journey, he wrote in self-congratulation that he and his men had 'attacked and destroyed 28 large towns and three or four score villages, fought 32 battles on land and water, contended with 52 Falls and Rapids, constructed about 30 miles of tramway through Forests, hauled our canoes and boat up a mountain 1,500 feet high, then over mountains 6 miles, then lowered them down the slope to the river, lifted by rough mechanical skill our canoes up gigantic boulders, 12, 15 and 20 feet high ... [and] obtained as booty in wars over $50,000 worth of ivory.' All this had come about thanks to his extraordinary physical toughness and determination. It was also due to the bravery of the Zanzibaris and other Africans, who had faced great hardship, constant danger, and not only the risk but the actuality of death, while helping their white employer find the goal he had set himself.

On 31 July the expedition was within six days' march of Boma. With four more cataracts to go, Stanley abandoned the canoes and the *Lady Alice* – 'to bleach and rot to dust' – and led the men overland. Unfortunately, his few remaining trade goods had no value this far west, and after three foodless days the column was starving. Stanley sent four messengers ahead, with a plea for help from any European who might be in Boma. He asked first for grain or rice 'to fill [my men's] pinched bellies immediately', secondly for cloth that he could use as barter, and thirdly for any spare luxuries that might appeal to a man who had been without them for so long. The messengers returned with all he required. ('Ye Gods! Just think, three bottles of pale ale,' Stanley marvelled.) And on 17 October 1877, precisely 1,000 days after it had left Zanzibar, the column limped into Boma.

From Boma it took them two days by steamboat to reach the mouth of the Congo, where Stanley sent dispatches to the *Telegraph* and *Herald* announcing his completion of the first east-west traverse of the continent, in which he had not only settled (barring unforeseen eventualities) the question of the Nile but had traced the Congo from start to finish. Never one to undersell himself, he also sent an article outlining the benefits that would spring from his discoveries. Forgetting conveniently the horrors of the cataracts, he painted the Congo as 'the great highway of commerce to broad Africa'. In due course these words would come back to haunt him.

After eight days' rest he and the remainder of his team caught a Portuguese gunboat to Luanda, the capital of Angola, where Stanley rejected the offer of speedy transport to Europe. It would be dereliction of duty, he explained, if he went home without seeing his men safely back to Zanzibar. More than two-thirds of them were sick, and all suffered from what Stanley described as 'a state of torpid brooding from which it was impossible to arouse them'. To this peculiar malady – whose symptoms resemble shellshock – he ascribed the deaths of a further eight men on the long journey via Cape Town and Durban to the coast of East Africa. More likely, however, they died from the various diseases, ranging from dropsy to dysentery, that they had contracted during their trek. When the British warship HMS *Industry* finally dropped anchor at Zanzibar, the expedition had been reduced to less than a third of its original strength: of the original 347 there remained only 88 men and 13 women, along with six children who had been born on the way. They all disappeared into obscurity, leaving Stanley to collect the honours on their behalf.

Stanley was, himself, in a state of shock and disability after the epic journey. In a photograph taken shortly after his return he appears little more than a skeleton: his normally fleshy jowls are drawn tight to the jaw; his cheekbones protrude; his nose is pinched and hook-like; his semi-hooded eyes stare hauntedly into the distance; and his hair is white. The only indi-cation that he is in his mid-thirties rather than his fifties is the black, drooping moustache that covers his upper lip.

In August 1879 Stanley was back at the mouth of the Congo. King Leopold II of Belgium had noted his earlier remarks about the river being a highway of African commerce, and was further intrigued by reports of the region's wealth – particularly in rubber, which was then a boom commodity. He asked Stanley to explore the Congo basin and claim as much of it as he could for Belgium before a rival explorer, Pierre Savorgnan de Brazza, did the same for France. Actually, the land would belong to Leopold personally rather than to Belgium, but the king assured Stanley of his good intentions and offered him a high-ranking post in the future colony. Stanley drove his men with such ferocity that he became known as *Bula Matari*, 'Breaker of Stones'. The so-called 'Congo Free State' that he helped create became a byword for oppression, in which Leopold's lieutenants operated without restraint, encouraging their workers with the threat of amputation if they did not meet quotas. Leopold reneged on his promise, fobbing him off with a medal and a consultancy fee. Eighteen eighty-seven found Stanley yet again on the Congo, leading an armed force to the other side of Africa, where a minor governor of the Sudan, Emin Pasha, needed assistance. Emin Pasha having been rescued in typically forceful style, and the continent having been traversed yet again, this time from west to east, Stanley returned to London.

It was his last foray into Africa. Retiring to an uneasy marriage, recurring bouts of malaria and a limp political career, Stanley found himself the subject of controversy. Members of the 1887–9 rescue mission made public horrendous acts that, although committed neither by Stanley nor with his approval, had nevertheless been part of the undertaking. One officer described how some of their African associates had butchered and eaten a young girl before his very eyes. Then, in the early 1900s, reports began to emerge of Leopold's 'Congo Free State' – of the millions killed and the millions more maimed in order to line the King of Belgium's pockets. Stanley had had little to do with the colony's day-to-day operations and, like much of the rest of the world, had been taken in by Leopold's assertion that he was engaged in a worthy programme of enlightenment. But his association with the place – and his support of Leopold's programme in the press – left an indelible stain.

Stanley suffered a stroke in 1903 and died of pleurisy the following year. He had always wanted to be remembered in the same breath as Livingstone, and on his deathbed asked his wife where she thought he should be buried. 'Westminster,' she replied supportively. 'Yes,' he replied, 'they will put me beside Livingstone.' But they never did. He was cremated and his ashes were buried near his home in Pirbright, Surrey. Arguably Britain's most effective – if also one of its most ruthless – African explorer, he had survived just long enough to see his life's work exposed as one of the more unsavoury episodes in Europe's scramble for Africa.

Carl Weyprecht and Julius von Payer (1872–4)

August Petermann was not disappointed by the *Hansa* calamity of 1869–70. If anything, it vindicated his theory: the current that had carried Hegemann south was clearly a branch of the Gulf Stream, but one so diminished as to make northward progress impracticable in that area. If Teutonic navigators were to find a true 'thermometric gateway' they should try for the point where the Gulf Stream hit the Arctic pack somewhere above Scandinavia or Russia. He appreciated that Germany had its hands full, what with the Franco-Prussian War, but Austria-Hungary was free – not only free but keen, if Captain Carl Weyprecht was to be believed.

In 1871 Weyprecht took a ship to the seas above the Siberian coast and found that the Arctic pack was considerably weaker than he had anticipated. Indeed, north of the islands of Novaya Zemlya it comprised a jumble of loose floes through which he would have been able to barge with ease had he had a steam vessel. In December of that year, before a congress of German and Austrian scientists, he declared publicly his faith in Petermann: 'The Gulfstream theory of Dr. Petermann ... has been fully confirmed ... we are convinced that a well-managed and energetically-managed expedition *must succeed* in reaching far higher latitudes in this sea than on any other point of the earth.' It was time, he said, for the Habsburg Empire to join the race for the North Pole.

On 14 July 1872 the newly built *Admiral Tegetthoff* left Bremerhaven with a crew selected from every corner of the Austro-Hungarian Empire – Slavs, Austrians, Hungarians, Italians and even a couple of alpine guides from the Tyrol who spoke a dialect quite incomprehensible to the others. The expedition had two commanders: at sea, Weyprecht was in charge; but when they reached land (as he was sure they would) Julius von Payer, who had participated in Germany's 1869 foray to Greenland, was to take control. Officers and crew were supremely confident that this would be the most successful polar expedition to date. They had supplies to last 1,000 days, their ship had a 100-horsepower engine, making it one of the most powerful vessels to have entered Arctic waters, and their route had been chosen by Germany's most respected geographer. A support ship had deposited a cache of food and fuel on Novaya Zemlya just in case they were forced to retreat

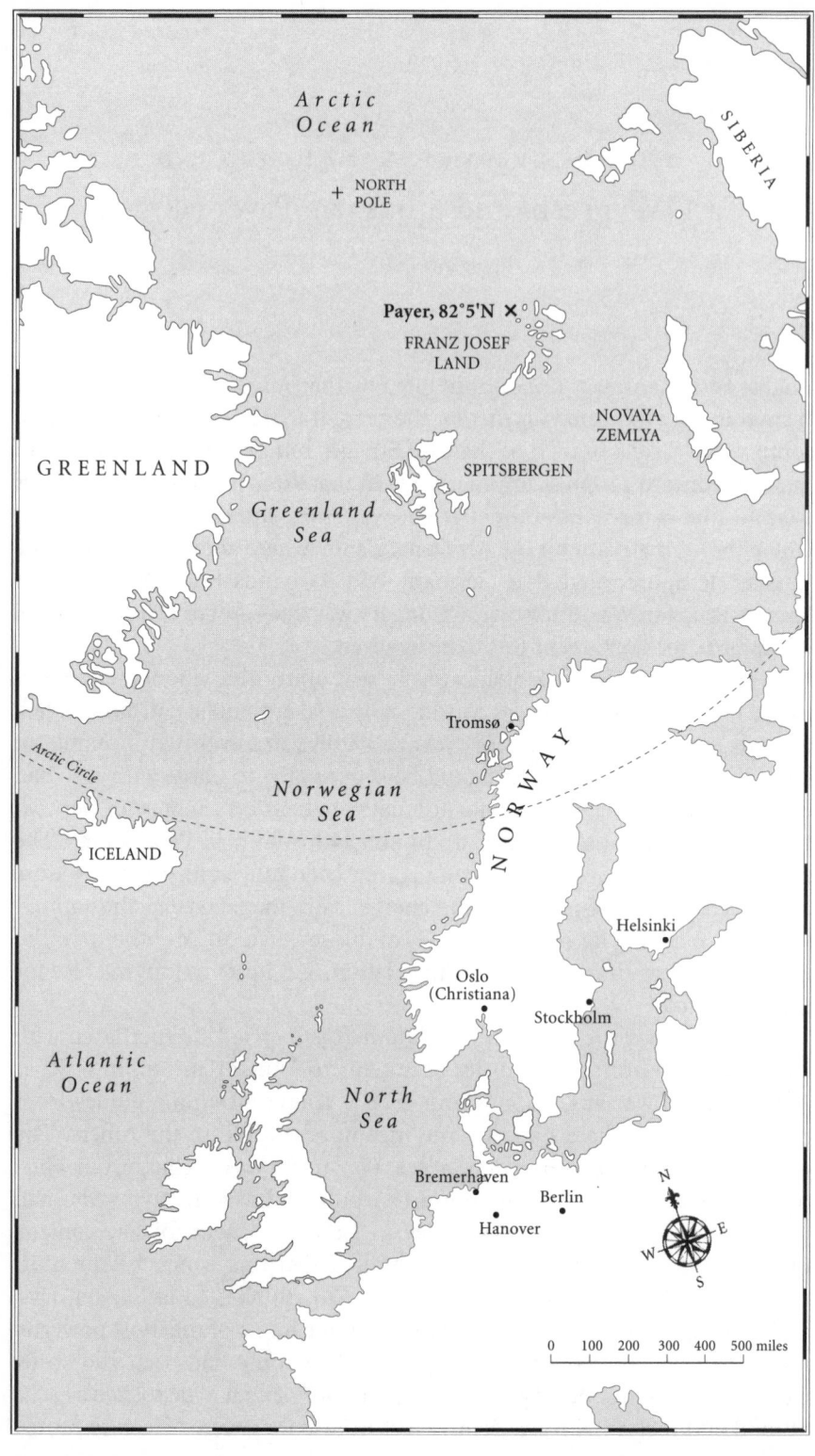

Arctic
Ocean

+ NORTH
POLE

SIBERIA

Payer, 82°5'N ✕

FRANZ JOSEF
LAND

NOVAYA
ZEMLYA

GREENLAND

Greenland
Sea

SPITSBERGEN

Tromsø

N O R W A Y

Norwegian
Sea

Arctic Circle

ICELAND

Helsinki

Oslo
(Christiana)

Stockholm

Atlantic
Ocean

North
Sea

Bremerhaven

Berlin

Hanover

N

W   E

S

0   100 200 300 400 500 miles

in their boats. But they were certain they would not need it. The sea was going to be clear all the way to the top of the world.

By 21 August the *Tegetthoff* was frozen solidly in the pack and being carried helplessly north. Petermann had been right: the Gulf Stream did continue towards the Pole. He had also been wrong: it very palpably did not melt the ice as it went. The *Tegetthoff* was in the worst position a ship could be: unable to move, at the mercy of every random whim of the pack, and heading into uncharted seas from which there was no obvious means of escape. 'We were no longer discoverers, but passengers against our will,' wrote Payer. 'From day to day we hoped for the hour of our deliverance! At first we expected it hourly, then from week to week; then at seasons of the year and changes of the weather, then in the chances of new year! But that hour never came.'

After two months of drifting the *Tegetthoff* met its first test. On 13 October a pressure ridge rose up and threatened to crush it. The two commanders ordered every man on deck, prepared boats, sledges and provisions, and waited for the moment when they would have to abandon ship. Four suspenseful days later the ice subsided and they were able to return to quarters. But it was not long before another pressure ridge came their way and the procedure had to be repeated. No sooner had that ridge abated than a new one arose. It continued month after month. 'Daily – for one hundred and thirty days – we went through the same experience in greater or lesser measure, almost always in sunless darkness,' Payer wrote. By March 1873 the ice had calmed and the sun had reappeared. But they were engulfed by mists so thick that they could not see where the current was taking them. Come summer they were at latitude 79° 43' N and should by rights have encountered open water – Weyprecht had penetrated to 79° in 1871 – but still the pack held them. Weyprecht and Payer were pondering an escape over the ice when, on 30 August, a miracle happened: at midday, for a brief moment, the mists cleared and they saw a chain of mountains on the north-eastern horizon. Abruptly they forgot their suffering and broke out the grog. Here was a landmass – which they christened Franz Josef Land after their emperor – that would lead to the Pole.

Payer, who had become increasingly impatient while at sea, was beside himself with excitement. But the pack was too broken for sledge or boat travel and, to his frustration, the wind now began to blow them south. When they eventually resumed their northward course it was with such impetuosity that they were nearly crushed against the ice surrounding Franz Josef Land. The *Tegetthoff* splintered beneath their feet as they rushed on to the deck clutching their escape bundles. 'As we watched the advancing wall of ice, and heard the too well-known howl it sent forth, and saw how fissures were formed at the edge of the floe, the days of the ice-pressures were painfully recalled,' Payer wrote. 'And the thought constantly returned – what will be the end of all this?'

It was November before the pack settled and Payer managed to set foot on Franz Josef Land. It was utterly barren, apparently lifeless and possessed of only the meagrest vegetation. But after so many months at sea '[it] had to us all the charms of a landscape in Ceylon'. Moreover, 'there was something sublime to the imagination in the utter loneliness of a land never before visited'. Payer made a brief examination of the immediate coast, erected a cairn in which he placed a note claiming this desolate spot for the emperor, and raised a silk flag bearing the Habsburg double-headed eagle. Then he returned to the *Tegetthoff* to await the arrival of spring, when improved weather conditions would allow a fuller examination of Austria-Hungary's latest possession.

Weyprecht did not share Payer's enthusiasm. While the discovery of Franz Josef Land made their harrowing drift worthwhile, it was not the end of their voyage – that would come only when his ship and his men were safely home. How, though, was this to be achieved? Their supplies were now at a point where they would have to leave by May 1874 at the latest. If the ice was as unrelenting the following year as it had been the previous two, there was no hope of the *Tegetthoff* breaking free. Therefore, they would have to man-haul their boats over the pack until they met open water – a journey of at least 100 miles, fraught with pressure ridges and uncertain floes – then sail for Novaya Zemlya, where the caches that they had never expected to use now seemed increasingly important. But would the men be equal to such a monumental task? Most of them were suffering from mild scurvy, and although there were polar bears to be shot off Franz Josef Land – that winter they killed 67 – the fresh meat was insufficient to keep the disease at bay for long. Accordingly, Weyprecht gave Payer the following ultimatum: he could lead three expeditions in spring; if the ice broke, however, the *Tegetthoff* would sail; if he was aboard, fair and good; if he was not, they would leave a boat and a stock of food; from that point he would be on his own.

Payer was beginning to detest Weyprecht. A poet and alpinist at heart, he had little in common with the stern naval man who was his superior. They had already quarrelled so fiercely that at one point Weyprecht had pulled a revolver on him. In a fit of defiance Payer accepted the conditions. But he accepted too the gravity of their situation. By 15 January the ship's engineer, one Otto Krisch, was so weakened by scurvy that he no longer had the strength to write his daily journal. By February the sick ward was filling up. On 10 March 1874 Payer took his first party out. It was not a success. They met temperatures so low that their breath fell to the ground with an audible tinkle – a phenomenon known as 'angels' tears' in Siberia. Their woollen outfits turned to stone, their eyelids froze shut, their beards became bleached, and in between bouts of constipation and diarrhoea they urinated blood. One scorbutic man had to be sent back to the ship. When he arrived he was speechless with cold, and blood was seeping from his pores. Weyprecht raised the man's arm, swivelled him until he pointed in the direction from which he had come, and leaped forthwith onto Franz Josef Land. Wearing no protective clothing, he trudged after the bedraggled party. To Payer he appeared like an apparition from the Bible: 'Suddenly I saw Weyprecht coming towards me among the crags of ice: a figure in white – beard, hair, eyebrows, clothing, all stiff with ice. The shawl around his mouth had frozen fast.' Weyprecht turned them about and personally – if irritably – escorted them back to the ship.

Payer's next foray was no more successful. Roped to a single Tyrolean guide, he was crossing a glacier when he felt a tug on his rope. He dropped at once to the ground and dug his ice-axe as deep as it would go. Behind him the rope broke as the guide fell into a crevasse, carrying with him the sledge, the dogs that were pulling it, and all their supplies. Looking into the hole, Payer heard a stream of Tyrolean invective and a faint howl from the dogs. Reassured that they were still alive, he leaped the gap – ten feet across – and ran for assistance. His previous journey had been cold, but now, by freak chance, the weather was hot and his Arctic gear hindered him. As he ran he discarded items of clothing. Off went his leggings, then his boots (feather-lined, from Greenland), then his hat, scarf and gloves. Sprinting through the snow in his stockings, he saw a small black dot – the tent in which he had left the three men who were his reserve party. For an age, it seemed, he ran, and the black dot looked no bigger – then suddenly he was upon it. Pausing only for a gulp of brandy, he led his men back to the crevasse, where they pulled the guide, the dogs and the sledge to the surface. After toasting themselves on a successful mission – Payer noticed that the guide had enjoyed a toast or two himself while down the crevasse – they forged onwards.

It was a dispiriting journey. At every turn they expected to make some momentous discovery, to see something – anything – that would reward them for their effort. But they never did. Of one mountain Payer wrote: 'We climbed up onto its ice-covered spine; full of high expectation we stood on its summit. To the north lay an indescribable wasteland, more desolate than any I ever met in the Arctic.' Wherever they went the same frigid scene presented itself. On 12 April, at a latitude of 82° 5' N, Payer finally abandoned the quest. There was nothing to be gained by continuing. In Payer's esti-mation Franz Josef Land was an archipelago, of approximately the same size as Spitsbergen, and certainly did not lead to a larger polar landmass. Nor did he believe for one minute that if he travelled to its furthest tip he would find anything other than ice. Petermann, and others, had conjectured that there might be an open sea at the pole, but Payer condemned this as a 'venial exaggeration', an 'antiquated hypothesis'. He built another cairn to mark their furthest north and deposited a message detailing his discoveries. To it he appended a terse note: 'After [the sledge party's] return to the ship it is the intention of the whole crew to leave this land and return home. The hopeless condition of the ship and the numerous cases of sickness constrain them to this step.'

As they struggled back to the *Tegetthoff* they were hampered by another burst of warm weather. The snow turned to slush, in which they sank to their waists. Sometimes, when skirting the coast, they fell through the ice. This was good news in a way, because it meant the *Tegetthoff* would be able to steam to freedom. It was also bad news: the ship might have already left, as Weyprecht had threatened. Redoubling their efforts, they reached the coast on 19 April, so exhausted that they could hardly stand. To their dismay their path was blocked by open sea. 'Pieces of ice tossed and tumbled about as if playing some carefree game for our amusement,' wrote Payer, 'as if nothing had changed in the least for this small band of men, who in reality found themselves before an impassable abyss.' He climbed a nearby mountain, from whose peak he saw the familiar outline of the *Tegetthoff* and a string of floes that led towards it. Picking their way over the pack, they at last regained the safety of their ship. The ice may have melted around Franz Josef Land, but the *Tegetthoff* was still fast. Weyprecht permitted Payer one last expedition – to investigate a nearby island – but after that their bargain was complete. On 20 May he ordered the evacuation to Novaya Zemlya.

Nobody in the annals of Arctic exploration has ever undertaken a journey such as that of the Austro-Hungarians during their retreat from Franz Josef Land. It was approximately 400 miles to Novaya Zemlya. Across this distance Weyprecht expected his men to drag three heavy whaling boats, burdened with 4,000 pounds of supplies. Even in winter, when the ice was firm, this would have been a hard task. In the spring, with the floes separating and the ice mushy, it was nigh impossible. The boats were so overladen that they could only haul one at a time. They chopped through pressure ridges so high that by the time they returned to the boats the ice had shifted and a new path had to be cut. Here they waded thigh-deep through a bog of newly melted snow. There they unloaded a boat to cross a few score yards of open water. And they had to repeat it all three times, once for each boat. The magnitude of their ordeal can be gauged by the fact that after two months' backbreaking toil they had travelled only nine miles.

On they went. Weyprecht enticed them with the prospect of Novaya Zemlya. There they would surely meet ships. If there were no ships then they would sail their boats to Norway. It was only 1,000 miles or so, and the provisions their supply ship had deposited were more than enough for the journey. What Weyprecht did not reveal was that the pack was moving north faster than they trudged south. 'Every lost day is not a nail but a whole plank in our coffin,' he wrote. 'Dragging the sledges over the ice is only a bluff, for the few miles we gain are of no importance to our purpose. The slightest breeze moves us about in random directions far more than the most exhausting day of labour ... I put on an unconcerned face to all this, but I am very much aware that we are probably lost if conditions do not change radically.' In his own mind there was only one solution: he and the other officers had pistols; when the time came they would use them on themselves. The crew would have to look to their own salvation. 'I sometimes feel as if I were not involved at all. I have resolved what I shall do if worse comes to worst, which is why I am so calm. But the fate of the sailors lies heavy on my heart.'

As the trek progressed the men began to fight with each other. Then they fought with the officers. After a while the officers fought among themselves. Their anger was directed at Weyprecht for having made them undertake such a march. Payer told him to his face that he intended to kill him as soon as it became clear they would not reach safety. Weyprecht must have been an extraordinary leader, for not only did he put Payer in his place, but he also cajoled the crew into continuing their journey. His efforts were rewarded on 15 August when the pack suddenly opened before them. They clambered into their boats and rowed for Novaya Zemlya. When the wind and ice allowed, they raised sail, but mostly they rowed, 24 hours a day, through mist and storm. After ten days, and having been blown past their carefully stashed depots on Novaya Zemlya, they rounded a cape and saw two Russian whalers. Weyprecht climbed aboard the largest ship, the *Nicolai*, and from his uniform pocket withdrew a tattered piece of paper. It was a letter of safe conduct signed by Tsar Alexander II three years previously. The Russian captain and his sailors stood silently on deck as the rest of the Austro-Hungarian expedition followed their commander.

Their return was greeted with jubilation. When they landed at Hamburg fireworks exploded in the night. Crowds cheered as a garlanded train carried them to Vienna. In the Austro-Hungarian capital a throng of at least a quarter of a million mobbed the route to the centre, where ancient balconies threatened to collapse under the weight of handkerchief-waving wellwishers. Emperor Franz Josef greeted them in person, and within weeks of their arrival 'Payer coats' and 'Weyprecht cravats' were being sported by everyone with pretensions to style. And why not? The creaky old empire had at last done something to prove that it was the equal of modern states. And it had done so in powerful fashion. Its subjects had opened a whole new sector of the Arctic. They may have lost their ship, but they had come back alive, and they had done so against odds that no one had hitherto surmounted.

Unfortunately, Weyprecht and Payer did not feel the same way. The two men, who had been such ardent exponents of polar exploration when they set out, returned disillusioned and shaken. They had not found the Pole; Petermann's theories were wrong; and the journey had been a nightmare. Their experiences destroyed them physically and mentally. Neither one was ever the same again. Weyprecht thought the expedition had been a waste of time. 'As a scientific goal,' he wrote, 'the pole itself is of perfect indifference. To have approached it serves at most the gratification of vanity.' Payer said much the same: 'We discovered (after our return from the north) that we were honoured far beyond our due . . . As to the discovery of a land unknown before, I personally place no value in it today.'

Their sense of hollowness reflected, presciently, the state of Austria-Hungary as a whole. On their way north, past Novaya Zemlya, the two commanders had thrown out bottles containing messages. Forty years later the bottles made their way home. They were addressed to dead men in redundant offices, ghostly servants of a navy that had no ships and an empire that had ceased to exist.

George Nares (1875–6)

Following the huge amount of money it had spent on the Franklin search – not to mention the loss of men and equipment that had occasioned that search – the British government had declared a moratorium on Arctic exploration. Neither it nor the public could see the point in risking further lives in what seemed a futile pursuit. A North-West Passage, of sorts, had been discovered by McClure and found to be unnavigable; the Canadian Arctic had been all but completely mapped with no sign of there being an alternative sea route to the Pacific; and such further scientific and geographical findings as were to be had seemed not worth the expense. As for the North Pole, standard wisdom declared that it was probably unreachable and, even if it wasn't, there was little to be gained by going there.

Some, however, urged strenuously that the Admiralty should take the process to its logical conclusion. Among them was an officer named Clements Markham, who had been involved in the Franklin search and who was convinced that Britain's reputation depended upon it finding the North Pole. He thought it outrageous that the world's greatest naval power, with its unequalled knowledge of Arctic conditions, should stand by while others stole a lead. Markham and his supporters battered away throughout the 1860s, garnering public support with blatantly one-sided propaganda – Markham, for example, published a number of popular accounts to prove that polar exploration was the safest, healthiest and most congenial pursuit imaginable to humankind – until, in the end, the government succumbed. In November 1874 Prime Minister Disraeli announced that a new expedition would be sent north the following spring. It would comprise two of the Royal Navy's strongest steam-powered ice-ships – the *Alert* under Captain George Nares and the *Discovery* under Commander Henry Stephenson. It would be equipped with sledges and Inuit hunters, and its provisions would be such as to obviate any possibility of scurvy. (In one of his books Clements Markham had announced scurvy to be a disease of the past.) Nares's orders were to make copious scientific observations, but above all to find the North Pole – or, failing that, to go further north than anyone yet.

When Nares and Stephenson left Portsmouth on 29 May 1875 Markham was certain that they would beat all records. And they did. Nares steamed

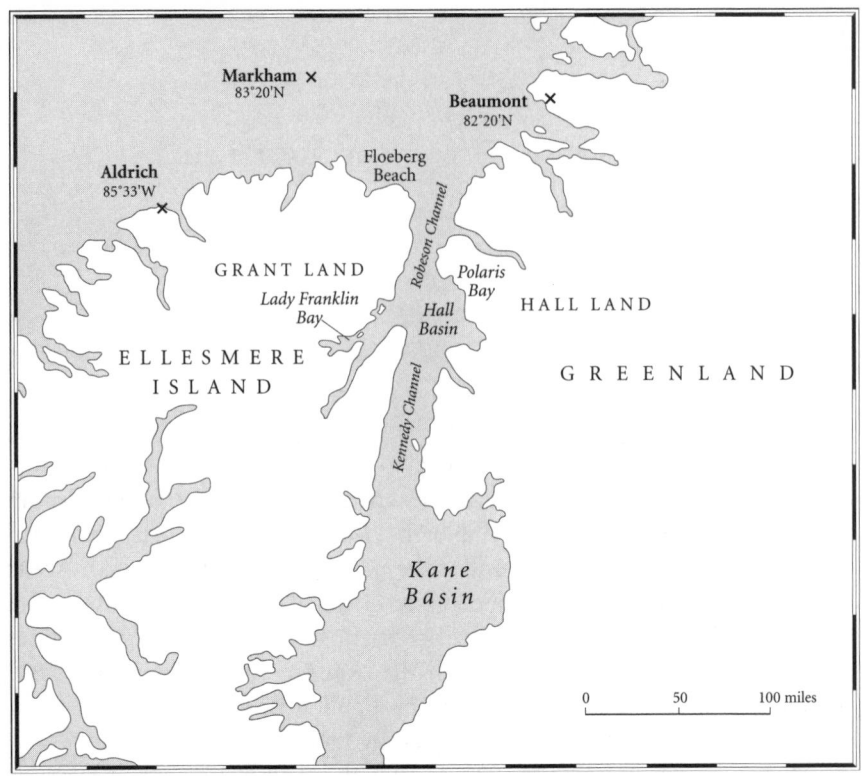

through Smith Sound, recharted the coasts on either side, then smashed his way into the ice to reach the top of Robeson Channel. Here, at 82° 27' N, the furthest north anyone had yet travelled by ship, he dropped anchor at a spot he named Floeberg Beach. Against the possibility of his becoming stuck and having to evacuate overland, he ordered the *Discovery* to winter in Lady Franklin Bay, to the south of Robeson Channel. Throughout that first winter the crews of both ships were in high spirits. They did not succumb to the depression that plagued most Arctic expeditions, thanks largely to a constant round of entertainments: skating, boxing matches, concerts and plays. They also made a number of sledge journeys to prepare themselves for the big push the following spring. They had come with dogs, but the only people who knew how to handle them were their Inuit hunters, Hans, and a Greenlander named Petersen; moreover, Nares was a man-hauler at heart (he, like Markham, had taken part in the Franklin search and had accompanied McClintock on his sledging forays), so the men went draped in harness. It was an experience for which they were unprepared. A junior lieutenant, Wyatt Rawson, recorded Nares's warning before they set out: '[He said] the hardest days work we had ever *imagined*, let alone *had*, would not hold a patch on the work we should have sledging.' When they returned, shattered and so badly frostbitten that several men underwent amputations (one officer's wounds did not heal for five months), Rawson commented, 'Captain Nares was right ... he was perfectly right.'

The going was no easier in the spring. On a preliminary trip to the *Discovery* Petersen lost both feet to frostbite and died not long after his return. The two officers who accompanied him were also badly frostbitten in the hands – simply from having tried to chafe Petersen's feet back to life. Nevertheless, Nares's men remained optimistic. And with good reason, for they belonged to the largest, best equipped and best provisioned Arctic expedition the world had ever seen. It is often tempting to regard Victorian explorers as bearded, pipe-smoking desperadoes, semi-primitives clad in unsuitable garments, who struggled ignorantly against the forces of nature. But the photos of the Nares expedition tell a different story. They show fit, healthy men, wearing clothes that would be instantly recognizable to their compatriots even 50 years later. These men lounge insouciantly against their sledges, with numbers on their clothes to indicate which sledge team they belong to. One or two of them wear white, cowboy-style hats. Their sledges look lightweight and efficient, the loads expertly wrapped. The images are of order, purpose and determination. They are startlingly modern.

Nares had planned three sledge parties: one, under Lieutenant Albert Markham (a cousin of Clements) and Lieutenant Alfred Parr, would head for the Pole, carrying two boats in case they met the open polar sea; a second, under Lieutenant Pelham Aldrich, would chart the north coast of Ellesmere Island; and a third, under Lieutenant Lewis Beaumont from the *Discovery*, would head over the frozen sea to investigate the glaciers and mountains of Greenland. When they assembled for the grand departure on 2 April 1876, heraldic emblems flying from their sledges, they had no reason to fear the coming ordeal. They had food, they had fuel to melt water, they had concentrated lemon juice to counteract scurvy, and there was safety in numbers: the combined roster came to 53 officers and men.

Of the three parties, Markham's faced the hardest grind. Their route led north through the jumbled hillocks and ridges of the polar pack. Sometimes they raised sail on their sledges and let the wind blow them along. But mostly they had to clear a path with picks and shovels. Their woollen clothes, which looked so splendid in the photographs, soon showed their limitations, absorbing perspiration and then freezing hard as boards. In the mornings they had to beat their trousers with axe-heads to make them bend at the knees. Blizzards confined them for days inside their communal sleeping bags – which, like their tents, had been built to the lightest specification for ease of transport. As their occupants thawed, the sleeping bags became saturated; and when they were packed onto the sledges they froze. Soon the entire outfit was hauling and sleeping in material as rigid as iron. The pack, meanwhile, was unrelenting: the tortuous icescape sent them on long diversions; for every real mile north they travelled at least another three; on one occasion they chopped through a hillock more than a quarter of a mile wide; on 7 May they took a whole day to cross 100 yards; typically the snow was knee-deep; sometimes the boats they were hauling sank from sight. Added to their discomfort was a worrying plague of 'seediness'. It manifested itself first on 6 March and then spread until, on 12 May, two thirds of Markham's men were feeling 'seedy'. Their legs tightened up, their gums swelled, and their limbs bled for no obvious reason. It was painful for most of them to walk, and some of the worst affected had to be dragged on the sledges. Reluctantly, Markham had to admit that the 'seediness' was scurvy. How this could have happened he did not understand. They had been taking regular sips from their bottles of lemon juice; by rights they should be perfectly healthy.

Markham planted the Union Jack at 83° 20' N. It was the furthest north any human being had travelled, and with this he was satisfied. In fact, after the past months' torture, he declared it 'a higher latitude, I predict, than will ever be attained'. The Pole was *totally and utterly impracticable*, and the open polar sea was such a ludicrous concept that 'its existence can only be in the brain of a few insane theorists'. He gave his men a day's rest, during which they broached a magnum of champagne and toasted their victory amidst jagged lumps of ice. Then he took them home as fast as they could go.

The track they had built on the way north allowed them to haul faster than they had on their way towards the Pole. But by 7 April only Markham, Parr and two others were still capable of hauling. The rest were either on the sledges or stumbling alongside. Markham threw out every inessential item and heaped the casualties and all his supplies on a single sledge, with which he led his party home. 'Every day, every hour, is important to us,' he wrote in his journal, 'as we know not when we might, one and all, be attacked and rendered useless.'

On 7 June they collapsed. They were 30 miles from the *Alert*, with no hope of covering that distance on their own before the summer thaw made sledge travel impossible. If, however, they received assistance from the *Alert* they might yet make it. Parr volunteered to fetch help. He covered the 30 miles in 24 hours, and on the evening of 8 June staggered aboard the *Alert*. He was so blackened with filth that at first nobody recognized him. Smoothly, Nares's men went into action, and by 14 June Markham's contingent was home. One man died before the rescuers arrived. Of the remaining 13 only three were still capable of walking.

Aldrich's party fared little better. They reached 82° 16' N, 85° 33' W on Ellesmere Island before they too were hit by scurvy. Their return journey, over disintegrating ice, was as horrific as Markham's. When men from the *Alert* came to their rescue (marching though snow so thick that sometimes they had to crawl) they discovered Aldrich and one other man trying valiantly to haul *both* their sledges, on which, apart from their supplies, were strapped four casualties. Two others, incapable of hauling, limped after them.

By mid-June practically every man aboard the *Alert* was suffering from scurvy. Realizing that they might all die before the thaw released them, Nares laid gunpowder charges and blew the *Alert* out of the ice. Then he steamed south to join the *Discovery*, where they would surely find relief. But conditions were little better in Lady Franklin Bay. Like the *Alert*, the *Discovery* had been hit by scurvy. But they could not leave, because Beaumont and his Greenland party had yet to return.

Of all Nares's sledge parties, that under Beaumont suffered the most. They traversed glaciers so steep that their sledge runners buckled. They trudged through drifts that swamped the sledge and where, with each step, their legs sank thigh-deep. In four feet of snow they had to climb out of each step they took. Sometimes they hauled their sledges over open rock. At best they made two miles per day. And, like the others, they began to show signs of scurvy. They halted on 23 May, having reached a place that Beaumont christened Sherard Osborn Fjord. The following day he climbed a 3,700-foot hill to scan the terrain, then led his men home. It had taken them 32 days to reach that spot. Three decades later the same distance would be covered by dog sled in eight days. Future explorers could only marvel at what Beaumont's men had done. 'How they managed to pull their sledges up Gap Valley,' Knud Rasmussen wrote in 1921, 'is a perfect riddle to all of us who have looked at the stony pass . . . We others can only bow our heads to those who did it.'

The journey back was even ghastlier than the journey out. To the uncompromising nature of the landscape was added gales that confined them to their thin, inadequate tents for days on end. One by one, the seven-strong team succumbed to scurvy. By 24 June Beaumont was the only man capable of walking, let alone hauling. Alone, he set out for the *Discovery* to find help. Fortunately, a rescue party was already on its way. It intercepted Beaumont, collected the remainder of his men, and helped them back to the coast of Greenland. By the end of their journey two men had died and, thanks to the thaw, the sledge-bound remainder were being dragged across bare shingle.

Beaumont and his party were taken aboard the *Discovery* on 15 August 1876, whereupon both ships fled the Arctic as swiftly as they could. It had been a horrendous and puzzling experience. Why should they have contracted scurvy when they had not only lemon juice but the best provisions the Royal Navy could offer? Nares did not know the answer. But he did know that he had done his best to fulfil his orders, and if anyone wanted to better him they were welcome to try. He had no expectation that they would succeed. On reaching Ireland he sent a terse, three-word telegram to his superiors: 'NORTH POLE IMPRACTICABLE.'

The message went down badly. The expedition's failure was a blow to the Royal Navy's reputation – indeed, a blow to the whole Empire. Some suggested that the Pole was impracticable only because Nares had been incompetent. Others wanted him court-martialled for lack of patriotic spirit. On his return to London he sat through a lengthy inquiry whose main object was to ascertain why his men had caught scurvy when every authority (i.e. Clements Markham) had said it was impossible. That his inquirers – and science – had no idea what caused scurvy was considered irrelevant. Some people linked it to the direction of the wind in Borneo, others said it derived from a lack of eggs, and others put it down to 'general filth'. In fact, the outbreak had sprung directly from the Navy's attempts to prevent it. Nares's lemon juice had been issued in concentrated form, so that when it froze it did not crack the bottles in which it was stored. The concentrating process involved boiling the juice in copper containers. Heat destroys Vitamin C and copper leaches it. But nobody knew that lack of Vitamin C was responsible for the disease; indeed, they did not even know that Vitamin C existed. The inquiry concluded that Nares had been guilty of inadequate provisioning and non-specific unsuitability for the job. It was all his fault.

The Nares expedition marked the end of the Royal Navy's long involvement with the Arctic. With its many commitments elsewhere, it had no desire to waste more time on North Polar exploration. Clements Markham tried his hardest to change the Admiralty's mind, publishing article after pamphlet to explain why Nares had not been at fault and why his failure should be considered only a temporary setback. When his pleading produced no results he eventually gave up. But he never forgot what he saw as Britain's destiny – to be first to the world's axis. For several decades he remained quiet, and then, at the turn of the century, by which time he was President of the Royal Geographical Society, he returned to his bone. If Britain was unwilling to take the North Pole it could surely make an attempt on the South. This time people listened, thereby sealing the fate of a young torpedo officer named Robert Falcon Scott.

George De Long (1879–82)

If there was one man who was satisfied by the failure of the Nares expedition it was Dr August Petermann. After the calamitous outcomes of the last two forays he had sponsored into the Arctic he had become the butt of British derision. Britain, like the US, favoured attacking the Pole via Greenland; Petermann's so-called 'thermometric gateways' were ridiculous. Humiliatingly, Petermann had been forced to make a semi-retraction. But now, as Britain itself was forced to retract, Petermann belaboured his antagonists with glee. They were wrong and he was right. The German and Austrian expeditions had merely proved his point: that the Gulf Stream exited on the east coast of Greenland was indisputable; what other current could have carried the *Hansa* south? That it entered the ice above Novaya Zemlya with power was equally certain: look how the pack had been concertina'd into a mass so impenetrable that the *Tegetthoff* had been unable to break through it.

Polar explorers, said Petermann, would never succeed unless they adopted his theories. If the Gulf Stream was too weak to melt a thermometric gateway off the east coast of Greenland, and too strong to create one at Novaya Zemlya, he had discovered another current that was just right. The Kuro Siwo flowed from the Pacific, past Japan, and through the Bering Strait to the Arctic. It was as warm as the Gulf Stream, but not as overwhelming. Navigators should therefore take their ships through the Bering Strait, whereupon they would be crowned with success. Unfortunately, governments in Europe and America no longer cared about the North Pole. It had caused them considerable misfortune and great expense; if it had defeated even the Royal Navy then why bother trying? Others could seek it if they liked, and good luck to them. They themselves were done with it.

One man listened to Petermann. He was James Gordon Bennett, a ruinous, alcoholic playboy and one of the richest men in America. He was also the owner of the *New York Herald*, a newspaper that had the largest circulation in the world. Like Petermann, he too had theories concerning the North Pole. Unlike Petermann, however, his theories were based on fact: the discovery of the Pole would be news; news sold copies; and if the *Herald* discovered the Pole it would be an unprecedented scoop. After a brief interview with the

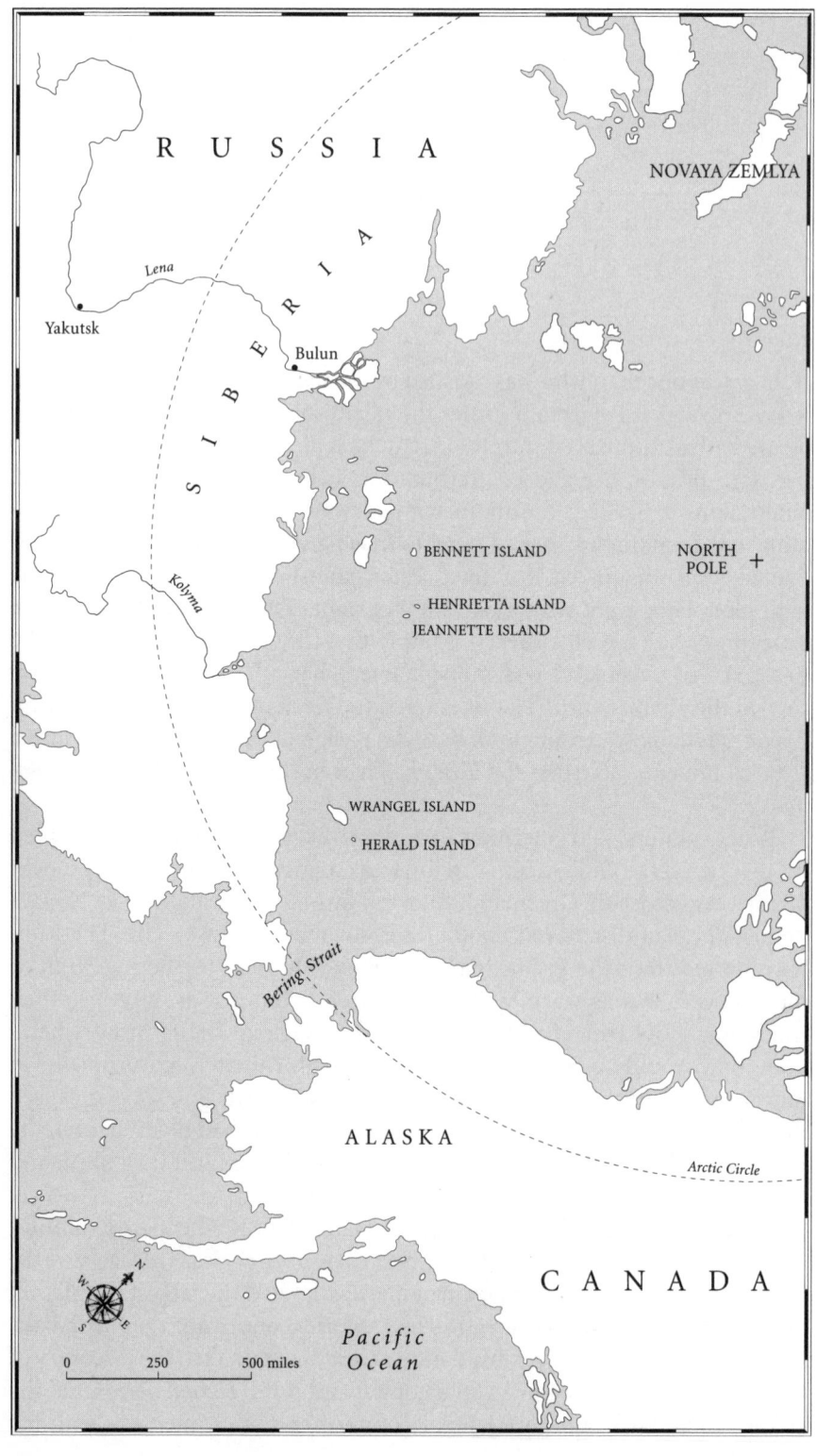

RUSSIA

NOVAYA ZEMLYA

Lena

Yakutsk

SIBERIA

Bulun

Kolyma

◊ BENNETT ISLAND

◦ HENRIETTA ISLAND
JEANNETTE ISLAND

NORTH
POLE +

WRANGEL ISLAND

◦ HERALD ISLAND

Bering Strait

ALASKA

Arctic Circle

CANADA

*Pacific
Ocean*

0   250   500 miles

'Sage of Gotha' – as Petermann was known – he set matters in motion. A ship was purchased from Britain, the US government was cajoled into strengthening it for the ice, and a crew was selected. Some were experienced sailors; most, however, were not; and the obligatory scientist was the *Herald*'s weather correspondent. (He was ordered to study Arctic meteorology and was put in charge of the onboard telephonic and lighting systems which, purchased from Bell and Edison, were untested but newsworthy novelties.) Their commander was an ex-naval officer named George Washington De Long, who had been once, briefly, to the Arctic.

Petermann committed suicide in September 1878, which might have been considered a bad omen by anyone other than Bennett. The proprietor of the *Herald* did not care. If the expedition came to grief he would move heaven and earth to save it. That was what he told De Long. What he did not tell him was that his rescue would sell as many copies as his success. Either way, circulation would rise.

The ship, christened *Jeannette* after Bennett's sister, left San Francisco on 8 July 1879. Stopping at an Alaskan port, De Long was discouraged by veterans who told him that scores of ships had vanished in the sea he was entering and that although there were polynyas, or stretches of open water, there was unlikely to be an ice-free passage to the Pole. A grizzled whaling captain by the name of Nye gave an honest assessment of his prospects: 'Put her into the ice and let her drift, and you may get through or you may go to the devil, and the chances are about equal.' Actually, Nye was being over-generous with his odds. There was no chance whatsoever of De Long getting through. That winter the US Coast and Geodetic Survey reported that: 'The [Bering] Strait is *incapable* of carrying a current of warm water of sufficient magnitude to have any marked effect on the condition of the Polar basin ... Nothing in the least tends to support the widely spread but unphilosophical notion that in any part of the Polar Sea we may look for large areas free from ice.' De Long, however, knew nothing of their findings. By the time they were delivered he was already in the ice. 'Do not give me up for I shall one day or another come back,' he wrote in a final letter to his wife.

On his way to the Pole, De Long had hoped to investigate Wrangel and Herald Islands, two lumps of rock that had been sighted some decades earlier by the Russian navigator Baron von Wrangel and had yet to be properly surveyed. They lay north-west of Bering Strait in roughly the same latitude as Novaya Zemlya, and should theoretically have presented no problem. But even this relatively simple goal was beyond De Long. Thanks to a series of time-wasting orders from Bennett, he arrived too late in the season. Barely had he sighted Herald Island when he found himself trapped in the floes. Like the *Tegetthoff* in 1872, the *Jeannette* was now a prisoner of the Arctic pack.

De Long expected constantly that the shifting pack would carry the ship into warmer water. But it did not happen. The currents and winds pushed the

Jeannette in a triangle, now north, now south, now east, while simultaneously carrying it slowly to the west. After a while he despaired of Petermann's theories. 'I pronounce a thermometric gateway to the North Pole a delusion and a snare,' he wrote in his journal. The realization came as little comfort. During the winter of 1879 and throughout 1880 he was plagued by far greater problems.

The first was the crew. They did not get on. The *Herald* 'scientist' became the object of everyone's mockery when it was discovered that he could not operate the lights or the telephone. That he was also in charge of photography and had left behind the developing chemicals occasioned further jeers. De Long's first officer, a socialite named Danenhower who had been foisted on him because his family knew Bennett's, was going blind from syphilis and had to endure repeated operations by candlelight to drain the mucus that collected round his corneas. Another man was diagnosed as insane. None of them could stand the long, tense days except the mate, George Melville, who performed a thousand tiny miracles to keep the expedition functioning.

De Long's second concern was the ice, which attacked them with almost human malevolence. Vast pressure ridges ground noisily towards the *Jeannette*, turning it on its side. Small eruptions came at it from beneath the keel. Like the crew of the *Tegetthoff*, that of the *Jeannette* spent days on end huddled on deck with their survival kits. At one point a floe punctured the *Jeannette* below the waterline. The two men whom De Long sent to battle the flood spent several hours waist-deep in freezing water. When they emerged, successful, De Long was so impressed that he recommended them for the Congressional Medal of Honor.

By July 1880 they were using 30 pounds of coal per day just to heat the ship and to keep the pumps going. If they continued at this rate they would have enough fuel for only five days' steaming. The idea of their reaching the Pole was now so far-fetched as to be laughable. Indeed, De Long seemed to fear the prospect of public derision far more than the ice itself. 'We and our narratives [will be] thrown into the world's dreary wastebasket and recalled ... only to be vilified and ridiculed,' he wrote. From his readings he noticed that the ice was pushing them south towards the Russian coast, where in due course he expected they would be ignominiously deposited. 'The knowledge that we have done nothing [is] almost enough to make me tear my hair in impotent rage.'

By the spring of 1881, with his dogs killing each other, his officers barely on speaking terms and his ship being twisted and squeezed by the ice, De Long began reluctantly to consider their escape. If they survived long enough to reach Siberia there was still hope that they could bring the *Jeannette* home in one piece. According to Petermann, the sea off Russia's northern coast was bound to be open even in winter. His reasoning was that the great rivers such as the Lena and Kolyma, which had their origins in central Asia, would be warm enough to melt the Arctic pack and thus provide a navigable channel between the Atlantic and the Pacific. There was, in fact, such a waterway – the North-East Passage – which had been traversed by a Swede named Nordenskiöld in the year De Long set out. Unfortunately, it was not open every year. De Long did not know this, but past experience had taught him to distrust anything Petermann said. 'This is about the only Arctic theory that we have not exploded,' he remarked caustically. In the event, he did not have a chance to put it to the test.

That summer De Long made a new discovery: two pimples of rock and ice that he named Henrietta and Jeannette Islands. 'Thank God we have at last landed upon a newly discovered part of this earth,' he wrote jubilantly. 'And now where next?' The pack gave him his answer. On 12 June 1881 the *Jeannette* was squeezed remorselessly. De Long evacuated the crew onto the ice, where they awaited the inevitable. It came at 4.00 the following morning when the ship suddenly rose up, folded in upon itself and then, its yardarms and masts clasped together 'like [the hands of] a great gaunt skeleton', slid vertically into the sea. The situation was not entirely bleak. De Long had saved their sledges, ample food and fuel, rifles, ammunition, compasses and sextants, plus three sledge-mounted boats. From where they stood it was only 200-odd miles to Siberia and, equipped as they were for travel on both ice and sea, there was no reason why they should not reach land.

Their journey over the pack was as heartbreaking and exhausting as it had been for Weyprecht's men in 1874. Their sledges were so overloaded that they travelled back and forth 26 miles to make just two. And, as was so often the case in Arctic exploration, no sooner had they decided to go south than the pack moved in the opposite direction. Not long into their trek De Long discovered they were 28 miles north of where they had started. Changing course from south to south-west, the party began to make progress against the drift. On 25 July they discovered another lump of rock – Bennett Island – which boosted morale enormously. Another fillip came soon afterwards when the pack disintegrated sufficiently for them to take to their boats. By 11 September they were 90 miles from land and had a week's rations left. Before them, if De Long's calculations were correct, lay the Lena delta. Consulting a map drawn by Petermann, he saw that the channels were easily navigable and dotted with towns and hamlets. Possibly there was a chance they might reach safety.

That night, however, they were hit by a violent storm. It was, in Melville's words, 'an incubus of horrors'. In the darkness and fury the three boats became separated, one of them never to be seen again. It was a tribute to De Long's seamanship that when the waves abated he was able to beach his craft in the middle of the delta. But the other boat, under Melville, was blown to the east. Separately, therefore, the two commanders began to pick their way through the 260-mile-wide maze of boggy islets that comprised the Lena delta. Melville was the luckier of the two. By pure chance he found a channel broader than the others, up which he and his men were able to row until they reached a village. Here, again by chance, they met one of the Cossack messengers who plied the region, and were able to send word of their plight, via the nearest large town, Yakutsk, to Siberia's capital Irkutsk, which had a telegraph link to the outside world. But Irkutsk was thousands of miles away. It would be a long time before help arrived, and until then Melville had no idea if De Long was alive, let alone where he might be.

De Long, too, had no idea where he was. As he led his 11 men through the Lena delta, it became obvious that Petermann's map was a nonsense. Nothing on it accorded with reality: the channels led in completely different directions; and the settlements simply did not exist or, if they did, they were not where Petermann said they were. Melville had found the same, writing: 'Bitterly we cursed Petermann and all his works which had led us astray.' Faced with a far harder task than Melville, De Long cursed his dead mentor with even more vehemence. Resorting to the compass, he travelled due south, now by water, now dragging the boat over swampy protuberances, hoping that in this fashion they would stumble sooner or later on a village. Alas, this was the worst course he could follow. From where he had landed, in the centre of the delta, south led only to the heart of the maze. Here, the best he could expect was to find a hunter's shack. But this was a distant hope, for winter was closing in and the hunters were already leaving for home.

Their food began to run out, but they were able to supplement their rations by shooting the occasional deer. This, combined with De Long's judicious provisioning aboard the *Jeannette*, ensured they stayed free of scurvy. But as the deer migrated before the oncoming winter, it was starvation rather than disease that occupied their minds – that and frostbite. Their clothes offered little protection against the intense, wind-chilled cold of Siberia. Neither did the thin canvas tent in which they huddled at night. To aggravate the situation, their clothes began to fall to pieces and they were forced to cut up the tent to make replacements. On 6 October frostbite claimed its first fatality.

By the end of the first week of October they had consumed their last scraps of food and were living on three ounces of alcohol per man per day. In these circumstances De Long took a gamble. Realizing, belatedly, that their southward march was leading them nowhere, he reverted to Petermann's map; unreliable it might have been, but it was now their only hope. According to his estimates, they were 25 miles away from a village called Kumakh-Surt. He therefore ordered two of his strongest men – Nindemann and Noros – to go ahead for assistance, while he and the others followed as best they could. He gave them a small amount of alcohol, a rifle, and strict instructions that if they shot a deer they were to bring it back before continuing to Kumakh-Surt. The two men left on 9 October. On the 17th one of De Long's men died of starvation. Three days later the others came to a halt, having covered perhaps 12 miles since the 9th. Too exhausted to continue, they lay under the last scrap of their tent, emerging only to stoke a signal fire with sections of their redundant boat. They took hypothetical comfort from the two men's non-appearance. Perhaps it meant they had got through to Kumakh-Surt and were even now on their way back with food and assistance? By the 29th Nindemann and Noros had not returned, and all but four of De Long's men had died. Two days later there was only De Long.

Nindemann and Noros were still alive. They had reached Kumakh-Surt – which lay not 25 miles distant but 80 – by dint of eating their shoes and their leather breeches, only to find it was an abandoned collection of shacks. Then on the 29th they met two hunters, who helped them to the nearest town, Bulun, from where they sent a message of distress to Yakutsk. On 2 November Melville also arrived in Bulun. During the last weeks he had agitated for a rescue mission, but had been discouraged by his Lena hosts: the weather was turning; if he waited awhile the ground would be frozen and he could make as many missions as he liked. Melville knew that he didn't have the time. Commandeering a team of dogs and drivers, he forced his way to Bulun and then, on hearing the news from Noros and Nindemann, retraced his steps to find De Long. He searched for 23 days, but when the weather became so bad that his dog-handlers refused to go any further he gave up. De Long was surely dead by now. 'Corpses,' he wrote, 'I could find with safety in the early spring.'

James Gordon Bennett had not forgotten his charge. In a spate of circulation-boosting activity he sent his journalists after De Long. They attacked Siberia by ship (it sank), by train, by foot and by sledge. It was Melville, however, who discovered the remains of De Long's party. In 1882 he took a team of local hunters and, with Nindemann as a guide, traipsed through the delta in search of his captain. Nindemann had a poor recollection of his trek the previous season, added to which was the fact that he had no idea how far the survivors had travelled since he left them. Also, snow had just fallen, turning the landscape into a uniform blank. Contrarily, it was this last handicap that helped them locate De Long. Protruding from the whiteness were four black poles, which Melville judged correctly were the remains of De Long's tent. Hurrying to the spot, he cleared the ground. One by one, the bodies came to light. Some rested peacefully; one, partially singed, lay by the remains of a campfire; others were contorted in death throes. De Long was on his back, one arm raised (Melville almost tripped over it), and not far distant, as if he had thrown it over his shoulder, was his journal. Its pages ended on 30 October with the words: 'Boyd and Gortz died during the night – Mr. Collins dying.' It was impossible to tell when De Long had died – mysteriously, the page for the 31st had been ripped out – but it was clear that he had been the last.

Melville collected every bit of evidence he could find – including a cache of maps and journals that De Long had placed on a nearby rise – then ordered his men to give the bodies a decent burial. The spot he chose was a 400-foot hillock 15 miles away. De Long and his party were interred in a communal coffin measuring 22 feet by 7. Above them, Melville raised a massive wooden cross on which he had inscribed their names. It was visible for 20 miles in every direction.

Siberia, however, was not to be their final resting place. After Melville came one of Bennett's correspondents, who opened the coffin, rummaged through it for papers that might be damaging to his employer's reputation, then arranged for the bodies' transportation to the United States. The Tsar supplied a railway cortège, draped in black, which carried them to the coast. They were then taken by ship to New York, where thousands came out to attend their funeral march. De Long was buried in the Bronx cemetery on 20 February. Fittingly, the occasion was marked by a violent snowstorm.

Bennett did not attend the funerals. Neither did he attend the subsequent inquiry, which disclosed several unpalatable facts about his organization and equipping of the *Jeannette* expedition. Instead, he took to his private yacht and sailed for Europe. In his wake, the US government came to three conclusions: first, that De Long had been immeasurably brave; second, that his voyage had been futile from the start; and third, that it would never again support futilities of this nature. Like the British before them, the Americans decided that a line should be drawn. Let who liked go to the Pole – but they would do so at their own peril and at their own expense.

Adolphus Greely (1881–4)

The International Year of Polar Cooperation was the world's response to the deaths and disasters that had been such a conspicuous element of its forays into the Arctic. First proposed by Carl Weyprecht following his return in 1874 from Franz Josef Land, it was founded on the sensible notion that if Arctic exploration was to benefit science (as had so often been claimed) then it was pointless despatching murderous expeditions to reach the North Pole – a spot that Weyprecht, among others, was convinced was not worth the finding. Instead, it would be far better to establish a series of research stations around the rim of the Arctic, from where teams of scientists could study the ice and its weather patterns in relative safety. Die-hard members of the exploring fraternity objected: if the North Pole was the culmination, so to speak, of the Arctic, then that was where efforts should be directed; fiddling at the fringes was a waste of time and money. Weyprecht, however, was backed by the influential Iron Chancellor of Germany, Bismarck, and, after a long gestation, the International Year of Polar Cooperation was agreed upon. In the winter of 1882–3 11 different countries sent their scientists to the polar rim. Weyprecht, alas, was not there to see them go: he had died of tuberculosis on 31 March 1881. Perhaps it was as well, because he would not have liked what became of his plan.

Of the 15 sub-polar stations the northernmost was in Lady Franklin Bay, where Nares's *Discovery* had wintered in 1875–6. Its establishment and operation was allotted to the United States of America. The man in charge was not a scientist, but a stern marine officer, Lieutenant Adolphus Greely, who was given responsibility for a 26-strong team including two Inuit hunters-cum-sledge-drivers. None of the Americans had ever been to the Arctic before. Greely, however, had long had his eyes on the ice, and so had his leading scientist, Dr Octave Pavy. For these two men, and for many of their subordinates, the International Polar Year had nothing to do with science. It was an excuse to try for the North Pole.

Greely's outfit sailed aboard the *Proteus* and reached its destination in late 1881. This was 12 months too soon, but it was agreed that the extra time would help them acclimatize to conditions and construct a base from which to make their observations. Using materials they had brought with them,

Greely's men constructed a large, barn-like edifice – Fort Conger – on the western shore of Lady Franklin Bay and settled down for their first winter. They had no ship with them, for the *Proteus* had returned to Newfoundland for refuelling and reprovisioning. But they had nothing to fear. Robeson Channel, off which Lady Franklin Bay lay, was by now so well known that its navigation was just a matter of waiting for the right moment. It had been arranged that support ships would bring them fuel and provisions, and

Greely had no reason to suspect they would not arrive. Indeed, it didn't much matter if they didn't, for his stores held enough food to last the men three years on full rations; they had plenty of lemon juice to keep scurvy at bay; and there was ample game to be shot in the region.

During that first winter the inhabitants of Fort Conger fell prey to the usual Arctic ennui. Greely, a hard, puritanical man, did not get on with Pavy, whom he suspected of being 'Bohemian'. Their mutual mistrust infected the others. In the officers' quarters, Lieutenant James Lockwood wrote that: 'We often sit silent during the whole day and even a meal fails to elicit anything more than a chance remark or two'. As for the crew, he complained that they 'have no desire to make discoveries and that if they could return next year, they will do so'. The Inuit, meanwhile, were ready to leave at once. One, Jens, took his dog team out in December just to escape the rancour of Fort Conger. The other, Frederick, told Greely that the men wanted to shoot him and all he wanted to do was go into the ice and die. He was persuaded, forcibly, to remain.

In April 1882 Greely sent his first two expeditions towards the Pole. One, under Pavy, went north along the coast of Ellesmere Island, the other, under Lockwood, crossed the frozen sea towards Greenland. Pavy returned shortly, having been blocked by open water. Lockwood took a little longer. Conditions were so bad that four of his men had to be sent back in the first week. But Lockwood, accompanied by a 24-year-old marine, Sergeant David Brainard, and Frederick the Inuit sledge driver, pressed on up the coast. On 4 May they reached Cape Britannia, one of the northernmost points sighted by Beaumont during his trek through Greenland in 1876. Beaumont had been prevented from reaching the cape by scurvy and atrocious weather. Lockwood and Brainard faced similar weather, but their superior provisions saved them from illness. On they pressed until, on 14 May, their supplies allowed them to go no further. Here, at 83° 24' N, they built a cairn to mark the victorious culmination of their journey, then turned for home.

When they reached Fort Conger on 11 June they brought Greely good news: they had travelled 100 nautical miles further than Beaumont, had explored 85 miles of uncharted coastline and, most importantly, had beaten Markham's record by four miles. Admittedly, those four miles, when transposed to an atlas, were barely visible to the naked eye; but what seemed small on the page went an astonishingly long way in the Arctic. Brainard, Lockwood and Frederick had done well. They had overcome snowblindness, they had endured gales that pelted them with ice as if they were walking through walls of flying gravel, and they had traversed some of the most inhospitable terrain on earth. Every single man had returned alive. Above all, they had shown that when it came to ice the US could equal, if not surpass, Great Britain.

Having done what he set out to do, Greely now did what he had been ordered to do – which was to make scientific observations. Even here, however, his exploring instinct got the better of him. During that summer he personally led a party into the interior of Ellesmere Island, a journey which could be justified on geographical grounds but which was really an excuse to find a northern alternative to the North-West Passage. When he and his men emerged from the rugged landscape they carried maps of territories that had never before been visited by humankind. But they had not found the sought-for seaway, and their journey had been so arduous that when they arrived at Fort Conger their boots were practically nonexistent.

By August 1882 the men were looking forward to the arrival of their first support ship. The promise of these shuttles, with their change of personnel, supplies and, above all, mail, had played a large part in reducing the psychological torment of that first Arctic winter. However, the expected ship did not appear. The *Jupiter*, which had been primed with every necessity for the men in Fort Conger, was unable to break through the ice in Kane Basin, so had dropped a couple of food caches, one at Littleton Island off the coast of Greenland, the other at Cape Sabine on Ellesmere Island, before returning to Newfoundland. Greely's men waited patiently and then, as the new ice began to form, resigned themselves to a second winter on Ellesmere Island.

Nobody had ever spent such a long time so far north, and the atmosphere in Fort Conger, which had never been good, deteriorated markedly as the long nights drew in. Lockwood likened it to life in the Bastille: 'no amusements, no recreations, no event to break the monotony'. In this respect they were no different from any other US crew that had entered the Arctic – as opposed to the British, who had made it a point to keep everybody busy, the history of American exploration was one of grim and silent suffering that often led to mutiny and madness. The men in Fort Conger, however, had extra cause for despair. Whereas their predecessors had had a ship, or a remnant of a ship, or at the very least some sturdy boats with men who knew how to handle them, Greely's contingent had only a small steam launch and three boats; none of these was suitable for navigation in the ice, and only two men had the vaguest notion of how to operate them. The Greely expedition, therefore, was dependent for its evacuation on its supply vessels. If no ship appeared – which now seemed a possibility – they would be forced either to take to the ice with their inadequate boats or to withdraw overland. Neither option appealed.

Greely was not despondent. They still had ample food and fuel, and if salvation had not appeared by 1 September 1883 – the date on which he had been ordered to quit Fort Conger – he had no qualms about escaping in the boats. On the way north he had laid depots along the west coasts of Smith Sound and Kane Basin with just such an eventuality in mind, and had instructed the supply vessels to do likewise. He had also ordered a station to be established at Littleton Island, whose telescope-wielding officers could send help to his party when it hove into view. It was, he reasoned, just a few days' journey from Lady Franklin Bay to Littleton Island. Buoyed by the prospect, he – or more accurately Lockwood, who loathed life in Fort Conger and had taken a particular dislike to Dr Pavy – flung sledge parties hither and thither during the spring of 1883. In March 1883 Lockwood went north again, in an attempt to better his previous best. He withdrew only when the ice began to break under his feet in Repulse Haven on the north coast of Greenland. A second attempt, in which he promised to be there and back within 44 days, was quashed at the outset by Greely, who declared it too risky. Greely did, however, let him take Brainard and Frederick on journeys through Ellesmere Island, during the course of which they ranged far and wide, at one point discovering a grove of fossilized trees whose slender, nine-inch thick trunks proved beyond doubt that the Arctic had once been a lot warmer than it was now.

By his last summer in Lady Franklin Bay Greely could congratulate himself on the fact that his expedition had gone further north, west and east than any other to date. He had beaten the British on all counts. At Fort Conger, however, there was less to brag about. Dr Pavy, in particular, seemed to have done very little for the International Year of Polar Cooperation. His cabin, when inspected by Greely, was a mess of rocks, skins, and pressed flowers which, far from being organized and catalogued – as he had assured Greely they would be – were simply scattered about the place. Greely invoked the law: Pavy's contract expired on 20 July; from that day he was discharged of all duties and ordered to give his records to Lockwood, who would thereafter take charge of the scientific programme. Lockwood, who was not a scientist, did as he was told. When Pavy protested he was placed under arrest, awaiting the arrival of that year's ship.

Not one but two ships were on their way. Following the failure of the *Jupiter*, the authorities had become uneasy about Greely's situation. In 1883, therefore, they sent not only the *Proteus* but a smaller ship, the *Yantic*, into Smith Sound. The *Proteus* was instructed to batter its way to Lady Franklin Bay at any cost; the smaller *Yantic*, meanwhile, was to wait at Littleton Island, as a back-up in case anything happened to the *Proteus*. As a further failsafe, the commanders of both ships were ordered to replenish the existing depots on either side of Smith Sound. So far so good, and exactly as Greely had wished. Unfortunately, the rescue operation descended into chaos. The *Proteus* offloaded only a handful of supplies before it was crushed by the ice and sank, forcing its crew to escape by boat to Littleton Island. Here, finding that the *Yantic* had not arrived (and suspecting that it never would, because of its size), the *Proteus* party sailed for a prearranged rendezvous at Cary Islands, south of Smith Sound. They missed the *Yantic* by a day. It had reached Cary Islands and had then continued to Littleton Island where, discovering that the survivors had left for Cary Islands, it promptly turned around. The two groups chased each other north and south, from rendezvous to rendezvous, at each point missing each other by a matter of days until, at last, after 15 days and 900 miles, they were reunited at Disko Island. The

Proteus survivors were taken aboard the *Yantic* and the whole operation retired in disarray to Newfoundland.

While these farcical proceedings were afoot, Greely was preparing to move out. On 9 August 1883, while his would-be rescuers were busy rescuing themselves, the steam launch *Lady Greely* puttered into Robeson Channel, towing three boats containing the men from Fort Conger, their scientific data and a limited amount of food. Behind them they left their dogs and enough supplies to see them through a third winter in case they were forced to retreat. Greely's men thought their commander had gone mad: it would have been much more sensible to winter at Fort Conger and then sledge south in the spring. Indeed, Greely did seem to be teetering on the brink of insanity: he flew into unreasoning rages, ranted, raved and at one point threatened to shoot the *Lady Greely's* mechanic for insubordination. When he hatched the lunatic idea of abandoning the steam launch and floating to safety on a large ice floe, some of his men began seriously to consider mutiny.

In the end Greely abandoned his plan. But it made little difference because, by 26 August, by which time they were more than halfway to Littleton Island, the flotilla was firmly embedded in the ice. After 15 days, during which they had drifted only 22 miles south, Greely called a meeting of his officers. It was agreed that they should abandon the steam launch and drag two of their three boats over the ice to the coast of Ellesmere Island, which was visible just 11 miles to the west. Off they set, 25 men hauling a total weight of 6,500 pounds. Within two days they had jettisoned one of their boats in the hope of easing their task. But the haul seemed, if anything, more arduous still. The remaining, overloaded boat was too heavy to be dragged in one go, so it and its contents had to be shuttled in three separate stages. For every mile they advanced Greely and his men had to cover five. And as if this was not bad enough, the floe began to drift north. 'Misfortune and calamity, hand in hand, have clung to us along the entire line of this retreat,' wrote Brainard. Round and round Kane Basin they circled until, at the end of September, more than six weeks after leaving Fort Conger, they struggled on to Ellesmere Island.

Their position was only marginally better than it had been. It was clearly impossible to cross the jumble of loose floes to Littleton Island, which meant that they would have to winter where they were. Fortunately, there were the supplies at Cape Sabine (which now lay to their north), and while Greely oversaw the construction of three miserable stone hovels, two men trekked to ascertain what the caches had to offer. When they returned eight days later it was with mixed news: the Cape Sabine depots contained 50 days' food; together with what remained after their drift, this meant they could survive 100 days at the maximum. On the other hand, a note left by the *Proteus* suggested that more supplies had been laid down at Littleton Island. When the sea froze they could reprovision by sledge: it was only 44 miles there and back, and although the going was hard it was not impossibly so.

Cheered by the prospect, Greely decided to decamp at once with their remaining possessions to Cape Sabine. He was under no illusions, however, as to what the coming months would be like: 'Privation, partial starvation, and possible death for the weakest,' he predicted.

At Cape Sabine they erected a rudimentary stone shelter, roofed by the oars from their boats, and consolidated their position. Some men were sent back to collect the remaining stores from the landing point and others were ordered to itemize the contents of the caches. The stocktaking revealed unwelcome deficiencies: some of the food had been laid down more than eight years ago by the Nares expedition and had gone so mouldy as to be inedible. Greely at once reduced rations to 14 ounces of food per person per day. On this amount he reckoned they would be able to survive until March, when it would be possible to sledge to Littleton Island. Lockwood spoke for them all when he wrote, 'Whether we can live on such a driblet of food remains to be seen'.

Even this driblet, however, rested on the recovery of 144 pounds of preserved meat that Nares had deposited at Cape Isabella to the south. On 2 November Greely despatched four men to collect these vital supplies. Eight days later one of them staggered back to camp to announce that the mission had failed. One of their number, a man named Elison, had become frostbitten. Without his help hauling the sledge, they had had to abandon the meat. In addition, Elison had become incontinent and had saturated the sleeping bag, with the result that he and the other two were now frozen in place. When a six-man party under Brainard and Lockwood hastened to their rescue they had to chop the sleeping bag open before they could bring its occupants back to safety. On their return Greely reduced rations to ten ounces per day – four of meat, six of bread.

Greely did his best to maintain morale – he organized uplifting lectures on the states of America – but it was impossible to conceal the dire straits they were in. Elison had one foot amputated, then the other, then his fingers one by one. People began to pilfer from the stores and to fight among themselves. Greely himself became increasingly short-tempered. On 18 January a man died, from scurvy and starvation. An attempt to reach Littleton Island by sledge on 1 February was thwarted by open seas. On 5 April Frederick the Inuit hunter died. The next day, so did another man. On 9 April Lockwood died, to be followed shortly afterwards by another two men. The pilfering continued. A few days after Lockwood's death they managed to shoot a bear, which saved them from immediate starvation. But on 29 April Jens, the other Inuit hunter, drowned while chasing a seal, taking with him their best rifle. On 10 May Greely estimated they had three days' food left. Those who had the strength shot a few dovekies or trawled for shrimp – minuscule things, little larger than a grain of wheat and mostly shell: 700 provided an ounce of meat. With this, and even tighter rationing, they managed to postpone the inevitable for a while longer. Still the channel refused to freeze, but even if it had they would not have been strong enough to cross it. It was as much as they could do to extricate themselves from their sleeping bags; for some, even this was too great an effort. As the weeks passed, and more men died, the survivors no longer bothered to bury their companions: they simply dragged the cadavers round the back.

By the beginning of June the thaw had made their hut uninhabitable, so they erected a tent some 150 yards from their original encampment. Nobody any longer expected to survive. To alleviate their constant hunger they chewed on their oilskin sleeping bags and scraped lichen from the rocks. When Brainard spotted a caterpillar he swallowed it whole. The only one who showed any sign of health was, perversely, the handless, footless Elison, who had been carefully nursed by Pavy. (Pavy, who for a while had seemed the fittest of them all, had gone in early May, having accidentally poisoned himself.) Greely, who had already written his last will and testament, was in as bad a shape as any of them, but he managed to maintain a semblance of military discipline. When one man was caught repeatedly stealing from their communal supplies Greely convened an impromptu firing squad and had him shot. Soon, however, they were all so weak that discipline became a meaningless concept. Besides, there was hardly anyone left to maintain it. At the end of the third week of June 1884 only seven men remained alive. When the tent partially collapsed they did not bother to put it back up, but lay under its folds, waiting for death.

While Greely's expedition was withering at Cape Sabine, the authorities were ponderously examining its plight. First there came a lengthy inquiry into why the *Proteus* and *Yantic* had made such a mess of things, which occasioned a mild censure of the two officers responsible. Then Congress and Senate spent weeks debating just how much should be spent on Greely's rescue and who should be allowed to take part in the mission. The deliberation was prolonged by petty squabbles over procedure and errors of wording. When a resolution was eventually passed it transpired that few ice-going ships were available and the two they bought – the *Proteus*'s sister ship, the *Bear*, and a whaler, the *Thetis* – were so expensive that there was no money left for a third. In desperation, they broadcast an alert to the whaling fleet: whoever found Greely's expedition would be entitled to a bounty of $25,000. Fortunately, Britain remembered how much the US had spent in the Franklin search and donated the *Alert*, which was re-equipped under the supervision of its erstwhile commander, George Nares. In April 1884, therefore, three ships sailed for Smith Sound under the overall command of Captain Winfield Scott Schley. Behind them came a line of eight bounty-hungry whalers.

On 21 June 1884 the first of the ships, Schley's *Thetis*, reached Littleton Island. They found nothing save traces of earlier expeditions and a single, untouched cache left by the *Proteus*. When the *Bear* arrived the following day Schley decided to snoop around Cape Sabine before pressing on to Lady

Franklin Bay. He did not really expect to find Greely on Ellesmere Island, but the effort had to be made; besides, it would be wise to deposit a new cache at Cape Sabine just in case he should miss Greely's party on his way north – and just in case, if the *Thetis* sank, as had the *Proteus*, he himself had need of the food.

Schley reached Cape Sabine on 22 June and divided his men into four groups, three of which were to investigate the existing cairns for messages, while the fourth was to comb the shoreline for any signs of Greely's presence. Almost at once the first returned with a bundle of papers that gave details of the journey from Fort Conger and the whereabouts of Greely's camp. Soon afterwards the second returned with Greely's journal, various scientific documents and confirmation of his present whereabouts When they reached the survivors' camp they were greeted by a surreal sight. One man seemed already dead. Another, who lay handless and footless, with a spoon attached to his forearm, seemed on the point of death. Two others were fumbling with a rubber bottle and a tin can. Stranger than all the rest was a bearded creature in a skullcap and dressing-gown, who crouched at the back of the tent. One of Schley's officers crawled in, took his hand, and asked if he was Greely. 'Yes,' came the faltering reply. 'Seven of us left – here we are – dying – like men. Did what I came to do – beat the best record.'

As the starving men were carried to the ships, Schley began a thorough – almost forensic – examination of the scene. The bodies were exhumed (or, in some cases, simply lifted off the ground) and the debris of the camp was picked over with care. Logs, scientific records, instruments, any objects of value – all were carefully retrieved and brought aboard the *Bear*. Two days later, on 24 June, Schley's little fleet sailed for home. It reached Portsmouth, New Hampshire, on 1 August, to be greeted by a 15,000-strong crowd. By then, however, there were only six of Greely's expedition left. Elison, who had hung on so miraculously, had had to undergo further amputations; too weak to survive the operation, he had died on 8 July.

Greely's expedition had in some respects been very successful. It had reached a new furthest north, and it had brought back a fund of data concerning meteorology, geology, astronomy, oceanography and biology. When published, his discoveries filled a two-volume, 13,000-page report, accompanied by charts and photographs, which comprised one of the most comprehensive bodies of Arctic research to date. In human terms, however, it had been a disaster. On every side, and at every opportunity, since August 1883 the expedition had been marked by incompetence and ill-judgement. Not only had Greely led his men into danger, from which the authorities had failed to rescue them, but he had actually shot one of them. (He was officially exonerated on this count, it being treated as a case of mutiny.) Even worse, it was found that some of the bodies had been eaten. Six of the corpses bore clear signs of having been tampered with. Someone had taken a knife, or scalpel, and cut strips of flesh from their limbs, carefully stripping the skin and then folding it back to disguise the incisions. Greely and the rest denied all knowledge of it. In retrospect, Dr Pavy was a possible culprit: he had the necessary surgical skills; he had (now the survivors thought of it) made a number of trips to fetch water from a pool near where the bodies had been buried; and before his death he had been in suspiciously good health. But maybe it had been someone else. Without evidence it was impossible to say.

Combined with the casualty rate, the evidence of cannibalism among Greely's men brought Arctic exploration into even further disrepute. If this was what happened to even a scientific expedition then the whole business was not worth the candle. 'The scientific information secured,' declaimed the President, 'could not compensate for the loss of human life.' The press agreed. 'Let there be an end to this folly,' said the *New York Times*. Needless to say, nobody in the Arctic fraternity paid the slightest attention. And after a while, neither did the public.

Fridtjof Nansen (1893–6)

In 1888, almost on a whim, a young Norwegian neuroscientist named Fridtjof Nansen decided to become the first person to cross Greenland on skis. The casual ease with which he completed the task changed his life. Abandoning his studies, he began to raise funds for an expedition to the North Pole – an expedition, as he explained to would-be sponsors, that would be unlike any other. He proposed not to fight the Arctic, as others had done, but to go (quite literally) with the flow. Noting that debris from De Long's *Jeannette*, which had sunk off Siberia in 1881, had washed up on the shores of Greenland, he concluded that an east-west current ran beneath the ice; therefore, if he set a ship in the pack above Siberia it would eventually be deposited in the Atlantic, having traversed the Arctic Ocean and possibly, even, having touched the North Pole. His plan met with approval, the money was raised, and on 24 June 1893 he left Christiania (modern Oslo) aboard the *Fram* on a journey that would change the face of polar exploration and make him one of the greatest celebrities of the age.

The *Fram* was no ordinary vessel. Rounded at prow and stern, and in cross-section shaped somewhat like an egg, it was constructed specifically for Arctic travel: if squeezed by the ice it would simply pop up and rest on the surface. It also contained a generator that could be driven by wind-power, a store of provisions so varied as to supply whatever magical ingredient was necessary to fend off scurvy, plus a 600-volume library to provide intellectual stimulus during the five years the journey was expected to last. There was the usual collection of compasses, chronometers, pendulums, reels of line for sounding the ocean floor and a host of other instruments – for, as Nansen swore, the *Fram*'s voyage was primarily scientific. But there were other items too, none of which had an obvious scientific application: some portable paraffin stoves by the name of 'Primus' that were 600 per cent more efficient than standard coal- or oil-fuelled models; a stock of skis to suit every snow condition; several light and flexible sledges designed by Nansen himself; a new type of conical tent, also designed by Nansen, which could be erected and dismantled in seconds; and a couple of kayaks similar to the Inuit versions he had encountered in Greenland but with watertight compartments in the bows. In addition, the *Fram* carried a team of dogs. This

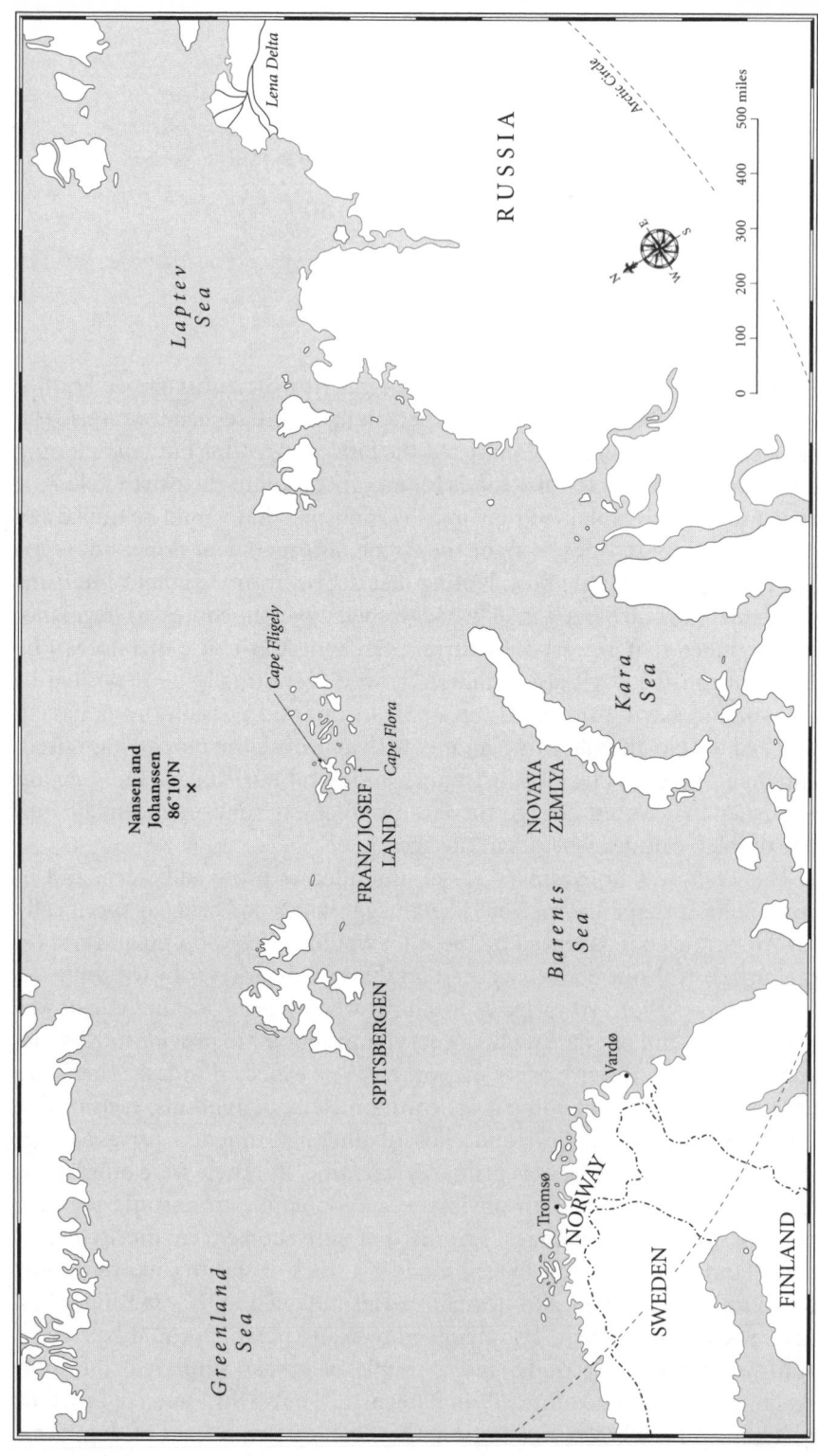

supercargo was included for one reason only: if the *Fram* did not reach the North Pole Nansen intended to jump ship and ski there.

On 25 September 1893 the *Fram* entered the ice north of the Lena Delta and began its long voyage west. Everything worked to perfection: the ship rose from every nip as it had been designed to do, the crew were not attacked by scurvy, the wind generator did its job faultlessly – everything was fine. Caught, initially, in the triangular drift that had bedevilled Weyprecht and De Long, the *Fram* worked its way slowly north. The months passed, the crew became bored and complacent, the ship's doctor began to dabble with drugs. The inaction made Nansen furious: 'Can't something happen?' he wrote in his journal. But nothing did happen, beyond the occasional ice-squeeze, from which the *Fram* emerged, as always, intact. During the first long winter Nansen roamed the pack, peering ever northwards. On 15 January 1894 he saw a flat icescape that stretched to the horizon and, for all he knew, to the Pole itself. 'It might almost be called an easy expedition for two men,' he wrote.

Throughout that year he prepared for the forthcoming odyssey. The sledges and kayaks, which had been packed in kit form, were assembled, the skis were treated with Stockholm pitch and, after much moody perusal, Nansen selected a travelling companion. His name was Hjalmar Johanssen, a dour but capable drifter who, before signing on as a stoker, had been among other things a prison warden and an international gymnast. On 14 March 1895, with the *Fram* sittingly slightly above the 84th parallel – a record north for a ship – Nansen and Johanssen departed for the Pole.

Nansen's plan was scary. He and Johanssen would ski north with a couple of dog teams hauling their kayaks and supplies for 100 days. As the food ran out they would feed the dogs to each other and then, when they had gone as far they could, they would retreat to Franz Josef Land, where they hoped to meet a whaler. If no whaler was to hand they would paddle – and maybe sail, for Nansen had equipped his kayaks with bamboo masts – to Norway. It was 350 nautical miles to the Pole, another 500 back to Franz Josef Land and yet another 1,000 to Norway. To call the proposed journey foolhardy would have been an understatement. It was a monumental gamble, involving unsupported travel in one of the world's coldest and most unpredictable climates, across an unexplored ocean riddled with potential hazards, with an escape route so uncertain as scarcely to merit the name.

Initially it looked as if the gamble would pay off. The ice was smooth, and the two Norwegians swept over it at an unprecedented rate, covering 20 miles per day for the first week. By 29 March they were at a record north of 85° 09'; if conditions held good and they continued at the same pace they would be at the top of the earth within a fortnight. Conditions did not hold. During the second week they encountered rough ice interspersed with leads of open water; the tents, which had been made of light material for ease of transport, provided chilly shelter, despite the use of the Primus stoves; at the same time the pack started drifting south; in the course of five days they made only 50 miles. By 8 April they had crossed the 86th parallel and Nansen called a halt. It was just conceivable that they would reach the Pole if they carried on, but if they did they would never return to tell the tale; as it was, their provisions were barely sufficient to last them back to Franz Josef Land. They allowed themselves a congratulatory feast of 'lobscouse, bread-and-butter, dry chocolate, stewed whortle berries, and our hot whey drink', before crawling into the tent in preparation for the trek home.

Extraordinarily, the ice that had given them so much trouble during the last ten days was now a flat plain over which they sped south as rapidly as they had travelled north during that first halcyon week. On 13 April, however, Johanssen found that his chronometer had stopped. Of itself this was no cause for worry; both men carried a chronometer and, as had happened in the past, if one stopped all they had to do was reset it against the one that still ticked. But when they came to do so they discovered that Nansen's chronometer had stopped too. The consequences were potentially disastrous: without knowing the exact Greenwich Meridian Time, to which their chronometers had been set in Christiania, they could not calculate their longitude. Without knowing their longitude they could not chart their east-west progress, and unless they could do that they would be unable to steer accurately for Franz Josef Land. Hesitantly, Nansen reset his chronometer to what he thought was the right time, but with a deliberate eastward bias, so that when they hit the latitude of Franz Josef Land all they had to do was march west until they reached safety. Even so, without knowing when the timepiece had stopped he had no idea if the exaggeration was sufficient. If it was not, and they arrived at the correct latitude but to the *west* of Franz Josef Land, they would walk until they either starved or fell into the Atlantic.

On that same day Nansen also found he had left their compass behind at the last stop. He skied back to fetch it, leaving Johanssen on his own. A follower rather than a leader, Johanssen was immediately struck by doubts. Would Nansen fall through the ice? Would he be able to find his way back through the wilderness? If he did not return what would Johanssen do next? Johanssen's description of his wait is a terrifyingly evocative description of Arctic solitude. 'Never have I felt anything so still,' he wrote. 'Not the slightest sound of any kind disturbed the silence near or far; the dogs lay as if lifeless with their heads on their paws in the white snow, glistening in the gleaming sun. It was so frighteningly still, I had to remain where I sat, I dared not move a limb; I hardly dared to breathe.' When he heard the swish of Nansen's skis he was overcome with relief – testimony both to the loneliness of their position and the power of Nansen's presence.

Nansen's was, indeed, a gigantic personality. Tall, fit, single-minded, possessed of tremendous drive and supreme self-confidence, he conquered everyone he met with sheer force of charisma and intellect. Yet, at the same time, he was prone to dark mood shifts in which he identified with ancient

Norse gods. Inspirational on first acquaintance, overpowering on prolonged contact, dangerous in confined spaces, Nansen was not a man with whom one dealt lightly. Johanssen found him self-centred, humourless, 'unsociable and clumsy in the smallest things; egoistic in the highest degree'. Then again, Johanssen was a born complainer, physically strong but psychologically weak, who depended upon the guidance of others. (He would later become an alcoholic, whose directionless career ended in suicide.) Probably this was why Nansen chose him for the North Pole journey in the first place. He could not brook a travelling companion who might voice opinions or, unthinkably, question his decisions. And firm decisions were needed if they were ever to get home.

On 4 June, at 82° 17' N, Nansen judged Franz Josef to be 25 miles distant. It was a guess, of course, because nothing was certain now the chronometers had stopped. In recent days their progress had been pitifully slow, hampered by poor weather, uneven ice and open leads. On 3 June they had travelled less than a mile. On the bright side, they were now so far south that they could augment their diminishing supplies by shooting seals, walruses and polar bears. But having enough to eat was of little use if they could not find their way home. 'Here we are then,' Nansen wrote during a blizzard, 'hardly knowing what to do next. What the going is like outside I do not know yet, but probably not much better than yesterday, and whether we ought to push on the little we can, or go out and try to capture a seal, I cannot decide.' In the event they did both and, on 24 July, they saw land. The trouble was, it was not like any land on their maps. As described by Julius von Payer in 1873, the northernmost point of Franz Josef Land, Cape Fligely, looked nothing like what rose from the sea before them. Had they reached Franz Josef Land or an undiscovered island to its west? They no longer cared. Shooting their last dogs, they abandoned their sledges and took to the kayaks (damaged during the long journey, but repaired hastily with candle wax) and paddled towards what had to be at least interim salvation. It was 146 days since they had left the *Fram*.

The island on which they landed in early August 1895 *was* part of Franz Josef Land, and as they made their way through the archipelago they met more and more territory that accorded with their maps. There were no whaling ships in the vicinity, however, and by the end of the month, as the weather began to deteriorate, Nansen realized they would have to spend the winter in the Arctic. They therefore set up camp on a desolate and uncharted spit of land and resigned themselves to a long, cold wait.

The shelter in which they intended to survive the winter comprised a three-foot-deep trench surrounded by a parapet of stones, roofed with walrus hides on a ridge-pole of driftwood. Before the cold came in earnest they were able to shoot enough polar bears, seals and walruses to see them through the season. Then, their larder amply stocked, they crawled into what they called 'The Hole', and resigned themselves to an imprisonment that would not end until the arrival of spring. The situation was not life-threatening: they had enough meat to keep starvation and scurvy at bay; and the blubber on the carcases provided fuel to cook their meals, melt snow into drinking water, and give them light. But life was dull, uncomfortable and unhygienic. The diet made them constipated and, after a while, gave them piles; in the absence of washing facilities they were reduced to scraping the grease from their underwear and adding it to the blubber lamps; they had nothing to do except talk, read over and over again Nansen's navigational tables (the only printed material they possessed) and, when those stimuli were exhausted, sleep. For Nansen the enforced stillness presented an opportunity to reflect upon Scandinavian mythology. For Johanssen it was a time of undistilled loneliness: the only sign that he existed as a person rather than an adjunct to his leader's ambition came when Nansen addressed him in the familiar tense for the first time in the entire journey. In this manner they passed eight long months in a snow-covered ditch on a strip of land whose existence was unknown to anybody save themselves.

On 19 May the ice cleared and they resumed their journey. But within a month they were struggling: on 12 June Nansen had to swim after their kayaks when they drifted into the sea while he and Johanssen took bearings from an iceberg; and on 13 June both vessels were fatally punctured by a pack of irate walruses. Dragging the craft on to yet another strip of uncharted land, they spent four days over the repairs and then, as they were about to re-embark, Nansen heard dogs barking. Johanssen listened closely, but said it was nothing: just seabirds, he assured his commander. Nansen was insistent, and skied inland to investigate. The decision saved both their lives.

Nansen and Johanssen were not the only people on Franz Josef Land during the winter of 1895–6. A British expedition under Frederick Jackson had been at Cape Flora throughout the season. When Jackson was alerted by a team member to an unusual human outline on the ice he pooh-poohed it. 'Oh nonsense,' he said, 'it is a walrus, surely?' Like Nansen, however, he thought it best to make sure. So he, too, donned his skis. If nothing else the trip would be good exercise. What he found was not a walrus but a black, greasy, shaggy-haired, foul-smelling creature whom he took at first for a shipwrecked Scandinavian whaler. Yet something about the man's bearing seemed familiar. As Jackson drew closer, he realized that the ragamuffin looked remarkably like a polar fundraiser he had met at the Royal Geographical Society four years previously. When their skis were almost touching, Jackson put a name to the memory. 'Aren't you Nansen?' he asked.

On a par with Stanley's 'Dr Livingstone, I presume?' Jackson's understated query was one of the great moments of 19th-century exploration. It was sheer luck that the only two parties in Franz Josef Land that year had bumped into each other. No fiction writer could have contrived such an encounter, each group initially dismissing the other as a chimera until, driven respectively by curiosity and desperation, their leaders came together in the heart of the Arctic. And what made their meeting so incredible was the fact that Nansen and Johanssen had spent three-quarters of a year in 'The Hole' while, just around the corner, Jackson and his men had been quartered in fully provisioned, wooden-hutted splendour. If not for the walrus attack, Nansen and Johanssen might never have known there were other explorers in the region and would have perished in their battered, leaky kayaks. As Jackson wrote: 'I can positively state that not a million to one chance of Nansen reaching Europe existed, and that but for our finding him on the ice, as we did, the world would never have heard of him again.' He was so amazed by the encounter that, when Johanssen was also rescued, he refused to let either man change their clothes so that he could take staged photographs of their arrival.

Jackson's support ship arrived on 25 July, and by 9 September the two Norwegians were home. Here they learned that the *Fram* had completed its drift and had arrived intact at Spitsbergen. Nansen's theories had been proved correct, his rash adventure to the Pole had ended without casualty, and he had proved indisputably that the best means of polar exploration was by skis and dog sled, carrying the lightest, most efficient equipment and taking as few team members as possible. Beneath the mountains that circled Christiania, smoke belched from yachts, tugs and steamers as every available ship, private or public, came to greet them. Nansen was invited to dine at the royal palace, and two months later published a 300,000-word account of the expedition. Well written, with photographs, drawings and colour illustrations by Nansen himself, the two-volume journal was a bestseller. When the British mountaineer Edward Whymper reviewed it he wrote: 'almost as great an advance as has been accomplished by all other voyages in the nineteenth century put together ... He is a Man in a Million.'

Salomon Andrée (1897)

Air travel, it was agreed by almost every explorer, was the technology of the future. This opinion was shared very particularly by those who had experienced the harsh climates and landscapes of the polar regions. If one could only fly, distances that would otherwise take years could be covered in days and the back-breaking business of sledging could be obviated. Unfortunately, at the end of the 19th century humankind could not fly. Or, more precisely, it could not fly very well. For centuries enthusiasts had tried to make ballooning a dependable means of getting from A to B, but the secret had always eluded them. The trouble lay first in the technology that kept the balloon aloft – the use of hot air meant that fire was an omnipresent threat – and secondly, the impossibility of steering, for however much balloonists claimed that they flew, all they really did was drift at the mercy of the wind. Nor could they drift very far, because their supply of hot air was limited by the amount of fuel they carried in the basket. By the late 1800s the first problem had been solved: by using hydrogen instead of hot air, balloonists could stay up for as long as gas remained within the canopy. But steering remained a problem. Until, that is, Salomon August Andrée turned his mind to it.

An employee of Sweden's Patent Department, Andrée was a born tinkerer, fascinated by technology and particularly by ballooning. In a series of experiments he found that if he draped ropes over the basket so that they dragged along the ground he could make a balloon drift in more or less whatever direction he wished. A rope to one side led the balloon one way, a rope to the other led it another way. These drag ropes also acted as ballast, ensuring that the balloonist was always in control: if the balloon tried to rise the weight of the ropes and their friction against the ground would bring it back to a safe and controllable distance above the surface. Perchance the drag ropes might catch on an obstacle, but Andrée had the answer: his ropes were equipped with screw fittings; all one had to do was lean over the basket and twist until the trapped section came free. After several experiments, in which Andrée discovered he could do almost anything with a balloon save go into reverse, he announced his intention to fly to the North Pole from Spitsbergen.

The Arctic community was sceptical. What would happen if the wind

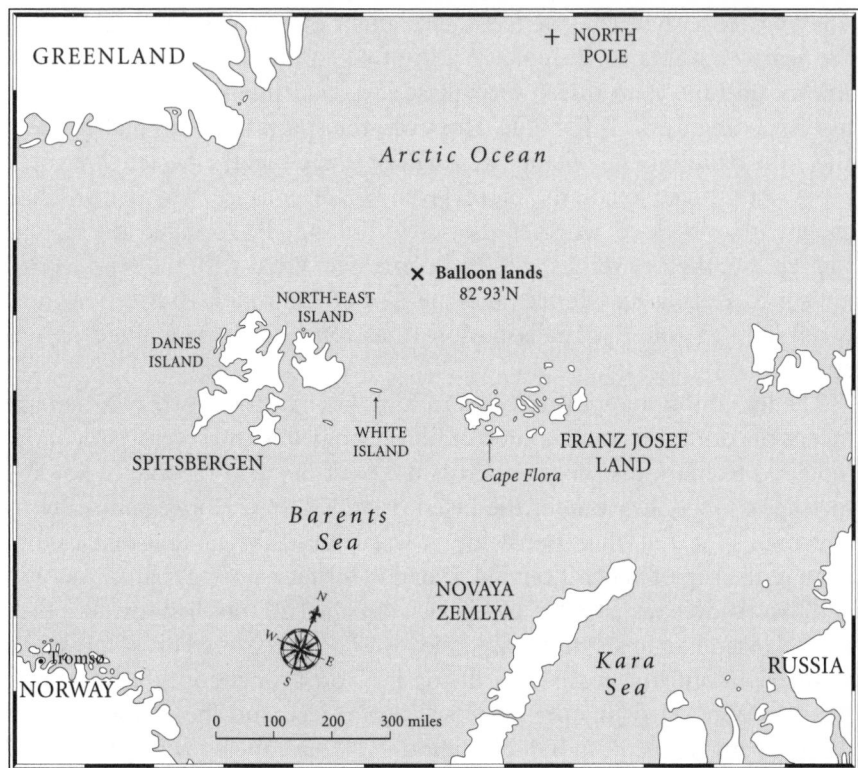

GREENLAND

+ NORTH POLE

Arctic Ocean

✕ **Balloon lands**
82°93'N

NORTH-EAST ISLAND

DANES ISLAND

WHITE ISLAND

SPITSBERGEN

FRANZ JOSEF LAND

Cape Flora

Barents Sea

NOVAYA ZEMLYA

N
W E
S

Tromsø

NORWAY

Kara Sea

RUSSIA

0   100   200   300 miles

changed direction, if the balloon lost gas, if it crashed? Andrée replied that he would take sledges with which he could travel over the pack to the nearest landmass, be it Spitsbergen, Franz Josef Land or an as yet undiscovered Arctic continent. But what if he was unable to reach land? In that case, Andrée said forthrightly, he would drown. Amidst the oohs and aahs he took the opportunity to criticize previous expeditions: over the last 70 years Arctic exploration had cost hundreds of lives and millions of pounds; his expedition was relatively cheap, and even if it failed the only casualties would be himself and the two others he intended to take with him. Why should anyone object? When they did object Andrée silenced them with an irrefutable argument: 'Dangerous? Perhaps. But what am I worth?'

In the summer of 1897 the *Eagle* – the largest balloon the world had ever seen – rose within a wooden scaffold on Danes Island, to the north of Spitsbergen. For miles around the seabed was stained red from the effluent of iron filings and sulphuric acid that had created the 170,000 cubic feet of hydrogen necessary to inflate the 818 square feet of silk squares linked by 86 miles of stitching. Andrée and his two companions, Knut Fraenkel and Nils Strindberg, waited impatiently for the right flying conditions until finally, on 11 July, the wind swung to the north. At 1.43 p.m. the three Swedes climbed into the basket and Andrée gave orders for the ground crew to cut the ropes.

The *Eagle* rose swiftly to 300 feet then, caught in an icy downdraught from the nearby mountains, dropped so abruptly that the basket touched the sea. Andrée and his team threw out ballast and soon the balloon was at 1,600 feet, speeding towards the Pole. However, the spectators who had come to cheer the balloonists to victory were aghast to see that the *Eagle's* three drag ropes were still coiled on the shore. From whatever cause, whether they had caught on a rock or whether the screw linkings had rotated during the sudden dip, their lower sections had come free. What with the sand he had jettisoned during his plunge, and the loss of the ropes, Andrée was now bereft of 1,500 pounds of ballast. More disastrously, he was no longer able to steer.

The loss did not appear to concern him. He had taken two rudimentary means of communication: a coop of homing pigeons and several cork buoys intended to mark his progress across the pack but also capable of holding messages. On 15 July one of the pigeons landed on a Norwegian sealer. A crewman shot it at once, but before it was cooked the captain managed to retrieve the slip of paper it carried. Dated 13 July, it reported that all was well and that Andrée was at 82° 2' N – in two days he had travelled further north than Nansen had in six months. A buoy was later recovered by a Norwegian woman combing the beach for driftwood. It, too, brought optimistic tidings. At 10.00 p.m. on 11 July the *Eagle* was at 830 feet, and the going was fine: 'Weather magnificent. In best of humours ...' Alas, the buoy was not found until August 1900, by which time nothing had been seen of the *Eagle* for three years. It would be another three decades before the world discovered what had happened to a flight that Andrée had estimated would take only a few days.

In 1930 a Norwegian sealer, the *Bratvaag*, dropped anchor off White Island to the east of Spitsbergen. It would not have done so were it not for a group of scientists who had come along for the ride and who insisted that they needed to study the island's glaciers and rock formations. Their investigation stopped before it had even started. On landing, they found the remains of a campsite. Its contents had been scattered by polar bears, but amidst the debris were three skeletons, several rolls of undeveloped film and a number of waterlogged journals. Here were the remains of Andrée's expedition to the North Pole.

From what forensic specialists were able to piece together, Andrée, Fraen- kel and Strindberg had been unfazed by the loss of their guide ropes. They had whisked northwards in complete confidence that they would soon be at the top of the globe. They joked, laughed, cooked a Chateaubriand steak on a special device that they lowered from the basket (fire being inadvisable directly beneath so much hydrogen) and had the very best of times. They were disconcerted by the way their balloon reacted to drops in temperature: when the sun was obscured by cloud the gas contracted and the basket bumped over the ice; but when the cloud passed they jumped hundreds of feet into the air. These shifts were of brief duration, and any discomfort caused by the bouncing of the basket could be avoided by climbing into the ring that connected it to the balloon. When Strindberg did so he declared the experience 'confoundedly pleasant'. On 12 July, however, a mass of dark cloud appeared on the horizon. Unable to steer, Andrée could only wait and watch as the *Eagle* drifted into it. As before, the basket began to strike the ice. The distance between each bounce depended on a wind that was now strong, now weak, and which switched at random from north to south. They threw out ballast and, when that failed to lift them, equipment and provisions. It did little good. At 11.20 p.m. the *Eagle* sank low enough for the stubs of its guide ropes to wrap themselves around a block of ice, and came to a halt less than 200 feet above the pack. Andrée told Fraenkel and Strindberg to get some rest while he kept watch through the wee hours. Amidst the rattling of the lines, the flap of fabric and the dispiriting patter of rain on the canopy, he composed his journal entry. The first lines were a masterpiece of understatement. 'It is not a little strange,' he wrote, 'to be floating here above the Polar Sea.'

It was not only strange but perilous. They were stranded above an unexplored sector of the Arctic, had jettisoned most of their food to keep themselves in the air, and, worst of all, the balloon was beginning to sink. Ever since it had been inflated, hydrogen had been seeping from the miles of stitching that linked the balloon's silk squares. Of itself, this was not a worry: Andrée was confident that their journey would be over before the loss became apparent. More distressing was the way the hydrogen contracted in the cold, and how, despite every precaution, rain and fog froze on the canopy. The balloon's reduced lifting power could not cope with the accumulation of ice. On 13 July the wind switched, the ropes disentangled themselves and the *Eagle* resumed its course. But the weight on the canopy had become so great that its progress could hardly be called flying. By 5.30 on the morning of 14 July, after four and a half hours scraping over the ice, Andrée released the remaining gas and all three jumped out of the basket.

They were at 82° 56' N, 29° 52' E, on a field of ice riven by open leads and pressure ridges. The temperature was below zero. Their thin ballooning clothes offered no protection against the wind. They had no experience of life on the Arctic pack and their supplies were sufficient for a few months at most. It was 192 miles to Spitsbergen and 210 miles to Franz Josef Land, the two places where they could be sure of finding provisions and, eventually, transport to safety. Andrée was not a man to panic. Reviewing their situation, he decided to head for Franz Josef Land where, although the journey might be longer, the chance of meeting a whaler was greater and where, even if the fleet had left for the winter, they could at least find shelter in the remains of Frederick Jackson's camp at Cape Flora. Accordingly, they loaded three sledges with 200 pounds of food and a canvas boat, and began the long haul south.

It was hard going yet, remarkably, they had no doubt they would survive. 'I am in excellent health,' Strindberg wrote in his journal. 'We are sure to come home by and by.' By 4 August, however, Andrée found that, although they were walking south-east, the pack was carrying them due west. Accordingly, he changed his plan. They would head instead for Spitsbergen, which he expected to reach in six or seven weeks. Turning about, they plodded north-west. Aided initially by favourable winds and good conditions, they became even more confident. 'We asked ourselves in silence if we might not possibly journey on in this glorious way to the end,' Strindberg wrote. Not if the Arctic could help it. Six weeks into their trek the drift changed direction, pushing them south-east at tremendous speed – in the course of three days they were carried 60 nautical miles in the direction from which they had come – and by mid-September Andrée announced they could no longer expect to reach either of their goals. They would have to winter on the ice.

It could have been worse, Andrée judged. Their sledges were in reasonable shape, and they still had the canvas boat for emergencies. They were fit and healthy, apart from Fraenkel, who suffered from unaccountable bouts of diarrhoea. All they had to do was make a shelter and shoot enough seals and polar bears to last them until spring. This they did, constructing an ice-brick igloo on the thickest, solidest-looking floe they could find, and bunkered down for the season. In his ingenious fashion Andrée constructed a net with which, if their stocks of meat ran out, he proposed to trawl for plankton. 'Our humour is pretty good,' he wrote, 'although joking and smiling are not of ordinary occurrence.'

On 17 September, the drift having carried them capriciously to the west, salvation appeared. It manifested itself as a block of white that remained in the same position no matter how the pack moved. If it was a glacier, and it could be nothing else, they were approaching an island. Once on solid land, their chances of survival would be greatly improved. Consulting his charts, Andrée saw that it was called New Iceland or, more commonly, White Island. The floe drifted slowly towards it, hovered at a distance of 1,000 yards and then, capriciously, sped south-east until the island vanished over the horizon. On 1 October the floe broke up, forcing the three Swedes on to a fragment that measured no more than 80 feet in diameter. A few days later, however, the drift was carrying them north-west, and once again the glacier was within sight. 'No one had lost courage,' Andrée wrote. 'With such comrades one should be able to manage under, I may say, any circumstances.' It was the last sentence that the experts in Tromsø were able to decipher.

From the remaining scraps of paper and the evidence collected by the *Bratvaag*, a sorrowful tale unfolded. Andrée's team had erected a tent, had secured it with boulders, had lit a signal fire, and had begun their long wait. Then they had died. The cause was probably trichinosis, a parasitical disease carried by many animals, including the polar bears whose flesh they had been eating for several months. Strindberg had gone first: his body was discovered beneath a tomb of boulders. Fraenkel had maybe been next: he was found on the shore, possibly having expired while dragging driftwood to the fire. Andrée's skeleton, knocked about by bears, lay against the rocks that had once supported the tent. His bones gave no clue as to how, or when, the ever-optimistic aeronaut realized that his dream had become a nightmare.

Fernand Foureau (1899–1900)

By the end of the 19th century France very much wished to link its colony of Algeria with those in Central and West Africa. Unfortunately, the intervening stretch of territory was the Sahara, the world's largest and bleakest desert. So far every attempt to raise the tricolour over this inhospitable waste had ended in disaster. Singly and in groups, French travellers had either been thwarted by the terrain or, more usually, murdered by its nomadic inhabitants, the Tuareg. When, in 1880, a column of French infantry under Colonel Paul Flatters marched south to negotiate with the Tuareg it was slaughtered almost to a man. In an age of imperial progress this was an unheard-of state of affairs: if other nations, Britain in particular, could seize countries around the world – in the case of India a whole subcontinent – seemingly at will and with little hindrance, then France should be able to do likewise with the Sahara. That it had not yet managed to do so was considered, in some quarters, an insult to national honour.

But even the most jingoistic supporters of Saharan conquest agreed that the task would be difficult. This dry wilderness was nigh impassable to a conventional army with its many men and long supply trains. And however great such an army's firepower might be, it was of little use against the hit-and-run tactics favoured by the Tuareg, and of no use at all against the dunes. The mountain stronghold of the Hoggar, for example, lay almost 1,000 miles south of Algiers and was surrounded by acre upon acre of trackless sand and rock in which only the Tuareg knew how to survive. With their knowledge of the wells, their skill with camels, their ability to navigate by the stars and the sun, and their centuries-old experience of life in one of the world's most hostile climates, they were absolute masters of their environment. No European could match them. Yet if the Sahara could not for the moment be conquered, it could at least be crossed. This was the dream of many men, but none pursued it so avidly as Fernand Foureau.

An Algerian settler turned explorer, Foureau made his first foray into the Sahara in 1879. Since then he had mounted 11 expeditions, and had crossed more than 13,000 miles of uncharted wilderness. But although acknowledged as France's most seasoned desert hand, he had never been able to reach the Hoggar and had never realized his greatest ambition: to traverse the Sahara

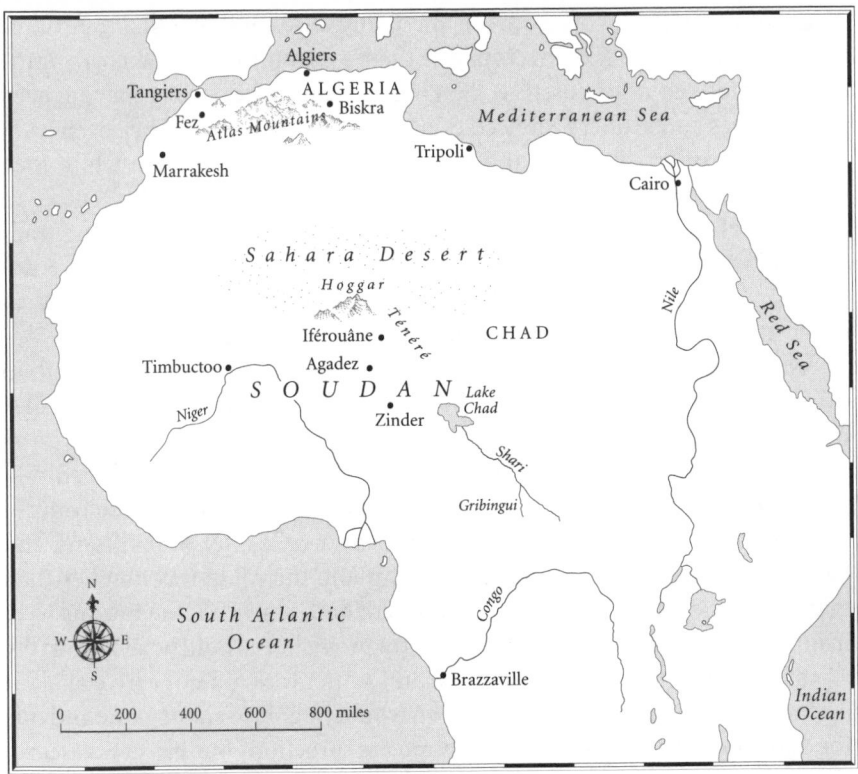

from top to bottom. In the late 1890s, however, thanks to a bequest from the Geographical Society of Paris, and with the offer of arms and money from the French government, he embarked on a journey that was to take him not only across the desert but thousands of miles further to the Congo River.

On paper, Foureau's expedition was a scientific one; and he did, indeed, take several scientists with him. Most of his assistants were later found to be too young, too incompetent or simply surplus to requirements, and were therefore sent home. Their absence did not worry him overmuch (he was quite capable of making the trip without them), but it laid bare the expedition's true, covert purpose. While Foureau wanted to make a peaceful journey from one side of the Sahara to the other, his military escort, under the command of Major François Lamy, had different objectives: the first was to show the Tuareg that French soldiers could cross the desert if they wanted to; and the second was to reach Lake Chad, where Lamy's force would combine with two other columns – one sent from Senegal, the other from the Congo – to establish French sovereignty over the region.

The Foureau-Lamy expedition that left the northern oasis of Biskra in October 1898 comprised 381 men, two Hotchkiss 42-mm cannon with 200 shells apiece, and an assemblage of 1,004 camels to carry food, water and ammunition. As leaders of the largest, most powerful foray France had ever made into the desert, both Foureau and Lamy were confident that the Tuareg would not dare attack them. Initially, their assumption proved correct: the caravan plodded unopposed to the Hoggar, where the Tuareg, having eyed Lamy's rifles and artillery, showed every sign of friendliness. They even went so far as to offer advice for the next stage of the journey: the white men should be careful, they said, because they were about to enter the Ténéré, an exceptionally cruel stretch of desert; also, if they survived the crossing, they should be aware that the people on the other side of the Ténéré were not necessarily as friendly as themselves. Neither Foureau nor Lamy paid as much attention to the Tuareg's warnings as they should have.

Foureau and Lamy had fallen prey to the old delusion that size was all. In Europe this might have held true, but in the Sahara, where wells were infrequent and often foul, and where pasture was minimal, it was small, rapid parties that had the best chance of survival. The Foureau-Lamy expedition was vast and slow, travelling only as fast as its troops could march. En route to the Hoggar, camels died as they struggled over mile after mile of sand and harsh rock. The men, too, started to complain: the route was tougher than they had anticipated; the water was tainted; and, above all, the rations were insufficient. It had been arranged that extra provisions would be sent from the north, but they never arrived on time and sometimes did not arrive at all. It had also been hoped that the expedition would be able to shoot game and buy food from caravans moving in the opposite direction. But game was scarce and the few caravans they met sold them only dates and the occasional sheep. As the men became hungrier and hungrier they devoured the newly dead camels with avidity – often without cooking them properly, for firewood, like everything else in the desert, was in short supply. To hunger was added the boredom of routine: the same loading of the camels in the morning, the same dreary slog during the day, and then the same unloading of the camels in the evening, to be repeated the next day and the one after. To tedium was added physical hardship: boiling days, nights so cold that their water froze in its containers, and a terrain so rugged that sometimes they had to blast a passage with dynamite. There weighed on them, too, the oppression of moving through a landscape of black outcrops and sandy ravines, in which the only signs of humanity were circles of fist-sized stones that marked the graves of those who had died there thousands of years before.

If the journey to the Hoggar had been hard, their discomfort increased a thousandfold once they entered the Ténéré. Here was a 100-mile stretch of sand without pasture or game, whose wells were unreliable and whose only comfort was the uncertain prospect of reaching the other side. Already weakened by ill-treatment and lack of food, the camels died *en masse*. Sometimes they did so with grace, sinking to their knees mid-journey and refusing to budge, peering hopefully after the caravan until they became just a dark blot on the horizon. Sometimes they collapsed at the evening stop. 'The camp had the appearance of a slaughterhouse,' one of Lamy's sergeants wrote in his diary. 'We saw nothing but camels lying outstretched, agonising, the neck twisted and between their legs.' During the course of six days almost 100 camels perished. Foureau had brought his own hardened mounts, but even they fell by the wayside. After a week in which a further 140 beasts died, he became seriously worried. 'In the conditions in which we find ourselves, these numbers are terrible and alarming. It has to be said that, in the middle of the desert, a group of men who see their caravan, or their animals, disappear, is irrevocably lost; nothing can save them; there is nothing left but to lie down in the shade of a boulder and wait for the final deliverance, that is to say, death.'

Even when the expedition crossed the Ténéré and reached the relative prosperity of the Soudan – as the semi-arid territory between the desert and the tropics was then known – the camels continued to die. Forty-three went at their first stop, 35 at the next, then another 19, then 15. By the time the expedition reached Iférouâne, a dusty, godforsaken town in modern Niger, it had only 585 camels to its name. In the expectation of being able to buy replacements, Foureau and Lamy settled down for a well-deserved rest. (By this time they had marched across 1,800 miles of desert.) The rest lasted longer than they would have wished. No fresh mounts were forthcoming, and for two months they sat in Iférouâne while their supplies ran out and the Tuareg launched piecemeal raids that on one occasion escalated into a frontal assault that was repelled only by the use of Lamy's artillery. And still the camels died – 'wax models placed by a fire could not melt away faster,' Foureau recorded in dismay. Soon their caravan numbered less than 200 beasts. The Frenchmen sent messages to the Sultan of Agadez, 200 miles to the south, asking for replacements. The sultan replied that he had none. Would some millet be of use? By 5 June 1899 there remained only 75 beasts of the 1,004 with which they had set out nine months before. In despair, Lamy raided the surrounding countryside for pack animals – donkeys, mostly, and a few camels – and then, having destroyed every inessential piece of equipment, the expedition set out for Agadez on 10 June.

Misled by their guides, they meandered across the Soudan, discarding baggage as their camels and donkeys died. Sometimes they buried their cartridges in the hope of retrieving them, but mostly they just blew them up. Personal belongings were burned, as were clothes. Men and officers alike went barefoot. One sergeant made a pair of trousers from date sacks, but he was an exception. Hunger stalked them. When the column reached Agadez on 28 July, firing a cannon to announce its arrival, it was in a sorry state. Most of the men were naked, and Foureau, stricken by fever and dressed in a purple vest, hung feebly from his saddle. Their spirits rose, however, when the sultan, riding out to greet them, promised both food and camels.

Ten days later, by which time nothing had materialized save a small quantity of millet, Lamy became angry. And when he discovered that he had not been dealing with the sultan after all, but with one of his viziers, he lost his temper. On 9 August he trained his cannon on the town and announced that unless he received camels and a guide forthwith he would level every building in sight. The sultan immediately produced several hundred donkeys which, he protested, was all he had in the way of transport. Lamy accepted the gift reluctantly. On 10 August, to the relief of all, the French column left Agadez for the town of Zinder, 300 miles to the south.

The wells were dry, the heat unbearable and the pasture nonexistent. The donkeys died, and the guide led them in the wrong direction (Lamy shot him when he found out). Forced to retreat, the expedition was then hit by one of the most violent sandstorms Foureau had ever experienced. One minute they were plodding through the scrub under clear skies; the next they felt a gust of wind and looked up to see the horizon covered in huge, plumed clouds, of a sinister copper colour. 'They advanced with fantastic speed and swept over us with a force that nothing could resist,' Foureau wrote, 'blinding everybody, blowing the baggage from the camels' backs, knocking over the mules. It was impossible to turn your back to it. Sand and gravel flew from every direction. We could not see farther than a few metres.' The storm lasted five and a half hours, and when they returned to Agadez on 18 August Lamy was in such a vile temper that he had to be restrained from blowing the sultan and his town to bits. Even Foureau, who normally took these things in his stride, acknowledged that they had suffered. As he later recalled, in a lecture to London's Royal Geographical Society, 'This march, made under a high temperature by men heavily loaded, without a drop to drink . . . has hardly a parallel in the history of exploration'.

Foureau and Lamy spent another two months at Agadez, negotiating with the sultan for food and camels, until in mid-October Lamy lost patience. He occupied the town's wells and offered the sultan a swap: water for transport. Once again, force worked. The sultan assembled a motley of animals – cows, donkeys and a few camels – and on 17 October the expedition left again for Zinder. Rain had fallen in the interim, making their second journey considerably easier than the first. They had a hard time, nonetheless. The newly verdant countryside was full of thorns and nettles, which were agony to the semi-naked men who pushed through them. And their camels kept dying: on 28 October they lost the last of the original batch.

They reached Zinder on 2 November 1899, parched, hungry and so ragged that they looked more like a collection of bandits than representatives of a European great power. They were greeted by cavalcades of trumpet-blowing African cavalry and – to their astonishment – by a troop of neatly dressed, well-fed troops from French Senegal. During their ordeal Foureau and Lamy had all but forgotten that they were part of a three-pronged attack on Lake Chad. The Senegalese, who were part of that attack, had been left at Zinder to accompany Lamy on his route south. They had food, clothes and, above all, women, all of which the newcomers were cordially invited to share. As the expedition was helped gently into town, some of its members began to cry.

Re-equipped and reinvigorated, the expedition proceeded on its march. On 21 January 1900 Foureau caught his first glimpse of Lake Chad. 'Here it really is,' he exulted, 'the long hoped for lake, the goal of our efforts during these past months, my dream for more than twenty years!' He wrote lyrically of glittering expanses of water, interspersed with islets of reeds, whose shores teemed with game. One day he watched for ten whole minutes as a herd of antelope passed by. His excitement evaporated as the expedition circled Chad to rendezvous with the rest of the force from Senegal. Less a lake than a large, swampy soakaway, Chad was surrounded by marshes and bogs, through which the soldiers waded, cursing. It was only marginally better than being in the desert.

In March they made contact with the Senegalese detachment. And then, to their wonder, they were joined by the Congolese, who had been struggling north to make the Chad rendezvous for more than two years. Both the Congolese and the Senegalese had suffered severely to get where they were and having reached their objective they released their frustration in an orgy of violence. Foureau took no part in the ensuing deplorable bloodshed. Before the action started he had already left Lamy to his devices and was canoeing up one of Lake Chad's tributaries, the River Shari, from whose headwaters he crossed to those of the Gribingui and thence down to the Congo. He reached Brazzaville on 21 July 1900. By 2 September, having caught a steamer from the mouth of the Congo, he was back in France.

Foureau's journey was without parallel in the annals of either French colonialism or Saharan exploration. No European had crossed the desert from top to bottom with such a large body of men. It was near miraculous that they had reached the other side with so few (human) casualties. And although he devoted only 70-odd pages of an 829-page-long journal to the final leg from Chad to the Congo, this part of the journey was in itself a considerable achievement. Admittedly, the military side of his expedition had been less than glorious – Lamy was among the many men who fell in the carnage that brought Chad under French control – but Foureau distanced himself from these unsavoury acts. He stressed, instead, the sheer distance he had covered – 2,500 miles – and the amount of scientific data he had recorded. When his data was eventually published and presented to the Geographical Society of Paris its substance – rock and soil analyses, observations concerning the proportions of African women's breasts, and a number of poorly developed photographs – may have seemed disproportionate to the time, money and lives expended on its collection. Nobody, however, really cared. Foureau had shown that Frenchmen could cross the Sahara, and this was what mattered.

'The circle is now completed,' he wrote in conclusion, 'the work is accomplished, the dream so long pursued has been realised. Farewell Africa. Be kind and hospitable to those who come after us.' He never went to the Sahara again.

The Duke of Abruzzi (1899–1900)

Europe's royal families were no strangers to exploration, having for centuries lent their name (and sometimes their money) to ventures of every conceivable nature. But sponsorship was as far as they cared to go: actually to participate in an expedition was unthinkable. By the end of the 19th century, however, a disturbing trend had become apparent: many of the younger members showed an eagerness for exotic locations, exposing themselves to unhealthy climates and dangerous wildlife in the pursuit of unnecessary adventure. Fortunately for their parents, they were so cosseted that even when hunting tigers or rhinos they were never placed in much discomfort, let alone danger. The Duke of Abruzzi, however, was an exception to the rule.

Luigi Amadeo Giuseppe Mario Fernando Francesco di Savoia-Aosta, Duke of Abruzzi, Prince of the ancient House of Savoy, third son of the King of Spain, cousin to the King of Italy, was a devotee of danger. In 1894, aged 21, he mastered the Matterhorn's perilous Zmutt Ridge and three years later became the first person to climb Alaska's Mount St Elias. Fresh from this triumph, he set his hat at the North Pole. In 1898 he visited Norway in order to quiz Fridtjof Nansen about his recent journey over the ice, and then, in quick succession, sent an order to Siberia for 120 sledge dogs, purchased an Arctic steamer which he rechristened *Stella Polare*, hired a Norwegian crew to man it, scoured the Italian navy for a team of would-be explorers, and informed an old mountaineering colleague, Captain Umberto Cagni, that he was to prepare for a new excursion. There was none of the usual flummery involving governmental permission, the approval of geographical societies and the long, tedious business of fundraising. When a man of Abruzzi's wealth and connections wanted something to happen it happened. By mid-August 1899 the *Stella Polare* was at Franz Josef Land, and by the beginning of September it was ice-bound in Teplitz Bay on Prince Rudolf Island, the northernmost landmass of the archipelago.

Not everything had gone to plan. When Abruzzi collected his dogs from Archangel they were smaller and unhealthier than he had anticipated, and required much bringing on. (Their individual characters and state of health would be a recurring theme of his journal.) And while making its way into

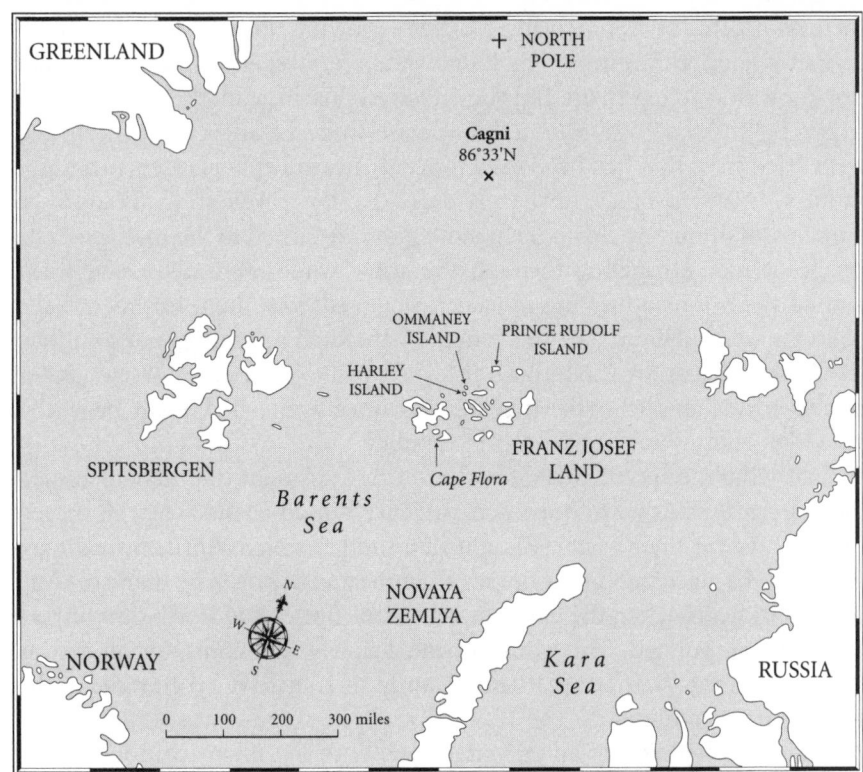

Teplitz Bay the *Stella Polare* had been stabbed by a pressure ridge. It was now uninhabitable thanks to the inflow of water and, worse, was perhaps mortally crippled. But Abruzzi did not care. Ordering Cagni to fix it, he sprang ashore and oversaw the construction of their winter quarters.

In the past, Arctic explorers had either wintered aboard ship, had constructed wooden huts near the shore or, *in extremis*, had huddled in igloos or stone dens. Abruzzi was having none of this. He erected two tents, complete with campbeds and feather mattresses, for sleeping quarters. Around these he erected a marquee that contained their stoves and cooking equipment. Enclosing it all was an even larger, grander marquee, in which they stacked their provisions. The triple-insulated pavilion kept them so warm that some nights Abruzzi had to douse the fires.

Abruzzi's attack on the Pole was well thought out. Three sledge parties would depart the following spring, two of them carrying supplies and the third being the group that would make the final assault on the Pole. The support teams would drop out, in carefully calculated stages, leaving the third to continue until its provisions were exhausted – except, that is, for what was necessary for the return journey. At what point the final team would have to turn back Abruzzi could not guess. They would probably not reach the Pole itself, but he hoped ardently that they would reach a new furthest north. It was much like Nansen's journey, but in reverse and with certain vital modifications. The Italians took kayaks, even though they did not know how to use them. But they rejected skis: instead, the sledgers were to run behind the dogs in *finneskoes*, canoe-shaped leather galoshes stuffed with dried grass that had been used for centuries in Lapland. Also, in a flight of Jules Verne-like fancy, Abruzzi had decided the travellers' loads could be lightened if miniature hydrogen balloons were attached to their sledges. The image of men struggling through the snow while their sledges bobbled behind them is as appealing now as it obviously was then. In practice the balloons were a failure, but the generator that had been designed to inflate them came in handy; Cagni used it to pump the *Stella Polare* free of water and was thus able to make it seaworthy once again. 'I did not believe it possible!' enthused Abruzzi on 15 November.

That winter, in preparation for the spring onslaught, the Italians honed their sledging skills with forays across Prince Rudolf Island. They all passed muster save for their leader. Caught in a sudden storm, Abruzzi sped over the edge of a glacier and into the sea. Clambering to safety, he made his way in the darkness back to the pavilion, where the tips of two frostbitten fingers had to be amputated. The wounds healed slowly, and come spring he was still unfit for the journey north. Reluctantly, he transferred command of the sledge parties to Cagni.

Cagni left Teplitz Bay on 11 March 1900 with ten men, 102 dogs and 13 sledges, each of which carried 510 pounds of food and equipment. After the supply teams had turned back, Cagni and three others would be left with five sledges, 48 dogs and food for 60 days. During the first stages of their march the cold was frightful. At 80° F below freezing the metal in their sledge runners and their ice-axes turned brittle as glass. They went to bed in sleeping bags that were frozen stiff and, on waking, donned clothes that within 30 minutes 'had already become a cuirass of ice'. They moved so slowly that Cagni sent the support teams home ahead of time. And then, in a burst of madness, he decided to make a dash for the Pole once the last party had left. If they reduced their rations there was a chance they might make it. For a while the Arctic led them onwards. With smooth ice and warm days, they ran for up to 12 hours per day, clocking off the miles in a mania of exhilaration. 'We did not feel the fatigue,' Cagni wrote, 'it seemed that life on that endless white plain consisted of placing one foot before the other, and we seemed to find in this mechanical movement peace of mind and repose for the body.'

On 24 April sanity returned. They were at 86° 34' N, had beaten Nansen by 21 miles and had 30 days' food remaining – plus their dogs. Cagni wandered alone over the pack and stared into the distance. 'On the clear horizon, in the form of a crown extending from east to west, was a bluish wall, which, seen from afar, appeared insurmountable.' Was it the edge of the North Pole, the brink of a tremendous landmass? All Cagni knew was that 'It was for us

Terrae ultima thule. They had no choice but to turn south for Teplitz Bay.

It was 250 miles to Franz Josef Land, and Cagni estimated that their provisions would carry them 360 miles if conditions held good. There was a deadline of sorts to be met: if they did not reach solid land by the end of May they were likely to be stranded by the summer thaw. But as they sped over the pack they had no doubt they would be at Teplitz Bay before the ice melted. On 28 April Cagni judged that another four or five days would see them to safety. Even if they went at their slowest ever rate the *Stella Polare* could not be a month distant. Over the following days they were hampered by storms and freezing temperatures. At one point Cagni became so badly frostbitten that he had to amputate the tip of his little finger using nothing more sophisticated than a pair of scissors. Even so, by 8 May they were at 83° and the ship was only 120 miles away. 'From this moment we feel we can live free of anxiety,' Cagni wrote.

The Arctic was not letting them escape so easily. From this moment it attacked them with an almost personal ferocity. On 10 May Cagni's readings revealed that the drift had carried them to a longitude almost 60 miles west of Prince Rudolf Island. It was an irritating setback, but not a life-threatening one: all they had to do was change course to the east. Still, it meant adding an unwelcome few days to their journey. As if it had read his mind, the drift increased its speed. On 12 May, having walked a good 40 miles to the east, Cagni's readings put them some 12 miles *west* of their position on the 10th. Even so, he estimated that they would be at Teplitz Bay within two weeks, and they had food for another 23 days on three-quarter rations. Moroeover, he had good reason to suspect the thaw might be late that year, which would give them extra leeway. The Arctic promptly began to thaw early. They struggled on through wet snow, their path obstructed ever more frequently by open leads, but making good mileage nonetheless – until they checked their position. On 18 May they were even further west than they had been nine days previously. Redoubling their efforts, the Italians made two degrees east by the 29th. In response, the ice began to melt faster. On 30 May it took them 12 hours to travel 1,000 yards. Then the drift pushed them back again. 'In seven days of severe toil we have not advanced three feet to the east!' Cagni wrote on 7 June. 'What will become of us?'

They reduced their rations, eked out their fuel, started eating the dogs, and changed direction so that instead of heading east to Teplitz Bay they would be travelling south towards Cape Flora on the tip of the archipelago. The Arctic responded immediately. Previously the going east had been difficult, whereas the ice to the south had always been smooth. Now the ice to the south was broken while that to the east was good. 'It seems as though it were done on purpose,' Cagni despaired. Battling eastwards, they were greeted at 2.00 p.m. on 9 June by their first glimpse of land in almost three months. They recognized it as Cape Mill, a headland they had spied during the journey north. There was no mistaking it: Cagni had even made a sketch of it from the deck of the *Stella Polare*. By dint of supreme effort they were at last within striking distance of Franz Josef Land. It took them an hour to find a hummock from which to take their bearings relative to Cape Mill, but no sooner had they reached its summit than the Arctic gave them another surprise: Cape Mill was no longer there. As far as the horizon there was nothing but a jumble of ice.

How or why Cape Mill had disappeared was something that Cagni could not explain. It had not been a hallucination; neither had it been a trick of refraction, a phenomenon common in the Arctic whereby distant objects seem much nearer than they actually are. No, they had seen it very clearly and in too fine a definition to be mistaken. Possibly the pack had drifted west, but surely not with such velocity as to place Cape Mill beyond sight in the space of 60 minutes. To this day there is no explanation of what happened to Cape Mill. That night they lay mystified and despondent in their tent, unable to sleep. Then, at 10.30 the following morning, Cape Mill rematerialized just 20 miles away. Cagni did not question how this could be. He simply ordered his men to run for Franz Josef Land. And run they did, for three whole days, while the Arctic teased them with banks of fog. Sometimes they could see where they were going, sometimes they were in a bank of white vapour. Cape Mill and other features flickered in and out of sight, according to Cagni, like slides in a magic lantern.

On 13 June they reached the tortoise-shaped hump of Harley Island, just off Cape Mill, but did not stop. They reached Ommaney Island on 14 June, then continued over the ice to Prince Rudolf Island, which was now only 30 miles to the north. They had two sledges and 12 dogs. If they rationed still further the supplies on the sledges, and ate the dogs, they could maybe last another two weeks. Once again they ran. The Arctic did its best to thwart them. It presented hummocks so hard that their ice-axes snapped. It shifted in random fashion, so that they never knew on reaching a floe whether it might suddenly drift into the ocean. One minute they could see their goal, the next it was hidden by fog. When the fog cleared it was replaced by snowstorms. The final torment came on 20 June. Encamped on a 60-foot-diameter floe, they were being carried slowly east towards Prince Rudolf Island when the current changed and dragged them west. Cagni had had enough. The wind was still blowing from the north-east and land was almost within touching distance. Raising the sails of the battered kayaks that he was still hauling on the sledges, he planted them on the floe. They caught the wind and, very slowly, the floe moved towards Prince Rudolf Island. Cagni and his team anticipated a safe landing, but the Arctic was ahead of them. The current changed direction, hurling them at the shore so fast that they had just enough time to jump off and run for their lives before the floe crumpled behind them. After three days climbing the ridges and mountains of Prince Rudolf Island they finally reached Teplitz Bay.

Abruzzi was appalled. Cagni and his team were black with cooking smoke and the accumulation of three months' personal grease. Their clothes were rags, they carried a single cooking pot smeared with dog fat, and the seven remaining dogs were skin and bone. The sledges had been mended and re-mended. Everything spoke of ruin: these were not the fit men he had sent out. And if their furthest north was good news, it had been bought at an unacceptable price. Although the first support team had returned safely, the second had not. Somewhere, on the journey home, three Italians, their dogs and sledges had vanished. Maybe they had become lost and had strayed on to a distant part of Franz Josef Land. If so, Abruzzi's search parties had not been able to locate them. Maybe they had fallen through the ice. Or maybe, as had almost happened to Cagni, the drift had carried them so far west that they had starved on the pack. When Cagni heard the news he bowed his head in dismay.

That August Abruzzi detonated 70 gunpowder and gun-cotton mines in the 17-foot-thick ice that encased his ship, and by September 1900 the *Stella Polare* was back in Tromsø. He sent telegrams to the King of Italy and to Christiania, the last of which was addressed to Nansen, informing him that his record had been beaten. But Abruzzi took little joy in his achievement. He had lost too many men and had caused too much suffering to feel triumphant. Instead, he raged against the Arctic and wrote with feeling of 'the day when a small band of men, subduing these inhospitable and repellent lands, shall avenge all the past sacrifices and the lives so sadly lost in this obstinate struggle, which has lasted centuries'. He would not be one of the conquerors. In later years he climbed the Ruwenzori Mountains and forged a new route up K2 in the Himalayas. But he never returned to the Pole.

Robert Peary and Frederick Cook (1908–9)

When he was in his twenties Robert Edwin Peary described himself thus: 'Tall, erect, broad-shouldered, full-chested, tough, wiry-limbed, clear-eyed, full-mustached, clear-browed complexion, a dead shot, a powerful, tireless swimmer, a first-class rider [and] a skilful boxer and fencer.' In most cases such a statement would be treated as egotistical bravado. Alarmingly, if anything Peary was being slightly modest. Not only was he as physically fit as he suggested, but he had an iron will to match. There was nothing he did not dare, nothing he could not endure and nothing that he was unwilling to attempt. All these extraordinary attributes, however, were dwarfed by his towering ambition.

Born in 1856 of New England stock, Peary lost his father at the age of two and spent the rest of his life trying to fill the gap. 'I do not wish to live and die without accomplishing anything,' he told his mother, at the age of 24. 'I must be the peer or superior of those about me to be comfortable.' He enlisted in the US Navy, but this was too slow and dull for his liking. Exploration seemed a more profitable route to glory and, having read the Arctic journals of men like Elisha Kane, he took leave in 1886 with the aim of becoming the first man to cross Greenland from west to east. He failed, penetrating less than 100 miles into the ice cap, but the setback did not worry him. He could always try again. And if somebody beat him to it – as Nansen did in 1888 – there was always more of Greenland to explore, and beyond Greenland one of the greatest prizes within the grasp of humankind: the North Pole. 'Remember, Mother, I *must* have fame,' he wrote, 'and I cannot reconcile myself to years of commonplace drudgery and a name late in life when I see an opportunity to gain it now and sip the delicious draught while I yet have youth and strength and capacity to enjoy it to the utmost ... I want my fame now.'

In 1891–2 he attacked Greenland again, sledging from the east coast of Robeson Channel to a spot he called Independence Bay, which he believed to be the northernmost tip of the island. Beyond, he saw a landmass stretching towards the Pole, to which he gave the name Peary Land. In fact, he had not reached Greenland's northern tip, and Peary Land, which he described as separated from the mainland by a body of water (Peary Channel), was an extension of Greenland. But the authorities were too amazed by his methods to quibble with his findings. Accompanied by one white companion, using dogs instead of manpower – unlike previous expeditions in the region – he had sledged 1,100 miles in 85 days. In 1888 Nansen had taken 40 days to cover a paltry 235 miles. Peary had broken every record in the book.

On his return he received the fame for which he yearned. In the course of 103 days he gave 165 lectures at a top rate of $2,000 per appearance. It was not enough to satisfy a man like himself. In 1893 he went in search of greater acclaim. Landing once again in Robeson Channel, he led an expedition into the ice cap, only to be thwarted by conditions so abominable that he had no choice but to retreat. The temperature hovered between −50 and −60° F which, with winds of 50 miles per hour, became an effective −125° F. 'The fates and all hell are against me,' Peary wrote, '*but I'll conquer yet!*'

In 1895 he made another journey to Independence Bay to examine its suitability as a staging post for an attack on the Pole. Taking his black manservant Matthew Henson, and a white volunteer named Hugh Lee, Peary departed on 1 April, from the west coast of Greenland, with 42 dogs and three sledge-loads of provisions. Accompanying them for the first 100 miles were six Inuit, whose sledges carried extra supplies in order to leave the others untouched for the final push. In order to save weight, Peary had trimmed his supplies to a minimum. But he had miscalculated. Five hundred miles into Greenland there were only 11 dogs left alive and the food had dwindled to the point where they had enough for the return journey but insufficient to last them to Independence Bay and back. If they continued they might be able to restock by shooting the game that was normally to be found along the coast. But if there was no game, or if the seals and walruses proved elusive, then they would die. Peary went forward. 'I felt,' he later wrote, 'that in that cool, deliberate moment we took the golden bowl of life in our hands, and that the bowl had suddenly become very fragile.'

Leaving Lee to be collected on their return, Peary and Henson dashed for Independence Bay, which they reached in mid-May. On 1 June, after two weeks during which they were too busy hunting to do any surveying, they retraced their steps to the camp where they had left Lee, and then headed for the west coast. Peary drove them at incredible speeds – sometimes covering more than 20 miles a day – steering such a reckless course through the crevasses that Lee was convinced he wanted to kill them all. Indeed, at one point Lee cracked under the strain and begged to be left behind. Peary's reply was that they either all got home or none of them did. And, true to his word, the three men staggered into base-camp in the last week of June. They were half-starved, half-mad and had just one dog remaining; but they were alive.

It had been a remarkable journey, an outstanding example of toughness and stamina – and of leadership too, if one ignored Peary's initial under-provisioning of the expedition. But beyond proving how far a human being could push himself, it had achieved nothing. The map of Greenland was

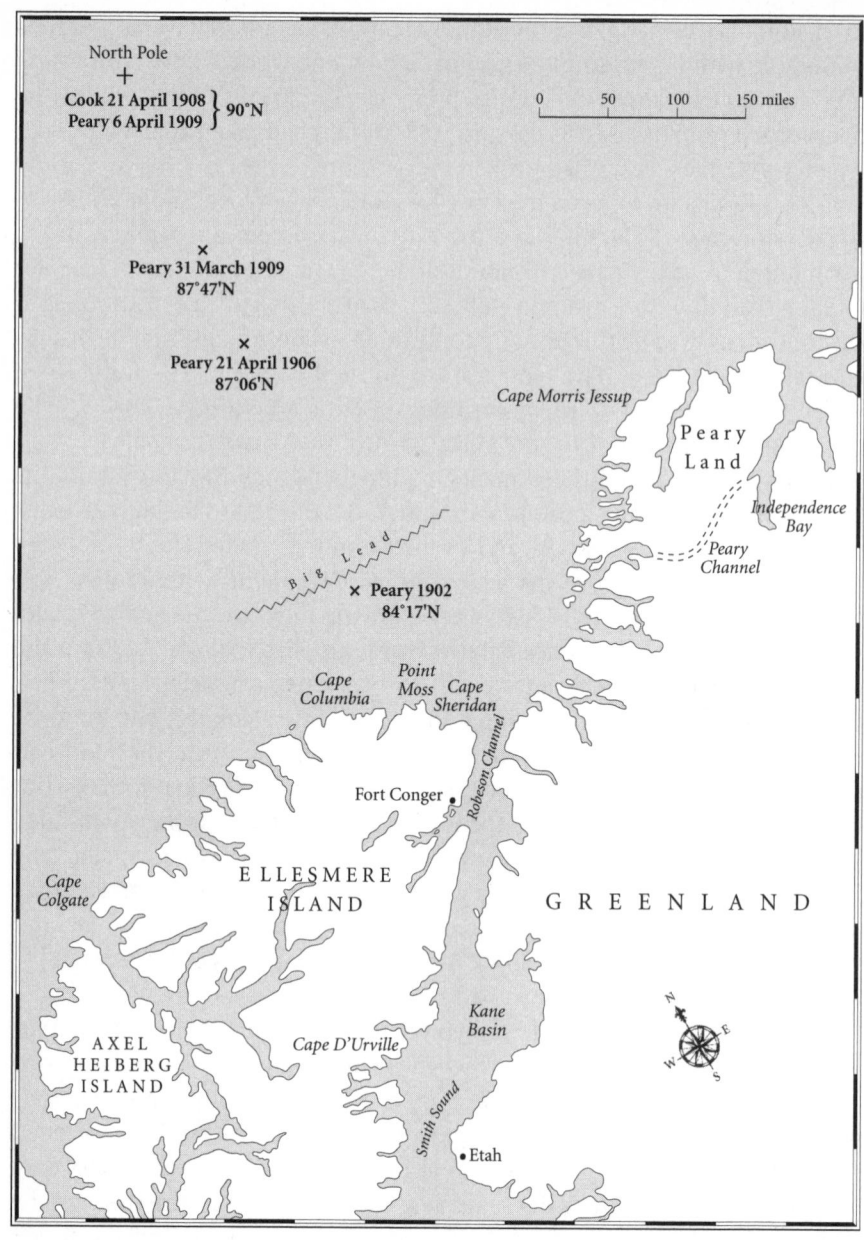

North Pole
+
Cook 21 April 1908 } 90°N
Peary 6 April 1909 }

0   50   100   150 miles

×
Peary 31 March 1909
87°47'N

×
Peary 21 April 1906
87°06'N

Cape Morris Jessup

Peary
Land

Independence
Bay

Peary
Channel

Big Lead

× Peary 1902
84°17'N

Cape
Columbia

Point
Moss Cape
Sheridan

Robeson Channel

Fort Conger

ELLESMERE
ISLAND

Cape
Colgate

GREENLAND

Kane
Basin

AXEL
HEIBERG
ISLAND

Cape D'Urville

Smith Sound

• Etah

little fuller than it had been, the North Pole was no nearer than before, and a large sum of money had been spent to no great purpose. Moreover, the expedition concluded with an act of supreme cultural vandalism. Steaming down the west coast of Greenland en route for the States, Peary stopped at the Inuit settlement of Etah. Here he took aboard three meteorites which for centuries had been the only available source of iron in the Arctic and which the Inuit believed to have souls. The Inuit had no further use for them, Peary announced; if they needed iron they could buy it from people like himself. These irreplaceable items were ultimately sold to the Smithsonian Institution where, on the discovery that they were no different from any other meteorite, they were consigned to the basement. Peary also took aboard a human cargo: six Inuit, to whom he promised a life of untold luxury with 'nice warm houses in the sunshine land, and guns and knives and needles and many other things'. They, too, were sold to the Smithsonian and, like the meteorites, were housed in the basement. By May 1898 four of them were dead. The remaining two, both children, eventually made their way back to the Arctic – but not before one of them discovered that his father's skeleton was now a museum display.

Peary did not care. Garlanded with gold medals from geographical societies in America and Britain, hailed as 'without exception, the greatest glacial traveller in the world', his one concern when he returned was that he was in his 41st year and that unless he galvanized himself a younger person might steal the prize he coveted so fiercely. There were a few stumbling-blocks to be overcome: the first was money; the second was permission from the Navy, from which he was still receiving officer's pay and in which he had not served for almost a decade. The matter of funding was solved by a collection of wealthy industrialists who later became known as the Peary Club. The second was solved by President Theodore Roosevelt, who was so impressed by Peary's determination to conquer the Pole (or rather his declaration that he wanted to conquer it for America) that he personally signed the papers giving him indefinite paid leave until he had achieved his goal. In July 1898 he was once more steaming for the Arctic.

His destination this time was not Greenland but Ellesmere Island, to the west of Kane Basin and Robeson Channel. Here, having established a forward base, he would wait until the opportunity presented itself before firing himself at the Pole 'like a ball from a cannon'. He would do so with only two American companions – Henson and a doctor named Tom Dedrick – and whatever Inuit he managed to recruit en route. And he would succeed by means of what he called 'The Peary System'. This system (which was not entirely new, but to which Peary gave his name nevertheless) involved a tripartite method whereby one sledge party prepared the trail and built shelters, a second laid down caches of food, and a third followed in their wake relying on the work of their predecessors to leave them fresh for the final push to the Pole. The truly novel, and possibly more important, aspect of Peary's system was that all members of the expedition were required to wear furs, sleep in igloos and, whenever possible, supplement their provisions with walrus, seal or any other game they might shoot – in short, it eschewed Western technology in favour of traditional Inuit survival skills.

The Peary System looked good in theory and was even better in practice. Peary's choice of Ellesmere Island over Greenland was also good. Unfortunately, this was not the expedition in which he was able to prove their worth. Landing at Cape D'Urville, on the west coast of Kane Basin, he became fixated by the notion that a team of Norwegians, led by Otto Sverdrup, Nansen's second-in-command on the *Fram*, were trying to steal a lead on him. In fact they had no interest in the Pole and were engaged in purely scientific and geographical research – and when the two parties met, they told him so – but Peary was jealous of his glory. Fearing that he might be thwarted by Sverdrup, he drove his men overland to Greely's old redoubt at Fort Conger. He did so in the middle of winter, a time when no sane person would venture into the Arctic gloom. In temperatures lower than −70° F he, Dedrick, Henson and two Inuit battled over the ice and snow until, in January 1899, they fell into Fort Conger.

The barn-like wooden building was in good condition. On entering it Peary lit a lamp – the last of his oil – and peered about. There were tables, chairs, crates of food and enough fuel to see them through the winter. He lit the kitchen range and a stove in the officers' quarters before admitting to Henson that he no longer had any feeling in his legs. Henson took a knife and sliced through Peary's sealskin boots and the rabbit-skin undershoes beneath. His legs were frostbitten to the knees. When Henson pulled away the undershoes the tips of several of Peary's toes came with them. Dedrick amputated six toes on the spot. Later, as they festered in the darkness of Fort Conger, Dedrick removed another two, leaving him with just a little toe on each foot. Peary was philosophical: 'A few toes aren't much to give to achieve the Pole,' he said. But he did not achieve the Pole this time. Forced to turn back by his Inuit, who had already begun to desert, he returned to Cape D'Urville. Here he recuperated until the spring of 1900, when he turned again to his task. As he explained, 'There is something beyond me, something outside of me, which impels me irresistibly to the work.' That year he crossed to Greenland, from where he shuffled to its northernmost point, Cape Morris Jessup, before turning back. In 1902, from Fort Conger, he and Henson sledged north through Ellesmere Island and onto the pack. They reached 84° 17′ N, but the wilderness of ice was more than they could cope with. 'The game is off ...' Peary wrote. 'I have made the best fight I knew. I believe it has been a good one. But I cannot accomplish the impossible.' Retreating to ice-free waters in August 1902, he was picked up by the expedition ship and carried to America.

'Peary Failed to Reach the Pole' was how the *New York Times* greeted his return. There it was in black and white: he was a failure. Nothing could be more galling for a man who strove so desperately to succeed. More infuriatingly still, while Peary had been toiling uselessly in the ice above Ellesmere Island, an Italian expedition under the Duke of Abruzzi had been breaking records in the ice above Franz Josef Land, trumping even Nansen with a furthest north of 86° 33′. If sometimes Peary had considered abandoning his quest – and there had been many such times – the news of Abruzzi's triumph gave him renewed vigour. 'Next time I'll smash all that to bits,' he told

Henson. 'Next time!' But would there be a next time? After so many failures, Peary was not quite the hero he had been. Funding was no longer so easy to find, and the Navy was adamant that he do the work for which it was still paying him. The spirit of patriotism came to his rescue. The Peary Club saw no reason why America should be beaten to the Pole by any other nation and dug into its collective pockets to furnish their man with all the equipment he required. The President, too, let it be known that he wanted Peary to try again. Bowing to Roosevelt's wishes, the Navy informed Peary not only that he had paid leave but that he was actively instructed to try for the Pole. 'Our national pride is involved in this undertaking,' the Navy Secretary wrote, 'and this department expects that you will accomplish your purpose and bring further distinction to a service of illustrious traditions.'

Peary left Manhattan on 16 July 1905 aboard the *Roosevelt*, a specially constructed, 1,000-horsepower, prototype icebreaker. Its captain was Bob Bartlett, an irascible but competent Arctic hand, who had commanded Peary's ship on the 1898–1902 expedition. Below decks were 12 crew and a scientist named Ross Marvin, who were later joined by 200 dogs and 50 Inuit men, women and children. Barging through the floes, the *Roosevelt* navigated Robeson Channel and reached its winter resting place, Cape Sheridan, on 5 September. Cape Sheridan was some two miles north of Nares's 1875 anchorage, but it was not the spot from which Peary intended to depart for the Pole; that was Point Moss, one of the northernmost headlands of Ellesmere Island. Throughout the winter the expedition prepared itself for the epic journey: the Inuit men hunted whenever possible, and their wives made the boots, leggings and furs that would be needed on the ice. In February 1906 Peary ordered the first parties to move out. Throughout that month the sledge parties shuttled to and fro, from Cape Sheridan to Point Moss and from Point Moss out onto the frozen Arctic Sea. The advance teams led by Henson smashed a route through the hummocks and ridges, and the support teams came in their wake, laying down caches of food at 50-mile intervals. When Peary himself reached Point Moss on 5 March to bring up the rear of the column, there were no less than 28 men and 120 dogs moving through the polar twilight towards the North Pole.

They reached their first major obstacle on 26 March, 124 miles from Point Moss. Here, where the continental shelf dropped into deeper waters, the pack was split by a stretch of open water that Peary called the 'Big Lead'. For seven infuriating days they waited by the Big Lead until the temperature fell, a film of ice materialized, and they were able to continue for the Pole. Three days later, however, they were pinned down for another week by a blizzard so fierce that it was sometimes impossible to stand upright. By now the support teams had all turned back for Cape Sheridan, leaving Peary and Henson accompanied by six Inuit. It was obvious that the supplies they carried could not last the two months Peary estimated it would take to reach the Pole, but if they could not snatch the ultimate prize they could at least claim a furthest north. On 13 April Peary abandoned everything but essentials and raced north with his men. A week later they stood at 87° 06' N, having bettered the Italian record by 36 miles. Exhausted though they were, they did not stop to rest but turned immediately for home. 'As I looked at the drawn faces of my comrades,' Peary wrote, 'I felt I had cut the margin as narrow as could reasonably be expected.'

The drift had by now carried them so far to the east, and their supplies were so low, that Peary decided not to follow his outward path but to cut down the 50th meridian to Greenland, on whose game-rich coast they could recuperate before proceeding to Cape Sheridan. The return journey showed just how finely Peary had cut his margin. They reached the Big Lead and scrambled over a series of ice blocks that had conveniently drifted together to form a bridge. But two days later they met a second Big Lead, half a mile across. This time there was no bridge; nor, with summer approaching, was it likely that the water would freeze; their one hope was that the drift might bring the two sides together. But as they camped on the northern shore, roasting their dogs over fires made of redundant sledges, the lead showed no signs of closing; if anything it opened wider. Finally, by a stroke of fortune, the temperature fell far enough for a skin of ice to form. Under normal circumstances Peary would have waited for it to thicken, but he had no time to spare. The chance was there. He took it.

As he described it, the crossing was hair-raising. 'Once started we could not stop, we could not lift our snowshoes. It was a matter of constantly and smoothly gliding one past the other with utmost care and evenness of pressure, and from every man as he slid a snowshoe forward, undulations went out in every direction through the thin film incrusting the black water. The sledge was preceded and followed by a broad swell. It was the first and only time in my Arctic work that I felt doubtful as to the outcome, but when near the middle of the lead the toe of my rear [boot] as I slid forward from it broke through twice in succession I thought to myself, "this is the finish," and when a little while later there was a cry from someone in the line, the words sprang from me of themselves: "God help him, which one is it?" but I dared not take my eyes from the steady, even gliding of my snowshoes, and the fascination at the glossy swell at the toes of them.' They crossed safely to the other side, but when they looked back they realized how close they had come to disaster. Behind them the Big Lead slowly began to open.

They were 113 miles from Greenland, and ahead of them was what Peary described as such 'a hell of shattered ice as I have never seen before and hope never to see again'. Reduced to one sledge and dog team, they heaved and hauled their way through the wilderness. Then, very much to their surprise, on 9 July they met a group of four humans. They were one of Peary's support parties that had turned back at the Big Lead; they had lost their way in a storm and were now cooking their last dogs over a fire made from their last sledges, before resigning themselves to death on an eastward-drifting pack that would eventually tip them into the Atlantic. Peary barely paused to hear their story before adding them to his team and driving the whole lot over the ice until they reached Greenland, from where they made the relatively easy passage to Cape Sheridan.

Whether Peary actually attained his furthest north is open to question. Experts have discovered a remarkable series of inconsistencies in his account, starting from 13 April when he made his dash for the record. Until then he had made six or seven miles per day. But over the next two days he claimed to have covered 60 miles, and from then until the 21st it was an average of 19 miles per day. How had he suddenly been able to go so fast, over bad ice (on one of his 30-mile days he encountered 11 leads) and in conditions no better than before? And when he reached his purported north he offered no calculations, and gave no proof to support his assertion. Had there been a trained navigator with him the story might have been different. But there was no such back-up. Indeed, he had specifically told Bartlett – who he had earlier promised could be part of the polar team – that he could not come with him. The return journey, too, is mysterious. How could Peary have travelled so far north and yet still have been able to catch up with a support team that had been walking south from the Big Lead since 26 March? The suspicion is that from 13 April to 9 June much of Peary's account is a fabrication.

If Peary did lie about his journey it might explain his subsequent actions. Instead of returning to the States that summer, he spent a second winter at Cape Sheridan and embarked the following spring on a prolonged survey of Ellesmere Island's northern coast. Having failed to achieve anything certain on the ice, he felt obliged to provide tangible proof of his presence on land. Outstripping (just) the efforts of the Nares and Greely expeditions, he reached a western cape that he named Colgate after one of his most influential sponsors. He recorded it with unseemly glee: 'What I saw before me in all its splendid, sunlit savageness was *mine*, mine by the right of discovery, to be credited to me, and associated with my name, generations after I ceased to be.' If he had already gone further north than any other human, why the desperate self-justification? And why, having reached Cape Colgate – which he undoubtedly did – did he feel the need to embellish his account? On 26 June 1907 he described a mountainous land to the north, whose summits he described with yearning. He called it Crocker Land after another of his sponsors. No such land existed, or ever has, as was revealed in 1914 when an expedition went specifically to find it. Peary may have been fooled by Arctic refraction; more likely Crocker Land was part of the wishful thinking that was beginning to epitomize his expeditions.

On returning to the *Roosevelt*, Peary found that it had been badly damaged by the ice: the rudder was broken, two of its four propellers had snapped and its hull was pocked with holes, some of them below the waterline. When the ship left Cape Sheridan in late summer 1906 it was, in Bartlett's words, 'a complete wreck'. Bartlett would have liked to steam directly south while his hasty repairs still held. But Peary had promised he would return the Inuit to their homes. As Bartlett said, '[He] had given his word and he never broke it, so the thing was done. It is no wonder these people loved and respected Peary. No other man in the past or present can or will get these people to do what he did.' However, no amount of admiration could disguise the ruinous state of the *Roosevelt*. Bereft of fuel, the crew burned the very beams of their ship, then went ashore to dynamite the frozen deposits of coal left by past expeditions, before finally stoking their furnace with seal and walrus blubber. Battered by floes, impeded by gales, leaking constantly, its makeshift rudder long since lost, the *Roosevelt* was unworkable by the time it reached ice-free waters. Only by heroic seamanship did Bartlett finally bring it to safety. At Cape Breton Island, in St Peter's Canal, the *Roosevelt* charged into a mudbank, over a fence and into a field, where a hysterical milkmaid ran in horror, followed by her cows. In Bartlett's words, the ship and its crew were 'ready for the insane asylum or the dump heap'.

For all his claims to a new furthest north, and for all the horrors and excitement of the expedition, Peary was once again a failure. His backers were disappointed and the public was indifferent. He had hoped to make at least $100,000 dollars from his published journal, but so scant was popular interest that he was unable even to pay off his $5,000 advance. The President was more understanding and granted him another three years' leave in which to finish the job. This time, however, the money was harder to find. What guarantee did people have that Peary would be any more successful than he had been before? In fact, was the Pole even worth finding? Gradually, though, the funds trickled in. The Peary Club stumped up tens of thousands of dollars and, by emphasizing not only the patriotic but the commercial advantages of being associated with his quest, Peary was able to raise still more in sponsorship deals. By July 1908, with the *Roosevelt* repaired and strengthened, Peary sailed once more for Smith Sound.

It was his strongest, most powerful expedition yet (as well as Henson, Bartlett, Marvin and most of the crew from his last trip, he also took three Americans chosen specifically for their fitness) but it was underpinned by a sense of desperation. Peary was in his fifties, and after two decades in the Arctic even his granite physique was beginning to show the strain. Whatever happened, this would be his last voyage to the north. There was also another source of worry: Peary had a rival. His name was Dr Frederick Cook, and he was already on his way to the Pole.

Cook was one of the up-and-coming stars of American exploration. Having served with Peary on his 1891–2 expedition, he had since led several expeditions of his own to Greenland, had taken part in the 1898–9 *Belgica* expedition to Antarctica, and in 1906 had climbed Mount McKinley, North America's highest peak. Charming, easygoing and unflappable, he was liked by all. The Norwegian explorer Roald Amundsen, who had been with him on the *Belgica*, described him as 'a man of unfaltering courage, unfailing hope, endless cheerfulness and unwearied kindness'. In July 1907 he went to Greenland with a wealthy sponsor named John Bradley, ostensibly for a few weeks' game hunting. But at the end of the summer Bradley returned alone. Cook had decided to stay for an attempt at the Pole.

To Peary, who considered the Pole his own private domain, this was an unforgivable breach of etiquette. As he told the press before his departure, Cook's plan 'for the admitted purpose of forestalling me [is] one of which no man possessing a sense of honour would be guilty'. His indignation, however, meant nothing. Cook was out there and, unless Peary moved fast, might indeed forestall him. Luckily, Peary could move very fast. Pausing briefly at Etah to annexe Cook's stash of game trophies, he pushed on to Cape Sheridan, which he reached on 5 September 1908. The supplies were unloaded, the crates being formed into houses that could hold his crew, 69 Inuit and 246 dogs for the winter. For more than a quarter of a mile the coast was strewn with box-huts, piles of coal and crate upon crate of provisions. It was, for the Arctic, a small city.

The plan was the same as last time, except that the sledge parties would depart from Cape Columbia, marginally further north than Point Moss, where during the winter they constructed a second city of boxes. By 1 March 1909 Peary was on the ice, and the trailblazers led by Henson and Bartlett were smashing a route for the 19 sledges, 24 men and 133 dogs that followed behind. They met the Big Lead, waited a week for it to close, then pressed on, Peary calling urgently for more fuel from his support teams. The fuel (vital for melting water) was delivered by Marvin, 'men and dogs steaming like a squadron of battleships', who accompanied them for a short distance before turning back.* By 28 March Peary had reached his (supposed) furthest north and was ploughing through unknown territory. 'I had believed that the thing could be done and that my destiny was to do it,' he exulted. On 31 March they were at 87° 47' N. This was Bartlett's calculation. On 1 April Peary sent Bartlett home. Despite having promised once again that he could go to the Pole, Peary decided that he was too junior and had put in too little Arctic time to be worthy of the honour. Or so he said. Maybe it was an excuse to be rid of a man who knew how to take readings with a sextant. On 6 April 1909 Peary was at the Pole. From a series of 13 separate observations he calculated that they were at 89° 57' N. He therefore continued north until he was certain that he had passed 90° N, raised the Stars and Stripes and formally took possession of the Pole and the surrounding region in the name of the President of the United States. 'The prize of 3 centuries, my dream and ambition for 23 years,' he wrote in his diary. '*Mine* at last! I cannot bring myself to realize it.'

---

* He never reached Cape Columbia. His Inuit companions claimed that he had fallen into the Big Lead. Much later they admitted that he was a stern taskmaster who refused repeatedly to let them ride on the sledge. So they shot him and tipped him into the sea.

They rested at the Pole for 24 hours, then began the journey home at 4.00 p.m. on 7 April. On the 9th they were at the camp where they had parted company with Bartlett, having covered the intervening distance of 133 miles in just 56 hours. By 23 April they were at Cape Columbia. Four days later they were safely aboard the *Roosevelt*. 'My life work is accomplished,' Peary exulted. 'The thing which it was intended from the beginning that I should do, the thing which I believed could be done, and that I could do, I have done ... This work is the finish, the cap and climax of nearly four hundred years of effort, loss of life, and expenditure of fortunes by the civilized nations of the world, and it has been accomplished in a way that is thoroughly American. I am content.'

His contentment did not last long. In mid-August, when the *Roosevelt* reached Etah, he heard an unwelcome piece of news. Dr Frederick Cook had beaten him to the North Pole. Departing from Etah early in 1908, Cook had travelled via Axel Heiberg Island, west of Ellesmere Island, and then had sledged north with a few Inuit until he reached the Pole on 21 April 1908. Above Ellesmere Island he had seen a body of land (as Peary had done on his last expedition) and had spent the rest of 1908 trying to find it before returning to Axel Heiberg Island; thence, having survived a winter in stone-age conditions, he had made his way the following spring to Etah, from where he had travelled overland to the Greenland port of Upernavik. He had an American witness to prove that he had been to Axel Heiberg Island, and that he had made the journey from Etah to Upernavik, and although he had no witnesses to show that he had been to the Pole during the spring of 1908 he had certainly been somewhere. And why should that somewhere not be the Pole? In the absence of proof (proof being taken as the presence of white men) his claim was as valid as Peary's.

Peary, whose polar career had been spent in defiance of competitors, had, to use one of his favourite words, been forestalled. He had been forestalled not by a day or a week but by almost 12 months. And he had been forestalled not by a recognized polar giant, such as Roald Amundsen, Robert Scott or Ernest Shackleton, to whom he had often been compared, but by a relative newcomer. Cook was the name on everyone's lips. From New York to Copenhagen, he was fêted as a hero. People mobbed him to grab a button, a cuff or a hat. He was awarded gold medals and was congratulated by learned societies throughout the world.

Immediately, Peary and his supporters launched a counterattack. Where were Cook's journals? Where were his calculations, his observations, and the instruments with which he had made them? Where was his proof? Cook fumbled and stuttered. His journals were with the authorities in Copenhagen. No, they were with a friend in America. No, only *some* were with the friend. In fact he, Cook, had all the papers but he needed a few months to make them ready for scrutiny. But he had also left valuable records and instruments at Etah, so perhaps he should be allowed a few more months in which to retrieve them. Actually, when he thought about it, all his papers were under guard in an iron-bound chest to prevent them being stolen by his detractors. When the records were eventually presented for inspection they consisted of 77 typed pages and no diary. 'No schoolboy could make such calculations,' fumed one explorer. 'It is a most childish attempt at cheating.' But his *real* diary was on its way, said Cook; his wife was bringing it in secret. The neatly handwritten diary duly arrived and was branded as a manufacture from beginning to end. When Cook produced photographs of his polar journey it was discovered that they were cropped versions of ones he had taken six years previously in Greenland. To cap it all, evidence emerged to prove that Cook had lied about his 1906 ascent of Mount McKinley: he had got nowhere near the summit, but had photographed himself standing on a much lower hill that had the same outline. Cook fled to South America. On his return to America he became an oil-field salesman and was jailed for fraud (though he was later pardoned when the 'fraudulent' oil field struck rich).

Such was the outrage at Cook's deception that nobody bothered to examine Peary's own proof in much depth. After a cursory look at his diaries and instruments, the National Geographic Society proclaimed that he had reached the Pole. Britain's Royal Geographical Society came to a similar opinion, but with reservations: he had no better evidence than Cook that he had stood at 90° N, and his mileage seemed incredible, varying at times from 30 to 50 miles per day; but to cast doubt on his achievement would be to call him a liar and, as everyone knew, Peary was a man of his word. The medals and awards that had been given to Cook were bestowed a thousandfold on Peary. Not until later in the 20th century did experts acknowledge that his proofs were insufficient and that the evidence pointed overwhelmingly to his not having reached the Pole. According to the British explorer Wally Herbert, who became in 1969 the first person to traverse the polar pack on foot, he might at best have come within 60 miles of his goal.

However, Peary's achievement should not be sneered at. In a region where every bit of ice looks the same, where every lead and every pressure ridge is indistinguishable from every other, does it matter if he turned back sooner than he should? What would he have found had he continued to the Pole? Nothing but more of the same monotonous ice. The marvel is that he got so far with the men and equipment he had. In awarding him the prize, geographical societies were guilty of self-deception, but little else.

Peary died on 19 February 1920 and was interred with full honours in Arlington Cemetery. Cook died in 1940. His last words were that he did not care what people said. 'I state emphatically that I, Frederick A. Cook, discovered the North Pole.' Both men were probably liars, but nobody will ever know for certain whether one or, fantastically, both might have been speaking the truth.

Robert Scott and Roald Amundsen (1911–12)

For a long while, following the voyage to Antarctica in 1839–43 by Captain James Clark Ross, the world paid little attention to its southernmost continent. Unlike the Arctic, with its promise of a sea passage to the Orient and the lure of rescuing Sir John Franklin, Antarctica was of slight interest to governments. True, its outer waters offered a natural bounty of whales and seals, but Antarctica itself was reckoned a dead and pointless place. What purpose would it serve sending expeditions over an endless expanse of ice? They might find the South Magnetic Pole, or even the South Pole itself, but these were goals of relatively small importance. Anyway, the severity of the climate made it very doubtful that anyone could survive a winter on the continent, let alone progress far into its interior. By the end of the 19th century, however, scientists and adventurers were turning their eyes south. As early as the 1870s Britain despatched *HMS Challenger* (captained by George Nares) to investigate the effects Antarctica had on the meteorology and currents of the southern hemisphere. The *Challenger* had brought back much valuable information, but there remained a host of questions yet to be answered. As developments in the Arctic seemed to prove with every passing year, ice was no longer the insuperable foe it had once appeared. If humankind could overcome the northern pack then it could do the same for the southern and, possibly, make inroads on the polar ice cap itself.

That this was no pipedream was shown in 1897–9, when the *Belgica* made the first wintering in Antarctic ice. It was not something its commander, Lieutenant Adrien de Gerlache, or crew had intended to do, nor was it an experience any of them wished to repeat. They very nearly died of scurvy and, as a young Norwegian, Roald Amundsen, reported, it was only the skill of an experienced Arctic hand, Dr Frederick A. Cook, that brought them home alive. Overlapping with the *Belgica* was the *Southern Cross* expedition, sponsored by a British news magnate and captained by a Norwegian whaler named Carsten Borchgrevink. Between 1898 and 1900 Borchgrevink established the first land base on the continent and sledged some distance over the Ross Ice Shelf, accumulating several pieces of rock and a reputation as one of the more unpleasant people with whom to be stuck in the ice.

These two voyages were of special interest to Sir Clements Markham,

President of Britain's Royal Geographical Society. A man of the John Barrow stamp, Markham had been urging Britain to reclaim its place at the forefront of polar exploration ever since the 1860s. The failure of the 1875–6 Nares expedition to the North Pole – of which he had been an ardent supporter – and subsequent success in the same field by other nationalities had dampened his ambitions in that direction. The Antarctic, on the other hand, was a clean slate on which Britain had every right to inscribe its superiority. And not only a right but a duty: was it not a Briton who had first set foot on the place? (Actually, it was not: an American sealer discovered the Antarctic peninsula, and the first continental landing had been made by a Frenchman; but this was by the by.) Let others do as they wished, Britain would be first to the South Pole. A year after Borchgrevink's return Markham orchestrated a multi-national assault on Antarctica, in which Swedes were sent to the peninsula, Germans to the eastern coast and Britons to the Ross Shelf. In 1902 a Scottish expedition would depart, and in 1903 a French. But it was the 1901 British voyage that excited him the most. He had chosen its destination with care: the Ross Shelf offered the best chance of reaching the Pole. And he had personally selected its leader as the man best qualified to do so.

Once the most powerful country on the globe, by 1900 Britain felt itself woefully under strength. Medical experts pronounced that since the Industrial Revolution its population of underpaid and undernourished workers were smaller and weaker than at any time in its history – a fact that was proved by the measurements of those who enlisted in 1899 to fight in the Boer War. Strong men and brave deeds were required to buck the trend. Markham already had his brave deed in mind: all he needed was a strong man to see it through. He chose Robert Falcon Scott. A young torpedo officer in the Royal Navy, Scott was one of those men who could only have existed at a certain time and in a certain place. The first decade of the 20th century was his time and Britain was his place. Unlike many of his compatriots, Scott was physically fit and had all his own teeth. He believed in God, but included king and country in his faith. He was daring, brave, intelligent, exceptionally tough, and single-minded in a grit-jawed sort of manner. He was, in Markham's opinion, the perfect man to raise the Union Jack over the South Pole. This would dispel the image of Britain's weakness and encourage others to follow suit.

Scott's voyage aboard the *Discovery* was a disappointment. Although the expedition explored the area around the Ross Ice Shelf and discovered King Edward VII Land, it made little progress across the ice. In 1907 Scott's second-in-command, Ernest Shackleton, sailed in the *Nimrod* to make his own stab at the Pole. He forged a route up the Beardmore Glacier, discovered the South Magnetic Pole and came within 100 miles of the Pole itself before being driven back by exhaustion and scurvy. By 1910 Markham was no longer President of the Royal Geographical Society, but his influence on Antarctic exploration remained strong. In that year Scott sailed aboard the *Terra Nova*

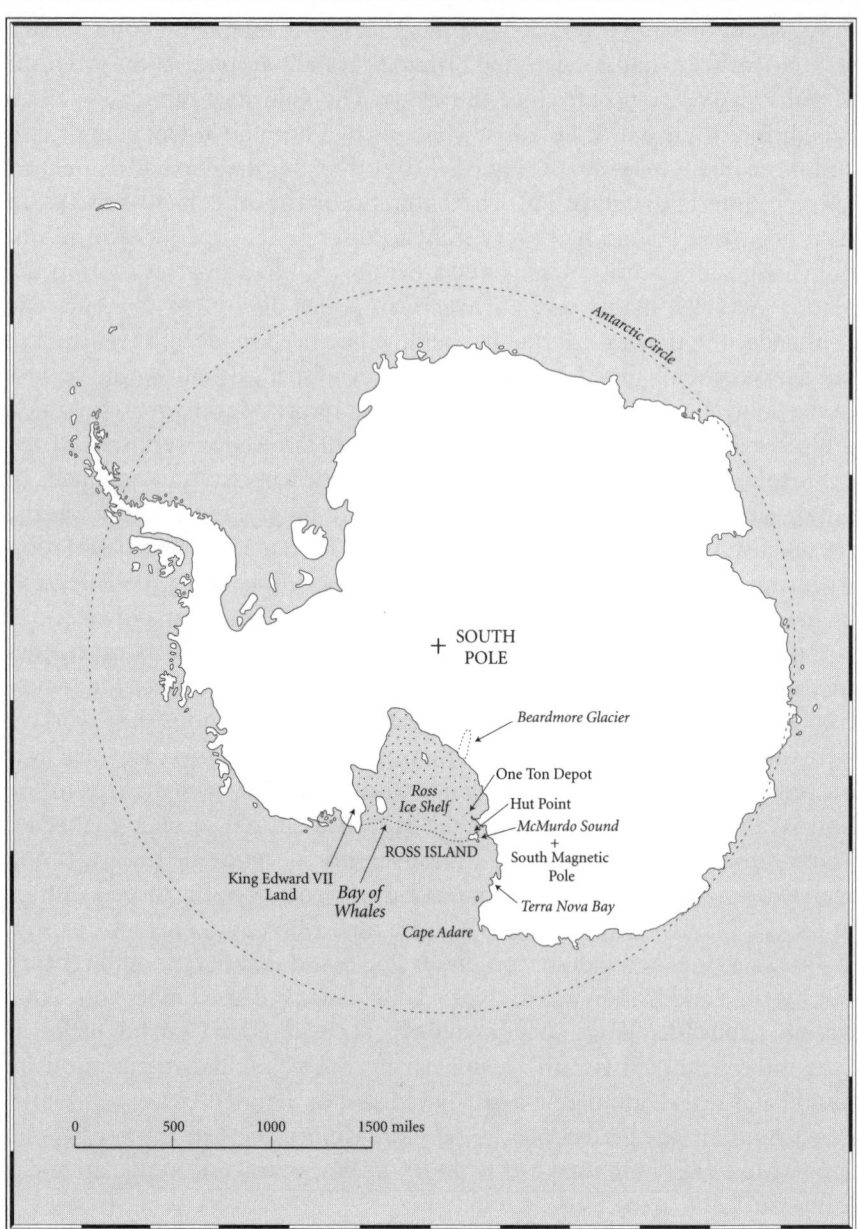

for what would be Britain's last and most successful push for the Pole.

When the *Terra Nova* expedition landed at Cape Evans in McMurdo Sound on 4 January 1911 it was the biggest, best provisioned, best equipped and most expensive assemblage ever to set foot on Antarctica. Its 49 members had pemmican and tinned food to last 36 months; they had the material to build wooden houses; they had skis, dogs and sledges; as an experiment they also took ponies and caterpillar-tracked mechanical sledges; they had experience of the ice – many of them had been south before – and they had a fit, fearless, inspirational leader.

Scott's aim was not only to reach the Pole. He wanted also to shed more light on the nature of Antarctica. His prospects in this respect were limited: he did not have an endless amount of time; his scientific officers would be able to do little more than record data and collect specimens for analysis at home; and there was so much of the continent that remained untouched – for all the activity in recent years, the interior was an almost pristine blank and the coast had been visited in few and isolated spots. Regardless of these limitations, Scott made a start before the austral winter of 1911. While he and his polar party remained at McMurdo Sound to take readings, perfect their ice-travelling skills and lay the depots that would be needed for their journey the following season, a group under Raymond Priestley was taken by ship to investigate the Bay of Whales, on the other side of the Ross Ice Shelf. Later, another party under Edward Wilson sledged to Ross Island to collect eggs from a rookery of emperor penguins (a theory held that at an embryonic stage they resembled fish, and might therefore offer clues as to how life emerged from the sea). Of the two travelling parties it was hard to say which had the worst experience. Wilson's left in winter, when the eggs would be at the required stage of development, and had an appalling time in temperatures as low as −75°F – one member, Apsley Cherry-Garrard, called it 'the worst journey in the world' – returning with five eggs, two of which they dropped. The men of Priestley's so-called northern party did not return at all that year. When they arrived at the Bay of Whales they found their anchorage occupied by a Norwegian expedition. Unwilling to share the spot with others, they steamed west to Cape Adare, landing at a spot they called Terra Nova Bay while their ship stood out to sea. The extra days' journey ate into the time allotted them. The pack ice formed early that year and the *Terra Nova* was unable to break through to the coast. Cut off from their support ship, Priestley's men built a shelter on a lump of rock they named Inexpressible Island and settled down to a lonely winter in which starvation and scurvy was kept at bay (just) by a monotonous diet of penguin meat.

Meanwhile, at McMurdo Sound, Scott's group was having its own troubles. The expensive mechanized sledges seized up in the Antarctic cold; the ponies floundered helplessly in the snow; and although the dogs worked perfectly, their mastery was beyond most of the men. These difficulties meant that the most important food cache, One Ton Depot, which was to greet Scott on the Ross Ice Shelf following his journey to the Pole, was placed considerably further north than had been planned. For the Pole attempt the following year Scott decided to take the dogs and ponies to the foot of the Beardmore Glacier, but from there, rather than risk using methods with which he was unfamiliar, it would be man-hauling – a time-honoured practice at which Britons had traditionally, if unfruitfully, excelled. Scott's first season could not, therefore, be called an unqualified success. And the prospects for his second were unfavourable: not only had his meteorologist predicted exceptionally bad weather for the coming summer, but he now found himself engaged in a race for the Pole. As the *Terra Nova* reported, the leader of the Norwegian expedition at the Bay of Whales was Roald Amundsen.

Amundsen was one of the most thrusting polar travellers of the age. Born in 1872, he was four years younger than Scott himself and was, if possible, even tougher and more determined. At an early age he had read Franklin's journals and had been so impressed that he had determined to carve a name (and career) for himself as an explorer. He devoted himself to the cause, building his muscles with repetitive exercises and testing his stamina with long winter ski journeys across the high plateaux of Norway. He first came to the world's attention in 1906 after a three-year voyage in which he traversed the North-West Passage in a small ship named the *Gjoa*, demonstrating with embarrassing ease that the key to success in the Arctic was to take a small group and live, as Inuit did, off the region's natural resources. His next goal was the North Pole, which he would undoubtedly have reached had not Robert Peary (supposedly) beaten him to it in 1909. When the news came Amundsen was momentarily disappointed. 'This was a blow indeed!' he wrote. 'If I was to maintain my prestige as an explorer, I must quickly achieve a sensational success of some sort.' Success of the kind he sought could only be found at the South Pole. So there he went, but in secret. Borrowing Fridtjof Nansen's *Fram* for what he explained would be a voyage through the Bering Strait, he steamed instead to the Antarctic. His arrival disturbed Scott partly because it was unannounced, partly because he was trespassing on what the British considered their territory, and partly because he was there purely to reach the South Pole. He had no intention of wasting time and money on scientific observations; he simply wanted to bag the globe's southernmost axis. And he wasn't going to man-haul his sledges but use dog teams, which his fellow countryman Nansen and the American Peary had shown were the most effective means of polar travel. He was a small, beaky-nosed, beady-eyed, ultra-efficient campaigner who had yet to lose any battle he had steeled himself to fight. His presence 80 miles nearer the Pole than themselves was, to the British, unnerving.

The following summer the two polar expeditions set out. Amundsen was the first to go, on 19 October 1911, with four men, four sledges and 52 dogs, travelling on skis and wearing the light, warm furs that had already proved such a boon in the Arctic. Scott left two weeks later with 15 men wearing unwieldy, moisture-absorbent woollens, and accompanied by 10 sledges dragged by ponies and dogs; after a while they shot the horses (which were either eaten or placed in caches for the return journey) and dragged the sledges themselves. Amundsen went fast and unencumbered, covering 90 miles in the first four days. The British party moved slowly and in harness, gathering rocks from nearby outcrops and piling them on their sledges. Scott's route took him up the Beardmore Glacier, a massive chequerboard of crevasses through which he picked his way with care, marking the route for his return journey and, once he had reached the top, depositing caches to sustain his team on their return. Amundsen, who had eschewed the Beardmore in favour of a short, hard climb over an adjoining, steeper glacier, was laying only the occasional cache: his security lay in speed – that and the dogs which, as the sledges lightened and became redundant, would be eaten. Throughout his journey Amundsen averaged 17 miles per day; Scott trudged on at a rate that was sometimes as low as 6 miles a day.

On 7 December Amundsen passed Shackleton's furthest south. 'I find it impossible to express the feelings that possessed me at that moment,' he later wrote. 'All the sledges had stopped, and from the foremost of them the Norwegian flag was flying. It shook itself out, waved and flapped so that the silk rustled; it looked wonderfully well in the pure, clear air and the shining white surroundings. 88 degrees 23 minutes was past; we were farther south than any human being had been.' On the same date Scott was still hauling his rock-laden sledges over the Beardmore Glacier. By 9 December Amundsen was confident of success, but without knowing Scott's whereabouts could not be entirely sure that the British had not, in some fantastic fashion, stolen the lead. 'Every step we now took in advance brought us rapidly nearer the goal,' he wrote. 'We could feel fairly certain of reaching it on the afternoon of the fourteenth ... None of us would admit that he was nervous, but I am inclined to think that we all had a little touch of that malady. What should we see when we got there? A vast, endless plain that no eye had yet seen and no foot yet trodden, or – No, it was an impossibility; with the speed at which we had travelled, we must reach the goal first, there could be no doubt about that. And yet – and yet ...'

Amundsen need not have worried. Scott's party did not reach the top of the Beardmore until 4 January – and when it did it was struggling with more than just overladen sledges and poor clothes. One man, Edgar Evans, had fallen into a crevasse and injured his head; he protested that it was nothing, but from that point he lagged continually. While his weakness may have been the result of brain damage, it was also a sign of incipient scurvy. Unlike Amundsen's team, who had moved fast enough to avoid the disease and had, anyway, been eating the flesh of their dogs, Scott's group had subsisted on pemmican and the various tinned foods that their nation produced and packaged with such efficiency. (Vitamin C had been discovered in 1911 by the London-based scientist Casimir Funk, but its anti-scorbutic properties – and its presence in fresh meat – were unknown to Scott when he provisioned the *Terra Nova*.) Blithely ignorant of Evans's disease, Scott drove his team forward.

At the top of the Beardmore Scott made a curious decision. The initial plan had been that the polar party would start large, then shed members as it went until only a select group of four remained for the last leg to the Pole: himself, 'Titus' Oates, Edward Wilson and Edgar Evans. One group had already turned back at the bottom of the Beardmore, and a second now departed at the top. But for some reason, Scott chose to increase the final group from four to five. The fifth man was Lieutenant 'Birdie' Bowers, an officer who was extremely fit but had no previous experience of polar travel. At a stroke, therefore, Scott reduced the space in their single tent and compromised the rationing. Why he made the choice remains a mystery: it could have been that he valued Bowers's navigational skills and physical strength, or it could just have been one of the sudden impulses to which he was prone. He did not acknowledge, however, that Bowers's lack of experience might be a hindrance. Nor did he realize how badly injured Evans was or how far his scurvy had progressed. Arguably, from this point, the expedition was doomed.

On 14 December Amundsen reached the South Pole. In anticipation of his arrival, the weather that morning was fine – it had been relatively warm throughout the journey, so much so that, despite a few blizzards, the fur-clad Norwegians 'sweated as if running races in the tropics' – and although the sky was overcast by 3.00 p.m., it was clear enough for them to tell from their instruments that they were at the Pole or at worst a few miles from it. Amundsen was surprised and a little disappointed: surprised because the journey had seemed so easy and uncomplicated; disappointed because he had always wanted to reach the North Pole but had, almost by default, conquered the South. He wrote: 'I cannot say – though I know it would sound more effective – that the object of my life was attained . . . I had better be honest and admit straight out that I have never known any man to be placed in such a diametrically opposite position to the goal of his desires as I was at that moment.' The Norwegians raised the flag, spent three days scouting the ice to make sure that they had actually reached the Pole, then sledged home on 17 December. 'The going was splendid and we were in good spirits, so we went along at a great pace . . . A mild, summer-like wind . . . was our last greeting from the Pole.' On 25 January 1912, at 4.00 a.m., they returned safely to the Bay of Whales with two sledges and 11 dogs. All five men were alive and well. Amundsen's summary of their record-breaking trip was terse: 'Ninety-nine days the trip had taken. Distance about 1,860 miles.'

On 17 January 1912 Scott's party limped on to the Pole. They found a Norwegian flag and a tent containing letters of encouragement, epistles which he was asked to carry back to the King of Norway, and, cheekily, a set of navigational instruments. It was hardly worth their while casting about to find the exact whereabouts of the Pole, but from a sense of duty they removed a sledge runner with which Amundsen had marked the spot and erected instead a Union Jack at what they calculated was a more precise location, about three-quarters of a mile north. Scott estimated its height as 9,500 feet above sea level, some 1,000 feet lower than the altitude he had measured at 88° S. Then, drearily, they mounted their camera on its tripod and posed for a self-portrait. The resulting exposure, of five men dressed in limp, black rags, their clothes and faces stained by soot and grease, is one of the most harrowing images of disappointment in the history of photography. Their despair is exacerbated by a squint, which gives the impression that the sun was shining; but although the ice cast its omnipresent glare, the weather on that day was cloudy and threatening; the temperature was −21°F and, as Scott recorded, 'there is that curious, damp feeling in the air which chills one to the bone in no time'. Whereas Amundsen had seen a shell of shining ice, Scott saw nothing but windswept emptiness. 'Great God!' he wrote. 'This is an awful place.'

They left on 18 January. Scott – who was an accomplished diarist – remarked: 'Well, we have turned our back now on the goal of our ambition and must face our 800 miles of solid dragging – and goodbye to most of our day-dreams!' Their sledges were still piled with rock, their food was low, Edgar Evans was growing weaker by the day, and the Antarctic was brewing a storm so horrendous that later commentators would give odds of its occurrence at twice in a hundred years. The winds poured from the interior towards the coast, giving the first indication of their violence while Scott's men were on the Beardmore. In the blizzards they lost their carefully positioned markers and had to find a new path through the crevasses. They were all starving, but Evans, scorbutic and damaged by his earlier fall, was the worst affected. He became incapable of movement and died on 18 February. Oates, meanwhile, had severely frostbitten feet and by 11 March was, as Scott wrote, 'very near the end. What we or he will do, God only knows ... Nothing could be said but to urge him to march as long as he could.' How long any of them could march was dictated by their provisions. They had a week's food, which would carry them at their present rate of six miles per day a distance of 42 miles. Their nearest cache, One Ton Depot, was 55 miles away. Even if the weather improved, Scott did not see how they could make the last 13 miles, given their current weakness and the rough nature of the ice. On that day Scott ordered Wilson to 'hand over the means of ending our trouble to us, so that any one of us may know how to do so ... We have 30 opium tabloids apiece and he is left with a tube of morphine. So far the tragical side of our story.'

The tragedy progressed. On 14 March the temperature sank to −43°F. 'It must be near the end,' Scott wrote, 'but a pretty merciful end ... No idea there could be temperatures like this at this time of the year with such winds. Truly awful outside the tent. Must fight it out to the last biscuit, but can't reduce rations.' On the 15th or 16th (Scott had lost track of time) Oates left the tent. 'He was a brave soul,' Scott recorded. 'This was the end. He slept through the night before last, hoping not to wake; but he woke in the morning – yesterday. It was blowing a blizzard. He said, "I am just going outside and may be some time." He went out into the blizzard and we have not seen him since.' They tried to dissuade him, but their appeal was in vain. 'We knew it was the act of a brave man and an English gentleman. We all hope to meet the end with similar spirit, and assuredly the end is not far.'

Oates's sacrifice very nearly saved the others. On the 19th they were 11 miles from One Ton Depot, had food for two days and enough fuel to melt snow for two cups of tea per person. It was just possible they might reach safety. But they did not. A ferocious storm hit them on the 20th, and nine days later Scott wrote his last diary entry. 'Every day we have been ready to start for our depot 11 *miles* away, but outside the door it remains a scene of whirling drift. I do not think we can hope for any better things now. We shall stick it out to the end, but we are getting weaker, of course, and the end cannot be far. It seems a pity, but I do not think I can write more.' At some later date he added, 'For God's sake look after our people'. After that there was nothing.

In late October Scott's base party sledged in search of their leader. Eleven miles south of One Ton Depot, on 12 November, they saw a black stick protruding from a smooth plateau of snow. It was the pole of Scott's tent. Digging down, they opened the canvas and discovered the three remaining members of the polar party. Bowers and Wilson lay peacefully in their sleeping bags, the tops closed down as if they were asleep. Scott was halfway out of his bag, with his coat open and one arm thrown over Wilson. Under his shoulders were the three notebooks in which he had scribbled his last thoughts. There were also two letters, one to Wilson's widow and another to his son's godfather, J. M. Barrie, both written a few days before his death. The former was a standard letter of regret. The latter was a personal testament to triumph and sorrow: 'We are showing that Englishmen can still die with a bold spirit, fighting it out to the end. It will be known that we have accomplished our object in reaching the Pole, and that we have done every-thing possible, even to sacrificing ourselves in order to save sick companions. I think this makes an example for Englishmen of the future ... Goodbye, I am not at all afraid of the end, but sad to have missed many a humble pleasure which I had planned for the future ... I may not have proved a very great explorer, but we have done the greatest march ever made and come very near to great success. Goodbye, my dear friend. Yours, R. SCOTT.'

They took the diaries, the undeveloped rolls of film, the personal effects, and then collapsed the tent, leaving as a memorial a cross of skis. When the northern party dug itself free in January 1913 and marched over the ice to McMurdo Sound – an awful journey in itself – its members could not believe what had happened. The greatest, most powerful expedition to have left Britain had ended in disaster. They packed their bags, boarded the *Terra Nova* and sailed home. Behind them they left their hut, their provisions, the skeletons of their mechanized sledges and all the impedimenta with which they had sailed so optimistically.

When news of the tragedy reached Britain the sensation was immense. Amundsen's prodigious achievement in reaching the Pole was drowned in a tidal wave of British national sentiment. It seemed almost as if the

Norwegians' efficiency was a form of cheating. Indeed, many felt that they *had* cheated: coming south without warning, trespassing on another man's continent, deliberately setting out to foil his effort. It was outrageous. And what had Amundsen done, other than place his foot on a piece of ice distinguished from its neighbours only by its coordinates? Scott, in contrast, had conducted a proper scientific expedition – had died, in fact, for the benefit of humankind. Ultimately, however, no one could deny how effective Amundsen had been, and once the mourning had ended a more sober appraisal of Scott's expedition took place. There were so many stages at which his death could have been averted: he could have trained himself to drive dogs rather than relying on ponies and man-hauling; he could have placed One Ton Depot further south; at the top of the Beardmore he could have stuck to his original plan instead of adding Bowers to the polar party; he could have left his sledge-load of rocks behind instead of dragging them to the end; he could have worn furs instead of woollens; he could have provisioned the men more effectively. All these criticisms came, of course, after the event. Whatever Scott might or might not have done, in doing what he did he became a legend.

It was not just the fact of his dying that gave him legendary status – others had died, just as bravely, in the ice – but the manner in which he did so. His was an age in which everything was writ large: empires, fortunes, machines, concepts, ambitions, deeds and disasters. To Britons such as Scott, of a certain class and a certain upbringing, life was governed by a straightforward set of rules: women and children went first, a captain went down with his ship, fights were fair and one shook the opponent's hand afterwards. Taking part was as important as winning, and the game was a vast and exciting one. If death came one faced it in the knowledge that one was doing one's duty. When the *Titanic* sank in April 1912 it was noted with approval that the band played to the last and that not only the captain but the owner went down with the ship. (Scott's nickname was, fittingly, 'The Owner'.) In later years these values would be caricatured, along with so many aspects of the Edwardian era, as mindless and self-deluding, a pompous exercise in self-righteousness divorced from reality. Maybe they were all these things. But they were also the code by which many people lived. According to the quasireligious ethos that gave Britain faith in its empire, Scott's death was not that of a simple explorer: he was a martyr.

Douglas Mawson (1911–13)

When Scott selected his men for the *Terra Nova's* last voyage, there was one he very much wanted to join the group: Dr Douglas Mawson from the University of Adelaide, a 30-year-old geologist who weighed 15 stone, not an ounce of which was fat. One contemporary described him as 'an Australian Nansen, of infinite resource, splendid physique, [and] astonishing indifference to frost'. Mawson had gained this accolade while a member of Shackleton's 1907–9 expedition, during which he not only became one of the first to scale Mount Erebus, but made a remarkable 1,260-mile sledge journey to reach the South Magnetic Pole. No sooner had he returned than he heard of Scott's forthcoming attempt at the Pole. Immediately he caught a ship to Britain, cabling Scott that he would pay a visit 'relative to Antarctic matters soon after arrival'. To Scott's surprise, the matters Mawson wanted to discuss had very little to do with the South Pole. The Australian advocated a separate expedition to chart the undiscovered coast west of Cape Adare, as well as to conduct a more thorough investigation of the South Magnetic Pole. As he pointed out, the region was closer to Hobart than was Perth. Its discovery was a matter not only of Australian national honour but of great scientific importance: everyone had been to the Ross Ice Shelf, but the region beyond Cape Adare, which formed the western promontory of the gulf in which the shelf sat, was a mystery. He had men willing to accompany him. All he needed was transport. If Scott would take him there on the *Terra Nova* he would consider his expedition subsidiary to Scott's, and his findings – which would surely be many – would be published as part of Scott's own.

Scott's response was negative. The *Terra Nova* had enough to do as it was, and a mission to Cape Adare was beyond its capabilities. But if Mawson wanted to join his own group he would be paid £800 per annum for the two years he expected to be away and would be guaranteed a place among the party Scott intended to take with him to the Pole. Mawson rejected his offer, and continued to do so despite Scott's persistence. He turned instead to Shackleton who, although not personally planning an expedition, was interested enough in the Cape Adare proposal to lend it his support. As with most polar ventures, finding the funds was almost as tiresome as the voyage itself; but with Shackleton's help Mawson raised enough to purchase a 280-

ton sealer, the *Aurora*, and provide 26 explorers with the provisions and equipment they would require for the journey in hand. In most respects his expedition was like Scott's: the men wore Jaeger woollens and waterproofs from the London clothiers Burberry; they took the same cans of pemmican and relied on the same conical tents. Unlike Scott, however, he did not expect to man-haul: instead, Mawson put his trust in dogs.

The *Aurora* left Hobart on 2 December 1911 and anchored off Antarctica on 8 January 1912. The pack ice had prevented them reaching Cape Adare, so they landed to the west, on a headland that sat within a 50-mile-wide stretch of water (Mawson called these respectively Cape Denison and Commonwealth Bay). Here the party split, 18 men under Mawson remaining at Cape Denison while the remaining eight under Frank Wild, a veteran of the first Scott expedition, sailed west, hoping to land about 500 miles from Cape Denison but in fact being forced 1,400 miles round Antarctica to the Shackleton Ice Shelf. Having dropped Wild's party, the *Aurora* steamed back to Hobart, not to return until the following year.

The Cape Denison party were well equipped. They had food for two years, building materials (including drills and dynamite) to construct three huts, 25 tons of coal, drums of oil, electric motors, batteries, furnaces, stoves, radios and even a small aircraft (though its wings had been damaged in transit and it could only be used for towing). During the autumn months they took scientific measurements, learned the rudiments of sledge travelling and climbed the steep slopes that rose from Commonwealth Bay, in early March making an exploratory foray five and a half miles across the plateau above. Anything more adventurous was precluded by the weather, whose ferocity astonished Mawson. The temperature sank to 60° F below freezing, and several times gales of up to 150 miles per hour devastated their camp, blowing away boats, sledges and any item that was not buried under the snow. 'The elements are trying to destroy us by hurricane,' he wrote. Later, 'The winds have a force so terrific as to eclipse anything previously known in the world. We have found the kingdom of blizzards. We have come to an accursed land.'

The following spring Mawson attacked the plateau. At the point they had reached in March they excavated a cavern in the ice – Aladdin's Cave, they called it – which was to act as their forward base. From here parties of three men would fan out to explore the surrounding plateau, dragging their sledges behind them or, in the case of one group that went west in the hope of connecting with Wild's party, using the crippled aeroplane as (in Mawson's words) an 'air-tractor'. The dogs, meanwhile, were reserved for the longest of the proposed journeys: a 500-mile march east along the uncharted coastline towards Cape Adare. This was Mawson's pet project, and it was he who was to undertake it, accompanied by two others: a Swiss mountaineer and ski champion, Dr Xavier Mertz, and a fresh-faced army officer, Lieutenant Belgrave Ninnis. By November the storms had abated slightly and on the 6th

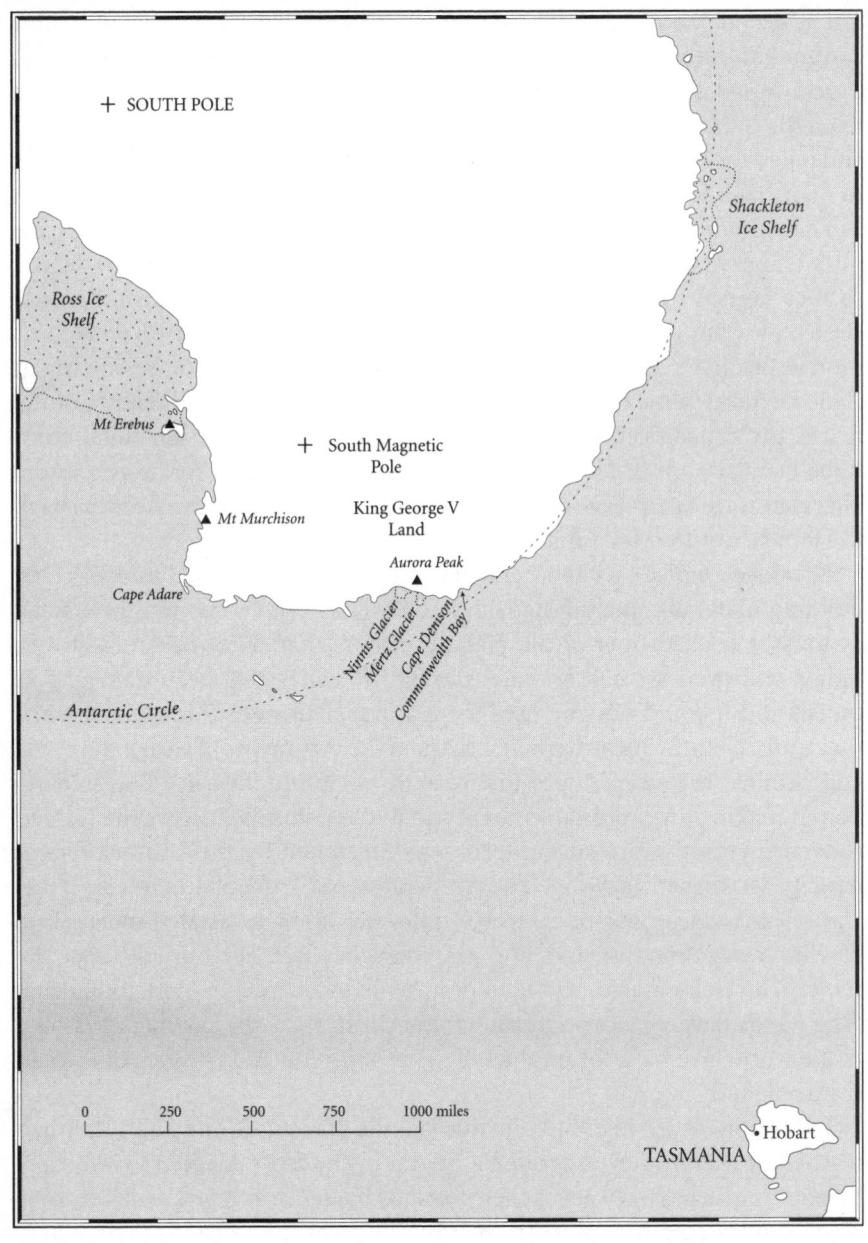

+ SOUTH POLE

Shackleton
Ice Shelf

Ross Ice
Shelf

Mt Erebus

+ South Magnetic
Pole

▲ *Mt Murchison*

King George V
Land

Aurora Peak
▲

Cape Adare

Ninnis Glacier
Mertz Glacier
Cape Denison
Commonwealth Bay

Antarctic Circle

0   250   500   750   1000 miles

TASMANIA • Hobart

of that month Mawson gave the order to depart. If all went well, he expected
the parties to cover 1,500 miles of unexplored coast and hinterland. They
had, however, only a limited time in which to do so. The *Aurora* was due
back in the first week of January, and if Wild's group was also to be picked
up before the ice closed in it would have to leave Commonwealth Bay by the
15th. This was the date, Mawson stressed, by which everyone must be back
at Cape Denison.

Mawson, Mertz and Ninnis had 17 dogs to pull three sledges weighing a total of 1,723 pounds. From this cargo each man drew a daily allowance of 40 ounces of food to see them over a distance that Mawson set at 15 miles per day. His estimate proved optimistic. Hampered by gales, crevasses and rippling plains of sastrugi – hard ridges of wind-carved ice that made sledging a nightmare – they rarely achieved their target. Two weeks into the journey they had covered only 120 miles, approximately half what Mawson had hoped for. During that time, however, they had climbed to a height of 2,600 feet, had discovered a mountain that they named Aurora Peak and had traversed the crater of an extinct volcano 1,000 feet deep and three miles in diameter. In the following weeks they made more discoveries: two huge glaciers, the first of which Mawson named after Mertz and the second after Ninnis. Once again, though, they lagged sadly behind schedule, taking seven days to cross the Ninnis Glacier alone. Beyond the Ninnis Glacier their speed picked up, and for several days they were able to cover 15 miles at a stretch. On 12 December, Mawson announced that their journey was almost at an end: two more days in these conditions would bring them a distance of 340 miles from Cape Denison. At that point he proposed they abandon one of the sledges, cache a quantity of surplus equipment, and make a lightweight sprint to the 155th meridian, the point he had reached on his last expedition with Shackleton. In this fashion he hoped they could cover a further 60 miles before turning for home.

Mawson's decision was rash. They would travel faster on the return journey, their food consumption having lightened the load on the sledges. But by the time they turned around they would have been on the ice for more than a month. They would have less than that to retrace the 400 miles to Commonwealth Bay. Even with lightened loads they would still face the same crevasses, gales and sastrugi that had slowed them down on the outward journey. Their sledges were battered, they had already lost several dogs and the remainder were exhausted. The men, too, were at the limits of their strength. Ninnis, the weakest of the party, had suffered frequent bouts of snowblindness and had, in addition, a badly frostbitten finger. In these conditions they were cutting their margin very fine if they wanted to catch the *Aurora* before it sailed on 15 January.

On 13 December, after just one day's travel, Ninnis's finger became so bad that Mawson had to lance it. Although it was a day earlier than planned, they took the chance while he was recovering to discard their worst sledge, redivide the load between the remaining two, and throw aside various pieces of broken or superfluous equipment. When they started again it was with Mertz skiing ahead to find a path, Mawson following on the lightest sledge and Ninnis trailing third with the bulk of their supplies, notably their tent and most of their food. Ninnis's sledge was considerably heavier than the others, but had been placed last on safety grounds: if by mistake Mertz led them over a weak snow bridge it would be Mawson's sledge, with its inconsequential burden, that fell into the crevasse, not Ninnis's valuable one. The fallacy in this reasoning became evident on 14 December. That day, at about 1.00 p.m., Mertz waved his ski stick to signal that he had passed over a crevasse. Mawson, seated on his sledge writing his journal, was unconcerned: they had survived countless snow bridges already and this one looked no more dangerous than any of the others. He crossed it without mishap, casually passed Mertz's warning back to Ninnis, then continued with his journal. Unlike Mawson, however, Ninnis was on foot; his weight, concentrated on a small area rather than spread over the broad runners of a sledge, broke the snow bridge. He, his six dogs, his sledge and everything upon which the expedition's survival depended fell into the crevasse.

Mawson and Mertz travelled a full quarter of a mile before they realized what had happened. Returning to the hole they saw two dogs, one fatally wounded, the other dead, lying on a shelf 150 feet down. Beside them were the remains of Ninnis's sledge. Of Ninnis himself there was no trace, and despite waiting for three hours they heard no calls for help. He was obviously dead – which was some consolation, for had he been alive there was nothing they could have done to rescue him: all their ropes joined together were insufficient to reach the bottom of the crevasse; they had to use field glasses just to spot the dogs. Mawson read the burial service over the hole, then concentrated on his and Mertz's own predicament. They had one week's rations for three men, a small bag of raisins and a box of chocolate, a Primus stove, a very light tent that they had been using as a sledge cover and, of course, Mawson's sledge. Fourteen miles behind them were the bits and pieces they had deposited the previous day. This, plus their six dogs, was all they had to see them the 300 miles back to base. As Mawson wrote, 'May God help us.'

They did not camp where they were, partly because it would have been too chilling to sleep alongside their companion's grave, but mainly because their tent had no supports. The only way to keep it upright was to cannibalize the sledge they had earlier abandoned. They departed at 9.00 p.m., and five and a half hours later were at the cache where Mawson produced their one tool – a 'Bonzer' knife, whose blade could be swapped for a hammer, a file or a miniature saw – and hacked the broken sledge into tentpoles. The entire stock of dog food having fallen into the crevasse, he fed the animals a pair of discarded wolfskin gloves and two worn-out shoes. As for himself and Mertz, they agreed to cut their daily rations from 40 to 8 ounces of food. In Mawson's words, 'It was to be a fight with Death and the Great Providence would decide the issue.'

The following morning Mawson cut another strip of wood from the sledge and tacked a Union Jack to it. Planting his makeshift flag in the snow, he formally took possession of the territory in the name of the British Crown. To this forbidding part of the world he gave the name King George V Land. The day was marked by another, far more symbolic event: they shot and ate their first dog, feeding the least palatable parts to the rest of the team and roasting the haunches for themselves on an upturned pot lid balanced over the Primus. No explorers had ever relished killing a dog, but most accepted it with equanimity. Mertz, however, was particularly affected by the act. It was not just that the dogs were loyal workers and friends, the only other living beings on the ice apart from themselves; it was also that they made a revolting meal. The meat had no fat, so was charred on the outside and raw in the middle. It also had an indefinable musty taste. The liver was a bit better, braised lightly so as to conserve goodness and make it easier to swallow (the legs required heavy chewing).

The dog meat gave them strength to travel the 15 miles a day that Mawson had stipulated as their minimum goal. But it was debatable how long their walking larder would last. By 18 December another two animals became so weak that Mawson had no option but to shoot them. On the 21st a fourth went the same way. What they did not eat immediately they stored on the sledge for the future. With only two dogs left, their progress became notice-ably slower, even though Mawson and Mertz were now harnessed to the sledge. To compound matters, both men felt unaccountably ill. They were seized by a weariness that could not be accounted for by the extra toil alone. Their stomachs hurt, their skin started peeling and their hair fell out. It did not seem to be scurvy: the telltale symptoms of swollen gums and aching joints were absent. Mawson assumed it was merely the effect of general malnutrition. Then, as the days passed, he wondered whether it might not be the absence of some particular element in their diet. Whatever the cause, there was nothing they could do about it at the moment. He could only hope that the disease got no worse.

In fact, their illness was caused not by an element missing from their diet but by something they had recently added to it: the dogs' livers. It was common knowledge that the livers of polar bears were dangerous to eat. Nobody knew why this should be, but the effects were so unpleasant that nobody was ever foolish enough to try it twice. The reason, which was not discovered for another 30 years, was that bear livers contain a toxic amount of Vitamin A. If taken in excess Vitamin A causes nausea, dizziness and a peeling of the skin as if badly sunburned. With repeated doses, these symp-toms are supplemented by hair loss, the opening of fissures around the eyes, nose and mouth, dysentery, weight loss, stomach pain, lassitude, irritability, dementia, delirium, convulsions and, finally, death from brain haemorrhage. Mawson and Mertz were well into the initial stages of Vitamin A poisoning. Why they should have contracted this disease was a puzzle, the solution to which was not found until 1971. In that year scientists proved that the husky liver was a miniature version of the bear's. Its Vitamin A content was not as great as that of the bear, but at an average weight of two pounds contained ten times the amount reckoned safe for human consumption. Ironically, Mawson and Mertz counted for their survival on a food that was steadily killing them. Already they had taken an overdose of Vitamin A.

By Christmas they were struggling through fresh snow on the Ninnis Glacier and had only one dog left, a bitch named Ginger. As the crow flew, they were 180-odd miles from Cape Denison, theoretically within a fortnight's march of safety if they covered 15 miles a day. But the crevasses of the Ninnis Glacier had already reduced their daily average to less than half that, and there was one more glacier and a crater to cross, not to mention stretches of sastrugi. Moreover, the mystery illness still plagued them, for some reason affecting Mertz more powerfully than Mawson. The only means they had of increasing their speed, and of reaching Commonwealth Bay before the 15 January deadline, was to lighten their load. Out went the camera, along with most of its film. The hypsometer that Mawson had used to take their altitude on every day of the march was dumped, as were the thermometers, the rifle and the ammunition. They tossed aside their logbooks and almanacs, keeping only their diaries. The sledge runners that had acted as tent supports were likewise jettisoned: from now on the canvas would be kept up by the telescopic legs of the theodolite. As for the dog carcases, they stewed them to a jelly and fed the bones to Ginger. To celebrate the new regime they put a pat of butter in their cocoa and gave themselves a slice of dog liver. While they were eating it, Mertz noticed something dangling from Mawson's head. Leaning over, he removed a piece of skin that was a perfect cast of his ear. Mawson remarked that their bodies were falling apart. Mertz, who still resented the loss of their dogs, said they should never have eaten them in the first place.

Three days later Ginger collapsed. Lacking a rifle, Mawson killed her with a much patched and mended spade. 'I can never forget the occasion,' he wrote. 'As there was nothing available to divide it, the skull was boiled whole ... after which we took it in turns eating to the middle line, passing the skull from one to the other.' His distress, however, did not diminish his appreciation of the food: 'Had a great breakfast off Ginger's skull – thyroid and brian.'

On the evening of New Year's Day 1913 they camped on the Mertz Glacier. Its namesake confided to his diary that he and Mawson had made just five miles, the sky so overcast and the light so poor that they could hardly see their way – not that they were strong enough in any case to make decent progress. Instinctively, he suspected the cause of their weakness. 'I cannot eat of the dogs any longer. Yesterday the flesh made me feel very sick.' They were the last words he wrote. From that date he became more and more apathetic. Rather than make a day's march, he preferred to lie in the sleeping bag until the weather improved. He also refused to touch another scrap of dog meat. When Mawson coaxed him to his feet he managed only a few miles before subsiding with frostbitten fingers. He rode on the sledge, but even that did not seem to help. Soon he was so weak that it took Mawson three hours to dress him for the day's journey. By 6 January Mawson was in a predicament. 'I could perhaps pull through – with the provisions at hand – but I cannot leave him. His heart seems to have gone. It is very hard for me – to be within 100 miles of the hut and in such a position is awful ... If only I could get on. But I must stop with Xavier, and he does not appear to be improving – both our chances are going now.'

On 7 January Mertz descended into madness, shouting in English and German, fouling himself intermittently and thrashing so violently that he broke one of the legs of the theodolite. Occasionally he fell unconscious, only to wake clutching his head and complaining of earache. Perhaps his brain was already beginning to haemorrhage. 'Obviously we can't go on today,' Mawson wrote in his diary. 'This is terrible.' At midnight Mertz slipped into a coma. By 2.00 on the morning of 8 January he was dead.

Mawson had neither the strength nor the means to dig a grave. The best he could do was drag the body out of the tent, erect a small cairn of snow, and place in Mertz's sleeping bag a short note describing the tribulations he had faced and the manner in which he had died. Then, as with Ninnis, he read the burial service. In his journal he wrote a sad epitaph: 'My comrade has been accepted into "the peace that passeth all understanding". It was my fervent hope that he had been received where sterling qualities and a high mind reap their due reward ... [Myself,] I seemed to stand alone on the wider shores of the world – and what a short step to enter the unknown future!'

So much time had been lost during Mertz's illness that Mawson doubted very much if he could reach the hut before the *Aurora*'s deadline – it was unlikely he would make it back to Cape Denison at all – but he resolved to press on regardless. If he had to die, the least he could do was die as near the coast as possible, making it easier for a rescue party to find his body and the expedition journals. Alone on the world's most inhospitable continent, Mawson, prepared for the trek with calm efficiency. As with the last reorganization of the sledge, many things now seemed superfluous. He cooked the remaining dog meat in a single batch and, wondering why he had not done so before, threw out the two gallons of fuel which had thereby become redundant. Using the 'Bonzer' knife, he sawed the sledge in half, using the left-overs to make a mast, to which he attached a sail made by sewing Mertz's coat to an old food bag. The excess pieces of wood and metal were stuck on Mertz's cairn to make a cross. With the same knife he mended the theodolite leg that Mertz had broken. Then, on 11 January, with an estimated 20 days' subsistence rations, he pulled his sledge over the glacier towards Cape Denison.

Why Mertz and not he should have succumbed to the strange ailment Mawson could not tell. But there was no mistaking the signs that he would soon go the same way. When he undressed to see how far the disease had progressed, long strips of skin and hair fell around him. At every point where his clothes had rubbed against him – his knees, shoulders, armpits, back and genitals – there was raw flesh. Here and there, clusters of boils were coming to a head. 'My whole body is apparently rotting from the want of proper nourishment,' he lamented. The seriousness of his condition became even more obvious during the first day's march from Mertz's cairn. As he laboured over the ice, he noticed a lumpy, squelching sensation in his boots: when he removed them he saw that the hard soles of his feet had fallen off. Grimly, he smeared the flesh with lanolin, stuck the soles back on and bandaged them tightly into place.

As he adjusted to the new horror, the sun emerged. Hoping that sunlight might do something for his condition, he spread the sledge sail on the ground, stripped naked and became probably the first person in history to sunbathe on Antarctica. 'I felt the good of the sun as I have never done before,' he wrote. 'A tingling sensation seemed to spread throughout my whole body, and I felt stronger and better.' By the end of the day, however, he had covered only six and a quarter miles, and on changing his bandages discovered that he was in even worse condition than he had suspected: his feet and ankles were covered in blisters; his mouth and nose had dried up; he no longer had any sense of taste and smell; his fingers and toes were blackened by frostbite. Later he found his watch had stopped. Then, as he was comforting himself that at least the sun was out, he was hit by a 30-hour blizzard.

At midday or thereabouts on 13 January he resumed the march. He could now see Aurora Peak, but it seemed hopelessly distant. For a moment he dithered between descending the glacier to the sea or continuing overland. If he went to the coast he might, even without his rifle, be able to kill seals and penguins, and would at last be able to recuperate. If he carried on, there was a chance he might be met by a rescue party. Wisely – for the Antarctic wildlife would vanish come winter and a journey round the coast to Cape Denison was beyond him – he opted for the latter.

On 15 January, the deadline he had set for the *Aurora*'s departure, he was still on the Mertz Glacier. 'I don't know what is on ahead at all,' he wrote. 'Trust the sky will clear ... It takes quite a while dressing my feet each day now.' Two days later he fell through a snow bridge. Luckily, the sledge stuck a yard from the lip and, luckier still, he had been dragging it with a sturdy alpine rope, up which he was able to climb to safety. 'Exhausted, weak and chilled ... I hung with the firm conviction that all was over ... it would be but the work of a moment to slip from the harness, then all the pain and the toil would be over. It was a rare situation, a rare temptation – a chance to quit small things for great – to pass from the petty exploration of a planet to the contemplation of vaster worlds beyond.' After another fall he made his tow-line into a rope ladder. Again and again he fell into crevasses, blinded by the constant drift. 'If only I had light,' he raged. If only I could get out of this hole.'

On 19 January Mawson emerged from the Mertz Glacier, the snow falling so thickly that he could barely see the ground underfoot. On the 21st he made two and a half miles over steep slopes, and at the end of the day threw away his crampons. He would need spikes for the final descent to Cape Denison, but there were a pair of good steel crampons in Aladdin's Cave. To reduce the load he even tore the cardboard covers from his journals. On the 22nd, he caught a glimpse of the eastern coast of Commonwealth Bay. Three days later, however, with less than 50 miles to go, a blizzard made further progress impossible. How long the storm would last he could not tell. Nor had he any idea what he would find when the snow cleared. Given his earlier instructions, it was unlikely the *Aurora* would still be in Commonwealth Bay. But as he wrote, 'I am full of hope and reliance on the great Providence which has pulled me through so far.'

In fact the *Aurora was* still in Commonwealth Bay, its captain having delayed his departure until the 30th; and on the 24th a rescue team was already climbing the slope to Aladdin's Cave. Pinned down by the same blizzard that hit Mawson, they were able to advance only 21 miles over the ice. They turned back at 9.00 a.m. on the 29th. Behind them they left a cairn of ice wrapped in black cloth, beneath which they placed a cache of food containing a message giving the position of Aladdin's Cave and the date they expected the ship to leave. While the rescuers had been marching west, Mawson had been hauling east. He reached the cairn six hours after their departure. On the previous night their two camps could not have been more than five miles apart.

Mawson struggled after the rescue party, over slopes so steep and icy as to be insurmountable without the crampons that he now wished he had not discarded. Once again the 'Bonzer' knife came into play. Dismantling the theodolite case, Mawson cut some planks to length, banged nails through them, and strapped them to his feet. In this manner he scraped his way into Aladdin's Cave on the evening of Saturday 1 February. After 80 days under canvas the ice-hole seemed to Mawson a haven of luxury. It was sheltered, warm and silent. Its floor was strewn with a cornucopia of valuable rubbish – half-eaten cans of pemmican, a tin of biscuits, old shoes and socks, sacks, boxes, a copy of some Sherlock Holmes stories, even a pineapple. He could have rested happily for several days, but he dared not. Possibly the *Aurora* was still in Commonwealth Bay. If he made a swift overnight descent, using the steel crampons he had left in Aladdin's Cave, he might just reach the coast before the ship raised anchor. But, having left so much behind, his rescuers had taken the one item he needed most. The crampons were not there. For a moment Mawson was tempted to start straightaway with his own nail-and-plank crampons; but when he looked at the ice and realized how weak he was he decided to delay his departure until early the following morning. If the *Aurora* had left, so be it; if it was still there, it would not be leaving before daybreak. It would be good, too, to come home on a Sunday. That night the katabatic winds flowed from the interior, inaugurating a blizzard that did not break for six days.

On the afternoon of Saturday 8 February Mawson limped down the slope on his makeshift crampons. He had 'changed' his soles religiously every night, but they had become too horny and painful to bear, so he had discarded them: as a result the nails of the theodolite planks now dug into his unprotected flesh. He comforted himself that, although it should have left long since, the *Aurora* might have been delayed by the same blizzard that had imprisoned him in Aladdin's Cave. He was right: it had been. But the *Aurora* had left, like him, as soon as the weather cleared. Mawson was 2,000 feet down the slope, a mile and a half from the hut at Cape Denison, when he spotted a plume of smoke at the far edge of Commonwealth Bay. It was the *Aurora,* and it was moving west.

The captain of the *Aurora* had not entirely abandoned his explorers. The base hut had supplies for two years, and he had left five men at Cape Denison to wait another Antarctic winter before sledging in search of the party's remains. It was these five who greeted the greasy figure – weighing less than 100 pounds – that hobbled down the hill that afternoon. Peering into Mawson's hood they discerned no recognizable features. Their first question was to ask which one he was. 'What a grand relief!' Mawson wrote in his diary. 'To have reached civilisation after what appeared utterly impossible. What a feeling of gratitude to Providence for such a deliverance. I had intended to push on to the utmost in the hope of reaching a point where my remains would be likely to be found by a relief expedition, but I had always hoped against hope for more. Now I had arrived at the goal of my utmost hopes ... I was overcome by a soft and smooth feeling of thanksgiving.'

Once Mawson had been carried to the base hut his first task was to radio the *Aurora* for assistance. But when the *Aurora* returned the following day it was met by an 80-mile-per-hour gale that blew the ship backwards into its wake. Throughout the afternoon the *Aurora* struggled against the wind but never came closer than 15 miles from the shore. 'Am most anxious to get off,' Mawson radioed. 'Hope you can wait a few days longer but cannot command you to do so and give you the option to decide whether or not to remain.' The *Aurora's* captain had little choice. The men at Cape Denison had food to last another winter and could be collected the following spring. Wild's party would die if they were left where they were. If he battled a gale that might last for a week he would not have enough coal both to retrieve Wild and to steam back to New Zealand. As it was, his fuel was dangerously low. He sailed that night for the Shackleton Ice Shelf. Having a receiver but no transmitter, he was unable to tell them of his decision, so it was only when Mawson's men woke on the morning of 10 February that they saw the ship had gone. A few hours later the wind fell and Commonwealth Bay assumed a glassy calmness. For Mawson it was the last in a sequence of tantalizing near-misses that had dogged him ever since 29 January. Once again he had just missed the boat.

Mawson's disease puzzled the expedition's doctor, Archie McLean, almost as much as it mystified Mawson himself. McLean tried everything, down to constructing an electrical scalp massager to restore his hair, but it did not work. Helpless, all he could do was watch as Mawson lay in his bunk complaining of pains in the side of his head while his bowels gave way. These were the symptoms that had preceded Mertz's death, but Mawson's iron constitution prevented him lapsing into delirium. At times, however, he came close: 'I find my nerves in a serious state,' he wrote, 'and from the feeling I have in the base of my head I have suspicion that I may go off my rocker soon!' He defied the notion that mental weakness might have a bodily cause: 'Too much writing today has brought this on.' He sought release in physical activity, cutting one of the hut's thick roof beams into a cross which he erected in the rocks of Cape Denison and on which he nailed a wooden plaque dedicating it to the memory of Ninnis and Mertz. Mawson was not McLean's only patient. As the winter wore on, the radio operator, Sidney Jeffryes, broke under the strain of solitude and began transmitting messages in which he told how he was being attacked by a pack of lunatics. He had to be forcibly restrained.

The *Aurora* returned in mid-December 1913 to find the Cape Denison party in poor shape. Jeffryes was still mad, and was eventually committed to an asylum. Mawson's hair returned, partially, as did some of his former bulk, but he was not the same confident character who had left Australia in 1911. He was, as one man said, 'a noticeably chastened man – quieter, humble, and I think very much closer to his God'. Everyone had been affected by two winters in the Antarctic. None of them recovered fully from the experience – particularly Mawson, who rarely spoke of it in later life, and only with difficulty divulged to a few academics the details of his march to Aladdin's Cave. He was unconcerned that the expedition had been overshadowed by Scott's disaster: he knew only too well what Scott must have endured.

He led further expeditions to the Antarctic, but never attacked it with the fervour he had shown in 1911. His remarkable accomplishments – the charting of some 2,000 miles of undiscovered coastline, the mapping of mountains, glaciers and craters, the crippling, solitary trek over ice and snow – never received the popular acclaim they were due. Of all the sorties that departed for the Antarctic in that strange, Scott-*Titanic* era, his was among the most effective, the most productive and yet the most ignored. He devoted the rest of his life to conservation, advocating the cessation of whale-hunting long before it became fashionable. He died in 1958, still pondering the cause of Mertz's death. He thought it might have been peritonitis.

Ernest Shackleton (1914–16)

The cataclysmic events of 1911–12 effectively cured the world of its obsession with Antarctica. The Pole had been captured, martyrs and heroes had been made, and the confident, gung-ho attitude of previous years had been replaced by wary respect. For one man, however, the continent could never be conquered until he himself stood at the South Pole. His name was Ernest Henry Shackleton.

A short, thickset man of Anglo-Irish descent, Shackleton had extraordinary physical presence and was an outstanding leader – a man who, according to a contemporary, 'could look you straight in the eyes and tell you to go to hell if you stood in his path'. He had first visited Antarctica as a member of Scott's 1901–3 expedition and in 1908 had led his own, hugely successful expedition, during which he forged a route up the Beardmore Glacier and came within 97 miles of the Pole. Other members of his party, among them the Australian Douglas Mawson, charted much new territory and discovered the Magnetic South Pole. For a while Shackleton was the most famous explorer in Britain, if not the world. The widespread belief was that if anyone was going to reach the Pole it would be him. Then came 1912, after which the only names on the public's lips were Amundsen and Scott. Eclipsed but undaunted, Shackleton came up with a way of re-establishing his preeminence: he would lead a party from one side of the continent to the other via the Pole. Such a journey, he argued, would be of enormous scientific benefit, for while the route south from the Ross Ice Shelf was relatively well documented (mostly by himself) the area beyond was as mysterious as the dark side of the moon. In reality his arguments were a figleaf. All he wanted to do was reach the Pole – as he admitted, it was 'the last spot of the world that counts as worth the striving for, though ungilded by aught but adventure'.

Winston Churchill, for one, was not fooled. As First Lord of the Admiralty, and one of the first people to whom Shackleton turned for support, he wrote disparagingly: 'Enough life and money has been spent on this sterile quest. The Pole has already been discovered. What is the use of another expedition?' Shackleton was not only a man of charisma and determination but an accomplished fundraiser. He took Churchill's rebuff in his stride, and by 1914 everything was in place for what he dubbed grandiosely – and pointedly – The Imperial TransAntarctic Expedition. Two separate parties would land on Antarctica. One, comprising six men, would sail to the Ross Ice Shelf on Mawson's old ship, *Aurora*, from where they would lay a string of food depots to the top of the Beardmore. The other, Shackleton's, would make its way through the Weddell Sea on the *Endurance*, a 350-ton ship designed expressly for polar service. Once *Endurance* reached the mainland, a group of three men would explore the coast west to Graham Land, another three would go east to Enderby Land, and two would remain at base. The six-strong polar party, meanwhile, would traverse the continent with dogs and a brace of propeller-driven sledges carrying enough supplies to see them to the first of the *Aurora*'s caches. From there, Shackleton and his companions would descend the Beardmore and cross the Ross Ice Shelf to complete their victorious, record-breaking trek.

Many things were wrong with Shackleton's plan. For a start, he hoped to reach the coast in November 1914. But the Weddell Sea was notoriously hostile, and he had no certainty of reaching the coast at all, let alone by November – Mawson had not been able to make a landing until January, and that was through relatively straightforward pack ice rather than the rotating gyre of the Weddell Sea. And if he did reach it he intended to start immediately on a 1,800-mile trek that he estimated would take five months. This was stretching the limits. Scott had started in October and had died in January. Mawson had started in November and had been lucky to get back by February. Were March and April 1915 meant to be sunnier for Shackleton than they had been for his predecessors? Moreover, how would Shackleton know whether the *Aurora* party had laid the caches on which his survival depended? Both ships had radios, but they were primitive and underpowered, quite incapable of transmitting to each other acoss the ice. If the *Aurora* failed in its task Shackleton would be marching to his death. And then there was scurvy. Scott's party had contracted the disease, and Mawson had suspected it might have afflicted him. On what grounds did Shackleton expect to remain immune? For all its fanfare, the Imperial TransAntarctic Expedition was a venture that strained the limits of logistical possibility. One can admire Shackleton's audacity. But the inescapable question remains: what on earth did he think he was doing?

He very nearly did nothing – or, at least, nothing to do with Antarctica. When the *Endurance* left London on Friday 1 August 1914 war was at hand, and by Monday a general mobilization had been announced. At anchor off Margate, Shackleton wired the Admiralty, volunteering the entire expedition for service. All he asked was that the company be kept together. 'There were enough trained and experienced men among us to man a destroyer,' he later wrote. But the Admiralty was sanguine. Given that the forthcoming conflict would be over by Christmas, it seemed silly to disrupt a project that had taken so long to arrange and on which substantial sums had already been

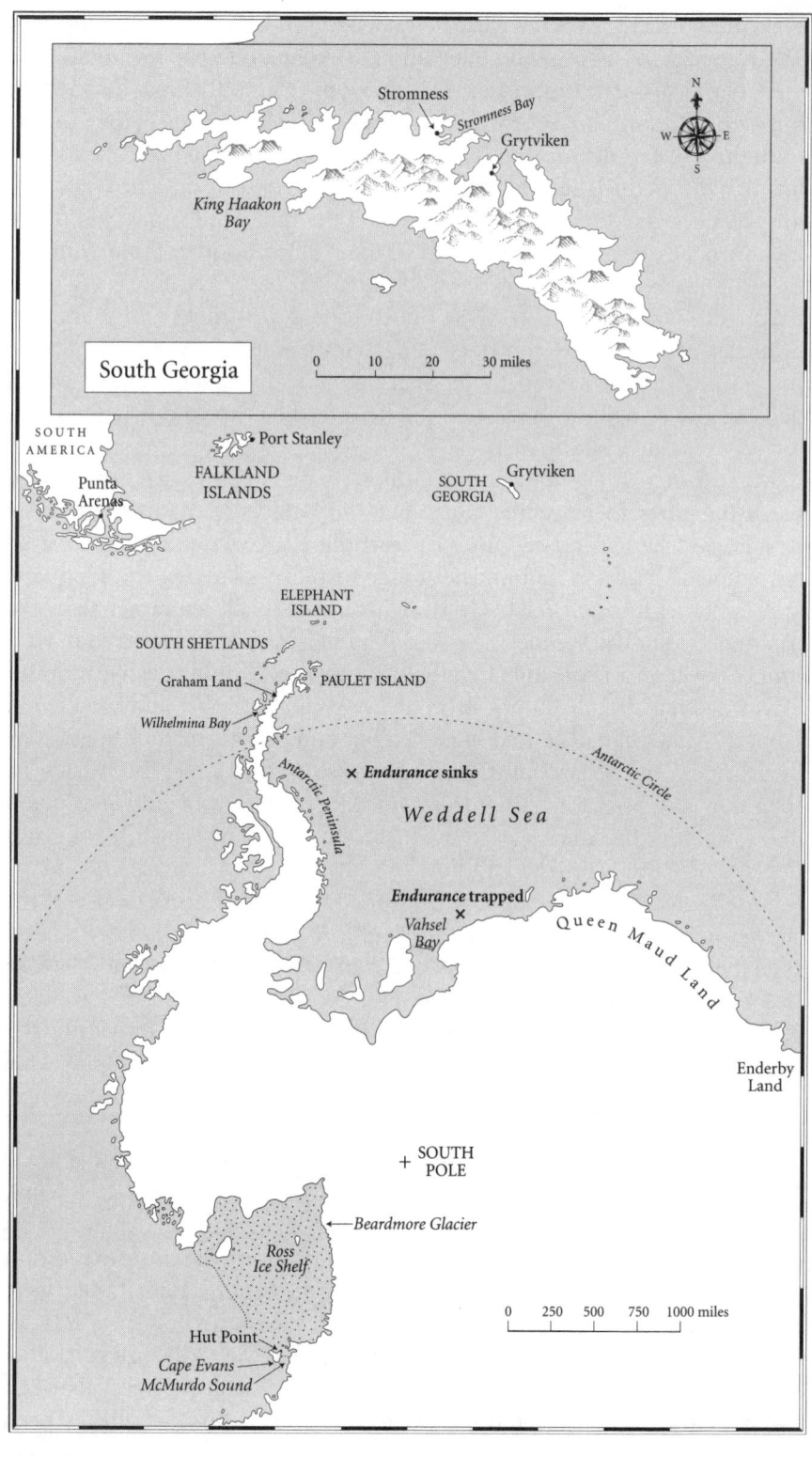

Stromness
Stromness Bay
Grytviken
King Haakon Bay

N
W E
S

South Georgia

0   10   20   30 miles

SOUTH AMERICA

Port Stanley
FALKLAND ISLANDS
Punta Arenas

SOUTH GEORGIA
Grytviken

ELEPHANT ISLAND

SOUTH SHETLANDS

Graham Land
Wilhelmina Bay
PAULET ISLAND

Antarctic Peninsula

× Endurance sinks

Antarctic Circle

Weddell Sea

Endurance trapped ×

Vahsel Bay

Queen Maud Land

Enderby Land

+ SOUTH POLE

Beardmore Glacier

Ross Ice Shelf

Hut Point
Cape Evans
McMurdo Sound

0   250   500   750   1000 miles

spent. Churchill himself was of that opinion. Within the hour a laconic telegram reached Margate: 'Proceed.' So Shackleton did.

On Tuesday he met King George V, who handed him a Union Jack to plant at the Pole. Queen Alexandra gave him a Bible, in which she wrote: 'May the Lord help you to do your duty and guide you through all dangers by land and sea. May you see all the works of the Lord and all his wonders in the deep.' That midnight, war was declared. *Endurance* left Plymouth on 8 August and, having touched at Buenos Aires and South Georgia, steamed for the ice on 5 December. Already it was a month behind schedule. It did not cross the Antarctic Circle until 11.00 p.m. on 30 December, by which time Shackleton had abandoned his idea of traversing the continent before April.

The Weddell Sea was harder, icier and stormier than they had imagined. The *Endurance* had to retreat, wait, divert and, when thwarted by the constantly changing leads, was forced to batter its way through sheets more than three feet deep. They were bedevilled by refraction, a familar foe from expeditions past: 'From the masthead the mirage is continually giving us false alarms. Everything wears an aspect of unreality. Icebergs hang upside down in the sky; the land appears as layers of silvery or golden cloud. Cloud banks look like land, icebergs masquerade as islands or nunataks, and the distant barrier to the south is thrown into view, though it is really outside our range of vision. Worst of all is the appearance of open water, caused by the refraction of distant water, or by the sun shining at an angle on a field of smooth snow or the face of ice cliffs below the horizon.' On 17 February the sun set, and though the pack reflected enough light to maintain a semblance of normality, winter was at hand. 'The summer had gone,' Shackleton lamented. 'Indeed, the summer had scarcely been with us at all.' Five days later the ship was fast in the ice, at 77° S, 60 nautical miles from its destination. The temperature was −10° F. They could see land now and then, but it was beyond their reach. As Shackleton was forced to admit, they would have to endure a season in the ice. 'This calm weather with intense cold in the summer is surely exceptional. My chief anxiety is the drift. Where will the vagrant winds and currents carry the ship during the long winter months that are ahead of us?'

On the other side of the continent the *Aurora* party was struggling to lay the depots on which the transcontinental travellers' survival depended. Their task, hard enough at the best of times, was made even harder by a combination of ill fortune and poor planning. Although they had been provided with the material for a base hut, they had not had time to build it, and were therefore forced to live in Scott's old quarters at Cape Evans. Similarly, they had insufficient food – no pemmican at all – so had to scrounge what they could from Scott's left-overs. The *Aurora* had been blown from the shore and was now sitting in McMurdo Sound, prevented by ice from delivering them the supplies they needed. They had arrived too late to train the dogs for the journey, with the result that they were unfit and unacclimatized.

Ernest Joyce, the only man among them who had solid experience of Antarctic travel, had been assured at the outset that he would be in charge of the overland part of the expedition. At the same time, however, Shackleton had given the *Aurora*'s captain, a one-eyed man named Aeneas Mackintosh, the authority to override him – which he did, insisting that he direct the sledge party. Organizational and personal problems were compounded by evil weather. By 12 February, after less than a fortnight on the Ross Ice Shelf, the depot-layers had advanced a mere 40 miles. That day, trapped in his tent by a blizzard, Mackintosh wrote, 'What on earth am I doing here?' One of the group, a chaplain named Spencer-Smith, was already ill from scurvy and frostbite, and was sent back with two others. Mackintosh, Joyce and Ernest Wild – whose brother Frank was on the *Endurance* – plugged on. The three men reached 80° S on 20 February, constructed cairns to direct Shackleton to their caches, then turned back four days later. They had ten days' food for the 150 miles it had taken them three weeks to cover. On 25 February, in the middle of yet another gale, Joyce wrote: 'trekking out of the question . . . The blizzard – fury. We are now on half rations. My heart aches for the dogs . . . Our sleeping bags are soaked; clothes in a smiliar condition.' On 25 March they arrived at Hut Point – across the bay from Cape Evans, on Ross Island, so-called because of the hut built by Scott and later used by Shackleton that still stood there – where they waited disconsolately for the sea to freeze, and on 2 June reached Cape Evans and – or so they expected – the safety of the *Aurora*. But the ship was not there. On 6 May it had been blown from its anchorage and was now beset in the pack. From this disastrous season the only consolation Mackintosh could derive was that Shackleton had surely been unable to start his journey and that next year he would be able to complete the chain of depots to the top of the Beardmore.

On 24 March, the day before Mackintosh reached Hut Point, it had been Empire Day. This holiday, invented ten years previously by the Earl of Meath, was intended to instil in British subjects the notion of a benevolent, all-wise institution that would last for as long as the sun never set on its far-flung domains. It was celebrated on the *Aurora* and, in the Weddell Sea, on the *Endurance*. Perhaps both ships' companies sensed the irony of drinking to a day that the Earl of Meath had meant 'to be spent by children in exercise of a patriotic and agreeable character'.

Clamped in the ice, *Endurance* drifted north through the Weddell Sea, threatened constantly by the shifting pack. Although a powerful icebreaker, it was not, like Nansen's *Fram*, round enough to rise above the floes, and by late October it was so badly squeezed that Shackleton ordered his men onto the ice. 'Our sadness,' wrote photographer Frank Hurley, 'is for the familar scene from which we are being expelled. The clock is ticking on the wall as we take a final leaving of our cosy wardroom.' They bade farewell to the *Endurance* at teatime on 27 October. That evening 28 men crawled into their tents. They had 18 reindeer sleeping bags among them and three boats containing 56 days' food for a journey to nobody was sure where. They could march to their intended destination, Vahsel Bay, which would be the first place a rescue party would search, or they could go overland 450 miles to Wilhelmina Bay, in Graham Land, where whalers occasionally stopped. Shackleton chose the latter, heading first for Paulet Island, where the explorer Nordenskiöld had left a hut and supplies 12 years earlier. From there he intended to cross to Wilhelmina Bay to fetch help. Fitting two of his boats with sledges, he led his men north-west (or, rather, west to counteract the due north drift of the pack) in a column of dogs, sledges and boats that stretched half a mile across the ice. To save weight each man was restricted to two pounds of personal possessions – Shackleton showed the way by flinging a handful of gold sovereigns onto the ice. 'I pray God,' he wrote, 'I can manage to get the whole party to civilisation.'

After a few days, during which they advanced only a few miles, Shackleton changed his mind. It would be better, he decided, to camp on the floe where they were – Ocean Camp, they called it – and wait for the ice to melt before taking to the boats. More supplies were retrieved from the *Endurance*, along with their third boat, and brought to Ocean Camp. For a month the *Endurance* remained visible, drifting north behind them. Finally, on 21 November, they saw its funnel tilt forwards. The stern rose in the air and then the whole ship crumpled into the sea. Some were glad to see it go, for it had long been, in Frank Hurley's words, 'an object of depression to all who turned their eyes in that direction.' Shackleton was distressed. It had been his command, and even in its decrepitude it had been a token of security. When it vanished, so did their last reminder of more optimistic times. 'I cannot write about it,' he recorded.

The Weddell Sea is shaped like an open hand, the fingers being Queen Maud Land and the thumb the Antarctic Peninsula. Ice collects within its grasp, but, unlike the ice of the Ross Shelf, which is anchored to the mainland by glaciers, the Weddell pack is in constant motion, rotated by the currents that flow past its mouth. It is best approached along the coast, where the ice tears free from the mainland and is at its loosest. Shackleton, however, had driven the *Endurance* into the centre of the Weddell Sea. Now he was trapped in its circle. In a way this was fortunate: the pack was carrying him north to open seas. In another way it was not: if he wanted to reach Paulet Island he would have to be on the outer, most hazardous rim of the pack and to judge precisely the right moment for his departure.

From camp to camp the *Endurance* men moved that winter across the Weddell Sea, readjusting their position as the pack drove north. The staleness of camp life, combined with inevitable clashes of personality, produced little squabbles that threatened to become major arguments. At every potential breach of discipline, however, Shackleton exerted his powerful personality. Singlehandedly he maintained morale, at one point speaking so convincingly of a future expedition to the Arctic that the men forgot their travails. He insisted so vehemently that they would be home by Christmas that most people believed him – and those who didn't dared not draw attention to the lie. Come Christmas, however, they were still in the Weddell Sea, and some of the men became so sick of hauling – they were then midway between camps – that Shackleton had to quell a nascent mutiny.

Life was little better for the *Aurora* party. The previous season's exertion had killed most of the dogs, and Mackintosh now displayed the bleeding gums and swollen joints of scurvy. It was Joyce, therefore, who became the expedition's effective leader, as he, Mackintosh and three others – assisted by the four remaining dogs – trudged over the Beardmore to lay, at 83° S, on 21 January, the last of the food caches. They had been joined at the outset by Spencer-Smith, but had been forced to leave him in a tent because he too had scurvy. In honesty, they would have liked to have left Mackintosh behind as well, not only because his absence would have made their progress faster, but because he could have kept the crippled chaplain company. But Mackintosh, refusing to acknowledge his condition or relinquish his nominal responsibility, had insisted he accompany them.

The return journey was a marvel of endurance and self-discipline. When they reached Spencer-Smith's tent the chaplain was too weak to walk and had to be put on a sledge. As Joyce and the others hauled resolutely Mackintosh could hardly keep pace. Soon they were all showing signs of scurvy. Their supplies were low, but they dared not take too much from the depots they had laid because, as they knew, Shackleton would need the food more desperately than they. 'Poor dogs & selves,' Joyce wrote on 15 February, 'practically done up ... it seems we are pulling over 300 lbs per man instead of about 130 lbs. I suppose we are getting a bit shaken up & want some fresh meat.' A week later, having been trapped in their tents for five days by a blizzard, they were almost out of food. Like Scott – about whom they spoke often, and remnants of whose trek they had met along the way – they were about ten miles from their next depot; indeed, they were not that far from his grave. Lest they suffer the same fate, Joyce and two of the healthiest men went into the storm to fetch supplies from the cache. The first day they covered a couple of hundred yards before having to turn back. 'Conditions were impossible,' wrote one man. 'Wind was of hurricane force and extremely gusty making it difficult to retain our feet. We could only see a few yards and even the sky was no different in appearance to anywhere else. There seemed to be no up or down.'

In the early hours of 26 February they attained the depot, so exhausted that it took them two hours to cover the last three-quarters of a mile and an hour more to pitch their tent – a process that was normally a matter of five minutes. Then, after a short rest, they loaded their sledge and started back. They reached the others on 29 February, the twelfth day of the storm and the sixth since they had had a decent meal. Once again the party started for Hut Point. Within a week Mackintosh was so enfeebled that the haulers left him in a tent, promising to come back when they themselves had reached safety and were stronger. Two days later Spencer-Smith died. He had maintained a glorious optimism right to the end – on 1 March, when Mount Erebus was in sight, he had written, 'it is homely to see the old place once again' – but he was too scorbutic to last the distance. One of his haulers wrote an irritable epitaph: 'We have pulled him helpless for 40 days, over a distance of 300 miles.'

Joyce and his men reached Hut Point on 11 March, gorged themselves on seal meat that they had laid down the previous year, then set forth to retrieve Mackintosh. By 18 March the company was safely home. During their depot-laying journeys they had covered more miles than any Antarctic sledgers to date and, in Joyce's words, '[had] suffered hardships that I did not think was possible for man to exist under the same conditions. I think the irony of fate was poor Smith going under a day before we arrived in.' Now, at Hut Point, they faced further months of discomfort before the sea froze and they could cross to Cape Evans, where life was slightly better and food more plentiful. But even when – or if – they reached Cape Evans there was no certainty that they would ever leave it, for the *Aurora* had vanished. Joyce wrote resignedly: 'As there is no news of the ship, & we cannot see her, we surmise she has gone down with all hands.'

Beyond the horizon, the *Aurora* was still afloat, in ice-free seas, but it was in poor shape: its rudder had been damaged, its anchors had been lost and its fuel was low. Less than a week after Joyce's final return to Hut Point the ship was steaming back to New Zealand. An Australian radio station picked up a transmission to that effect on 24 March, bringing the world its first news of the Imperial TransAntarctic Expedition. As the press interrupted its coverage of the Western Front to speculate on events in Antarctica, Churchill frothed with indignation. Currently in Flanders, he found it hard to see beyond the slaughter that surrounded him. 'Fancy that ridiculous Shackleton & his South Pole – at the crash of the world,' he wrote to his wife. When the papers began to agitate for a rescue mission – assuming, wrongly, that Shackleton must have completed his journey – Churchill put the expedition in what he saw as its proper context: 'When all the sick and wounded have been tended, when all their impoverished & broken hearted homes have been restored, when every hospital is gorged with money, & every charitable subscription is closed, then & not until then wd I concern myself with those penguins. I suppose, however, something will have to be done.'

Yes, something had to be done. But however Churchill puffed and ranted, Shackleton was the only man capable of doing it. At the beginning of March the *Endurance* survivors were alive and healthy, thanks to a diet of penguin and seal that had prevented their contracting scurvy. But they were still in the Weddell pack – after his brush with mutiny, Shackleton had decided that waiting rather than hauling was the best policy; he called their present site Patience Camp – and the ice was too dangerous for them to sail for Paulet Island, now less than 100 miles distant. On 27 March the northward drift carried them within sight of land: it was just 40 miles away, but the ice was too loose for sledging, too tight for sailing. The next day it was gone. They had now been at the mercy of the pack for six months and 2,000 miles. Their food was coming to an end, they had not washed since October, and for toothpaste had been using an improvised mix of snow and soot. The urgency of reaching land was overwhelming. They had missed their window, and once winter set in they would either be in seas so stormy that their boats would likely sink, or be heading towards Antarctica as the Weddell Sea drew them back into its clasp.

By the first week of April they were well past Paulet Island and their floe was breaking up. On the 9th Shackleton ordered the boats to be launched. To the north was a desolate outcrop of rock and ice, a distant relation of the South Shetlands, to which their maps gave the name Elephant Island. He hoped they might be able to make Graham Land, on the peninsula, but failing that Elephant Island was their last chance. They were not yet free of the pack, so they had to row rather than sail, hampered constantly by the vagrant movements of the ice. Now it tightened, forcing them to drag their three boats onto a floe, now it split beneath them. One night, as Shackleton prowled the camp, kept awake by 'an intangible feeling of uneasiness', he saw a tent stretch as the floe separated beneath it. 'I rushed forward, helped some men to come out from under the canvas ... The crack had widened to about 4 feet and ... I saw a whitish object floating in the water. It was a sleeping bag with a man inside. I was able to grasp it, and, with a heave, lifted man and bag on the floe. A few seconds later the ice-edges came together again with tremendous force.'

As ice and currents swept them beyond reach of Graham Land, they were forced, as Shackleton had anticipated, to head for Elephant Island, unexplored since American sealers had first discovered it in 1830. They beached on 11 April, after a week in which they had not slept for four consecutive days. 'Most of us,' a crew-member wrote, 'hardly knew whether to laugh or cry ... We took childish joy in looking at the black rocks & picking up the stones, for we had stepped on no land since Dec. 5 1914.' Their euphoria soon vanished as they realized they were not much better off than before. They had a better chance of shooting wildlife, but that was all. Their position, on a spit of gravel, was damp and exposed. Winter was not far off. They were no nearer salvation, had no shelter, no means of communication and no hope of being rescued. Even if a ship had been sent after them – they had no idea if it had; in fact it had not – why should its captain bother with Elephant Island when there were other, more likely places to search? After all their travails on the pack, it seemed they were doomed at best to another winter, at worst to starvation. One of the officers, the navigator Frank Worsley, tried to console Shackleton, saying that whatever their fate, they would be grateful for his superhuman efforts on their behalf. The response was gruff. 'Superhuman effort isn't worth a damn unless it achieves results.'

Worsley was surprised. 'My view was that we were all grown men, going of our own free will on this expedition, and that it was up to us to bear whatever was coming to us. Not so Shackleton. His idea was that we had trusted him, that we had placed ourselves in his hands, and that should anything happen to us he was morally responsible.'

Shackleton already had a result in mind: a journey on one of their boats to find help. Wilhelmina Bay was out of the question: the winds and currents were in the wrong direction. Cape Horn was a possibility, as were the Falkland Islands, both of them being relatively close. But once again the winds in that latitude were wrong. His best bet was the permanently manned whaling stations of South Georgia, 700 miles away over seas that were famously bad but ran where he wanted to go. 'The hazards,' he wrote, 'were obvious, but I calculated that at worst this venture would add nothing to the risks of the men left on the island.' It took more than a week to fit their largest boat, the *James Caird*, with watertight decking for ocean travel – a process that involved partially dismantling the other two vessels – and on 24 April it sailed for South Georgia. With him Shackleton took five men: Worsley, Vincent the bosun, McNeish the carpenter, McCarthy a seaman and, at the last moment, Crean, the second-officer of the *Endurance*.

It was a journey of inconceivable discomfort. The *James Caird* was just 22 feet long and, once the stores had been stowed, there was room for only three men at a time to sleep beneath the decking, switching with their companions above at four-hour intervals. Not that being below was any great privilege, however, for the boat leaked and had to be regularly bailed, mostly by hand but, when the level subsided, with a homemade pump. Their clothes – which they had been wearing for seven months – were designed for the dry cold of Antarctica rather than the constant, salt-water showers of sea travel. Their reindeer sleeping bags moulted, shedding damp hairs into the men's noses, mouths and food, and two of them began to rot, filling the boat with such a nauseating stench that they had to be thrown overboard. The boulders they had taken aboard as ballast had to be shifted to trim the boat and to gain access to the pump – which, like everything else, became clogged with reindeer hair. 'The moving of the boulders was weary and painful work,' Shackleton later recorded. 'We came to know every one of the stones by sight and touch, and I still have vivid memories of their angular peculiarities even today ... As weights to be moved about in cramped quarters they were simply appalling. They spared no portion of our poor bodies.' As they toiled, their wet clothes rubbed the insides of their thighs raw. Conversely, when they did not move, the cold, waterlogged, restricted conditions impeded their circulation, and turned their feet into puffy masses of white flesh. On the tenth night Worsley was so hunched after a stint at the tiller that he had to be massaged straight before he could fit in his sleeping bag.

And then there was the sea itself. In the first days they spent hours chipping at frozen spray lest the *James Caird* founder beneath its weight. In the wake of ice and snow came gales and waves so high that when in the valleys their sail flapped idly. On the eleventh day, 5 May, Shackleton saw an awesome spectacle: 'At midnight I was at the tiller and suddenly noticed a line of clear sky between the south and the southwest. I called to the other men that the sky was clearing, and then a moment later I realised that what I had seen was not a rift in the clouds but the white crest of an enormous wave. During twenty-six years' experience of the ocean in all its moods I had not encountered a wave so gigantic. It was a mighty upheaval of the ocean, a thing quite apart from the big white-capped seas that had been our tireless enemies for many days. I shouted, "For God's sake, hold on! It's got us!" Then came a moment of suspense that seemed drawn out into hours.' The *James Caird* was tossed about like a cork but survived – just. 'We baled with the energy of men fighting for life, flinging the water over the sides with every receptacle that came to our hands, and after ten minutes of uncertainty we felt the boat renew her life beneath us.' Possibly the surge had been caused by a massive calving of one of Antarctica's glaciers. If so, it was a vicious farewell. With dry understatement Shackleton wrote: 'Earnestly we hoped that never again would we encounter such a wave.'

In all conditions, and through every setback, Worsley kept them on course for South Georgia. The only navigational aids he possessed were a compass, a well-thumbed book of tables and a sextant that he used on the rare occasions when the sky was clear, hanging on to the boat with one hand while shooting his position with the other. How he did it was a marvel. When the German explorer Arved Fuchs replicated Shackleton's journey in 2000, he was baffled how anyone could plot a course with such limited equipment, in such heavy seas and in such dire conditions (Worsley made his calculations by candlelight in the dank and wretched space under the decking). Nevertheless, Worsley managed by skill, perseverance and the odd bit of luck to steer them towards South Georgia. They saw its cliffs on 8 May, their fifteenth day in the boat – and the last but one before their water ran out.

At Hut Point Captain Aeneas Mackintosh was fretting. It had been almost two months since he had been dragged back from the Beardmore expedition and, although not fully recovered, he was strong enough to exercise his old authority. He was tired of the food, the claustrophobic shelter that was barely windproof, and the blubber that supplied their light and fuel, pervading the whole hut with soot and stench. He had never lived in such conditions before, could not stand the thought of being trapped, and wanted to get out – a syndrome common today, even in the comfort of modern research stations, to those who spend any length of time in Antarctica. On 8 May, while the *James Caird* was on its last run to South Georgia, Mackintosh told Joyce that he was going to walk across McMurdo Sound to Cape Evans. Joyce told him not to – all but ordered him not to: the ice looked firm but could not be relied upon, being too young to resist the winds that might, without warning, pour from the interior; the sky showed every sign of a blizzard; if he waited another two months the company could evacuate in safety together. Mackintosh ignored the advice. That day, accompanied by a fellow convalescent named Hayward, he set out for Cape Evans. Hitherto, neither man had been able to walk two miles unattended. The distance to Cape Evans was 13 miles.

Joyce gave up: 'I don't know why these people are so anxious to risk their lives again, but it seems they are that way inclined.' Another man was more explicit: 'As I stood watching the two figures ... disappearing into the gloom of midday, there was a tinge of bitterness in my thoughts at the tremendous effort we had made to get these two men back.' Thirty minutes after Mackintosh's and Hayward's departure a blizzard came on. On 10 May, as soon as the wind abated, Joyce and the remaining two men went in search of them. They followed their footprints for about three miles until brought to a halt by an expanse of water, covered by a film of ice, running north for as far as the eye could see. As Joyce had predicted, part of the bay ice had been blown out to sea; but it was impossible to tell if Mackintosh and Hayward had gone with it or had managed to reach Cape Evans before the break-up. Hoping for the best, they retired to Hut Point. 'We are quite happy here,' Joyce wrote, 'and do not intend to leave until safe.'

On the same day, the seventeenth since he had left Elephant Island, Shackleton completed his boat journey. When Worsley sighted South Georgia on 8 May they were jubilant. But the shore was so rugged and inhospitable that it took another two days, skirting in a rough figure of eight, before they landed, in cold, drizzling rain, on a beach in King Haakon Bay on the southern coast of the island. Thirstily, they drank the glacial water that poured from the hills above. It could only be a temporary stop, for the beach was surrounded on all sides by cliffs, so after two days they sailed for a better berth at the mouth of the bay. Taking stock, they had good reason to be proud of themselves: they had covered 700 miles in foul weather; they had reached their goal with ten days' rations remaining; they had landed at a spot where there was water, wildlife and, when they up-ended the boat, shelter. Their feet were frostbitten, but they had survived the journey without death or serious injury. It was a magnificent accomplishment, flawed only by one very important detail: they were on the wrong side of the island.

To reach the whaling stations on the north-east coast they had two options: to sail round South Georgia or to take a short-cut overland. The first was impractical, for even if the crew could be persuaded to leave the relative luxury of their camp neither they nor the *James Caird* were in any condition to undertake a journey of some 130 miles. The second option was hardly more attractive: South Georgia's mountainous interior was unknown and unmapped; nobody had penetrated further than a mile inland; and received opinion held the crags and glaciers to be insurmountable. They had neither the clothes nor the equipment for mountaineering, and some of them were too weak to contemplate walking, let alone climbing, any distance. But, according to Worsley's calculations, the station of Husvik in Stromness Bay was only 17 miles from their present position. Given the right weather, and assuming they encountered nothing too difficult, a small party of the fittest might be able to cross South Georgia in a day or two.

Shackleton left with Worsley and Crean in the early hours of Friday 19 May, beneath a full moon, strung about with ropes and provisions – Crean had constructed a sledge from driftwood, but it was abandoned as being too unwieldy – and with screws from the *James Caird* driven through the soles of their boots to act as crampons. For alpenstocks they had lengths of the boat's strakes; and for an ice-axe they took the last item from McNeish's toolbox, an adze. Within two hours they had climbed 2,500 feet – a fair time by any standard, miraculous given their state – and were face to face with South Georgia's mountains. 'High peaks, impassable cliffs, steep snow slopes, and sharply descending glaciers were prominent features in all directions,' Shackleton wrote. They roped up and marched on. To and fro they went, taking wrong turnings, retracing their steps, cutting their way up and down ice slopes with the adze. At 11.00 a.m. they broached a crest, only to be faced by a precipice of 1,500 feet. They skirted around it, and an hour later made their way across a bergschrund a mile and a half long and 1,000 feet deep – 'two battleships could have been hidden in it', Worsley recorded in awe – before climbing an ice slope of 45 degrees to a 4,500-foot pass from which, at last, they could see the north coast. Before they could reach it, however, they first had to climb down another slope and then up a ridge of 2,000 feet. By now fog was beginning to creep over the peaks behind them. They had no tent, no sleeping bags, and were wearing the same threadbare clothes in which they had left the *Endurance*. 'It was of the utmost importance for us to get down . . . before dark,' Shackleton recorded. Recklessly, they coiled their ropes into bucket-sledges and slid down the hill. 'We seemed to shoot into space,' Worsley wrote. 'For a moment my hair fairly stood on end. Then quite suddenly I was grinning! I was actually enjoying it . . . I yelled with excitement, and found that Shackleton and Crean were yelling too.' In two or three minutes they descended 900 feet* to land in a pile of soft snow. Behind them, grey fingers of fog crept over the ridge on which they had been standing.

On they went, over snowfields and down glaciers, laughing and congratulating themselves, until, in the early morning of 20 May, the sea was beneath them. But it was not Stromness Bay. Somewhere they had taken a wrong turning. 'Wearily and mechanically', they retraced their steps. As lack of sleep, dehydration and sheer exhaustion took their toll, the trek assumed a hallucinatory quality. They misjudged distances, mistook one glacier for another and, for a while, could not remember whether their party numbered three or four. When, having stumbled down yet another hill, towards yet another bay, they heard at 6.30 a.m. a steam-whistle, at first they thought it

---

* The distance of 900 feet is as judged by Shackleton. His biographer, Roland Huntford, puts it at 1,500 feet. Worsley thought it was nearer 3,000 feet.

was a dream. Might it, however, be the Husvik whalers' wake-up alarm? If so, there would be another blast in half an hour. At 7.00 the whistle sounded again. This time there could be no mistake: they were within reach of safety. 'It was a moment hard to describe,' Shackleton wrote. 'Pain and ache, boat journeys, marches, hunger and fatigue seemed to belong to the limbo of forgotten things, and there remained only the perfect contentment that comes of work accomplished.'

The three men descended a sharp incline, cutting footsteps with the adze for thousands of feet until they were almost on top of the beach. 'The last lap of the journey proved extraordinarily difficult,' Shackleton wrote. 'Vainly we searched for a safe, or reasonably safe, way down from the steep ice-clad mountainside. The sole possible pathway seemed to be a channel cut by water running from the upland. Down through icy water we followed the course of this stream.' It terminated in a cascade that cut through a 30-foot cliff. They could not climb down the cliff and there was no way out to left or right. Retreat being impossible they wrapped one of their ropes round a boulder and lowered themselves into the waterfall itself. At 4.00 p.m., having stumbled over a mile of shale, they reached the whaling station. The first people they encountered were two young boys, who fled at the sight of them.

Six hours later they had been fed, washed and clothed, and a whaler was steaming to rescue the castaways in King Haakon Bay. 'We had ceased to be savages,' Shackleton wrote, 'and had become civilised men again.' While they acclimatized themselves to the unaccustomed comfort of sleeping in a bed for the first time in six months, a gale blew up. They had arrived just in time. In Worsley's opinion, 'Had we been crossing that night, nothing could have saved us.' For Shackleton it was the final confirmation that they had survived not by skill or luck but by divine intervention. When his journal was published in 1919 it contained the following passage: 'When I look back at those days I have no doubt that Providence guided us, not only across those snow fields, but across the storm-white sea that separated Elephant Island from our landing place on South Georgia. I know that during that long and racking march of thirty-six hours over the unnamed mountains and glaciers of South Georgia it seemed to me often that we were four, not three. I said nothing to my companions on the point, but afterwards Worsley said to me, "Boss, I had a curious feeling on the march that there was another person with us."' Crean confessed to the same impression. 'One feels "the dearth of human words, the roughness of mortal speech" in trying to describe things intangible,' Shackleton wrote, 'but a record of our journeys would be incomplete without a reference to a subject very near to our hearts.'*

* This strange phenomenon might have been invented to give the journal a religious touch – to lend it, perhaps, some of the 'Great God' grandeur of Scott's diaries. From a medical viewpoint, it might be explained as a delusion produced by dehydration. (Like Mawson, who had also expressed his thanks to Providence, Shackleton's men had been short of water during the last leg of their journey. Similar experiences were soon to be recorded on the first ascents of Everest.) Or it could be diagnosed as a shared

While the men of the King Haakon Bay party were being rescued, Shackleton had already organized a ship and crew to take him to Elephant Island. He sailed aboard the *Southern Sky* on Tuesday 23 May, taking Crean and Worsley with him. En route he stopped at the South Georgian whaling station of Grytviken, where a wireless operator sent a message to London. Received by the Admiralty on 31 May, it read, 'Sir Ernest Shackleton arrived today'. It was a welcome diversion for British newspapers which, fed up with the slaughter in Flanders, ran Antarctic headlines for a week, relegating the 100-day-plus battle of Verdun to the side columns.

Three days into the journey it became clear that the pack was too thick for the *Southern Sky* to reach Elephant Island. Repairing to the Falklands, Shackleton sought in vain for a strong enough vessel among the ships in Port Stanley. A relief ship was being prepared in Britain, but it could not be there before October, which was too late. A flurry of radio messages to South America produced a Uruguayan trawler, *Instituto de Pesca No. 1*, which arrived in Port Stanley on 10 June. But once again the pack was too thick; the trawler was forced to turn back after three days, with the peaks of Elephant Island tantalizingly visible on the horizon. A second attempt was made with two Chilean ships – the schooner *Emma* and the steamer *Yelcho* – but this too failed. A third try with the *Emma* alone likewise came to nothing. Back in Port Stanley on 8 August, Shackleton learned that the relief ship would now be with him in mid-September. The obvious course, as suggested by the Governor, was to wait for its arrival. Shackleton, however, had had his fill of Port Stanley: 'The street of that port is about a mile and a half long,' he wrote. 'It has the slaughterhouse at one end and the graveyard at the other. The chief distraction is to walk from the slaughterhouse to the graveyard. For a change one may walk from the graveyard to the slaughterhouse ... I could not content myself to wait for six or seven weeks, knowing that six hundred miles away my companions were in dire need.'

By 14 August he was in Chile, scouring Punta Arenas for a suitable ship. Finding none, he begged the Chilean government to lend him the *Yelcho* and its crew for one final voyage. It was a steel-hulled vessel 'quite unsuitable for work in the pack' (he had previously used it only to tow the *Emma* through Magellan Strait), but there was a small chance that, if the sea was clear, it could make Elephant Island. Generously, the Chileans acceded to his request, and on 25 August Shackleton steamed south for his fourth stab at the Antarctic pack in two months. This time he was successful. A gale had temporarily blown the ice northwards, leaving the *Yelcho* with open water. At noon on 30 August it was off Elephant Island.

The 22 castaways were coming to the end of their strength. For months

hallucination, akin to 'The Angel of Mons' which so many soldiers said they had seen during the retreat of 1914. On the other hand, it may have been a genuine spiritual experience. No explanation can be dismissed. The image was so powerful that it was adopted by T. S. Eliot in *The Wasteland* (1922), since when it has entered the religious and literary canon.

they had been living under two upturned boats, eking out their rations with whatever wildlife they could shoot. Their lives had devolved into a dreary continuum of food and sleep. Ernest Wild, their commander, did his best to keep them alert: if, for example, the sea was clear when they woke he would have them pack their kit in anticipation of Shackleton's arrival. When groundwater seeped into their living quarters he had them bail it out and dig drainage channels (before the channels were finished they bailed 410 gallons in 48 hours). But nothing he did could compensate for their sordid living conditions. 'Our shingle floor will scarcely bear examination by strong light,' Wild wrote, 'without causing even us to shudder and express our disapprobation as to its state. Oil mixed with reindeer hair, bits of meat, sennegrass [which they used as insulation in their boots], and penguin feathers form a conglomeration which cements the stones together ... All joints are aching through being compelled to lie on the hard, rubbly floor which forms our bedsteads.' Many days the wind and snow compelled them to stay indoors, either sleeping 'in the attic' or creeping on all fours in a space that was four foot six inches at its highest and made even lower by the damp clothes they draped from their bunk-shelves. 'From all parts,' wrote one inmate, 'there dangles an odd collection of blubbery garments, hung up to dry, through which one crawls, much as a chicken in an incubator.'

The day of 30 August was like any other. They prepared their gear for evacuation then slumped into routine. 'We were just assembling for lunch to the call of "Lunch O!"' wrote Wild, 'and I was serving out the soup, which was particularly good that day, consisting of boiled seal's backbone, limpets, and seaweed, when there was another hail from Marston of "Ship O!" Some of the men thought it was "Lunch O!" over again, but when there was another yell from Marston, lunch had no further attractions.' Shackleton approached on one of the *Yelcho*'s boats and threw them packets of cigarettes. Within an hour the men, their equipment, the expedition's logs and its scientific records were aboard. On 2 September the *Yelcho* docked at Punta Arenas. The police were alerted, the fire alarms were rung, and most of the population – of whom a proportion was, at that time, British – came out in welcome. 'It was a great reception,' Shackleton recorded, 'and with the strain of long, anxious months lifted at last, we were in a mood to enjoy it.'

Shackleton could not relax fully: he had yet to rescue the *Aurora* party at McMurdo Sound. He caught a ship to New Zealand, arriving in December 1916. At Wellington he found the government had already outfitted *Aurora* for a return journey and had placed John King Davis in charge. Davis – who has since been described as 'arguably the greatest ship's captain of this age of Antarctic discoveries' – had been a member of Shackleton's 1907–9 expedition, had commanded the *Aurora* on Mawson's expedition, and was a man whom Shackleton trusted implicitly. Shackleton joined the crew at a nominal one shilling per month as an advisor for overland travel. The *Aurora* touched Antarctica on 10 January. Shackleton sledged over the ice but saw nothing. Then, as he was returning to the ship, Joyce and his survivors hove into view. They were hustled into the safety of the ship. Of the original ten, only seven remained.

Spencer-Smith, the chaplain, could be accounted for immediately. But the whereabouts of Mackintosh and Hayward were less certain. When Joyce's group had reached Cape Evans on 15 July the one-eyed captain was not there. The likelihood was that he and Hayward had been blown out to sea in the storm of 8 May; it was just conceivable, however, that they might have reached land before the break-up. 'There was no possibility of either man being alive,' Shackleton wrote. 'They had been without equipment when the blizzard broke the ice they were crossing. It would have been impossible for them to have survived more than a few days, and eight months had now elapsed without news of them.' Nevertheless, he felt it his duty to make every effort to retrieve their bodies. A search of the coast produced nothing: 'There was no sign of . . . any person having visited the vicinity.' A laborious trudge inland was similarly fruitless: 'there was nothing to be seen but blue ice, crevassed, showing no protuberances . . . I could see there was not the slightest chance of finding any remains owing to the enormous snow drifts wherever the cliffs were accessible.' By 16 January he conceded that even had the two men reached land – which he doubted – he would never find their bodies. The *Aurora* sailed the following day for New Zealand, Shackleton examining the coast for cairns or markers as they went, and on 8 February it reached Wellington.

The Imperial TransAntarctic Expedition dissolved in an atmosphere of anticlimax. There was none of the triumphant flag-waving and speech-giving that normally followed an expedition's return. Instead, the 53 survivors were sucked into the various branches of Britain's war machine – three of them died, five were wounded, four were decorated for gallantry, many were mentioned in despatches – and it was two years before Shackleton finally embarked on the money-raising that was, traditionally, an explorer's right. He published his journal, titled simply *South*; and from December 1919 to May 1920 he lectured twice daily, at the Philharmonic Hall in London's Great Portland Street, on the horrors and the heroism of his expedition. His talk, accompanied by a film made by Frank Hurley, was surely the most memorable show-and-tell in history. The exploring community was impressed. Apsley Cherry-Garrard wrote glowingly (and with perhaps a dig at Scott), 'I know why it is that every man who has served under Shackleton swears by him. I believe Shackleton has never lost a man: he must have had some doubts as to whether he would save one then. But he did, he saved every one of them.' Roald Amundsen was unstinting in his praise: 'Do not let it be said that Shackleton has failed. No man fails who sets an example of high courage, of unbroken resolution, of unshrinking endurance.' The British public, however, did not share their enthusiasm. *South* sold well, but not nearly as well as it should have; and most of the time the Philharmonic

Hall was filled far below capacity. The truth was, people no longer cared.

When Shackleton sailed in 1914 explorers were considered heroes; if not for the war he could have achieved the status of men like Nansen, Scott and Amundsen. But in 1919 the very concept of heroism was in disrepute. Everyone in Europe could tell of bravery, of suffering, of good and bad leadership. Davis had warned of this in New Zealand, telling him that 'he seemed unable to realise, yet, that the war was engrossing the thoughts and emotions of the majority of civilised man and that, consequently, people were apt to be impatient with polar exploration. And, when every man in uniform was either a real, or at least a potential hero, people were also a little impatient of polar explorers in general.' Shackleton tried to link his expedition to the war. 'Mackintosh, Hayward, and Spencer-Smith died for their country as surely as any who gave up their lives on the fields of France and Flanders,' he insisted. The claim was patently false. They had died because of incompetence, bad planning and bad luck – in this respect maybe they did share something with the dead of Flanders – but they had not given their lives for their country: they had given them for the ill-conceived ambition of one man. True, it was only because of Shackleton's quite remarkable leadership qualities that so many had survived; had another been in charge the entire expedition might have perished. On the other hand, with a different leader they might never have been put in jeopardy. Standing in the half-empty Philharmonic Hall, Hurley's film flickering on the screen behind him, Shackleton must have been painfully aware that he was a redundant commodity.

He tried to claw back some stature, proposing first an Arctic expedition (it fell through) and then, more successfully, a circumnavigation of Antarctica. He departed in 1921 aboard the *Quest* on a voyage that according to one man 'seemed to have a beginning but, somehow, no end'. His justification was a search for undiscovered sub-Antarctic islands and a possible exploration of the unknown Enderby quadrant. But he had other adventures in mind: he wanted to search Trinidad for Captain Kidd's buried treasure and investigate the South Pacific for a rumoured lagoon of pearls. His crew, many of whom were veterans of the 1914–16 expedition, were worried: he was less confident, more diffident, than usual; and he was physically weaker. He had suffered for a long time from chest problems, which he refused to have inspected, let alone treated, and when the *Quest* stopped at Rio de Janeiro he had a massive heart-attack. Broken in health and spirit, he continued towards the Antarctic. 'The Boss,' wrote one man, 'says ... quite frankly that he does not know what he will do after S. Georgia.' Perhaps Shackleton did not care what he would do. Before leaving he had written to a friend, 'We ... go into the ice into the life that is mine and I do pray that we will make good, it is my last time'. His heart gave way on 5 January 1922. He was buried at Grytviken, South Georgia, beneath the mountains he had crossed just six years before.

George Mallory and Sandy Irvine (1924)

Ever since 1852, when the Survey of India had recognized Everest as the highest mountain in the world, the British had been wondering what to do about it. First they gave it a number – Peak XV – then in 1865 they gave it a name, and then, inevitably, in the 1890s they decided to climb it. The decision was purely academic, for Nepal and Tibet, on whose borders the mountain lay, still resisted British incursions. Even after the 1904 Treaty of Tibet, Everest remained practicably inaccessible. In part this was because of the ruggedness of its surrounding terrain; but predominantly it was because travellers were required to obtain permission from Lhasa, Peking (which claimed suzerainty over Tibet and maintained garrisons in the country) and the India Office, all of whom guarded their interests jealously. By 1913 the nearest a foreigner had come to the mountain was 40 miles, and the most anyone had seen of it was the top 1,000 feet or so. Following World War I, however, the political situation had eased, and an attempt on Everest was at last possible. Naturally, it would be a British attempt. To the members of the Royal Geographical Society and the Alpine Club, who joined forces to plan the first ascent, Everest had to be climbed not, as one mountaineer would explain, because it was there, but because it was theirs.

Sir Francis Younghusband, soldier, imperial administrator and regional expert, justified the action in typically British terms. The conquest of Everest would produce no tangible benefit at all, he warned his audience at a Royal Geographical Society lecture. But it would be of inestimable value to one's character: 'The accomplishment of such a feat will elevate the human spirit and will give man, especially us geographers, a feeling that we really are getting the upper hand on the earth, and that we are acquiring a true mastery of our surroundings. As long as we impotently creep about at the foot of these mighty mountains without attempting to ascend them, we entertain towards them a too excessive feeling of awe ... if man stands on earth's highest summit, he will have an increased pride and confidence in himself in the struggle for ascendancy over matter. This is the incalculable good which the ascent of Mount Everest will confer.' Younghusband's was the sort of archaic speech that might have gone down well before the war but it did not fit with the present mood. As the *Daily News* remarked sarcastically, it would be a proud moment indeed for the man who stood on top of the world, 'but he will have the painful thought that he has queered the pitch for posterity'. Nonetheless, few serious mountaineers could resist Young-husband's call to arms.

The necessary permissions were obtained and a two-year programme was outlined. In 1921 a party of climbers would conduct a reconnaissance of the area. Then, in 1922, a proper assault would be made by a second team. This approach was necessary for three reasons, the first of which was logistical. From Darjeeling, in British India, the only way to reach Everest was by foot and on pony, a journey that would take at least a month. Along the way it would be necessary to hire numerous mules and donkeys, plus porters who were willing (and more importantly, able) to tackle snow and extreme height. Any number of problems might arise, from malaria, dysentery, altitude sickness and food poisoning in the men to recalcitrance, illness and death among the pack animals. Also, a chain of procedure had to be established, for this was not the standard, lightweight, scramble of alpine mountaineering, but a siege that required reinforcements at every stage, up to and including Everest itself. Secondly, the mountain had to be scouted, and its perils calculated at first hand. One could not contemplate it from the safety of a village as one could, say, with the Matterhorn. It was so distant, so tall – at more than 29,000 feet it was six miles higher than Mont Blanc – that a survey was needed simply to establish where it was, let alone how best to find a way through its cliffs and snow slopes. Thirdly, it was important to show that Everest's conquest was not just an example of nationalistic peak-bagging. A full geographical survey was to be conducted and, although opportunities could be seized, members should bear in mind that 'attempts on a particular route must not be prolonged to hinder the completion of the reconnaissance'.

The 1921 expedition yielded mixed results. The chain of command and the forwarding of supplies worked reasonably well. However, of the two most senior and experienced Himalayan hands one died from exhaustion and another was broken by illness. The approach was mapped and the area surveyed in a rudimentary fashion, and by climbing the surrounding peaks they spied a potential route to the summit. It was not an easy one. At the bottom of the North Face one member wrote despairingly: 'The long imagined snow slopes of this Northern Face of Everest with their gentle and inviting angle turn out to be the most appalling precipice, nearly 10,000 feet high ... The prospect of ascent in any direction is about nil and our present job is to rub our noses against the impossible in such a way as to persuade mankind that some noble heroism has failed once again.' On the other hand, if they could skirt the precipices and reach a saddle that they named the North Col, it would be possible to attain the North-East Ridge and from there the way looked clear to the top. A party did climb successfully to the North Col from where they reported that: 'No obstacle appeared, or none

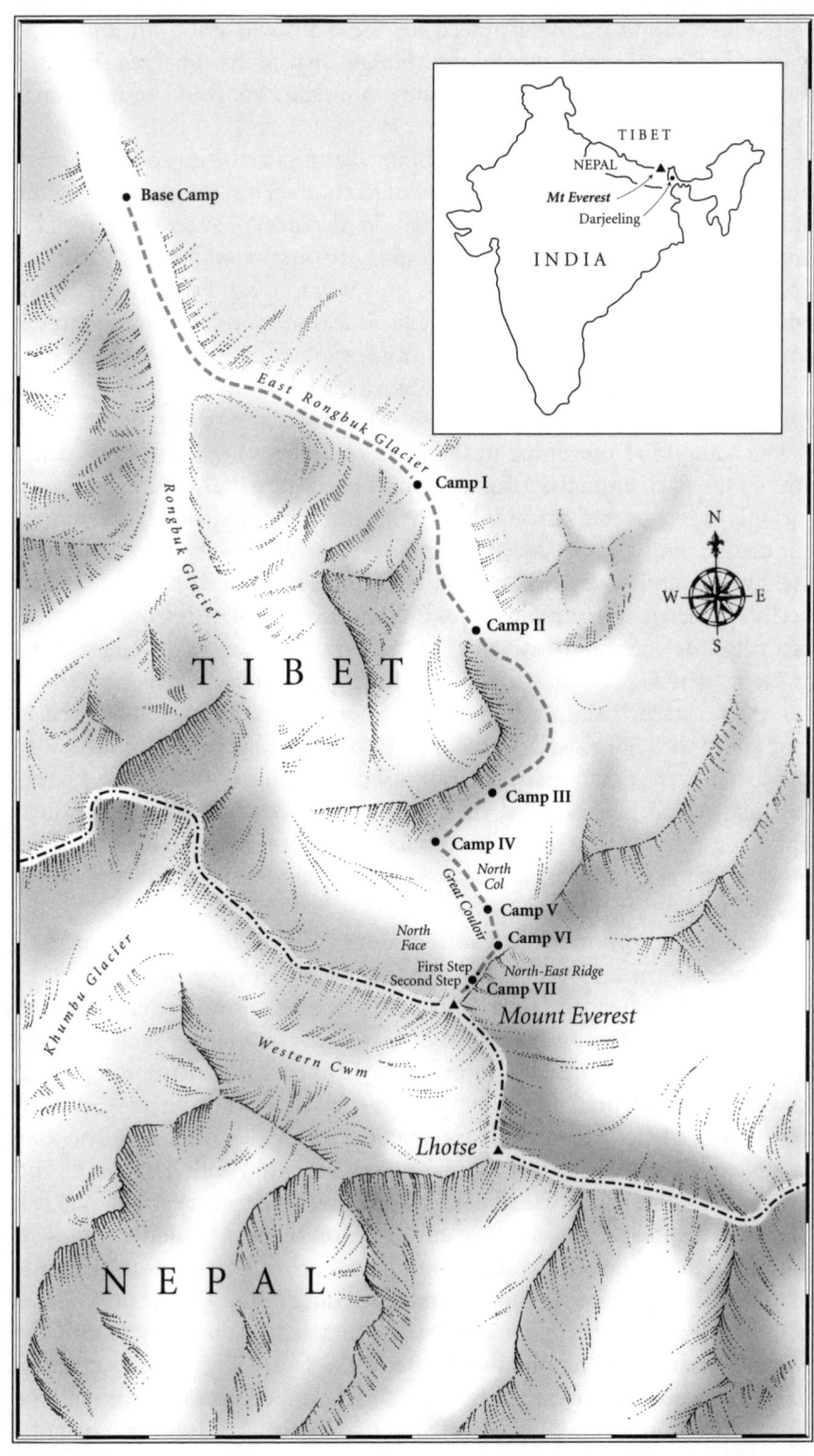

Base Camp

East Rongbuk Glacier

Rongbuk Glacier

TIBET

Camp I

Camp II

Camp III

Camp IV

North Col

Great Couloir

Camp V

Camp VI

North Face

First Step
Second Step

North-East Ridge

Camp VII

Mount Everest

Khumbu Glacier

Western Cwm

Lhotse

NEPAL

TIBET

NEPAL

Mt Everest

Darjeeling

INDIA

N
W E
S

so formidable that a competent party would not easily surmount it or go around it. If one harboured a doubt about this way before, it was impossible to keep it any longer.' They had neither the time nor the supplies to cover the final distance. Nor did they have the weather. A gale came from the north-west, so strong that they had to lean forward in order to remain upright. Peering through their goggles, they saw that 'the powdery fresh snow on the great face of Everest was being swept along in unbroken spindrift and the very ridge where our route lay was marked out to receive its unmitigated fury. We could see the blown snow deflected upwards for a moment where the wind met the ridge, only to rush violently down in a frightful blizzard on the leeward side.' They turned back, satisfied at having reached a height of 23,000 feet and in the knowledge that they had opened the way for the summit expedition of 1922.

The Mount Everest Committee chose a strange assortment of men for the 1922 attempt. On the grounds that youthful enthusiasm should be tempered by wisdom, the party comprised old buffers and youthful daredevils. Among the buffers was General Charles Bruce, an Indian Army officer who had been discharged in 1919 on grounds of 'cardiac debility with great enlargement', but who was given overall control of the expedition despite his obviously weak health. (As he later joked, 'Even my liver was found to be so large that it required two men and a boy to carry it'.) Several other members were past their prime, including the climbing leader Lieutenant-Colonel Edward Strutt, and at least one of them had been classified medically as 'not a very good specimen'. Of the daredevils there was Howard Somervell, a Cambridge-educated surgeon, amateur musician and artist who was 32, and a climber of great ability. Major 'Teddy' Norton was another: the grandson of alpine pioneer Sir Alfred Wills, he had grown up in the Alps, had superb organizational and diplomatic skills, could speak several Indian dialects, and exuded quiet authority. Then there were George Finch and George Mallory, who would become the expedition's leading figures.

On paper, the two Georges had much in common: they were both in their thirties, they were expert mountaineers and they had proved their ability over numerous seasons in the Alps. In personality and background, however, they were very different. Born in 1888, Finch had led an unusual life, moving from Australia to France and then to Switzerland before finding a job in Britain as a research chemist. He was a strong, fast climber, with a particular interest in the technical aspects of mountaineering – the various states of snow, ice and rock, the effects of cold and altitude on the human frame. But to the stuffier members of Britain's mountaineering establishment he was uncouth, unconventional and not quite the right sort. His supporters had had some difficulty persuading the Mount Everest Committee to accept him. Mallory, on the other hand, was the Alpine Club's darling. Two years older than Finch, he was the son of a vicar, had been educated at Cambridge, had served as a gunner in World War I, and was a schoolteacher. He was well known in literary circles – the Bloomsbury Group adored him for his physical beauty and mental purity – and as a mountaineer was renowned for his elastic agility on rock. Mallory's technique, however, was more spiritual than technical: he had an almost Victorian attitude to climbing, in that he did it for the thrill and the beauty alone. He was, however, notorious for his absent-mindedness – he could forget even the most basic things, such as tying himself on to the rope – and in the eyes of some could be too impetuous for his own good.

Finch and Mallory differed in more than character. Finch was an advocate of oxygen, which he said was vital where they would be going. As he explained to the Mount Everest Committee, they could only guess at the conditions ahead and had no idea if humans could even survive at that altitude. Italy's Duke of Abruzzi had matched his furthest north of 1900 with a furthest skyward in 1909, attaining 24,600 feet in the Karakorams, but this was the highest anybody had been. At the peak of Everest, nearly a mile above Abruzzi's furthest, the air would be so thin and so cold that climbers would have a hard time staying alive, let alone moving with any strength. The debilitating effects of altitude had been well attested ever since the first person climbed Mont Blanc; there was every reason to suppose they would become intolerable on Everest. Mallory, the muscular Christian, rejected the idea of oxygen on aesthetic grounds: it was not possible to appreciate beauty or to climb effectively with artificial assistance. Besides, he was of the firm opinion that the thinness of the air could be overcome by a combination of acclimatization and proper breathing. In the end a typically British compromise was reached: the expedition would take oxygen but would not necessarily use it.

The expedition surmounted the lower slopes of Everest without difficulty, and on 14 May 1922 the first party, comprising Mallory, Norton and Somervell, plus a surveyor named Morshead, set out for the North Col. Four days later they had not only reached their goal but were at a height of 25,000 feet. Here, at Camp V, the cold was so intense that they had to send the porters back. The following morning, with Morshead suffering from a combination of frostbite and exhaustion, the other three left him in the tent and departed on their own for the summit. The terrain was not technically difficult, but it was awkward, and steep enough to mean death if they slipped. Their greatest difficulty, however, was the atmosphere. Determined to defeat the mountain the old-fashioned way, they had come without oxygen and were soon prey to a lethargy worse than anything they had encountered in their careers. 'Our whole power seemed to depend on the lungs,' Mallory wrote. 'The air, such as it was, was inhaled through the mouth and expired again to some sort of tune in the unconscious mind, and the lungs beat time, as it were, for the feet. An effort of the will was required not so much to induce any movement of the limbs as to set the lungs to work and keep them working.' By 2.00 p.m., at a new record of 26,800 feet, it became obvious that they were not going to reach the top. Also, it was important that they get Morshead to a more sheltered position before nightfall. In Mallory's opinion, 'the only wisdom was in retreat'. That evening they arrived safely at Camp IV, on the edge of the North Col, dehydrated and in a state of semi-stupefaction from lack of oxygen. Of his decision to turn back Mallory wrote: 'Wonderful as such an experience would be, I had not even the desire to look over the North-East Ridge; I would have gladly got to the North-East Shoulder as being the sort of place one ought to reach, but I had no strong desire to get there, and none at all for the wonder of being there ... Our minds were not behaving as we would wish them to behave.' The following day, as they made their way down the North Col to Camp III, they met Finch leading a party in the opposite direction.

It had originally been planned that Finch would make a second attempt with Norton. But Norton had gone with the first group – without telling him – leaving Finch with no experienced mountaineers fit enough for the ascent. Unfazed, Finch selected two of the strongest remaining men – a Gurkha named Tejbir and a novice climber named Geoffrey Bruce – and set off with a team of ten porters plus three oxygen sets. At 25,500 feet they pitched a new Camp V, sent the porters back, and settled down for a uncomfortable night of gales. Sleep was impossible, as they spent the hours holding down the groundsheet to stop the wind getting underneath. 'We knew,' Finch wrote, 'that once the wind got a hold upon it, the tent would belly out like a sail, and nothing would save it from stripping away from its moorings and being blown, with us inside it, over the precipices.' Before the storm died, on the afternoon of the next day, the tent was in tatters: three guy ropes had snapped, a wind-blown rock had knocked a hole in the canvas, and the door could no longer be fastened. Six porters climbed heroically to their rescue, bringing thermoses of tea and Bovril. They would have liked to escort them down the mountain to safety, but Finch waved the offer aside. After another night in their tent, taking gulps of oxygen – in Finch's case interspersed with puffs on a cigarette – the three men continued upwards. After 500 feet Tejbir collapsed. In an act for which he would later be soundly criticized, Finch gave him a few bottles of oxygen and let him make his way home.

Forsaking the route that Mallory had taken, Finch and Bruce donned their masks and hacked across the North Face towards a couloir, or snow-filled gully, that seemed to offer an easy way to the ridge. Here was a remarkable situation: Bruce, a beginner who had to be taught as he went along, was helping pioneer a route up the world's highest mountain, and doing so with a primitive, cumbersome and weighty apparatus that had never seen proper service and was little more than a prototype. Neither he nor Finch was afflicted by the hallucinatory dullness that had bedevilled Mallory's group, and they were moving swiftly – at their best they averaged 900 feet per hour. It was almost too good to be true. Only three things could stop them: Bruce, the weather or the oxygen. Bruce was still going strong; the weather could have been better, but was reasonable; and the oxygen was working perfectly – so far.

In Britain, scientists had given solemn advice on the use of oxygen. When used properly it would help climbers reach the summit. But once it had been employed there was no going back. If they took the masks off at high altitude, or if the supply failed for any other reason, they would die. At about midday Bruce stumbled against a rock and broke one of the glass tubes leading from his canisters. Within a few steps he was gasping for air. 'I saw him struggling ineffectually to climb up towards me,' Finch recorded. 'Quickly descending the few intervening feet, I was just in time to grasp his right shoulder with my left hand as he was on the point of falling backwards over the precipice. I dragged him face forwards against the rock, and, after a supreme effort on the part of both, we gained the ledge where I swung him round into a sitting position against the slope above.' Perched on the North Face of Everest, clad in tweeds and woollen shirts, and wearing solar topees to protect them from the effects of high-altitude radiation, they took turns breathing from Finch's oxygen tube. Finch contrived a T-piece so that they could both breathe from his own canisters while he mended Bruce's equipment. Freshly aerated, they climbed on. But the shock, and the draining effect of the stop, had done for Bruce. Finch wrote: 'Now I saw that [he], like Tejbir, had driven his body almost to the uttermost. A little more would spell breakdown. My emotions are eternally my own, and I will not put down on paper a cold-blooded, psychological analysis of the cataclysmic change they underwent, but will merely indicate the initial and final mental positions . . . Never for a moment did I think we would fail; progress was steady, the summit was there before us; a little longer and we should have been at the top. And then – suddenly, unexpectedly, the vision was gone.'

They had beaten Mallory to a new record of 27,300 feet. The difference was only 500 feet, but in percentage terms it was huge. Finch and Bruce had 1,600 feet to go, and could have covered it, theoretically, in three or four hours. They would then have had just enough time to descend to a camp before nightfall. In the lore of Everest it has been suggested that had Finch been on his own he might have reached the summit. Like Mallory, however, he rightly took responsibility for the weakest member and led Bruce down the hill in a superb 6,000-foot descent that took them below the North Col to Camp III, where they arrived before the day was out, mildly frostbitten and, in Finch's words, 'dead, dead beat'. The expedition's supplies were plundered to their most extravagant limit. 'The brightest memory that remains with me of that night is dinner,' Finch recalled. 'Four quails truffled in *pâté de foie gras*, followed by nine sausages, only left me asking for more. With the remains of a tin of toffee tucked away in the crook of my elbow, I fell asleep in the depths of my warm sleeping bag.'

Finch's triumph left Mallory unsettled. He had to make one final stab at Everest. 'Frankly the game is not good enough: the risks of getting caught are too great; the margin of strength when men are at great heights is too small. Perhaps it's mere folly to go up again. But how can I be out of the hunt?' Mallory's assessment of his rashnesss was accurate. When he departed with Finch, Somervell and 14 porters on 3 June the monsoon season was upon them – as they discovered on waking one morning to find a fresh fall of snow on the hill above. For Finch, who had not fully recovered from his last ascent, this was a peril too far. Instructing the others in the use of oxygen, he returned to camp. Mallory and Somervell declined to follow him, and instead led the porters upwards. On the slopes of the North Col the inevitable happened: the fresh snow gave way beneath them in an avalanche that carried nine porters over a cliff and into a crevasse. Only two men survived. A length of rope protruding from a packed mass of snow marked their companions' grave.

It was an unpleasant coda to what had been, in many respects, a successful year. Somervell, in particular, felt the loss of these men who had done so much to help them, with little enough reward, and whose names most people would never know. 'Why, oh why could not one of us Britishers have shared their fate?' he cried in anguish. Mallory was equally moved: 'I'm quite knocked out by this accident,' he wrote to a friend. 'Seven of these brave men killed, and they were ignorant of mountain dangers, like children in our care. And I'm to blame . . . Do you know that sickening feeling that one can't go back and have it undone and that nothing will make good?'

He *was* to blame, as many people did not hesitate to point out in the subsequent evaluation of the expedition's achievements. One eminent member wrote: 'Mallory is a very good, stout hearted baby, but quite unfit to be placed in charge of anything, including himself . . . [He] cannot even observe the conditions in front of him. To attempt such a passage in the Himalaya after new snow is idiotic. What the hell did they think they could do *on Everest* in such conditions even if they did get up to the North Col?' What indeed? As for Somervell, he was 'the most urbanely conceited youth I have ever struck – and quite the toughest . . . He was honestly prepared to chuck his life away on the most remote chance of success.' In contrast, Norton received unanimous acclaim: 'a huge success in every direction . . . Always on for *any* job and always did the job well.' Finch, too, was given his due share of praise, albeit in a backhanded way: 'We so dreaded [him] that we were relieved to find his manners very passable: his temper agreeable: his mountain knowledge not overrated. He had *very* bad luck on his climb. With any reasonable conditions he would have stood on top of the final ridge. With luck he would have got to the top. But he is very Australian.'

With these accolades, it might have been expected that Norton and Finch would be included in the next expedition – set for 1924 – and Mallory and Somervell, if not left behind, then at least reconsidered. Britain's mountaineering establishment, however, moved in mysterious ways. They selected Norton without a moment's hesitation, not only for his mountaineering but for his organizational skills. But Finch, they learned, had used photographs of Everest while lecturing in Switzerland in June 1923. He had, it was true, signed a standard form assigning all pictorial and written results of the 1922 expedition to the Mount Everest Committee. But given that he had taken the pictures himself, that he had used his own camera, that he had not been the official expedition photographer, and that the agreement was in any case too restrictive to be legally binding, he saw no reason why he should be barred, a year after the event, from making money from his own photographs. The Mount Everest Committee saw it otherwise. General Charles Bruce voiced the general prejudice: 'He's torn it now ... I think this action on his part definitely rules him out of the next expedition ... What a swine the man is.' On these piffling grounds Finch was dropped. The same perverse reasoning worked in favour of the bad boys, Mallory and Somervell. The latter, everyone agreed, had shown exceptional stamina and should definitely be part of the 1924 expedition. As for Mallory, his social standing and mountaineering skills were sufficient for him not only to be selected but to be a member of the selecting panel.

To give the Committee its due, there were very few people other than Mallory and Somervell whom they could have chosen (apart from the reviled Finch). The elasticity and strength of youth were important factors in an attack on Everest, as was experience of the mountain itself. Nobody else of that age fitted the bill so perfectly. Indeed, the Committee was so strapped for climbers that, when it completed the 1924 roster, it chose a man with virtually no mountaineering qualifications at all. 'Sandy' Irvine was a Cambridge engineering undergraduate, a rowing 'Blue', resourceful, robust and with an apparently endless supply of good humour. An adventurous youth, he had joined a university expedition to Spitsbergen in the summmer of 1923 (without any previous Arctic experience) and had performed so well that his more experienced mentors had been flabbergasted. He seemed not to know the meaning of fear, and was willing to try anything.* In his energy and determination to succeed he displayed a brand of innocent optimism that had been in short supply since 1914 and which endeared him to the veterans on the selecting panel. Most importantly, he was practical and inventive, possessing a technical ingenuity that was foreign to those with whom he would climb – Germany was at that time the prime exponent of mechanical climbing aids – and these skills would be useful, for the 1924 expedition was going to take oxygen.

The establishment's dislike of oxygen had lessened since 1922. The alpinist Sir Douglas Freshfield, President of the Royal Geographical Society, favoured

* In winter 1923 Arnold Lunn invited him to Murren – the Swiss resort at which Lunn had established the sport of downhill and slalom skiing – and after a few lessons tried him on a short test run. The result was impressive. 'Sandy pointed his ski straight down the slope, and let go. By a miracle he stood up for most of the way then, at top speed, he came an almighty purler and vanished into a cloud of snow. To the astonishment of the spectators (who all thought he must be badly hurt) he was up in a moment, shook himself and finished the course ... in 40 seconds. On that day the next best time was five minutes.'

the use of new technology. He drew uncomfortable parallels between Everest and the Poles, noting that Britain's unwillingness to use skis and dogs had been the cause of its many failures in both the Arctic and Antarctica. If one was to insist on the physical purity of an ascent, without any artificial aids, one might as well ban goggles, protective clothes and sturdy boots. And why not caffeine, nicotine and food into the bargain? 'So long as the summit of Everest is gained, who cares whether it is with or without the use of oxygen?' he declaimed. Mallory, though he did not say so outright, shared his views. After Finch's success in 1922, he was now a convert to what Tibetan porters called 'English air'. On the steamer to India, and on the 300-mile journey to Tibet, he made a point of befriending Irvine.

When the expedition reached Everest the spirit of fair play overrode the banalities of technology. Mallory – now the climbing leader as well as the leading climber – agreed with Norton that attempts should be made, as in 1922, with and without oxygen. He himself was in favour of 'English air' but could not deny the others their desire to reach the summit without it. So concurrent parties would leave for the summit, staggered as in a school handicap. The oxygenless men were to start from an undetermined Camp VI and the oxygenated ones from a proposed Camp VII. Nobody had ever spent a night higher than Camp V, but Mallory was sure that Camps VI and VII could be achieved.

During the journey to Tibet Irvine established himself up as a jack-of-all-trades. Erecting a workshop tent, he mended countless bits of gear: cameras, tripods, tables, stools, torches, beds, saddles, ice-axes and crampons. When the cardboard lampshades burned he constructed new ones from tin. When people mentioned the difficulties of the North Col he produced a 60-foot rope ladder. While the others discussed routes, Irvine inspected, dismantled and reconstructed the oxygen kit – which was woefully bad. Of the 90 cylinders they had been issued, 15 were empty and 24 leaked; their tubes were uniformly fragile. 'Ye Gods!' Irvine wrote home. 'I broke one today taking it out of its packing case.' He tinkered with the valves and connecting tubes to make them more reliable, and turned the apparatus on its head so that the delicate connections pointed downwards rather than being at shoulder level where they could be broken – as Geoffrey Bruce's had been in 1922 – by a chance blow against rock. He was not much of a conversationalist, but everyone agreed that his presence was a bonus.

Norton and Somervell led the first, oxygenless, attempt, establishing Camp VI at 26,800 feet and departing on the morning of 5 June for the summit. Rather than follow the ridge, they attempted a face climb through a gully – the Great Couloir – that ran from the Rongbuk Glacier to bisect the North-East Ridge at the final pyramid. This meant a shallower ascent over uncertain terrain, whose rocks offered fewer handholds. But in Norton's eyes it was preferable to the ridge, which was not only exposed but interrupted by two difficult faces, to which they gave the names First and Second Steps. The weather was fine and nearly windless, but in the thin atmosphere they moved slowly. As Norton later recalled, his simple aim was to take 20 paces without stopping for a rest: the most he ever managed was 13. It was bitterly cold and, despite being wrapped in layers of tweed and woollens, they shivered so fiercely that Norton wondered if he was suffering an attack of malaria. (Finch had experimented with goose-down-insulated jackets in 1922, but they were considered far too radical by the British.) Also, the chilled air made them cough continually. This was a phenomenon they had encountered before; by midday, however, when they were almost at the Great Couloir, Somervell was hacking so fiercely that he told Norton to proceed on his own. Norton was not gone long. The snow in the Great Couloir was too deep and too soft, so he continued up the rocks on one side. By 1.00 p.m. he was at 28,126 feet, and the summit was less than 1,000 feet away. He was certain he could reach it, even without oxygen – a point on which he was later adamant – but he was less sure that he could do so *and* climb back to safety before nightfall. Also, he was beginning to see double, having made the mistake of removing his goggles earlier in the day. The risk was too great. Turning back, he rejoined Somervell and started down for the North Col.

They reached Camp VI, where they collapsed the tents and weighted them with stones before continuing to Camp V. Here the slope was safe enough for them to unrope and begin a series of glissades. Somervell was still coughing badly. What had started as a dryness in the throat had developed into an obstruction of some kind; after a while he began to lag, and then he stopped altogether. Norton, whose mind was wandering from lack of oxygen, assumed he had paused to sketch the view. In fact, Somervell was on the point of asphyxiation. The mysterious lump in his throat had dislodged itself and now prevented him breathing. Sinking to his knees, he hammered on his chest with both hands, and at last the thing came free. He spat it into the snow, coughed a bit of blood, and ran after Norton. 'I once more breathed really freely,' he exulted, 'more freely than I had done for some days.' At some point he had over-exerted himself and had inhaled too deeply for too long; his airways had become frostbitten, and the lump he coughed up was the dead mucous lining of his larynx.

It was dark by the time they reached the North Col, so they made their way through the crevasses by torchlight, shouting down to Camp IV for an escort. A reply came back that help would be with them soon – also some oxygen. But it wasn't oxygen they needed, it was water. At that altitude it took so long to melt snow that they had done so only when strictly necessary. Dehydration, rather than hypoxia, was their problem. In Norton's words, 'I remember shouting again and again, "We don't want the damned oxygen; we want drink." My own throat and voice were in none too good a case, and my feeble wail seemed swallowed up in the dim white expanse below glimmering in the starlight.'

Back at Camp IV the pair had every reason to congratulate themselves. It was only by an avoidable accident that Somervell had stopped before the Great Couloir; had they been together they might have bivouacked on a ledge and reached the summit the following day. The distance involved was 902 feet – four or five hours' climbing at most, judging by their earlier speed, with perhaps another hour for unseen difficulties. Using the same route and the same equipment, and given the same conditions, there was no reason why a similarly fit team should not do better.

Mallory and Irvine were next. On 7 June, with four porters, they left for Camp VI. For support they had Noel Odell, a competent mountaineer and geologist who had shown on previous climbs a complete indifference to the absence or presence of oxygen – when given a set of bottles he took a few sniffs and then, finding it made no impact, had handed it to his porter – and who was to wait for them at Camp V. Mallory and Irvine, however, were taking no chances. They donned Irvine's refined oxygen apparatus and left Camp VI early on 8 June, having sent their four porters back with two notes, one for Odell and another for the cameraman, John Noel, who was waiting at the North Col to capture their triumph on celluloid. The note to Odell said they'd lost their stove and had forgotten their compass. The one to Noel read: 'We'll probably start early tomorrow (8th) in order to have clear weather. It won't be too early to start looking for us either crossing the rock band or going up skyline at 8.0 p.m. Yours Ever, G. Mallory.' He meant 'a.m.' Already hypoxia had taken hold.

Unlike Norton, Mallory decided to follow the ridge, preferring the technique that he knew to an icy scramble up the rocks of the Great Couloir. He and Irvine travelled light, carrying two oxygen cylinders apiece, a light lunch, a couple of waterproofs and a Kodak Vestpocket camera to snap the view from the top. Whether from genuine confidence or from misjudgement, they seemed to believe that the climb would only take a few hours. So certain were they of reaching the summit and returning to Camp VI before dusk that they did not bother with a Camp VII. There were no obvious hazards in view: as Mallory wrote in his letter to Odell, 'Perfect weather for the job!'

Odell climbed from Camp V and caught a last glimpse of them at about 1.00 p.m. It was misty, but the clouds parted briefly, allowing him a clear view of the ridge. 'My eyes became fixed upon one tiny black spot silhouetted on a small snow-crest beneath a rock-step in the ridge; the black spot moved. Another black spot became apparent and moved up the snow to join the other on the crest. The first then approached the great rock-step and shortly emerged at the top; the second did likewise. Then the whole fascinating vision vanished, enveloped in cloud.' Continuing to Camp VI, he left some food for the two men's return, then descended (as instructed by Mallory) to await their arrival at Camp IV. On the journey down he was struck by the speed with which he was able to cover the distance between Camps V and IV – it took a mere 30 minutes. From this he drew two reassuring conclusions: that oxygen was not strictly necessary in order to make good time; and no matter how long it took Mallory and Irvine to reach the summit, their margin of safety was considerably greater than anticipated. If, say, they reached the top with only an hour to spare, they might still be able to return to Camp VI before sundown.

That night the occupants of Camp IV kept watch for lights or distress flares to show the whereabouts of Mallory and Irvine. They saw nothing, but in itself this was not a cause for worry: the sky was clear and the moon bright enough for the pair to have made a night-time descent; and anyway, in addition to forgetting his compass the absent-minded Mallory had also left behind his torch and lantern. They kept their binoculars trained on Camp V throughout the morning of the 9th, but saw no signs of movement. By midday Odell could stand it no longer and went to investigate. He spent that night at Camp V, and on the morning of 10 June departed for Camp VI. He did so alone, having sent his two porters back on the previous evening, and in a mood of growing despair. If Mallory and Irvine were alive and fit they should surely by now have returned to Camp V; if they were still at Camp VI they must be ill or wounded; and if they were not at Camp VI they were certainly dead. It was two days since they had left for the summit, and the night of the 9th had been so cold that Odell had been unable to sleep despite wearing all his clothes and being wrapped in two sleeping bags. Nobody could have survived those conditions in the open. His hope was that they were at Camp VI. Perhaps one of them had broken a limb. Perhaps they were waiting for rescue. But when he reached Camp VI it was exactly as he had last seen it, except that a tentpole had collapsed. For two hours – without oxygen – he followed the route Mallory and Irvine had taken, searching without success for their bodies.

As he went, Odell was overwhelmed by the power and majesty of the mountain. 'This upper part of Everest must be indeed the remotest and least hospitable spot on earth,' he wrote, 'but at no time more emphatically and impressively so than when a darkened atmosphere hides its features and a gale races over its cruel face ... I realised that the chances of finding the missing ones were indeed small on such a vast expanse of crags and broken slabs.' Wherever the remains of Mallory and Irvine might be, they could only be found by a large group of determined men, and the chances of that were slim. The current expedition was played out, and it was unlikely that another would be despatched, at great expense, to scour the great bulk of Everest for two small bodies. He returned to Camp V, where he laid out two sleeping bags in a 'T', the prearranged signal to show that Mallory and Irvine were dead, then he turned for one last look at the peak. 'It seemed to look down with cold indifference on me, mere puny man, and howl derision in windgusts at my petition to yield up its secrets – this mystery of my friends.' At the end of June the 1924 Everest expedition slunk back to India, from where it caught a ship to Britain and took a long, introspective look at its failings.

Physically, they had been right to withdraw: when doctors examined the survivors they found that most members of the high-altitude teams had dangerously enlarged hearts and had suffered some degree of frostbite to their throats. They had also done some remarkable things. They had proved that, with acclimatization and a degree of fitness, it was possible to go higher without oxygen than had been believed feasible: Norton's climb had set a record – only 902 feet to the top! – and possibly Odell's had too. But what of Mallory and Irvine? It was impossible to blame anyone but themselves – or Everest – for their deaths. What had happened to them, though? Had they summitted the mountain and died on the way down, or had they fallen before they reached the top? If they had been at the Second Step when Odell saw them, then they might have done it; and if their bodies could be found, the film inside the little Kodak camera would reveal all. But the whereabouts of their bodies remained a mystery.

Over succeeding decades people hurled themselves at Everest. Trusting to the experiences of Norton and Odell, they refused to take oxygen and they all failed. In 1952 a British expedition finally overcame the various cols and ridges to stand on top of the world. They used the same siege technique that the 1924 expedition had pioneered, and they used oxygen. Not until 1978 did Reinhold Messner and Peter Habeler complete an oxygen-free ascent, to be followed by Messner's famous solo climb in 1981. Between 1924 and 1952 there was a large gap; between 1924 and 1978 an even larger one. What had happened during those years to make the last thousand feet so insurmountable? Was it the mountain, the weather or the men? Had the national – or international – stock diminished so rapidly that nobody had the same powers of endurance as climbers like Norton, Somervell and Odell? The answer was probably Mallory and Irvine. They were the first to die at high altitude on Everest, and their deaths were a psychological block to those who came after. It did not matter that Mallory was a terminally forgetful climber, nor that Irvine was an amateur. They hovered, like Banquo's ghost, behind every Everest expedition.

When Edmund Hillary famously said, 'We knocked the bastard off', there was a brief hiatus before Everest became everyone's. Its conquest was not easy, but if it had been done once it could be done again. Like the Matterhorn, it had lost its mystique and the road was open for all. It remained a difficult hill – as witnessed by the scores of frozen corpses that can still be found on its slopes – but it was now seen much as it had been in 1924: high, but not impossible. By the late 1990s it had become an extreme tourist destination, where people who had never climbed a hill in their lives could be escorted to the summit for a sizeable sum of dollars, with every expectation of returning alive.

Still the search for Mallory and Irvine went on. An ice-axe was found below the North-East Ridge in 1933. In 1975 a Chinese climber reported an 'English dead' at approximately the same height as Camp VI. In 1991 two oxygen bottles were found at the foot of the First Step. Odell's report had led optimists to assume that the pair were on the Second Step, but perhaps they were far lower, as was suggested in 1999 when an American research expedition found Mallory's bleached but perfectly preserved corpse on a field of rubble below the First Step. It lay face down, and its right leg was badly broken. Poignantly, they were able to establish its identity by the name-tape sewn into the jacket.

The images of Mallory's remains make rough viewing. For how long had he survived with his broken leg? How, why and when had he fallen? And what had happened to Irvine? None of these questions can be answered. The 1975 Chinese expedition mentioned a body sitting, or sleeping, with a hole in its face. This was clearly not the body the Americans had found. Was it Irvine? If so, what had happened to the two men? Had Irvine become stuck, whereupon Mallory had gone down on his own? Or had Mallory fallen first, leaving the inexperienced Irvine stranded on a ledge? And when, above all, had they fallen? Was it before or after the summit? The Americans did not find Mallory's Kodak camera – he might have given it to Irvine, or it might have bounced down the hill – but when somebody does find it, and if its film has not perished, it will answer one of the great questions in the history of exploration: did Mallory and Irvine get there first?

Umberto Nobile (1928)

In 1903 the Wright brothers' *Kittyhawk* made its first tentative leap into the air. Two decades later, following a period of astoundingly rapid technological advance, humankind's mastery of the skies was established. The aeroplanes that clattered above Europe and America during the 1920s were unreliable, uncomfortable and dangerous. Their supremacy, however, could not be denied. They made mockery of the land below. What did an aeronaut care for mountains, rivers and jungles? All distances were now 'as the crow flies'. Indeed, the crow barely got a look-in, given the speeds at which modern planes flew. Planes, however, had one drawback: the size of their fuel tanks limited them to short hops between prearranged depots. For sustained, long-distance flights, therefore, people turned to dirigibles. Better known as Zeppelins, after the German who had pioneered their development, these propeller-driven behemoths were, to many, the way of the future. A honey-comb of hydrogen-filled bubbles, contained within a carapace of silk and powered by an internal combustion engine, the Zeppelin combined the economy of a balloon with the directional capability of a plane. It had its own problems: it could make little headway against adverse winds, and the hydrogen was dangerously flammable. Nevertheless, disasters were rare, and by the mid-1920s Zeppelins were a common sight above every major Western city.

Mechanized air travel was a boon to Arctic explorers. In 1925 Roald Amundsen and his American sponsor, Lincoln Ellsworth, made an attempt on the North Pole in two Dornier seaplanes. Taking off from Spitsbergen, they reached 88° N before engine failure forced them to return (leaving one Dornier behind on the ice). The following year Richard Evelyn Byrd followed their route in a Fokker and was awarded a Congressional Medal of Honour as the first airman to reach the Pole. Doubts were cast on his claim, and the consensus today is that he did not reach his goal. A few days after Byrd's return, however, a joint American–Italian–Norwegian expedition left Spits-bergen on a three-day flight that took them safely across the Pole to Alaska. The craft in question was a Zeppelin, the *Norge*, purchased second-hand by Amundsen and Ellsworth, and piloted by the Italian dirigible expert Colonel Umberto Nobile. The expedition was hailed as a triumph: it had made the

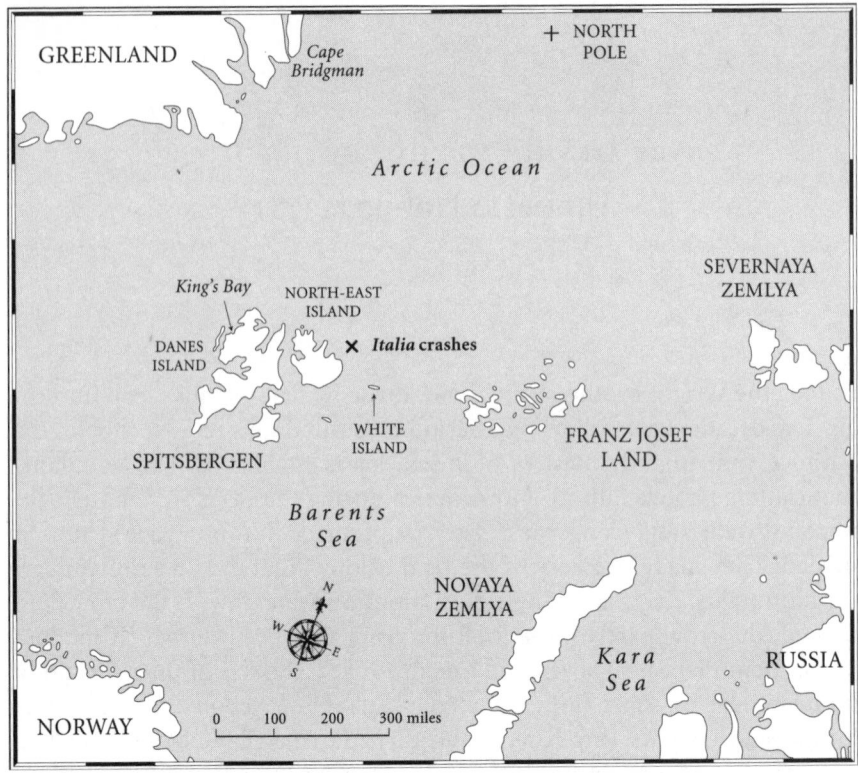

first Arctic crossing, had made the first undisputed sighting of the North Pole, had proved the durability and overall excellence of Zeppelins, had boosted the international standing of Mussolini's infant fascist state (on landing, Nobile was ordered to make a tour of immigrant communities in the US – 'Italian colonies', as Il Duce called them), and had demonstrated how puny the earth's natural obstacles were to men of the air. It had also answered a nagging question: did there exist a continental landmass in the vicinity of the Pole? Peary had reported no such thing, and Amundsen believed firmly that he had attained 90°N. But Peary had been a crawler on the ice; Amundsen was now a gladiator of the sky. In the *Norge* he had hoped to cap his traverses of the North-West and North-East Passages, and his attainment of the South Pole, with the discovery of the world's northernmost island – perhaps even to lower a rope ladder and name it after himself. However, when the *Norge* reached the North Pole Amundsen could see nothing but ice. It was maybe this disappointment that sparked a bizarre animosity towards Nobile. On his return Amundsen accused the Italian of being a nervous, incompetent pilot who knew nothing about the Arctic, was ignorant of the most basic survival skills and was a dwarfish popinjay to boot. Nobile was, certainly, small in stature, excitable and fond of uniforms, and had no experience at all of surface travel in the Arctic. He had, also, a sentimental attachment to his pet terrier, which accompanied him everywhere and which, in times of emotion, he would clasp to his chest. But he was a reasonably confident pilot and knew more about Zeppelins than Amundsen ever would. Ignoring the latter's attack, Nobile left the now bankrupt Amundsen to fulminate while he prepared his own, purely Italian expedition to the polar regions.

Nobile's plan was not to make a second headline dash to the Pole (though another visit might be useful) but to undertake a series of flights from Spitsbergen which, over time, would explore the 1,500,000 square miles of pack that remained unknown to science. Besides scanning the ice from above, he also wanted – weather permitting – to land small teams on the relatively uncharted islands, such as Severnaya Zemlya, that lay above the Russian coast. These teams could be picked up at a later date or could make their way home across Siberia. The craft in which he intended to perform these deeds was the *Italia*, a 384-foot-long dirigible whose three engines totalled 750 horsepower and produced a top speed of 70 miles per hour. It was not the machine he had had in mind: he had envisaged a dirigible three times the size, with a bigger gondola and far greater lifting power; but the Italian Air Ministry had refused him the resources. Still, the *Italia* was slightly more efficient than the *Norge*, and once Nobile had made a few modifications – new anti-freeze, new gas valves, better insulation, rubber strips to protect the canopy from ice shards spat out by the propellers – it was fit for Arctic service.

Nobile attracted his share of critics. Russian scientists, whose experience of the theory and practicalities of Arctic flight stemmed from before the Great War, pointed out that the *Italia* was undersized: its gondola was too small, its engines could not match the force of Arctic gales. They said, repeatedly, that Nobile should reconsider his idea of landing parties on Siberian islands: the winds would be too strong for a safe landing, let alone a safe retrieval; he did not realize how hard it was in the Arctic to spot men from the air; a retreat through Siberia was difficult at the best of times and without proper preparation equivalent to a death sentence. In all, they concluded, the enterprise was 'extraordinarily risky'. The air minister, Italo Balbo, thought the programme a waste of time: Italy's new fascist regime could be promoted more effectively and with far greater pomp by, say, sending a squadron of planes to Argentina. Even Mussolini had doubts: when Nobile first outlined his ambitions, he replied, 'Perhaps it would be better not to tempt Fate a second time'.

In the end, however, Mussolini signalled his approval. The prospect of demonstrating yet again Italy's aerial supremacy in the Arctic was too tempting. Equally alluring was the fact that the Italian government had nothing to lose: the idea was Nobile's; the funding was supplied almost entirely by the city of Milan and the Royal Geographical Society. If Nobile succeeded the government could bask in his glory; if he failed it could deny responsibility – after all, it was a private enterprise to which it had contributed little more than its good wishes. And the project did have a certain altruistic attraction: unlike so many of his predecessors, who had pretended to be acting in the name of science when really they were engaged in a race for the Pole, Nobile hoped his programme would be of genuine scientific and geographical benefit. As Mussolini told him, 'This enterprise is not one of those destined to strike the popular imagination, like your 1926 expedition. But it will attract the attention of the scientific world. I see that there is a great deal of interest in it abroad.'

Nobile hired three scientists – one Italian, one Czech and one Swede – plus two Italian journalists, an Italian wireless operator, four Italian navigators and 18 Italian crew. Having learned from his experience on the *Norge*, he wanted as few foreigners as possible. He approached the polar veteran Fridtjof Nansen, who advised him on equipment for the land parties, the provisions he should take to combat scurvy, and the basic necessities he would require for survival should the *Italia* crash on the pack. Nobile followed the broad thrust of his instructions – with the exception of Amundsen, Nansen was the most experienced polar traveller alive – but made a few amendments of his own. He did not take dogs, for example, because although they were indisputably the best means of sledge travel he had no space for them in the *Italia*. Neither did he take the lightweight tents suggested by Nansen, preferring instead heavier and better insulated models. Similarly, he rejected the Norwegian and British brand of pemmican for a recipe more suited to Italian tastes, substituting peas for rice, oatmeal for raisins, potatoes for sugar and onions for vegetables, and increasing the percentage of dried meat and fat.

Nobile's final piece of cargo was an oak cross, dedicated by the Pope, with which he was to consecrate the North Pole. With this aboard, and having had final audiences with the King of Italy and Mussolini, Nobile was ready to fly. On the evening of 19 April 1928 the *Italia* rose from its moorings at Milan airfield and steered north for Spitsbergen. Eighteen days later, having flown a total of 3,200 miles through unexpectedly rough weather, it was at King's Bay – the spot from which Nobile had departed two years previously on his trip to the Pole – where two ships, the *Hobby* and the *Citta di Milano*, were unloading the fuel and provisions he would need during the coming months.

For his first flight, on 11 May, Nobile planned an epic journey across Greenland to the mouth of Canada's Mackenzie River. Unfortunately, bad weather and a broken rudder cable forced him back to King's Bay after only eight hours. His second flight, to Severnaya Zemlya, was more successful. The *Italia* took to the air on 15 May and returned three days later after a journey of more than 2,000 miles. To Nobile's chagrin, strong winds had prevented him reaching his goal, but he had flown over the north coasts of Franz Josef Land and Novaya Zemlya and had traversed some 48,000 square kilometres of undiscovered ice. Moreover, the *Italia* had behaved perfectly, and during much of its flight had been navigated by radio – the bearings being sent from a transmitter at King's Bay – a relative novelty for the time and of enormous value in the featureless Arctic pack.

Five journalists had assembled at King's Bay to report on Nobile's expeditions. But as Mussolini had pointed out, the *Italia*'s programme was not the stuff of headlines. However successful the flight to Severnaya Zemlya may have been, it was of limited interest to the wider world. It was Nobile's third foray that caught the journalists' attention: a voyage over the quadrant of ice stretching north from a line between Spitsbergen and Greenland. That Nobile would be traversing an unknown part of the globe was immaterial. What *was* news was that he would be crossing the North Pole, where he would deposit the Pope's cross, the flag of Milan and a five-pound note that an English woman had sent him with the request that it be left on top of the world.

At 4.00 a.m. on 23 May the *Italia* again rose into the air, carrying a reduced crew of 16 men and Nobile's pet dog. Within 14 hours it was above Cape Bridgman on the north coast of Greenland, and shortly after midnight on 24 May it was at the Pole. The crew toasted their success in mugs of egg nog, dropped flags, offloaded the Pope's wooden cross – so bulky that they had some difficulty pushing it through the door – played patriotic songs on a portable gramophone and cried, 'Nobile for ever! Long Live Italy!' They shook hands solemnly and sent victorious radio messages to Spitsbergen. Then at 2.20 a.m. they turned south, following the 25th meridian that would lead them back to Spitsbergen. They expected no difficulties – a view that was shared by the press at King's Bay: 'To fly in the polar zone is like eating bread and butter,' remarked one man. 'In Europe the natural conditions are considerably more difficult.'

The *Italia* flew uneventfully south, the weather seemingly in its favour. There was a north-west wind and, despite banks of thin fog and the formation of ice on the radio antennae, the journey proceeded smoothly. After a few hours, however, the weather turned sour. The wind changed to the south-west, thick mist obscured their vision and, after a brief debate as to whether they should abandon Spitsbergen and head for Alaska or Siberia – the decision was no – Nobile took the ship to within sight of the pack in order to check their speed and drift. The news was not good: they were down to 25 miles per hour (despite an airspeed indication of 60) and they were being pushed to the east. The wind had now turned into a gale, covering the craft with ice and hampering radio transmission. At 10.30 on the morning of 25 May the operators at King's Bay received a message that the *Italia* had been delayed by strong winds, was low on petrol, and could not be expected home until later that afternoon. It was the last message they would receive. About what happened next there is an extraordinary lack of information. As a contemporary historian lamented, 'No one could explain exactly how the catastrophe occurred'.

By 3.00 a.m. on 25 May Nobile's navigators estimated they were within 120 miles of the north coast of Spitsbergen, but were being pushed continually east. At about 9.30 a.m. the elevating rudders jammed – nobody knew why – sending the ship nose-first towards the pack. When they were 250 feet above the ice they managed to fix the rudders, at the same time throwing out ballast so that they rose to perhaps 2,500 feet before restabilizing at 1,500 feet. It must have been about this time that the *Italia* transmitted its last situation report, detailing a position of 180 miles north-east of King's Bay. But then there were inexplicable difficulties with the gas, one end of the *Italia* – by some accounts the bow, by others the stern – rising higher than the other. Despite adjusting the valves, nothing seemed to stabilize the dirigible and, to everyone's bewilderment, although gas pressure remained high the *Italia* began to sink rapidly. All three engines were turning at their fastest, the rudders were at maximum elevation, but still they descended. Of the succeeding minutes there survives only a picture of confusion. Unable to believe the rate of descent, Nobile threw out a glass ball of red dye and counted the seconds until it burst on the snow. This rudimentary altimeter, which he had packed in case his instruments proved faulty, showed only too well how accurate they were. Within minutes of its impact the *Italia* collided with the pack. The stern engine broke off, as did the control cabin, whose occupants were flung onto the ice. Relieved of its burden, the *Italia* rose lopsidedly into the air and skittered northwards, trailing lengths of fabric and twisted metal. Before it vanished from sight Nobile saw the face of Sub-Lieutenant Ettore Arduino peering from one of the broken catwalks.

Nobile had been badly gashed on the head and had broken both an arm and a leg. His second officer, Filippo Zappi, had broken a wrist. A Swedish scientist, Finn Malmgren, had sustained heavy bruising down his left side and had possibly broken an arm. A mechanic, Natale Cecioni, had broken a leg. Five others, however, had escaped without injury, and Nobile's dog scampered happily about the place. Around them were strewn the contents of the control cabin and, not far off, the cabin itself, a crumpled aluminium box. A 50-metre red stain showed where the *Italia*'s glass altimeter balls had burst, one by one, as the cabin had been dragged over the snow. Among the wreckage were bits and pieces of the survival kit Nobile had packed on Nansen's advice, including a tent, an 18-kilogram box of pemmican, a Very pistol with flares, boxes of matches, a Colt revolver with 100 cartridges and, best of all, a radio. Near the remains of the stern engine and its accompanying gondola sat a mechanic, Vincenzo Pomella, who was, to judge by his posture, reaching for a shoe that had been torn off his foot. But when they came closer it was apparent that he was dead. Of the *Italia*'s 16-strong crew, nine in all were definitely alive. Of the remainder, except for Pomella, they had no clue. Shortly after the crash a column of smoke rose on the horizon. Some said that the airship had blown up. Others, optimistically, suggested the crew were offloading excess petrol drums to keep the ship in the air. The truth was beyond their reckoning. They had no means of transport and no travelling gear, and were too battered even to contemplate a rescue mission. Nothing was ever found of the *Italia*, nor of the half-dozen men it contained.

The survivors' first act was to erect the tent and carry the invalids to shelter. Their second was to radio an SOS to Spitsbergen. There was no answer. When next they tried, the instrument went dead. They spent that first night huddled in discomfort – nine men and a dog in a tent designed for four, the space being further cramped by the bulky radio, which they had brought inside in the hope that their body heat would warm up the batteries. It was a misty night and bitterly cold. That it wasn't raining and the wind was mild were their only comforts.

The following morning they made two important discoveries. The first was a case of astronomical instruments, complete with tables, which would allow them to find their position once the mist cleared. The second was that the radio had responded well to its night in the tent and was now working perfectly. A brief opening in the cloud allowed them to take a sighting – they were just north of 81°, between the 26th and 27th meridian, which placed them 180 miles from King's Bay and 50 miles north-east of Spitsbergen's second largest island. The radio operator, Giuseppe Biagi, sent an SOS to this effect; but once again there was no reply. In order to conserve the batteries he did not transmit continuously, but sent a message at five minutes to the hour, every other hour, throughout the day and night. Still there was no answer. Biagi ran tests to see if the transmitter was faulty, but everything seemed to be in order. He was puzzled that no one heard their calls, particularly as the reception was so clear that, on the evening of the 26th, they were able to pick up the nine o'clock news from Rome. Nothing had been heard from the *Italia* for 24 hours, said the announcer, and there was concern as to its fate. Receiving cost nothing in terms of battery power, so Biagi listened frequently. He was even able to pick up a message from the *Citta di Milano*. 'We imagine you are ... between the 15th and 20th meridians E. of Greenwich,' it ran. 'Trust us. We are organising help.' Any relief expedition in that direction would have been fruitless, as Biagi tried to transmit. Again there was no answer.

They cooked their first meal of pemmican. The result was an unpleasant yellowish gruel. They had experimented with it in Italy and were so disgusted that they had given it to a dog – which had also rejected it. It tasted no better now, but in the circumstances they devoured it ravenously. That same evening the wind swung to the north-west. If they had still been in the air it would have brought them to King's Bay within two or three hours. But they were not in the air, as they were reminded when there came a long roar and a juddering of the tent. The same wind that might have carried them to safety was now disrupting the floe on which they were camped. Ideally, they would have moved to a safer place, but no piece of ice could be guaranteed firmer than another and, besides, they had no transport. A sun sighting the following day showed they were being pushed east towards Franz Josef Land. They had food for two months, at a ration of 300 grams per man per day, but without boats, skis, dogs or sledges all they could do was sit passively and consume their daily allowance. Their only hope lay in the radio, from which Biagi continued to transmit at two-hourly intervals. If just one message got through, the rescuers would be able to send a plane to collect them. If, that is, a plane was available.

Back at King's Bay, Captain Giuseppe Romagna of the *Citta di Milano* was uncertain how to act. He did have a plane, but had been forbidden to use it by Italo Balbo, the air minister who had previously sneered at Nobile's flight and was unwilling to aid it in any way. Despite his transmission, Romagna had no real idea of Nobile's whereabouts and, even if he had, he had no authority to search for him. There were others, however, who saw the *Italia*'s disappearance as a call to arms. Across Scandinavia and Europe, aeronauts gathered with serious intent. Amidst their ranks, Roald Amundsen suddenly materialized. Casting aside his detestation of Nobile, he persuaded the governments of Norway and Sweden that they had the expertise to rescue the castaways. The veteran explorer urged 'the utmost speed and urgency' in launching a sea–air expedition to search for the *Italia*. The governments listened and towards the end of May seven ships left Sweden, each equipped with an aircraft. The Russians chipped in with a massive icebreaker, the *Krassin*; and Italy donated a small 350-ton sealer, the *Braganza*.

The pilots had one objective: to find Nobile. Amundsen had, maybe, another: to find whatever polar landmass the Italians might have missed. There was a sadness to his resolve: he had made polar exploration his life's career; now there was so little left to explore he wanted one last moment of glory on the ice. 'If only you knew how splendid it is up there,' he remarked to an Italian journalist. 'That's where I want to die. I shan't complain if death takes me in the fulfilment of a high mission, quickly and without suffering.'

The news that the survivors received on the radio was discouraging. They were heartened to learn that rescue was on its way, but they were downcast when they heard that the search would extend no further than North-East Island, whose outline they could just discern to the west. On 28 May the Swedish scientist Malmgren approached Nobile with a plan: he and two others would walk over the ice to North-East Island, from where they would try to intercept the rescuers. His arm was not broken, just badly bruised, so he was fit for the journey. He estimated it would take them 15 or 16 days to cover the 20 miles. Nobile was at first reluctant but, with the ice being carried towards Franz Josef Land at a rate of 14 miles per day, Malmgren's suggestion seemed their best hope. Not that it was much of a hope, however: when he asked the Swede in private how he rated his chances compared with those of the men who were to stay at the tent, Malmgren replied, 'Both parties will die.'

Malmgren left on the evening of 30 May with two of the *Italia*'s navigators,

Commanders Filippo Zappi and Adalberto Mariano. They carried a small amount of pemmican, a knife, an axe and a pack of letters from those they left behind. They could also have taken a sledge. Cecioni, despite his injuries, had manufactured one from the debris of the control cabin. But it was too unwieldy; on an experimental trip it took them more than an hour to drag a 100-pound load a distance of 40 yards. Even without it they made poor enough headway. For two days Nobile followed their progress through binoculars. When he lost sight of them they had advanced less than three miles. As he recorded, drily, 'That wasn't much'.

While Malmgren's group vanished towards Spitsbergen, Biagi continued to send SOS signals, in both English and Italian. To optimize the chance of somebody – anybody – hearing, he used the same wavelength as that of the Eiffel Tower, then not just a tourist attraction but a functioning radio mast, to which most Europeans tuned for the 8.00 p.m. time signal. He received no answer – the men on Spitsbergen and on the *Citta di Milano*, assuming the *Italia* was lost, had jammed the air with speculative reports of Nobile's death – but on 3 June he caught a garbled message from Rome. The Soviet embassy had informed the government that a farmer in Archangel, who happened to be an amateur radio ham, had picked up one of Biagi's signals. He had been able to make little of it, but had heard what he thought was the word 'Petermann'. The nearest place of that name was Petermann Land – which did not in fact exist, but which was believed to be near Franz Josef Land. It was of no help to the castaways. Neither was a second report that they caught on 7 June, in which an American ham claimed to have received a message saying that the *Italia* had crashed on a mountain and the crew were living in its wreckage. He gave their position as north of the 84th parallel. On the same day, however, they received a message from the *Citta di Milano*: 'Heard you clearly, receiving your SOS and coordinates.' Anticipating an air rescue, the survivors found an unbroken glass ball of red dye and smeared its contents over the tent to make it more visible. The colour faded after a few days, but from then on their home became known as the 'Red Tent'.

By now a total of six nations had joined the search for Nobile. Eighteen ships, 22 planes and 1,500 men were searching the pack. And they were looking not only for the Italians but for Amundsen. He had taken off in mid-June and had not been heard of since. Presumably he too was stranded on the ice. On 18 June an Italian pilot, Major Umberto Maddalena, spotted the Red Tent, and five days later a Fokker ski-plane landed on the ice to airlift Nobile and his dog to safety. The pilot, Lieutenant Einar Lundborg of the Swedish Air Force, apologized for not being able to take more than one man, but promised to return in a short while to evacuate the others. When Nobile protested that he should not be the first to leave, Lundborg assured him that all would be fine: within a day and a half the entire contingent would be at Spitsbergen. It would take, at most, four easy flights. Lundborg was overconfident. He delivered Nobile safely, but on his next landing the Fokker overturned, and although he escaped without injury the plane was beyond repair. Thus, in his leather flying gear, the Swedish pilot found himself an inhabitant of the Red Tent.

Lundborg's stay was brief and unsettling. To everyone's bewilderment, he immediately advocated a retreat over the ice to Spitsbergen. When that was rejected, he hovered restlessly until 6 July, when a second Swedish plane, piloted by Lieutenant Birger Schyberg, landed near the Red Tent. Abandoning most of his belongings, Lundborg 'fled almost in panic' to the plane, assured the stunned survivors that he would be back, and then took off, never to be seen again. There were to be no more plane landings. By now the weather was so unpredictable and the ice so slushy that the pilots refused to fly. The same conditions, however, would assist the Russian icebreaker. It was on the *Krassin*, therefore, that the rescuers pinned their hopes.

The *Krassin* had left the Vega on 24 June, carrying a stern order from Moscow: '[with] energy, discipline, staying power, zest and courage on the part of all . . . there must be unconditional success'. It also carried a commissar to make sure there would be no backsliding. The Soviets' fear of failure was greater than their fear of the ice. Where the Swedes had considered conditions too treacherous for safe flying, the captain of the *Krassin* simply unloaded a Junkers ski-plane onto the ice and told its pilot, Boris Tchukhnovsky, to find the Red Tent. The huge five-crew Junkers took off on 10 July, and by the following morning it had crashed on one of Spitsbergen's remote eastern capes. Its occupants were alive and unhurt, with plenty of food, but it meant that yet another party was marooned. Before his descent, however, Tchukhnovsky had spotted a column of smoke from the Red Tent, and radioed its coordinates to the icebreaker. He had also seen a group of men on a floe surrounded by open water. At first they were unsure how many men there were: one crewman thought he had seen five, in which case it could be either Amundsen and his crew or the lost men of the *Italia*; another said he saw only one; but when Tchukhnovsky circled the floe he saw two men waving makeshift flags, and a dark shape that he presumed was a third lying motionless on the ice. It could only be Malmgren's party. His last message was, 'Don't stop for us. Go to Malmgren's aid soonest.'

From where the *Krassin* lay the men were at most 18 miles distant. The ice, however, was six feet thick, and initially they moved at an average of one and a half miles per hour, sounding the ship's siren at regular intervals. Later the pack opened, and at 5.20 a.m. on 12 July they spotted the men. It was Malmgren's party, as Tchukhnovsky had guessed, but Malmgren was not there, only Zappi and Mariano. They were surrounded by debris, some of which Tchukhnovsky had obviously mistaken for a man because, when questioned, the Italians said that Malmgren had been dead for a month: he had collapsed from his wounds and from the exhaustion of walking over the pack. They also said that they had not eaten since 30 June. While Zappi and

Mariano were bathed and fed, the *Krassin* steamed towards Tchukhnovsky's coordinates for the Red Tent. Late on the afternoon of the same day they dropped a ladder and took aboard the last surviving members of the *Italia*.

The postmortem of Nobile's expedition was a sad business. Nobody talked of the new ground he had covered. Nobody, even, took much interest in the cause of the *Italia*'s crash. They were more excited by Nobile having been the first to be evacuated by Lundborg. It was held widely in Italy that this was not how a leader should act and that the only honourable course of action was for him to shoot himself. Those on the scene protested that he had 'been coaxed out on false premises', but their voices counted for nothing. The pressure was so intense that Nobile fled Italy and accepted a post as airship designer in the Soviet Union. His disgrace was eclipsed only by the rumours surrounding Malmgren's fate. Malmgren had died: that much was clear. How he had died, however, and what had happened to his body, remained a mystery. The *Krassin*'s doctor noted a peculiar discrepancy between Zappi and Mariano: the former had 12 items of clothing, the latter only five; Zappi seemed well-fed and, despite claiming not to have eaten for almost a fortnight, was discovered to have had a meal the day before his rescue (the doctor examined his faeces); on interrogation, the Soviets learned that Mariano had spent much of the time snowblind; they also reported that the Italians had held hurried, secretive conversations before collaborating on their story of Malmgren's death. The suspicion – unproven – was that Zappi might have eaten Malmgren.

Most damning was the extraordinary manner in which the *Italia*'s rescue had been carried out. The bravery of those who took part could not be questioned; but when the statistics were examined it was hard to tell where valour stopped and foolhardiness began. Of the pilots who had gone in search of Nobile no less than three had had to be rescued themselves: apart from Lundborg and Tchukhnovsky, a Russian named Babuskin had also gone missing. Largely forgotten in the aerial drama was a two-man sledge party that had crossed the ice from Spitsbergen to find Malmgren: it, too, had become stranded and needed rescuing. On the journey from Spitsbergen to Europe an Italian plane also crashed, killing all three men on it. And then there was Amundsen. Since he left Spitsbergen on 18 June in a Latham float plane, with one Norwegian and four Frenchmen, nothing had been heard of him. It was presumed he must have crashed; but nobody thought he was dead, merely that his radio – far weaker than the little emergency set carried by the *Italia* – had put him beyond contact. After all, other planes had come down and their crews had survived despite having no knowledge of survival on the ice. Amundsen was undoubtedly on a floe or some distant cape, using his much-vaunted Arctic skills to keep himself and his companions alive. On 31 July, however, one of the Latham's floats was discovered on a small island off Norway. Later a fuel tank also bobbed ashore. It had been punctured and repaired with a wooden plug, and had probably been used as a replacement for the lost float. The trick had been known to work before; but this time, obviously, it had not. Amundsen and his five companions were dead. More people had died trying to rescue Nobile and his men than had died on the *Italia* itself.

Nobile's expedition provided a fitting coda to the heroic age of polar exploration. The heroes – men like Amundsen, Nansen and Scott – had been inspired partly by Sir John Franklin, whose tribulations and ultimate disappearance in search of the North-West Passage had set a benchmark for those who would follow. Amundsen had admitted openly that Franklin had been his role model, the man whose example started him on a career as an explorer. In terms of men lost and of the expense and incompetence of the multi-national rescue missions, Nobile's expedition had been an abbreviated version of Franklin's. And like Franklin's it had ushered in a new era. By 1928 most of the heroes were either dead or in retirement; of the few still in service Amundsen had been the last remaining giant. Amundsen was now gone, as were the goals that he and his fellows had set themselves and the methods they had used to achieve them. After centuries of human endeavour, future exploration would rely on the combustion engine.

SELECT BIBLIOGRAPHY

In the absence of source notes it seems redundant to itemize every letter, diary and scrap of archive material. The following, therefore, is a list of books that I have found most directly helpful. Those wishing to research any explorer in greater depth should first address the secondary sources: they are not only accessible but contain fuller bibliographies than can be given here. Alternatively the primary sources will take you straight to the horse's mouth.

PRIMARY SOURCES

Abbruzzi, L. *Farther North than Nansen*, Howard Wilford Bell, London, 1901
—(trans. W. Le Queux), *On the 'Polar Star' in the Arctic Sea* (2 vols), Hutchinson, London, 1903
Amundsen, R., *The South Pole* (2 vols), John Murray, London, 1912
—*My Life as an Explorer*, Heinemann, London, 1927
Armstrong, A., *A Personal Narrative of the Discovery of the North-West Passage*, Hurst & Blackett, London, 1857
Andrée, S., *The Andrée Diaries*, John Lane, London, 1931
Burton, R., *The Lake Regions of Central Africa* (2 vols), Longman, London, 1860
Caillié, R., *Le Voyage de René Caillié à Tombouctou et à travers L'Afrique 1824–28*, Librairie Plon, Paris, 1832
Clapperton, H., *A Journal of a Second Expedition into the Interior of Africa*, John Murray, London, 1829
Cook, F., *My Attainment of the Pole*, The Polar Publishing Co., New York, 1911
Cook, J. (ed. J. Beaglehole), *The Journals of Captain James Cook on his voyages of discovery* (5 vols), Cambridge University Press, Cambridge, 1955–74
Collinson, R., *Journal of HMS* Enterprise *on the expedition in search of Sir John Franklin's ships by Behring Strait 1850–55*, Sampson Low, Marston, Searle & Rivington, London, 1889
Cummins, J., *The Voyage of Christopher Columbus*, Weidenfeld and Nicolson, London, 1992

De Long, G. (ed. E. De Long), *The Voyage of the Jeannette* (2 vols), Kegan Paul, Trench & Co., London, 1883

Denham, D., Clapperton, H. & Oudney, W., *A Narrative of Travels and Discoveries in northern and central Africa in the years 1822, 1823 and 1824* (2 vols), John Murray, London, 1828

Foureau, F., *D'Alger au Congo*, Editions L'Harmattan, Paris, 1990

Foxe, L., *North-west Fox; or Fox from the North-west Passage*, Hakluyt Society, London, 1893

Franklin, J., *Narrative of a journey to the shores of the Polar Sea in the years 1819–20–21–22*, John Murray, London, 1823

—*Narrative of a Second Expedition to the shores of the Polar Sea in the years 1825, 1826 and 1827*, John Murray, London, 1828

Greely, A., *Three Years of Arctic Service* (2 vols), Richard Bentley, London, 1886

Hood, R. (ed. S. Houston), *To the Arctic by Canoe, 1819–1821.* McGill-Queen's University Press, Montreal, 1974

Huish, R. (ed.), *The Travels of Richard and John Lander into the Interior of Africa*, John Saunders, London, 1828

Humble, R., *Marco Polo*, Weidenfeld and Nicolson, London, 1975

Humboldt, A., and Bonpland, A., *Personal Narrative of Travels to the Equinoctial Regions of the New Continent during the years 1799–1804* (7 vols), Longman, London, 1814–29

Jackson, F., *A Thousand Days in the Arctic* (2 vols), Harper, London, 1899

James, T., *The voyages of Captain Luke Foxe of Hull and Captain Thomas James of Bristol in Search of a North-West Passage in 1631–32*, Hakluyt Society, London, 1893

Joutel, H., *La Salle's Last Voyage*, Joseph McDonough, Albany N.Y., 1906

Koldewey, K. (trans. C. Mercier; ed. H. Bates), *The German Arctic Expedition of 1869–70*, Sampson Low, Marston, Low & Searle, London, 1874

Lander, R., *Records of Captain Clapperton's last expedition to Africa* (2 vols), Colburn & Bentley, London, 1830

Lander, R. & J., *Journal of an expedition to explore the course and termination of the Niger*, (3 vols), John Murray, London, 1833

Livingstone, D., *Narrative of an Expedition to the Zambezi and its Tributaries; and of the Discoveries of the Lakes Shirwa and Nyassa, 1858–1864*, John Murray, London, 1865

Lyon, G., *Private Journal During the Recent Voyage of Discovery Under Captain Parry*, John Murray, London, 1824

McClure, E. (ed. S. Osborn), *The Discovery of the North-West Passage by HMS* Investigator, Longman, London, 1856

McCormick, R., *Voyages of Discovery in the Arctic and Antarctic and Round the World* (2 vols), Sampson, London, 1884

Markham, A., *The Great Frozen Sea: A personal narrative of the voyage of the 'Alert'*, Dalby, Isbister & Co., London, 1878

Mawson, D., *The Home of the Blizzard* (2 vols), Heinemann, London, 1915

—(eds. F. & E. Jacka), *Mawson's Antartic Diaries*, Unwin Hyman, London, 1988

Melville, G., *In the Lena Delta*, Longmans, Green & Co., London, 1885

Nansen, F. (trans. M. Grepp), *Farthest North* (2 vols), Constable & Co., London, 1897

Nares, G., *Narrative of a Voyage to the Polar Sea* (2 vols), Sampson Low, Marston, Searle & Rivington, London, 1878

Nobile, U., *With the 'Italia' to the North Pole*, Allen & Unwin, London, 1930

Nourse, J. (ed.), *Narrative of the Second Arctic Expedition made by Charles F. Hall*, Government Printing Office, Washington, 1879

Parry, W. E., *Journal of a Voyage for the Discovery of a North-West Passage...in the years 1819–20*, John Murray, London, 1821

—*Journal of a Second Voyage for the Discovery of the North-West Passage...in the years 1821–22–23*, John Murray, London, 1824

—*Narrative of an Attempt to Reach the North Pole...in the year 1827*, John Murray, London, 1828

Payer, J., *New Lands Within the Arctic Circle* (2 vols), Macmillan, London, 1876

Peary, R., *Northwards over the Great Ice* (2 vols), Methuen, London, 1898

—*Nearest the Pole*, Hutchinson, London, 1907

—*The North Pole*, Dover, New York, 1986

Pigafetta, A., *Primo viaggio intorno al globo sulla squadra del capit. Magellianes, 1519–22*, Milan, 1800

Richardson, J. (ed. S. Houston), *Arctic Ordeal. The Journal of John Richardson...1820–22*, McGill-Queen's University Press, Montreal, 1984

Ross, James, *A Voyage of Discovery and Research in the Southern Antarctic Regions during the years 1839–43* (2 vols), John Murray, London, 1847

Ross, John, *A Voyage of Discovery...inquiring into the probability of a North-West Passage*, John Murray, London, 1819

—*Narrative of a Second Voyage in Search of a North-West Passage...during the years 1829, 1830, 1831, 1832, 1833*, Webster, London, 1835

Saussure, H.-B., *Voyages Dans Les Alpes* (4 vols), Barde Manget, Geneva, 1786–96

Scott, R., *Scott's Last Expedition* (2 vols), Smith, Elder & Co., London, 1913

Shackleton, E., *South*, Penguin, London, 2002

Stanley, H., *How I Found Livingstone: travels, adventures and discoveries in Central Africa, including four months' residence with Dr. Livingstone*, Sampson Low, Marston, Low & Searle, London 1872

—*Through the Dark Continent, or the sources of the Nile, around the great lakes of equatorial Africa and down the Livingstone River to the Atlantic Ocean*, Sampson Low, Marston, Searle & Rivington, London, 1890

Steller, G., *Journal of a Voyage with Bering, 1741–1742*, Stanford University Press, Stanford, 1988

Tyndall, J., *Hours of Exercise in the Alps*, Longman, London, 1872

Whymper, E., *Scrambles Amongst the Alps in the years 1860–69*, Murray, London, 1871

Wiggins, J. (ed.), *The Austro-German Polar Expedition under the command of Lieut. Weyprecht*, William Carr, London, 1875

SECONDARY SOURCES

Adams, A., *The Eternal Quest*, Constable, London, 1970

Allan, T. (ed.), *Voyages of Discovery*, Time-Life Books, Amsterdam, 1989

Allen, B., *The Faber Book of Exploration*, Faber and Faber, London, 2002

Ambrose, S., *Undaunted Courage: Meriwether Lewis, Thomas Jefferson, and the Opening of the American West*, Simon & Schuster, New York, 1996

Berton, P., *The Arctic Grail*, Viking, London, 1988

Bickel, L., *This Accursed Land*, Birlinn, Edinburgh, 2001

—Shackleton's Forgotten Men, Pimlico, London, 2001

Boyle, C. (ed.), *The Colonial Overlords*, Time-Life Books, Amsterdam, 1990

Brody, H., *Living Arctic*, Faber and Faber, London, 1987

Bierman, J., *Dark Safari: the Life behind the Legend of Henry Morton Stanley*, Hodder & Stoughton, London, 1991

Botting, D., *Humboldt and the Cosmos*, Michael Joseph, London, 1973

Cameron, I., *Magellan*, Weidenfeld and Nicolson, London, 1974

Dunn, R., *The Adventures of Ibn Battuta*, UCL Press, Los Angeles, 1989

Edwards, P. (ed.), *Last Voyages*, Clarendon Press, Oxford, 1988

Fisher, E., *Bering's Voyages*, C. Hurst & Co., London, 1977

Flannery, T., *The Explorers*, Phoenix, London, 1999

Fleming, F., *Barrow's Boys*, Granta, London, 1998

—Killing Dragons, Granta, London, 2000

—Ninety Degrees North, Granta, London, 2001

Fleming, F. (ed.), *The Pulse of Enterprise*, Time-Life Books, Amsterdam, 1990

—The Mongol Conquests, Time-Life Books, Amsterdam, 1989

Fulford, T., and Kitson P. (eds.), *Travels, Explorations and Empires: 1770–1835*, Vols I–IV, Pickering & Chatto, London, 2001

Gardner, B., *The Quest for Timbuctoo*, Cassell, London, 1968

Guadalupi, G., & Shugaar, A., *Latitude Zero*, Robinson, London, 2002

Giudici, D., *The Tragedy of the Italia*, D. Appleton & Co., New York, 1929

Granzotto, G. (trans. S. Sartarelli), *Christopher Columbus*, Collins, London, 1986

Hopkirk, P., *The Great Game*, Oxford University Press, Oxford, 1991

Holzel, T., & Salkeld, A., *The Mystery of Mallory and Irvine*, Cape, London, 1986

Hough, R., *Captain James Cook*, Hodder and Stoughton, London, 1994

Howgego, R., *Encyclopedia of Exploration to 1800*, Hordern House, Sydney, 2002

Huntford, R., *Shackleton*, Cardinal, London, 1989

Keay, J., *The Great Arc*, Harper Collins, London, 2000

Lambert, K., '*Hell With A Capital H*', Pimlico, London, 2002

Latham, E., *The Travels of Marco Polo*, Abaris Books, New York, 1982

Lopez, B., *Arctic Dreams*, Picador, London, 1987

McDermott, J., *Martin Frobisher: Elizabethan Privateer*, Yale University Press, New Haven, 2001

McKee, A., *Ice Crash*, Souvenir Press, London, 1979

McLynn, F., *Snow Upon the Desert*, Murray, London, 1990

Mitchell, J., & Gibbon, L., *Nine Against The Unknown*, Jarrolds, London, 1934

Moorehead, A., *Cooper's Creek*, White Lion, London, 1973

O'Brian, P., *Joseph Banks*, Collins Harvell, London, 1987

Parkman, F., *France and England in North America*, Vol. III *The Discovery of the Great West*, Little, Brown & Co., Boston, 1875

Parry, J., *The Age of Reconnaissance*, Weidenfeld and Nicolson, London, 1963

Porch, D., *The Conquest of the Sahara*, Cape, London, 1985

Preston, D., *A First Rate Tragedy*, Constable, London, 1997

Pyne, S., *The Ice*, Weidenfeld & Nicolson, London, 2003

Roditi, E, *Magellan of the Pacific*, Faber and Faber, London, 1972

Sattin, A., *The Gates of Africa*, Harper Collins, London, 2003

Savours, A., *The Search for the North West Passage*, Chatham Publishing, London, 1999

Scott, J., *Icebound: Journeys to the Northwest Sea*, Gordon & Cremonesi, London, 1977

Sobel, D., *Longitude*, Fourth Estate, London, 1996

Thompson, B., *Imperial Vanities*, Harper Collins, London, 2001

Unwin, R., *A Winter Away From Home: William Barents and the North-east Passage*, Seafarer Books, London, 1995

Venables, S., *Everest: Summit of Achievement*, Bloomsbury, London, 2003

Von Hagen, V., *South America Called Them*, Robert Hale, London, 1949

Watkins, R., *Unknown Seas: How Vasco da Gama Opened the East*, John Murray, London, 2003

Weise, A., *The Discoveries of America*, Richard Bentley, London, 1884

Wood, F., *The Silk Road*, British Library, London, 2003

INDEX